Formal Languages and Computation

Models and Their Applications

Formal Languages and Computation

Models and Their Applications

Alexander Meduna

CRC Press
Taylor & Francis Group
Boca Raton London New York

CRC Press is an imprint of the
Taylor & Francis Group, an **informa** business
AN AUERBACH BOOK

CRC Press
Taylor & Francis Group
6000 Broken Sound Parkway NW, Suite 300
Boca Raton, FL 33487-2742

First issued in paperback 2019

ISBN-13: 978-0-367-37887-5 (pbk)

Library of Congress Cataloging-in-Publication Data

Meduna, Alexander, 1957-
Formal languages and computation : models and their applications / Alexander Meduna.
pages cm
Includes bibliographical references and index.

1. Formal languages. 2. Machine theory. I. Title.

QA267.3.M43 2013
005.13'1--dc23 2013025935

Visit the Taylor & Francis Web site at
http://www.taylorandfrancis.com

and the CRC Press Web site at
http://www.crcpress.com

To Ivana and Zbyněk and

in memory of Meister Eckhart and Gustav Mahler

Contents

Preface xiii
Acknowledgments xvii
Author xix

SECTION I INTRODUCTION

1 Mathematical Background 3
- 1.1 Logic 3
- 1.2 Sets and Sequences 4
- 1.3 Relations 6
- 1.4 Graphs 7

2 Formal Languages and Rewriting Systems 13
- 2.1 Formal Languages 13
- 2.2 Rewriting Systems 15
  - 2.2.1 Rewriting Systems in General 16
  - 2.2.2 Rewriting Systems as Language Models 17
  - 2.2.3 Rewriting Systems as Computational Models 21
- 2.3 Synopsis of the Book 25

SECTION II REGULAR LANGUAGES AND THEIR MODELS

3 Models for Regular Languages 31
- 3.1 Finite Automata 31
  - 3.1.1 Representations of Finite Automata 32
- 3.2 Restricted Finite Automata 34
  - 3.2.1 Removal of ε-Rules 34
  - 3.2.2 Determinism 38
    - 3.2.2.1 Complete Specification 42
  - 3.2.3 Minimization 43
- 3.3 Regular Expressions and Their Equivalence with Finite Automata 45
  - 3.3.1 Regular Expressions 45
  - 3.3.2 Equivalence with Finite Automata 47
    - 3.3.2.1 From Finite Automata to Regular Expressions 47
    - 3.3.2.2 From Regular Expressions to Finite Automata 49

4 Applications of Regular Expressions and Finite Automata: Lexical Analysis 61
4.1 Implementation of Finite Automata 62
4.1.1 Table-Based Implementation 62
4.1.2 Case-Statement Implementation 64
4.2 Introduction to Lexical Analysis 66
4.2.1 Lexical Units and Regular Expressions 66
4.2.2 Scanners and Finite Automata 66
4.3 Implementation of a Scanner 67

5 Properties of Regular Languages 73
5.1 Pumping Lemma for Regular Languages 73
5.1.1 Applications of the Pumping Lemma for Regular Languages 75
5.2 Closure Properties 77
5.2.1 Applications of Closure Properties 80

SECTION III CONTEXT-FREE LANGUAGES AND THEIR MODELS

6 Models for Context-Free Languages 85
6.1 Context-Free Grammars 85
6.2 Restricted Context-Free Grammars 89
6.2.1 Canonical Derivations and Derivation Trees 90
6.2.1.1 Leftmost Derivations 90
6.2.1.2 Rightmost Derivations 92
6.2.1.3 Derivation Trees 92
6.2.1.4 Ambiguity 94
6.2.2 Removal of Useless Symbols 96
6.2.3 Removal of Erasing Rules 99
6.2.4 Removal of Single Rules 103
6.2.5 Chomsky Normal Form 104
6.2.6 Elimination of Left Recursion 106
6.2.7 Greibach Normal Form 110
6.3 Pushdown Automata 113
6.3.1 Pushdown Automata and Their Languages 113
6.3.2 Equivalence with Context-Free Grammars 114
6.3.2.1 From Context-Free Grammars to Pushdown Automata 114
6.3.2.2 From Pushdown Automata to Context-Free Grammars 115
6.3.3 Equivalent Types of Acceptance 119
6.3.4 Deterministic Pushdown Automata 121

7 Applications of Models for Context-Free Languages: Syntax Analysis 131
7.1 Introduction to Syntax Analysis 132
7.1.1 Syntax Specified by Context-Free Grammars 133
7.1.2 Top-Down Parsing 134
7.1.3 Bottom-Up Parsing 136

7.2 Top-Down Parsing 141
7.2.1 Predictive Sets and LL Grammars 142
7.2.1.1 LL Grammars 145
7.2.2 Predictive Parsing 146
7.2.2.1 Predictive Recursive-Descent Parsing 146
7.2.2.2 Predictive Table-Driven Parsing 149
7.2.2.3 Handling Errors 153
7.2.2.4 Exclusion of Left Recursion 154
7.3 Bottom-Up Parsing 155
7.3.1 Operator-Precedence Parsing 155
7.3.1.1 Operator-Precedence Parser 156
7.3.1.2 Construction of Operator-Precedence Parsing Table 158
7.3.1.3 Handling Errors 159
7.3.1.4 Operator-Precedence Parsers for Other Expressions 162
7.3.2 LR Parsing 163
7.3.2.1 LR Parsing Algorithm 164
7.3.2.2 Construction of LR Table 167
7.3.2.3 Handling Errors in LR Parsing 173

8 Properties of Context-Free Languages 187
8.1 Pumping Lemma for Context-Free Languages 187
8.1.1 Applications of the Pumping Lemma 189
8.2 Closure Properties 189
8.2.1 Union, Concatenation, and Closure 190
8.2.2 Intersection and Complement 190
8.2.3 Homomorphism 192
8.2.4 Applications of the Closure Properties 192

SECTION IV TURING MACHINES AND COMPUTATION

9 Turing Machines and Their Variants 199
9.1 Turing Machines and Their Languages 199
9.2 Restricted Turing Machines 202
9.2.1 Computational Restrictions 203
9.2.2 Size Restrictions 205
9.3 Universal Turing Machines 206
9.3.1 Turing Machine Codes 206
9.3.2 Construction of Universal Turing Machines 208

10 Applications of Turing Machines: Theory of Computation 213
10.1 Computability 214
10.1.1 Integer Functions Computed by Turing Machines 214
10.1.2 Recursion Theorem 217
10.1.3 Kleene's s-m-n Theorem 219

10.2 Decidability ... 220
10.2.1 Turing Deciders ... 220
10.2.2 Decidable Problems ... 223
10.2.2.1 Decidable Problems for Finite Automata ... 223
10.2.2.2 Decidable Problems for Context-Free Grammars ... 225
10.2.3 Undecidable Problems ... 227
10.2.3.1 Diagonalization ... 228
10.2.3.2 Reduction ... 230
10.2.3.3 Undecidable Problems Not Concerning Turing Machines ... 233
10.2.4 General Approach to Undecidability ... 234
10.2.4.1 Rice's Theorem ... 237
10.2.5 Computational Complexity ... 238
10.2.5.1 Time Complexity ... 238
10.2.5.2 Space Complexity ... 240

11 Turing Machines and General Grammars ... 245
11.1 General Grammars and Their Equivalence with Turing Machines ... 245
11.1.1 General Grammars ... 245
11.1.2 Normal Forms ... 246
11.1.3 Equivalence of General Grammars and Turing Machines ... 248
11.1.3.1 From General Grammars to Turing Machines ... 248
11.1.3.2 From Turing Machines to General Grammars ... 249
11.2 Context-Sensitive Grammars and Linear-Bounded Automata ... 250
11.2.1 Context-Sensitive Grammars and Their Normal Forms ... 250
11.2.1.1 Normal Forms ... 251
11.2.2 Linear-Bounded Automata and Their Equivalence with Context-Sensitive Grammars ... 251
11.2.2.1 From Context-Sensitive Grammars to Linear-Bounded Automata ... 251
11.2.2.2 From Linear-Bounded Automata to Context-Sensitive Grammars ... 252
11.2.3 Context-Sensitive Languages and Decidable Languages ... 253
11.3 Relations between Language Families ... 254

SECTION V CONCLUSION

12 Concluding and Bibliographical Remarks ... 261
12.1 Summary ... 261
12.2 Modern Trends ... 263
12.2.1 Conditional Grammars ... 263
12.2.2 Regulated Grammars ... 263
12.2.3 Scattered Context Grammars ... 264
12.2.4 Grammar Systems ... 264
12.3 Bibliographical and Historical Remarks ... 264

Appendix I: Index to Special Symbols 269
Appendix II: Index to Language Models 271
References 273
Bibliography 279
Index 289

Preface

This book is designed to serve as a text for a one-semester introductory course in the theory of formal languages and computation. It covers all the traditional topics of this theory, such as automata, grammars, parsing, computability, decidability, computational complexity, and properties of formal languages. Special attention is paid to the fundamental models for formal languages and their applications in computer science.

Subject

Formal language theory defines languages mathematically as sets of sequences consisting of symbols. This definition encompasses almost all languages as they are commonly understood. Indeed, natural languages, such as English, are included in this definition. Of course, all artificial languages introduced by various scientific disciplines can be viewed as formal languages; perhaps most illustratively, every programming language represents a formal language in terms of this definition. It thus comes as no surprise that formal language theory, which represents a mathematically systematized body of knowledge concerning formal languages, is important to all the scientific areas that make use of these languages to a certain extent.

The theory of formal languages represents the principal subject of this book. The text focuses its attention on the fundamental models for formal languages and their computation-related applications in computer science, hence its title *Formal Languages and Computation: Models and Their Applications.*

Models

The strictly mathematical approach to languages necessitates introducing formal models that define them. Most models of this kind are underlain by *rewriting systems*, which are based on rules by which they repeatedly change sequences of symbols, called strings. Despite their broad variety, most of them can be classified into two basic categories—generative and accepting language models. Generative models, better known as *grammars*, define strings of their language, so their rewriting process generates them from a special start symbol. On the other hand, accepting models, better known as *automata*, define strings of their language by a rewriting process that starts from these strings and ends in a prescribed set of final strings.

Applications

The book presents applications of language models in both practical and theoretical computer science.

In practice, the text explains how appropriate language models underlie computer science engineering techniques used in *language processors*. It pays special attention to *programming language analyzers* based on four language models—regular expressions, finite automata, context-free grammars, and pushdown automata. More specifically, by using *regular expressions* and *finite automata*, it builds up *lexical analyzers*, which recognize lexical units and verify that they are properly formed. Based on *context-free grammars* and *pushdown automata*, it creates *syntax analyzers*, which recognize syntactic structures in computer programs and verify that they are correctly written according to grammatical rules. That is, the text first explains how to specify the programming language syntax by using context-free grammars, which are considered the most widely used specification tool for this purpose. Then, it describes how to write syntax analyzers based on pushdown automata.

In theory, the book makes use of language-defining models to explore the very heart of the *foundations of computation*. That is, the text introduces the mathematical notion of a *Turing machine*, which has become a universally accepted formalization of the intuitive notion of a procedure. Based on this strictly mathematical notion, it studies the general limits of computation. More specifically, it performs this study in terms of two important topics concerning computation—computability and decidability. Regarding *computability*, it considers Turing machines as computers of functions over nonnegative integers and demonstrates the existence of functions whose computation cannot be specified by any procedure. As far as *decidability* is concerned, it formalizes problem-deciding algorithms by Turing machines that halt on every input. The book formulates several important problems concerning the language models discussed earlier in this book and constructs algorithms that decide them. On the other hand, it describes several problems that are not decidable by any algorithm. Apart from giving several specific undecidable problems, this book builds up a general theory of undecidability. Finally, the text approaches decidability in a much finer and realistic way. Indeed, it reconsiders problem-deciding algorithms in terms of their computational complexity measured according to time and space requirements. Perhaps most importantly, it shows that although some problems are decidable in principle, they are intractable for absurdly high computational requirements of the algorithms that decide them.

Use

As already stated, this book is intended as a textbook for a one-term introductory course in formal language theory and its applications in computer science.

Second, the book can also be used as an accompanying textbook for a compiler class at an undergraduate level because the text allows the flexibility needed to select only the topics relevant to compilers.

Finally, this book is useful to all researchers, including people out of computer science, who somehow deal with formal languages and their models in their scientific fields.

Approach

Primarily, this book represents a theoretically oriented treatment of formal languages and their models. Indeed, it introduces all formalisms concerning them with enough rigor to make all results quite clear and valid. Every complicated mathematical passage is preceded by its intuitive explanation so that even the most complex parts of the book are easy to grasp. Every new concept or algorithm is preceded by an explanation of its purpose and followed by some examples with comments to reinforce its understanding. All applications are given in a quite realistic way to clearly demonstrate a strong relation between the theoretical concepts and their uses.

Secondarily, as already pointed out, the text also presents several significant applications of formal languages and their models in practice. All applications are given in a quite realistic way to clearly show a close relation between the theoretical concepts and their uses.

Prerequisites

On the part of the student, no previous knowledge concerning formal languages is assumed. Although this book is self-contained, in the sense that no other sources are needed for understanding the material, a familiarity with the rudiments of discrete mathematics is helpful for a quick comprehension of formal language theory. A familiarity with a high-level programming language helps to grasp the material concerning applications in this book.

Organization

Synopsis

The entire text contains 12 chapters, which are divided into 5 sections.

Section I, which consists of Chapters 1 and 2, gives an introduction to the subject. Chapter 1 recalls the basic mathematical notions used in the book. Chapter 2 gives the basics of formal languages and rewriting systems that define them.

Section II, which consists of Chapters 3 through 5, studies regular languages and their models. Chapter 3 gives the basic definitions of these languages and their models, such as regular expressions and finite automata. Chapter 4 is application oriented; specifically, it builds lexical analyzers by using models for regular languages. Chapter 5 studies properties concerning regular languages.

Section III, which consists of Chapters 6 through 8, discusses context-free languages and their models. To a large extent, its structure parallels Section II. Indeed, Chapter 6 defines context-free languages and their models, including context-free grammars and pushdown automata. Chapter 7 explains how to construct syntax analyzers based on these grammars and automata. Chapter 8 establishes certain properties concerning context-free languages.

Section IV, which consists of Chapters 9 through 11, concerns Turing machines as a formalization of algorithms. Chapter 9 defines them. Based on Turing machines, Chapter 10 gives the basic ideas, concepts, and results underlying the theory of computation and its crucially important parts, including computability, decidability, and computational complexity. Simultaneously, this chapter establishes important properties concerning languages defined by Turing machines. Chapter 11 presents the essentials concerning general grammars, which represent grammatical counterparts to Turing machines.

Section V consists of Chapter 12. This chapter summarizes the entire textbook, points out selected modern trends, makes many historical and bibliographical remarks, and recommends further reading to the serious student.

Finally, the book contains two appendices. Appendix I gives the index to mathematical symbols used in the text. Appendix II contains the alphabetic index that lists all important language models introduced in the book.

Numbering

Regarding the technical organization of the text, algorithms, conventions, corollaries, definitions, lemmas, and theorems are sequentially numbered within chapters. Examples and figures are organized similarly. The end of conventions, corollaries, definitions, lemmas, and theorems is denoted by ■.

Exercises

At the end of each chapter, a set of exercises is given to reinforce and augment the material covered. Selected exercises, denoted by S, have their solutions or parts of them at the end of the chapter.

Algorithms

This textbook contains many algorithms. Strictly speaking, every algorithm requires a verification that it terminates and works correctly. However, the termination of the algorithms given in this book is always so obvious that its verification is omitted throughout. The correctness of complicated algorithms is verified in detail. On the other hand, we most often give only the gist of the straightforward algorithms and leave their rigorous verification as an exercise. The text describes the algorithms in Pascal-like notation, which is so simple and intuitive that even the student unfamiliar with the Pascal programming language can immediately pick it up. In this description, a Pascal **repeat** loop is sometimes ended with **until no change**, meaning that the loop is repeated until no change can result from its further repetition. As the clear comprehensibility is a paramount importance in the book, the description of algorithms is often enriched by an explanation in words.

Support on the World Wide Web

Further backup materials, including lecture notes, are available at http://www.fit.vutbr.cz/~meduna/books/flc.

Acknowledgments

For almost a decade, I taught the theory of formal languages and computation at the University of Missouri-Columbia in the United States back in the 1990s, and since 2000, I have taught this subject at the Brno University of Technology in the Czech Republic. The lecture notes I wrote at these two universities underlie this book, and I have greatly benefited from conversations with many colleagues and students there. In addition, this book is based on notes I have used for my talks at various American, Asian, and European universities over the past three decades. Notes made at the Kyoto Sangyo University in Japan were particularly helpful.

Writing this book was supported by the European Regional Development Fund in the IT4Innovations Centre of Excellence project (CZ.1.05/1.1.00/02.0070). This work was also supported by the Visual Computing Competence Center (TE01010415).

My thanks to Martin Čermák and Jiří Techet for their comments on a draft of this text. Without the great collaboration, encouragement, and friendship with Zbyněk Křivka, I would have hardly started writing this book, let alone complete it. I am also grateful to John Wyzalek at Taylor & Francis for excellent editorial work. Finally, I thank my wife Ivana for her patience and, most importantly, love.

Author

Alexander Meduna, PhD, is a full professor of computer science at the Brno University of Technology in the Czech Republic, where he earned his doctorate in 1988. From 1988 until 1997, he taught computer science at the University of Missouri-Columbia in the United States. Even more intensively, since 2000, he has taught computer science and mathematics at the Brno University of Technology. In addition to these two universities, he has taught computer science at several other American, European, and Japanese universities for shorter periods of time. His classes have been primarily focused on formal language theory and its applications in theoretical and practical computer science. His teaching has also covered various topics including automata, discrete mathematics, operating systems, and principles of programming languages. Among many other awards for his scholarship and writing, he received the Distinguished University Professor Award from Siemens in 2012. He very much enjoys teaching classes related to the subject of this book.

Dr. Meduna has written several books. Specifically, he is the author of two textbooks—*Automata and Languages* (Springer, 2000) and *Elements of Compiler Design* (Taylor & Francis, 2008; translated into Chinese in 2009). Furthermore, he is the coauthor of three monographs—*Grammars with Context Conditions and Their Applications* (along with Martin Švec, Wiley, 2005), *Scattered Context Grammars and Their Applications* (with Jiří Techet, WIT Press, 2010), and *Regulated Grammars and Automata* (with Petr Zemek, Springer, 2014). He has published over 90 studies in prominent international journals, such as *Acta Informatica* (Springer), *International Journal of Computer Mathematics* (Taylor & Francis), and *Theoretical Computer Science* (Elsevier). All his scientific work discusses the theory of formal languages and computation, the subject of this book, or closely related topics, such as compiler writing.

Alexander Meduna's website is http://www.fit.vutbr.cz/~meduna. His scientific work is described in detail at http://www.fit.vutbr.cz/~meduna/work.

INTRODUCTION I

In this two-chapter introductory section, we first review the mathematical notions, concepts, and techniques used throughout this book to express all the upcoming theory of formal languages clearly and precisely. Then, we introduce formal languages defined by rewriting systems, and we also explain how these systems underlie important models used in both practical and theoretical computer science. We conclude this section by giving a synopsis of the entire book.

Chapter 1 reviews the principal ideas and notions underlying some mathematical areas because they are needed for understanding this book. These areas include logic, set theory, discrete mathematics, and graph theory.

Chapter 2 gives an introduction to this work. It defines its two central notions—formal languages and rewriting systems—and demonstrates how to use them as language-defining models and models of computation. In terms of these models, this chapter closes its discussion by presenting a synopsis of the entire book.

Chapter 1

Mathematical Background

This chapter reviews rudimentary concepts from logic (Section 1.1), set theory (Section 1.2), discrete mathematics (Section 1.3), and graph theory (Section 1.4). For readers familiar with them, this chapter can be skipped and treated as a reference for notation and definitions.

1.1 Logic

In this section, we review the basics of elementary logic. We pay a special attention to the fundamental proof techniques used in this book.

In general, a *formal mathematical system S* consists of basic *symbols*, *formation rules*, *axioms*, and *inference rules*. Basic symbols, such as constants and operators, form components of *statements* that are composed according to formation rules. Axioms are primitive statements, whose validity is accepted without justification. By inference rules, some statements infer other statements. A *proof* of a statement s in S consists of a sequence of statements $s_1, \ldots, s_i, \ldots, s_n$ such that $s = s_n$ and each s_i is either an axiom of S or a statement inferred by some of the statements $s_1, \ldots, s_{i-1}$ according to the inference rules; s proved in this way represents a *theorem* of S.

Logical connectives join statements to create more-complicated statements. The most common logical connectives are *not*, *and*, *or*, *implies*, and *if and only if*. In this list, *not* is unary while the other connectives are binary. That is, if s is a statement, then *not* s is a statement as well. Similarly, if s_1 and s_2 are statements, then s_1 *and* s_2, s_1 *or* s_2, s_1 *implies* s_2, and s_1 *if and only if* s_2 are statements, too. We often write $\neg$, $\wedge$, and $\vee$ instead of *not*, *and*, and *or*, respectively. The following *truth table* presents the rules governing the *truth* or *falsity* concerning statements connected by the binary connectives. Regarding the unary connective $\neg$, if s is true, then $\neg s$ is false, and if s is false, then $\neg s$ is true.

Convention 1.1 Throughout this book, *truth* and *falsity* are denoted by **1** and **0**, respectively. ■

By the truth table (Figure 1.1), s_1 *and* s_2 is true if both statements are true; otherwise, s_1 *and* s_2 is false. Analogically, we can interpret the other rules governing the truth or falsity of a statement containing the other connectives from this table. A statement of *equivalence*, which has the form

s_1	s_2	$\wedge$	$\vee$	*implies*	*if and only if*
0	0	0	0	1	1
0	1	0	1	1	0
1	0	0	1	0	0
1	1	1	1	1	1

Figure 1.1 Truth table.

s_1 *if and only if* s_2, sometimes abbreviated to s_1 *iff* s_2, plays a crucial role in this book. A proof that it is true usually consists of two parts. The *only-if* part demonstrates that s_1 *implies* s_2 is true although the *if* part proves that s_2 *implies* s_1 is true.

Example 1.1 There exists a useful way of representing ordinary *infix arithmetic expressions* without using parentheses. This notation is referred to as *Polish notation* that has two fundamental forms—*postfix* and *prefix notation*. The former is defined recursively as follows:

Let Ω be a set of binary operators, and let Σ be a set of operands.

1. Every $a \in \Sigma$ is a postfix representation of a.
2. Let AoB be an infix expression, where $o \in \Omega$, and A, B are infix expressions. Then, CDo is the postfix representation of AoB, where C and D are the postfix representations of A and B, respectively.
3. Let C be the postfix representation of an infix expression A. Then, C is the postfix representation of (A).

Consider the infix logical expression $(\mathbf{1} \vee \mathbf{0}) \wedge \mathbf{0}$. The postfix expressions for $\mathbf{1}$ and $\mathbf{0}$ are $\mathbf{1}$ and $\mathbf{0}$, respectively. The postfix expression for $\mathbf{1} \vee \mathbf{0}$ is $\mathbf{1}\ \mathbf{0} \vee$, so the postfix expression for $(\mathbf{1} \vee \mathbf{0})$ is $\mathbf{1}\ \mathbf{0} \vee$, too. Thus the postfix expression for $(\mathbf{1} \vee \mathbf{0}) \wedge \mathbf{0}$ is $\mathbf{1}\ \mathbf{0} \vee \mathbf{0} \wedge$.

The prefix notation is defined analogically, except that in the second part of the definition, o is placed in front of AB; the details are left as an exercise.

There exist many logic laws useful to demonstrate that an implication is true. Specifically, the *contrapositive law* says (s_1 *implies* s_2) *if and only if* (($\neg s_2$) *implies* ($\neg s_1$)), so we can prove s_1 *implies* s_2 by demonstrating that ($\neg s_2$) *implies* ($\neg s_1$) holds true. We also often use a *proof by contradiction* based on the law saying (($\neg s_2$) *and* s_1) *implies* $\mathbf{0}$ is true. Less formally, if from the assumption that s_2 is false and s_1 is true, then we obtain a false statement, s_1 *implies* s_2 is true. A *proof by induction* demonstrates that a statement s_i is true for all integers $i \geq b$, where b is a nonnegative integer. In general, a proof of this kind is made in the following way:

Basis. Prove that s_b is true.

Inductive Hypothesis. Suppose that there exists an integer n such that $n \geq b$ and s_m is true for all $b \leq m \leq n$.

Inductive Step. Prove that s_{n+1} is true under the assumption that the inductive hypothesis holds.

A proof by contradiction and a proof by induction are illustrated in the beginning of Section 1.2 (see Example 1.2).

1.2 Sets and Sequences

A *set*, Σ, is a collection of elements that are taken from some prespecified *universe*. If Σ contains an element a, then we symbolically write $a \in \Sigma$ and refer to a as a *member* of Σ. On the other hand, if a is not in Σ, then we write $a \notin \Sigma$. If Σ has a finite number of members, then

Σ is a *finite set*; otherwise, Σ is an *infinite set*. The finite set that has no member is the *empty set*, denoted by $\varnothing$. The *cardinality* of a finite set, Σ, *card*(Σ), is the number of Σ's members; note that *card*($\varnothing$) = 0.

Convention 1.2 Throughout this book, $\mathbb{N}$ denotes the set of *natural numbers*—that is, $\mathbb{N} = \{1, 2, \ldots\}$, and ${}_0\mathbb{N} = \{0\} \cup \mathbb{N}$. ■

Example 1.2 The purpose of this example is twofold. First, we give examples of sets. Second, as pointed out in the conclusion of Section 1.1, we illustrate how to make proofs by contradiction and by induction.

Let P be the set of all primes (a natural number n is prime if its only positive divisors are 1 and n).

A proof by contradiction. By contradiction, we next prove that P is infinite. That is, assume that P is finite. Set $k = card(P)$. Thus, P contains k numbers, $p_1, p_2, \ldots, p_k$. Set $n = p_1 p_2 \ldots p_k + 1$. Observe that n is not divisible by any p_i, $1 \leq i \leq k$. As a result, either n is a new prime or n equals a product of new primes. In either case, there exists a prime out of P, which contradicts that P contains all primes. Thus, P is infinite. Another proof by contradiction is given in Example 1.3.

A proof by induction. As already stated, *by induction*, we prove that a statement s_i holds for all $i \geq b$, where $b \in \mathbb{N}$. To illustrate, consider $\{i^2 \mid i \in \mathbb{N}\}$, and let s_i state

$$1 + 3 + 5 + \ldots + 2i - 1 = i^2$$

for all $i \in \mathbb{N}$; in other words, s_i says that the sum of odd integers is a perfect square. An inductive proof of this statement is as follows:

Basis. As $1 = 1^2$, s_1 is true.

Inductive Hypothesis. Assume that s_m is true for all $1 \leq m \leq n$, where n is a natural number.

Inductive Step. Consider $s_{n+1} = 1 + 3 + 5 + \ldots + (2n - 1) + (2(n + 1) - 1) = (n + 1)^2$. By the inductive hypothesis, $s_n = 1 + 3 + 5 + \ldots + (2n - 1) = n^2$. Hence, $1 + 3 + 5 + \ldots + (2n - 1) + (2(n + 1) - 1) = n^2 + 2n + 1 = (n + 1)^2$. Consequently, s_{n+1} holds, and the inductive proof is completed.

A finite set, Σ, is customarily specified by listing its members; that is, $\Sigma = \{a_1, a_2, \ldots, a_n\}$, where a_1 through a_n are all members of Σ; as a special case, we have $\{\} = \varnothing$. An infinite set, Ω, is usually specified by a property, π, so that Ω contains all elements satisfying π; in symbols, this specification has the following general format $\Omega = \{a \mid \pi(a)\}$. Sets whose members are other sets are usually called *families* of sets rather than sets of sets.

Let Σ and Ω be two sets. Σ is a *subset* of Ω, symbolically written as $\Sigma \subseteq \Omega$, if each member of Σ also belongs to Ω. Σ is a *proper subset* of Ω, written as $\Sigma \subset \Omega$, if $\Sigma \subseteq \Omega$ and Ω contains an element that is not in Σ. If $\Sigma \subseteq \Omega$ and $\Omega \subseteq \Sigma$, then Σ *equals* Ω, denoted by $\Sigma = \Omega$. The *power set* of Σ, denoted by *power*(Σ), is the set of all subsets of Σ.

For two sets, Σ and Ω, their *union*, *intersection*, and *difference* are denoted by $\Sigma \cup \Omega$, $\Sigma \cap \Omega$, and $\Sigma - \Omega$, respectively, and defined as $\Sigma \cup \Omega = \{a \mid a \in \Sigma \text{ or } a \in \Omega\}$, $\Sigma \cap \Omega = \{a \mid a \in \Sigma \text{ and } a \in \Omega\}$, and $\Sigma - \Omega = \{a \mid a \in \Sigma \text{ and } a \notin \Omega\}$. If Σ is a set over a universe U, then the *complement* of Σ is denoted by $\sim\Sigma$ and defined as $\sim\Sigma = U - \Sigma$. The operations of union, intersection, and complement are related by *DeMorgan's laws* stating that $\sim(\sim\Sigma \cup \sim\Omega) = \Sigma \cap \Omega$ and $\sim(\sim\Sigma \cap \sim\Omega) = \Sigma \cup \Omega$, for any two sets Σ and Ω. If $\Sigma \cap \Omega = \varnothing$, then Σ and Ω are *disjoint*. More generally, n sets $\Delta_1, \Delta_2, \ldots, \Delta_n$, where $n \geq 2$, are *pairwise disjoint* if $\Delta_i \cap \Delta_j = \varnothing$ for all $1 \leq i, j \leq n$ such that $i \neq j$.

A *sequence* is a list of elements from some universe. A sequence is *finite* if it consists of finitely many elements; otherwise, it is *infinite*. The *length of* a finite sequence x, denoted by $|x|$, is the number of elements in x. The *empty sequence*, denoted by ε, is the sequence consisting of no element; that is, $|\varepsilon| = 0$. For brevity, finite sequences are specified by listing their elements throughout. For instance, (0, 1, 0, 0) is shortened to 0100; notice that $|0100| = 4$.

1.3 Relations

For two objects, a and b, (a, b) denotes the *ordered pair* consisting of a and b in this order. Let A and B be two sets. The *Cartesian product* of A and B, $A \times B$, is defined as $A \times B = \{(a, b)|\ a \in A$ and $b \in B\}$. A *binary relation* or, briefly, a *relation*, ρ, from A to B is any subset of $A \times B$; that is, $\rho \subseteq A \times B$. If ρ represents a finite set, then it is a *finite relation*; otherwise, it is an *infinite relation*. The *domain of* ρ, denoted by *domain*(ρ), and the *range of* ρ, denoted by *range*(ρ), are defined as *domain*(ρ) = $\{a|\ (a, b) \in \rho$ for some $b \in B\}$ and *range*(ρ) = $\{b|\ (a, b) \in \rho$ for some $a \in A\}$. If $A = B$, then ρ is a *relation on A*. A relation σ is a *subrelation* of ρ if $\sigma \subseteq \rho$. The *inverse of* ρ, denoted by *inverse*(ρ), is defined as *inverse*(ρ) = $\{(b, a)|\ (a, b) \in \rho\}$. A *function* from A to B is a relation φ from A to B such that for every $a \in A$, *card*($\{b|\ b \in B$ and $(a, b) \in \varphi\}$) ≤ 1. If *domain*(φ) $= A$, then φ is *total*. If we want to emphasize that φ may not satisfy *domain*(φ) $= A$, then we say that φ is *partial*. If for every $b \in B$, *card*($\{a|\ a \in A$ and $(a, b) \in \varphi\}$) ≤ 1, then φ is an *injection*. If for every $b \in B$, *card*($\{a|\ a \in A$ and $(a, b) \in \varphi\}$) ≥ 1, then φ is a *surjection*. If φ is a total function that is both a surjection and an injection, then φ represents a *bijection*.

As relations and functions are defined as sets, the set operations allied to them, too. For instance, if $\rho \subseteq A \times B$ is a function, then its complement, $\sim\rho$, is defined as $(A \times B) - \rho$.

Convention 1.3 Let $\rho \subseteq A \times B$ be a relation. To express that $(a, b) \in \rho$, we usually write $a\rho b$. If ρ represents a function, then we often write $\rho(a) = b$ instead of $a\rho b$. If $\rho(a) = b$, then b is the *value* of ρ for *argument a*. ■

If there is a bijection from an infinite set ψ to an infinite set Ξ, then ψ and Ξ have the *same cardinality*. An infinite set, Ω, is *countable* or, synonymously, *enumerable*, if Ω and $\mathbb{N}$ have the same cardinality; otherwise, it is *uncountable* (according to Convention 1.2, $\mathbb{N}$ is the set of natural numbers).

Example 1.3 Consider the set of all even natural numbers, E. Define the bijection $\varphi(i) = 2i$, for all $i \in \mathbb{N}$. Observe that φ represents a bijection from $\mathbb{N}$ to E, so they have the same cardinality. Thus, E is countable.

Consider the set ς of all functions mapping $\mathbb{N}$ to $\{\mathbf{0}, \mathbf{1}\}$. By contradiction, we prove that ς is uncountable. Suppose that ς is countable. Thus, there is a bijection from ς to $\mathbb{N}$. Let ${}_if$ be the function mapped to the ith positive integer, for all $i \geq 1$. Consider the total function g from $\mathbb{N}$ to $\{\mathbf{0}, \mathbf{1}\}$ defined as $g(j) = \mathbf{0}$ if and only if ${}_jf(j) = \mathbf{1}$, for all $i \geq 1$, so $g(j) = \mathbf{1}$ if and only if ${}_jf(j) = \mathbf{0}$. As ς contains g, $g = {}_kf$ for some $k \geq 1$. Specifically, $g(k) = {}_kf(k)$. However, $g(k) = \mathbf{0}$ if and only if ${}_kf(k) = \mathbf{1}$, so $g(k) \neq {}_kf(k)$, which contradicts $g(k) = {}_kf(k)$. Thus, ς is uncountable.

The proof technique by which we have demonstrated that ς is uncountable is customarily called *diagonalization*. To see why, imagine an infinite table with ${}_1f$, ${}_2f$, … listed down the rows and 1, 2, … listed across the columns (see Figure 1.2). Each entry contains either $\mathbf{0}$ or $\mathbf{1}$. Specifically, the

	1	2	...	k	...
${}_1f$	**0**	**1**		**0**	
${}_2f$	**1**	**1**		**1**	
⋮					
$g = {}_kf$	**0**	**0**		**0** *iff* **1**	
⋮					

Figure 1.2 Diagonalization.

entry in row ${}_if$ and column j contains **1** if and only if ${}_if(j) = \mathbf{1}$, so this entry contains **0** if and only if ${}_if(j) = \mathbf{0}$. A contradiction occurs at the diagonal entry in row ${}_kf$ and column k because $g(k) = \mathbf{0}$ if and only if ${}_kf(k) = \mathbf{1}$ and $g(k) = {}_kf(k)$; in other words, this diagonal entry contains **0** if and only if it contains **1**, which is impossible. We make use of this proof technique several times in this book.

Let A be a set, ρ be a relation on A, and a, $b \in A$. For $k \geq 1$, the *k-fold product* of ρ, ρ^k, is recursively defined as (1) $a\rho^1 b$ iff $a\rho b$, and (2) $a\rho^k b$ iff there exists $c \in A$ such that $a\rho c$ and $c\rho^{k-1}b$, for $k \geq 2$. Furthermore, $a\rho^0 b$ if and only if $a = b$. The *transitive closure* of ρ, ρ^+, is defined as $a\rho^+ b$ if and only if $a\rho^k b$, for some $k \geq 1$, and the *reflexive and transitive closure* of ρ, ρ^*, is defined as $a\rho^* b$ if and only if $a\rho^k b$, for some $k \geq 0$.

1.4 Graphs

Let A be a set. A *directed* graph or, briefly, a *graph* is a pair $G = (A, \rho)$, where ρ is a relation on A. Members of A are called *nodes*, and ordered pairs in ρ are called *edges*. If $(a, b) \in \rho$, then edge (a, b) *leaves* a and *enters* b. Let $a \in A$; then, the *in-degree* of a and the *out-degree* of a are $card(\{b| \ (b, a) \in \rho\})$ and $card(\{c| \ (a, c) \in \rho\})$. A sequence of nodes, $(a_0, a_1, \ldots, a_n)$, where $n \geq 1$, is a *path of length n* from a_0 to a_n if $(a_{i-1}, a_i) \in \rho$ for all $1 \leq i \leq n$; if, in addition, $a_0 = a_n$, then $(a_0, a_1, \ldots, a_n)$ is a *cycle of length n*. In this book, we frequently *label* the edges of G with some attached information. Pictorially, we represent $G = (A, \rho)$ so we draw each edge $(a, b) \in \rho$ as an arrow from a to b possibly with its label as illustrated in Example 1.4.

Example 1.4 Consider a program p and its *call graph* $G = (P, \rho)$, where P represents the set of subprograms in p, and $(x, y) \in \rho$ iff subprogram x calls subprogram y. Specifically, let $P = \{a, b, c, d\}$, and $\rho = \{(a, b), (a, c), (b, d), (c, d)\}$, which says a calls b and c, b calls d, and c calls d as well (see Figure 1.3).

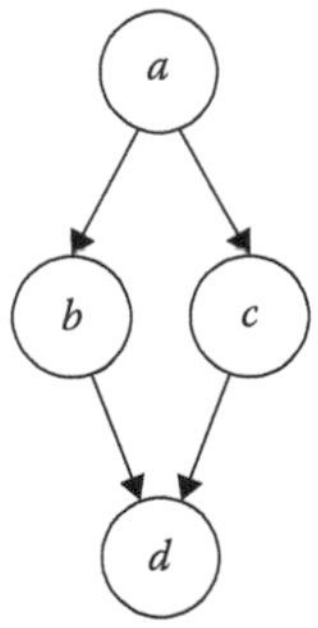

Figure 1.3 Graph.

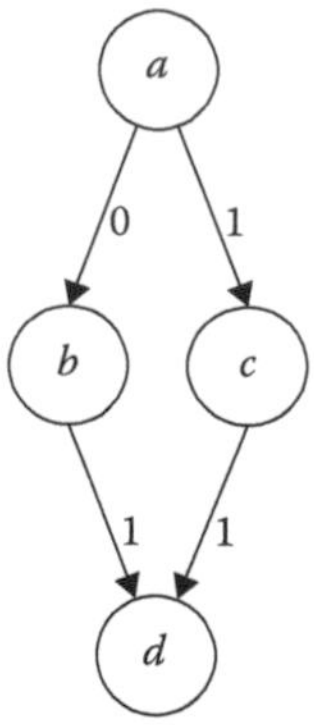

Figure 1.4 Labeled graph.

The in-degree of a is 0, and its out-degree is 2. Notice that (a, b, d) is a path of length 2 in G. G contains no cycle because none of its paths starts and ends in the same node.

Suppose we use G to study the value of a global variable during the four calls. Specifically, we want to express that this value is zero when call (a, b) occurs; otherwise, it is one. We express this by labeling the edges of G in the way given in Figure 1.4.

Let $G = (A, \rho)$ be a graph. G is an *acyclic graph* if it contains no cycle. If $(a_0, a_1, \ldots, a_n)$ is a path in G, then a_0 is an *ancestor* of a_n and a_n is a *descendant* of a_0; if in addition, $n = 1$, then a_0 is a *direct ancestor* of a_n and a_n a *direct descendant* of a_0. A *tree* is an acyclic graph $T = (A, \rho)$ such that A contains a specified node, called the *root* of T and denoted by $root(T)$, and every $a \in A - root(T)$ is a descendant of $root(T)$ and its in-degree is one. If $a \in A$ is a node whose out-degree is 0, then a is a *leaf*; otherwise, it is an *interior node*. In this book, a tree T is always considered as an *ordered tree* in which each interior node a $\in A$ has all its direct descendants, b_1 through b_n, where $n \geq 1$, ordered from the left to the right so that b_1 is the leftmost direct descendant of a and b_n is the rightmost direct descendant of a. At this point, a is the *parent* of its *children* b_1 through b_n, and all these nodes together with the edges connecting them, (a, b_1) through (a, b_n), are called a *parent-children portion of T*. The *frontier* of T, denoted by $frontier(T)$, is the sequence of T's leaves ordered from the left to the right. The *depth* of T, $depth(T)$, is the length of the longest path in T. A tree $S = (B, \upsilon)$ is a *subtree of T* if $\emptyset \subset B \subseteq A$, $\upsilon \subseteq \rho \cap (B \times B)$, and in T, no node in $A - B$ is a descendant of a node in B; S is an *elementary subtree* of T if $depth(S) = 1$.

Like any graph, a tree T can be described as a two-dimensional structure. To simplify this description, however, we draw a tree T with its root on the top and with all edges directed down. Each parent has its children drawn from the left to the right according to its ordering. Drawing T in this way, we always omit all arrowheads.

Apart from this two-dimensional representation, however, it is frequently convenient to specify T by a one-dimensional representation, denoted by $odr(T)$, in which each subtree of T is represented by the expression appearing inside a balanced pair of $\langle$ and $\rangle$ with the node that is the root of that subtree appearing immediately to the left of $\langle$. More precisely, $odr(T)$ is defined by the following recursive rules:

1. If T consists of a single node a, then $odr(T) = a$.
2. Let (a, b_1) through (a, b_n), where $n \geq 1$, be the parent-children portion of T, $root(T) = a$, and T_k be the subtree rooted at b_k, $1 \leq k \leq n$, then $odr(T) = a\langle odr(T_1)\ odr(T_2) \ldots odr(T_n)\rangle$.

Example 1.5 illustrates both the one-dimensional *odr*-representation and the two-dimensional pictorial representation of a tree. For brevity, we prefer the former throughout this book.

Example 1.5 Graph G discussed in Example 1.4 is acyclic. However, it is no tree because the in-degree of node d is two. By removing edge (b, d), we obtain a tree $T = (P, \tau)$, where $P = \{a, b, c, d\}$ and $\tau = \{(a, b), (a, c), (c, d)\}$. Nodes a and c are interior nodes while b and d are leaves. The root of T is a. We define b and c as the first and the second child of a, respectively. A parent-children portion of T is, for instance, (a, b) and (a, c). Notice that $frontier(T) = bd$, and $depth(T) = 2$. Following the recursive rules (1) and (2), we obtain the one-dimensional representation of T as $odr(T) = a\langle bc\langle d\rangle\rangle$. Its subtrees are $a\langle bc\langle d\rangle\rangle$, $c\langle d\rangle$, b, and d. In Figure 1.5, we pictorially describe $a\langle bc\langle d\rangle\rangle$ and $c\langle d\rangle$.

Exercises

1. A *tautology* is a statement that is true for all possible truth values of the statement variables.
   a. Prove that the contrapositive law represents a tautology.
   b. State and prove five more tautologies.
   c. Finally, from a more general viewpoint, prove that every theorem of a formal mathematical system represents a tautology, and conversely, every tautology is a theorem.
2. A *Boolean algebra* is a formal mathematical system, which consists of a set Σ and operations $\vee$, $\wedge$, and $\neg$. The axioms of Boolean algebra are as follows.
   Associativity:

   $$a \vee (b \vee c) = (a \vee b) \vee c, \text{ and } a \wedge (b \wedge c) = (a \wedge b) \wedge c, \text{ for all } a, b, c \in \Sigma.$$

   Commutativity:

   $$a \vee b = b \vee a, \text{ and } a \wedge b = b \wedge a, \text{ for all } a, b \in \Sigma.$$

   Distributivity:

   $$a \wedge (b \vee c) = (a \wedge b) \vee (a \wedge c), \text{ and } a \vee (b \wedge c) = (a \vee b) \wedge (a \vee c), \text{ for all } a, b \in \Sigma.$$

   In addition, Σ contains two distinguished members, 0 and 1, such that for all $a \in \Sigma$,

   $$a \vee 0 = a,\ a \wedge 1 = a,\ a \vee (\neg a) = 1,\ a \wedge (\neg a) = 0$$

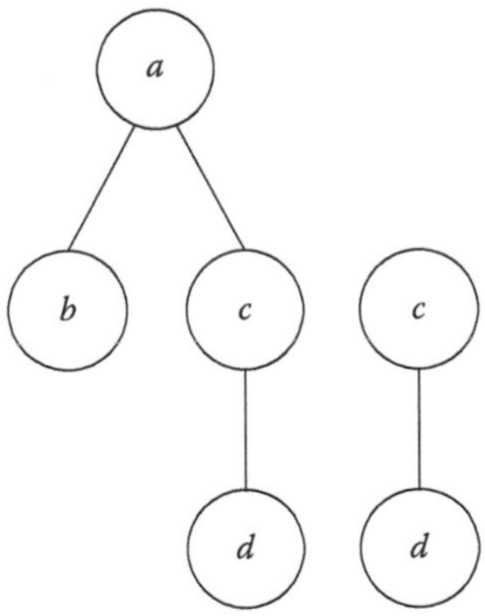

Figure 1.5 A tree and a subtree.

The rule of inference is substitution of equals for equals.

a. Consider the Boolean algebra in which $0 = \mathbf{0}$ and $1 = \mathbf{1}$, where $\mathbf{1}$ and $\mathbf{0}$ denote truth and falsity according to Convention 1.1, and $\Sigma - \{\mathbf{1}, \mathbf{0}\} = \emptyset$. Furthermore, consider this statement

$$a \vee (b \wedge \neg a) = a \vee b$$

where $a, b \in \Sigma$. Prove that this statement represents a theorem in the Boolean algebra.

b. Reformulate (a) so Σ is any superset of $\{\mathbf{1}, \mathbf{0}\}$. Does the above-mentioned statement necessarily represent a theorem in the Boolean algebra generalized in this way? Prove your answer rigorously.

c. Give five statements and prove that they are theorems in terms of the Boolean algebra generalized in (b).

3. By induction, prove that for any set Σ, $card(power(\Sigma)) = 2^{card(\Sigma)}$ (see Section 1.1 for $power(\Sigma)$).
4. Let $\Sigma \subseteq {}_0\mathbb{N}$, and let φ be the total function from ${}_0\mathbb{N}$ to $\{\mathbf{0}, \mathbf{1}\}$ defined by $\varphi(i) = \mathbf{1}$ iff $i \in \Sigma$, for all $i \in {}_0\mathbb{N}$; then, φ is the *characteristic function* of Σ. Express basic set operations, such as union, in terms of characteristic functions.
5. Let Σ and Ω be two sets, and let ρ and ρ' be two relations from Σ to Ω. If ρ and ρ' represent two identical subsets of $\Sigma \times \Omega$, then ρ *equals* ρ', symbolically written as $\rho = \rho'$.
   Perform (a) and (b), given as follows.
   a. Illustrate this definition by five examples in terms of relations over ${}_0\mathbb{N}$.
   b. Reformulate this definition by using characteristic functions.
6. Let Σ be a set, and let ρ be a relation on Σ. Then,
   a. If for all $a \in \Sigma$, $a\rho a$, then ρ is *reflexive*.
   b. If for all $a, b \in \Sigma$, $a\rho b$ implies $b\rho a$, then ρ is *symmetric*.
   c. If for all $a, b \in \Sigma$, ($a\rho b$ and $b\rho a$) implies $a = b$, then ρ is *antisymmetric*.
   d. If for all $a, b, c \in \Sigma$, ($a\rho b$ and $b\rho c$) implies $a\rho c$, then ρ is *transitive*.

   Consider relations (i) through (ix), given as follows. For each of them, determine whether it is reflexive, symmetric, antisymmetric, or transitive.
   i. $\emptyset$
   ii. $\{(1, 3), (3, 1), (8, 8)\}$
   iii. $\{(1, 1), (2, 2), (8, 8)\}$
   iv. $\{(x, x) \mid x \in \Sigma\}$
   v. $\{(x, y) \mid x, y \in \Sigma, x < y\}$
   vi. $\{(x, y) \mid x, y \in \Sigma, x \leq y\}$
   vii. $\{(x, y) \mid x, y \in \Sigma, x + y = 9\}$
   viii. $\{(x, y) \mid x, y \in \Sigma, y$ is divisible by $x\}$
   ix. $\{(x, y) \mid x, y \in \Sigma, x - y$ is divisible by $3\}$

   Note that x is divisible by y if there exists a positive integer z such that $x = yz$.
7. Let Σ be a set, and let ρ be a relation on Σ. If ρ is reflexive, symmetric, and transitive, then ρ is an *equivalence relation*. Let ρ be an equivalence relation on Σ. Then, ρ partitions Σ into disjoint subsets, called *equivalence classes*, so that for each $a \in \Sigma$, the equivalence class of a is denoted by $[a]$ and defined as $[a] = \{b \mid a\rho b\}$.

   Prove that for all a and b in Σ, either $[a] = [b]$ or $[a] \cap [b] = \emptyset$.
8. Let Σ be a set, and let ρ be a relation on Σ. If ρ is reflexive, antisymmetric, and transitive, then ρ is a *partial order*. If ρ is a partial order satisfying either $a\rho b$ or $b\rho a$, for all $a, b \in \Sigma$ such that $a \neq b$, then ρ is a *linear order*.

   Let Σ be a set. Define the relation ρ on $power(\Sigma)$ as $\rho = \{(A, B) \mid A, B \in power(\Sigma), A \subseteq B\}$ (see Section 1.1 for $power(\Sigma)$). Prove that ρ represents a partial order.

9 S. Prove the following two theorems.

Theorem Let Σ be a set, ρ be a relation on Σ, and ρ^+ be the transitive closure of ρ. Then, (i) ρ^+ is a transitive relation, and (ii) if ρ' is a transitive relation such that $\rho \subseteq \rho'$, then $\rho^+ \subseteq \rho'$. ■

Theorem Let Σ be a set, ρ be a relation on Σ, and ρ^* be the transitive-reflexive closure of ρ. Then, (i) ρ^* is a transitive and reflexive relation, and (ii) if ρ' be a transitive and reflexive relation such that $\rho \subseteq \rho'$, then $\rho^* \subseteq \rho'$. ■

10. Generalize the notion of a binary relation to the notion of an n-ary relation, where n is a natural number. Similarly, generalize the notion of a binary function to the notion of an n-ary function. Illustrate these generalized notions by several examples.
11 S. Define the prefix Polish notation rigorously. In a step-by-step way, describe the translation of $(\mathbf{1} \vee \mathbf{0}) \wedge \mathbf{0}$ into the prefix Polish notation.
12. Consider the one-dimensional representation of trees *odr* (see Section 1.4). Prove that the prefix Polish notation is actually the same as *odr* with parentheses deleted.
13. Design an alternative one-dimensional representation for trees, different from *odr*.
14. Consider the directed graphs defined and discussed in Section 1.4. Intuitively, *undirected graphs* are similar to these graphs, except that their edges are undirected. Define them rigorously.
15. Consider the definition of a tree in Section 1.4. Reformulate this definition based on the notion of a partial order.

Solutions to Selected Exercises

9. We prove only the first theorem.

Theorem Let Σ be a set, ρ be a relation on Σ, and ρ^+ be the transitive closure of ρ. Then, (i) ρ^+ is a transitive relation, and (ii) if ρ' is a transitive relation such that $\rho \subseteq \rho'$, then $\rho^+ \subseteq \rho'$.

Proof. To prove (i), we demonstrate that if $a\rho^+b$ and $b\rho^+c$, then $a\rho^+c$, which means that that ρ^+ is a transitive relation. As $a\rho^+b$, there exist $x_1, \ldots, x_n$ in Σ so $x_1\rho x_2, \ldots, x_{n-1}\rho x_n$, where $x_1 = a$ and $x_n = b$. As $b\rho^+c$, there also exist $y_1, \ldots, y_m$ in Σ so $y_1\rho y_2, \ldots, y_{m-1}\rho y_m$, where $y_1 = b$ and $y_m = c$. Consequently, $x_1\rho x_2, \ldots, x_{n-1}\rho x_n, y_1\rho y_2, \ldots, y_{m-1}\rho y_m$, where $x_1 = a$, $x_n = b = y_1$, and $y_m = c$. As a result, $a\rho^+c$.

To prove (ii), we demonstrate that if ρ' is a transitive relation such that $\rho \subseteq \rho'$, then $\rho^+ \subseteq \rho'$. Less formally, (ii) says that ρ^+ is the smallest transitive relation that includes ρ. Let ρ' be a transitive relation such that $\rho \subseteq \rho'$, and let $a\rho^+b$. Then, there exist $x_1, \ldots, x_n$ in Σ so $x_1\rho x_2, \ldots, x_{n-1}\rho x_n$, where $x_1 = a$ and $x_n = b$. As $\rho \subseteq \rho'$, $x_1\rho' x_2, \ldots, x_{n-1}\rho' x_n$ where $x_1 = a$ and $x_n = b$. Because ρ' is transitive, $a\rho'b$. Consequently, $a\rho^+b$ implies $a\rho'b$. ■

11. Let Ω be a set of binary operators, and let Σ be a set of operands.
   a. Every $a \in \Sigma$ is a prefix representation of a.
   b. Let AoB be an infix expression, where $o \in \Omega$, and A, B are infix expressions. Then, oCD is the prefix representation of AoB, where C and D are the prefix representations of A and B, respectively.
   c. Let C be the prefix representation of an infix expression A. Then, C is the prefix representation of (A).

   Consider the infix logical expression $(\mathbf{1} \vee \mathbf{0}) \wedge \mathbf{0}$.
   a. The prefix expressions for $\mathbf{1}$ and $\mathbf{0}$ are $\mathbf{1}$ and $\mathbf{0}$, respectively.
   b. The prefix expression for $\mathbf{1} \vee \mathbf{0}$ is $\vee\ \mathbf{1}\ \mathbf{0}$, so the prefix expression for $(\mathbf{1} \vee \mathbf{0})$ is $\vee\ \mathbf{1}\ \mathbf{0}$, too.
   c. Thus, $\wedge \vee \mathbf{1}\ \mathbf{0}\ \mathbf{0}$ is the prefix expression for $(\mathbf{1} \vee \mathbf{0}) \wedge \mathbf{0}$.

Chapter 2

Formal Languages and Rewriting Systems

The purpose of this chapter is threefold. First, Section 2.1 introduces the terminology concerning formal languages. Second, Section 2.2 introduces rewriting systems. Then, based upon these systems, in an intuitive and preliminary way, it outlines major topics discussed later in this book in a more rigorous and thorough way. Third, Section 2.3 gives a synopsis of this book.

2.1 Formal Languages

An *alphabet* Σ is a finite nonempty set, whose members are called *symbols*. Any nonempty subset of Σ is a *subalphabet* of Σ. A finite sequence of symbols from Σ is a *string* over Σ; specifically, ε is referred to as the *empty string*—that is, the string consisting of zero symbols. By Σ^*, we denote the set of all strings over Σ; $\Sigma^+ = \Sigma^* - \{\varepsilon\}$. Let $x \in \Sigma^*$. Like for any sequence, $|x|$ denotes the *length of x*—that is, the number of symbols in x. For any $a \in \Sigma$, $occur(x, a)$ denotes the number of occurrences of as in x, so $occur(x, a)$ always satisfies $0 \leq occur(x, a) \leq |x|$. Furthermore, if $x \neq \varepsilon$, $symbol(x, i)$ denotes the ith symbol in x, where $i = 1, \ldots, |x|$. Any subset $L \subseteq \Sigma^*$ is a *formal language* or, briefly, a *language* over Σ. Set $symbol(L, i) = \{a |\ a = symbol(x, i), x \in L - \{\varepsilon\}, 1 \leq i \leq |x|\}$. Any subset of L is a *sublanguage* of L. If L represents a finite set of strings, L is a *finite language*; otherwise, L is an *infinite language*. For instance, Σ^*, which is called the *universal language* over Σ, is an infinite language while $\emptyset$ and $\{\varepsilon\}$ are finite; noteworthy, $\emptyset \neq \{\varepsilon\}$ because $card(\emptyset) = 0 \neq card(\{\varepsilon\}) = 1$. Sets whose members are languages are called *families of languages*.

Example 2.1 The English alphabet, consisting of 26 letters, illustrates the definition of an alphabet as stated earlier, except that we refer to its members as symbols in this book. Our definition of a language includes all common artificial and natural languages. For instance, programming languages represent formal languages in terms of this definition, and so do English, Navaho, and Japanese. Any family of natural languages, including Indo-European, Sino-Tibetan, Niger-Congo, Afro-Asiatic, Altaic, and Japonic families of languages, is a language family according to the definition.

Convention 2.1 In strings, for brevity, we simply juxtapose the symbols and omit the parentheses and all separating commas. That is, we write $a_1a_2...a_n$ instead of $(a_1, a_2, ..., a_n)$.

Let ${}_{fin}\Phi$ and ${}_{infin}\Phi$ denote the families of finite and infinite languages, respectively. Let ${}_{all}\Phi$ denote the family of all languages; in other words, ${}_{all}\Phi = {}_{fin}\Phi \cup {}_{infin}\Phi$. ■

Operations. Let $x, y \in \Sigma^*$ be two strings over an alphabet Σ, and let $L, K \subseteq \Sigma^*$ be two languages over Σ. As languages are defined as sets, all set operations apply to them. Specifically, $L \cup K$, $L \cap K$, and $L - K$ denote the union, intersection, and difference of languages L and K, respectively. Perhaps most importantly, the *concatenation of x with y*, denoted by xy, is the string obtained by appending y to x. Notice that for every $w \in \Sigma^*$, $w\varepsilon = \varepsilon w = w$. The concatenation of L and K, denoted by LK, is defined as $LK = \{xy|\ x \in L, y \in K\}$.

Apart from binary operations, we also make some unary operations with strings and languages. Let $x \in \Sigma^*$ and $L \subseteq \Sigma^*$. The *complement* of L is denoted by $\sim L$ and defined as $\sim L = \Sigma^* - L$. The *reversal of x*, denoted by *reversal*(x), is x written in the reverse order, and the *reversal* of L, *reversal*(L), is defined as *reversal*$(L) = \{$*reversal*$(x)|\ x \in L\}$. For all $i \geq 0$, the ith *power of x*, denoted by x^i, is recursively defined as (1) $x^0 = \varepsilon$, and (2) $x^i = xx^{i-1}$, for $i \geq 1$. Observe that this definition is based on the *recursive definitional method*. To demonstrate the recursive aspect, consider, for instance, the ith power of x^i with $i = 3$. By the second part of the definition, $x^3 = xx^2$. By applying the second part to x^2 again, $x^2 = xx^1$. By another application of this part to x^1, $x^1 = xx^0$. By the first part of this definition, $x^0 = \varepsilon$. Thus, $x^1 = xx^0 = x\varepsilon = x$. Hence, $x^2 = xx^1 = xx$. Finally, $x^3 = xx^2 = xxx$. By using this recursive method, we frequently introduce new notions, including the *ith power of L*, L^i, which is defined as (1) $L^0 = \{\varepsilon\}$ and (2) $L^i = LL^{i-1}$, for $i \geq 1$. The *closure of L*, L^*, is defined as $L^* = L^0 \cup L^1 \cup L^2 \cup \dots$, and the *positive closure of L*, L^+, is defined as $L^+ = L^1 \cup L^2 \cup \dots$. Notice that $L^+ = LL^* = L^*L$, and $L^* = L^+ \cup \{\varepsilon\}$. Let $w, x, y, z \in \Sigma^*$. If $xz = y$, then x is a *prefix* of y; if in addition, $x \notin \{\varepsilon, y\}$, x is a *proper prefix* of y. By *prefixes*(y), we denote the set of all prefixes of y. Set *prefixes*$(L) = \{x|\ x \in$ *prefixes*(y) for some $y \in L\}$. For $i = 0, \dots, |y|$, *prefix*(y, i) denotes y's prefix of length i; notice that *prefix*$(y, 0) = \varepsilon$ and *prefix*$(y, |y|) = y$. If $zx = y$, x is a *suffix* of y; if in addition, $x \notin \{\varepsilon, y\}$, x is a *proper suffix* of y. By *suffixes*(y), we denote the set of all suffixes of y. Set *suffixes*$(L) = \{x|\ x \in$ *suffixes*(y) for some $y \in L\}$. For $i = 0, \dots, |y|$, *suffix*(y, i) denotes y's suffix of length i. If $wxz = y$, x is a *substring* of y; if in addition, $x \notin \{\varepsilon, y\}$, x is a *proper substring* of y. By *substrings*(y), we denote the set of all substrings of y. Observe that for all $v \in \Sigma^*$, *prefixes*$(v) \subseteq$ *substrings*(v), *suffixes*$(v) \subseteq$ *substrings*(v), and $\{\varepsilon, v\} \in$ *prefixes*$(v) \cap$ *suffixes*$(v) \cap$ *substrings*(v). Set *symbols*$(y) = \{a|\ a \in$ *substrings*(y), $|a| = 1\}$. Furthermore, set *substrings*$(L) = \{x|\ x \in$ *substrings*(y) for some $y \in L\}$ and *symbols*$(L) = \{a|\ a \in$ *symbols*(y) for some $y \in L\}$.

Example 2.2 Consider the alphabet $\{0, 1\}$. For instance, ε, 1, and 010 are strings over $\{0, 1\}$. Notice that $|\varepsilon| = 0$, $|1| = 1$, and $|010| = 3$. The concatenation of 1 and 010 is 1010. The third power of 1010 equals 101010101010. Observe that *reversal*(1010) = 0101. We have *prefixes*(1010) = $\{\varepsilon, 1, 10, 101, 1010\}$, where 1, 10, and 101 are proper prefixes of 1010 while ε and 1010 are not. We have *suffixes*(1010) = $\{\varepsilon, 0, 10, 010, 1010\}$, *substrings*(1010) = $\{\varepsilon, 0, 1, 01, 10, 010, 101, 1010\}$, and *symbols*(1010) = $\{0, 1\}$.

Set $K = \{0, 01\}$ and $L = \{1, 01\}$. Observe that $L \cup K$, $L \cap K$, and $L - K$ are equal to $\{0, 1, 01\}$, $\{01\}$, and $\{1\}$, respectively. The concatenation of K and L is $KL = \{01, 001, 011, 0101\}$. For L, $\sim L = \Sigma^* - L$, so $\sim L$ contains all strings in $\{0, 1\}^*$ but 1 and 01. Furthermore, *reversal*$(L) = \{1, 10\}$ and $L^2 = \{11, 101, 011, 0101\}$. The strings in L^* that consists of four or fewer symbols are ε, 1, 01, 11, 011, 101, 111, 0101, 0111, 1011, 1101, and 1111. $L^+ = L^* - \{\varepsilon\}$. Notice that *prefixes*$(L) = \{\varepsilon, 1, 0, 01\}$, *suffixes*$(L) = \{\varepsilon, 1, 01\}$, *substrings*$(L) = \{\varepsilon, 0, 1, 01\}$, and *symbols*$(L) = \{0, 1\}$.

Letter	μ	Letter	μ	Letter	μ	Letter	μ
A	· –	*H*	· · · ·	*O*	– – –	*V*	· · · –
B	– · · ·	*I*	· ·	*P*	· – – ·	*W*	· – –
C	– · – ·	*J*	· – – –	*Q*	– – · –	*X*	– · · –
D	– · ·	*K*	– · –	*R*	· – ·	*Y*	– · – –
E	·	*L*	· – · ·	*S*	· · ·	*Z*	– – · ·
F	· · – ·	*M*	– –	*T*	–		
G	– – ·	*N*	– ·	*U*	· · –		

Figure 2.1 Morse code.

Let T and U be two alphabets. A total function τ from T^* to $power(U^*)$ such that $\tau(uv) = \tau(u)\tau(v)$ for every $u, v \in T^*$ is a *substitution* from T^* to U^*. By this definition, $\tau(\varepsilon) = \{\varepsilon\}$ and $\tau(a_1a_2\ldots a_n) = \tau(a_1)\tau(a_2)\ldots\tau(a_n)$, where $a_i \in T$, $1 \leq i \leq n$, for some $n \geq 1$, so τ is completely specified by defining $\tau(a)$ for every $a \in T$. A total function υ from T^* to U^* such that $\upsilon(uv) = \upsilon(u)\upsilon(v)$ for every $u, v \in T^*$ is a *homomorphism* from T^* to U^*. As any homomorphism is obviously a special case of a substitution, we simply specify υ by defining $\upsilon(a)$ for every $a \in T$; if $\upsilon(a) \neq \varepsilon$ for all $a \in T$, υ is said to be an *ε-free homomorphism*. It is worth noting that a homomorphism from T^* to U^* may not represent an injection from T^* to U^* as illustrated in Example 2.3.

Example 2.3 Let ${}_{English}\Delta$ denote the English alphabet. The *Morse code*, denoted by μ, can be seen as a homomorphism from ${}_{English}\Delta^*$ to $\{\cdot, –\}^*$ (see Figure 2.1). For instance,

$$\mu(SOS) = \cdot\cdot\cdot – – – \cdot\cdot\cdot$$

Notice that μ is no injection from ${}_{English}\Delta^*$ to $\{\cdot, –\}^*$; for instance, $\mu(SOS) = \mu(IJS)$.

We conclude this section by Example 2.4, which demonstrates how to represent nonnegative integers by strings in a very simple way. More specifically, it introduces function *unary*, which represents all nonnegative integers by strings consisting of *a*s. Later in this book, especially in Section IV, we frequently make use of *unary*.

Example 2.4 Let a be a symbol. To represent nonnegative integers by strings over $\{a\}$, define the total function *unary* from ${}_0\mathbb{N}$ to $\{a\}^*$ as $unary(i) = a^i$, for all $i \geq 0$. For instance, $unary(0) = \varepsilon$, $unary(2) = aa$, and $unary(1000000) = a^{1000000}$.

2.2 Rewriting Systems

Rewriting systems, defined and discussed in this section, are used in many mathematical and computer science areas, ranging from purely theoretically oriented areas, such as the investigation of computational principals in terms of logic, up to quite pragmatically oriented areas, such as the construction of translators. Considering the subject of this book, it comes as no surprise that we primarily make use of rewriting systems as language-defining models and computational models.

This section is divided into three subsections. Section 2.2.1 introduces rewriting systems in general. Section 2.2.2 treats them as language-defining models. Finally, Section 2.2.3 formalizes the intuitive notion of a procedure by them.

2.2.1 Rewriting Systems in General

Definition 2.2 A *rewriting system* is a pair, $M = (\Sigma, R)$, where Σ is an alphabet, and R is a finite relation on Σ^*. Σ is called the *total alphabet of M* or, simply, the *alphabet of M*. A member of R is called a *rule of M*, and accordingly, R is referred to as the *set of rules* in M.

The *rewriting relation* over Σ^* is denoted by $\Rightarrow$ and defined so that for every $u, v \in \Sigma^*$, $u \Rightarrow v$ in M iff there exist $(x, y) \in R$ and $w, z \in \Sigma^*$ such that $u = wxz$ and $v = wyz$. As usual, $\Rightarrow^*$ denotes the transitive and reflexive closure of $\Rightarrow$. ■

Convention 2.3 Let $M = (\Sigma, R)$ be a rewriting system. Each rule $(x, y) \in R$ is written as $x \rightarrow y$ throughout this book. We often denote $x \rightarrow y$ with a label r as $r: x \rightarrow y$, and instead of $r: x \rightarrow y \in R$, we just write $r \in R$. For $r: x \rightarrow y \in R$, x and y represent the *left-hand side of r*, denoted by ***lhs***(r), and the *right-hand side of r*, denoted by ***rhs***(r), respectively.

R^* denotes the set of all *sequences of rules* from R; accordingly, by $\rho \in R^*$, we briefly express that ρ is a sequence of rules from R. By analogy with strings (see Convention 2.1), in sequences of rules, we simply juxtapose the rules and omit the parentheses as well as all separating commas in them. That is, if $\rho = (r_1, r_2, \ldots, r_n)$, we simply write ρ as $r_1 r_2 \ldots r_n$. To explicitly express that Σ and R represent the components of M, we write ${}_M\Sigma$ and ${}_MR$ instead of Σ and R, respectively. To explicitly express that $\Rightarrow$ and $\Rightarrow^*$ concern M, we write ${}_M\Rightarrow$ and ${}_M\Rightarrow^*$ instead of $\Rightarrow$ and $\Rightarrow^*$, respectively. Furthermore, by $u\ {}_M\Rightarrow v\ [r]$, where $u, v \in \Sigma^*$ and $r \in R$, we express that M directly rewrites u as v according to r. To express that M makes $u\ {}_M\Rightarrow^* w$ according to a sequence of rules, $r_1 r_2 \ldots r_n$, we write $u\ {}_M\Rightarrow^* v\ [r_1 r_2 \ldots r_n]$. Of course, whenever the information regarding the applied rules is immaterial, we omit these rules; in other words, we simplify $u\ {}_M\Rightarrow v\ [r]$ and $u\ {}_M\Rightarrow^* v\ [r_1 r_2 \ldots r_n]$ to $u\ {}_M\Rightarrow v$ and $u\ {}_M\Rightarrow^* v$, respectively. Most often, however, M is understood, so we just write $\Rightarrow$ and $\Rightarrow^*$ instead of ${}_M\Rightarrow$ and ${}_M\Rightarrow^*$, respectively.

By underlining, we specify the substring rewritten during a rewriting step, if necessary. More formally, if $u = wxz$, $v = wyz$, $r: x \rightarrow y \in R$, where $u, v, x, y \in \Sigma^*$, then $w\underline{x}z \Rightarrow wyz\ [r]$ means that the x occurring behind w is rewritten during this step by using r (we usually specify the rewritten occurrence of x in this way when other occurrences of x appear in w and z). ■

Example 2.5 Let us introduce a rewriting system M that translates all strings $x \in {}_{English}\Delta^*$ to the corresponding Morse code $\mu(x)$, where ${}_{English}\Delta$ and μ have the same meaning as in Example 2.3. That is, we define $M = (\Sigma, R)$ with $\Sigma = {}_{English}\Delta \cup \{\cdot, -\}$ and $R = \{a \rightarrow \mu(a) \mid a \in {}_{English}\Delta\}$. Labeling the rules by l_1 through l_{26}, we list them in Figure 2.2.

Define the function $T(M)$ from ${}_{English}\Delta^*$ to $\{\cdot, -\}^*$ as

$$T(M) = \{(s, t) \mid s \Rightarrow^* t,\ s \in {}_{English}\Delta^*,\ t \in \{\cdot, -\}^*\}$$

Observe $T(M) = \mu$, so M actually translates strings from ${}_{English}\Delta^*$ to the corresponding Morse codes. For instance, $T(M)$ contains $(SOS, \ldots --- \ldots)$. Indeed, making use of Convention 2.3, we have

$$
\begin{aligned}
SO\underline{S} &\Rightarrow \underline{S}O \ldots && [l_{19}]\\
&\Rightarrow \ldots \underline{O} \ldots && [l_{15}]\\
&\Rightarrow \ldots --- \ldots && [l_{19}]
\end{aligned}
$$

Thus, $SOS \Rightarrow^* \cdots --- \cdots\ [l_{19}l_{15}l_{19}]$. Therefore, $(SOS, \cdots --- \cdots) \in T(M)$. To rephrase this less mathematically, M translates SOS to its Morse code $\cdots --- \cdots$ as desired.

Rules in R			
l_1: $A \to \cdot -$	l_8: $H \to \cdot\cdot\cdot\cdot$	l_{15}: $O \to - - -$	l_{22}: $V \to \cdot\cdot\cdot -$
l_2: $B \to - \cdot\cdot\cdot$	l_9: $I \to \cdot\cdot$	l_{16}: $P \to \cdot - - \cdot$	l_{23}: $W \to \cdot - -$
l_3: $C \to - \cdot - \cdot$	l_{10}: $J \to \cdot - - - -$	l_{17}: $Q \to - - \cdot -$	l_{24}: $X \to - \cdot\cdot -$
l_4: $D \to - \cdot\cdot$	l_{11}: $K \to - \cdot -$	l_{18}: $R \to \cdot - \cdot$	l_{25}: $Y \to - \cdot - -$
l_5: $E \to \cdot$	l_{12}: $L \to \cdot - \cdot\cdot$	l_{19}: $S \to \cdot\cdot\cdot$	l_{26}: $Z \to - - \cdot\cdot$
l_6: $F \to \cdot\cdot - \cdot$	l_{13}: $M \to - -$	l_{20}: $T \to -$	
l_7: $G \to - - \cdot$	l_{14}: $N \to - \cdot$	l_{21}: $\mathrm{U} \to \cdot\cdot -$	

Figure 2.2 Rules of *M*.

2.2.2 Rewriting Systems as Language Models

In this book, we frequently discuss languages that are infinite, so we cannot specify them by an exhaustive enumeration of all their elements. Instead, we define them by formal models of finite size, and we base these models upon rewriting systems (see Definition 2.2).

Whenever we use a rewriting system, $M = (\Sigma, R)$, as a language-defining model, then for brevity, we denote the language that M defines by $L(M)$. In principal, M defines $L(M)$, so it either *generates* $L(M)$ or *accepts* $L(M)$. Next, we explain these two fundamental language-defining methods in a greater detail. Let $S \subseteq \Sigma^*$ and $F \subseteq \Sigma^*$ be a *start language* and a *final language*, respectively.

I. The *language generated by M* is defined as the set of all strings $y \in F$ such that $x \Rightarrow^* y$ in M for some $x \in S$. M used in this way is generally referred to as a *language-generating model*.
II. The *language accepted by M* is the set of all strings $x \in S$ such that $x \Rightarrow^* y$ in M for some $y \in F$. M used in this way is referred to as a *language-accepting model*.

Convention 2.4 Let D be the notion of a language model defined as a rewriting system, $M = ({}_M\Sigma, {}_MR)$, whose components ${}_M\Sigma$ and ${}_MR$ satisfy some prescribed properties, referred to as D-properties. By ${}_D\Psi$, we denote the entire set of all possible rewriting systems whose components satisfy D-properties; mathematically,

$${}_D\Psi = \{M \mid M = ({}_M\Sigma, {}_MR) \text{ is a rewriting system with } {}_M\Sigma \text{ and } {}_MR \text{ satisfying } D\text{-properties}\}.$$

By ${}_D\Phi$, we denote the family of languages defined by all the rewriting systems contained in ${}_D\Psi$; mathematically:

$${}_D\Phi = \{L(M) \mid M \in {}_D\Psi\}$$ ■

Example 2.6 To illustrate method I, we define the notion of a *parenthesis-generating language model* (*PGLM*) as a rewriting system, $M = ({}_M\Sigma, {}_MR)$, where ${}_M\Sigma$ consists of (and), and ${}_MR$ is a finite set of rules of the form $\varepsilon \to x$ with $x \in {}_M\Sigma^*$. Let $S = \{\varepsilon\}$ and $F = {}_M\Sigma^*$. We define the language generated by M as

$$L(M) = \{t \mid s \Rightarrow^* t, s \in S, t \in F\}$$

In other words,

$$L(M) = \{t|\ \varepsilon \Rightarrow^* t,\ t \in \Sigma^*\}$$

Following Convention 2.5, by ${}_{PGLM}\Psi$, we denote the set of all rewriting systems that represent a *PGLM*—that is, their alphabets consist of (and), and each of their rules has ε as its left-hand side. Furthermore, we set ${}_{PGLM}\Phi = \{L(Z)|\ Z \in {}_{PGLM}\Psi\}$.

Next, we consider $X \in {}_{PGLM}\Psi$ defined as $X = ({}_X\Sigma, {}_XR)$, ${}_X\Sigma$ consists of (and), and

$${}_XR = \{\varepsilon \rightarrow ()\}$$

For example,

$$\varepsilon \Rightarrow () \Rightarrow ()() \Rightarrow (())() \Rightarrow (()())()$$

in X, so $(()())() \in L(X)$. Observe that $L(X)$ consists of all properly nested parentheses; for instance, $() \in L$, but $(() \notin L$.

To illustrate method II, we define the notion of a *parenthesis-accepting language model* (*PALM*) as a rewriting system $M = ({}_M\Sigma, {}_MR)$, where ${}_M\Sigma$ is an alphabet consisting of (and), and ${}_MR$ is a finite set of rules of the form $x \rightarrow \varepsilon$ with $x \in \Sigma^*$. Let $S = \Sigma^*$ and $F = \{\varepsilon\}$. We define the language accepted by M as

$$L(M) = \{s|\ s \Rightarrow^* t,\ s \in S,\ t \in F\}$$

In other words,

$$L(M) = \{s|\ s \Rightarrow^* \varepsilon,\ s \in \Sigma^*\}$$

Let ${}_{PALM}\Psi$ denote the set of all rewriting systems that represent a *PALM*, and let ${}_{PALM}\Phi = \{L(W)|\ W \in {}_{PALM}\Psi\}$.

Next, we consider $Y \in {}_{PALM}\Psi$ defined as $Y = ({}_Y\Sigma, {}_YR)$, where ${}_Y\Sigma$ consists of (and), and

$${}_YR = \{() \rightarrow \varepsilon\}$$

For instance, Y accepts $(())()$

$$(())\underline{()} \Rightarrow (\underline{()}) \Rightarrow \underline{()} \Rightarrow \varepsilon$$

where the underlined substrings denote the substrings that are rewritten (see Convention 2.3). On the other hand, observe that $((\underline{()} \Rightarrow (($, and ((cannot be rewritten by Y, so $((()$ is not accepted by Y. Observe that $L(X) = L(Y)$. More generally, as an exercise, prove that

$${}_{PGLM}\Phi = {}_{PALM}\Phi$$

If some language models define the same language, they are said to be *equivalent*. For instance, in Example 2.6, X and Y are equivalent. More generally, suppose we have defined two language-defining models, referred to as C and D. Let ${}_C\Phi = {}_D\Phi$ (see Convention 2.4); then, Cs and Ds are *equivalent*, or synonymously, Cs and Ds are *equally powerful*. If Cs and Ds are equivalent, we also say that Cs *characterize* ${}_D\Phi$. For instance, in Example 2.6, *PGLM*s and *PALM*s are equivalent because ${}_{PGLM}\Phi = {}_{PALM}\Phi$, so *PGLM*s characterize ${}_{PALM}\Phi$.

For brevity, *language-generating models* are often called *grammars* in this book; for instance, in Example 2.6, the PGLM could be referred to as a *parenthesis grammar* for brevity.

Let $G = ({}_G\Sigma, {}_GR)$ be a grammar. The symbols occurring in $L(G)$ are referred to as *terminal symbols* or, briefly, *terminals*, denoted by ${}_G\Delta$ in this book, so ${}_G\Delta \subseteq {}_G\Sigma$. We set ${}_GN = {}_G\Sigma - {}_G\Delta$, whose members are called *nonterminal symbols* or *nonterminals*. The start language of G always consists of a single symbol; more precisely, ${}_GN$ contains a special *start symbol*, denoted by ${}_GS$, so we always have ${}_G\Delta \subset {}_G\Sigma$. In ${}_GR$, at least one nonterminal occurs on the left-hand side of every rule. If $v \Rightarrow^* w$ in G, where $v, w \in \Sigma^*$, then we say that G *makes a derivation from* v *to* w. The *language generated by* G, $L(G)$, is defined as

$$L(G) = \{w \in {}_G\Delta^* \mid {}_GS \Rightarrow^* w\}$$

Example 2.7 discusses grammars in which the left-hand side of every rule consists of a single nonterminal. As a result, these grammars rewrite nonterminals regardless of the context in which they appear in the strings, hence their name *context-free grammars* (CFGs). Section III of this book is primarily dedicated to them and their languages, naturally referred to as *context-free languages*.

As illustrated in Example 2.7, in a CFG, $G = (\Sigma, R)$, there may exist many different derivations from v to w, where $v, w \in \Sigma^*$. Since a derivation multiplicity like this obviously complicates the discussion of G and $L(G)$, we often reduce it by considering only *leftmost derivations* in which G always rewrites the leftmost nonterminal occurring in the current rewritten string. Unfortunately, even if we reduce our attention only to these derivations, we may still face a derivation multiplicity of some sentences, and this undesirable phenomenon is then referred to as grammatical *ambiguity*.

Convention 2.5 Let $G = (\Sigma, R)$ be a grammar. By analogy with Convention 2.3, to explicitly express that Σ, Δ, N, S, and R represent the above-mentioned components in G, we write ${}_G\Sigma$, ${}_G\Delta$, ${}_GN$, ${}_GS$, and ${}_GR$ instead of plain Σ, Δ, N, S, and R, respectively. ■

Example 2.7 We define the notion of a CFG as a rewriting system, $G = ({}_G\Sigma, {}_GR)$, where ${}_G\Sigma = {}_GN \cup {}_G\Delta$, which satisfy the properties stated previously. Specifically, ${}_GN$ always contains a special start symbol, denoted by ${}_GS$, shortened to S throughout this example. ${}_GR$ is a finite set of rules of the form $A \rightarrow x$ with $A \in {}_GN$ and $x \in {}_G\Sigma^*$. We define the language generated by G as

$$L(G) = \{w \in {}_G\Delta^* \mid S \Rightarrow^* w\}$$

Set ${}_{CFG}\Psi = \{G \mid G \text{ is a CFG}\}$ (see Convention 2.4). Next, we consider two specific instances, U and V, from ${}_{CFG}\Psi$.

Let $U \in {}_{CFG}\Psi$ be defined as $U = ({}_U\Sigma, {}_UR)$, ${}_U\Delta = \{a, b\}$, ${}_UN = \{S, A\}$, and ${}_UR = \{S \rightarrow SS, S \rightarrow A, A \rightarrow aAb, A \rightarrow \varepsilon\}$. For example, U makes

$$\underline{S} \Rightarrow \underline{S}S \Rightarrow \underline{A}S \Rightarrow aAb\underline{S} \Rightarrow aAb\underline{A} \Rightarrow aAba\underline{A}b \Rightarrow a\underline{A}bab \Rightarrow aa\underline{A}bbab \Rightarrow aabbab$$

in U; recall that we specify the rewritten symbols by underlining (see Convention 2.3). Thus, $S \Rightarrow^* aabbab$, so $aabbab \in L(U)$. As an exercise, prove that

$$L(U) = K^*$$

with

$$K = \{a^i b^i \mid i \geq 0\}$$

In words, the language generated by U is the closure of K (see Section 2.1 for the definition of closure).

As already stated, a leftmost derivation is a derivation in which G always rewrites the leftmost nonterminal occurring in every string. While the above-mentioned derivation is not leftmost, the next derivation represents a leftmost derivation from S to *aabbab*:

$$\underline{S} \Rightarrow \underline{S}S \Rightarrow \underline{A}S \Rightarrow a\underline{A}bS \Rightarrow aa\underline{A}bbS \Rightarrow aabb\underline{S} \Rightarrow aabb\underline{A} \Rightarrow aabba\underline{A}b \Rightarrow aabbab$$

Notice, however, that there exist infinitely many other leftmost derivations from S to *aabbab*, including these two leftmost derivations:

$$\underline{S} \Rightarrow \underline{S}S \Rightarrow \underline{S}SS \Rightarrow \underline{A}SS \Rightarrow \underline{S}S \Rightarrow \underline{A}S \Rightarrow a\underline{A}bS \Rightarrow aa\underline{A}bbS \Rightarrow aabb\underline{S} \Rightarrow aabb\underline{A} \Rightarrow aabba\underline{A}b \Rightarrow aabbab$$

$$\underline{S} \Rightarrow \underline{S}S \Rightarrow \underline{A}S \Rightarrow a\underline{A}bS \Rightarrow aa\underline{A}bbS \Rightarrow aabb\underline{S} \Rightarrow aabb\underline{S}S \Rightarrow aabb\underline{A}S \Rightarrow aabba\underline{A}bS \Rightarrow aabbab\underline{S} \Rightarrow aabbab\underline{A} \Rightarrow aabbab$$

Thus, U is ambiguous, which usually represents a highly undesirable property in practice. Therefore, we may prefer using an equivalent unambiguous CFG, such as $V \in {}_{CFG}\Psi$ defined next.

Let $V = ({}_V\Sigma, {}_VR)$, where ${}_V\Delta = \{a, b\}$, ${}_VN = \{S, A\}$, and ${}_VR = \{S \rightarrow AS, S \rightarrow \varepsilon, A \rightarrow aAb, A \rightarrow ab\}$. For example, V generates *aabbab* by this unique leftmost derivation:

$$\underline{S} \Rightarrow \underline{A}S \Rightarrow a\underline{A}bS \Rightarrow aabb\underline{S} \Rightarrow aabb\underline{A}\underline{S} \Rightarrow aabbab\underline{S} \Rightarrow aabbab$$

Clearly, U and V are equivalent; however, U is ambiguous while V is not.

In this book, we often introduce a new notion of a grammar as a special case of the notion of a grammar that has already been defined. To illustrate, we define the notion of a *linear grammar* (*LG*) as a CFG, $H = ({}_H\Sigma, {}_HR)$, in which the right-hand side of every rule contains no more than one occurrence of a nonterminal. In other words, ${}_HR$ is a finite set of rules of the form $A \rightarrow uBv$ with $A \in {}_HN$, $B \in {}_HN \cup \{\varepsilon\}$, and $u, v \in {}_H\Delta^*$. We set ${}_{LG}\Psi = \{G \mid G \text{ is an LG}\}$ (see Convention 2.4).

For instance, consider $W \in {}_{LG}\Psi$ defined as $W = ({}_W\Sigma, {}_WR)$, ${}_W\Delta = \{a, b\}$, ${}_WN = \{S\}$, and ${}_WR = \{S \rightarrow aSb, S \rightarrow \varepsilon\}$. For example,

$$S \Rightarrow aSb \Rightarrow aaSbb \Rightarrow aabb$$

in W. Thus, $aabb \in L(W)$. Observe that $L(W) = K$, where $K = \{a^ib^i \mid i \geq 0\}$ as explained earlier.

We close this example by taking a more general view at CFGs, LGs, and the language families they generate. Following Convention 2.4, set

$${}_{CFG}\Phi = \{L(C) \mid C \in {}_{CFG}\Psi\} \text{ and } {}_{LG}\Phi = \{L(D) \mid D \in {}_{LG}\Psi\}$$

LGs are special cases of CFGs, so ${}_{LG}\Phi \subseteq {}_{CFG}\Phi$. To prove that this inclusion is proper, take

$$K^2 = KK = \{a^ib^ia^jb^j \mid i, j \geq 0\}$$

Observe that no more than one occurrence of a nonterminal appears in any string generated by an LG. As an exercise, make use of this property to prove that no LG generates K^2, so $K^2 \notin {}_{LG}\Phi$. Clearly, $K^2 \in {}_{CFG}\Phi$. Since $K^2 \in {}_{CFG}\Phi - {}_{LG}\Phi$ and ${}_{LG}\Phi \subseteq {}_{CFG}\Phi$, ${}_{LG}\Phi \subset {}_{CFG}\Phi$.

Let M and N be two language models. If ${}_M\Phi \subset {}_N\Phi$ (see Convention 2.4), then we say that Ns are *stronger* or, equivalently speaking, *more powerful* than Ms. For instance, in Example 2.7, we have proved that CFGs are stronger than LGs because ${}_{LG}\Phi \subset {}_{CFG}\Phi$.

Regarding properties of language families, this book pays its principal attention to *closure properties*, which are helpful to answer some important questions concerning these families, such as whether a given language belongs to a language family. To give an insight into them, let o be an n-ary operation. Let Ξ be a language family. We say that Ξ *is closed under* o or, synonymously, *o preserves* Ξ if the application of *o* to any *n* languages in Ξ results into a language that is also in Ξ.

We demonstrate most closure properties *effectively* in this book. To explain what this means, let M be a language-defining model, ${}_M\Psi = \{X \mid X$ is an instance of $M\}$, and ${}_M\Phi = \{L(X) \mid X \in {}_M\Psi\}$. Giving an effective proof that ${}_M\Phi$ is closed under *o* consists in constructing an algorithm that converts any *n* models in ${}_M\Psi$ to a model in ${}_M\Psi$ so that the resulting model defines the language resulting from *o* applied to the languages defined by the *n* models.

In this introductory book, closure properties are discussed only in terms of n-ary operation for $n = 1$ and $n = 2$—that is, only unary and binary operations are considered.

Example 2.8 Let ${}_{CFG}\Phi$ and ${}_{LG}\Phi$ have the same meaning as in Example 2.7. As operation, consider closure (see Section 2.1). Recall that the closure of a language L is denoted by L^*.

First, we effectively prove that ${}_{CFG}\Phi$ is closed under this operation. Let L be any language in ${}_{CFG}\Phi$, and let $X = ({}_X\Sigma, {}_XR)$ be a CFG that generates L, mathematically written as $L = L(X)$. Next, we give an algorithm that converts X to a CFG $Y = ({}_Y\Sigma, {}_YR)$ so Y generates the closure of $L(X)$, symbolically written as $L(Y) = L(X)^*$. Introduce a new symbol, A. Turn X to $Y = ({}_Y\Sigma, {}_YR)$ so ${}_Y\Sigma = {}_X\Sigma \cup \{A\}$, ${}_Y\Delta = {}_X\Delta$, ${}_YR = \{A \rightarrow {}_XSA, A \rightarrow \varepsilon\} \cup {}_XR$, where ${}_XS$ is the start symbol of X. Define A as the start symbol of Y—that is, $A = {}_YS$ (see Convention 2.5). As an exercise, prove that $L(Y) = L(X)^*$. Since $L = L(X)$, $L^* \in {}_{CFG}\Phi$. Hence, ${}_{CFG}\Phi$ is closed under this operation.

Second, we prove that ${}_{LG}\Phi$ is not closed under this operation. Take $K = \{(^i)^i \mid i \geq 0\}$. In Example 2.7, we give an LG W such that $L(W) = K$, so $K \in {}_{LG}\Phi$. Just like in the conclusion of Example 2.7, prove that $K^j \notin {}_{LG}\Phi$, for any $j \geq 2$. By using this result, show that $K^* \notin {}_{LG}\Phi$. Hence, ${}_{LG}\Phi$ is not closed under this operation.

Finally, in I and II given next, we illustrate how to use closure properties to establish results concerning ${}_{CFG}\Phi$ and ${}_{LG}\Phi$.

I. In Example 2.7, we have constructed CFGs that generate K^*. As a consequence, we have actually proved that $K^* \in {}_{CFG}\Phi$ in a constructive way. Now, we demonstrate that closure properties may free us from grammatical constructions in proofs like this. Indeed, as $K \in {}_{LG}\Phi$ and every LG is a special case of a CFG, $K \in {}_{CFG}\Phi$. Since ${}_{CFG}\Phi$ is closed with respect to closure, $K^* \in {}_{CFG}\Phi$, which completes the proof.
II. In Example 2.7, we have also proved that ${}_{LG}\Phi \subset {}_{CFG}\Phi$. By using closure properties, we can establish this proper inclusion in an alternative way. Indeed, by definition, ${}_{LG}\Phi \subseteq {}_{CFG}\Phi$. Since ${}_{CFG}\Phi$ is closed under closure while ${}_{LG}\Phi$ is not, ${}_{LG}\Phi \subset {}_{CFG}\Phi$, and we are done.

2.2.3 Rewriting Systems as Computational Models

While Section 2.2.2 has primarily dealt with language-generating models, this section bases its discussion upon language-accepting models, frequently referred to as *automata* or *machines* for brevity. More specifically, in this section, automata are primarily seen as models of computation. To introduce this important topic, Example 2.9 gives an automaton, which accepts strings just like any other language-accepting model. In addition, however, it acts as a computational model, too.

Example 2.9 We introduce a rewriting system, $M = (\Sigma, R)$, which acts as a computer of well-written postfix Polish expressions, defined in Example 1.1. Set

- $\Sigma = \{\mathbf{0}, \mathbf{1}, \vee, \wedge\}$;
- $R = \{\mathbf{11}\vee \rightarrow \mathbf{1}, \mathbf{10}\vee \rightarrow \mathbf{1}, \mathbf{01}\vee \rightarrow \mathbf{1}, \mathbf{00}\vee \rightarrow \mathbf{0}, \mathbf{11}\wedge \rightarrow \mathbf{1}, \mathbf{10}\wedge \rightarrow \mathbf{0}, \mathbf{01}\wedge \rightarrow \mathbf{0}, \mathbf{00}\wedge \rightarrow \mathbf{0}\}$.

Observe that for all $x \in \Sigma^*$ and $i \in \{\mathbf{0}, \mathbf{1}\}$,

$$x \Rightarrow^* i \text{ iff } x \text{ is a postfix polish expression whose logical value is } i$$

For instance, $\mathbf{10\vee0\wedge} \Rightarrow \mathbf{10\wedge} \Rightarrow \mathbf{0}$, so $\mathbf{10\vee0\wedge} \Rightarrow^* \mathbf{0}$, and observe the logical value of $\mathbf{10\vee0\wedge}$ is indeed $\mathbf{0}$. On the other hand, $\mathbf{101\wedge} \Rightarrow \mathbf{10}$, and from $\mathbf{10}$, M can make no further rewriting step; notice that $\mathbf{101\wedge}$ is no postfix polish expression.

In Example 2.9, M can be viewed as a highly stylized procedure, which evaluates all well-constructed postfix logical expressions over $\{\mathbf{0}, \mathbf{1}, \vee, \wedge\}$. This view brings us to considering rewriting systems as computational models that formalize the intuitive notion of an *effective procedure* or, briefly, a *procedure*—the central notion of computation as a whole. We surely agree that each procedure is finitely describable and consists of discrete steps, each of which can be executed mechanically. That is, throughout this book, we understand the *intuitive notion of a procedure* as a finite set of instructions, each of which can be executed in a fixed amount of time. When executed, a procedure reads input data, executes its instructions, and produces output data. Of course, both the input data and the output data may be nil. An *algorithm* is a special case of a procedure that halts on all inputs. For instance, every computer program represents a procedure, and if the program never enters an endless loop, then it is an algorithm.

In this introductory book, we restrict our attention only to rewriting systems that act as computational models of nonnegative integer functions. To use rewriting systems to compute the numeric functions, we obviously need to represent all nonnegative integers by strings. Traditionally, they are represented in unary. More specifically, every $i \in {}_0\mathbb{N}$ is represented as *unary*(i), where *unary* is defined in Example 2.4. Consequently, $unary(j) = a^j$ for all $j \geq 0$; for instance, *unary*(0), *unary*(2), and *unary*(999) are equal to ε, aa, and a^{999}, respectively.

Example 2.10 describes rewriting systems that act as integer function computers. The way by which they perform their computation strongly resembles the way by which *Turing machines* (TMs) compute integer functions in Section IV of this book. The example also illustrates that just like grammars use some auxiliary symbols, so do automata, whose alphabets often contain some *delimiter* and *state* symbols.

Example 2.10 Let $M = (\Sigma, R)$ be a rewriting system, where $\Sigma = \{\rhd, \lhd, \blacktriangleright, \blacksquare, a\}$, and R is a finite set of rules of the form $x \rightarrow y$, where either $x, y \in \{\rhd\}W$ or $x, y \in W$ or $x, y \in W\{\lhd\}$ with $W = \{a\}^*\{\blacktriangleright, \blacksquare\}\{a\}^*$. Let f be a function over ${}_0\mathbb{N}$. *M computes f* iff the next equivalence holds true:

$$f(i) = j \text{ iff } \rhd\blacktriangleright unary(i)\lhd \Rightarrow^* \rhd\blacksquare unary(j)\lhd \text{ in } M$$

where $i, j \in {}_0\mathbb{N}$. Considering the definition of *unary* (see Example 2.4), we can rephrase this equivalence as

$$f(i) = j \text{ iff } \rhd\blacktriangleright a^i\lhd \Rightarrow^* \rhd\blacksquare a^j\lhd \text{ in } M$$

Notice that the string of *a*s is delimited by $\rhd$ and $\lhd$. M always starts its computation from $\blacktriangleright$, referred to as the *start state*, and finalizes it in $\blacksquare$, referred to as a *final state*.

Let g be the *successor function* defined as $g(i) = i + 1$, for all $i \geq 0$. Informally, we construct a rewriting system, $X = ({}_X\Sigma, {}_XR)$, that computes g so $\rhd\blacktriangleright a^i\lhd \Rightarrow^* \rhd\blacksquare a^{i+1}\lhd$ so it moves $\blacktriangleright$ across a^i to the $\lhd$ and replaces it with $a\lhd$. As a result, in between $\rhd$ and $\lhd$, X increases the number of *a*s by one, so X constructed in this way computes g. Formally, ${}_X\Sigma = \{\rhd, \lhd, \blacktriangleright, \blacksquare, a\}$ and

$${}_XR = \{\blacktriangleright a \rightarrow a\blacktriangleright, \blacktriangleright\lhd \rightarrow \blacksquare a\lhd, a\blacksquare \rightarrow \blacksquare a\}$$

For instance, X computes $g(2) = 3$ as

$$\triangleright\blacktriangleright aa\triangleleft \Rightarrow \triangleright a\blacktriangleright a\triangleleft \Rightarrow \triangleright aa\blacktriangleright\triangleleft \Rightarrow \triangleright aa\blacksquare a\triangleleft \Rightarrow \triangleright a\blacksquare aa\triangleleft \Rightarrow \triangleright\blacksquare aaa\triangleleft$$

Modify X by introducing a new rule of the form $a\blacktriangleright \rightarrow \blacktriangleright a$. Denote the rewriting system modified in this way by Y. Formally, $Y = ({}_Y\Sigma, {}_YR)$, ${}_Y\Sigma = \{\triangleright, \triangleleft, \blacktriangleright, \blacksquare, a\}$, and

$${}_YR = \{\blacktriangleright a \rightarrow a\blacktriangleright,\ a\blacktriangleright \rightarrow \blacktriangleright a,\ \blacktriangleright\triangleleft \rightarrow \blacksquare a\triangleleft,\ a\blacksquare \rightarrow \blacksquare a\}$$

As a simple exercise, prove that Y also computes g. However, Y can move $\blacktriangleright$ across as between $\triangleright$ and $\triangleleft$ in either direction while X cannot. For instance, Y computes $g(2) = 3$ by infinitely many sequences of rewriting steps, including these three sequences:

I. $\triangleright\blacktriangleright aa\triangleleft \Rightarrow \triangleright a\blacktriangleright a\triangleleft \Rightarrow \triangleright aa\blacktriangleright\triangleleft \Rightarrow \triangleright aa\blacksquare a\triangleleft \Rightarrow \triangleright a\blacksquare aa\triangleleft \Rightarrow \triangleright\blacksquare aaa\triangleleft$

II. $\triangleright\blacktriangleright aa\triangleleft \Rightarrow \triangleright a\blacktriangleright a\triangleleft \Rightarrow \triangleright\blacktriangleright aa\triangleleft \Rightarrow \triangleright a\blacktriangleright a\triangleleft \Rightarrow \triangleright aa\blacktriangleright\triangleleft \Rightarrow \triangleright aa\blacksquare a\triangleleft \Rightarrow \triangleright a\blacksquare aa\triangleleft \Rightarrow \triangleright\blacksquare aaa\triangleleft$

III. $\triangleright\blacktriangleright aa\triangleleft \Rightarrow \triangleright a\blacktriangleright a\triangleleft \Rightarrow \triangleright\blacktriangleright aa\triangleleft \Rightarrow \triangleright a\blacktriangleright a\triangleleft \Rightarrow \triangleright\blacktriangleright aa\triangleleft \Rightarrow \triangleright a\blacktriangleright a\triangleleft \Rightarrow \triangleright\blacktriangleright aa\triangleleft \Rightarrow \triangleright a\blacktriangleright a\triangleleft \Rightarrow$
$\triangleright\blacktriangleright aa\triangleleft \Rightarrow \triangleright a\blacktriangleright a\triangleleft \Rightarrow \triangleright\blacktriangleright aa\triangleleft \Rightarrow \triangleright a\blacktriangleright a\triangleleft \Rightarrow \triangleright\blacktriangleright aa\triangleleft \Rightarrow \triangleright a\blacktriangleright a\triangleleft \Rightarrow \triangleright\blacktriangleright aa\triangleleft \Rightarrow \triangleright a\blacktriangleright a\triangleleft \Rightarrow$
$\triangleright aa\blacktriangleright\triangleleft \Rightarrow \triangleright aa\blacksquare a\triangleleft \Rightarrow \triangleright a\blacksquare aa\triangleleft \Rightarrow \triangleright\blacksquare aaa\triangleleft$

We say that X works deterministically while Y does not, and we return to the topic of *determinism* from a more general viewpoint after closing this example.

Let us now demonstrate that we can approach the discussion of rewriting systems acting as computers of functions in the other way around. That is, given a rewriting system, we can naturally ask what function the system computes. Consider, for instance, $Z = ({}_Z\Sigma, {}_ZR)$, ${}_Z\Sigma = \{\triangleright, \triangleleft, \blacktriangleright, \blacksquare, a\}$ and

$${}_ZR = \{\blacktriangleright a \rightarrow aa\blacktriangleright,\ \blacktriangleright\triangleleft \rightarrow \blacksquare\triangleleft,\ a\blacksquare \rightarrow \blacksquare a\}$$

For example, notice that

$$\triangleright\blacktriangleright aa\triangleleft \Rightarrow \triangleright aa\blacktriangleright a\triangleleft \Rightarrow \triangleright aaaa\blacktriangleright\triangleleft \Rightarrow \triangleright aaaa\blacksquare\triangleleft \Rightarrow \triangleright aaa\blacksquare a\triangleleft \Rightarrow \triangleright aa\blacksquare aa\triangleleft \Rightarrow$$
$$\triangleright a\blacksquare aaa\triangleleft \Rightarrow \triangleright\blacksquare aaaa\triangleleft$$

More generally, M deterministically computes the function $f(i) = 2i$ for all $i \geq 0$; for instance, $f(1) = 2$ and $f(9) = 18$. Indeed, starting from $\triangleright\blacktriangleright a^i\triangleleft$, it computes $\triangleright\blacktriangleright a^i\triangleleft \Rightarrow^* \triangleright\blacksquare a^{2i}\triangleleft$ for all $i \geq 0$.

Finally, let us point out that we can approach computational models in a more fundamental way. Return to the definition given in the beginning of this example, and assume that f may be, in a general case, a partial function. Under this assumption, literally every rewriting system with $\{\triangleright, \triangleleft, \blacktriangleright, \blacksquare, a\}$ as its alphabet computes a function. At a glance, this statement sounds almost incredible because we may have rewriting systems with rules by which they can never compute anything (for instance, this is the case whenever they have no rule containing $\blacksquare$); consequently, the computed function is undefined for all arguments. However, realize that functions that are everywhere undefined are mathematically legitimate instances of partial functions, too. When discussing models of computation later in Chapter 10, we will also approach them in such a general way—that is, we will consider the entire set of them all as well as the corresponding set of functions computed by them. Indeed, we will define functions computed by aforementioned TMs. We will investigate the set of all these functions in order to find out what is computable by computers and what is not, which is obviously a problem area of general mathematical as well as philosophical interest.

Consider X and Y in the previous example. They both compute the same function by rewriting strings over K, where $K = \triangleright\{a\}^*\{\blacktriangleright, \blacksquare\}\{a\}^*\triangleleft$. As already pointed out in the example, however, in terms of the way they work, there exists a fundamental difference between X and Y—the former works deterministically over K while the latter does not. That is, X rewrites any string from K by no more than one rule while Y does not satisfy this property.

Definition 2.6 Let $M = (\Sigma, R)$ be a rewriting system and $K \subseteq \Sigma^*$. M is *deterministic over* K if for every $w \in K$, there is no more than one $r \in R$ such that $w\ {}_M\!\Rightarrow v\ [r]$ with $v \in K$ (when K is understood, we usually just say that M is *deterministic*). ■

Consequently, if M is deterministic over K, then ${}_M\!\Rightarrow$ represents a function over K—that is, for all $u, v, w \in K$, if $u\ {}_M\!\Rightarrow v$ and $u\ {}_M\!\Rightarrow w$, then $v = w$. In general, the basic versions of various types of rewriting systems are always introduced quite generally and, therefore, nondeterministically in the theory of computational and language models. That is also why we first define the basic versions of these models in a nondeterministic way throughout this book. In practice, however, we obviously prefer their deterministic versions because they are easier to implement. Therefore, we usually place a restriction on their rules so that the models with rules restricted in this way necessarily work deterministically. Of course, we always study whether all the nondeterministic versions can be converted to equivalent deterministic versions, and if so, we want to perform this conversion algorithmically. As determinism obviously represents such an important investigation area, we pay a special attention to this topic throughout this book.

As pointed out in the conclusion of Example 2.10, when discussing models of computation, we are inescapably lead to a certain *metaphysics of computation*, trying to find out what computers can compute and what they cannot. To narrow this investigation to mathematics, we obviously want to know whether there is a procedure that computes any function. Unfortunately, the answer is no. To justify this answer, we need a formalization of the intuitive notion of a procedure, and any formalization of this kind obviously has to satisfy the essential property that each of its instances is finitely describable. Suppose we have a general mathematical model Γ formalizing the intuitive notion of a procedure that satisfies this property. All the instances of Γ are countable because we can make a list of all their finite descriptions, for instance, according to length and alphabetic order, so the set of these descriptions is equal in cardinality to $\mathbb{N}$. However, we already know that the set of all functions is uncountable (see Example 1.3), so there necessarily exist functions that cannot be computed by any procedure. Simply put, the number of all functions is uncountable while the number of formalized procedures is countable.

More surprisingly, even if we narrow our attention to the set ϕ containing all total functions over $\mathbb{N}$, by using the diagonalization proof technique (see Example 1.3), the theory of *computability*, which studies questions of this kind, can easily demonstrate a specific function $g \in \phi$ that cannot be computed by any Γ-formalized procedure. Indeed, since each function $h \in \phi$ is total, it has to be computed by an algorithm, which always halts and produces $h(j)$ for all $j \in \mathbb{N}$. For the sake of contradiction, suppose that all functions in ϕ are computed by an algorithm formalized by an instance of Γ. Consider all the descriptions of the Γ instances that compute the functions in ϕ. Let ${}_1F, {}_2F, \ldots$ be an enumeration of these finite descriptions. By ${}_iF\text{-}f$, we denote the function computed by the algorithm formalized by the model described as ${}_iF$ in the enumeration. Define the function g as $g(k) = {}_kF\text{-}f(k) + 1$, for all $k \in \mathbb{N}$. As $g \in \phi$, the enumeration ${}_1F, {}_2F, \ldots, {}_jF, \ldots$ contains ${}_jF$ such that ${}_jF\text{-}f$ coincides with g, for some $j \geq 1$. Then, ${}_jF\text{-}f(j) = g(j) = {}_jF\text{-}f(j) + 1$, which is a contradiction. Thus, no Γ-formalized algorithm computes g.

Apart from uncomputable functions, there also exist undecidable problems, which cannot be decided by any algorithm. More regretfully and surprisingly, the theory of *decidability* has even proved that there will never exist algorithms that decide problems with genuine significance in computer science as a whole. For instance, it is undecidable whether a program always halts; that is, the existence of a general algorithm that decides this problem is ruled out once and for all.

However, even if we restrict our attention only to decidable problems and take a closer look at them, we find out that they significantly differ in terms of their *time and space computational complexity*. Indeed, two decidable problems may differ so the computation of one problem takes reasonable amount of time while the computation of the other does not—that is, compared to the first problem, the other problem is considered as *intractable* because its solution requires an unmanageable amount of time. Thus, apart from theoretically oriented investigation, this study of computational complexity is obviously crucially important to most application-oriented areas of computer science as well.

2.3 Synopsis of the Book

In this section, we link all the terminology introduced in this chapter to the rest of this book and, thereby, make its synopsis. The book is divided into Sections I through V. Section I is concluded by this chapter. The others are outlined next.

In this book, the most important language-defining models are finite automata, CFGs, and TMs, which define the language families denoted by ${}_{FA}\Phi$, ${}_{CFG}\Phi$, and ${}_{TM}\Phi$, respectively. Accordingly, Sections II, III, and IV cover models, applications, and properties concerning ${}_{FA}\Phi$, ${}_{CFG}\Phi$, and ${}_{TM}\Phi$, respectively. Each of these sections consists of three chapters.

Section II

Section II consists of Chapters 3 through 5. Chapter 3 introduces finite automata and regular expressions as the basic language models that characterize ${}_{FA}\Phi$, whose languages are usually referred to as regular languages. Chapter 4 demonstrates how to apply these models to text processing. Specifically, based upon them, it builds up lexical analyzers. Finally, Chapter 5 establishes several properties, including closure properties, which are helpful to prove or disprove that some languages are regular.

Section III

Section III consists of Chapters 6 through 8. Chapter 6 defines already mentioned CFGs, which characterize ${}_{CFG}\Phi$—the family of context-free languages. In addition, it defines pushdown automata, which also characterize ${}_{CFG}\Phi$, so these grammars and automata are equivalent. Chapter 7 applies these models to syntax analysis. It explains how to describe programming language syntax by CFGs and, then, convert these grammars to efficient syntax analyzers that act as pushdown automata. In many respects, Chapter 8 parallels Chapter 5; however, Chapter 8 obviously studies language properties in terms of ${}_{CFG}\Phi$. That is, it establishes many properties concerning CFGs and explains how to use them to answer certain important questions concerning them.

Section IV

While Sections II and III make use of various rewriting systems as language-defining models, Section IV uses them primarily as computational models. It consists of Chapters 9 through 11. Chapter 9 defines already mentioned TMs. Based upon them, Chapter 10 outlines the theory of computability, decidability, and computational complexity. To link these machines to the theory of formal languages, Chapter 11 considers them as language-accepting models, defines their grammatical counterparts, and establishes the relation between several subfamilies of ${}_{TM}\Phi$. Perhaps most importantly, it states that

$${}_{fin}\Phi \subset {}_{FA}\Phi \subset {}_{CFG}\Phi \subset {}_{TM}\Phi \subset {}_{all}\Phi$$

Section V

The purpose of the final one-chapter section is fourfold. First, it summarizes this book. Second, it places all its material into a historical and bibliographical context. Third, it selects several modern and advanced topics, omitted in this introductory book, and gives their overview. Finally, Section V suggests further reading for the serious student.

Exercises

1. Let Σ be an alphabet. Let $x = aaabababbb$, where $a, b \in \Sigma$. Determine $prefix(x)$, $suffix(x)$, and $substring(x)$.
2. Give a nonempty string x such that $x^i = reversal(x)^i$, for all $i \geq 0$.
3 S. Let $L = \{a^n | \; n \geq 2\}$ be a language over an alphabet, Σ. Determine $\sim L$ with (i) $\Sigma = \{a\}$ and (ii) $\Sigma = \{a, b\}$.
4. Let Σ be an alphabet. Prove that every $x \in \Sigma^*$ satisfies (a) through (c), given next.
   a. $prefix(x) \subseteq substring(x)$
   b. $suffix(x) \subseteq substring(x)$
   c. $\{\varepsilon, x\} \subseteq prefix(x) \cap suffix(x) \cap substring(x)$
5. Select some common components of your favorite programming language. Specify them by using the notions introduced in Section 2.1, such as various language operations. For instance, consider integers in C and specify them by using such simple operations as concatenation and closure.
6 S. Formalize the usual dictionary order as a *lexicographic order* based upon a linear order, defined in Exercise 8 in Chapter 1. Write a program that implements the lexicographic order. Test this program on a large file of English words.
7. Let Σ be an alphabet. Prove or disprove each of the following four statements.
   a. For all $i \geq 0$, $\varepsilon^i = \varepsilon$.
   b. For all $x \in \Sigma^*$, $x\varepsilon = \varepsilon x = x$.
   c. For all $x \in \Sigma^*$, $x^i x^j = x^j x^i = x^{i+j}$.
   d. For all $x, y \in \Sigma^*$, $reversal(xy) = reversal(y)reversal(x)$.
8. Consider the language $L = \{011, 111, 110\}$. Determine $reversal(L)$, $prefix(L)$, $suffix(L)$, L^2, L^*, and L^+.
9. Prove that every language L satisfies $L\{\varepsilon\} = \{\varepsilon\}L = L$, $L\varnothing = \varnothing L = \varnothing$, $L^+ = LL^* = L^*L$, and $L^* = L^+ \cup \{\varepsilon\}$.
10. Let Σ be an alphabet. Determine all languages L over Σ satisfying $L^* = L$; for instance, Σ^* is one of them.
11. Let Σ be an alphabet. Prove that the family of all finite languages over Σ is countable, but the family $power(\Sigma^*)$—that is, the family of all languages over Σ—is not countable.
12. Let K and L be two finite languages over $\{0, 1\}$ defined as $K = \{00, 11\}$ and $L = \{0, 00\}$. Determine KL, $K \cup L$, $K \cap L$, and $K - L$.
13 S. Prove or disprove that the following two equations hold for any two languages J and K.
   a. $(J \cup K)^* = (J^*K^*)^*$
   b. $(JK \cup K)^* = J(KJ \cup J)^*$
14. Consider each of the following equations. Prove or disprove that it holds for any three languages J, K, and L.
   a. $(JK)L = J(KL)$
   b. $(J \cup K)L = JL \cup KL$
   c. $L(J \cup K) = LJ \cup LK$

d. $(J \cap K)L = JL \cap KL$
e. $L(J \cap K) = LJ \cap LK$
f. $L(J - K) = LJ - LK$

15. Let Σ be an alphabet. In terms of formal languages, *DeMorgan's law* says that $\sim(\sim K \cup \sim L) = K \cap L$ for any two languages K and L over Σ. Prove this law.

16 S. Recall that a rewriting system is a pair, $M = (\Sigma, R)$, where Σ is an alphabet, and R is a finite relation on Σ^* (see Definition 2.2). Furthermore, the rewriting relation over Σ^* is denoted by $\Rightarrow$ and defined so that for every $u, v \in \Sigma^*$, $u \Rightarrow v$ in M iff there exist $x \rightarrow y \in R$ and $w, z \in \Sigma^*$ such that $u = wxz$ and $v = wyz$. For every $n \geq 0$, the n-fold product of $\Rightarrow$ is denoted by $\Rightarrow^n$. Determine $m \in {}_0\mathbb{N}$ satisfying for all $u, v \in \Sigma^*$ and $n \geq 0$, $u \Rightarrow^n v$ in M implies $|v| \leq nm|u|$.

17. Let $G = (\Sigma, R)$ be a rewriting system (see Definition 2.2), $v, w \in \Sigma^*$, and $v \Rightarrow^* w$. If w cannot be rewritten by any rule from R—in other words, $w \Rightarrow z$ is false for any $z \in \Sigma^*$, then $v \Rightarrow^* w$ is said to be *terminating*, symbolically written as $v\ {}_t\!\Rightarrow^* w$. Let $S \in \Sigma$ be a special start symbol. Set ${}_tL(G) = \{w \in \Sigma^* \mid S\ {}_t\!\Rightarrow^* w\}$.

Consider each of the following languages over $\{a, b, c\}$. Construct a rewriting system G such that ${}_tL(G)$ coincides with the language under consideration.

a. $\{a^i b a^j b a^i \mid i, j \geq 1\}$
b. $\{a^i b a^i \mid i \geq 0\}$
c. $\{a^i b^i a^{2i} \mid i \geq 0\}$
d. $\{a^i b^j c^i \mid i \geq 0 \text{ and } j \geq 1\}$
e. $\{b^i a^j b^i c^j \mid i, j \geq 0\}$
f. $\{b^i a^k b^k a^l b^k \mid i, j \geq 0,\ i = k \text{ or } l = k\}$
g. $\{x \mid x \in \{a, b, c\}^*, occur(x, a) > occur(x, b) > occur(x, c)\}$
h. $\{x \mid x \in \{a, b, c\}^*, occur(x, a) = occur(x, b) = occur(x, c)\}$
i. $\{a^i \mid i = 2^n, i \geq 0\}$
j. $\{xx \mid x \in \{a, b\}^*\}$

18. Return to Example 2.7.
a. Modify CFGs so S is a finite language, not a single symbol. Formalize this modification. Are the CFGs modified in this way as powerful as CFGs?
b. Rephrase and solve (a) in terms of LGs.

19 S. Is every formal language defined by a language-defining rewriting system? Justify your answer.

20 S. Define the notion of a rewriting system that acts as computers of functions over Σ^*, where Σ is any alphabet. Then, based on this definition, introduce a specific rewriting system that acts as a computer of the function f over $\{\mathbf{0}, \mathbf{1}, \vee, \wedge\}^*$ defined for all $x \in \Sigma^*$ and $i \in \{\mathbf{0}, \mathbf{1}\}$, by this equivalence: $f(x) = i$ iff x is a prefix Polish expression whose logical value is i.

21 S. Consider Example 2.5 and Definition 2.6.
a. Consider M in Example 2.5. Demonstrate that M rewrites strings nondeterministically in terms of Definition 2.6.
b. Modify Example 2.5 as follows. Redefine $M = (\Sigma, R)$ so $\Sigma = {}_{English}\Delta \cup \{\cdot, -, \#\}$ and $R = \{a \rightarrow \mu(a)\# \mid a \in {}_{English}\Delta\}$. Define the function ν from ${}_{English}\Delta^*$ to $\{\cdot, -, \#\}^*$ as $\nu = \{(s, t) \mid s \Rightarrow^* t \text{ in } M, s \in {}_{English}\Delta^*, t \in \{\cdot, -, \#\}^*\}$; for instance, ν contains $(SOS, \cdots\# - - - \# \cdots \#)$. Construct deterministic rewriting systems D and E that define ν and $inverse(\nu)$, respectively.

Solutions to Selected Exercises

3. If $\Sigma = \{a\}$, $\sim L = \{\varepsilon, a\}$. If $\Sigma = \{a, b\}$, $\sim L = \{a, b\}^* - \{a\}\{a\}^+$.

6. Let Σ be a set, and let β be a linear order on Σ. We extend β to Σ^* so that for any $x, y \in \Sigma^*$, $x\beta y$ if $x \in prefixes(y) - \{y\}$, or for some $k \geq 1$ such that $|x| > k$ and $|y| > k$, $prefix(x, k - 1) = prefix(y, k - 1)$ and $symbol(x, k)\beta symbol(y, k)$. This extended definition of β is referred to as the *lexicographic order* β on Σ^*. Take, for instance, Σ as the English alphabet and β as its alphabetical order. Then, the lexical order β extended in the above-mentioned way represents the usual dictionary order on Σ^*.

13. To disprove (ii), take J and K as any two languages such that $\varepsilon \notin J$ and $\varepsilon \in K$; then, $\varepsilon \in (JK \cup K)^*$, but $\varepsilon \notin J(KJ \cup J)^*$.
16. Take m as the minimal nonnegative integer satisfying $m \geq |x| - |y|$, for all $x \rightarrow y \in R$. By induction on $n \geq 0$, prove that for all $u, v \in \Sigma^*$, $u \Rightarrow^n v$ in M implies $|v| \leq nm|u|$.
19. In the conclusion of Section 2.2, there is an explanation why some functions cannot be computed by any procedure, which has a finite description. Make use of a similar argument to prove that some formal languages are not defined by any language-defining rewriting systems.
20. Let Σ be an alphabet. Without any loss of generality, suppose that Σ and $\{\triangleright, \triangleleft, \blacktriangleright, \blacksquare\}$ are disjoint. Let $M = (W, R)$ be a rewriting system, where $W = \Sigma \cup \{\triangleright, \triangleleft, \blacktriangleright, \blacksquare\}$, and R is a finite set of rules of the form $x \rightarrow y$, where either $x, y \in \{\triangleright\}X$ or $x, y \in X$ or $x, y \in X\{\triangleleft\}$ with $X = \Sigma^*\{\blacktriangleright, \blacksquare\}\Sigma^*$. Let f be a function over Σ^*. M *computes* f iff this equivalence holds true: $f(x) = y$ iff $\triangleright\blacktriangleright x\triangleleft \Rightarrow^* \triangleright\blacksquare y\triangleleft$ in M, where $x, y \in \Sigma^*$.

    Define the rewriting system $M = (W, R)$ with $W = \{\mathbf{0}, \mathbf{1}, \vee, \wedge, \triangleright, \triangleleft, \blacktriangleright, \blacksquare\}$ and

$$\begin{aligned} R = {} & \{\blacktriangleright\vee ij \rightarrow \blacktriangleright k \mid i, j, k \in \{\mathbf{0}, \mathbf{1}\}, k = \mathbf{0} \text{ iff } i = j = \mathbf{0}\} \\ & \cup \{\blacktriangleright\wedge ij \rightarrow \blacktriangleright k \mid i, j, k \in \{\mathbf{0}, \mathbf{1}\}, k = \mathbf{1} \text{ iff } i = j = \mathbf{1}\} \\ & \cup \{\blacktriangleright i \rightarrow i\blacktriangleright \mid i \in \{\mathbf{0}, \mathbf{1}, \vee, \wedge\}\} \\ & \cup \{i\blacktriangleright \rightarrow \blacktriangleright i \mid i \in \{\mathbf{0}, \mathbf{1}, \vee, \wedge\}\} \\ & \cup \{\blacktriangleright i\triangleleft \rightarrow \blacksquare i\triangleleft \mid i \in \{\mathbf{0}, \mathbf{1}\}\} \end{aligned}$$

    Observe that for all $x \in \Sigma^*$ and $i \in \{\mathbf{0}, \mathbf{1}\}$, $f(x) = i$ iff x is a prefix Polish expression whose logical value is i. For instance, $\triangleright\blacktriangleright\wedge\vee\mathbf{100}\triangleleft \Rightarrow \triangleright\wedge\blacktriangleright\vee\mathbf{100}\triangleleft \Rightarrow \triangleright\wedge\blacktriangleright\mathbf{10}\triangleleft \Rightarrow \triangleright\blacktriangleright\wedge\mathbf{10}\triangleleft \Rightarrow \triangleright\blacktriangleright\mathbf{0}\triangleleft \Rightarrow \triangleright\blacksquare\mathbf{0}\triangleleft$.
21. Consider (a). Notice that, for instance, $SO\underline{S} \Rightarrow SO\cdots$ and $\underline{S}OS \Rightarrow \cdots OS$ in M, so M rewrites strings nondeterministically in terms of Definition 2.6.

    Consider (b). Define $D = ({}_D\Sigma, {}_DR)$ with ${}_D\Sigma = {}_{English}\Delta \cup \{S, \cdot, -, \#, \$\}$ and ${}_DR = \{Sa \rightarrow \mu(a)S \mid a \in {}_{English}\Delta\} \cup \{S\$ \rightarrow \$\}$. Define $T(D) = \{(s, t) \mid Ss\$ \Rightarrow^* t\$, s \in {}_{English}\Delta^*, t \in \{\cdot, -, \#\}^*\}$. Prove that $T(D) = \nu$.

    Define $E = ({}_E\Sigma, {}_ER)$ with ${}_E\Sigma = {}_D\Sigma$ and ${}_ER = \{S\mu(a) \rightarrow aS \mid a \in {}_{English}\Delta\} \cup \{S\$ \rightarrow \$\}$. Define $T(E) = \{(s, t) \mid Ss\$ \Rightarrow^* t\$, s \in \{\cdot, -, \#\}^*, t \in {}_{English}\Delta^*\}$. Prove that $T(E) = inverse(\nu)$.

REGULAR LANGUAGES AND THEIR MODELS

II

A language over an alphabet is regular if it can be obtained from the empty string and the symbols in the alphabet by, finitely, many applications of three language operations—union, concatenation, and closure. Defined in this way, regular languages are obviously very simple. Nevertheless, these languages and their models come up in a large number of application areas within computer science. Indeed, they are used to design various computer-science units, ranging from many hardware components, such as switching circuits, to software tools, such as various text processing programs and lexical analyzers. Consequently, these languages are central to much of the formal language theory, so this three-chapter section of the book explores them in detail.

Chapter 3 introduces two fundamental models for regular languages—finite automata and regular expressions. A finite automaton represents a language-accepting rewriting system (see Section 2.2). Based on, finitely, many states and rules, it works by making moves on an input string in a left-to-right symbol-by-symbol way. During a move, the finite automaton reads a symbol and changes the current state according to one of its rules. If it reads the entire string and enters a final state, the automaton accepts the input string, and the set of all accepted strings in this way forms the language that the automaton defines. Compared to this language-accepting approach, in a more straightforward way, a regular expression defines its language without involving any rewriting systems. Indeed, it is a rather simple language-denoting formula consisting of ε, the symbols, and three operators that denote union, concatenation, and closure. We prove that both models, including some of their variants, are equivalent—that is, they characterize the family of regular languages.

Chapter 4 describes applications of regular expressions and finite automata in lexical analysis as a typical software-oriented application area underlain by these models.

Chapter 5 establishes fundamental properties of regular languages. It concentrates its attention on establishing properties that allow us to prove or, in contrast, disprove that a given language is regular, which obviously represents perhaps the most essential information about the language.

Chapter 3

Models for Regular Languages

In this three-section chapter, we discuss finite automata and regular expressions as basic models for regular languages. In Section 3.1, we define the basic model of a finite automaton. Then, in Section 3.2, we introduce several restricted, but equivalent versions of this basic model. Finally, in Section 3.3, we define regular expressions and demonstrate the equivalence between them and finite automata.

3.1 Finite Automata

We next define finite automata as special cases of rewriting systems, introduced in Section 2.2. Therefore, we straightforwardly apply the terminology concerning rewriting systems to finite automata. Perhaps, most significantly, we apply relations $\Rightarrow$, $\Rightarrow^n$, $\Rightarrow^+$, and $\Rightarrow^*$ to them.

Definition 3.1 A *finite automaton* (*FA* for short) is a rewriting system $M = (\Sigma, R)$, where

- Σ contains subsets Q, F, and Δ such that $\Sigma = Q \cup \Delta$, $F \subseteq Q$, and $Q \cap \Delta = \emptyset$
- R is a finite *set of rules* of the form $qa \rightarrow p$, where $q, p \in Q$ and $a \in \Delta \cup \{\varepsilon\}$

Q, F and Δ are referred to as the *set of states*, the *set of final states* and the *alphabet of input symbols*, respectively. Q contains a special state called the *start state*, usually denoted by s. M *accepts* $w \in \Delta^*$ if $sw \Rightarrow^* f$ in M with $f \in F$. The *language accepted by M* or, briefly, the *language of M* is denoted by $L(M)$ and defined as the set of all strings that M accepts; formally,

$$L(M) = \{w \mid w \in \Delta^*, sw \Rightarrow^* f, f \in F\}$$ ■

Every string an FA M rewrites has the form qav, where $q \in Q$, $a \in \Delta \cup \{\varepsilon\}$, and $v \in \Delta^*$. By using a rule of the form $qa \rightarrow p$, where $q, p \in Q$ and $a \in \Delta \cup \{\varepsilon\}$, M reads a and changes q to p. By repeatedly performing rewriting steps like this, M reads the string of input symbols in a left-to-right way and, simultaneously, moves the current state closer toward its right end. M accepts $w \in \Delta^*$ if starting from sw, it reads all the input string and ends up in a final state.

We next introduce some specific terminology concerning finite automata. We use this terminology throughout this book whenever finite automata are under discussion.

Convention 3.2 We denote the set of all finite automata by ${}_{FA}\Psi$. Set ${}_{FA}\Phi = \{L(M)| \ M \in {}_{FA}\Psi\}$. For every $M \in {}_{FA}\Psi$, a *configuration* of M is a string of the form qv, where $v \in \Delta^*$ and $q \in Q$. ${}_{M}X$ denotes the set of all configurations of M. If $\beta \Rightarrow \chi$ in M, where $\beta, \chi \in {}_{M}X$, M makes a *move* or a *computational step* from β to χ. M makes a *sequence of moves* or a *computation* from β to χ if $\beta \Rightarrow^* \chi$ in M, where $\beta, \chi \in {}_{M}X$. A computation of the form $sw \Rightarrow^* f$, where $w \in \Delta^*$ and $f \in F$, is called an *accepting computation*.

Furthermore, we automatically assume that Σ, Δ, Q, s, F, and R denote its total alphabet, the alphabet of input symbols, the set of states, the start state, the set of final states, and the set of rules of M, respectively. ■

Let us point out that apart from Convention 3.2, we frequently apply the previously introduced Convention 2.3 to FAs as well. That is, for any $M \in {}_{FA}\Psi$, whenever there exists any danger of confusion concerning its components, we mark Σ, Δ, Q, s, F, and R with M as ${}_{M}\Sigma$, ${}_{M}\Delta$, ${}_{M}Q$, ${}_{M}s$, ${}_{M}F$, and ${}_{M}R$, respectively, to explicitly relate these components to M (in particular, we make these marks when several automata are simultaneously discussed).

3.1.1 Representations of Finite Automata

Throughout this book, we represent any $M \in {}_{FA}\Psi$ in one of the following five ways.

1. The *formal description* of M spells out the states, symbols, and rules of M strictly according to Definition 3.1.
2. M is defined by simply *listing its rules* together with specifying the start state and the final states of M.
3. M is specified by its *state table* whose columns and rows are denoted with the members of $\Delta \cup \{\varepsilon\}$ and the states of Q, respectively. The start state denotes the first row. The final states are specified by underlining. For each $q \in Q$ and each $a \in \Delta \cup \{\varepsilon\}$, the entry in row q and column a contains $\{p| \ qa \rightarrow p \in R\}$. For brevity, we omit the braces in the sets of these entries; a blank entry means $\emptyset$.
4. M is specified by its *state diagram* in a pictorial way. That is, this diagram is a labeled directed graph such that each node is labeled with a state $q \in Q$, and for two nodes $q, p \in Q$, there is an edge (q, p) labeled with $\{a| \ qa \rightarrow p \in R, a \in \Delta \cup \{\varepsilon\}\}$. For simplicity, we entirely omit every edge labeled with $\emptyset$ in the diagram. Furthermore, in the specification of edge-labeling nonempty sets, we omit the braces; for instance, instead of $\{a, b\}$ as an edge label, we just write a, b. To symbolically state that a state s is the start state, we point to it with a short arrow like in Figure 3.1. Final states are doubly circled.
5. We give an *informal description* of M. That is, we describe it as a procedure, omitting various details concerning their components. Describing M in this way, we always make sure that the translation from this description to the corresponding formal description represents a straightforward task.

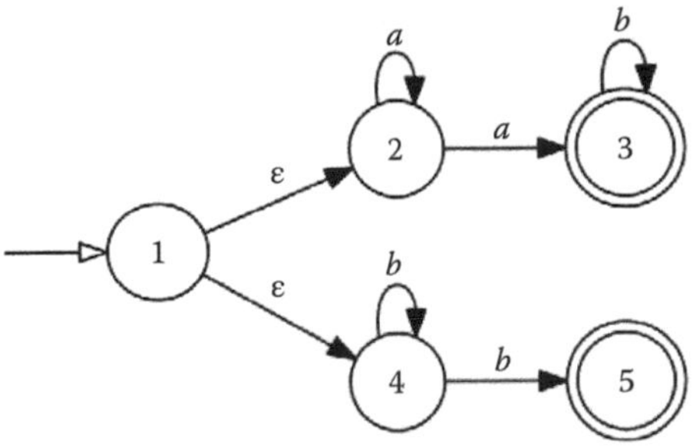

Figure 3.1 State diagram.

Example 3.1 In this example, we design an FA M that accepts $\{a\}^+\{b\}^* \cup \{b\}^+$, symbolically written as

$$L(M) = \{a\}^+\{b\}^* \cup \{b\}^+$$

We describe M in all five ways sketched earlier.

Informal description. We design M so it accepts either w_1w_2 or w_3, where $w_1 \in \{a\}^+$, $w_2 \in \{b\}^*$, $w_3 \in \{b\}^+$; therefore, $L(M) = \{a\}^+\{b\}^* \cup \{b\}^+$. From its start state 1, without reading any input symbol, M moves either to states 2 to accept w_1w_2 or to state 4 to accept w_3. Looping 2, M can read any number of *a*s. In addition, M can make a move from 2 to state 3 while reading a. In 3, M reads any number of *b*s. As 3 is a final state, M completes the acceptance of w_1w_2 in this way. To accept w_3, in 4, M reads any number of *b*s. In addition, M can make a move from 4 to state 5 with b. Since 5 is a final state, M completes the acceptance of w_3.

List of Rules. M is defined by the following seven rules:

$$1 \to 2,\ 1 \to 4,\ 2a \to 2,\ 2a \to 3,\ 3b \to 3,\ 4b \to 4,\ 4b \to 5$$

where 1 is the start state while 3 and 5 are final states.

Formal description. Let $M = (\Sigma, R)$, where $\Sigma = Q \cup \Delta$ with $Q = \{1, 2, 3, 4, 5\}$, $\Delta = \{a, b\}$, $F = \{3, 5\}$, and 1 is the start state. Furthermore, R contains the seven rules listed earlier.

State Table. In Figure 3.2, we describe M by its state table.

State Diagram. In Figure 3.1, we describe M by its state diagram.

For instance, M accepts aab in this way

$$1aab \Rightarrow 2aab \Rightarrow 2ab \Rightarrow 3b \Rightarrow 3$$

Considering the design of M in terms of its implementation, we see that it deserves an improvement. Indeed, M can be redesigned, so it contains fewer rules and states. Even more importantly, the current version of M can perform several different computations on the same input, and this nondeterminism obviously complicates its use in practice. To put it more generally, we obviously

State	a	b	ε
1			2, 4
2	2, 3		
<u>3</u>		3	
4		4, 5	
<u>5</u>			

Figure 3.2 State table.

prefer implementing FAs that work deterministically. Therefore, mostly from this pragmatically oriented perspective, we give several useful algorithms that convert FAs to their equivalent versions that are easy to implement and apply in practice.

3.2 Restricted Finite Automata

FAs introduced in Section 3.1 represent a mathematically convenient rewriting system (see Definition 3.1). On the other hand, they are so general that they are difficult to implement and apply in practice as already pointed out in the conclusion of Section 3.1. Therefore, in the present section, we simplify FAs so that they are more convenient to implement than their general versions. That is, we introduce several restricted versions of these automata and explain how to transform FAs to them so that they accept the same languages. Consequently, all the upcoming restricted versions are as powerful as FAs, so they also accept ${}_{FA}\Phi$ (see Convention 3.2).

3.2.1 Removal of ε-Rules

FAs may contain *ε-rules*, by which they make *ε-moves* during which they change states without reading any symbols. Consequently, on some input strings, they may loop endlessly. As obvious, in practice, we prefer using FAs without any ε-rules because during every move, they read a symbol, so they cannot loop endlessly. Therefore, we next explain how to remove ε-rules from any FA without disturbing its language.

Definition 3.3 Let $M \in {}_{FA}\Psi$. M is an *ε-free finite automaton*(${}_{\varepsilon\text{-}free}FA$ for short) if every rule in ${}_{M}R$ is of the form $qa \to p$, where $q, p \in {}_{M}Q$ and $a \in {}_{M}\Delta$ (see Convention 3.2). ■

Before transforming any FA to an equivalent ${}_{\varepsilon\text{-}free}$FA, we explain how to construct the set of states E that an FA can reach by ε-moves from a given set of states E because this construction plays an important role in the transformation.

Convention 3.4 Let $M \in {}_{FA}\Psi$ and $E \subseteq {}_{M}Q$. By *ε-moves*(E), we denote the set of states that M can reach by sequences of ε-moves from states in E; formally,

$$\varepsilon\text{-}moves(E) = \{q \mid o \Rightarrow^{*} q, \text{ where } o \in E, q \in {}_{M}Q\}$$

We often omit the braces in E if E contains a single state; in other words, *ε-moves*($\{p\}$) is shortened to *ε-moves*(p), where $p \in {}_{M}Q$. ■

Basic Idea. Given $M \in {}_{FA}\Psi$ and $E \subseteq {}_{M}Q$, we determine *ε-moves*(E) in the following way. Initially, set *ε-moves*(E) to E because M can reach any state in E by performing zero ε-moves. If ${}_{M}Q$ contains a state p such that $q \to p \in {}_{M}R$ with $q \in$ *ε-moves*(E), add p to *ε-moves*(E), and in this way, keep extending *ε-moves*(E) until no more states can be included into *ε-moves*(E). The resulting set *ε-moves*(E) satisfies *ε-moves*(E) $= \{q \mid o \Rightarrow^{*} q, \text{ where } o \in E, q \in {}_{M}Q\}$ as desired.

Algorithm 3.5 States Reachable without Reading.

Input. An FA $M = ({}_M\Sigma, {}_MR)$ and $E \subseteq {}_MQ$.

Output. ε-$moves(E) = \{q \mid o \Rightarrow^* q$, where $o \in E, q \in {}_MQ\}$.

Method.

begin

set ε-$moves(E)$ to E
repeat
ε-$moves(E) = \varepsilon$-$moves(E) \cup \{p \mid q \rightarrow p \in {}_MR$ **and** $q \in \varepsilon$-$moves(E)\}$
until no change {ε-$moves(E)$ cannot be further extended}

end.

Lemma 3.6 Algorithm 3.5 is correct.

Proof. To establish this lemma, we prove Claims A and B, in which ε-$moves(E_i)$ denotes the set of states that ε-$moves(E)$ contains after the ith iteration of the **repeat** loop, where $i = 0, 1, \ldots, h$, for some $h \leq card({}_MQ)$.

Claim A. For every $j \geq 0$ and every $p \in {}_MQ$, if $p \in \varepsilon$-$moves(E_j)$, then there exists $q \in \varepsilon$-$moves(E)$ such that $q \Rightarrow^* p$ in M.

Proof of Claim A (by induction on $j \geq 0$).

Basis. Let $j = 0$. Observe that $p \in \varepsilon$-$moves(E_0)$ implies $p \in \varepsilon$-$moves(E)$. As $p \Rightarrow^0 p$, the basis holds.

Induction Hypothesis. Assume that Claim A holds for all $j = 0, \ldots, i$, where i is a non-negative integer.

Induction Step. Let $p \in \varepsilon$-$moves(E_{i+1})$. Next, we distinguish two cases—$p \in \varepsilon$-$moves(E_j)$, for some $j \leq i$ and $p \in \varepsilon$-$moves(E_{i+1}) - \varepsilon$-$moves(E_i)$.

1. Let $p \in \varepsilon$-$moves(E_j)$, for some $j \leq i$. By the induction hypothesis, there exists $q \in {}_MQ$ such that $q \Rightarrow^* p$ in M, so the inductive step holds in this case.
2. Let $p \in \varepsilon$-$moves(E_{i+1}) - \varepsilon$-$moves(E_i)$. Examine the **repeat** loop. Observe that there exists $o \rightarrow p \in {}_MR$ for some $o \in \varepsilon$-$moves(E_i)$. By the induction hypothesis, $q \Rightarrow^* o$ in M for some $q \in \varepsilon$-$moves(E)$, so $q \Rightarrow^* o \Rightarrow p$ in M. Thus, $q \Rightarrow^* p$ in M, and the inductive step holds in this case as well.

Claim B. For all $j \geq 0$, if $q \Rightarrow^j p$ in M with $q \in E$, then $p \in \varepsilon$-$moves(E)$.

Proof of Claim B (by induction on $j \geq 0$).

Basis. Let $j = 0$. That is, $q \Rightarrow^0 p$ in M with $q \in E$, so $q = p$. Then, the algorithm includes p into ε-*moves*(E) even before the first iteration of the **repeat** loop; formally, $p \in \varepsilon\text{-}moves(E_0)$. Thus, the basis holds.

Induction Hypothesis. Assume that Claim B holds for all $j = 0, \ldots, i$, where i is a nonnegative integer.

Induction Step. Let $q \Rightarrow^{i+1} p$ in M with $q \in E$. Next, we first consider $p \in \varepsilon\text{-}moves(E_j)$, for some $j \leq i$; then, we study the case when $p \notin \varepsilon\text{-}moves(E_j)$, for any $j \leq i$.

1. Let $p \in \varepsilon\text{-}moves(E_j)$, for some $j \leq i$. Recall that no iteration of the **repeat** loop removes any states from ε-*moves*(E). Therefore, $p \in \varepsilon\text{-}moves(E)$.
2. Let $p \notin \varepsilon\text{-}moves(E_j)$, for any $j \leq i$. As $i + 1 \geq 1$, we can express $q \Rightarrow^{i+1} p$ in M as $q \Rightarrow^{i} o \Rightarrow p$, and the induction hypothesis implies $o \in \varepsilon\text{-}moves(E)$. ${}_MR$ contains $o \rightarrow p$ because $o \Rightarrow p$ in M. As $o \in \varepsilon\text{-}moves(E)$ and $o \rightarrow p \in {}_MR$, the **repeat** loop adds p to E during iteration $i + 1$, so $p \in \varepsilon\text{-}moves(E)$.

By Claims A and B, $q \Rightarrow^* p$ in M with $q \in E$ if and only if $p \in \varepsilon\text{-}moves(E)$. Hence, Algorithm 3.5 correctly determines $\varepsilon\text{-}moves(E) = \{q \mid o \Rightarrow^* q, \text{ where } o \in E, q \in {}_MQ\}$, so the lemma holds. ■

We are now ready to convert any FA I to an equivalent ${}_{\varepsilon\text{-}free}$FA O.

Basic Idea. By using Algorithm 3.5, we find out whether ${}_Is \Rightarrow^* f$ with $f \in {}_IF$ (${}_Is$ denotes the start state of I according to Convention 3.2), which implies that I accepts ε, and if this is the case, we include ${}_Is$ into ${}_OF$ in order that O accepts ε as well. Furthermore, set

$${}_OR = \{qa \rightarrow p \mid q \in {}_IQ, a \in {}_I\Delta, oa \rightarrow p \in {}_IR \text{ for some } o \in \varepsilon\text{-}moves(\{q\})\}$$

where ε-*moves*($\{q\}$) is constructed by Algorithm 3.5; therefore, by $qa \rightarrow p \in {}_OR$, O simulates $qa \Rightarrow^* oa \Rightarrow p$ in I.

Algorithm 3.7 Removal of ε-Rules.

Input. An FA $I = ({}_I\Sigma, {}_IR)$.

Output. ${}_{\varepsilon\text{-}free}$FA O satisfying $L(I) = L(O)$.

Method.

begin

set ${}_O\Sigma$ to ${}_I\Sigma$ with ${}_O\Delta = {}_I\Delta$, ${}_OQ = {}_IQ$, and ${}_Os = {}_Is$
set ${}_OF$ to $\{q \mid q \in {}_IQ, \varepsilon\text{-}moves(q) \cap {}_IF \neq \emptyset\}$
set ${}_OR$ to $\{qa \rightarrow p \mid q \in {}_IQ, a \in {}_I\Delta, oa \rightarrow p \in {}_IR \text{ for some } o \in \varepsilon\text{-}moves(q) \text{ in } I\}$

end.

Theorem 3.8 Algorithm 3.7 is correct. Therefore, for every FA I, there exists an equivalent ${}_{\varepsilon\text{-}free}$FA O.

Proof. Notice that Algorithm 3.7 produces ${}_O\Delta = {}_I\Delta$, ${}_OQ = {}_IQ$, and ${}_Os = {}_Is$. Therefore, for simplicity, we just write Δ, Q, and s throughout this proof because there exists no danger of confusion. However, we carefully distinguish ${}_IF$ from ${}_OF$ because they may differ from each other.

As obvious, ${}_OR$ contains no ε-rules. To establish $L(O) = L(I)$, we first prove the following claim.

Claim. For every $q, p \in Q$ and $w \in \Delta^+$, $qw \Rightarrow^+ p$ in O iff $qw \Rightarrow^+ p$ in I.

Proof of the Claim.

Only if. By induction on $|w| \geq 1$, we next prove that for every $q, p \in Q$ and $w \in \Delta^+$, $qw \Rightarrow^+ p$ in O implies $qw \Rightarrow^+ p$ in I.

Basis. Let $|w| = 1$ and $qw \Rightarrow^+ p$ in O. Since $|w| = 1$, w is a symbol in Δ. As ${}_OR$ contains no ε-rules, $qw \Rightarrow^+ p$ is, in effect, a one-move computation of the form $qw \Rightarrow p$ in O. Thus, $qw \rightarrow p$ in ${}_OR$. By the definition of ${}_OR$, $ow \rightarrow p \in {}_IR$ for some $o \in \varepsilon\text{-}moves(\{q\})$ in I, so $q \Rightarrow^+ o$ and $ow \Rightarrow p$ in I. Consequently, $qw \Rightarrow^+ p$ in I.

Induction Hypothesis. Assume that the *only-if* part of this claim holds for all $w \in \Delta^+$ with $|w| \leq n$, where n is a nonnegative integer.

Induction Step. Let $qw \Rightarrow^+ p$ in O, where $q, p \in Q$ and $w \in \Delta^+$ with $|w| = n + 1$, so $|w| \geq 2$. Because $|w| \geq 2$ and ${}_OR$ contains no ε-rules, we can express $qw \Rightarrow^+ p$ as $qva \Rightarrow^+ ha \Rightarrow p$, where $h \in Q$, $a \in \Delta$, v is a prefix of w, and $|v| = n$. As $qv \Rightarrow^+ h$ in O and $|v| = n$, $qv \Rightarrow^+ h$ in I by the inductive hypothesis. Since $ha \Rightarrow p$ in O, $ha \rightarrow p \in {}_OR$. By the definition of ${}_OR$, $ha \Rightarrow^+ oa \Rightarrow p$ in I, where $o \in Q$. Putting $qv \Rightarrow^+ h$ and $ha \Rightarrow^+ oa \Rightarrow p$ in I together, $qva \Rightarrow^+ ha \Rightarrow^+ p$ in I. Because $va = w$, $qw \Rightarrow^+ p$ in I. Thus, the *only-if* part of the claim holds.

If. The *if* part of the claim is left as an exercise.

To prove that $L(O) = L(I)$, consider the above claim for $q = s$. That is, $sw \Rightarrow^+ p$ in O iff $sw \Rightarrow^+ p$ in I for all $w \in \Delta^+$, so $L(O) - \{\varepsilon\} = L(I) - \{\varepsilon\}$. As ${}_OF = \{q | \; q \in {}_IQ, \varepsilon\text{-}moves(q) \cap {}_IF \neq \emptyset\}$, $s \Rightarrow^* p$ in O with $p \in {}_OF$ iff $s \Rightarrow^* p \Rightarrow^* f$ in I with $f \in {}_IF$. Therefore, $L(O) = L(I)$, and the lemma holds. ■

Example 3.2 Return to the FA in Figure 3.2. By Algorithm 3.5, we next determine ε-*moves*(1), which denotes the set of states reachable from state 1 by ε-moves. The first iteration of the **repeat** loop adds 2 and 4 to ε-*moves*(1) because $1 \rightarrow 2$ and $1 \rightarrow 4$ are ε-rules in this FA, so this iteration produces ε-*moves*(1) = {1, 2, 4}. During the second iteration of the **repeat** loop, this iteration adds no new state to ε-*moves*(1), so the **repeat** loop exits. As $1 \rightarrow 2$ and $1 \rightarrow 4$ are the only ε-rules in the FA, ε-*moves*(i) = {i} for all the other states i = 2, ..., 5. Having constructed these sets, we use Algorithm 3.7 to transform the finite automaton to an equivalent ${}_{\varepsilon\text{-}free}$FA. For instance, as ε-*moves*(1) = {1, 2, 4} and $2b \rightarrow 2$ is a rule of the input automaton, Algorithm 3.7 introduces a rule of the form $1b \rightarrow 2$ into the output automaton. The complete list of the resulting output ${}_{\varepsilon\text{-}free}$FA, displayed in Figure 3.3, follows next:

$$1a \rightarrow 2,\ 1a \rightarrow 3,\ 1b \rightarrow 4,\ 1b \rightarrow 5,\ 2a \rightarrow 2,\ 2a \rightarrow 3,\ 3b \rightarrow 3,\ 4b \rightarrow 4, \text{ and } 4b \rightarrow 5$$

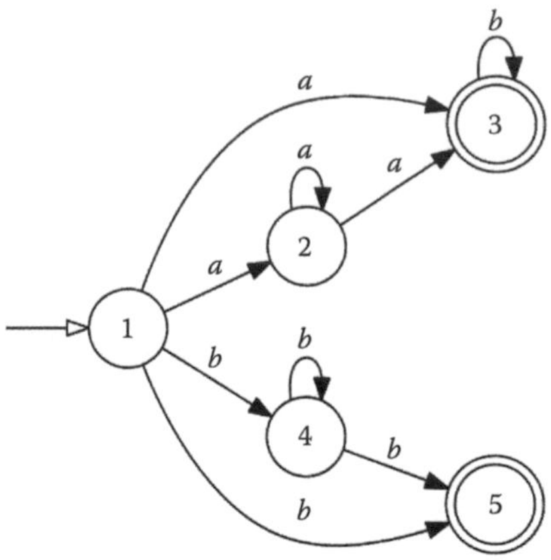

Figure 3.3 $_{\varepsilon\text{-}free}$**FA.**

3.2.2 Determinism

An $_{\varepsilon\text{-}free}$FA can make several different moves on the same symbol from the same state. For instance, take the $_{\varepsilon\text{-}free}$FA in Figure 3.3; from 1, it can enter states 2 or 3 on a. As obvious, this nondeterminism represents an undesirable phenomenon in practice. Therefore, in this section, we explain how to convert any $_{\varepsilon\text{-}free}$FA to its deterministic version that makes no more than one move on every symbol from the same state. In other words, a deterministic FA makes a unique sequence of moves on every input string, and this property clearly simplifies its use in practice.

Definition 3.9 Let $M = ({}_M\Sigma, {}_MR)$ be an $_{\varepsilon\text{-}free}$FA. M is a *deterministic FA* (a *DFA* for short) if for every $q \in Q$ and every $a \in \Delta$, there exists no more than one $p \in Q$ such that $qa \rightarrow p \in {}_MR$. ■

Next, we explain how to convert any $_{\varepsilon\text{-}free}$FA to an equivalent DFA.

Basic Idea. Consider any $_{\varepsilon\text{-}free}$FA $I = ({}_I\Sigma, {}_IR)$. To turn I to an equivalent DFA $O = ({}_O\Sigma, {}_OR)$, set ${}_OQ = \{\langle W\rangle \mid W \subseteq {}_IQ\}$—that is, any set $W \subseteq {}_IQ$ is represented by a unique symbol $\langle W\rangle$. Furthermore, if $W \cap {}_IF \neq \emptyset$, include $\langle W\rangle$ into ${}_OF$. For every $\langle X\rangle \in {}_OQ$ and every $a \in \Delta$, add $\langle X\rangle a \rightarrow \langle Y\rangle$ to ${}_OR$ with $Y = \{q \mid xa \rightarrow q \in {}_IR$, for some $x \in X$ and $a \in {}_I\Delta\}$. Consequently, $\langle\{{}_Is\}\rangle w \Rightarrow^* \langle Z\rangle$ in O iff ${}_Isw \Rightarrow^* p$, for all $p \in Z$ and $w \in \Delta^*$. Specifically, for every $\langle E\rangle \in {}_OF$, $\langle\{{}_Is\}\rangle w \Rightarrow^* \langle E\rangle$ in O iff ${}_Isw \Rightarrow^* f$ in I, for some $f \in E \cap {}_IF$. In other words, O accepts w iff I accepts w, so $L(O) = L(I)$.

Algorithm 3.10 $_{\varepsilon\text{-}free}$FA to DFA Conversion.

Input. An $_{\varepsilon\text{-}free}$FA $I = ({}_I\Sigma, {}_IR)$.

Output. A DFA $O = ({}_O\Sigma, {}_OR)$ such that $L(O) = L(I)$.

Method.

begin

set ${}_O\Delta = {}_I\Delta$
set ${}_OQ = \{\langle W\rangle \mid W \subseteq {}_IQ\}$

set $_OF = \{\langle U\rangle \mid \langle U\rangle \in {_OQ}$ and $U \cap {_IF} \neq \emptyset\}$
set $_Os = \langle\{_Is\}\rangle$
for every $\langle X\rangle \in {_OQ}$ and every $a \in \Delta$, add $\langle X\rangle a \rightarrow \langle Y\rangle$ to $_OR$ with $Y = \{q \mid pa \rightarrow q \in {_IR}, p \in X\}$

end.

Theorem 3.11 Algorithm 3.10 is correct. Therefore, for every $_{\varepsilon\text{-}free}$FA, there exists an equivalent DFA.

Proof. Clearly, for any subset $O \subseteq {_IQ}$ and any input symbol $a \in {_I\Delta}$, there exists a single set, $P \subseteq {_IQ}$, satisfying this equivalence

$$p \in P \text{ iff } oa \rightarrow p \in {_IR} \text{ for some } o \in O$$

Notice that $_I\Delta = {_O\Delta}$. Consequently, for any $\langle O\rangle \in {_OQ}$ and $a \in {_O\Delta}$, there exists a unique state $\langle P\rangle \in {_OQ}$, such that $\langle O\rangle a \rightarrow \langle P\rangle \in {_OR}$, so O is deterministic. A rigorous proof that $L(I) = L(O)$ is left as an exercise. ■

Algorithm 3.10 works simply, but this simplicity is perhaps its only advantage. Observe that it produces $O = ({_O\Sigma}, {_OR})$ with $card({_OQ}) = card(power({_IQ}))$ and $card({_OR}) = card(power({_IQ}) \times \Delta)$. This exponential increase in the number of states and rules represents an indisputable drawback as illustrated by the next example.

Convention 3.12 For simplicity, we omit braces in the states of the form $\langle\{\ldots\}\rangle$ and write $\langle\ldots\rangle$ instead; for example, $\langle\{2, 3\}\rangle$ is simplified to $\langle 2, 3\rangle$. ■

Example 3.3 Reconsider $_{\varepsilon\text{-}free}$FA in Figure 3.3. Recall its rules

$$1a \rightarrow 2,\ 1a \rightarrow 3,\ 1b \rightarrow 4,\ 1b \rightarrow 5,\ 2a \rightarrow 2,\ 2a \rightarrow 3,\ 3b \rightarrow 3,\ 4b \rightarrow 4, \text{ and } 4b \rightarrow 5$$

in which states 3 and 5 are final. This automaton works nondeterministically. For instance, from 1 on b, it can make a move to 4 or 5. With this automaton as its input, Algorithm 3.10 produces the equivalent DFA in which every state that contains 3 or 5 is final. The automaton has 32 states because $2^5 = 32$.

Notice that Algorithm 3.10 may introduce some states completely uselessly. Specifically, it may introduce states that the output DFA can never reach from its start state. For instance, in Figure 3.4, $\langle 1, 2\rangle$ is obviously unreachable as follows from their absence in the table columns denoted by either of the two input symbols.

Definition 3.13 In a DFA, $M = (\Sigma, R)$, a state $q \in Q$ is *reachable* if there exists $w \in \Delta^*$ such that $sw \Rightarrow^* q$ in M; otherwise, q is *unreachable* in M. ■

Algorithm 3.14 converts any $_{\varepsilon\text{-}free}$FA to its deterministic version that contains only reachable states.

Basic Idea. Take any $_{\varepsilon\text{-}free}$FA, $I = ({_I\Sigma}, {_IR})$. The following algorithm transforms I to an equivalent DFA, $O = ({_O\Sigma}, {_OR})$, so it parallels the previous algorithm except that a new state is introduced into $_OQ$ only if it is reachable. Initially, $_OQ$ contains only the start state $\langle {_Is}\rangle$. Then, if $_OQ$ already contains $\langle W\rangle$, where $W \subseteq {_IQ}$, and $P = \{p \mid oa \Rightarrow p$ for some $o \in W\}$ is nonempty, where $a \in \Delta$, then we add $\langle P\rangle$ to $_OQ$ and include $\langle W\rangle a \rightarrow \langle P\rangle$ into $_OR$.

State	a	b
⟨∅⟩	⟨∅⟩	⟨∅⟩
⟨1⟩	⟨2, 3⟩	⟨4, 5⟩
⟨2⟩	⟨2, 3⟩	⟨∅⟩
⟨3⟩	⟨∅⟩	⟨3⟩
⟨4⟩	⟨∅⟩	⟨4, 5⟩
⟨5⟩	⟨∅⟩	⟨∅⟩
⟨1,2⟩	⟨2, 3⟩	⟨4, 5⟩
⟨1,3⟩	⟨2, 3⟩	⟨3, 4, 5⟩
⟨1,4⟩	⟨2, 3⟩	⟨4, 5⟩
⟨1,5⟩	⟨2, 3⟩	⟨4, 5⟩
⟨2, 3⟩	⟨2, 3⟩	⟨3⟩
⟨2, 4⟩	⟨2, 3⟩	⟨4, 5⟩
⟨2, 5⟩	⟨2, 3⟩	⟨∅⟩
⟨3, 4⟩	⟨∅⟩	⟨3, 4, 5⟩
⟨3, 5⟩	⟨∅⟩	⟨3⟩
⟨4, 5⟩	⟨∅⟩	⟨4, 5⟩

State	a	b
⟨1, 2, 3⟩	⟨2, 3⟩	⟨3, 4, 5⟩
⟨1, 2, 4⟩	⟨2, 3⟩	⟨4, 5⟩
⟨1, 2, 5⟩	⟨2, 3⟩	⟨4, 5⟩
⟨1, 3, 4⟩	⟨2, 3⟩	⟨3, 4, 5⟩
⟨1, 3, 5⟩	⟨2, 3⟩	⟨3, 4, 5⟩
⟨1, 4, 5⟩	⟨2, 3⟩	⟨4, 5⟩
⟨2, 3, 4⟩	⟨2, 3⟩	⟨3, 4, 5⟩
⟨2, 3, 5⟩	⟨2, 3⟩	⟨3⟩
⟨2, 4, 5⟩	⟨2, 3⟩	⟨4, 5⟩
⟨3, 4, 5⟩	⟨∅⟩	⟨3, 4, 5⟩
⟨1, 2, 3, 4⟩	⟨2, 3⟩	⟨3, 4, 5⟩
⟨1, 2, 3, 5⟩	⟨2, 3⟩	⟨3, 4, 5⟩
⟨1, 2, 4, 5⟩	⟨2, 3⟩	⟨4, 5⟩
⟨1, 3, 4, 5⟩	⟨2, 3⟩	⟨3, 4, 5⟩
⟨2, 3, 4, 5⟩	⟨2, 3⟩	⟨3, 4, 5⟩
⟨1, 2, 3, 4, 5⟩	⟨2, 3⟩	⟨3, 4, 5⟩

Figure 3.4 DFA state table.

Algorithm 3.14 $_{\varepsilon\text{-}free}$FA to DFA Conversion without Unreachable States.

Input. An $_{\varepsilon\text{-}free}$FA $I = ({}_I\Sigma, {}_IR)$.

Output. A DFA $O = ({}_O\Sigma, {}_OR)$ such that $L(O) = L(I)$ and ${}_OQ$ contains only reachable states.

Method.

begin
  set ${}_O\Delta = {}_I\Delta$
  set ${}_OQ = \{\langle {}_Is\rangle\}$
  set ${}_Os = \langle {}_Is\rangle$
  set ${}_OR = \varnothing$
  repeat
    if $a \in {}_I\Delta$, $X \subseteq {}_IQ$, $\langle X\rangle \in {}_OQ$, $Y = \{p \mid qa \Rightarrow p$ in I with $q \in X\}$, $Y \neq \varnothing$ **then**
    begin
      add $\langle Y\rangle$ to ${}_OQ$
      add $\langle X\rangle a \to \langle Y\rangle$ to ${}_OR$
    end
  until no change
    set ${}_OF = \{\langle Y\rangle \mid \langle Y\rangle \in {}_OQ, Y \cap {}_IF \neq \varnothing\}$
end.

Example 3.4 Convert $_{\varepsilon\text{-}free}$FA from Figure 3.3 to an equivalent DFA by using Algorithm 3.14, which initializes the start state of the DFA to ⟨1⟩. From 1 on a, the $_{\varepsilon\text{-}free}$FA enters 2 or 3, so introduce ⟨2, 3⟩ as a new state and $\langle 1\rangle a \to \langle 2, 3\rangle$ as a new rule in the output DFA. From 2, on a, the $_{\varepsilon\text{-}free}$FA enters 2 or 3, and from 3, on a, it does not enter any state; therefore, add $\langle 2, 3\rangle a \to \langle 2, 3\rangle$ to the set of rules in the DFA. Complete the construction of the DFA as an exercise. The resulting DFA is defined by its rules

$$\langle 1\rangle a \to \langle 2, 3\rangle,\ \langle 1\rangle b \to \langle 4, 5\rangle,\ \langle 2, 3\rangle a \to \langle 2, 3\rangle,\ \langle 2, 3\rangle b \to \langle 3\rangle,\ \langle 3\rangle b \to \langle 3\rangle, \text{ and } \langle 4, 5\rangle b \to \langle 4, 5\rangle$$

where states ⟨2, 3⟩, ⟨3⟩, and ⟨4, 5⟩ are final. Figure 3.5 gives the state diagram of the resulting output DFA.

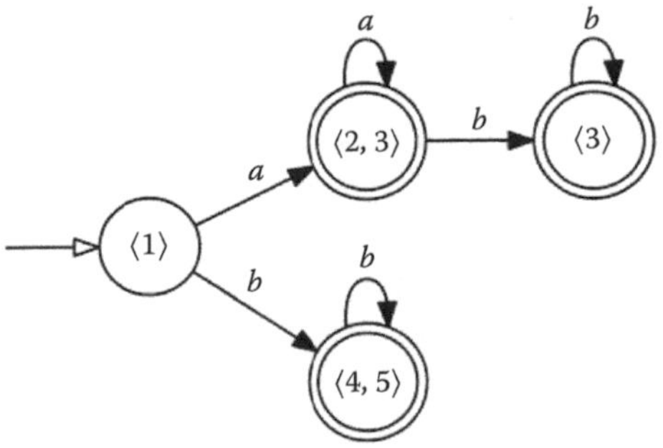

Figure 3.5 State diagram of DFA.

Besides unreachable states, a DFA may contain useless states from which there is no computation that terminates in a final state. In the rest of this section, we explain how to detect and remove states like these. We give only a gist of this removal while leaving its detailed description to the Exercises.

Definition 3.15 In a DFA, $M = (\Sigma, R)$, a state $q \in Q$ is *terminating* if there exists $w \in \Delta^*$ such that $qw \Rightarrow^* f$ in M with $f \in F$; otherwise, q is *nonterminating*. ■

Next, we sketch a two-phase transformation of any DFA to an equivalent DFA in which each state is both reachable and terminating.

Basic Idea. Consider any DFA, $I = ({}_I\Sigma, {}_IR)$. For I, we construct a DFA, $O = ({}_O\Sigma, {}_OR)$, such that $L(O) = L(I)$ and each state in ${}_OQ$ is both reachable and terminating by performing steps (1) and (2) as follows.

1. Determine the set of all terminating states ${}_IQ_{term} \subseteq {}_IQ$. Observe that all final states are automatically terminating because ε takes I from any final state to the same state by making zero moves. Therefore, initialize ${}_IQ_{term}$ to F. If there exists $a \in \Delta$ and $p \in {}_IQ_{term}$ such that $oa \rightarrow p \in {}_IR$ with $o \in {}_IQ - {}_IQ_{term}$, then o is also terminating, so add o to ${}_IQ_{term}$. Repeat this extension of ${}_IQ_{term}$ until no more states can be added into ${}_IQ_{term}$. The resulting set ${}_IQ_{term}$ contains all terminating states in I.
2. Without any loss of generality, suppose that ${}_IQ$ contains only reachable states. Having determined all terminating states ${}_IQ_{term}$ in step (1), we are now ready to construct O from I. If ${}_Is \notin {}_IQ_{term}$, $L(I) = \emptyset$, and the construction of O is trivial. If ${}_Is \in {}_IQ_{term}$, remove all nonterminating states from ${}_IQ$ and eliminate all rules containing nonterminating states in ${}_IR$. Take the resulting automaton as O.

In the exercises, we turn the basic idea given earlier to a precisely described algorithm, illustrate its use by several examples, and prove Theorem 3.16 in a fully rigorous way.

Theorem 3.16 For every DFA I, there exists an equivalent DFA O in which all states are both reachable and terminating. ■

3.2.2.1 Complete Specification

In a general case, a DFA, $M = ({}_M\Sigma, {}_MR)$, may get stuck on some input strings. Indeed, for a state $q \in {}_MQ$ and an input symbol $a \in {}_M\Delta$, ${}_MR$ may have no rule with qa on its left-hand side. As a result, when occurring in q and reading a somewhere in the middle of an input string, M gets stuck, so it never completes reading the string. As obvious, this phenomenon is ruled out if M contains a rule for every state and every input symbol because it always completely reads every single input string, which is a property often highly appreciated in theory as well as in practice. Indeed, from a theoretical viewpoint, this property simplifies achieving some significant results concerning DFAs, such as their minimization (see Section 3.2.3). Form a practical viewpoint, it makes their implementation easier (see Section 4.2). Therefore, we explain how to adapt any DFA so that it satisfies this property.

Definition 3.17 A DFA, $M = ({}_M\Sigma, {}_MR)$, is a *completely specified DFA* (a *${}_{cs}$DFA* for short) if for every $q \in {}_MQ$ and every $a \in {}_M\Delta$, there exists precisely one $p \in {}_MQ$ such that $qa \rightarrow p \in {}_MR$. ■

We next sketch a transformation of any DFA, $I = ({}_I\Sigma, {}_IR)$, to a completely specified DFA, $O = ({}_O\Sigma, {}_OR)$, satisfying $L(O) = L(I)$.

Basic Idea. If I is completely specified, we take O as I, and we are done. Suppose that I is not completely specified. To obtain an equivalent ${}_{cs}$DFA O, set ${}_OQ$ to ${}_IQ \cup \{o\}$ and ${}_OR$ to ${}_IR \cup \{qa \rightarrow o \mid q \in {}_OQ, a \in {}_I\Delta$, and $qa \rightarrow p \notin {}_IR$ for any $p \in {}_IQ\}$, where o is a new state.

It is worth noticing that ${}_OQ = {}_IQ \cup \{o\}$, where o represents a new nonterminating state. By Theorems 3.16 and 3.18, for any FA, there is an equivalent DFA that has only reachable and terminating states. As a result, we obtain Theorem 3.18, whose rigorous proof is left as an exercise.

Theorem 3.18 For every DFA, $I = ({}_I\Sigma, {}_IR)$, there exists a ${}_{cs}$DFA, $O = ({}_O\Sigma, {}_OR)$, such that

I. $L(O) = L(I)$;
II. $card({}_IQ) \leq card({}_OQ) \leq card({}_IQ) + 1$;
III. in ${}_OQ$, all states are reachable and no more than one state is nonterminating. ■

Example 3.5 Return to the DFA from Example 3.4 (see Figure 3.5). Recall its rules

$$\langle 1\rangle a \rightarrow \langle 2, 3\rangle, \langle 1\rangle b \rightarrow \langle 4, 5\rangle, \langle 2, 3\rangle a \rightarrow \langle 2, 3\rangle, \langle 2, 3\rangle b \rightarrow \langle 3\rangle, \langle 3\rangle b \rightarrow \langle 3\rangle, \text{ and } \langle 4, 5\rangle b \rightarrow \langle 4, 5\rangle$$

To convert this DFA to an equivalent ${}_{cs}$DFA, follow the previous basic idea. That is, by using a new nonfinal state o, change this DFA to the ${}_{cs}$DFA defined as

$$\langle 1\rangle a \rightarrow \langle 2, 3\rangle, \langle 1\rangle b \rightarrow \langle 4, 5\rangle, \langle 2, 3\rangle a \rightarrow \langle 2, 3\rangle, \langle 2, 3\rangle b \rightarrow \langle 3\rangle, \langle 3\rangle a \rightarrow o, \langle 3\rangle b \rightarrow \langle 3\rangle,$$

$$\langle 4, 5\rangle a \rightarrow o, \langle 4, 5\rangle b \rightarrow \langle 4, 5\rangle, oa \rightarrow o, \text{ and } ob \rightarrow o$$

3.2.3 Minimization

Even a DFA M may contain some states that can be merged together without affecting $L(M)$. By merging these states, we can minimize the size of M with respect to the number of the states; as obvious, a minimization like this is frequently highly appreciated in practice. Before explaining how to achieve it, we need some terminology.

Definition 3.19 Let $M = ({}_M\Sigma, {}_MR)$ be a DFA.

I. A string $w \in {}_M\Delta^*$ *distinguishes* p from q, where $p, q \in {}_MQ$, if $pw \Rightarrow^* u$ and $qw \Rightarrow^* v$ in M, for some $u, v \in {}_MQ$ satisfying either ($u \in F$ and $v \in Q - F$) or ($v \in F$ and $u \in Q - F$).
II. State p is *distinguishable* from q if there exists an input string that distinguishes p from q; otherwise, p and q are *indistinguishable.*
III. M is a *minimum-state finite automaton* (a ${}_{min}DFA$ for short) if each $q \in {}_MQ$ is reachable, terminating, and distinguishable from all $p \in {}_MQ - \{q\}$. ■

Next, we explain how to transform any DFA $I = ({}_I\Sigma, {}_IR)$ to an equivalent ${}_{min}$DFA $O = ({}_O\Sigma, {}_OR)$. Without any loss of generality, suppose that I represents a ${}_{cs}$DFA in which all states are reachable and no more than one state is nonterminating (see Theorem 3.18). Clearly, if ${}_MQ = {}_MF$, then $L(M) = {}_M\Delta^*$ because I is a ${}_{cs}$DFA, and if ${}_MF = \emptyset$, then $L(M) = \emptyset$. In either case, the ${}_{min}$DFA that accepts $L(M)$ has a single state; a trivial proof of this result is left as an exercise. Therefore, we assume that ${}_IQ \neq {}_IF$ and ${}_IF \neq \emptyset$ in the transformation sketched next.

Basic Idea. First, the transformation of I to O constructs the set of states ${}_OQ$ so ${}_OQ \subseteq \{\langle W\rangle|\ W \subseteq {}_IQ\}$. Initially, set ${}_OQ$ to $\{\langle {}_IF\rangle, \langle {}_IQ - {}_IF\rangle\}$ because ε obviously distinguishes $\langle {}_IF\rangle$ from $\langle {}_IQ - {}_IF\rangle$, so $\langle {}_IF\rangle$ and $\langle {}_IQ - {}_IF\rangle$ are necessarily distinguishable. Let $a \in {}_I\Delta$, $\emptyset \subset U \subset X \subset {}_IQ$, and $\langle X\rangle \in {}_OQ$. If $\{y|\ ua \Rightarrow y$ in I, $u \in U\}$ and $\{z|\ va \Rightarrow z$ in I, $v \in X - U\}$ are two nonempty disjoint sets, then any state $u \in U$ is distinguishable from any state $v \in X - U$, so replace $\langle X\rangle$ with two states, $\langle U\rangle$ and $\langle X - U\rangle$ in ${}_OQ$ and, thereby, increase $card({}_OQ)$ by one. Keep extending ${}_OQ$ in this way until no further extension is possible. As I may contain one nonterminating state (see Definition 3.17 and Theorem 3.18), the resulting output automaton may have a nonterminating state as well; if this is the case, remove it as well as all rules containing it. To complete the construction of O, set ${}_Os = \langle Y\rangle$, where $\langle Y\rangle \in {}_OQ$ with ${}_Is \in Y$, ${}_OF = \{\langle Y\rangle|\ Y \subseteq {}_IF\}$, and ${}_OR = \{\langle X\rangle a \rightarrow \langle Y\rangle|\ qa \Rightarrow p$ in I, $q \in X, p \in Y, a \in {}_I\Delta\}$.

Algorithm 3.20 DFA Minimization.

Input. A ${}_{cs}$DFA $I = ({}_I\Sigma, {}_IR)$ such that all states are reachable, no more than one state is nonterminating, ${}_IQ \neq {}_IF$, and ${}_IF \neq \emptyset$.

Output. A ${}_{min}$DFA $O = ({}_O\Sigma, {}_OR)$ such that $L(O) = L(I)$.

Method.

begin

set ${}_O\Delta = {}_I\Delta$
set ${}_OQ = \{\langle {}_IF \rangle, \langle {}_IQ - {}_IF \rangle\}$
while there exist $a \in {}_I\Delta$, $U, X \subset {}_IQ$ such that
$\emptyset \subset U \subset X$,
$\langle X \rangle \in {}_OQ$, and
$\{y \mid ua \Rightarrow y \text{ in } I, u \in U\}$ and $\{z \mid va \Rightarrow z \text{ in } I, v \in X - U\}$ are two nonempty disjoint sets **do**
begin
set ${}_OQ = ({}_OQ - \{\langle X \rangle\}) \cup \{\langle U \rangle, \langle X - U \rangle\}$
end
set ${}_Os = \langle Y \rangle$, where $\langle Y \rangle \in {}_OQ$ with ${}_Is \in Y$
set ${}_OR = \{\langle X \rangle a \rightarrow \langle Y \rangle \mid qa \Rightarrow p \text{ in } I, q \in X, p \in Y, a \in \Delta\}$
set ${}_OF = \{\langle Y \rangle \mid Y \subseteq {}_IF\}$
if $\langle Z \rangle \in {}_OQ - {}_OF$ **and** $\langle Z \rangle$ is nonterminating **then**
begin
set ${}_OR = {}_OR - \{\langle X \rangle a \rightarrow \langle Y \rangle \mid \{\langle X \rangle, \langle Y \rangle\} \cap \{\langle Z \rangle\} \neq \emptyset, a \in \Delta\}$
remove $\langle Z \rangle$ from ${}_OQ$
end

end.

As an exercise, based on the basic idea that precedes Algorithm 3.20, prove Theorem 3.21.

Theorem 3.21 Algorithm 3.20 is correct. Therefore, for every ${}_{cs}$DFA, there exists an equivalent ${}_{min}$DFA. ■

There exist many alternative algorithms that also minimize DFA; some of them are discussed in the exercises. Nevertheless, from any DFA, they all construct an essentially unique ${}_{min}$DFA O equivalent with I—that is, any other minimum-state finite automaton equivalent to I completely coincides with O except that its names of states may differ. A proof of this crucial result is omitted because it is beyond the scope of this introductory text.

Example 3.6 Return to the ${}_{cs}$DFA from Example 3.5. By Algorithm 3.20, convert this automaton to an equivalent minimum-state finite automaton O. This transformation first starts with two states—$\langle\{\langle 1 \rangle, o\}\rangle$ and $\langle\{\langle 2, 3 \rangle, \langle 3 \rangle, \langle 4, 5 \rangle\}\rangle$—which correspond to the sets of nonfinal and final states, respectively, in the ${}_{cs}$DFA. After this start, the **while** loop replaces $\langle\{\langle 2, 3 \rangle, \langle 3 \rangle, \langle 4, 5 \rangle\}\rangle$ with $\langle\{\langle 2, 3 \rangle\}\rangle$ and $\langle\{\langle 3 \rangle, \langle 4, 5 \rangle\}\rangle$ as follows from these rules:

$$\langle 2, 3 \rangle a \rightarrow \langle 2, 3 \rangle, \langle 2, 3 \rangle b \rightarrow \langle 3 \rangle, \langle 3 \rangle a \rightarrow o, \langle 3 \rangle b \rightarrow \langle 3 \rangle, \langle 4, 5 \rangle a \rightarrow o, \langle 4, 5 \rangle b \rightarrow \langle 4, 5 \rangle$$

Then, this loop replaces $\langle\{\langle 1 \rangle, o\}\rangle$ with $\langle\{\langle 1 \rangle\}\rangle$ and $\langle\{o\}\rangle$. After this replacement, the set of states can no longer be extended by the algorithm. For simplicity and readability, rename states $\langle\{\langle 1 \rangle\}\rangle$, $\langle\{\langle 2, 3 \rangle\}\rangle$, $\langle\{\langle 3 \rangle, \langle 4, 5 \rangle\}\rangle$, and $\langle\{o\}\rangle$ to 1, 2, 3, and 4, respectively. States 2 and 3 are final. Construct the set of rules

$$1a \rightarrow 2,\ 1b \rightarrow 3,\ 2a \rightarrow 2,\ 2b \rightarrow 3,\ 3a \rightarrow 4,\ 3b \rightarrow 3,\ 4a \rightarrow 4, \text{ and } 4b \rightarrow 4$$

State 4 is nonterminating. Remove it as well as all the rules that contain 4. The resulting ${}_{min}$DFA O is given in Figure 3.6.

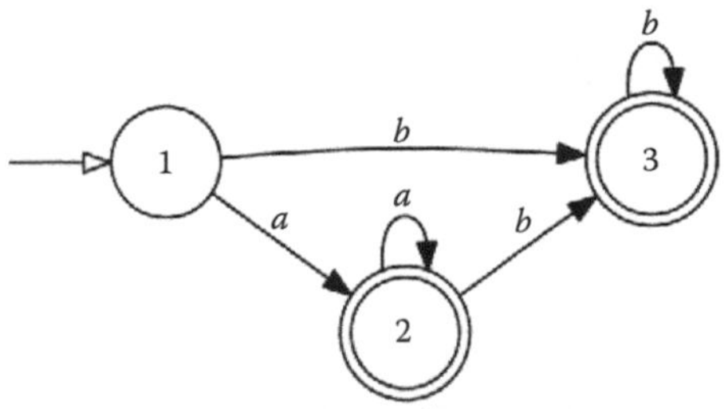

Figure 3.6 Minimum-state finite automaton.

To sum up the previous theorems of this chapter (see Theorems 3.8, 3.11, 3.16, 3.18, and 3.21), all the variants of FAs are equally powerful as stated in Corollary 3.22.

Corollary 3.22 FAs, ${}_{\varepsilon\text{-}free}$FAs, DFAs, ${}_{cs}$DFAs, and ${}_{min}$DFAs are equally powerful. They all characterize ${}_{FA}\Phi$. ■

3.3 Regular Expressions and Their Equivalence with Finite Automata

In this section, we introduce regular expressions and define regular languages by them (see Section 3.3.1). Then, we demonstrate that these expressions and finite automata are equivalent—more precisely, they both characterize the family of regular languages (see Section 3.3.2).

3.3.1 Regular Expressions

Regular expressions represent simple language-denoting formulas, based on the operations of concatenation, union, and closure.

Definition 3.23 Let Δ be an alphabet. The *regular expressions* (*RE* for short) over Δ and the *languages that these expressions denote* are defined recursively as follows:

I. $\emptyset$ is a regular expression denoting the empty set
II. ε is a regular expression denoting $\{\varepsilon\}$
III. a, where $a \in \Delta$, is a regular expression denoting $\{a\}$
IV. if r and s are regular expressions denoting the languages R and S, respectively, then
   i. $(r|s)$ is a regular expression denoting $R \cup S$
   ii. (rs) is a regular expression denoting RS
   iii. $(r)^*$ is a regular expression denoting R^*

The language denoted by a regular expression r is symbolically written as $L(r)$. A language $L \subseteq \Delta^*$ is *regular* iff there exists a regular expression r satisfying $L = L(r)$. The family of all regular languages is denoted by ${}_{reg}\Phi$. ■

In practice as well as in theory, REs sometimes use + instead of |. This book uses the latter throughout.

Regular expressions are said to be *equivalent* if they define the same language. For instance, as a simple exercise, prove that $(a)^*$ and $((a)^*\varepsilon)$ are equivalent, but $(a)^*$ and $((a)^*\varnothing)$ are not.

In practice, we frequently simplify the *fully parenthesized regular expressions* created strictly by this definition by reducing the number of parentheses in them. To do so, we introduce Convention 3.24 concerning the priority of the three operators.

Convention 3.24 We automatically assume that * has higher precedence than operation concatenation, which has higher precedence than |. In addition, the expression rr^* and r^*r is usually written as r^+. ■

Based on Convention 3.24, we can make regular expressions more succinct and readable. For instance, instead of $((a^*)(b(b^*)))$, we can write $(a^*)(b^+)$ or even a^*b^+ according to Convention 3.24. From a broader point of view, Convention 3.24 allows us to establish general equivalences between regular expressions. To illustrate, all the following regular expressions are equivalent:

$$(r)^*,\ (r^*),\ ((r|\varnothing)^*),\ (r|\varnothing)^*,\ r^*|\varnothing^*, \text{ and } r^*$$

Specifically, instead of (r^*), we can thus equivalently write $(r)^*$ or r^*, and we frequently make use of these equivalent expressions later in this section (see, for instance, the proof of Lemma 3.26). There exist a number of other equivalences as well as algebraic laws obeyed by regular expressions, and many of them allow us to further simplify regular expressions as demonstrated in the exercises.

We close this section by an example concerning REs applied to the English vocabulary.

Example 3.7 We open this example in terms of formal English. Let Δ be the English alphabet together with a hyphen (-). Let $W \subseteq \Delta^*$ be the set of all possible well-formed English words, including compound words, such as *made-up*. Notice that W is infinite. For instance, the subset $V \subseteq W$ containing infinitely many words of the form

$$(great\text{-})^i grandparents$$

for all $i \geq 0$. Purely theoretically speaking, they all represent well-formed English words although most of them, such as

great-great-great-great-great-great-great-great-great-great-great-grandparents

are rather uncommon words, which most people never utter during their lifetime. Although V represents an infinite set of rather bizarre English words, it is easily and rigorously defined by a short regular expression of the form

$$(great\text{-})^* grandparents$$

To illustrate the use of REs in terms of informal English, *blah* is a word that is repeatedly used to describe words or feelings where the specifics are considered unimportant or boring to the speaker or writer. It is usually seen in writing transcribing speech. An example of this use might be a sentence like the following:

He keeps making stupid excuses that he is tired and sleepy blah-blah-blah.

As the repetition of *blah* is unlimited, the set of all these compound words contains

blah, blah-blah, blah-blah-blah, blah-blah-blah-blah, blah-blah-blah-blah-blah, …

Simply put, this set represents the infinite language $\{blah\text{-}\}^*\{blah\}$. Observe that this language is denoted by an RE of the form

$$(blah\text{-})^* blah$$

3.3.2 Equivalence with Finite Automata

First, we explain how to transform any DFA to an equivalent RE. Then, we describe the transformation of any RE to an equivalent FA and, thereby, establish the equivalence between REs and FAs.

3.3.2.1 From Finite Automata to Regular Expressions

Next, we explain how to convert any DFA to an equivalent RE.

Basic Idea. Let $M = ({}_M\Sigma, {}_MR)$ be a DFA and $card(Q) = n$, for some $n \geq 1$. Rename states in M, so $Q = \{q_1, \ldots, q_n\}$ with $q_1 = s$. For all $i, j = 1, \ldots, n$ and all $k = 0, \ldots, n$, let $[i, k, j]$ denote the language consisting of all input strings on which M makes a computation from q_i to q_j during which every state q_l that M enters and leaves satisfies $l \leq k$. That is, for all $x \in \Delta^*$, $x \in [i, k, j]$ iff $q_i x \Rightarrow^+ q_j$ and for every $y \in prefix(x) - \{\varepsilon, x\}$, $q_i y \Rightarrow^+ q_l$ with $l \leq k$.

Definition 3.25 For all $k = 0, \ldots, n$, we recursively define $[i, k, j]$ as

1. $[i, 0, j] = \{a |\ a \in \Delta \cup \{\varepsilon\}, q_i a \Rightarrow^m q_j \text{ with } m \leq 1\}$
2. for $k \geq 1$, $[i, k, j] = [i, k-1, j] \cup [i, k-1, k][k, k-1, k]^*[k, k-1, j]$ ■

According to (1), $a \in [i, 0, j]$ iff $q_i a \rightarrow q_j \in R$, and $\varepsilon \in [i, 0, j]$ iff $i = j$. According to (2), $[i, k-1, j] \subseteq [i, k, j]$, so $[i, k, j]$ contains all input strings that take M from q_i to q_j during which it never passes through q_l with $l \geq k - 1$. Furthermore, $[i, k, j]$ includes $[i, k-1, k][k, k-1, k]^*[k, k-1, j]$, which contain all input strings $x = uvw$ such that (a) u takes M from q_i to q_k, (b) v takes M from q_k back to q_k zero or more times, and (c) w takes M from q_k to q_j. Observe that during (a) through (c), M never enters and leaves q_l with $l \geq k - 1$. Furthermore, notice that M performs (*b*) zero times iff $v = \varepsilon$. Based on these properties, the following lemma demonstrates that for every $[i, k, j]$, there is an RE ${}_{i,k,j}E$ such that $L({}_{i,k,j}E) = [i, k, j]$. From this lemma, Theorem 3.27 derives that $L(M)$ is denoted by the RE ${}_{1,n,j_1}E|{}_{1,n,j_2}E|\ldots|{}_{1,n,j_h}E$ with $F = \{q_{j_1}, q_{j_2}, \ldots, q_{j_h}\}$.

Lemma 3.26 For all $i, j = 1, \ldots, n$ and all $k = 0, \ldots, n$, there exists an RE ${}_{i,k,j}E$ such that $L({}_{i,k,j}E) = [i, k, j]$, where $[i, k, j]$ has the meaning given in Definition 3.25.

Proof (by induction on $k \geq 0$).

Basis. Let $i, j \in \{1, \ldots, n\}$ and $k = 0$. By (1) in Definition 3.25, $[i, 0, j] \subseteq \Delta \cup \{\varepsilon\}$, so there surely exists an RE ${}_{i,0,j}E$ such that $L({}_{i,0,j}E) = [i, 0, j]$.

Induction Hypothesis. Suppose that there exists $l \in \{1, \ldots, n\}$ such that for each $i, j \in \{1, \ldots, n\}$ and $k \leq l - 1$, there exists an RE ${}_{i,k,j}E$ such that $L({}_{i,k,j}E) = [i, k, j]$.

Induction Step. Consider any $[i, k, j]$, where $i, j \in \{1, \ldots, n\}$ and $k = l$. By the recursive formula (2), $[i, k, j] = [i, k-1, j] \cup [i, k-1, k][k, k-1, k]^*[k, k-1, j]$. By the induction hypothesis, there exist REs ${}_{i,k-1,j}E$, ${}_{i,k-1,k}E$, ${}_{k,k-1,k}E$, and ${}_{k,k-1,j}E$ such that $L({}_{i,k-1,j}E) = [i, k-1, j]$, $L({}_{i,k-1,k}E) = [i, k-1, k]$, $L({}_{k,k-1,k}E) = [k, k-1, k]$, and $L({}_{k,k-1,j}E) = [k, k-1, j]$. Thus, $[i, k, j]$ is denoted by the RE ${}_{i,k-1,j}E|{}_{i,k-1,k}E({}_{k,k-1,k}E)^*{}_{k,k-1,j}E$. ■

Theorem 3.27 For every DFA M, there exists an equivalent RE E.

Proof. By the definition of $[i, k, j]$ for $k = n$ (see Definition 3.25), where $i, j \in \{1, \ldots, n\}$, $[i, n, j] = \{x \mid x \in \Delta^*, q_i x \Rightarrow^* q_j\}$. Thus, $L(M) = \{x \mid x \in \Delta^*, x \in [1, n, j], q_j \in F\}$. Thus,

$$L(M) = {}_{1,n,j_1}E \mid {}_{1,n,j_2}E \mid \ldots \mid {}_{1,n,j_h}E$$

where $F = \{q_{j_1}, q_{j_2}, \ldots, q_{j_h}\}$. Consequently, the theorem holds true. ■

Example 3.8 Consider the DFA M defined by its rules

$$q_1a \rightarrow q_1,\ q_1b \rightarrow q_2, \text{ and } q_2b \rightarrow q_2$$

where q_1 is the start state and q_2 is the only final state. Notice that $L(M) = \{a\}^*\{b\}^+$. Following the idea in the preceding discussion, construct

$${}_{1,0,1}E = a|\varepsilon,\ {}_{1,0,2}E = b,\ {}_{2,0,2}E = b|\varepsilon,\ {}_{2,0,1}E = \varnothing$$

Furthermore, we obtain

$$\begin{aligned}
{}_{1,1,1}E &= {}_{1,0,1}E|{}_{1,0,1}E({}_{1,0,1}E)^*{}_{1,0,1}E = (a|\varepsilon)|(a|\varepsilon)(a|\varepsilon)^*(a|\varepsilon) = a^*\\
{}_{1,1,2}E &= {}_{1,0,2}E|{}_{1,0,1}E({}_{1,0,1}E)^*{}_{1,0,2}E = b|(a|\varepsilon)(a|\varepsilon)^*(b) = a^*b\\
{}_{2,1,1}E &= {}_{2,0,1}E|{}_{2,0,1}E({}_{1,0,1}E)^*{}_{1,0,1}E = \varnothing|\varnothing(a|\varepsilon)^*(a|\varepsilon) = \varnothing\\
{}_{2,1,2}E &= {}_{2,0,2}E|{}_{2,0,1}E({}_{1,0,1}E)^*{}_{1,0,2}E = (b|\varepsilon)|\varnothing(a|\varepsilon)^*b = b|\varepsilon\\
{}_{1,2,1}E &= {}_{1,1,1}E|{}_{1,1,2}E({}_{2,1,2}E)^*{}_{2,1,1}E = a^*|a^*b(b|\varepsilon)^*\varnothing = a^*\\
{}_{1,2,2}E &= {}_{1,1,2}E|{}_{1,1,2}E({}_{2,1,2}E)^*{}_{2,1,2}E = a^*b|a^*b(b|\varepsilon)^*(b|\varepsilon) = a^*b^+\\
{}_{2,2,1}E &= {}_{2,1,1}E|{}_{2,1,2}E({}_{2,1,2}E)^*{}_{2,1,1}E = \varnothing|(b|\varepsilon)(b|\varepsilon)^*\varnothing = \varnothing\\
{}_{2,2,2}E &= {}_{2,1,2}E|{}_{2,1,2}E({}_{2,1,2}E)^*{}_{2,1,2}E = (b|\varepsilon)|(b|\varepsilon)(b|\varepsilon)^*(b|\varepsilon) = b^*
\end{aligned}$$

M has two states q_1 and q_2, where q_1 is the start state and q_2 is the only final state. Therefore, ${}_{1,2,2}E$ denotes $L(M)$. Indeed, $L(M) = \{a\}^*\{b\}^+ = L({}_{1,2,2}E) = L(a^*b^+)$.

3.3.2.2 From Regular Expressions to Finite Automata

Consider fully parenthesized REs over an alphabet Δ—that is, REs constructed strictly according to Definition 3.23 without involving any simplification introduced in Convention 3.24. Next, we transform these expressions to equivalent FAs. To achieve this transformation, we first prove the following three statements.

I. There exist FAs equivalent to the trivial REs $\varnothing$, ε, and $a \in \Delta$.
II. For any pair of FAs, I and J, there exist FAs that accept $L(I) \cup L(J)$ and $L(I)L(J)$.
III. For any FA, I, there exists an FA that accepts $L(I)^*$.

By induction on the number of operators occurring in REs, we then make use of these statements to obtain the desired transformation that turns any RE to an equivalent FA.

Lemma 3.28 There exist FAs that accept the empty set, $\{\varepsilon\}$, and $\{a\}$ with $a \in \Delta$.

Proof. First, any FA with no final state accepts the empty set. Second, $\{\varepsilon\}$ is accepted by any one-state FA that contains no rule. Its only state is the start state; simultaneously, this state is final. As obvious, this automaton accepts $\{\varepsilon\}$. Third, let $a \in \Delta$. Consider a one-rule FA defined by one rule $sa \rightarrow f$, where s is the start nonfinal state and f is the only final state. Clearly, $L(M) = \{a\}$. ■

Next, we convert any two FAs, I and J, to an FA O satisfying $L(O) = L(I) \cup L(J)$.

Basic Idea (see Figure 3.7). Let us consider any two FAs, I and J. Without any loss of generality, we assume that I and J have disjoint sets of states (if I and J contain some states in common, we rename states in either I or J so that they have no state in common). Construct O so that from its start state ${}_Os$, it enters ${}_Is$ or ${}_Js$ by an ε-move. From ${}_Is$, O simulates I, and from ${}_Js$, it simulates J. Whenever occurring in a final state of I or J, O can enter its only final state ${}_Of$ by an ε-move and stop. Thus, $L(O) = L(I) \cup L(J)$.

Algorithm 3.29 FA for Union.

Input. Two FAs, $I = ({}_I\Sigma, {}_IR)$ and $J = ({}_J\Sigma, {}_JR)$, such that ${}_IQ \cap {}_JQ = \varnothing$.

Output. An FA, $O = ({}_O\Sigma, {}_OR)$, such that $L(O) = L(I) \cup L(J)$.

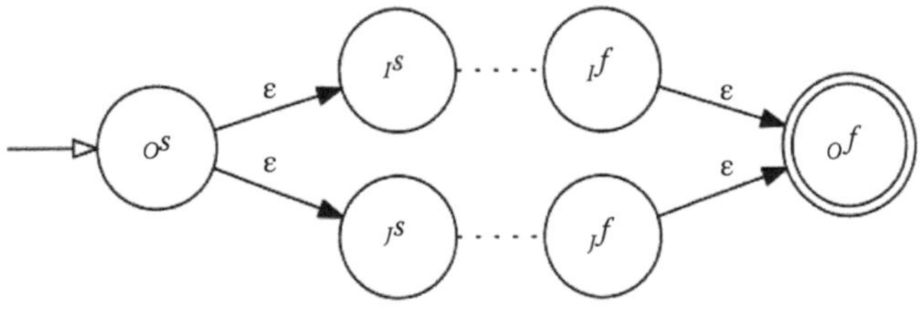

Figure 3.7 FA for union.

Method.

begin

set ${}_O\Delta = {}_I\Delta \cup {}_J\Delta$
set ${}_OQ = {}_IQ \cup {}_JQ$
introduce two new states, ${}_Os$ and ${}_Of$, into ${}_OQ$, and define ${}_Os$ as the start state in O;
set ${}_OF = \{{}_Of\}$
set ${}_OR = {}_IR \cup {}_JR \cup \{{}_Os \rightarrow {}_Is, {}_Os \rightarrow {}_Js\} \cup \{p \rightarrow {}_Of \mid p \in {}_IF \cup {}_JF\}$

end.

Lemma 3.30 Algorithm 3.29 is correct.

Proof. To establish $L(O) = L(I) \cup L(J)$, we first prove the following claim.

Claim. For every $w \in {}_O\Delta^*$, $qw \Rightarrow^* p$ in O iff $qw \Rightarrow^* p$ in K with $K \in \{I, J\}$, $q, p \in {}_KQ$.

Proof of the Claim.

Only if. By induction on $i \geq 0$, we prove for every $w \in {}_O\Delta^*$ and every $i \geq 0$,

$$qw \Rightarrow^i p \text{ in } O \text{ implies } qw \Rightarrow^i p \text{ in } K$$

where $K \in \{I, J\}$ and $q, p \in {}_KQ$. As obvious, the *only-if* part follows from this implication.

Basis. Let $i = 0$, so $qw \Rightarrow^0 p$ in O, where $q, p \in {}_KQ$, and $K \in \{I, J\}$. Then, $q = p$ and $w = \varepsilon$. Clearly, $q \Rightarrow^0 q$ in K, and the basis holds.

Induction Hypothesis. Assume that the implication holds for all $0 \leq i \leq n$, where $n \in {}_0\mathbb{N}$.

Induction Step. Let $qw \Rightarrow^{n+1} p$ in O, where $q, p \in {}_KQ$ for some $K \in \{I, J\}$ and $w \in {}_O\Delta^*$. Because $n + 1 \geq 1$, express $qw \Rightarrow^{n+1} p$ as $qva \Rightarrow^n oa \Rightarrow p$ in O, where $o \in {}_KQ$, $w = va$ with $a \in {}_O\Delta \cup \{\varepsilon\}$ and $v \in {}_O\Delta^*$. Since $oa \Rightarrow p$ in O, $oa \rightarrow p \in {}_OR$. Recall that $o, p \in {}_KQ$. Thus, by the definition of ${}_OR$ (see Algorithm 3.29), ${}_KR$ contains $oa \rightarrow p$, so $oa \Rightarrow p$ in K. By the inductive hypothesis, $qv \Rightarrow^n o$ in K. Putting $qv \Rightarrow^n o$ and $oa \Rightarrow p$ in K together, $qva \Rightarrow^n oa \Rightarrow p$ in K. Because $va = w$, $qw \Rightarrow^{n+1} p$ in K, which completes the induction step.

If. By analogy with the *only-if* part of the claim, prove its *if* part as an exercise.

Consequently, the Claim holds true.

Observe that O makes every accepting computation (see Convention 3.2) so that it starts by applying a rule from $\{{}_Os \rightarrow {}_Is, {}_Os \rightarrow {}_Js\}$ and ends by applying a rule from $\{p \rightarrow {}_Of \mid p \in {}_IF \cup {}_JF\}$. More formally, O accepts every $w \in L(O)$ by a computation of the form

$${}_Osw \Rightarrow {}_Ksw \Rightarrow^* {}_Kf \Rightarrow {}_Of$$

where $K \in \{I, J\}$ and ${}_Kf \in {}_KF$. Consider the previous claim for $q = {}_Ks$ and $p = {}_Kf$ to obtain

$${}_Ksw \Rightarrow^* {}_Kf \text{ in } O \text{ iff } {}_Ksw \Rightarrow^* {}_Kf \text{ in } K$$

Thus,

$$_Osw \Rightarrow {_K}sw \Rightarrow^* {_K}f \Rightarrow {_O}f \text{ iff } {_K}sw \Rightarrow^* {_K}f \text{ in } K$$

Hence, $w \in L(O)$ iff $w \in L(K)$. In other words, $L(O) = \{w \in L(K)|\ K \in \{I, J\}\}$. That is, $L(O) = L(I) \cup L(J)$, and the lemma holds. ■

Before going any further, we need the notion of a stop state, used in Algorithm 3.33.

Definition 3.31 Let M be an FA. In $_MQ$, a *stop state* is a state that does not occur on the left-hand side of any rule in $_MR$. ■

By this definition, any FA can never leave any of its stop states. By Lemma 3.32, without any loss of generality, we can always assume that an FA has precisely one final state, which is also a stop state.

Lemma 3.32 For every FA I, there exists an equivalent FA O such that $_OF = \{_Of\}$ and $_Of$ is a stop state.

Proof. Let I be an FA. Take any FA J such that $L(J) = \varnothing$ (see Lemma 3.28). By using Algorithm 3.29, convert I and J to an FA O satisfying $L(O) = L(I) \cup L(J) = L(I) \cup \varnothing = L(I)$. Observe that O constructed in this way has a single final state $_Of$, which is also a stop state. ■

We are now ready to convert any pair of FAs, I and J, to an FA O that accepts $L(O) = L(I)L(J)$.

Basic Idea (see Figure 3.8). Consider any two FAs, I and J, such that $_IQ \cap {_J}Q = \varnothing$. Without any loss of generality, suppose that I has a single final state, $_If$, such that $_If$ is also a stop state, and J has also only one final state, $_Jf$, and this state is a stop state (see Lemma 3.32). Construct O as follows. Starting from $_Is$, O simulates I until it enters $_If$, from which O makes an ε-move to $_Js$. From $_Js$, O simulates J until O enters $_Jf$, which is also the only final state in O. Thus, $L(O) = L(I)L(J)$.

Algorithm 3.33 FA for Concatenation.

Input. Two FAs, $I = ({_I}\Sigma, {_I}R)$ and $J = ({_J}\Sigma, {_J}R)$, such that $_IQ \cap {_J}Q = \varnothing$, $_IF = \{_If\}$, $_JF = \{_Jf\}$, $_If$ and $_Jf$ are both stop states (see Lemma 3.32).

Output. An FA, $O = ({_O}\Sigma, {_O}R)$, such that $L(O) = L(I)L(J)$.

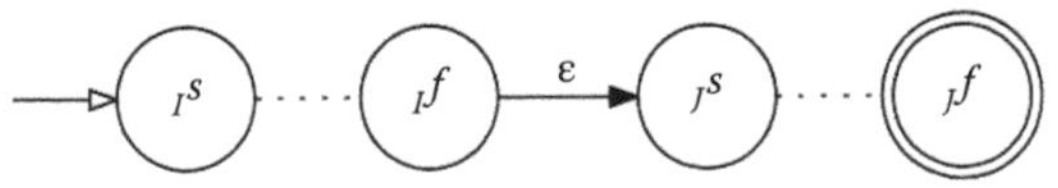

Figure 3.8 FA for concatenation.

Method.

begin

set ${}_O\Delta = {}_I\Delta \cup {}_J\Delta$
set ${}_OQ = {}_IQ \cup {}_JQ$
set ${}_Os = {}_Is$
set ${}_OF = \{{}_Jf\}$
set ${}_OR = {}_IR \cup {}_JR \cup \{{}_If \to {}_Js\}$

end.

Lemma 3.34 Algorithm 3.33 is correct.

Proof. Notice that O accepts every $w \in L(O)$ by a computation of the form

$$ {}_Isuv \Rightarrow^* {}_Ifv \Rightarrow {}_Jsv \Rightarrow^* {}_Jf $$

where $w = uv$. Thus, ${}_Isu \Rightarrow^* {}_If$ in I, and ${}_Jsv \Rightarrow^* {}_Jf$ in J. Therefore, $u \in L(I)$ and $v \in L(J)$, so $L(O) \subseteq L(I)L(J)$. In a similar way, demonstrate $L(I)L(J) \subseteq L(O)$. Hence, $L(O) = L(I)L(J)$. A rigorous version of this proof is left as an exercise. ■

We now convert any FA I to an FA O satisfying $L(I) = L(O)^*$.

Basic Idea (Figure 3.9). Consider an FA, I. Without any loss of generality, suppose that I has a single final state ${}_If$ such that ${}_If$ is also a stop state (see Lemma 3.32). Apart from all states from I, O has two new states, ${}_Os$ and ${}_Of$, where ${}_Os$ is its start state and ${}_Of$ is its only final state. From ${}_Os$, O can enter ${}_Of$ without reading any symbol, thus accepting ε. In addition, it can make an ε-move to ${}_Is$ to simulate I. Occurring in ${}_If$, O can enter ${}_Is$ or ${}_Of$ by making an ε-move. If O enters ${}_Is$, it starts simulating another sequence of moves in I. If O enters ${}_Of$, it successfully completes its computation. Therefore, $L(O) = L(I)^*$.

Algorithm 3.35 FA for Iteration.

Input. An FA, $I = ({}_I\Sigma, {}_IR)$, such that ${}_IF = \{{}_If\}$, and ${}_If$ is a stop state (see Lemma 3.32).

Output. An FA, $O = ({}_O\Sigma, {}_OR)$, such that $L(O) = L(I)^*$.

Method.

begin

set ${}_O\Delta = {}_I\Delta$
set ${}_OQ = {}_IQ$
introduce two new states, ${}_Os$ and ${}_Of$, into ${}_OQ$; define ${}_Os$ as the start state in O;
set ${}_OF = \{{}_Of\}$
set ${}_OR = {}_IR \cup \{{}_Os \to {}_Of, {}_Os \to {}_Is, {}_If \to {}_Is, {}_If \to {}_Of\}$

end.

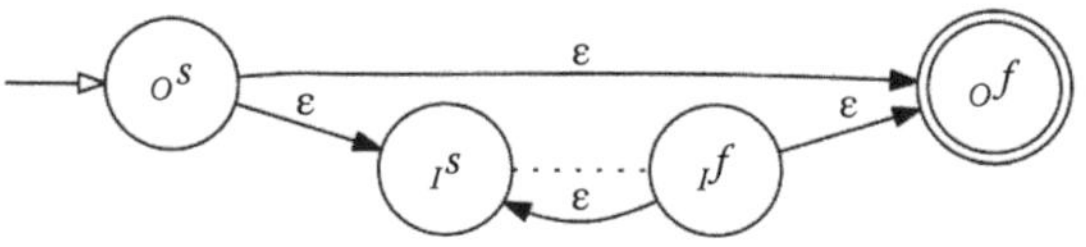

Figure 3.9 FA for iteration.

Lemma 3.36 Algorithm 3.35 is correct.

Proof. To see the reason why $L(O) = L(I)^*$, observe that O accepts every $w \in L(O) - \{\varepsilon\}$ in this way

$$
\begin{aligned}
{}_O s v_1 v_2 \ldots v_n &\Rightarrow {}_I s v_1 v_2 \ldots v_n \\
&\Rightarrow^* {}_I f v_2 \ldots v_n \\
&\Rightarrow {}_I s v_2 \ldots v_n \\
&\Rightarrow^* {}_I f v_3 \ldots v_n \\
&\vdots \\
&\Rightarrow {}_I s v_n \\
&\Rightarrow^* {}_I f \\
&\Rightarrow {}_O f
\end{aligned}
$$

where $n \in \mathbb{N}$, $w = v_1 v_2 \ldots v_n$ with $v_i \in L(I)$ for all $i = 1, \ldots, n$. Furthermore, O accepts ε as ${}_O s\varepsilon \Rightarrow {}_O f$. Therefore, $L(I)^* \subseteq L(O)$. Similarly, prove $L(O) \subseteq L(I)^*$. As $L(I)^* \subseteq L(O)$ and $L(O) \subseteq L(I)^*$, $L(O) = L(I)^*$. A rigorous version of this proof is left as an exercise. ■

We are now ready to prove that for any RE, there is an equivalent FA. In the proof, we will consider fully parenthesized REs defined strictly according to Definition 3.23 (i.e., we do not consider their simplified versions introduced in Convention 3.24).

Theorem 3.37 Let r be an RE; then, there exists an FA M such that $L(r) = L(M)$.

Proof (by induction on the number of operators in r). Let r be a fully parenthesized RE over an alphabet Δ (see Definition 3.23).

Basis. Let r be a fully parenthesized RE that contains no operator. By Definition 3.23, r is of the form $\emptyset$, ε, or a with $a \in \Delta$. Then, this basis follows from Lemma 3.28.

Induction Hypothesis. Suppose that Theorem 3.37 holds for every RE containing n or fewer operators, for some $n \in {}_0\mathbb{N}$.

Induction Step. Let e be any fully parenthesized RE containing $n + 1$ operators. Thus, e is of the form $(r|s)$, (rs), or $(r)^*$, where r and s are REs with no more than n operators, so for r and s, Theorem 3.37 holds by the induction hypothesis. These three forms of e are considered next.

I. Let $e = (r|s)$, so $L(e) = L(r) \cup L(s)$. As Theorem 3.37 holds for r and s, there are FAs I and J such that $L(r) = L(I)$ and $L(s) = L(J)$. By using Algorithm 3.29, verified by Lemma 3.30, convert I and J to an FA O satisfying $L(O) = L(I) \cup L(J)$, so $L(O) = L(e)$.
II. Let $e = (rs)$, so $L(e) = L(r)L(s)$. Let I and J be FAs such that $L(r) = L(I)$ and $L(s) = L(J)$. By using Algorithm 3.33, turn I and J to an FA O satisfying $L(O) = L(I)L(J)$, so $L(O) = L(e)$.
III. Let $e = (r)^*$, so $L(e) = L((r)^*)$. Let I be an FA such that $L(r) = L(I)$. By using Algorithm 3.35, convert I to an FA O satisfying $L(O) = L(I)^* = L(r)^* = L(e)$. ■

Taking a closer look at the proof of Theorem 3.37, we see that it actually presents a method of converting any fully parenthesized RE to an equivalent FA as sketched next.

Basic Idea. Consider any RE. Processing from the innermost parentheses out, determine how the expression is constructed by Definition 3.23. Follow the conversion described in the proof of Theorem 3.37 and simultaneously create the equivalent FAs by the algorithms referenced in this proof. More specifically, let r and s be two REs obtained during the construction.

1. Let r is an RE of the form $\emptyset$, ε, or a, where $a \in \Delta$. Turn r to an equivalent FA by the method given in the proof of Lemma 3.28.
2. Let r and s be two REs, and let I and J be FAs equivalent with r and s, respectively. Then,
   a. $(r|s)$ is equivalent to the FA constructed from I and J by Algorithm 3.29.
   b. (rs) is equivalent to the FA constructed from I and J by Algorithm 3.33.
   c. $(r)^*$ is equivalent to the FA constructed from I by Algorithm 3.35.

Leaving an algorithm that rigorously reformulates this method as an exercise, we illustrate it by Example 3.9.

Example 3.9 Consider $(a((b|c))^*)$ as a fully parenthesized RE. By Definition 3.23, we see that this expression is step-by-step constructed by making expressions a, b, c, $(b|c)$, $((b|c))^*$, and $(a((b|c))^*)$, numbered by 1, 2, 3, 4, 5, and 6, respectively, for brevity; in this example, we construct the six FAs, M_1 through M_6, so M_i is equivalent to RE i, where $i = 1, \ldots, 6$ (see Figure 3.10). During the construction of M_i, $1 \leq i \leq 5$, we always introduce two new states, denoted by ${}_is$ and ${}_if$ (during the construction of M_6, we need no new state).

Consider the first three elementary subexpressions a, b, and c that denote languages $\{a\}$, $\{b\}$, and $\{c\}$, respectively. Based on the construction given in the proof of Lemma 3.28, we construct M_1, M_2, and M_3 that accept $\{a\}$, $\{b\}$, and $\{c\}$, respectively. From expressions b and c, we make expression $(b|c)$ that denotes $\{b\} \cup \{c\}$. Recall that M_2 and M_3 are equivalent to expressions b and c, respectively; that is, $L(M_2) = \{b\}$ and $L(M_3) = \{c\}$. Thus, with M_2 and M_3 as the input of Algorithm 3.29, we construct M_4 that accepts $L(M_2) \cup L(M_3) = \{b\} \cup \{c\} = \{b, c\}$. From $(b|c)$, we can make $((b|c))^*$ that denotes $(\{b\} \cup \{c\})^* = \{b, c\}^*$. Recall that M_4 is equivalent to RE 4. Therefore, with M_4 as the input of Algorithm 3.35, we construct M_5 equivalent to RE 5. From RE 1 and RE 5, we make RE 6 that denotes $\{a\}(\{b\} \cup \{c\})^* = \{a\}\{b, c\}^*$. M_1 and M_5 are equivalent to expressions RE 1 and RE 5, respectively. Therefore, with M_1 and M_5 as the input of Algorithm 3.33, we construct an FA M_6 equivalent to RE 6 as desired. Figures 3.11 through 3.14 summarize this construction.

By algorithms given in Section 3.2, we can now turn M_6 to an equivalent ${}_{min}$DFA M_{min} depicted in Figure 3.15.

We close this chapter by a crucially important Theorem 3.38, which summarizes Theorems 3.27 and 3.37 and Corollary 3.22.

	RE	FA
1	a	M_1
2	b	M_2
3	c	M_3
4	$(b\|c)$	M_4
5	$((b\|c))^*$	M_5
6	$(a((b\|c))^*)$	M_6

Figure 3.10 REs and FAs.

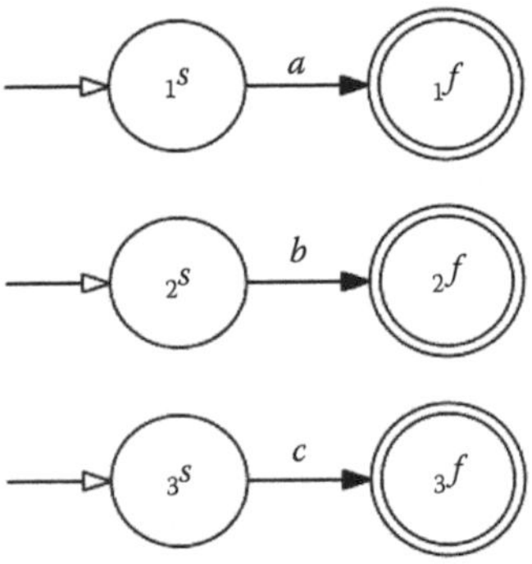

Figure 3.11 M_1, M_2, and M_3.

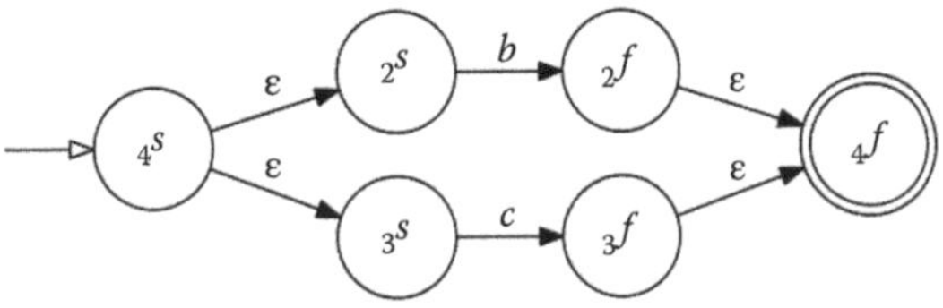

Figure 3.12 M_4.

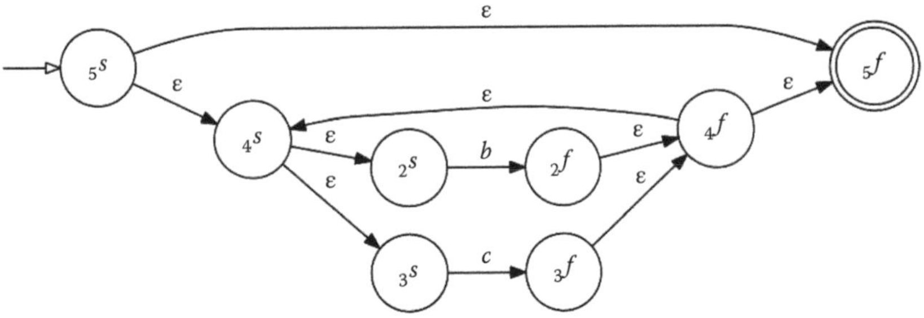

Figure 3.13 M_5.

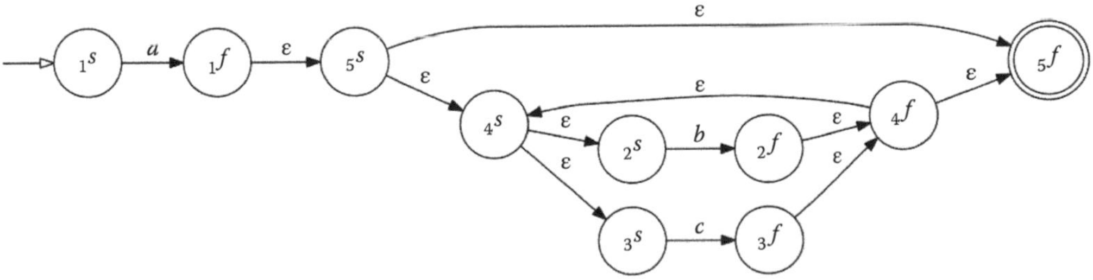

Figure 3.14 M_6.

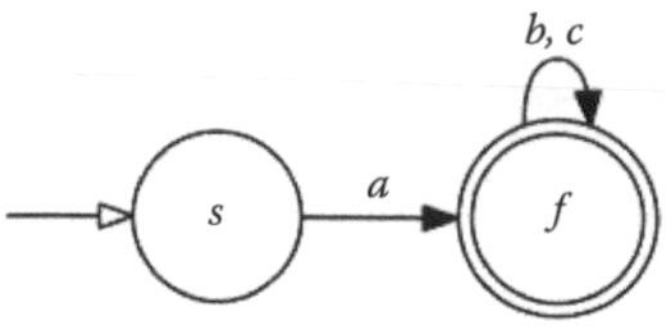

Figure 3.15 M_{min}.

Theorem 3.38 The REs and the FAs are equivalent—that is, they both characterize $_{reg}\Phi$. Consequently, all the restricted versions of FAs mentioned in Corollary 3.22 characterize $_{reg}\Phi$, too. ■

Exercises

1. Let L be the language consisting of all strings over {0, 1} such that 011 does not occur as a substring in them. Define L formally. Construct an FA that accepts L. Construct an RE that denotes L.
2. Consider each of the following languages: (i) through (x). Construct an FA that accepts the language and an RE that denotes it. Give a proof that verifies the construction.
   i. $\{a^i bba^j bb \mid i, j \geq 1\}$
   ii. $\{a^i b^j a \mid i \geq 0 \text{ and } j \geq 1\}$
   iii. $\{a^{2i} \mid i \geq 0\}$
   iv. $\{a^i b^j c^k \mid i, k \geq 0 \text{ and } j \geq 1\}$
   v. $\{bab^i a^j \mid i, j \geq 0\}$
   vi. $\{x \mid x \in \{a, b\}^*, aa \in substring(x)\}$
   vii. $\{x \mid x \in \{a, b\}^*, abb \in substring(x) \text{ iff } bba \notin suffixes(x)\}$
   viii. $\{x \mid x \in \{a, b\}^*, aa \in substring(x), aa \notin suffixes(x)\}$
   ix. $\{x \mid x \in \{a, b\}^*, ab \notin substring(x), |x| \text{ is divisible by } 3\}$
   x. $\{x \mid x \in \{a, b\}^*, bab \notin substring(x), |x| \text{ is divisible by } 3, bb \in suffixes(x)\}$

3 S. Consider the following FAs, (i) through (v), in which 1 is the start state and 4 is the only final state.
   i. $1a \rightarrow 2, 1b \rightarrow 1, 1b \rightarrow 2, 2a \rightarrow 2, 2b \rightarrow 2, 2b \rightarrow 3, 3a \rightarrow 3, 3a \rightarrow 4$
   ii. $1a \rightarrow 2, 1 \rightarrow 4, 1b \rightarrow 1, 1b \rightarrow 2, 2a \rightarrow 2, 2b \rightarrow 2, 2b \rightarrow 3, 3a \rightarrow 3, 3a \rightarrow 1$
   iii. $1a \rightarrow 2, 2a \rightarrow 3, 3b \rightarrow 2, 2b \rightarrow 1, 1c \rightarrow 4$
   iv. $1a \rightarrow 2, 1b \rightarrow 3, 2c \rightarrow 1, 3c \rightarrow 1, 1c \rightarrow 4$
   v. $1a \rightarrow 1, 1 \rightarrow 2, 2b \rightarrow 2, 2 \rightarrow 3, 3 \rightarrow 1, 3 \rightarrow 4$

   For each of them, give
   a. its state table
   b. the state diagram
   c. the accepted language and a proof verifying that the language is correctly determined
   d. an equivalent RE together with a proof that verifies the equivalence

4. Consider the following REs, (i) through (v).
   i. $ab(bb)^*ba$
   ii. $((ab)^*ba(ab)^*)$
   iii. $((ab|ba)^*|(aabb)^*)^*$
   iv. $aa(ba)^*|bb^*$
   v. $ba(bab)^*|ab(ab)^*$

   For each of them, give
   a. the language denoted by the RE and a proof verifying that the language is correctly determined
   b. an equivalent DFA together with a proof that verifies the equivalence
   c. if possible, a shorter equivalent RE together with a proof that verifies the equivalence
5. Consider the following identities for REs. Verify them by rigorous proofs.
   i. $r(s|t) = rs|rt$
   ii. $r(st) = (rs)t$

iii. $r|(s|t) = (r|s)|t$
iv. $r\varepsilon = \varepsilon r = r$
v. $r\varnothing = \varnothing r = \varnothing$
vi. $r^* = r^*\varepsilon = \varepsilon r^*$

6. How many different languages over {0, 1} are defined by two-state FAs? Reformulate and answer this question in terms of special versions of FAs, including $_{\varepsilon\text{-}free}$FAs and DFAs.
7. Chapter 3 contains results whose proofs were only sketched or even omitted. These results include Theorems 3.8, 3.11, 3.16, 3.18, and 3.21 and Lemmas 3.30, 3.34, and 3.36. Prove these results rigorously.
8. Section 3.2.3 explains how to minimize DFAs. Give some alternative methods of this minimization.
9. Example 3.9 is preceded by a sketch that describes the conversion of any RE to an equivalent FA. Reformulate this sketch as an algorithm and verify its correctness in a rigorous way.
10 S. Consider the standard definition of an FA (see Definition 3.1). Generalize it so that the FA can read an entire string during a single move to obtain the definition of a *long-reading FA* ($_{long}$*FA* for short). Formalize this generalization. Are $_{long}$FAs and standard FAs equivalent? If so, (i) design an algorithm that turns any $_{long}$FA to an equivalent FA and (ii) verify this algorithm by a rigorous proof. If not, give (i) a $_{long}$FA such that there is no FA equivalent with the $_{long}$FA and (ii) a proof that verifies this nonequivalence.
11. Let $M = (\Sigma, R)$ be a DFA (see Definition 3.9). A state $q \in {}_MQ$ is *looping* if there exists $w \in \Delta^+$ such that $qw \Rightarrow^* q$. M is *loop-free* if no state in $_MQ$ is looping. Prove that a language L is finite iff $L = L(M)$, where M is a loop-free DFA.
12 S. A *two-way finite automaton* is an FA generalized, so it can make moves right as well as left on the input string. Formalize this generalization. Are these automata and FAs equivalent? Justify your answer by a rigorous proof.
13 S. A *finite transducer* M is an FA modified, so it emits an output string during every move. Consider $a_1 \ldots a_n$, where each a_i is an input symbol or ε, $1 \le i \le n$, for some $n \ge 1$, and suppose that M emits a string x_i during a move on a_i. If M accepts $a_1 \ldots a_n$ by analogy with the standard FA way of acceptance (see Definition 3.1), then it translates $a_1 \ldots a_n$ to $x_1 \ldots x_n$. The *translation of* M is the relation consisting of all pairs (x, y) such that M translates x to y. Formalize this gist. That is, define the notion of a finite transducer and its translation rigorously.
14. Design a tabular and graphical representation of finite transducers by analogy with the FA state tables and state diagrams (see Section 3.1).

Solutions to Selected Exercises

3. Consider (v). Its state table is

State	a	b	ε
1	1		2
2		2	3
3			1, 4
4			

The accepted language equals L^* with $L = \{a^ib^j \mid i, j \ge 0\}$. Observe that L^* coincides with $\{a, b\}^*$, denoted by an RE of the form $(a|b)^*$. Complete the solution concerning (v). Solve (i) through (iv).

10. **Definition** A *long-reading FA* (${}_{long}FA$) is a rewriting system, $M = (\Sigma, R)$, where

- Σ is divided into two pairwise disjoint subalphabets Q and Δ;
- R is a finite *set of rules* of the form $qx \rightarrow p$, where $q, p \in Q$ and $x \in \Delta^*$.

Q and Δ are referred to as the *set of states* and the *alphabet of input symbols*, respectively. Q contains a state called the *start state*, denoted by s, and a *set of final states*, denoted by F. Like in any rewriting system, we define $u \Rightarrow v$, $u \Rightarrow^n v$ with $n \geq 0$, and $u \Rightarrow^* v$, where $u, v \in \Sigma^*$. If $sw \Rightarrow^* f$ in M, where $w \in \Delta^*$, *M accepts w*. The set of all strings that M accepts is the *language accepted by M*, denoted by $L(M)$. ■

FAs and ${}_{long}$FAs are equivalent. On the one hand, every FA is obviously a special case of a ${}_{long}$FA. On the other hand, we can convert any ${}_{long}$FA to an equivalent FA by the next algorithm. First, we give its gist.

Basic Idea. Take any ${}_{long}$FA, $I = ({}_I\Sigma, {}_IR)$. Construct an equivalent FA, $O = ({}_O\Sigma, {}_OR)$, so it simulates reading in I symbol by symbol. That is, if I applies a rule of the form $qa \rightarrow p \in {}_IR$, where $q, p \in {}_IQ$ and $a \in {}_I\Delta \cup \{\varepsilon\}$, O simulates this application by the same rule. If I applies a rule of the form $qa_1a_2 \ldots a_n \rightarrow p \in {}_IR$, where $q, p \in {}_IQ$ and each a_i is an input symbol, for some $n \geq 2$, O simulates this application by consecutively applying rules

$$q \rightarrow \langle p, a_1a_2 \ldots a_n \rangle, \langle p, a_2 \ldots a_n \rangle a_1 \rightarrow \langle p, a_2 \ldots a_n \rangle, \ldots, \langle p, a_n \rangle a_n \rightarrow \langle p, \varepsilon \rangle, \langle p, \varepsilon \rangle \rightarrow p,$$

where $\langle p, a_1a_2 \ldots a_n \rangle, \langle p, a_2 \ldots a_n \rangle, \ldots, \langle p, a_n \rangle, \langle p, \varepsilon \rangle$ are new states.

Algorithm ${}_{long}$FA to FA Conversion.

Input. A ${}_{long}$FA $I = ({}_I\Sigma, {}_IR)$.

Output. An FA $O = ({}_O\Sigma, {}_OR)$ such that $L(O) = L(I)$.

Method.

begin

set ${}_O\Delta = {}_I\Delta$
set ${}_OQ = {}_IQ$
set ${}_Os = {}_Is$
set ${}_OF = {}_IF$
set ${}_OR = \{qa \rightarrow p \mid qa \rightarrow p \in {}_IR, q, p \in {}_IQ, a \in {}_I\Delta \cup \{\varepsilon\}\}$;
for every $qa_1a_2 \ldots a_n \rightarrow p \in {}_IR$, $q, p \in {}_IQ$, $a_i \in {}_I\Delta$, $1 \leq i \leq n$, for some $n \geq 2$,
  include $\langle p, a_1a_2 \ldots a_n \rangle, \langle p, a_2 \ldots a_n \rangle, \ldots, \langle p, a_n \rangle, \langle p, \varepsilon \rangle$ into ${}_OQ$, and
  include $q \rightarrow \langle p, a_1a_2 \ldots a_n \rangle, \langle p, a_1a_2 \ldots a_n \rangle a_1 \rightarrow \langle p, a_2 \ldots a_n \rangle, \ldots,$
  $\langle p, a_n \rangle a_n \rightarrow \langle p, \varepsilon \rangle, \langle p, \varepsilon \rangle \rightarrow p$ into ${}_OR$;

end.

Verify this algorithm by analogy with the proof of Theorem 3.8.

12. **Definition** A *two-way finite automaton* is a rewriting system, $M = (\Sigma, R)$, where

- Σ is divided into two pairwise disjoint subsets Q and Δ;
- R is a finite *set of rules* of the form $x \rightarrow y$, where either $x = qa$ and $y = ap$ or $x = aq$ and $y = pa$, for some $q, p \in Q$ and $a \in \Delta$.

Q and Δ are referred to as the *set of states* and the *alphabet of input symbols*, respectively. Q contains a state called the *start state*, denoted by s, and a *set of final states*, denoted by F. Like in any rewriting system, we define $u \Rightarrow v$, $u \Rightarrow^n v$ with $n \geq 0$, and $u \Rightarrow^* v$, where $u, v \in \Sigma^*$

(see Definition 1.5). If $qw \Rightarrow^* wf$ in M with $f \in F$, *M accepts w*. The set of all strings that M accepts is the *language accepted by M*, denoted by $L(M)$. ■

Prove that these automata are as powerful as FAs.

13. **Definition** Let $M = (\Sigma, R)$ be an FA, O be an *output alphabet*, and o be a total *output function* from R to O^*. Then, $\Pi = (\Sigma, R, o)$ is a *finite transducer underlain by M*. Let $\Pi = (\Sigma, R, o)$ be a *finite transducer*, $v \in \Delta^*$, and $w \in O^*$. If *M accepts v according to $r_1r_2\ldots r_n$*, where $r_i \in R$, $1 \leq i \leq n$, for some $n \geq 0$, then *Π translates v to $o(r_1)o(r_2)\ldots o(r_n)$ according to $r_1r_2\ldots r_n$* (the case when $n = 0$ means that v, $r_1r_2\ldots r_n$, and $o(r_1)o(r_2)\ldots o(r_n)$ are equal to ε). The *translation of Π*, $T(\Pi)$, is defined as $T(\Pi) = \{(v, w) \mid v \in \Delta^*, w \in O^*, \Pi \text{ translates } v \text{ to } w\}$. ■

Convention For brevity, we often express $r \in R$ with $o(r) = y$ as ry; that is, if r: $qa \rightarrow p \in R$ and $o(r) = y$, we write r: $qa \rightarrow py$. ■

Informally, a finite transducer, $\Pi = (\Sigma, R, o)$, translates an input string, $a_1\ldots a_n$, to an output string, $x_1\ldots x_n$, as follows. In essence, it works by analogy with its underlying automaton $M = (\Sigma, R)$; moreover, Π writes a suffix of the produced output string during every step of this translation process. More exactly, assume that Π has already translated $a_1\ldots a_{i-1}$ to $x_1\ldots x_{i-1}$, so the current input symbol is a_i. At this point, Π can make a translation step according to a rule of the form $q \rightarrow px_i$ or $qa_i \rightarrow px_i$, where q is Π's current state. According to $q \rightarrow px_i$, Π changes q to p and writes x_i behind $x_1\ldots x_{i-1}$, so it actually extends $x_1\ldots x_{i-1}$ to $x_1\ldots x_{i-1}x_i$. According to $qa_i \rightarrow px_i$, Π does the same; in addition, however, it reads a_i, so a_{i+1} becomes the input symbol in the next step. If in this way Π translates $a_1\ldots a_n$ to $x_1\ldots x_n$ and M accepts $a_1\ldots a_n$, $(a_1\ldots a_n, x_1\ldots x_n) \in T(\Pi)$, which denotes the translation defined by Π.

Of course, the notion of a finite transducer and its translation can be formalized in other ways so the resulting notion has the same meaning as the notion defined above. Give an alternative formalization like this.

Chapter 4

Applications of Regular Expressions and Finite Automata: Lexical Analysis

Regular expressions (REs) and finite automata (FAs) underlie many computer science units, ranging from hardware components, such as switching circuits, to software tools, such as text editors. Out of this large variety, we explain how they are applied to the *lexical analysis* of high-level programming languages in this section.

Compared to Chapter 3, this application-oriented chapter differs in size as well as style. Indeed, this chapter is much shorter. Second, regarding its presentation style, all concepts underlying lexical analysis are presented in a more descriptive way rather than in the form of strictly rigorous mathematical notions used in Chapter 3. A special attention is paid to their implementation to reflect the pragmatically orientated focus of this chapter.

As far as its organization is concerned, this chapter consists of two sections. Section 4.1 explains how to implement completely specified deterministic finite automata ($_{cs}$DFAs) (see Section 3.2.2) because this implementation is needed in Section 4.2, which discusses the lexical analysis—the subject of this chapter. More precisely, Section 4.2 consists of two subsections. First, Section 4.2.1 gives an introduction to lexical analysis. Second, Section 4.2.2 explains how to implement a lexical analyzer.

Before this pragmatically oriented chapter is started, a note concerning its description of algorithms is in order. Just like the previous chapter, the present chapter describes them by using Pascal-like notation, which is very intuitive and readable. However, some of these algorithms, such as Algorithms 4.2 and 4.3, are actually meant as sample programs that implement components of lexical analyzers. All of them are straightforwardly convertible to any common programming language, such as Java.

4.1 Implementation of Finite Automata

This section explains how to implement $_{cs}$DFAs because grasping the construction of a lexical analyzer presupposes a familiarity with this implementation. As a matter of fact, we give two alternative algorithms that implement these automata. The first algorithm actually implements them based on their state tables. The other algorithm is based on a nested **case** statement; based on this algorithm, a lexical analyzer is implemented in Section 4.2.2. In both of them, we make use of Convention 4.1.

Convention 4.1 Algorithms 4.2 and 4.3 assume that a given input string w is followed by $\triangleleft$, which thus acts as an *input end marker*. As their output, the algorithms announces **ACCEPT** if $w \in L(M)$ and **REJECT** if $w \notin L(M)$. ■

As obvious, in practice, the end of a given input string is always somehow specified, so $\triangleleft$ only symbolically expresses this end. For instance, if the input string is written as a file, then the end of the file fulfills the role of $\triangleleft$.

4.1.1 *Table-Based Implementation*

First, we give the algorithm that implements any completely specified DFA, M, based on its state table. In this algorithm, we assume that its states are numbered by 1 through n, for some $n \in \mathbb{N}$, where 1 is the start state.

Algorithm 4.2 FA Implementation: A Tabular Method.

Input. A $_{cs}$DFA, $M = ({}_M\Sigma, {}_MR)$ with ${}_MQ = \{1, \ldots, n\}$, ${}_M\Delta = \{a_1, \ldots, a_m\}$, $s = 1$, and $w\triangleleft$ with $w \in {}_M\Delta^*$.

Output. **ACCEPT** if $w \in L(M)$, and **REJECT** if $w \notin L(M)$.

Note. Recall that ${}_MF$ denotes the set of final states in M according to Convention 3.2.

Method.

type

states = 1..n
symbols = 'a_1'..'a_m'
rules = **array**[*states*, *symbols*] **of** *states*
stateset = **set of** *states*

var

state: *states*
symbol: *symbols*
rule: *rules* {array *rule* represents the state table of M}
finalstates: *stateset*

begin

for all $i = 1, \ldots, n$ and all $j = 1, \ldots, m$, {filling in the state table}
  if $ia_j \rightarrow k \in {}_MR$ **then**
    set $rule[i, 'a_j'] = k$
set *finalstates* to ${}_MF$ {initialization of final states}
set *state* = 1 {1 is the start state}
read(*symbol*)
while $symbol \neq \triangleleft$ **do**
begin
  state = *rule*[*state*, *symbol*] {simulation of a move}
  read(*symbol*)
end
if $state \in finalstates$ **then** {decision of acceptance}
  ACCEPT $\{w \in L(M)\}$
else
  REJECT $\{w \notin L(M)\}$

end.

In Algorithm 4.2, a rule, $ia_j \rightarrow k \in {}_MR$, is represented by $rule[i, 'a_j'] = k$. If $state = i$, $symbol = a_j$, and $rule[i, 'a_j'] = k$, the **while** loop of this algorithm sets *state* to k to simulate the application of $ia_j \rightarrow k$. When this loop reads $\triangleleft$, it exits and the **if** statement tests whether *state* represents a final state. If so, $w \in L(M)$; otherwise, $w \notin L(M)$.

Example 4.1 Let us consider the $_{cs}$DFA represented by the state table given in Figure 4.1. Its start state is 1, and the final states are 2 and 3. As obvious, it accepts the language $\{a\}^*\{b\}^*$.

Following Algorithm 4.2, we give its implementation in Pascal.

```
program DFA(input, output);

{
Based on Algorithm 4.2, this program simulates the completely specified
DFA depicted in Figure 4.1. It reads an input string from file input.
The input string is terminated with #.
}

type
  states    = 1..4;
  stateset  = set of states;
  symbols   = Char;
  symbolset = set of symbols;
  rules     = array[states, symbols] of states;

var
  state       : states;
  finalstates : stateset;
  symbol      : symbols;
  rule        : rules;

const
  alphabet : symbolset = ['a'..'b'];
```

State	a	b
1	2	3
<u>2</u>	2	3
<u>3</u>	4	3
4	4	4

Figure 4.1 State table.

```
begin

  {initialization of rule according to the state table in Figure 4.1}
  rule[1, 'a'] := 2; rule[1, 'b'] := 3;
  rule[2, 'a'] := 2; rule[2, 'b'] := 3;
  rule[3, 'a'] := 4; rule[3, 'b'] := 3;
  rule[4, 'a'] := 4; rule[4, 'b'] := 4;

  finalstates := [2, 3];          {initialization of final states}
  state := 1;                     {1 is the start state}

  read(symbol);

  while symbol in alphabet do
  begin
    state := rule[state, symbol];  {simulation of a move}
    read(symbol)
  end;

  if symbol = '#' then            {the input has been completely read}
    if state in finalstates then  {decision of acceptance}
      writeln('ACCEPT')
    else
      writeln('REJECT')
  else
    writeln('ILLEGAL INPUT SYMBOL') {symbol differs from the symbols of
                                     alphabet or #}

end.
```

With *abb#* as its input, the **while** loop in the above-mentioned program makes these three iterations. The first iteration begins with *state* = 1 and *symbol* = '*a*'. Thus, it sets *state* to 2 because *rule*[1, '*a*'] = 2. The second iteration has *state* = 2 and *symbol* = '*b*', so it sets *state* to 3 because *rule*[2, '*b*'] = 3. The third iteration starts with *state* = 3 and *symbol* = '*b*', therefore it sets *state* = 3 because *rule*[3, '*b*'] = 3. The next symbol is '#', so the **while** loop exits and the **if** statement determines that *state* belongs to *finalstates* because *state* = 3 and *finalstates* = [2, 3]. Therefore, this statement writes ACCEPT.

4.1.2 Case-Statement Implementation

Algorithm 4.2 represents the state table of its input automaton by a two-dimensional array. Algorithm 4.3 is based on a nested **case** statement, which frees this implementation from using any array; indeed, the state table is hardwired into the program structure by using **case** statements. Later on, Section 4.3 illustrates this algorithm by several examples that put it firmly into the implementation of a lexical analyzer.

Algorithm 4.3 FA Implementation: A **case**-Statement-Based Method.

Input. A ${}_{cs}$DFA, $M = ({}_M\Sigma, {}_MR)$ with ${}_MQ = \{1, \ldots, n\}$, ${}_M\Delta = \{a_1, \ldots, a_m\}$, $s = 1$, and $w\triangleleft$ with $w \in {}_M\Delta^*$.

Output. **ACCEPT** if $w \in L(M)$, and **REJECT** if $w \notin L(M)$.

Method.

```
type
    states = 1..n
    symbols = 'a1'..'am'
    stateset = set of states
var
    state: states
    symbol: symbols
    finalstates: stateset

begin
    set finalstates to MF                  {initialization of final states}
    set state = 1
    read(symbol)
    while symbol ≠ ◁ do                    {simulation of moves}
    begin
        case state of
            1: ...
            ⋮
            i: case symbol of
                'a1': ...
                ⋮
                'aj': state = k if iaj → k ∈ MR
                ⋮
                'am': ...
            end {of the case statement corresponding to i}
            ⋮
            n: ...
        end {of the outer case statement}
        read(symbol)
    end {of the while loop}
    if state ∈ finalstates then            {decision of acceptance}
        ACCEPT                             {w ∈ L(M)}
    else
        REJECT                             {w ∉ L(M)}
end.
```

As further discussed in the Exercises, Algorithm 3.3 has an important advantage over Algorithm 3.2. Indeed, although Algorithm 3.2 strictly requires ${}_{cs}$DFA as its input automaton, Algorithm 3.3 does not—that is, the latter can also implement incompletely specified DFAs without any problems.

4.2 Introduction to Lexical Analysis

A lexical analyzer or, more briefly and customarily, a *scanner* breaks up a programming-language code into logically cohesive lexical entities, referred to as *lexical units*. That is, it reads the string of characters that make up the program to include the following:

1. Recognize the instances of lexical units the program consists of
2. Verify their correct construction according to REs that define them
3. Categorize them according to their types, such as identifiers or integers

This section shows how to define lexical units by REs and design a scanner based on FAs.

4.2.1 Lexical Units and Regular Expressions

The lexical units of a typical high-level programming language are usually specified by REs. Many of them contain several identical sub-expressions. Therefore, to simplify their specification, we often name some elementary expressions, such as l and d in Convention 4.4, and use these names in the definitions of more-complex REs.

Convention 4.4 Throughout this chapter, **letter** and **digit** stand for any letter and digit, respectively; furthermore, l and d are REs standing for (A|...|Z|a|...|z) and (0|...|9), so **letter** and **digit** are denoted by l and d, respectively. ■

In Figure 4.2, we define identifiers, positive integers, and positive real numbers by REs, which make use of l and d from Convention 4.4. First, identifiers are defined as arbitrarily long alphanumerical strings that begin with a letter. Second, integers are defined as arbitrarily long nonempty numerical strings. Finally, real numbers correspond to the positive real numbers in mathematics. That is, they have the form $x.y$, where x is a nonempty numeric string and y is a numeric string. The case when $y = \varepsilon$ means $y = 0$; for instance, 2. have the same meaning as 2.0.

4.2.2 Scanners and Finite Automata

A scanner recognizes every instance of a lexical unit occurring in the program, so it scans the sequence of characters that make up the program to recognize the next instance of a lexical unit, verify its correct form, and categorize it according to its type. It is usually based on completely specified DFAs (see Definition 3.17), described by their state diagrams in what follows.

Convention 4.5 In Figures 4.3 and 4.4, by labeling an edge leaving a state with **others**, we mean any symbol that denotes no other edge leaving or entering the state. ■

Lexical unit	Regular expression	Example
identifier	$l(d\|l)^*$	$a21$
integer number	d^+	10
real number	$d^+.d^*$	0.01

Figure 4.2 Definition of lexical units by regular expressions.

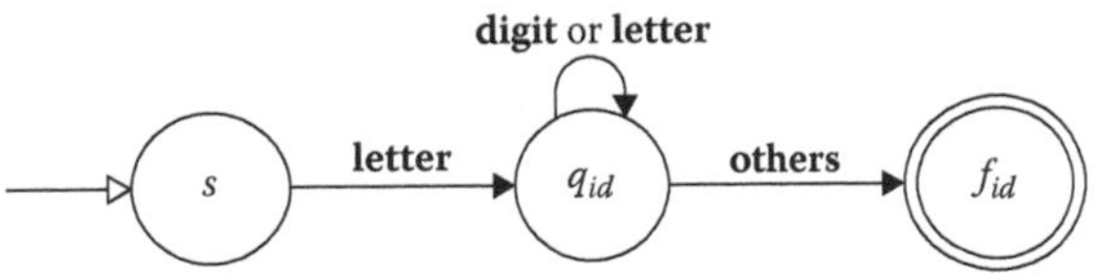

Figure 4.3 A scanner for identifiers.

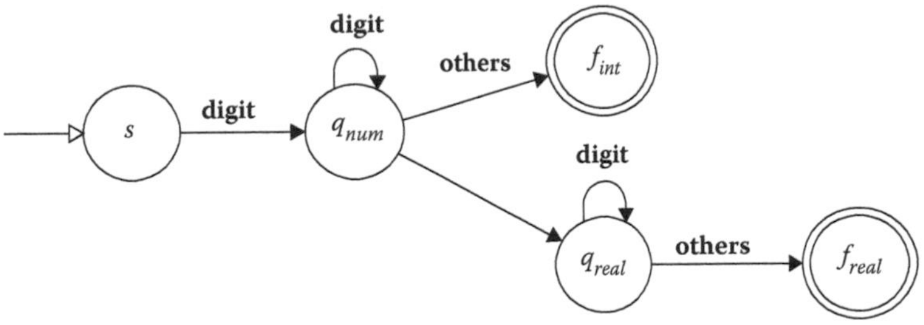

Figure 4.4 A scanner for integers and real numbers.

Figure 4.3 pictures a DFA that acts as a scanner for identifiers. In practice, a scanner is usually designed for several types of lexical units. To illustrate a multilexical-unit scanner like this, Figure 4.4 presents a DFA that acts as a scanner for both integer numbers and real numbers. It distinguishes these lexical units by its two final states—f_{int} and f_{real}. Indeed, ending in f_{int} means that an integer has been recognized whereas, ending in f_{real} implies the recognition of a real number.

A scanner recognizes a lexical unit as the longest possible string denoted by its regular expression. Indeed, as obvious, *ab* represents a single identifier, not two identifiers—*a* and *b*. However, recognizing the longest string of this kind necessitates reading an extra symbol that actually follows the string. As a result, the lexical analyzer has to return this extra character into the scanned file and start the next scan in front of it. To illustrate, notice that scanners in Figures 4.3 and 4.4 complete the recognition of a lexical unit by performing a move on **others** and, thereby, reading an extra character, which thus has to be returned.

On the other hand, the file that contains a high-level program code usually contains sequences of characters that are irrelevant as far as the lexical analysis is concerned. These irrelevant text passages include comments as well as sequences of characters that results in empty space when printed, such as white-space characters, including blanks, carriage returns, and line feeds. The scanner removes them all.

4.3 Implementation of a Scanner

In this section, we sketch an implementation of a scanner by using a Pascal-like pseudo-code. For simplicity, we suppose that any file that contains a program code consists of lexical units defined in Figure 4.2 and blanks are the only useless characters to be removed. Before the implementation, some conventions are needed.

Convention 4.6 A blank is denoted by □ throughout the book. Throughout this chapter, *ch* is a variable that stores a single *ch*aracter. Furthermore, *lu* is a string of characters, which represents a *l*exical *u*nit. ■

Based on Algorithm 4.3, we next sketch the scanner implementation as the procedure **SCANNER**, which makes use of two other procedures—**IDENTIFIER** and **NUMBER**. Typically, **SCANNER** is applied repeatedly to recognize a whole sequence of identifiers and numbers. Consequently, whenever *ch* contains an extra character, which follows the recognized lexical unit, it pushes it back onto the input, so the next application of **SCANNER** starts by reading it. For instance, $1A$ consists of integer 1 followed by identifier A. **SCANNER** actually recognizes 1 when it reads A, which is thus returned to the input; without this return, **SCANNER** would improperly omit A during its next application. We suppose that the input sequence of identifiers and numbers is ended by ◁ (see Convention 4.1).

As obvious, in practice, the end of a given input string is always somehow specified, so ◁ only symbolically expresses this end. For instance, if the input string is written as a file, then the end of the file fulfills the role of ◁.

Strictly speaking, Algorithm 4.3 requires that its input DFA is completely specified. In the implementation below, this complete specification is arranged by the **otherwise** branch in the **case** statement, which is entered in all cases corresponding to a lexical error.

```
procedure SCANNER;
begin
   repeat
      read(ch)                    {read the next input character and place it into ch}
   until ch ≠ □;                  {exit when a blank is read}
   if ch ≠ ◁ then                 {SCANNER has not reached ◁, which ends the input}
   begin
      set lu to ε;
      case ch of
         letter : IDENTIFIER;           {perform procedure IDENTIFIER (see below)}
         digit  : NUMBER;               {perform procedure NUMBER (see below)}
         otherwise writeln('lexical error')
      end {of the case statement}
   end {of the if statement}
end
```

IDENTIFIER, given next, implements a scanner that recognizes identifiers. **SCANNER** calls **IDENTIFIER** with *ch* containing a letter and *lu* set to ε.

```
procedure IDENTIFIER;
begin
  repeat
     extend lu by concatenating it with ch;
     read(ch)                  {read the next input character and place it into ch}
  until ch ∉ letter ∪ digit;   {exit when a non-alphanumeric symbol is read}
  push back ch onto the standard input; {ch contains a non-alphanumeric symbol}
  writeln('identifier ', lu, ' is recognized')
end
```

Based on Figure 4.4, procedure **NUMBER** recognizes and categorizes positive integer and real numbers.

```
procedure NUMBER;
begin
  repeat
      extend lu by concatenating it with ch;
      read(ch)                    {read the next input character and place it into ch}
  until ch ∉ digit;               {exit when a non-numeric symbol is read}
  if ch ≠ '.' then
  begin
      push back ch onto the standard input;      {ch contains a non-numeric symbol}
      writeln('integer ', lu, ' is recognized')
  end
  else
  begin
      repeat
          extend lu by concatenating it with ch;
          read(ch)
      until ch ∉ digit;           {exit when a non-numeric symbol is read}
      push back ch onto the standard input;      {ch contains a non-numeric symbol}
      writeln('real number ', lu, ' is recognized')
  end {of the if statement}
end
```

Example 4.2 This example gives a Pascal implementation of the scanner sketched previously.

```
program scanner(input, output);

{
This program implements the scanner whose pseudo-code precedes
Example 4.2. It reads an input string from the standard input. The input
string is terminated with #.
}

type
  symbols    = Char;
  symbolset  = set of symbols;

var
  ch        : symbols;  {the current read character}
  previous  : Boolean;  {auxiliary variable for pushing ch back to the
                         input}
  lu        : String;   {lexical unit}

const
  letters     : symbolset = ['a'..'z'];
  digits      : symbolset = ['0'..'9'];
  BLANK       : symbolset = [' ', #10, #13];
  ENDMARKER   : symbols   = '#';

procedure GETSYM;      {read a character from the input while supporting
                        push-back}
begin
  if previous then
    previous := false
  else
    read(ch)
end {of GETSYM procedure};
```

```
procedure UNGETSYM;        {pushing the last read symbol back to the input}
begin                      {so it is read in the next application of GETSYM}
  if not previous then
    previous := true
  else                {this implementation does not support double
                       push-back}
    writeln('internal error')
end {of UNGETSYM procedure};

procedure IDENTIFIER;
begin
  repeat
    lu := lu + ch;   {concatenate the string in lu and the character in ch}
    GETSYM
  until not ((ch in letters) or (ch in digits)); {exit when a
                                                   non-alphanumeric symbol is
                                                   read}
  UNGETSYM;        {the non-alphanumeric symbol in ch is pushed back onto
                    the standard input}
  writeln('identifier ', lu , ' is recognized');
end {of IDENTIFIER procedure};

procedure NUMBER;
begin
  repeat
    lu := lu + ch;    {concatenate the string in lu and the character in ch}
    GETSYM
  until not (ch in digits);      {exit when a non-numeric symbol is read}
  if ch <> '.' then
  begin
    UNGETSYM;      {the non-numeric symbol in ch is pushed back onto
                    the standard input}
    writeln('integer ', lu, ' is recognized');
  end
  else
  begin
    repeat
      lu := lu + ch;    {concatenate the string in lu and the character
                         in ch}
      GETSYM
    until not (ch in digits);      {exit when a non-numeric symbol is read}
    UNGETSYM;          {the non-numeric symbol in ch is pushed back onto
                        the standard input}
    writeln('real number ', lu, ' is recognized');
  end
end {of NUMBER procedure};

procedure SCANNER;
begin
  repeat
    GETSYM
  until not (ch in BLANK);        {continue when a non-blank character is
                                   read}
  if ch <> ENDMARKER then         {SCANNER has not reached the end marker}
  begin
    lu := '';
    case ch of
      'a'..'z':  IDENTIFIER;   {perform procedure IDENTIFIER}
      '0'..'9':  NUMBER;       {perform procedure NUMBER}
      otherwise writeln('lexical error')
```

```
    end {of the case statement}
  end {of the if statement}
end {of SCANNER procedure};

{Main program body}
begin
  while ch <> ENDMARKER do        {scan the standard input until the first
                                   end marker denoted by # is read}
    SCANNER;
end.
```

Exercises

1 S. Let L be the language consisting of all identifiers defined as alphanumeric strings containing a letter. Define L formally. Construct an FA that accepts L. Construct an RE that denotes L.

2. Choose your favorite programming language, such as C. Let L be the language consisting of all well-constructed identifiers in the chosen programming language. Construct an FA that accepts L and an RE that denotes L.

3. Consider the following Pascal program. Does the program contain any lexical errors? If so, specify them. If not, write all the instances of lexical units in this program.

```
program trivialprogram(input, output);
var i : integer;

   function result(k: integer): integer;
   begin
      result := k * k + k
   end;

begin
   read(i);
   writeln('For ', i, ', the result is ', result(i))
end.
```

4. Detect all lexical errors, if any, appearing in the following Pascal fragment.

```
while a <> 0.2+E2 do writeln(" ');

if a > 24. than
   write('hi')
else
   write ('bye);

for i := 1 through 10 todo writeln(Iteration: ', i:1);
```

5 S. Let L be the language consisting of programming-language comments delimited by { and } in a Pascal-like way. Suppose that such a comment may contain any number of either {s or }s; however, it does not contain both { and }. Construct an FA that accepts L. Construct an RE that denotes L.

6. Construct an RE that defines Pascal-like real numbers without any superfluous leading or trailing 0s; for instance, 10.01 and 1.204 are legal, but 01.10, 01.24, and 1.360 are not.

7. FORTRAN ignores blanks. Explain why this property implies that a FORTRAN lexical analyzer has to look ahead to determine how to scan a source program. Consider

```
DO 9 J = 1, 9
DO 10 J = 1. 9
DO 9 J = 1 9
```

Which of these FORTRAN fragments are correct? Justify your answer.

8. Consider the following Python program. Specify all lexical errors, if any, occurring in this program. List all well-formed lexical units in the program.

```
''' Short program in Python 3 with several lexical errors. '''
foo = 1.0e1.5
bar = 0e
if foo:
    if bar:
       x = "hello"\"
  else:
       print('world\ )
```

9. Consider the following C program. Specify all lexical errors, if any, in the program. List all well-formed lexical units in this program.

```
#include <stdio.h>
#include ""math.h"

int main(void) {
  double d = 1e+%;
  @
  if  (d > 0) {
      double a = 1e*3;
      double b = 123.45.33;
      int i = 09;
      char c = 'a;
  }
  /* Multi-line comment
     that is not ended
  printf("Program completed.);
}
```

10. Modify all Pascal lexical units by reversing them; for instance, identifiers are defined as alphanumerical strings that end with a letter. Write a program to implement a scanner that recognizes these modified lexical units. Notice that integers remain unchanged after this modification, but identifiers do not. List all lexical units that remain unchanged after this modification.
11. Modify Algorithm 4.3 so it has any DFA as its input automaton, so the DFA may be incompletely specified. Discuss advantages and disadvantages of this modification. Introduce an incompletely specified DFA and implement it based on this modified algorithm in your favorite programming language.
12. Write a program to simplify Pascal programs by converting all the uppercase letters to the lowercase letters and removing all comments and blanks.
13. Write a program that transforms the state table of any $_{cs}$DFA to a program that represents the implementation described in Algorithm 4.2 FA Implementation: A Tabular Method. Use your favorite programming language.
14. Write a program that transforms the state table of any $_{cs}$DFA to a program that represents the implementation described in Algorithm 4.3 FA Implementation: A **case**-Statement-Based Method. Use your favorite programming language.
15. Design a new scanner that recognizes all lexical units of a real programming language, such as Java. Write a program to implement it.

Solutions to Selected Exercises

1. Let l and d have the same meaning defined in Convention 4.4. For instance, $(d|l)^*l(d|l)^*$ is an RE that denotes L. Complete this solution by defining L formally and by constructing a DFA that accepts L.
5. Let s be an RE that denotes any symbol that may occur in the programming-language comments except for { and }. Then, $(\{(s|\{)^*\})|(\{(s|\})^*\})$ is an RE that denotes L. Complete this solution by constructing a DFA that accepts L.

Chapter 5

Properties of Regular Languages

Given a language and a language family, perhaps the most fundamental problem consists in determining whether or not the language belongs to the family. This chapter discusses this problem in terms of the family of regular languages, ${}_{reg}\Phi$ (see Definition 3.23). That is, it establishes several properties of regular languages that are helpful to prove or disprove that a language is in ${}_{reg}\Phi$.

First, Section 5.1 establishes a lemma, customarily referred to as the *pumping lemma* for regular languages, which represents a crucially important tool for demonstrating that certain languages are out of ${}_{reg}\Phi$. Then, Section 5.2 establishes basic closure properties concerning ${}_{reg}\Phi$. Roughly speaking, it demonstrates that ${}_{reg}\Phi$ is closed under most common language operations, including the operations defined in Section 2.1. It shows how to combine closure properties together with the pumping lemma to disprove that some languages are regular. On the other hand, it also demonstrates how to use closure properties to prove that some languages are regular.

5.1 Pumping Lemma for Regular Languages

To give an insight into this important lemma, consider any $L \in {}_{reg}\Phi$ and any deterministic finite automaton (DFA), $M = (\Sigma, R)$, satisfying $L(M) = L$. Set $k = card(Q)$. Suppose that $z \in L(M)$ with $|z| \geq k$. As M reads a symbol during every move, M accepts z by making a sequence of $|z|$ moves; therefore, there necessarily exists at least one state that M visits two or more times when accepting z. Take the first two visits of the same state, q, in this sequence of moves and decompose z according to them as follows. Set $z = uvw$ so that u, v, and w satisfy the following properties:

1. u takes M from the start state to the first visit of q.
2. v takes M from the first visit of q to the second visit of q.
3. Apart from the two visits of q in properties 1 and 2, M never visits any state twice on uv.
4. w takes M from the second visit of q to a final state f.

As M is deterministic and, therefore, makes no ε-moves, $0 < |v|$. By properties 1 through 3, $|uv| \leq k$. Most importantly, M can obviously iterate the sequence of moves between the two visits of q described in properties 1 and 2 m times, for any $m \geq 0$, and during each of these iteration, M reads v. Consequently, M accepts every string of the form $uv^m w$. Next, we state and prove this lemma rigorously.

Lemma 5.1 Pumping lemma for regular languages. Let $L \in {}_{reg}\Phi$. Then, there exists a positive integer $k \in \mathbb{N}$ such that every string $z \in L$ satisfying $|z| \geq k$ can be expressed as $z = uvw$, where $0 < |v| \leq |uv| \leq k$, and $uv^m w \in L$, for all $m \geq 0$.

Proof. Let $L \in {}_{reg}\Phi$. Let L be finite. Set k to any positive integer satisfying $|z| < k$, for all $z \in L$, so the lemma trivially holds simply because L contains no string whose length is greater than or equal to k. Therefore, suppose that L is infinite. Let $M = (\Sigma, R)$ be a DFA such that $L(M) = L$. Set $k = card(Q)$. Consider any string $z \in L$ with $|z| \geq k$. As $z \in L$, $sz \Rightarrow^* f[\rho]$, where s is the start state of M, $f \in F$, and $\rho \in R^*$ is a sequence of rules from R. Because M makes no ε-moves and, thus, reads a symbol on every step, $|\rho| = |z|$. As $|z| \geq k$ and $k = card(Q)$, $|\rho| \geq card(Q)$. Therefore, during $sz \Rightarrow^* f[\rho]$, M enters some states more than once. Consider the shortest initial part of this sequence of moves during which M visits the same state, $q \in Q$. More formally, express $sz \Rightarrow^* f[\rho]$ as

$$
\begin{aligned}
suvw &\Rightarrow^* qvw && [\sigma] \\
&\Rightarrow^+ qw && [\tau] \\
&\Rightarrow^* f && [\upsilon]
\end{aligned}
$$

where $\rho = \sigma\tau\upsilon$, $q \in Q$, $|\tau| \geq 1$, and during $suvw \Rightarrow^* qw$, M visits q precisely twice and any other state no more than once.

Claims A and B verify that uvw satisfies the conditions stated in the lemma.

Claim A. $0 < |v|$ and $|uv| \leq k$.

Proof of Claim A. As $|v| = |\tau|$ and $|\tau| \geq 1$, $0 < |v|$. Because during $suvw \Rightarrow^* qw\,[\sigma\tau]$, M visits q twice and any other state no more than once, $|\sigma\tau| \leq card(Q)$. As $|uv| = |\sigma\tau|$ and $card(Q) = k$, $|uv| \leq k$. Thus, $|uv| \leq k$.

Claim B. For all $m \geq 0$, $uv^m w \in L$.

Proof of Claim B. Let $m \geq 0$. M accepts $uv^m w$ by repeating the sequence of moves according to τ m times; formally,

$$
\begin{aligned}
suv^m w &\Rightarrow^* qv^m w && [\sigma] \\
&\Rightarrow^* qw && [\tau^m] \\
&\Rightarrow^* f && [\upsilon]
\end{aligned}
$$

Thus, for all $m \geq 0$, $uv^m w \in L$; notice that for $m = 0$, M actually accepts uw so it completely omits the sequence of moves made according to τ and, therefore, computes

$$
\begin{aligned}
suw &\Rightarrow^* qw && [\sigma] \\
&\Rightarrow^* f && [\upsilon]
\end{aligned}
$$

■

Example 5.1 To illustrate the technique used in the previous proof, take this regular language

$$L = \{a\}\{bc\}^*\{b\}$$

Consider the DFA M defined by the following three rules:

$$1: sa \to p,\ 2: pb \to f,\ 3: fc \to p$$

where s is the start state of M and $f \in F$. As obvious, $L(M) = L$. Since M has three states, set $k = 3$. Consider $z = abcb \in L$. As $|z| = 4$ and $k = 3$, z satisfies $|z| \geq k$. M accepts z as $sabcb \Rightarrow^* f\,[1232]$, which can be expressed in a move-by-move way as follows:

$$\begin{aligned} sabcb &\Rightarrow pbcb && [1] \\ &\Rightarrow fcb && [2] \\ &\Rightarrow pb && [3] \\ &\Rightarrow f && [2] \end{aligned}$$

The shortest initial part of this computation that contains two occurrences of the same state is

$$\begin{aligned} sabcb &\Rightarrow pbcb && [1] \\ &\Rightarrow fcb && [2] \\ &\Rightarrow pb && [3] \end{aligned}$$

where p is the state M visits twice. Following the above proof, we express $sabcb \Rightarrow^* f\,[1232]$ as

$$\begin{aligned} suvw &\Rightarrow^* qvw && [1] \\ &\Rightarrow^* qw && [23] \\ &\Rightarrow^* f && [2] \end{aligned}$$

with $u = a$, $v = bc$, and $w = b$. Observe that $0 < |v| = 2$ and $|uv| = 3 \leq k = 3$. As $a(bc)^m b = u(v)^m w \in L$, for all $m \geq 0$, all the conditions stated in Lemma 5.1 hold. Specifically, take $m = 2$ to obtain $a(bc)^m b = a(bc)^2 b = abcbcb$. M accepts $abcbcb$ by iterating the partial computation according to 23 twice as follows:

$$\begin{aligned} sabcbcb &\Rightarrow^* pbcbcb && [1] \\ &\Rightarrow^* pbcb && [23] \\ &\Rightarrow^* pb && [23] \\ &\Rightarrow^* f && [2] \end{aligned}$$

5.1.1 Applications of the Pumping Lemma for Regular Languages

As already pointed out, we primarily apply Lemma 5.1 to prove that a given language L is out of ${}_{reg}\Phi$. Of course, a proof like this is made by contradiction, and its typical structure follows:

1. Assume that $L \in {}_{reg}\Phi$.
   Consider the constant k from the pumping lemma, and select a string $z \in L$ whose length depends on k so $|z| \geq k$ is surely true.
2. Consider all possible decompositions of z into uvw satisfying $|uv| \leq k$ and $v \neq \varepsilon$, and for each of these decompositions, demonstrate that there exists $m \geq 0$ such that $uv^m w \notin L$, which contradicts the third condition in Lemma 5.1.
3. The contradiction obtained in (2) implies that the assumption in (1) was incorrect, so $L \notin {}_{reg}\Phi$.

Example 5.2 Let $L = \{x|\ x \in \{0, 1\}^*, occur(x, 0) = occur(x, 1)\}$. In other words, L is the language consisting of strings containing the same number of 0s and 1s. Following the proof scheme earlier almost literally, we easily demonstrate that $L \notin {}_{reg}\Phi$.

1. Assume that $L \in {}_{reg}\Phi$.
2. As $L \in {}_{reg}\Phi$, there exists a natural number k satisfying Lemma 5.1. Set $z = 0^k1^k$. Notice that $z \in L$. Notice that $|z| \geq k$ because $|z| = 2k \geq k$.
3. By Lemma 5.1, z can be expressed as $z = uvw$ so the conditions of the pumping lemma hold. As $0 < |v|$ and $|uv| \leq k$, $v \in \{0\}^+$. Consider $uv^0w = uw$. Then, $uw = 0^j1^k$ with $j = k - |v|$; therefore, $uw \notin L$. However, by the pumping lemma, $uv^mw \in L$, for all $m \geq 0$, including the case when $m = 0$, so $uw \in L$—a contradiction.
4. By the contradiction in (3), $L \notin {}_{reg}\Phi$.

Example 5.2 followed the recommended four-step proof idea, consisting of (1) through (4), almost literally. Example 5.3 makes use of the pumping lemma in a more original and ingenious way.

Example 5.3 Clearly, $\{a\}^+ \in {}_{reg}\Phi$. Consider its sublanguage $P \subseteq \{a\}^+$ defined as $P = \{a^n|\ n \text{ is prime}\}$ (a positive integer n is prime if its only positive divisors are 1 and n). As demonstrated next, $P \notin {}_{reg}\Phi$. Thus, from a more general viewpoint, we see that a sublanguage of a regular language may be nonregular.

Assume that P is regular. Then, there exists a positive integer k satisfying the pumping lemma. As P is infinite, there surely exists a string $z \in P$ such that $|z| \geq k$. By Lemma 5.1, z can be written as $z = uvw$, so the conditions of the pumping lemma hold. Consider uv^mw with $m = |uw| + 2|v| + 2$. As $|uv^mw| = |uw| + m|v| = |uw| + (|uw| + 2|v| + 2)|v| = (|uw| + 2|v|) + (|uw| + 2|v|)|v| = (|uw| + 2|v|)(1 + |v|)$, $|uv^mw|$ is no prime and, thus, $uv^mw \notin P$. By the pumping lemma, however, $uv^mw \in P$—a contradiction. Thus, $P \notin {}_{reg}\Phi$.

Observe that this result has its significant practical consequences. Indeed, as P is nonregular, no FA accepts P (see Theorem 3.38). Consequently, informally speaking, the FAs are not strong enough to handle the primes.

Lemma 5.1 is a powerful tool to disprove that certain languages are in ${}_{reg}\Phi$, but it cannot be applied in the positive sense. That is, it cannot be used to prove that certain languages are regular because some nonregular languages satisfy the pumping-lemma conditions as Example 5.4 illustrates. Consequently, proving that a language satisfies these conditions does not necessarily imply that the language is regular.

Example 5.4 Take

$$L = \{a^ob^nc^n|\ o \geq 1 \text{ and } n \geq 0\} \cup \{b^oc^n|\ o, n \geq 0\}$$

Observe that L satisfies the conditions of the pumping lemma for regular languages although $L \notin {}_{reg}\Phi$. To see that L satisfies the pumping lemma conditions, set $k = 1$. Consider any string $z \in L$ and $|z| = k$. As $z \in L$, either $z \in \{a^ob^nc^n|\ o \geq 1 \text{ and } n \geq 0\}$ or $z \in \{b^oc^n|\ o, n \geq 0\}$.

1. Let $z = a^ob^nc^n$, for some $o \geq 1$ and $n \geq 0$. Express z as $z = uvw$ with $u = \varepsilon$, $v = a$, and $w = a^{o-1}b^nc^n$. Clearly, $v \neq \varepsilon$ and $|uv| = k = 1$. Furthermore, notice that $a^mb^nc^n \in L$, for all $m \geq 1$, so $uv^mw \in L$, for all $m \geq 0$. Thus, the pumping lemma conditions are satisfied in this case.
2. Let $z = b^oc^n$, for some $o, n \geq 0$. Express z as $z = uvw$ with $u = \varepsilon$, v is the leftmost symbol of b^oc^n, and w is the remaining suffix of z. For $o = 0$, $v = c$ and $w = c^{n-1}$, and all the three conditions hold. For $o \geq 1$, $v = b$ and $w = b^{o-1}c^n$, and all the three conditions hold in this case as well.

Thus, L satisfies the conditions of the pumping lemma for regular languages.

Finally, prove that $L \notin {}_{reg}\Phi$ by contradiction. That is, assume that $L \in {}_{reg}\Phi$. Let $M = (\Sigma, R)$ be a DFA such that $L(M) = L$. As an exercise, show how to transform M to an FA N such that $L(N) = \{ab^nc^n \mid n \geq 0\}$, and by analogy with Example 5.2, prove that $\{ab^nc^n \mid n \geq 0\} \notin {}_{reg}\Phi$. From this contradiction, it follows that $L \notin {}_{reg}\Phi$.

5.2 Closure Properties

Based on the general concept of closure properties sketched in Section 2.2.2, we see that ${}_{reg}\Phi$ is closed under a language operation o if ${}_{reg}\Phi$ contains every language that results from o applied to any regular languages; equivalently, we say that o preserves ${}_{reg}\Phi$. Closure results concerning ${}_{reg}\Phi$ are obviously useful to prove that some languages are regular. Indeed, to prove that a relatively complicated language K belongs to ${}_{reg}\Phi$, we construct K from simpler regular languages by operations that preserve ${}_{reg}\Phi$, so K has to be in ${}_{reg}\Phi$. However, combined with the pumping lemma, the closure properties of regular languages are often very helpful in proofs that a language L is nonregular. Indeed, assuming that L is regular, we first transform this language to a simpler language K by using some operations under which ${}_{reg}\Phi$ is closed. Then, by using the pumping lemma, we prove that K is nonregular, so we conclude L is not regular either.

In this section, we prove that ${}_{reg}\Phi$ is closed under most common theoretical language operations, such as union, concatenation, closure, complement, intersection, regular substitution, finite substitution, and homomorphism. In fact, we demonstrate most of these closure properties *effectively* in terms of FAs. In other words, when proving that a given operation o preserves the family of regular languages, we actually present an algorithm that converts any FAs to another FA that accepts the language resulting from o applied to the languages accepted by the input automata.

Union, concatenation, and closure. We have already demonstrated that the family of regular languages is closed under union, concatenation, and closure (see Algorithms 2.19, 2.21, and 2.23, and Theorem 5.2).

Theorem 5.2 ${}_{reg}\Phi$ is closed under union, concatenation, and closure. ■

Complement and Intersection. To prove that ${}_{reg}\Phi$ is closed under complement, we explain how to turn any ${}_{cs}$DFA I to a ${}_{cs}$DFA O such that $L(O) = {\sim}L(I)$.

Theorem 5.3 Let I be a ${}_{cs}$DFA. Then, there exists a ${}_{cs}$DFA O such that $L(O) = {\sim}L(I)$. Consequently, ${}_{reg}\Phi$ is closed under complement.

Proof. Let $L \in {}_{reg}\Phi$. Without any loss of generality, suppose that $L = L(I)$, where I is a completely specified DFA (${}_{cs}$DFA) (see Definition 3.17 and Theorem 3.18). From I, construct a ${}_{cs}$DFA O by making every nonfinal state final and vice versa. As I is completely specified, so is O. Thus, O completely reads every input string over Δ. Consequently, O accepts a string iff I rejects it, so $L(O) = \Delta^* - L(I)$. As ${\sim}L = {\sim}L(I) = \Delta^* - L(I)$, $L(O) = {\sim}L$. Hence, ${}_{reg}\Phi$ is closed under complement. ■

Theorem 5.4 ${}_{reg}\Phi$ is closed under intersection.

Proof. Let $K, L \in {}_{reg}\Phi$. By DeMorgan's law (see Section 1.2), $\sim(\sim K \cup \sim L) = K \cap L$, so Theorem 5.4 follows from Theorems 5.2 and 5.3. ■

Regular substitution. As a special case of substitution (see Section 2.1), we next define the regular substitution and prove that ${}_{reg}\Phi$ is closed under it. This important closure property represents a powerful theoretical tool for proving several other closure properties as demonstrated later in this section.

Before proving this important closure property, let us recall that in an FA, a stop state is a state from which there exists no move (see Definition 3.31). Consequently, no FA can leave any of its stop states. Lemma 3.32 says that without any loss of generality, we can always assume that an FA has precisely one final state, which is also a stop state. Notice that the proof of Lemma 3.32 introduces no ε-rules. Consequently, considering Theorems 3.8 and 3.38, without any loss of generality, we can always assume that any regular language is accepted by an ε-free FA (${}_{\varepsilon\text{-}free}$FA) with a single final state, which is also a stop state. We make use of this result in the upcoming proof that ${}_{reg}\Phi$ is closed under regular substitution.

Definition 5.5 Let V and W be two alphabets, and let h be a substitution from V^* to W^* such that for all $a \in V$, $h(a) \in {}_{reg}\Phi$. Then, h is a *regular substitution*. ■

We plan to prove that ${}_{reg}\Phi$ is closed under regular substitution (see Theorem 5.8) in the following way. First, we consider any regular substitution h and any $K \in {}_{reg}\Phi$. Without any loss of generality, we assume that K is accepted by an ${}_{\varepsilon\text{-}free}$FA I such that ${}_IF = \{{}_If\}$, where ${}_If$ is a stop state. To demonstrate that ${}_{reg}\Phi$ is closed under the regular substitution, we explain how to convert h and I to an FA O such that $L(O) = h(L(I)) = h(K)$, which establishes the desired closure property. Before giving Algorithm 5.6 that performs this conversion, we sketch its basic idea.

Basic Idea. Let h, K, and I have the above meaning. More precisely, let h be a regular substitution such that for every $a \in {}_I\Delta$, $h(a) = L(a\text{−}I)$, where $a\text{−}I$ is an FA. We construct an FA O satisfying $a_1a_2\ldots a_n \in L(I)$ iff $w_1w_2\ldots w_n \in L(O)$ for every $w_i \in L(a_i\text{−}I)$, so $L(O) = h(L(I)) = h(K)$. In a greater detail, I has a single final state, ${}_If$, which is also a stop state. O works as follows. First, O simulates $a_1\text{−}I$. When O enters a final state of $a_1\text{−}I$ and, thereby, accepts w_1, O starts to simulate $a_2\text{−}I$, and so forth. After simulating all n automata $a_1\text{−}I$ through $a_n\text{−}I$ in this way, O has read $w_1w_2\ldots w_n$ with $w_i \in h(a_i)$. As $a_1a_2\ldots a_n \in L(I)$, $w_1w_2\ldots w_n$ takes O to its only final state, so at this point, O accepts $w_1w_2\ldots w_n$.

Note that the following algorithm requires that the state sets of I, $a_1\text{−}I$, ..., $a_n\text{−}I$ are pairwise disjoint. This requirement is obviously without any loss of generality; indeed, if two automata contain some states in common, we rename states in either of them to obtain two disjoint sets.

Algorithm 5.6 An FA for Regular Substitution.

Input. An ${}_{\varepsilon\text{-}free}$FA, $I = ({}_I\Sigma, {}_IR)$, such that ${}_IF = \{{}_If\}$ and ${}_If$ is a stop state, and a set of FAs $\varsigma = \{\text{a−}I \mid \text{a−}I \text{ is an FA}, a \in {}_I\Delta\}$ such that I and all the automata in ς have pairwise disjoint sets of states.

Output. An FA O such that $w_1w_2\ldots w_n \in L(O)$ iff $w_1w_2\ldots w_n \in L(a_1\text{−}I)L(a_2\text{−}I)\ldots L(a_n\text{−}I)$, where $a_1a_2\ldots a_n \in L(I)$, $a_i \in {}_I\Delta$, $a_i\text{−}I \in \varsigma$, $w_i \in L(a_i\text{−}I)$, $1 \leq i \leq n$, for some $n \in {}_0\mathbb{N}$ ($n = 0$ means $w_1w_2\ldots w_n = a_1a_2\ldots a_n = \varepsilon$).

Method.

begin

set ${}_OQ = {}_IQ \cup \{\langle qo\rangle \mid q \in {}_IQ,\ o \in {}_{a-I}Q \text{ with } a-I \in \varsigma,\ a \in {}_I\Delta\}$
set ${}_Os = {}_Is$
set ${}_OF = \{{}_If\}$
set ${}_O\Delta = \{a \mid a \in {}_{a-I}\Delta \text{ with } a-I \in \varsigma\}$
set ${}_OR = \{q \to \langle q_{a-I}s\rangle \mid q \in {}_IQ,\ a-I \in \varsigma, \text{ for some } a \in {}_I\Delta\}$
$\cup \{\langle qp\rangle b \to \langle qo\rangle \mid q \in {}_IQ,\ pb \to o \in {}_{a-I}R \text{ with } b \in {}_{a-I}\Delta \cup \{\varepsilon\},\ a-I \in \varsigma, \text{ for some } a \in {}_I\Delta\}$
$\cup \{\langle qf\rangle \to p \mid q, p \in {}_IQ,\ qa \to p \in {}_IR \text{ with } a \in {}_I\Delta,\ f \in {}_{a-I}F \text{ with } a-I \in \varsigma\}$

end.

Lemma 5.7 Algorithm 5.6 is correct.

Proof. Let I and ς have the same meaning as in Algorithm 5.6. We need to demonstrate that Algorithm 5.6 correctly constructs an FA O such that $w_1w_2\ldots w_n \in L(O)$ iff $w_1w_2\ldots w_n \in L(a_1-I)$ $L(a_2-I)\ldots L(a_n-I)$, where $a_1a_2\ldots a_n \in L(I)$, $a_i \in {}_I\Delta$, $w_i \in L(a_i-I)$, $a_i-I \in \varsigma$, $1 \leq i \leq n$, where $n \in {}_0\mathbb{N}$. We begin with the following important claim.

Claim. Let $q \in {}_IQ$, $a_1a_2\ldots a_n \in {}_I\Delta^*$, $a_i \in {}_I\Delta$, $1 \leq i \leq n$, where $n \in {}_0\mathbb{N}$. Then, ${}_Isa_1a_2\ldots a_n \Rightarrow^* q$ in I iff ${}_Osw_1w_2\ldots w_n \Rightarrow^* q$ in O with $w_i \in L(a_i-I)$, where $a_i-I \in \varsigma$.

Only if. By induction on $n \geq 0$, we next prove that for every $q \in {}_IQ$, $a_1a_2\ldots a_n \in {}_I\Delta^*$, $a_i \in {}_I\Delta$, $1 \leq i \leq n$, ${}_Isa_1a_2\ldots a_n \Rightarrow^* q$ in I implies ${}_Osw_1w_2\ldots w_n \Rightarrow^* q$ in O with $w_i \in L(a_i-I)$, where $a_i-I \in \varsigma$.

Basis. Let $n = 0$, so $w_1w_2\ldots w_n = a_1a_2\ldots a_n = \varepsilon$. As ${}_IR$ has no ε-rules, I accepts ε as ${}_Is \Rightarrow^0 {}_If$ in I, so ${}_Is = {}_If$. Since ${}_Os = {}_Is$ and ${}_OF = \{{}_If\}$, ${}_Is \Rightarrow^0 {}_If$ in I implies ${}_Os \Rightarrow^0 {}_If$ in O, so ${}_Os \Rightarrow^* {}_If$ in O.

Induction Hypothesis. Assume that the *only-if* part of the claim holds for all strings of length k, $1 \leq k \leq n$, for some $n \in {}_0\mathbb{N}$.

Induction Step. Let $q \in {}_IQ$, $a_1a_2\ldots a_na_{n+1} \in {}_I\Delta^*$, $a_i \in {}_I\Delta$, $1 \leq i \leq n+1$, and ${}_Isa_1a_2\ldots a_{n+1} \Rightarrow^* q$ in I. As I is without ε-rules, express ${}_Isa_1a_2\ldots a_{n+1} \Rightarrow^* q$ as

$$\begin{aligned} {}_Isa_1a_2\ldots a_na_{n+1} &\Rightarrow^* pa_{n+1} \\ &\Rightarrow q \qquad [pa_{n+1} \to q] \end{aligned}$$

in I, where $pa_{n+1} \to q \in {}_IR$ with $p \in {}_IQ$. Thus, ${}_Isa_1a_2\ldots a_n \Rightarrow^* p$ in I. By the induction hypothesis, ${}_Osw_1w_2\ldots w_n \Rightarrow^* p$ in O with $w_i \in L(a_i-I)$, $a_i-I \in \varsigma$, $1 \leq i \leq n$. For every $w_{n+1} \in L(a_{n+1}-I)$, $\sigma w_{n+1} \Rightarrow^* \varphi$ in $a_{n+1}-I$, where σ is the start state of $a_{n+1}-I$ and φ is a final state in $a_{n+1}-I$. At this point, Algorithm 5.6 introduces $p \to \langle p\sigma\rangle$ and $\langle p\varphi\rangle \to q$ to ${}_OR$. Furthermore, the algorithm includes the rules of $a_{n+1}-I$ into ${}_OR$ as well, so $\sigma w_{n+1} \Rightarrow^* \varphi$ in O. Thus,

$$\begin{aligned} pw_{n+1} &\Rightarrow \langle p\sigma\rangle w_{n+1} \quad [p \to \langle p\sigma\rangle] \\ &\Rightarrow^* \langle p\varphi\rangle \\ &\Rightarrow q \qquad\qquad [\langle p\varphi\rangle \to q] \end{aligned}$$

in O. Consequently, ${}_{O}sw_1w_2\ldots w_nw_{n+1} \Rightarrow^* \langle p\sigma\rangle w_{n+1} \Rightarrow^* \langle p\varphi\rangle \Rightarrow q$ in O with $w_i \in L(a_i{-}I)$, $1 \leq i \leq n+1$, so the induction step is completed. Thus, the *only-if* part of the proof holds.

If. A proof of this part of the claim is left as an exercise.

Considering the above claim for $q = {}_{I}f$, we see that for every $a_1a_2\ldots a_n \in {}_{I}\Delta^*$, $a_i \in {}_{I}\Delta$, $1 \leq i \leq n$, where $n \in {}_0\mathbb{N}$, ${}_{I}sa_1a_2\ldots a_n \Rightarrow^* {}_{I}f$ in I iff ${}_{O}sw_1w_2\ldots w_n \Rightarrow^* {}_{I}f$ in O with $w_i \in L(a_i{-}I)$, where $a_i{-}I \in \varsigma$. Recall that ${}_{O}F = \{{}_{I}f\}$. Therefore, $a_1a_2\ldots a_n \in L(I)$ iff $w_1w_2\ldots w_n \in L(O)$, so the lemma holds. ■

Theorem 5.8 ${}_{reg}\Phi$ is closed under regular substitution.

Proof. Let $K \in {}_{reg}\Phi$. Then, there exists an FA I such that $K = L(I)$ with ${}_{I}\Delta = symbols(K)$ (see Theorem 3.38). Without any loss of generality, assume that I satisfies the properties stated in Algorithm 5.6—that is, $I = ({}_{I}\Sigma, {}_{I}R)$ represents an ${}_{\varepsilon\text{-}free}$FA such that ${}_{I}F = \{{}_{I}f\}$, and ${}_{I}f$ is a stop state. Let h be a regular substitution from ${}_{I}\Delta^*$ to V^*. That is, for every $a \in symbols(K)$, $h(a)$ is regular, so there exists an FA $a{-}I$ such that $h(a) = L(a{-}I)$. Set $\varsigma = \{a{-}I \mid a{-}I$ is an FA, $a \in symbols(K)\}$. By Algorithm 5.6 and Lemma 5.7, there exists an FA O satisfying $w_1w_2\ldots w_n \in L(O)$ iff $w_1w_2\ldots w_n \in L(a_1{-}I)L(a_2{-}I)\ldots L(a_n{-}I)$, where $a_1a_2\ldots a_n \in L(I)$, $a_i \in {}_{I}\Delta$, $a_i{-}I \in \varsigma$, $w_i \in L(a_i{-}I)$, $1 \leq i \leq n$, where $n \in {}_0\mathbb{N}$ (as already noted, $n = 0$ means $w_1w_2\ldots w_n = a_1a_2\ldots a_n = \varepsilon$). Thus, $L(O) = h(L(I)) = h(K)$. Because O is an FA, $h(K) \in {}_{reg}\Phi$ (see Theorem 3.38). ■

Theorem 5.8 is a powerful result having many significant consequences as illustrated later.

Definition 5.9 Let V and W be two alphabets, and let h be a substitution from V^* and W^* such that for all $a \in V$, $h(a)$ is a finite language. Then, h is a *finite substitution*. ■

Notice that every finite substitution and every homomorphism (see Section 2.1) are special cases of regular substitution. Thus, Theorem 5.8 implies the next result.

Corollary 5.10 ${}_{reg}\Phi$ is closed under finite substitution and homomorphism. ■

5.2.1 Applications of Closure Properties

As already pointed out, together with the pumping lemma for regular languages, the closure properties are frequently used to prove that a language L is not regular. Typically, a proof of this kind is made by contradiction in the following way.

1. Assume that $L \in {}_{reg}\Phi$.
2. By using operations preserving ${}_{reg}\Phi$, construct a new language K from L, so $K \in {}_{reg}\Phi$; make this construction so that the following proof in (3) is as simple as possible.
3. By the pumping lemma, prove that $K \notin {}_{reg}\Phi$, which contradicts $K \in {}_{reg}\Phi$ as stated in (2).
4. The contradiction obtained in (3) implies $L \notin {}_{reg}\Phi$.

Example 5.5 Let $L = \{x|\ x \in \{0, 1\}^*, occur(x, 0) \neq occur(x, 1)\}$. Next, we prove that this language is nonregular.

1. Assume that $L \in {}_{reg}\Phi$.
2. Consider $\{0\}^*\{1\}^*$, which is obviously in ${}_{reg}\Phi$. Consider $K = {\sim}L \cap \{0\}^*\{1\}^* = \{0^n1^n|\ n \geq 0\}$. By Theorems 5.3 and 5.4, $K \in {}_{reg}\Phi$.
3. By analogy with Example 5.4, prove that $K \notin {}_{reg}\Phi$, which contradicts $K \in {}_{reg}\Phi$.
4. Having obtained the contradiction in (3), we conclude that $L \notin {}_{reg}\Phi$.

While the pumping lemma is of no use in proving that a language is in ${}_{reg}\Phi$ (see Example 5.1), closure properties are useful in this positive sense. Indeed, suppose a direct proof that a language L is regular would require a design of an enormously complicated FA, followed by a complex proof that this automaton indeed accepts L. Frequently, we can simplify this difficult proof so we define L by several simple regular languages combined by operations under which the family of regular languages is closed and, therefore, conclude that L is in ${}_{reg}\Phi$.

Example 5.6 Consider $L = \{a^ib^jc^kd^l|\ i, k \geq 0 \text{ and } j, l \geq 1\}$. To verify that $L \in {}_{reg}\Phi$, express this language as $L = h(\{a\})\{b\}h(\{c\})\{d\}$, where h is a regular substitution defined as $h(a) = \{a\}^*\{b\}^*$ and $h(c) = \{c\}^*\{d\}^*$. As $\{a\}$, $\{b\}$, $\{c\}$, and $\{d\}$ are obviously regular, $L = h(\{a\})\{b\}h(\{c\})\{d\}$ is also regular by Theorems 5.2 and 5.8.

Exercises

1 S. Example 5.3 demonstrates that $\{a^n|\ n \text{ is a prime}\}$ is not regular. Give an alternative proof of this result by using the pumping lemma for regular languages (see Lemma 5.1).

2. Consider each of the following languages. By the pumping lemma for regular languages, demonstrate that the language is not regular.
   a. $\{a^iba^i|\ i \geq 1\}$
   b. $\{a^ib^j|\ 1 \leq i \leq j\}$
   c. $\{a^{2^i}|\ i \geq 0\}$
   d. $\{a^ib^jc^k|\ i, j, k \geq 0 \text{ and } i = k + j\}$
   e. $\{a^ib^ic^j|\ i, j \geq 0 \text{ and } i \leq j \leq 2i\}$
   f. $\{a^ib^jc^k|\ i, j, k \geq 0,\ i \neq j,\ k \neq i, \text{ and } j \neq k\}$
   g. $\{a^ib^jc^jd^i|\ i, j \geq 0 \text{ and } j \leq i\}$
   h. $\{a^ib^{2i}|\ i \geq 0\}$
3. Prove the following modified version of the pumping lemma for regular languages.

   Lemma Let L be a regular language. Then, there is a natural number, k, such that if $xzy \in L$ and $|z| = k$, then z can be written as $z = uvw$, where $|v| \geq 1$ and $xuv^mwy \in L$, for all $m \geq 0$. ■

   Use this lemma to prove that $\{a^ib^jc^j|\ i, j \geq 1\}$ is not regular.
4. Consider the following languages. Use the closure properties of the regular languages and the regular pumping lemma to demonstrate that these languages are not regular.
   a. $\{w|\ w \in \{a, b\}^* \text{ and } occur(w, a) = 2occur(w, b)\}$
   b. $\{0^i10^i|\ i \geq 1\}$
   c. $\{wcv|\ w \in \{a, b\}^* \text{ and } v = reversal(w)\}$
5. Introduce a set of 10 languages from ${}_{reg}\Phi$ such that each of them contains infinitely many subsets that are not in ${}_{reg}\Phi$. For each language, L, in this set, define a nonregular language, K, such that $K \subseteq L$ and prove that K is not regular by the pumping lemma (Lemma 5.1). For instance, take L defined as $L = \{a, b\}^*$, and consider $K = \{a^nb^n|\ n \geq 0\}$. Clearly, $K \subseteq L$ and $L \in {}_{reg}\Phi$. By Lemma 5.1, it is easy to prove that $K \notin {}_{reg}\Phi$.
6. Prove the pumping lemma for regular languages in terms of REs rather than FAs.
7. Complete Example 5.4.
8. Give a rigorous proof of Lemma 5.6.
9. Prove that a language, L, over an alphabet Σ, is regular iff there exists a natural number, k, satisfying this statement: if $z \in \Sigma^*$ and $|z| \geq k$, then (1) $z = uvw$ with $v \neq \varepsilon$ and (2) $zx \in L$ if

and only if $uv^m wx \in L$, for all $m \geq 0$ and $x \in \Sigma^*$. Explain how to use this lemma to prove that a language is regular. Then, explain how to use this lemma to prove that a language is not regular.

10. Assume that L is a regular language over an alphabet Σ. Is it necessarily true that $\sim L$ is also regular under this assumption? Rephrase and answer this question in terms of *substrings*(L), *prefixes*(L), *suffixes*(L), *reversal*(L), L^*, and L^+.
11. Prove Theorem 5.2 in terms of regular expressions (REs.).
12. Let L be a regular language over an alphabet Σ. Define the next language operations. For each of these operations, prove or disprove that the family of regular languages is closed under the operation.
    a. $min(L) = \{w \mid w \in L \text{ and } (prefix(w) - \{w\}) \cap L = \emptyset\}$
    b. $max(L) = \{w \mid w \in L \text{ and } \{w\}\Sigma^+ \cap L = \emptyset\}$
    c. $sqrt(L) = \{x \mid xy \in L \text{ for some } y \in \Sigma^*, \text{ and } |y| = |x|^2\}$
    d. $log(L) = \{x \mid xy \in L \text{ for some } y \in \Sigma^*, \text{ and } |y| = 2^{|x|}\}$
    e. $cycle(L) = \{vw \mid wv \in L \text{ for some } v, w \in \Sigma^*\}$
    f. $half(L) = \{w \mid wv \in L \text{ for some } v \in \Sigma^*, \text{ and } |w| = |v|\}$
    g. $inv(L) = \{xwy \mid xzy \in L \text{ for some } x, y, w, z \in \Sigma^*, z = reversal(w)\}$
13. For a language L over an alphabet Σ and a symbol $a \in \Sigma$, ${}_aEraser(L)$ denotes the language obtained by removing all occurrences of a from the strings of L. Formalize this operation. Is ${}_{reg}\Phi$ closed under it?

14 S. Theorem 5.8 has stated that the family of regular languages is closed under regular substitution in terms of FAs. Prove this important closure property in terms of REs.

Solutions to Selected Exercises

1. Observe that $L = \{a^n \mid n \text{ is a prime}\}$ is infinite. Let z be any string in L such that $|z| \geq k$, where k is the constant from the regular pumping lemma (see Lemma 5.1). Express $z = uvw$, where u, v, and w satisfy the properties of the regular pumping lemma. If $|uw| \in \{0, 1\}$, then $|uv^0w| \in \{0, 1\}$, so $uv^0w \notin L$—a contradiction. Let $|uw| \geq 2$. Set $m = |uw|$. By the pumping lemma $uv^mw \in L$. However, $|uv^mw| = |uw| + |v^m| = m + m|v| = m(1 + |v|)$, so $uv^mw \notin L$. Thus, $L \notin {}_{reg}\Phi$.

14. Consider a regular substitution, η, and a regular language, L. To prove that $\eta(L)$ is regular, define L and η by REs. More precisely, consider a regular language, L, such that $L = L(E_0)$, where E_0 is a RE over an alphabet Σ_0. Let η be a regular substitution such that for each $a \in \Sigma_0$, $\eta(a) = L(E_a)$, where E_a is an RE. Observe that for every string $a_1a_2\ldots a_n \in L(E_0)$, where $a_i \in \Sigma_0$, $i = 1, \ldots, n$, for some $n \geq 0$,

$$w_1w_2\ldots w_n \in \eta(a_1a_2\ldots a_n) \text{ iff } w_i \in L(E_{a_i})$$

(the case when $n = 0$ implies $a_1a_2\ldots a_n = w_1w_2\ldots w_n = \varepsilon$). Construct a RE E, satisfying $w \in L(E_0)$ if and only if $w' \in L(E)$, where $w = a_1a_2\ldots a_n \in \Sigma_0^*$; $a_i \in \Sigma_0$; $w' = w_1w_2\ldots w_n$ with $w_i \in L(E_{a_i})$; $i = 1, \ldots, n$; for some $n \geq 0$. As $\eta(a) = L(E_a)$, for all $a \in \Sigma_0$, $L(E) = \eta(L(E_0)) = \eta(L)$ and, thus, $\eta(L)$ is regular.

III CONTEXT-FREE LANGUAGES AND THEIR MODELS

Section III covers context-free languages and their two fundamental models—context-free grammars and pushdown automata. First, it defines these models and establishes their theoretical basics. Then, it demonstrates their typical use in practice. Specifically, it explains how to apply them to syntax analysis. Finally, it establishes fundamental properties of context-free languages. This section consists of Chapters 6, 7, and 8.

Chapter 6 defines context-free grammars and pushdown automata. Context-free grammars represent language-generating rewriting systems while pushdown automata are language-accepting rewriting systems. Most importantly, it demonstrates that both models are equivalent, that is, they both characterize the family of context-free languages. In addition, Chapter 6 covers several transformations that make these models easy to implement and, thereby, use in practice.

Chapter 7 explains how to apply context-free grammars and pushdown automata to the syntax analysis of programming languages. First, it uses context-free grammars as specification tool for the syntactic structures of programming languages. Then, it constructs syntax analyzers based on pushdown automata.

Chapter 8 demonstrates basic properties of context-free languages. First, it proves a context-free pumping lemma and explains how to use it to prove certain languages not to be context-free. Then, it establishes fundamental closure properties concerning the family of context-free languages and uses them to prove or, in contrast, disprove that some languages belong to this family.

Chapter 6

Models for Context-Free Languages

Context-free grammars (CFGs) and pushdown automata (PDA), that is, two rudimental models for context-free languages (CFLs) represent special cases of rewriting systems, defined in Section 2.2. A CFG is a language-generating rewriting system. Each of its rewriting rules has a single symbol on its left-hand sides. By repeatedly applying these rules, the grammar generates sentences of its language. A PDA is a language-accepting rewriting system. In essence, consider the notion of a finite automaton (FA) (see Definition 3.1). A PDA represents an FA extended by a potentially infinite pushdown list. During a move, according to one of its rules, it reads a symbol, changes the current state, and rewrites a string of symbols occurring on the pushdown top. If it reads the entire input string, empties the pushdown list and enters a final state, the automaton accepts the input string; the set of all accepted strings in this way is the language that the automaton accepts.

This chapter, consisting of Sections 6.1 through 6.3, introduces and studies CFGs and PDA. Section 6.1 defines general versions of CFGs, after which Section 6.2 presents several grammatical transformations that can be applied to these general versions to make their representation more convenient. Section 6.3 defines PDA and proves their equivalence with CFGs; in other words, it demonstrates that they both characterize the family of CFLs.

It is noteworthy that some notions, such as the notion of a CFG and the notion of a linear grammar (LG), were already introduced in Section 2.2 in an informal way. This chapter defines them fully rigorously.

6.1 Context-Free Grammars

As already mentioned and illustrated in Section 2.2.2, a CFG represents a language-generating rewriting system based on finitely many terminal symbols, nonterminal symbols, and grammatical rules. Terminal symbols occur in the language generated by the grammar while nonterminal symbols do not. Each rule has a single nonterminal symbol on its left-hand side while its right-hand side is a string, which may contain both terminal and nonterminal symbols. Starting from a special start symbol, the grammar repeatedly rewrites nonterminal symbols according to its rules until it obtains a sentence, that is, a string that consists solely of terminal symbols. The set of all sentences represents the language generated by the grammar.

Definition 6.1 A *context-free grammar* (*CFG*) is a rewriting system $G = (\Sigma, R)$, where

- Σ is divided into two disjoint subalphabets, denoted by N and Δ.
- R is a finite *set of rules* of the form $A \to x$, where $A \in N$ and $x \in \Sigma^*$.

N and Δ are referred to as the *alphabet of nonterminal symbols* and the *alphabet of terminal symbols*, respectively. N contains a special *start symbol*, denoted by S.

If $S \Rightarrow^* w$, where $w \in \Sigma^*$, *G derives w*, and w is a *sentential form*. $F(G)$ denotes the set of all sentential forms derived by G. The *language generated by G*, symbolically denoted by $L(G)$, is defined as $L(G) = F(G) \cap \Delta^*$. Members of $L(G)$ are called *sentences*. If $S \Rightarrow^* w$ and w is a sentence, $S \Rightarrow^* w$ is a *successful derivation* in G. ■

To explain Definition 6.1 less formally, consider a string xAy and a rule $A \to u \in R$, where $A \in N$ and $x, y, u \in \Sigma^*$. By using $A \to u$, G makes a derivation step from xAy to xuy so it changes A to u in xAy, symbolically written as $xAy \Rightarrow xuy$. If G makes a sequence of derivation steps from S to a string $w \in \Sigma^*$, then w is a sentential form. Every sentential form over Δ is a sentence, and the set of all sentences is the language of G, denoted by $L(G)$. As a result, every sentence w satisfies $S \Rightarrow^* w$ with $w \in \Delta^*$, so $L(G) = \{w \in \Delta^* | \ S \Rightarrow^* w\}$.

Since any CFG, $G = (\Sigma, R)$, represents a rewriting system, all the notions introduced for rewriting systems are applicable to G as well (see Section 2.2). That is, by $u \Rightarrow v$ $[r]$, where $u, v \in \Sigma^*$, and $r \in R$, we say that G directly rewrites u to v by r or, as we customarily say in terms of CFGs, *G makes* a *derivation step from u to v by r*. Furthermore, to express that G makes $u \Rightarrow^* w$ according to a sequence of rules, $r_1r_2\ldots r_n$, we write $u \Rightarrow^* v$ $[r_1r_2\ldots r_n]$, which is read as a *derivation from u to v by using* $r_1r_2\ldots r_n$. On the other hand, whenever the information regarding the applied rules is immaterial, we omit these rules. In other words, we often simplify $u \Rightarrow v$ $[r]$ and $u \Rightarrow^* v$ $[r_1r_2\ldots r_n]$ to $u \Rightarrow v$ and $u \Rightarrow^* v$, respectively.

Convention 6.2 For any CFG G, we automatically assume that Σ, N, Δ, S, and R denote the total alphabet, the alphabet of nonterminal symbols, the alphabet of terminal symbols, the start symbol, and the set of rules, respectively. If there exists a danger of confusion, we mark Σ, N, Δ, S, and R with G as ${}_G\Sigma$, ${}_GN$, ${}_G\Delta$, ${}_GS$, and ${}_GR$, respectively, to clearly relate these components to G (in particular, we make these marks when several CFGs are simultaneously discussed). For brevity, we often abbreviate nonterminal symbols and terminal symbols to *nonterminals* and *terminals*, respectively. If we want to express that a nonterminal A forms the left-hand side of a rule, we refer to this rule as an *A-rule*. If we want to specify that A is rewritten during a derivation step, $xAy \Rightarrow xuy$, we underline this A as $x\underline{A}y \Rightarrow xuy$.

For brevity, G is often defined by simply listing its rules together with specifying its nonterminals and terminals, usually denoted by uppercases and lowercases, respectively.

We denote the *family of* CFGs by ${}_{CFG}\Psi$. We set ${}_{CFG}\Phi = \{L(G) | \ G \in {}_{CFG}\Psi\}$, and we refer to ${}_{CFG}\Phi$ as the *family of* CFLs, so any language in ${}_{CFG}\Phi$ is called a CFL. ■

Example 6.1 demonstrates how to determine the language generated by a CFG in a rigorous way. The CFG considered in the example is relatively simple; in fact, it represents an LG, in which every rule has no more than one occurrence of a nonterminal on its right-hand side as already stated in Example 2.7. As a result, every sentential form contains no more than one occurrence of a nonterminal, and this property makes the determination of the generated language relatively simple. Before giving the example, we repeat the notion of an LG (see Example 2.7) as a CFG in which the right-hand side of every rule contains no more than one occurrence of a nonterminal.

Definition 6.3 Let $G = (\Sigma, R)$ be a CFG such that each $A \rightarrow x \in R$ satisfies $x \in \Delta^*(N \cup \{\varepsilon\})\Delta^*$. Then, G is said to be a *linear grammar* (*LG*). ■

Example 6.1 Consider $L = \{a^k b^k | \ k \geq 1\}$. In principle, we generate the strings from L by a CFG, G, so G derives sentential forms

$$S, aSb, aaSbb, aaaSbbb, \ldots$$

in which G rewrites S with ab during the very last derivation step. Formally, $G = (\Sigma, R)$, where $\Sigma = \{a, b, S\}$ and $R = \{S \rightarrow aSb, S \rightarrow ab\}$. In Σ, $\Delta = \{a, b\}$ is the alphabet of terminals and $N = \{S\}$ is the alphabet of nonterminals, where S is the start symbol of G. Under Convention 6.2, we can specify G simply as

1: $S \rightarrow aSb$
2: $S \rightarrow ab$

Consider $aaSbb$. By using rule 1, G rewrites S with aSb in this string, so $aaSbb \Rightarrow aaaSbbb$ [1]. By using rule 2, G rewrites S with ab, so $aaSbb \Rightarrow aaabbb$ [2]. By using the sequence of rules 112, G makes

$$\begin{aligned} aaSbb &\Rightarrow aaaSbbb && [1] \\ &\Rightarrow aaaaSbbbb && [1] \\ &\Rightarrow aaaaabbbbb && [2] \end{aligned}$$

Briefly, we write $aaSbb \Rightarrow^* aaaaabbbbb$ [112] or, even more simply, $aaSbb \Rightarrow^* aaaaabbbbb$.

To verify that G generates $\{a^k b^k | \ k \geq 1\}$, recall that by using rule 1, G replaces S with aSb, and by rule 2, G replaces S with ab. Consequently, every successful derivation has the form

$$S \Rightarrow aSb \Rightarrow aaSbb \Rightarrow \ldots \Rightarrow a^k S b^k \Rightarrow a^{k+1} b^{k+1}$$

which G makes according to a sequence of rules of the form $1^k 2$, for some $k \geq 0$. In symbols, $S \Rightarrow^* a^{k+1} b^{k+1}$ [$1^k 2$]. From these observations, we see $L(G) = \{a^k b^k | \ k \geq 1\}$; a detailed verification of this identity is left as an exercise.

The two-rule linear CFG considered in Example 6.1 generates every sentence by a unique derivation, so the analysis of its derivation process is rather easy. As a result, the determination of its generated language represents a simple task as well. In a general case, however, $G \in {}_{CFG}\Psi$ may contain several occurrences of nonterminals on the right-hand sides of their rules and generate their sentences by a variety of different derivations. Under these circumstances, the determination of $L(G)$ may be more complicated as shown in Example 6.2. This example also illustrates a typical two-phase approach to achieving complicated results: (1) first, a more general result is established then (2) as its straightforward consequence, the desired result is derived.

Example 6.2 Consider L from Example 6.1. Let K be the set of all permutations of strings in L. Equivalently speaking, K contains all nonempty strings consisting of an equal number of as and bs. Formally,

$$K = \{w \mid w \in \{a, b\}^{+} \text{ and } occur(w, a) = occur(w, b)\}$$

In this example, we prove that K is generated by the CFG G defined as

$$1: S \to aB,\ 2: S \to bA,\ 3: A \to a,\ 4: A \to aS,\ 5: A \to bAA,\ 6: B \to b,\ 7: B \to bS,\ 8: B \to aBB$$

We first prove the following claim, which says something more than we actually need to establish $K = L(G)$. From this claim, we subsequently obtain $K = L(G)$ as a straightforward consequence of this claim.

Claim. For all $w \in \{a, b\}^*$, these three equivalences hold

I. $S \Rightarrow^* w$ iff $occur(a, w) = occur(b, w)$;
II. $A \Rightarrow^* w$ iff $occur(a, w) = occur(b, w) + 1$;
III. $B \Rightarrow^* w$ iff $occur(b, w) = occur(a, w) + 1$.

Proof. This claim is proved by induction on $|w| \geq 1$.

Basis. Let $|w| = 1$.

I. From S, G generates no sentence of length one. On the other hand, no sentence of length one satisfies $occur(a, w) = occur(b, w)$. Thus, in this case, the basis holds vacuously.
II. Examine G to see that if $A \Rightarrow^* w$ with $|w| = 1$, then $w = a$. For $w = a$, $A \Rightarrow^* w$ [3]. Therefore, II holds in this case.
III. Prove III by analogy with the proof of II.

Consequently, the basis holds.

Induction Hypothesis. Assume that there exists a positive integer $n \geq 1$ such that the claim holds for every $w \in \{a, b\}^*$ satisfying $1 \leq |w| \leq n$.

Induction Step. Let $w \in \{a, b\}^*$ with $|w| = n + 1$.

Consider I in the claim. To prove its *only-if* part, consider any derivation of the form $S \Rightarrow^* w$ [ρ], where ρ is a sequence of rules. This derivation starts from S. As only rules 1 and 2 have S on the left-hand side, express $S \Rightarrow^* w$ [ρ] as $S \Rightarrow^* w$ [$r\pi$], where $\rho = r\pi$ and $r \in \{1, 2\}$.

i. If $r = 1$, $S \Rightarrow^* w$ [1π], where $1: S \to aB$. At this point, $w = av$, and $B \Rightarrow^* v$ [π], where $|v| = n$. By the induction hypothesis, III holds for v, so $occur(b, v) = occur(a, v) + 1$. Therefore, $occur(a, w) = occur(b, w)$.
ii. If $r = 2$, $S \Rightarrow^* w$ [2π], where $2: S \to bA$. Thus, $w = bv$, and $A \Rightarrow^* v$ [π], where $|v| = n$. By the induction hypothesis, II holds for v, so $occur(a, v) = occur(b, v) + 1$. As $w = bv$, $occur(a, w) = occur(b, w)$.

To prove the *if* part of I, suppose that $occur(a, w) = occur(b, w)$. Clearly, $w = av$ or $w = bv$, for some $v \in \{a, b\}^*$ with $|v| = n$.

i. Let $w = av$. Then, $|v| = n$ and $occur(a, v) + 1 = occur(b, v)$. As $|v| = n$, by the induction hypothesis, we have $B \Rightarrow^* v$ iff $occur(b, v) = occur(a, v) + 1$ from III. By using $1: S \to aB$, we obtain $S \Rightarrow aB$ [1]. Putting $S \Rightarrow aB$ and $B \Rightarrow^* v$ together, we have $S \Rightarrow aB \Rightarrow^* av$, so $S \Rightarrow^* w$ because $w = av$.
ii. Let $w = bv$. Then, $|v| = n$ and $occur(a, v) = occur(b, v) + 1$. By the induction hypothesis, we have $A \Rightarrow^* v$ iff $occur(a, v) = occur(b, v) + 1$ (see II). By $2: S \to bA$, G makes $S \Rightarrow bA$. Thus, $S \Rightarrow bA$ and $A \Rightarrow^* v$, so $S \Rightarrow^* w$.

Take II in the claim. To prove its *only-if* part, consider any derivation of the form $A \Rightarrow^* w$ [ρ], where ρ is a sequence of rules in G. Express $A \Rightarrow^* w$ [ρ] as $A \Rightarrow^* w$ [$r\pi$], where $\rho = r\pi$ and $r \in \{3, 4, 5\}$ because rules 3: $A \rightarrow a$, 4: $A \rightarrow aS$, and 5: $A \rightarrow bAA$ are all the A-rules in G.

i. If $r = 3$, $A \Rightarrow^* w$ [$r\pi$] is a one-step derivation $A \Rightarrow a$ [3], so $w = a$, which satisfies $occur(a, w) = occur(b, w) + 1$.
ii. If $r = 4$, $A \Rightarrow^* w$ [4π], where 4: $A \rightarrow aS$. Thus, $w = av$, and $S \Rightarrow^* v$ [π], where $|v| = n$. By the induction hypothesis, from I, $occur(a, v) = occur(b, v)$, so $occur(a, w) = occur(b, w) + 1$.
iii. If $r = 5$, $A \Rightarrow^* w$ [5π], where 5: $A \rightarrow bAA$. Thus, $w = buv$, $A \Rightarrow^* u$, $A \Rightarrow^* v$, where $|u| \leq n$, $|v| \leq n$. By the induction hypothesis, from II, $occur(a, u) = occur(b, u) + 1$ and $occur(a, v) = occur(b, v) + 1$, so $occur(a, uv) = occur(b, uv) + 2$. Notice that $occur(b, uv) = occur(b, w) - 1$ implies $occur(a, uv) - 2 = occur(b, w) - 1$. Furthermore, from $occur(a, uv) - 2 = occur(b, w) - 1$, it follows that $occur(a, uv) = occur(a, w)$, so $occur(a, w) = occur(b, w) + 1$.

To prove its *if* part of II, suppose that $occur(a, w) = occur(b, w) + 1$. Obviously, $w = av$ or $w = bv$, for some $v \in \{a, b\}^*$ with $|v| = n$.

i. Let $w = av$. At this point, $|v| = n$ and $occur(a, v) = occur(b, v)$. As $|v| = n$, by the induction hypothesis, we have $S \Rightarrow^* v$. By using 4: $A \rightarrow aS$, $A \Rightarrow aS$ [4]. Putting $A \Rightarrow aS$ and $S \Rightarrow^* v$ together, we obtain $A \Rightarrow aS \Rightarrow^* av$, so $A \Rightarrow^* w$ because $w = av$.
ii. Let $w = bv$. At this point, $|v| = n$ and $occur(a, v) = occur(b, v) + 2$. Express v as $v = uz$ so that $occur(a, u) = occur(b, u) + 1$ and $occur(a, z) = occur(b, z) + 1$; as an exercise, we leave a proof that $occur(a, v) = occur(b, v) + 2$ implies that v can always be expressed in this way. Since $|v| = n$, $|u| \leq n \geq |z|$. Thus, by the induction hypothesis (see II), we have $A \Rightarrow^* u$ and $A \Rightarrow^* z$. By using 5: $A \rightarrow bAA$, $A \Rightarrow bAA$ [5]. Putting $A \Rightarrow bAA$, $A \Rightarrow^* u$, and $A \Rightarrow^* z$ together, we obtain $A \Rightarrow bAA \Rightarrow^* buz$, so $A \Rightarrow^* w$ because $w = bv = buz$.

Prove III by analogy with the proof of the inductive step of II, given earlier.

Having established this claim, we easily obtain the desired equation $L(G) = \{w|\ w \in \{a, b\}^+$ and $occur(w, a) = occur(w, b)\}$ as a consequence of I. Indeed, this equivalence says that for all $w \in \{a, b\}^*$, $S \Rightarrow^* w$ iff $occur(a, w) = occur(b, w)$. Consequently, $w \in L(G)$ iff $occur(a, w) = occur(b, w)$. As G has no ε-rules, $\varepsilon \notin L(G)$, so $L(G) = \{w|\ w \in \{a, b\}^+$ and $occur(w, a) = occur(w, b)\}$.

6.2 Restricted Context-Free Grammars

In this section, we introduce several reasonable restrictions placed on CFGs to simplify their investigation in theory and use in practice. We struggle to introduce all the restricted versions so they are as powerful as their general versions, defined in Section 6.1.

Section 6.2.1 reduces the derivation multiplicity of CFGs by restricting its attention only to canonical derivations and derivation trees. This section also explores the phenomenon of ambiguity in CFGs and their languages, and it points out the existence of CFLs that are always generated in an ambiguous way. Section 6.2.2 explains how to remove all redundant symbols from grammars in $_{CFG}\Psi$. Section 6.2.3 describes how to turn any CFG to an equivalent CFG in which no rule has ε as its right-hand side. Section 6.2.4 transforms any CFG to an equivalent CFG in which a single nonterminal does not form the right-hand side of any rule. Continuing with the same topic in a more restrictive way, Section 6.2.5 describes how to convert any grammar in $_{CFG}\Psi$ to an equivalent Chomsky normal form grammar in which every rule has on its right-hand side a terminal or two nonterminals. Section 6.2.6 discusses the grammatical phenomenon of left recursion, which causes the grammars to go into an infinite loop, and explains how to remove this phenomenon. Finally, Section 6.2.7 describes how to transform any grammar in ${}_{CFG}\Psi$ to an equivalent Greibach normal form grammar in which every rule has on its right-hand side a terminal followed by zero or more nonterminals.

6.2.1 Canonical Derivations and Derivation Trees

As illustrated by Example 6.2, in a general case, $G \in {}_{CFG}\Psi$ may generate the same sentence by many different derivations, and this derivation multiplicity obviously complicates the discussion of G and $L(G)$ in both theory and practice. To reduce this derivation multiplicity, we first introduce two special types of *canonical derivations*—namely, *leftmost derivations* and *rightmost derivations*—and demonstrate that $x \in L(G)$ iff G generates x by either of these two canonical derivations. In addition, in terms of graph theory, we simplify the discussion concerning grammatical derivations by *derivation trees*, which represent derivations by graphically displaying rules but suppressing the order of their applications.

During this section, the reader should carefully keep in mind that we frequently and automatically make use of Convention 6.2.

6.2.1.1 Leftmost Derivations

A derivation is *leftmost* if during its every single derivation step, the leftmost occurrence of a nonterminal is rewritten in the sentential form.

Definition 6.4 Let $G = (\Sigma, R)$ be a CFG.

I. Let $r: A \rightarrow z \in R$, $t \in \Delta^*$, $o \in \Sigma^*$. Then, G makes the *leftmost derivation step from tAo to tzo according to r*, symbolically written as $tAo \ {}_{lm}\!\Rightarrow tzo\ [r]$.

II. *Leftmost derivations in G* are defined recursively as follows:

  i. For all $u \in \Sigma^*$, then G makes the *leftmost derivation from u to u according to* ε, symbolically written $u \ {}_{lm}\!\Rightarrow^* u\ [\varepsilon]$.

  ii. If $u, w, v \in \Sigma^*$, $\rho = \sigma r$, $\sigma \in R^*$, $r \in R$, $u \ {}_{lm}\!\Rightarrow^* w\ [\sigma]$ and $w \ {}_{lm}\!\Rightarrow v\ [r]$ in G, then G makes the *leftmost derivation from u to v according to* ρ, symbolically written as $u \ {}_{lm}\!\Rightarrow^* v\ [\rho]$ in G. ■

To point out the crucial parts of Definition 6.4, notice that in I, A is the leftmost occurrence of a nonterminal in the rewritten string tAo. According to II, $u \ {}_{lm}\!\Rightarrow^* u\ [\varepsilon]$ in G, for every $u \in \Sigma^*$. If $\rho = r_1 r_2 \ldots r_n$, where $r_j \in R$, for some $n \in \mathbb{N}$, and there are $w_0, w_1, \ldots, w_n \in \Sigma^*$ such that $w_{j-1} \ {}_{lm}\!\Rightarrow w_j\ [r_j]$ in G (see I), for all $1 \leq j \leq n$, then G makes the leftmost derivation from w_0 to w_n according to ρ, $w_0 \ {}_{lm}\!\Rightarrow^* w_n\ [\rho]$. If ρ represents an immaterial piece of information, we omit it and simplify $w_0 \ {}_{lm}\!\Rightarrow^* w_n\ [\rho]$ to $w_0 \ {}_{lm}\!\Rightarrow^* w_n$. It is worth noting that apart from $w_0 \ {}_{lm}\!\Rightarrow^* w_n\ [\rho]$, there may exist $\sigma \in R^*$ such that $\rho \neq \sigma$ and $w_0 \ {}_{lm}\!\Rightarrow^* w_n\ [\sigma]$ in G as well. In fact, in a general case, G can make $w_0 \ {}_{lm}\!\Rightarrow^* w_n$ according to several different sequences of rules from R^*.

Next, we demonstrate that every CFG can generate each sentence by a leftmost derivation.

Theorem 6.5 Let $G \in {}_{CFG}\Psi$. Then, $w \in L(G)$ iff $S \ {}_{lm}\!\Rightarrow^* w$ in G.

Proof. The *if* part of the proof says that $S \ {}_{lm}\!\Rightarrow^* w$ implies $w \in L(G)$, for every $w \in \Delta^*$. As $S \ {}_{lm}\!\Rightarrow^* w$ is a special case of a derivation from S to w, this implication surely holds. Therefore, we need only to prove the *only-if* part that says that $w \in L(G)$ implies $S \ {}_{lm}\!\Rightarrow^* w$ in G. This implication straightforwardly follows from the next claim.

Claim. For every $w \in L(G)$, $S \Rightarrow^n w$ implies $S\ {}_{lm}\!\Rightarrow^n w$, for all $n \geq 0$.

Proof. (by induction on $n \geq 0$).

Basis. For $n = 0$, this implication is trivial.

Induction Hypothesis. Assume that there exists an integer $n \geq 0$ such that the claim holds for all derivations of length n or less.

Induction Step. Let $S \Rightarrow^{n+1} w\ [\rho]$, where $w \in L(G)$, $\rho \in R^+$, and $|\rho| = n + 1$. If $S \Rightarrow^{n+1} w\ [\rho]$ is leftmost, the induction step is completed. Assume that this derivation is not leftmost. Express $S \Rightarrow^{n+1} w\ [\rho]$ as

$$
\begin{array}{llll}
S & {}_{lm}\!\Rightarrow^* & uAv\underline{B}x & [\sigma] \\
 & \Rightarrow & uAvyx & [r\text{: } B \rightarrow y] \\
 & \Rightarrow^* & w & [\theta]
\end{array}
$$

where $\sigma, \theta \in R^*$, $\rho = \sigma r \theta$, r: $B \rightarrow y \in R$, $u \in$ *prefixes*(w), $A \in N$, and $v, x, y \in \Sigma^*$. In other words, $S\ {}_{lm}\!\Rightarrow^* uAv\underline{B}x$ is the longest leftmost derivation that begins $S \Rightarrow^{n+1} w$. As $w \in L(G)$ and $L(G) \subseteq \Delta^*$ (see Definition 6.1), $w \in \Delta^*$. Thus, $A \notin$ *symbols*(w) because $A \in N$. Hence, A is surely rewritten during $uAvyx \Rightarrow^* w$. Express $S \Rightarrow^{n+1} w$ as

$$
\begin{array}{llll}
S & {}_{lm}\!\Rightarrow^* & uAv\underline{B}x & [\sigma] \\
 & \Rightarrow & uAvyx & [r\text{: } B \rightarrow y] \\
 & \Rightarrow^* & u\underline{A}z & [\pi] \\
 & {}_{lm}\!\Rightarrow & utz & [p\text{: } A \rightarrow t] \\
 & \Rightarrow^* & w & [o]
\end{array}
$$

where $\pi, o \in R^*$, $\theta = \pi p o$, p: $A \rightarrow t \in R$, $vyx \Rightarrow^* z$, $z \in \Sigma^*$. Rearrange this derivation so the derivation step according to p is made right after the initial part $S\ {}_{lm}\!\Rightarrow^* uAvBx\ [\sigma]$; more formally written,

$$
\begin{array}{llll}
S & {}_{lm}\!\Rightarrow^* & u\underline{A}vBx & [\sigma] \\
 & {}_{lm}\!\Rightarrow & utv\underline{B}x & [p\text{: } A \rightarrow t] \\
 & \Rightarrow & utvyx & [r\text{: } B \rightarrow y] \\
 & \Rightarrow^* & utz & [\pi] \\
 & \Rightarrow^* & w & [o]
\end{array}
$$

The resulting derivation $S \Rightarrow^* w\ [\sigma p r \pi o]$ begins with at least $|\sigma p|$ leftmost steps, so its leftmost beginning is definitely longer than the leftmost beginning of the original derivation $S \Rightarrow^{n+1} w\ [\rho]$. If $S \Rightarrow^* w\ [\sigma p r \pi o]$ is leftmost, the induction step is completed. If not, apply the derivation rearrangement described above to $S \Rightarrow^* w\ [\sigma p r \pi o]$. After no more than $n - 2$ repetitions of this rearrangement, we necessarily obtain $S\ {}_{lm}\!\Rightarrow^* w$, which completes the induction step, so the proof of the claim is completed.

By this claim, we see that $w \in L(G)$ implies $S\ {}_{lm}\!\Rightarrow^* w$ in G, so the theorem holds. ■

We might naturally ask whether for every $G \in {}_{CFG}\Psi$, $G = (\Sigma, R)$, $S \Rightarrow^* w$ iff $S\ {}_{lm}\!\Rightarrow^* w$, for all $w \in \Sigma^*$. To rephrase this question less formally, we might ask whether Theorem 6.5 can be generalized in terms of all sentential forms, not just sentences. Surprisingly, the answer is no. Indeed, to give a trivial counterexample, consider a two-rule CFG defined as $S \rightarrow AA$ and $A \rightarrow a$. Observe that this grammar makes $S \Rightarrow AA \Rightarrow Aa$; however, there is no leftmost derivation of Aa in G.

6.2.1.2 Rightmost Derivations

As their name indicates, in *rightmost derivations*, the rightmost occurrence of a nonterminal is rewritten during its every derivation step.

Definition 6.6 Let $G = (\Sigma, R)$ be a CFG.

I. Let $r: A \rightarrow z \in R$, $t \in \Delta^*$, $o \in \Sigma^*$. Then, G makes the *rightmost derivation step from oAt to ozt according to r*, symbolically written as $oAt\ _{rm}\!\Rightarrow ozt\ [r]$.
II. *Rightmost derivations in G* are defined recursively as follows:
   i. For all $u \in \Sigma^*$, then G makes the *rightmost derivation from u to u according to* ε, symbolically written $u\ _{rm}\!\Rightarrow^* u\ [\varepsilon]$.
   ii. If $u, w, v \in \Sigma^*$, $\rho = \sigma r$, $\sigma \in R^*$, $r \in R$, $u\ _{rm}\!\Rightarrow^* w\ [\sigma]$ and $w\ _{rm}\!\Rightarrow v\ [r]$ in G, then G makes the *rightmost derivation from u to v according to* ρ, symbolically written as $u\ _{rm}\!\Rightarrow^* v\ [\rho]$ in G. ■

Let $u, v \in \Sigma^*$, $\rho \in R^*$, and $u\ _{rm}\!\Rightarrow^* v\ [\rho]$ in G. If ρ represents an immaterial piece of information, we usually simplify $u\ _{rm}\!\Rightarrow^* v\ [\rho]$ to $u\ _{rm}\!\Rightarrow^* v$. Of course, in a general case, G can make $u\ _{rm}\!\Rightarrow^* v$ according to several different sequences of rules from R^*.

As an exercise, by analogy with Theorem 6.5, prove Theorem 6.7.

Theorem 6.7 Let $G \in {}_{CFG}\Psi$. Then, $w \in L(G)$ iff $S\ _{rm}\!\Rightarrow^* w$. ■

6.2.1.3 Derivation Trees

Apart from the canonical derivations, we often simplify the discussion concerning grammatical derivations graphically by *derivation trees*, composed of *rule trees*. As their names indicate, rule trees describe grammatical rules while derivation trees represent derivations by specifying the rules, expressed as rule trees, according to which they are made together with the nonterminals to which the rules are applied. On the other hand, derivation trees suppress the order of the applications of the rules, so we make use of these trees when this order is immaterial.

A derivation tree in a CFG, $G = (\Sigma, R)$, is any tree such that its root is from Σ, and for each of its elementary subtrees (see Section 1.4), e, there is a rule, $l \in R$, such that e represents l (see I in Definition 6.8). Apart from the notion of a derivation tree, the following definition also specifies its correspondence to the derivation it represents. Let us note that this definition makes use of the terminology concerning trees introduced in Section 1.4.

Definition 6.8 Let $G = (\Sigma, R)$ be a CFG.

I. For $l: A \rightarrow x \in R$, $A\langle x\rangle$ is the *rule tree that represents l*.
II. The *derivation trees representing derivations* in G are defined recursively as follows:
   i. One-node tree X is the derivation tree corresponding to $X \Rightarrow^0 X$ in G, where $X \in \Sigma$.
   ii. Let d be the derivation tree representing $A \Rightarrow^* uBv\ [\rho]$ with $frontier(d) = uBv$, and let l: $B \rightarrow z \in R$. The derivation tree that represents

$$\begin{aligned} A &\Rightarrow^* u\underline{B}v \quad [\rho] \\ &\Rightarrow uzv \quad [l] \end{aligned}$$

   is obtained by replacing the $(|u|+1)$st leaf in d, B, with the rule tree corresponding to l, $B\langle z\rangle$.
III. A *derivation tree* in G is any tree t for which there is a derivation represented by t (see II). ■

Convention 6.9 Let $G = (\Sigma, R)$ be a CFG. For any $l: A \rightarrow x \in R$, ${}_G\clubsuit(l)$ denotes the rule tree corresponding to l. For any $A \Rightarrow^* x\ [\rho]$ in G, where $A \in N$, $x \in \Sigma^*$, and $\rho \in R^*$, ${}_G\clubsuit(A \Rightarrow^* x\ [\rho])$ denotes the derivation tree corresponding to $A \Rightarrow^* x\ [\rho]$. Just like we often write $A \Rightarrow^* x$ instead of $A \Rightarrow^* x\ [\rho]$ (see Convention 6.2), we sometimes simplify ${}_G\clubsuit(A \Rightarrow^* x\ [\rho])$ to ${}_G\clubsuit(A \Rightarrow^* x)$ in what follows if there is no danger of confusion. Finally, ${}_G\clubsuit_{all}$ denotes the set of all derivation trees for G. ■

Theorem 6.10 Let $G \in {}_{CFG}\Psi$, $G = (\Sigma, R)$, $A \in N$, and $x \in \Sigma^*$. Then, $A \Rightarrow^* x$ in G iff $t \in {}_G\clubsuit_{all}$ with $root(t) = A$ and $frontier(t) = x$.

Proof. Consider any CFG, $G = (\Sigma, R)$. The *only-if* part of the equivalence says that for every derivation $A \Rightarrow^* x$, where $A \in N$ and $x \in \Sigma^*$, there exists $t \in {}_G\clubsuit_{all}$ such that $root(t) = A$ and $frontier(t) = x$. From Definition 6.8, we know how to construct ${}_G\clubsuit(A \Rightarrow^* x)$, which satisfies these properties.

The *if* part says that for every $t \in {}_G\clubsuit_{all}$ with $root(t) = A$ and $frontier(t) = x$, where $A \in N$ and $x \in \Sigma^*$, there exists $A \Rightarrow^* x$ in G. We prove the *if* part by induction on $depth(t) \geq 0$.

Basis. Consider any $t \in {}_G\clubsuit_{all}$ such that $depth(t) = 0$. As $depth(t) = 0$, t is a tree consisting of one node, so $root(t) = frontier(t) = A$, where $A \in N$. Observe that $A \Rightarrow^0 A$ in G; therefore, the basis holds.

Induction Hypothesis. Suppose that the *if* part holds for all trees of depth n or less, where $n \in {}_0\mathbb{N}$.

Induction Step. Consider any $t \in {}_G\clubsuit_{all}$ with $depth(t) = n + 1$, $root(t) = A$, $frontier(t) = x$, $A \in N$, $x \in \Sigma^*$. Consider the topmost rule tree, ${}_G\clubsuit(p)$, occurring in t. That is, ${}_G\clubsuit(p)$ is the rule tree whose root coincides with $root(t)$. Let $p: A \rightarrow u \in R$. Distinguish these two cases—(a) $u = \varepsilon$ and (b) $u \neq \varepsilon$.

a. If $u = \varepsilon$, t has actually the form $A\langle\rangle$, which means $u = \varepsilon$ and $depth(t) = 1$, and at this point, $A \Rightarrow \varepsilon\ [p]$, so the induction step is completed.
b. Assume $u \neq \varepsilon$. Let $u = X_1X_2\ldots X_m$, where $X_i \in \Sigma$, $1 \leq i \leq m$, for some $m \geq 1$. Thus, t is of the form $A\langle t_1t_2\ldots t_m\rangle$, where each t_i is in ${}_G\clubsuit_{all}$ and satisfies $root(t_i) = X_i$, $1 \leq i \leq m$, with $depth(t_i) \leq n$. Let $frontier(t_i) = y_i$, where $y_i \in \Sigma^*$, so $x = y_1y_2\ldots y_m$. As $depth(t_i) \leq n$, by the induction hypothesis, $X_i \Rightarrow^* y_i$ in G, $1 \leq i \leq m$. Since $A \rightarrow u \in R$ with $u = X_1X_2\ldots X_m$, we have $A \Rightarrow X_1X_2\ldots X_m$. Putting together $A \Rightarrow X_1X_2\ldots X_m$ and $X_i \Rightarrow^* y_i$ for all $1 \leq i \leq m$, we obtain

$$\begin{aligned} A &\Rightarrow X_1X_2\ldots X_m \\ &\Rightarrow^* y_1X_2\ldots X_m \\ &\Rightarrow^* y_1y_2\ldots X_m \\ &\ \vdots \\ &\Rightarrow^* y_1y_2\ldots y_m \end{aligned}$$

Thus, $A \Rightarrow^* x$ in G, the induction step is completed, and the *if* part of the equivalence holds true. ■

Corollary 6.11 Let $G \in {}_{CFG}\Psi$. Then, $w \in L(G)$ iff ${}_G\clubsuit_{all}$ contains t such that $root(t) = S$ and $frontier(t) = w$.

Proof. This corollary follows from Theorem 6.10 for $S \Rightarrow^* w$ with $w \in {}_G\Delta^*$. ■

Theorem 6.10 and Corollary 6.11 imply the following important Corollary 6.12, which says that without any loss of generality, we can always restrict our attention to the canonical derivations or derivation trees when discussing the language generated by CFGs.

Corollary 6.12 For every $G \in {}_{CFG}\Psi$, I through III, as follows, coincide with $L(G) = \{w \in {}_G\Delta^* |\ S \Rightarrow^* w\}$.

I. $\{w \in {}_G\Delta^* |\ S\ {}_{lm}\Rightarrow^* w\}$;
II. $\{w \in {}_G\Delta^* |\ S\ {}_{rm}\Rightarrow^* w\}$;
III. $\{w \in {}_G\Delta^* |\ w = frontier(t)$, where $t \in {}_G\clubsuit_{all}$ with $root(t) = S\}$. ■

6.2.1.4 Ambiguity

Unfortunately, even if we reduce our attention only to canonical derivations or derivation trees, we may still face a derivation multiplicity of some sentences. Indeed, some CFGs make several different canonical derivations of the same sentences; even worse, some languages in ${}_{CFG}\Phi$ are generated only by CFGs of this kind.

Definition 6.13 Let $G \in {}_{CFG}\Psi$.

I. $G \in {}_{CFG}\Psi$ is *ambiguous* if $L(G)$ contains a sentence w such that $S\ {}_{lm}\Rightarrow^* w\ [\rho]$ and $S\ {}_{lm}\Rightarrow^* w\ [\sigma]$ for some $\rho, \sigma \in R^*$ with $\rho \neq \sigma$; otherwise, G is *unambiguous*.
II. $L \in {}_{CFG}\Phi$ is *inherently ambiguous* if every $G \in {}_{CFG}\Psi$ such that $L(G) = L$ is ambiguous. ■

Less formally, according to I in Definition 6.13, G is ambiguous if it generates a sentence by two different leftmost derivations. To rephrase I in terms of rightmost derivations, G is ambiguous if there exist $S\ {}_{rm}\Rightarrow^* w\ [\rho]$ and $S\ {}_{rm}\Rightarrow^* w\ [\sigma]$ with $\rho \neq \sigma$, for some $w \in L(G)$. In terms of ${}_G\clubsuit_{all}$ (see Convention 6.9), G is ambiguous if ${}_G\clubsuit_{all}$ contains t and u such that $t \neq u$ while $frontier(t) = frontier(u)$.

We close this section by illustrating its key notions—canonical derivations, rule trees, derivation trees, and ambiguity.

Example 6.3 Consider

$$Z = \{a^i b^j c^k |\ i, j, k \in \mathbb{N},\ i = j \text{ or } j = k\}$$

Observe that $Z = L(G)$, where $G \in {}_{CFG}\Psi$ is defined by the following 10 rules:

$$0: S \to AB, 1: A \to aAb, 2: A \to ab, 3: B \to cB, 4: B \to c,$$
$$5: S \to CD, 6: C \to aC, 7: C \to a, 8: D \to bDc, 9: D \to bc$$

Indeed, G uses rules 0 through 4 to generate $\{a^i b^j c^k |\ i, j, k \in \mathbb{N}, i = j\}$. By using rules 5 through 9, it generates $\{a^i b^j c^k |\ i, j, k \in \mathbb{N}, j = k\}$. As the union of these two languages coincides with Z, $L(G) = Z$.

Notice that G can generate every sentence by a variety of different derivations. For instance, consider $aabbcc \in L(G)$. Observe that G generates this sentence by the twelve different derivations, I through XII, listed in Figure 6.1 (according to Convention 6.2, we specify the rewritten symbols by underlining).

Figure 6.2 describes the rule trees ${}_G\clubsuit(0)$ through ${}_G\clubsuit(9)$ corresponding to the 10 rules in G. In addition, ${}_G\clubsuit(0)$ is pictorially shown in Figure 6.3.

Consider, for instance, the first derivation in Figure 6.1. Figure 6.4 presents this derivation together with its corresponding derivation tree constructed in a step-by-step way. In addition, the resulting derivation tree, $S\langle A\langle aA\langle ab\rangle b\rangle B\langle cB\langle c\rangle\rangle\rangle$, is pictorially shown in Figure 6.5.

In Figure 6.1, derivations I and VII represent two different leftmost derivations that generate $aabbcc$. Thus, G is an ambiguous CFG.

I		II		III		IV		V		VI	
$\underline{S}$		$\underline{S}$		$\underline{S}$		$\underline{S}$		$\underline{S}$		$\underline{S}$	
$\Rightarrow \underline{A}B$	[0]	$\Rightarrow \underline{A}B$	[0]	$\Rightarrow \underline{A}B$	[0]	$\Rightarrow A\underline{B}$	[0]	$\Rightarrow A\underline{B}$	[0]	$\Rightarrow A\underline{B}$	[0]
$\Rightarrow a\underline{A}bB$	[1]	$\Rightarrow aAb\underline{B}$	[1]	$\Rightarrow aAb\underline{B}$	[1]	$\Rightarrow \underline{A}cB$	[3]	$\Rightarrow Ac\underline{B}$	[3]	$\Rightarrow \underline{A}cB$	[3]
$\Rightarrow aabb\underline{B}$	[2]	$\Rightarrow a\underline{A}bcB$	[3]	$\Rightarrow aAbc\underline{B}$	[3]	$\Rightarrow a\underline{A}bcB$	[1]	$\Rightarrow \underline{A}cc$	[4]	$\Rightarrow aAbc\underline{B}$	[1]
$\Rightarrow aabbc\underline{B}$	[3]	$\Rightarrow aabbc\underline{B}$	[2]	$\Rightarrow a\underline{A}bcc$	[4]	$\Rightarrow aabbc\underline{B}$	[2]	$\Rightarrow a\underline{A}bcc$	[1]	$\Rightarrow a\underline{A}bcc$	[4]
$\Rightarrow aabbcc$	[4]	$\Rightarrow aabbcc$	[4]	$\Rightarrow aabbcc$	[2]	$\Rightarrow aabbcc$	[4]	$\Rightarrow aabbcc$	[2]	$\Rightarrow aabbcc$	[2]

VII		VIII		IX		X		XI		XII	
$\underline{S}$		$\underline{S}$		$\underline{S}$		$\underline{S}$		$\underline{S}$		$\underline{S}$	
$\Rightarrow \underline{C}D$	[5]	$\Rightarrow \underline{C}D$	[5]	$\Rightarrow \underline{C}D$	[5]	$\Rightarrow C\underline{D}$	[5]	$\Rightarrow C\underline{D}$	[5]	$\Rightarrow C\underline{D}$	[5]
$\Rightarrow a\underline{C}D$	[6]	$\Rightarrow aC\underline{D}$	[6]	$\Rightarrow aC\underline{D}$	[6]	$\Rightarrow \underline{C}bDc$	[8]	$\Rightarrow Cb\underline{D}c$	[8]	$\Rightarrow \underline{C}bDc$	[8]
$\Rightarrow aa\underline{D}$	[7]	$\Rightarrow a\underline{C}bDc$	[8]	$\Rightarrow aCb\underline{D}c$	[8]	$\Rightarrow a\underline{C}bDc$	[6]	$\Rightarrow \underline{C}bbcc$	[9]	$\Rightarrow aCb\underline{D}c$	[6]
$\Rightarrow aab\underline{D}c$	[8]	$\Rightarrow aab\underline{D}c$	[7]	$\Rightarrow a\underline{C}bbcc$	[9]	$\Rightarrow aab\underline{D}c$	[7]	$\Rightarrow a\underline{C}bbcc$	[6]	$\Rightarrow a\underline{C}bbcc$	[9]
$\Rightarrow aabbcc$	[9]	$\Rightarrow aabbcc$	[9]	$\Rightarrow aabbcc$	[7]	$\Rightarrow aabbcc$	[9]	$\Rightarrow aabbcc$	[7]	$\Rightarrow aabbcc$	[7]

Figure 6.1 Twelve derivations of *aabbcc*.

Rule	Rule tree
0: $S \rightarrow AB$	$S\langle AB\rangle$
1: $A \rightarrow aAb$	$A\langle aAb\rangle$
2: $A \rightarrow ab$	$A\langle ab\rangle$
3: $B \rightarrow cB$	$B\langle cB\rangle$
4: $B \rightarrow c$	$B\langle c\rangle$
5: $S \rightarrow CD$	$S\langle CD\rangle$
6: $C \rightarrow aC$	$C\langle aC\rangle$
7: $C \rightarrow a$	$C\langle a\rangle$
8: $D \rightarrow bDc$	$D\langle aDc\rangle$
9: $D \rightarrow bc$	$D\langle bc\rangle$

Figure 6.2 $_G♣(0)$ through $_G♣(9)$.

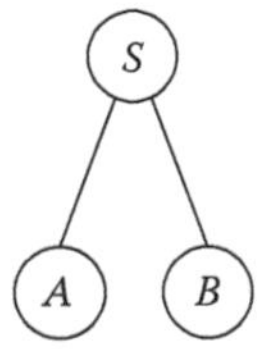

Figure 6.3 Rule tree $_G♣(0)$ of the form $S\langle AB\rangle$.

Derivation		*Derivation tree*
$\underline{S}$		S
$\Rightarrow \underline{A}B$	[0]	$S\langle AB\rangle$
$\Rightarrow a\underline{A}bB$	[1]	$S\langle A\langle aAb\rangle B\rangle$
$\Rightarrow aabb\underline{B}$	[2]	$S\langle A\langle aA\langle ab\rangle b\rangle B\rangle$
$\Rightarrow aabbc\underline{B}$	[3]	$S\langle A\langle aA\langle ab\rangle b\rangle B\langle cB\rangle\rangle$
$\Rightarrow aabbcc$	[4]	$S\langle A\langle aA\langle ab\rangle b\rangle B\langle cB\langle c\rangle\rangle\rangle$

Figure 6.4 Derivation I and its corresponding derivation tree.

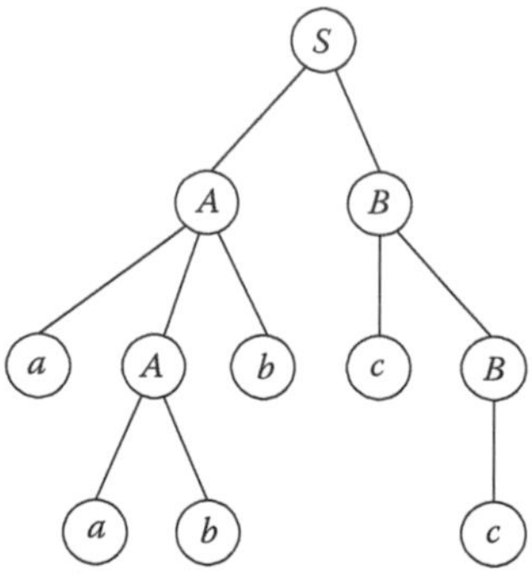

Figure 6.5 Derivation tree $S\langle A\langle aA\langle ab\rangle b\rangle B\langle cB\langle c\rangle\rangle\rangle$.

As a matter of fact, Z is inherently ambiguous because every CFG that generates Z is ambiguous. Leaving a fully rigorous proof of this inherent ambiguousness as an exercise, we next only sketch its two-step gist. Consider any $H \in {}_{CFG}\Psi$ satisfying $L(H) = Z$. Take any $l \in \mathbb{N}$ satisfying $l > |\boldsymbol{rhs}(r)|$ for all rules $r \in {}_{H}R$.

1. Show that H necessarily contains two disjoint subsets of rules, X and Y, such that by rules from X, H generates $\{a^i b^j c^k \mid i, j, k \in \mathbb{N}, i = j\}$, and by rules from Y, it generates $\{a^i b^j c^k \mid i, j, k \in \mathbb{N}, j = k\}$; otherwise, H would generate $a^i b^j c^k$ with $i \neq j \neq k$.
2. Consider $a^l b^l c^l \in Z$. By using rules from both X and Y, H necessarily makes two different leftmost derivations of $a^l b^l c^l$; consequently, Z is inherently ambiguous. ■

The conclusion of Example 6.3 implies a pragmatically negative result saying that some CFLs are generated only by ambiguous CFGs.

Corollary 6.14 Unambiguous CFGs generate a proper subfamily of ${}_{CFG}\Phi$. ■

6.2.2 Removal of Useless Symbols

CFGs may contain some symbols that are of no use regarding the generated languages. As a result, useless symbols like these only unnecessarily increase the size of CFGs and, thereby, obscure their specification. Therefore, we next explain how to remove these superfluous symbols from CFGs.

As completely useless, we obviously consider all symbols from which no terminal string is derivable, so we eliminate them first.

Definition 6.15 Let $G \in {}_{CFG}\Psi$. A symbol $X \in {}_{G}\Sigma$ is *terminating* if $X \Rightarrow^* w$ in G for some $w \in {}_{G}\Delta^*$; otherwise, X is *nonterminating*. ■

Basic Idea. Let $G = ({}_{G}\Sigma, {}_{G}R)$ be a CFG. We construct the set V containing all terminating symbols in G in the following way. First, set V to ${}_{G}\Delta$ because every terminal $a \in {}_{G}\Delta$ satisfies $a \Rightarrow^0 a$, so a is surely terminating by Definition 6.15. If $A \rightarrow x \in R$ satisfies $x \in V^*$, then $A \Rightarrow x \Rightarrow^* w$ in G, for some $w \in \Delta^*$; therefore, add A to V because $A \Rightarrow x \Rightarrow^* w$ and, consequently, A is terminating. In this way, keep extending V until no further terminating symbol can be added to V. The resulting set V contains only terminating symbols in G.

Algorithm 6.16, whose formal verification is left as an exercise, constructs V based on this idea.

Algorithm 6.16 Terminating Symbols.

Input. A CFG, $G = ({}_G\Sigma, {}_GR)$.

Output. The subalphabet, $V \subseteq {}_G\Sigma$, that contains all terminating symbols in G.

Method.

begin

set V to ${}_G\Delta$
repeat
if $A \rightarrow x \in {}_GR$ and $x \in V^*$ **then**
add A to V
until no change

end.

Example 6.4 Consider this CFG

$$S \rightarrow S\,o\,S,\ S \rightarrow S\,o\,A,\ S \rightarrow A,\ A \rightarrow A\,o\,A,\ S \rightarrow (S),\ S \rightarrow i,\ B \rightarrow i$$

where o, i, (, and) are terminals, and the other symbols are nonterminals. Intuitively, o and i stand for an *o*perator and an *i*dentifier, respectively. Notice that the CFG generates the set of expressions that can be built up using the terminal symbols; for instance, $S \Rightarrow^* i\,o\,(i\,o\,i)$.

With this CFG as its input, Algorithm 6.16 first sets $V = \{o, i, (,)\}$. Then, it enters the **repeat** loop.

As $B \rightarrow i$ with $i \in V$, it adds B to V. For the same reason, $S \rightarrow i$ leads to the inclusion of S to V, so $V = \{o, i, (,), B, S\}$. At this point, the **repeat** loop cannot further increase V, so it exits. As a result, A is nonterminating because $A \notin V$.

Apart from nonterminating symbols, a symbol is considered as useless in a CFG if starting from the start symbol, the grammar makes no derivation of a string that contains the symbol. To put it more formally and briefly, for $G \in {}_{CFG}\Psi$, $X \in {}_G\Sigma$ is inaccessible and, therefore, useless in G if $X \notin$ *symbols*$(F(G))$; recall that $F(G)$ denotes the set of all sentential forms of G (see Definition 6.1), and *symbols*$(F(G))$ denotes the set of all symbols occurring in $F(G)$ (see Section 2.1).

Definition 6.17 Let $G = ({}_G\Sigma, {}_GR)$ be a CFG, and let $X \in {}_G\Sigma$. X is *accessible* if $X \in$ *symbols*$(F(G))$; otherwise, X is *inaccessible*. ■

Basic Idea. Let $G = ({}_G\Sigma, {}_GR)$ be a CFG. To construct the alphabet, $W \subseteq {}_G\Sigma$, that contains all accessible symbols, initialize W with ${}_GS$. Indeed, the start symbol ${}_GS$ is always accessible because ${}_GS \Rightarrow^0 {}_GS$. If $A \rightarrow x \in {}_GR$ with $A \in W$, we include *symbols*(x) into W because we can always change A to x by $A \rightarrow x$ in any sentential form, so *symbols*$(x) \subseteq$ *symbols*$(F(G))$. Keep extending W in this way until no further symbols can be added to W to obtain the set of all accessible symbols. Algorithm 6.18 constructs W in this way.

Algorithm 6.18 Accessible Symbols.

Input. A CFG, $G = ({}_G\Sigma, {}_GR)$.

Output. The subalphabet, $W \subseteq {}_G\Sigma$, that contains all accessible symbols in G.

Method.

begin

set W to $\{{}_GS\}$
repeat
  if ***lhs***$(r) \in W$ for some $r \in {}_GR$ **then**
    add *symbols*(***rhs***(r)) to W
until no change

end.

Example 6.5 Consider the same CFG as in Example 6.4—that is,

$$S \rightarrow S\,o\,S,\ S \rightarrow S\,o\,A,\ S \rightarrow A,\ A \rightarrow A\,o\,A,\ S \rightarrow (S),\ S \rightarrow i,\ B \rightarrow i$$

With this CFG as its input, Algorithm 6.18 first sets $W = \{S\}$. As $S \rightarrow S\ o\ S$, the **repeat** loop adds o to W. Furthermore, since $S \rightarrow A$, this loop also adds A there. Continuing in this way, this loop exits with W containing all symbols but B, so B is the only inaccessible symbol in this CFG.

Definition 6.19 Let $G = ({}_G\Sigma, {}_GR)$ be a CFG. A symbol $X \in {}_G\Sigma$ is *useful* in G if $X \in$ *symbols*$(F(G))$ and $X \Rightarrow^* w$ with $w \in {}_G\Delta^*$; otherwise, X is *useless*. ■

In other words, X is *useful* if it is both accessible and terminating. Making use of Algorithms 6.16 and 6.18, we next explain how to turn any CFG to an equivalent CFG that contains only useful symbols.

Algorithm 6.20 Useful Symbols.

Input. A CFG $I = ({}_I\Sigma, {}_IR)$.

Output. A CFG $O = ({}_O\Sigma, {}_OR)$ such that $L(I) = L(O)$, and all symbols in ${}_O\Sigma$ are useful.

Method.

begin

1. by using Algorithm 6.16, find all terminating symbols in ${}_I\Sigma$; then, eliminate all nonterminating symbols and the rules that contain them from I;
2. consider the CFG obtained in (1); by using Algorithm 6.18, determine all its accessible symbols; then, remove all inaccessible symbols and the rules that contain them from the CFG; the resulting CFG is O;

end.

Theorem 6.21 Algorithm 6.20 is correct.

Proof. By contradiction, prove that every nonterminal in O is useful. Assume that $X \in {}_O\Sigma$ and X is a useless symbol. Consequently, (i) for every $y \in \Sigma^*$ such that $S \Rightarrow^* y$, $X \notin symbols(y)$, or (ii) for every $x \in \Sigma^*$ such that $X \Rightarrow^* x$, $x \notin {}_O\Delta^*$. Case (i) is ruled out because Algorithm 6.18 would eliminate X. Case (ii) is ruled out as well. Indeed, if for every $x \in \Sigma^*$ such that $X \Rightarrow^* x$, $x \notin {}_O\Delta^*$, then X would be eliminated by Algorithm 6.16. Thus, $X \notin {}_O\Sigma$, which contradicts $X \in {}_O\Sigma$. As a result, every symbol in ${}_O\Sigma$ is useful.

As an exercise, complete the proof. That is, prove that $L(I) = L(O)$. ■

Observe that the order of the two transformations in Algorithm 6.20 is crucially important. Indeed, if we reverse them, this algorithm does not work properly. To give a trivial counterexample, consider the CFG I defined as $S \rightarrow a$, $S \rightarrow A$, $A \rightarrow AB$, and $B \rightarrow a$. Notice that $L(I) = \{a\}$. If we apply the transformations in Algorithm 6.20 properly, we obtain an equivalent one-rule grammar O defined as $S \rightarrow a$. That is, in this way, Algorithm 6.20 rightly detects and eliminates A and B as useless symbols. However, if we improperly apply Algorithm 6.18 before Algorithm 6.16, we obtain a two-rule grammar $S \rightarrow a$ and $B \rightarrow a$, in which B is useless.

Example 6.6 Once again, return to the CFG

$$S \rightarrow S\,o\,S,\ S \rightarrow S\,o\,A,\ S \rightarrow A,\ A \rightarrow A\,o\,A,\ S \rightarrow (S),\ S \rightarrow i,\ B \rightarrow i$$

discussed in Examples 6.4 and 6.5. Eliminate the nonterminating symbols from this CFG by Algorithm 6.20. From Example 6.4, we already know that A is the only nonterminating symbol, so the elimination of all rules containing A produces the grammar defined as

$$S \rightarrow S\,o\,S,\ S \rightarrow (S),\ S \rightarrow i,\ B \rightarrow i$$

Apply Algorithm 6.18 to this CFG to find out that B is the only inaccessible symbol in it. By removing $B \rightarrow i$, we obtain

$$S \rightarrow S\,o\,S,\ S \rightarrow (S),\ S \rightarrow i$$

as the resulting equivalent CFG in which all symbols are useful.

6.2.3 Removal of Erasing Rules

It is often convenient to eliminate all erasing rules—that is, the rules that have ε on the right-hand sides—in a CFG. Indeed, without these rules, the CFG can never make any sentential form shorter during a derivation step, and this property obviously simplifies its exploration as well as application. In this section, we explain how to make this elimination.

Definition 6.22 Let $G = (\Sigma, R)$ be a CFG. A rule of the form $A \rightarrow \varepsilon \in R$ is called an *erasing rule* or, briefly, an *ε-rule.* ■

Before eliminating all ε-rules in any $G \in {}_{CFG}\Psi$, we explain how to determine all the nonterminals from which G can derive ε.

Definition 6.23 Let $G \in {}_{CFG}\Psi$. A nonterminal $A \in N$ is *ε-nonterminal* in G if $A \Rightarrow^* \varepsilon$ in G. ■

Basic Idea. Let $I \in {}_{CFG}\Psi$. To determine the set ${}_IE \subseteq {}_IN$ containing all ε-nonterminals in I, we initialize ${}_IE$ with the left-hand sides of all these ε-rules. Indeed, if for $A \in {}_IN$ and $A \rightarrow \varepsilon \in {}_IR$, then $A \Rightarrow \varepsilon$ in I. Then, we extend ${}_I E$ by every $B \in {}_I N$ for which there is $B \rightarrow x \in {}_I R$ with $x \in {}_I E^*$, which obviously implies $B \Rightarrow^* \varepsilon$. Repeat this extension until no further ε-nonterminals can be added to ${}_I E$.

Algorithm 6.24 Determination of ε-Nonterminals.

Input. A CFG, $I = ({}_I\Sigma, {}_I R)$.

Output. The subalphabet, ${}_I E \subseteq {}_I N$, containing all ε-nonterminals in I.

Method.

begin

  initialize ${}_I E$ with $\{A \mid A \rightarrow \varepsilon \in {}_I R\}$
  repeat
    if $B \rightarrow x \in {}_I R$ with $x \in {}_I E^*$ **then**
      add B to ${}_I E$
  until no change

end.

As an exercise, prove that Algorithm 6.24 is correct.

Example 6.7 Consider Algorithm 6.24. As the input CFG I, take

$$S \rightarrow AB, A \rightarrow aAb, B \rightarrow cBd, A \rightarrow \varepsilon, B \rightarrow \varepsilon$$

As obvious, $L(I) = \{a^n b^n \mid n \geq 0\}\{c^m d^m \mid m \geq 0\}$. Algorithm 6.24 initializes ${}_I E$ with A and B because both nonterminals occur as the left-hand sides of the two ε-rules in I, that is, $A \rightarrow \varepsilon$ and $B \rightarrow \varepsilon$. Then, it enters the **repeat** loop. As $S \rightarrow AB$ with $AB \in {}_I E^*$, it includes S into ${}_I E$. After this inclusion, the **repeat** loop cannot further increase ${}_I E$; therefore, it exits.

We are now ready to eliminate all ε-rules from any CFG. More exactly, since no CFG without ε-rules can generate ε, we explain how to turn any $I \in {}_{CFG}\Psi$ to $O \in {}_{CFG}\Psi$ so O generates $L(I) - \{\varepsilon\}$ without possessing any ε-rules.

Basic Idea. Let $I = ({}_I\Sigma, {}_I R)$ be a CFG. Determine all its ε-nonterminals by Algorithm 6.24. Take any $B \rightarrow y \in {}_I R$ with $y = x_0 A_1 x_1 \ldots A_n x_n$, where $n \in \mathbb{N}$, so that A_1 through A_n are ε-nonterminals. Add all possible rules of the form $B \rightarrow x_0 X_1 x_1 \ldots X_n x_n$ to ${}_O R$, where $X_i \in \{\varepsilon, A_i\}$, $1 \leq i \leq n$, and $X_1 X_2 \ldots X_n \neq \varepsilon$, because each A_i can be erased by $A_i \Rightarrow^* \varepsilon$ in I. Keep extending ${}_O R$ in this way until no further rules can be added to it.

Algorithm 6.25 Elimination of ε-Rules.

Input. A CFG, $I = ({}_I\Sigma, {}_I R)$.

Output. A CFG, $O = ({}_O\Sigma, {}_O R)$, such that $L(O) = L(I) - \{\varepsilon\}$ and ${}_O R$ contains no ε-rules.

Method.

begin

  set ${}_O R = \{A \rightarrow y \mid A \rightarrow y \in {}_I R, y \neq \varepsilon\}$
  use Algorithm 6.24 to determine ${}_I E \subseteq {}_I N$ containing all ε-nonterminals in I
  repeat

if $B \to x_0A_1x_1\ldots A_nx_n$ in ${}_IR$, where $A_i \in {}_IE$, $x_j \in ({}_I\Sigma - {}_IE)^*$, for all $1 \le i \le n$, $0 \le j \le n$, where $n \in \mathbb{N}$ **then**
extend ${}_OR$ by $\{B \to x_0X_1x_1\ldots X_nx_n| \; X_i \in \{\varepsilon, A_i\}, 1 \le i \le n, |X_1X_2\ldots X_n| \ge 1\}$
until no change

end.

As an exercise, prove that Algorithm 6.25 is correct.

Theorem 6.26 Algorithm 6.25 is correct. Therefore, for every $L \in {}_{CFG}\Phi$, there exists a CFG, $G = ({}_G\Sigma, {}_GR)$, such that $L(G) = L - \{\varepsilon\}$ and ${}_GR$ contains no ε-rules. ■

Example 6.8 Reconsider the CFG defined as

$$S \to AB, A \to aAb, B \to cBd, A \to \varepsilon, \text{ and } B \to \varepsilon$$

(see Example 6.7). Take this CFG as I in Algorithm 6.25. Initially, this algorithm sets ${}_OR = \{S \to AB, A \to aAb, B \to cBd\}$, then it enters the **repeat** loop. Consider $S \to AB$. Both A and B are ε-nonterminals, so Algorithm 6.25 adds $S \to AB$, $S \to B$, and $S \to A$ to ${}_OR$. Analogically, from $A \to aAb$ and $B \to cBd$, this algorithm constructs $A \to aAb$, $B \to cBd$, $A \to ab$, and $B \to cd$, respectively. In this way, as the resulting CFG O without ε-rules, Algorithm 6.25 produces

$$S \to AB, S \to A, S \to B, A \to aAb, B \to cBd, A \to ab, B \to cd$$

Observe that O generates $\{a^nb^n| \; n \ge 0\}\{c^nd^n| \; n \ge 0\} - \{\varepsilon\}$, so $L(O) = L(I) - \{\varepsilon\}$.

Before closing this section, we make two final remarks. First, we make a remark concerning the generation of ε. Then, we sketch an alternative method of eliminating erasing rules.

Generation of ε. As already pointed out, if a CFG contains no ε-rules, it cannot generate ε. That is, let $L = L(I)$, where $I = ({}_I\Sigma, {}_IR)$ be a CFG; then, Algorithm 6.25 converts I to a CFG, $O = ({}_O\Sigma, {}_OR)$, so $L(O) = L(I) - \{\varepsilon\}$. To generate L including ε, we can easily change O to $G = ({}_G\Sigma, {}_GR)$ so ${}_G\Sigma = {}_O\Sigma \cup \{{}_GS\}$ and ${}_GR = {}_OR \cup \{{}_GS \to {}_OS, {}_GS \to \varepsilon\}$, where the start symbol ${}_GS$ is a newly introduced symbol, which is not in ${}_O\Sigma$. As obvious, $L(G) = L$, which gives rise to Theorem 6.27, whose straightforward proof is left as an exercise.

Theorem 6.27 For every $L \in {}_{CFG}\Phi$ such that $\varepsilon \in L$, there is a CFG, $G = ({}_G\Sigma, {}_GR)$, such that G simultaneously satisfies properties I through III, given next.

I. $L(G) = L$;
II. ${}_GS \to \varepsilon$ is the only ε-rule in ${}_GR$, where is the start symbol of G;
III. ${}_GS$ does not occur on the right-hand side of any rule in ${}_GR$. ■

An alternative removal of ε-rules. The previously described method that removes ε-rules consists, in fact, of two algorithms. Indeed, Algorithm 6.25, which performs this removal, makes use of Algorithm 6.24, which determines the set of all ε-nonterminals in the input CFG. Next, we describe an alternative removal of ε-rules, which does not require any predetermination of ε-nonterminals.

Basic Idea. Let $I \in {}_{CFG}\Psi$ and $A \in {}_IN$. If A derives ε in I, then a derivation like this can be expressed in the following step-by-step way

$$A \Rightarrow x_1 \Rightarrow x_2 \Rightarrow \ldots \Rightarrow x_n \Rightarrow \varepsilon$$

where $x_i \in {}_GN^*$, for all $1 \leq i \leq n$, for some $n \in {}_0\mathbb{N}$ ($n = 0$ means $A \Rightarrow \varepsilon$). If a sentential form contains several occurrences of A, each of them can be erased in this way although there may exist many alternative ways of erasing A. Based on these observations, during an application of a rule, Algorithm 6.28 introduces a compound nonterminals of the form $\langle X, W\rangle$, in which X is a symbol that is not erased during the derivation and W is a set of nonterminals that is erased. Within the compound nonterminal, the algorithm simulates the erasure of nonterminals in W in the way sketched above. Observe that as W is a set, W contains no more than one occurrence of any nonterminal because there is no need to record several occurrences of the same nonterminal; indeed, as already pointed out, all these occurrences can be erased in the same way.

Algorithm 6.28 Alternative Elimination of ε-Rules.

Input. A CFG, $I = ({}_I\Sigma, {}_IR)$.

Output. A CFG, $O = ({}_O\Sigma, {}_OR)$, such that $L(O) = L(I) - \{\varepsilon\}$ and ${}_OR$ contains no ε-rules.

Method.

begin

set ${}_O\Sigma = \{\langle X, U\rangle \mid X \in {}_I\Sigma, U \subseteq {}_IN\} \cup {}_I\Delta$, ${}_O\Delta = {}_I\Delta$, and ${}_OS = \langle {}_IS, \varnothing\rangle$
set ${}_OR$ to $\varnothing$
repeat
if $B \rightarrow x_0X_1x_1X_2x_2\ldots X_nx_n$ in ${}_IR$, where $X_i \in {}_I\Sigma$, $x_j \in {}_IN^*$, for all $1 \leq i \leq n$, $0 \leq j \leq n$, where $n \in \mathbb{N}$ **then**
add $\langle B, \varnothing\rangle \rightarrow \langle X_1, \mathit{symbols}(x_0x_1\ldots x_n)\rangle X_2\ldots X_n$ to ${}_OR$
if $\langle X, U\rangle \in {}_ON$, where $X \in {}_I\Sigma$, $U \subseteq {}_IN$, $U \neq \varnothing$, and $C \rightarrow z \in {}_IR$ with $C \in U$ and $z \in {}_IN^*$ **then**
add $\langle X, U\rangle \rightarrow \langle X, (U - \{C\}) \cup \mathit{symbols}(z)\rangle$ to ${}_OR$
until no change
for all $a \in {}_G\Delta$, add $\langle a, \varnothing\rangle \rightarrow a$ to ${}_OR$

end.

As an exercise, prove that Algorithm 6.28 is correct.

Example 6.9 Reconsider the CFG defined as

$$S \rightarrow aSb \text{ and } S \rightarrow \varepsilon$$

Algorithm 6.28 converts this CFG to the next equivalent grammar without ε-rules

$$\langle S, \varnothing\rangle \rightarrow \langle a, \varnothing\rangle\langle S, \varnothing\rangle\langle b, \varnothing\rangle,\ \langle S, \varnothing\rangle \rightarrow \langle a, \{S\}\rangle\langle b, \varnothing\rangle,$$
$$\langle a, \{S\}\rangle \rightarrow \langle a, \varnothing\rangle,\ \langle a, \varnothing\rangle \rightarrow a,\ \langle b, \varnothing\rangle \rightarrow b$$

A detailed description of this conversion is left as an exercise.

As a rule, Algorithm 6.28 produces O with many rules having a single nonterminal on their right-hand sides, which often make the definition of O clumsy as Example 6.9 illustrates. Therefore, in Section 6.2.4, we explain how to eliminate these rules without affecting the generated language.

6.2.4 Removal of Single Rules

By using rules with a single nonterminal on the right-hand side, CFGs only rename their nonterminals; otherwise, they fulfill no role at all. Therefore, it is sometimes desirable to remove them. This section explains how to make this removal.

Definition 6.29 Let $G = ({}_G\Sigma, {}_GR)$ be a CFG. A rule of the form $A \rightarrow B \in {}_GR$, where A and B are in ${}_GN$, is called a *single rule.* ■

Basic Idea. To transform a CFG I to an equivalent CFG O without single rules, observe according to a sequence of single rules, every derivation is of the form $A \Rightarrow^* B$ in I, where A and B are nonterminals. Furthermore, notice that for any derivation of the form $A \Rightarrow^* B$, there exists a derivation from A to B during which no two identical rules are applied. Consider the set of all derivations that have the form $A \Rightarrow^* B \Rightarrow x$, where $x \notin {}_IN$ and $A \Rightarrow^* B$ is made according to a sequence of single rules so that this sequence contains no two identical rules. Notice that this set is finite because every derivation of the above form consists of no more than $card({}_IR)$ steps, and ${}_IR$ is finite. For any derivation $A \Rightarrow^* B \Rightarrow x$ in the set, which satisfies the above requirements, introduce $A \rightarrow x$ to obtain the resulting equivalent output CFG O without single rules.

Algorithm 6.30 Elimination of Single Rules.

Input. A CFG, $I = ({}_I\Sigma, {}_IR)$.

Output. A CFG, $O = ({}_O\Sigma, {}_OR)$, such that $L(O) = L(I)$ and ${}_OR$ contains no single rules.

Method.

begin

set ${}_O\Sigma = {}_I\Sigma$ and ${}_OR = \emptyset$
repeat
if $A \Rightarrow^n B \Rightarrow x$ in I, where $A, B \in {}_IN$, $x \in {}_I\Sigma^* - {}_IN$, $1 \leq n \leq card({}_IR)$, and
$A \Rightarrow^n B$ is made by n single rules **then**
add $A \rightarrow x$ to ${}_OR$
until no change

end.

As an exercise, prove that Algorithm 6.30 is correct.

Theorem 6.31 Algorithm 6.30 is correct. Therefore, for every $L \in {}_{CFG}\Phi$, there exists a CFG, $G = ({}_G\Sigma, {}_GR)$, such that $L(G) = L$ and ${}_GR$ contains no single rules. ■

Example 6.10 Reconsider the CFG obtained in Example 6.8. Recall its set of rules—

$$S \rightarrow AB, S \rightarrow A, S \rightarrow B, A \rightarrow aAb, B \rightarrow cBd, A \rightarrow ab, B \rightarrow cd$$

As obvious, $S \rightarrow A$ and $S \rightarrow B$ are single rules. Consider this CFG as I in Algorithm 6.30 to transform it to an equivalent CFG O without single rules. From $S \Rightarrow A \Rightarrow aAb$, the algorithm constructs $S \to aAb$. Similarly, from $S \Rightarrow A \Rightarrow ab$, it makes $S \to ab$. As the resulting CFG O, it produces

$$S \to AB,\ S \to aAb,\ S \to ab,\ S \to cBd,\ S \to cd,\ A \to aAb,\ B \to cBd,\ A \to ab,\ B \to cd$$

We close this section by summarizing all the useful grammatical transformations given earlier in this chapter to demonstrate how to obtain a properly defined CFG from any CFG. Of course, first, we state what we mean by this proper definition.

Definition 6.32 A CFG, $G = ({}_G\Sigma, {}_GR)$, is *proper* if

I. ${}_G\Sigma$ contains no useless symbols.
II. ${}_GR$ contains neither ε-rules nor single rules. ■

Theorem 6.33 For every CFG, $I = ({}_I\Sigma, {}_IR)$, there exists a proper CFG, $O = ({}_O\Sigma, {}_OR)$, such that $L(O) = L(I) - \{\varepsilon\}$.

Proof. Let $I = ({}_I\Sigma, {}_IR)$ be any CFG. Remove all useless symbols from ${}_I\Sigma$ (see Algorithm 6.20). Apply Algorithm 6.28 to the CFG without useless symbols to an equivalent CFG containing no ε-rules; then, by Algorithm 6.30, convert the CFG without ε-rules to a CFG without any single rules. Take the resulting CFG as O. Observe that O is proper and $L(O) = L(I) - \{\varepsilon\}$. ■

6.2.5 Chomsky Normal Form

In this section, we explain how to transform any CFG to an equivalent proper grammar in Chomsky normal form, in which each of its rule has on its right-hand side either a terminal or two nonterminals. We often make use of the Chomsky normal form to simplify proofs as demonstrated later in this chapter (see, for instance, Algorithm 6.38 and the proof of Theorem 6.39 in Section 6.2.6).

Definition 6.34 A CFG, $G = (\Sigma, R)$, is in *Chomsky normal form* if it is proper, and in addition, every rule $A \to x \in R$ satisfies $x \in \Delta \cup NN$. ■

Basic Idea. Let $I = ({}_I\Sigma, {}_IR)$ be a CFG. Without any loss of generality, suppose that I is proper (see Theorem 6.33). Start the transformation of I to an equivalent CFG, $O = ({}_O\Sigma, {}_OR)$, in Chomsky normal form by introducing nonterminal subalphabet $W = \{a' \mid a \in {}_I\Delta\}$ together with the bijection β from ${}_I\Sigma$ to $W \cup {}_IN$ that maps every $a \in {}_I\Delta$ to the nonterminal a' and every $A \in {}_IN$ to itself. Set ${}_O\Sigma = W \cup {}_I\Sigma$. For every $a \in {}_I\Delta$, include $a' \to a$ into ${}_OR$, and for every $A \to a \in {}_IR$, move $A \to a$ from ${}_IR$ to ${}_OR$. Furthermore, for each $A \to XY \in {}_IR$, where X and Y are in ${}_I\Sigma$, add $A \to \beta(X_1)\beta(X_2)$ to ${}_OR$ and, simultaneously, eliminate $A \to X_1X_2$ in ${}_IR$. Finally, for every $A \to X_1X_2X_3\ldots X_{n-1}X_n \in {}_IR$ with $n \geq 3$, include new nonterminals $\langle X_2\ldots X_n\rangle, \langle X_3\ldots X_n\rangle, \ldots, \langle X_{n-2}X_{n-1}X_n\rangle, \langle X_{n-1}X_n\rangle$ into ${}_ON$ and add the rules $A \to \beta(X_1)\langle X_2\ldots X_n\rangle$, $\langle X_2\ldots X_n\rangle \to \beta(X_2)\langle X_3\ldots X_n\rangle, \ldots, \langle X_{n-2}X_{n-1}X_n\rangle \to \beta(X_{n-2})\langle X_{n-1}X_n\rangle$, $\langle X_{n-1}X_n\rangle \to \beta(X_{n-1})\beta(X_n)$ to ${}_OR$; notice that the added rules satisfy the Chomsky normal form. In this way, $A \Rightarrow X_1X_2X_3\ldots X_{n-1}X_n$ $[A \to X_1X_2X_3\ldots X_{n-1}X_n]$ in I is simulated in O as

$$\begin{aligned}
A &\Rightarrow \beta(X_1)\langle X_2\ldots X_n\rangle \\
&\Rightarrow \beta(X_1)\beta(X_2)\langle X_3\ldots X_n\rangle \\
&\ \vdots \\
&\Rightarrow \beta(X_1)\beta(X_2)\ldots\beta(X_{n-2})\langle X_{n-1}X_n\rangle \\
&\Rightarrow \beta(X_1)\beta(X_2)\ldots\beta(X_{n-2})\beta(X_{n-1})\beta(X_n)
\end{aligned}$$

and $\beta(X_j) \Rightarrow X_j$ $[\beta(X_j) \to X_j]$ in O, for every $X_j \in {}_I\Delta$, where $1 \leq j \leq n$.

O constructed in this way may contain some useless nonterminals; if it does, remove these useless symbols and all rules that contain them by using Algorithm 6.20.

Algorithm 6.35 Chomsky Normal Form.

Input. A proper CFG, $I = ({}_I\Sigma, {}_IR)$.

Output. A CFG, $O = ({}_O\Sigma, {}_OR)$, in Chomsky normal form such that $L(I) = L(O)$.

Method.

begin

introduce $W = \{a' \mid a \in {}_I\Delta\}$ and the bijection β from ${}_I\Sigma$ to $W \cup {}_IN$ defined as
$\beta(a) = a'$ for all $a \in {}_I\Delta$, and $\beta(A) = A$ for all $A \in {}_IN$
set ${}_O\Sigma = W \cup {}_I\Sigma$ and ${}_OR = \varnothing$

for all $a \in {}_I\Delta$ **do**
add $a' \rightarrow a$ to ${}_OR$

for all $A \rightarrow a \in {}_IR$, $A \in {}_IN$, $a \in {}_I\Delta$ **do**
move $A \rightarrow a$ from ${}_IR$ to ${}_OR$

for all $A \rightarrow X_1X_2 \in {}_IR$, $A \in {}_IN$, $X_i \in {}_I\Sigma$, $i = 1, 2$ **do**
begin
add $A \rightarrow \beta(X_1)\beta(X_2)$ to ${}_OR$
remove $A \rightarrow X_1X_2$ from ${}_IR$
end

repeat
if for some $n \geq 3$, $A \rightarrow X_1X_2X_3\ldots X_{n-1}X_n \in {}_IR$, $A \in {}_IN$, $X_i \in {}_I\Sigma$, $i = 1, \ldots, n$ **then**
begin
introduce new nonterminals $\langle X_2\ldots X_n\rangle, \langle X_3\ldots X_n\rangle, \ldots, \langle X_{n-2}X_{n-1}X_n\rangle, \langle X_{n-1}X_n\rangle$ into ${}_ON$
add $A \rightarrow \beta(X_1)\langle X_2\ldots X_n\rangle, \langle X_2\ldots X_n\rangle \rightarrow \beta(X_2)\langle X_3\ldots X_n\rangle, \ldots,$
$\langle X_{n-2}X_{n-1}X_n\rangle \rightarrow \beta(X_{n-2})\langle X_{n-1}X_n\rangle, \langle X_{n-1}X_n\rangle \rightarrow \beta(X_{n-1})\beta(X_n)$ to ${}_OR$
remove $A \rightarrow X_1X_2X_3\ldots X_{n-1}X_n$ from ${}_IR$
end

until no change
remove all useless symbols and rules that contain them from O by Algorithm 6.20

end.

Following the basic idea that precedes Algorithm 6.35, prove Theorem 6.36 as an exercise.

Theorem 6.36 Algorithm 6.35 is correct. Therefore, for every $L \in {}_{CFG}\Phi$, there exists a CFG, $G = ({}_G\Sigma, {}_GR)$, such that $L(G) = L$ and G satisfies the Chomsky normal form. ■

Example 6.11 Return to the CFG obtained in Example 6.6, that is,

$$S \rightarrow S\,o\,S,\ S \rightarrow (S),\ S \rightarrow i$$

which obviously represents a proper CFG. Consider it as I in Algorithm 6.35, which converts this CFG to an equivalent CFG, $O = ({}_O\Sigma, {}_OR)$, in the Chomsky normal form as follows. Initially, Algorithm 6.35 introduces four new nonterminals; o', $('$, $)'$, and i'; and the bijection β from $\{S, o, (,), i\}$ to $\{S, o', (',)', i'\}$ that maps S, o, $($, $)$, and i to S, o', $('$, $)'$, and i', respectively. Then, it includes $o' \rightarrow o$, $(' \rightarrow ($, $)' \rightarrow)$, and $i' \rightarrow i$ into ${}_OR$. After this, it places $S \rightarrow i$ into ${}_OR$. From $S \rightarrow S\,o\,S$, this algorithm subsequently constructs $S \rightarrow S\langle oS\rangle$, $\langle oS\rangle \rightarrow o'S$. Analogously, from $S \rightarrow (S)$, it constructs $S \rightarrow ('\langle S)\rangle$, $\langle S)\rangle \rightarrow S)'$. Algorithm 6.35 exits from the **repeat** loop with O defined as

$$o' \rightarrow o,\ (' \rightarrow (,\ )' \rightarrow),\ i' \rightarrow i,\ S \rightarrow i,\ S \rightarrow S\langle oS\rangle,\ \langle oS\rangle \rightarrow o'S,\ S \rightarrow ('\langle S)\rangle,\ \langle S)\rangle \rightarrow S)'$$

This CFG contains an inaccessible symbol i'. Algorithm 6.20 detects this symbol as useless and removes it together with the rule $i' \rightarrow i$, which contains it. Rename S, $\langle oS\rangle$, o', $('$, $\langle S)\rangle$, and $)'$ to A_1, A_2, A_3, A_4, A_5, and A_6, respectively, and order the rules according to their left-hand sides as follows:

$$A_1 \rightarrow A_1A_2,\ A_1 \rightarrow A_4A_5,\ A_1 \rightarrow i,\ A_2 \rightarrow A_3A_1,\ A_3 \rightarrow o,\ A_4 \rightarrow (,\ A_5 \rightarrow A_1A_6,\ A_6 \rightarrow)$$

where A_1 is the start symbol. This CFG represents the resulting version of the CFG in the Chomsky normal form.

6.2.6 Elimination of Left Recursion

A CFG is *left-recursive* if it can make a derivation of the form $A \Rightarrow^+ Ax$ for a nonterminal A and a string x. Left recursion causes the CFG to enter an infinite loop during leftmost derivations, which often represents an undesirable grammatical phenomenon, whose removal is highly appreciated. Indeed, from a theoretical viewpoint, this removal is needed to turn CFGs to their Greibach normal form in Section 6.2.7. From a more practical point of view, most top-down parsing methods, discussed in Section 7.2, work only with non-left-recursive CFGs. Therefore, this section explains how to make this removal.

Definition 6.37 Let $G = ({}_G\Sigma, {}_GR)$ be a CFG and $A \in {}_GN$.

I. A rule of the form $A \rightarrow Ay \in {}_GR$, where $y \in {}_G\Sigma^*$, is a *directly left-recursive rule*, and A is a *directly left-recursive nonterminal*. G is *directly left-recursive* if ${}_GN$ contains a directly left-recursive nonterminal.
II. A derivation of the form $A \Rightarrow^+ Ax$, where $x \in {}_G\Sigma^*$, is a *left-recursive derivation*, and A is a *left-recursive nonterminal* in G. G is *left-recursive* if ${}_GN$ contains a left-recursive nonterminal. ■

Next, we give an insight into a transformation that converts any left-recursive CFG to an equivalent CFG that is not left-recursive.

Basic idea. As obvious, directly left-recursive nonterminals are special cases of left-recursive nonterminals. We first sketch how to remove them from any CFG without affecting the generated language.

Elimination of direct left recursion. Let $G = ({}_G\Sigma, {}_GR)$ be a directly left-recursive CFG. Without any loss of generality, suppose that G is proper (see Definition 6.32 and Theorem 6.33). Observe that for every nonterminal $A \in {}_GN$, there surely exists an A-rule that is not directly left-recursive; otherwise, A would be a useless symbol, which contradicts that G is proper.

For every directly left-recursive symbol A introduce a new nonterminal B into ${}_GN$, and for any pair of rules,

$$A \rightarrow Aw \text{ and } A \rightarrow u$$

where $u \in {}_G\Sigma^*$ and $A \rightarrow u$ is not a left-recursive rule, introduce

$$A \rightarrow u,\ A \rightarrow uB,\ B \rightarrow wB, \text{ and } B \rightarrow w$$

into ${}_GR$. Repeat this extension of G until nothing can be added to ${}_GN$ or ${}_GR$ in this way. Then, eliminate all the directly left-recursive A-rules in ${}_GR$, so the resulting CFG is not a directly left-recursive. Consider, for instance,

$$A \Rightarrow Aw \Rightarrow Aww \Rightarrow uww$$

made by two applications of $A \rightarrow Aw$ followed by one application of $A \rightarrow u$ in the original version of G. The modified version of G simulates the above derivation as

$$A \Rightarrow uB \Rightarrow uwB \Rightarrow uww$$

by applying $A \rightarrow u$, $B \rightarrow wB$, and $B \rightarrow w$. To illustrate this elimination by an example, take

$$S \rightarrow SoS,\ S \rightarrow (S),\ S \rightarrow i$$

as G (see Example 6.6). From this CFG, the transformation sketched above produces

$$S \rightarrow (S),\ S \rightarrow i,\ S \rightarrow (S)B,\ S \rightarrow iB,\ B \rightarrow oSB,\ B \rightarrow oS$$

For instance, $S \Rightarrow SoS \Rightarrow Soi \Rightarrow ioi$ in the original CFG is simulated by the transformed nondirectly left-recursive CFG as $S \Rightarrow iB \Rightarrow ioS \Rightarrow ioi$.

Elimination of general left recursion. We are now ready to eliminate general left recursion, which represents a more hidden grammatical trap. In essence, we make this elimination by the elimination of direct left recursion combined with a modification of rules so their right-hand sides start with nonterminals ordered in a way that rules out left recursion.

More precisely, without any loss of generality (see Theorem 6.36), we consider a CFG, $I = ({}_I\Sigma, {}_IR)$, in Chomsky normal form with ${}_IN = \{A_1, \ldots, A_n\}$, where $card({}_IN) = n$ (of course, we can always rename the nonterminals in I in this way). We next sketch how to turn I to an equivalent CFG, $O = ({}_O\Sigma, {}_OR)$, with ${}_ON = \{A_1, \ldots, A_n\} \cup \{B_1, \ldots, B_m\}$, where B_1 through B_m are new nonterminals ($m = 0$ actually means that ${}_ON = {}_IN$), and ${}_IR$ contains rules of these three forms:

I. $A_i \rightarrow au$ with $a \in {}_O\Delta$ and $u \in {}_ON^*$;
II. $A_i \rightarrow A_jv$, for some $A_i, A_j \in \{A_k |\ 1 \leq k \leq n\}$ such that $i < j$, and $v \in {}_ON^+$;
III. $B_i \rightarrow Cw$ with $C \in \{A_k |\ 1 \leq k \leq n\} \cup \{B_l |\ 1 \leq l \leq i - 1\}$ and $w \in {}_ON^*$.

As demonstrated shortly (see the proof of Theorem 3.69), I through III imply that O cannot make a derivation of the form $A_k \Rightarrow^+ A_kx$ or $B_l \Rightarrow^+ B_lx$, where $1 \leq k \leq n$ and $1 \leq l \leq i - 1$; in other words, O is a non-left-recursive CFG (of course, as opposed to I, O may not be in Chomsky normal form though).

The construction of O is based on repeatedly changing I by (1) and (2), given next, until I cannot be further modified. Then, O is defined as the final version of I, resulting from this repeated modification. To start with, set $k = 0$ and $i = 1$.

1. In ${}_IR$, for every rule of the form $A_i \rightarrow A_jy$, where $j < i$, $y \in {}_IN^*$, extend ${}_IR$ by all A_i-rules of the form $A_i \rightarrow zy$, where $A_j \rightarrow z \in {}_IR$, $z \in {}_IN^+$ (according to Convention 6.2, A_i-rule is a rule with A_i on its left-hand side). After this extension, remove $A_i \rightarrow A_jy$ from ${}_IR$.
2. Rephrase and perform the elimination of direct recursion described above in terms of I instead of G. That is, let $A_i \in {}_IN$ be a directly left-recursive nonterminal in I. Rephrase the above-described elimination of direct left recursion in terms of A_i as follows. Increase k by one and introduce a new nonterminal B_k into ${}_IN$. First, for every pair of rules,

$$A_i \rightarrow A_iw \text{ and } A_i \rightarrow u$$

where $A_i \to u$ is not a directly left-recursive rule, add

$$A_i \to u,\ A_i \to uB_k,\ B_k \to wB_k, \text{ and } B_k \to w$$

to ${}_IR$. Repeat this extension of ${}_IR$ until no more rules can be inserted into ${}_IR$ in this way. After this extension is completed, remove all directly left-recursive A_i-rules from ${}_IR$.

When ${}_IR$ cannot be modified by further repetition of (1) or (2), increase i by 1. If $i \leq n$, repeat (1) and (2) again in the same way; otherwise, set ${}_O\Sigma$ and ${}_OR$ to ${}_I\Sigma$ and ${}_IR$, respectively, to obtain $O = ({}_O\Sigma, {}_OR)$ as the resulting non-left-recursive CFG equivalent with the original version of I (of course, as opposed to I, O may not satisfy the Chomsky normal form).

Based on this basic idea, we give Algorithm 6.38 that turns I to O, satisfying the above properties.

Algorithm 6.38 Elimination of Left Recursion.

Input. A left-recursive CFG $I \in {}_{CFG}\Psi$ in Chomsky normal form with ${}_IN = \{A_1, \ldots, A_n\}$, for some $n \geq 1$.

Output. A non-left-recursive CFG $O \in {}_{CFG}\Psi$ such that $L(I) = L(O)$, ${}_ON = \{A_k | \ 1 \leq k \leq n\} \cup \{B_l | \ 1 \leq l \leq m\}$, for some $m \geq 0$, and each rule in ${}_OR$ has one of these three forms

I. $A_i \to au$ with $a \in {}_O\Delta$, and $u \in {}_ON^*$;
II. $A_i \to A_jv$, for some $A_i, A_j \in \{A_k | \ 1 \leq k \leq n\}$ such that $i < j$, and $v \in {}_ON^+$;
III. $B_i \to Cw$ with $C \in \{A_k | \ 1 \leq k \leq n\} \cup \{B_l | \ 1 \leq l \leq i-1\}$ and $w \in {}_ON^*$.

Method.

begin
  set $k = 0$

  for $i = 1, \ldots, n$ **do**
  begin
    repeat
      if $A_i \to A_jy \in {}_IR$, where $j < i$ and $y \in {}_IN^*$ **then**
      begin
        repeat
          if $A_j \to z \in {}_IR$, where $z \in {}_IN^+$ **then**
            add $A_i \to zy$ to ${}_IR$
        until no change
        remove $A_i \to A_jy$ from ${}_IR$
      end

      if $A_i \in {}_IN$ is a directly left-recursive nonterminal in I **then**
      begin
        $k = k + 1$
        introduce a new nonterminal B_k into ${}_IN$
        repeat
          if $A_i \to A_iw$ and $A_i \to u$ are in ${}_IR$, where $w, u \in {}_IN^+$ and
            $A_i \to u$ is not a directly left-recursive rule **then**
              add $A_i \to uB_k$, $B_k \to wB_k$, and $B_k \to w$ to ${}_IR$

until no change
remove all directly left-recursive A_i-rules from ${}_IR$ {notice that $A_i \to u$ remains in ${}_IR$}
end {of **if** statement}

until no change
end {of the **for** loop}

define $O = ({}_O\Sigma, {}_OR)$ with ${}_O\Sigma = {}_I\Sigma$ and ${}_OR = {}_IR$

end.

Theorem 6.39 Algorithm 6.38 is correct. Therefore, for every CFG I in Chomsky normal form, there exists an equivalent non-left-recursive CFG O.

Proof. By a straightforward examination of Algorithm 6.38, we see that each rule in ${}_OR$ has one of the forms I through III. Next, by contradiction, we prove that O is non-left-recursive. Suppose that O is left-recursive. We distinguish two cases—(a) $\{A_k | \ 1 \leq k \leq n\}$ contains a left-recursive nonterminal and (b) $\{B_l | \ 1 \leq l \leq m\}$ contains a left-recursive nonterminal.

a. Let A_i be left-recursive, for some $A_i \in \{A_1, \ldots, A_n\}$. That is, there exists $x \in {}_ON^+$ such that $A_i \Rightarrow^+ A_ix$ in O. Recall that the right-hand side of every A_i-rule starts with a terminal or a nonterminal from $\{A_k | \ i < k \leq n\}$ (see I and II in Algorithm 6.38), which rules out $A_i \Rightarrow^+ A_ix$ in O—a contradiction.
b. Let B_i be left-recursive, for some $B_i \in \{B_1, \ldots, B_m\}$. That is, there exists $x \in {}_ON^+$ such that $B_i \Rightarrow^+ B_ix$ in O. Recall that the right-hand side of every B_i-rule starts with a nonterminal from $\{A_k | \ 1 \leq k \leq n\} \cup \{B_l | \ 1 \leq l < i\}$ (see III in Algorithm 6.38). Furthermore, no right-hand side of any A_i-rule starts with a nonterminal from $\{B_l | \ 1 \leq l \leq m\}$, for all $1 \leq i \leq n$ (see II in Algorithm 6.38). Thus, O cannot make $B_i \Rightarrow^+ B_ix$—a contradiction.

Thus, O is a non-left-recursive CFG. As an exercise, complete this proof by demonstrating that $L(I) = L(O)$. ■

Example 6.12 Reconsider the CFG in the Chomsky normal form

$$A_1 \to A_1A_2, A_1 \to A_4A_5, A_1 \to i, A_2 \to A_3A_1, A_3 \to o, A_4 \to (, A_5 \to A_1A_6, A_6 \to)$$

from Example 6.11. Observe that this CFG is left-recursive because A_1 is a directly left-recursive nonterminal. Consider the CFG as the input grammar I in Algorithm 6.38. Observe that I satisfies all the properties required by Algorithm 6.38. Apply this algorithm to convert I to an equivalent non-left-recursive grammar O, satisfying the output properties described in Algorithm 6.38. In this application, $n = 6$ because I has six nonterminals—A_1 through A_6. For $i = 1$, the **for** loop replaces $A_1 \to A_1A_2$ with

$$A_1 \to A_4A_5, A_1 \to A_4A_5B_1, A_1 \to i, A_1 \to iB_1, B_1 \to A_2B_1, B_1 \to A_2$$

After this replacement, for $i = 2, \ldots, 4$, the **for** loop does not change any rule. For $i = 5$, this loop replaces $A_5 \to A_1A_6$ with

$$A_5 \to A_4A_5A_6, A_5 \to A_4A_5B_1A_6, A_5 \to iA_6, A_5 \to iB_1A_6$$

After this replacement, it replaces $A_5 \to A_4A_5A_6$ with $A_5 \to (A_5A_6$. Finally, it replaces $A_5 \to A_4A_5B_1A_6$ with $A_5 \to (A_5B_1A_6$. For $k = 6$, the **for** loop does not change any rule. Consequently, the resulting output grammar O produced by Algorithm 6.38 is defined as

I. $A_1 \to i, A_1 \to iB_1, A_3 \to o, A_4 \to (, A_5 \to (A_5A_6, A_5 \to (A_5B_1A_6, A_5 \to iA_6, A_5 \to iB_1A_6, A_6 \to)$
II. $A_1 \to A_4A_5, A_1 \to A_4A_5B_1, A_2 \to A_3A_1$
III. $B_1 \to A_2B_1, B_1 \to A_2$

Theorem 6.40 For every $L \in {}_{CFG}\Phi$, there exists a non-left-recursive $G \in {}_{CFG}\Psi$ satisfying $L(G) = L$.

Proof. If $\varepsilon \notin L$, this theorem follows from Theorems 6.36 and 6.39. Suppose that $\varepsilon \in L$. Let $G \in {}_{CFG}\Psi$ be non-left-recursive, and let $L(G) = L - \{\varepsilon\}$. Define $H = ({}_H\Sigma, {}_HR)$ in ${}_{CFG}\Psi$ so ${}_H\Sigma = {}_G\Sigma \cup \{{}_HS\}$ and ${}_HR = {}_GR \cup \{{}_HS \to {}_GS, {}_HS \to \varepsilon\}$, where the start symbol ${}_HS$ is a newly introduced symbol, ${}_HS \notin {}_G\Sigma$. Observe that $H \in {}_{CFG}\Psi$ is non-left-recursive, and $L(H) = L$. ■

Right Recursion. By analogy with left recursion, we define its right counterpart.

Definition 6.41 $G \in {}_{CFG}\Psi$ is *right-recursive* if $A \Rightarrow^+ xA$ in G, for some $A \in {}_GN$ and $x \in {}_G\Sigma^*$. ■

As an exercise, prove

Theorem 6.42 For every $L \in {}_{CFG}\Phi$, there exists a non-right-recursive $G \in {}_{CFG}\Psi$ satisfying $L(G) = L$. ■

6.2.7 Greibach Normal Form

A CFG in Greibach normal form has the right-hand side of every rule started with a terminal followed by zero or more nonterminals. This form often simplifies proofs of results concerning CFGs as discussed in Exercise 4 of Chapter 8.

Definition 6.43 A CFG, $G = (\Sigma, R)$, is in *Greibach normal form* if every rule $A \to x \in R$ satisfies $x \in \Delta N^*$. ■

Basic Idea. Without any loss of generality, suppose that a CFG, $I = ({}_I\Sigma, {}_IR)$, satisfies the properties of the output CFG produced by Algorithm 6.38 (see Theorem 6.39). That is, ${}_IN = \{A_k | \ 1 \le k \le n\} \cup \{B_l | \ 1 \le l \le m\}$, for some $n, m \ge 0$, and each rule in ${}_IR$ has one of these three forms

I. $A_i \to au$ with $a \in {}_I\Delta$, and $u \in {}_IN^*$;
II. $A_i \to A_jv$, for some $A_i, A_j \in \{A_k | \ 1 \le k \le n\}$ such that $i < j$ and $v \in {}_IN^+$;
III. $B_i \to Cw$ with $C \in \{A_k | \ 1 \le k \le n\} \cup \{B_l | \ 1 \le l \le i - 1\}$ and $w \in {}_IN^*$.

Consider all rules of the form $A_i \to au$ with $a \in {}_I\Delta$, and $u \in {}_IN^*$ (see I). As obvious, they are in Greibach normal form.

Consider any rule of the form $A_n \to u$ (see I and II). As n is the greatest number in $\{1, \ldots, n\}$, $A_n \to u$ is not of the form II, so it is of the form I. That is, u starts with a terminal and, therefore, $A_n \to u$ is in Greibach normal form. For every pair of rules $A_{n-1} \to A_nv$ and $A_n \to u$, introduce a rule $A_{n-1} \to uv$ into ${}_OR$, which is in Greibach normal form because so is $A_n \to u$. As a result, all the newly introduced A_{n-1}-rules are in Greibach normal form. Then, for every pair of rules $A_{n-2} \to A_jv$ and $A_j \to u$ in II with $n - 2 < j$—that is, $j = n - 1$ or $j = n$, make an analogical introduction of new rules. Proceeding down toward $n = 1$ in this way, we eventually obtain all A_k-rules in Greibach normal form.

Consider any rule $B_1 \to u$ from III. For B_1, u starts with A_j for some $j = 1, \ldots, n$, and all the A_j-rules in ${}_OR$ are in Greibach normal form. Therefore, for every pair of rules $B_1 \to A_jy$ in ${}_IR$

and $A_j \rightarrow v$ in ${}_OR$, add $B_1 \rightarrow vy$ to ${}_OR$. As a result, all the newly introduced B_1-rules in ${}_OR$ are in Greibach normal form. Then, for every pair of rules $B_2 \rightarrow Cw$ in ${}_IR$ with $C \in \{A_k | \ 1 \leq k \leq n\} \cup \{B_1\}$ and a C-rule $C \rightarrow z$ in ${}_OR$, which is already in Greibach normal form, add $B_2 \rightarrow zw$ to ${}_OR$. Proceeding from 1 to m in this way, we eventually obtain all the B_l-rules in Greibach normal form, $1 \leq l \leq m$. The resulting CFG is in Greibach normal form and generates $L(I)$.

Algorithm 6.44 Greibach Normal Form.

Input. A non-left-recursive CFG $I \in {}_{CFG}\Psi$ such that ${}_IN = \{A_k | \ 1 \leq k \leq n\} \cup \{B_l | \ 1 \leq l \leq m\}$, for some $n, m \geq 0$, and each rule in ${}_IR$ has one of these three forms

I. $A_i \rightarrow au$ with $a \in {}_I\Delta$, and $u \in {}_IN^*$;
II. $A_i \rightarrow A_jv$, for some $A_i, A_j \in \{A_k | \ 1 \leq k \leq n\}$ such that $i < j$, and $v \in {}_IN^+$;
III. $B_i \rightarrow Cw$ with $C \in \{A_k | \ 1 \leq k \leq n\} \cup \{B_l | \ 1 \leq l \leq i - 1\}$ and $w \in {}_IN^*$.

Output. A CFG $O \in {}_{CFG}\Psi$ such that $L(O) = L(I)$ and O is in Greibach normal form.

Method.

begin
  set ${}_ON = {}_IN$ and ${}_O\Delta = {}_I\Delta$
  set ${}_OR = \{A_i | \ A_i \rightarrow au$ with $a \in {}_I\Delta$ and $u \in {}_IN^*\}$
  for $i = n, n - 1, \ldots, 1$ **do**
    for each $A_i \rightarrow A_jy \in {}_IR$, where $A_i, A_j \in \{A_k | \ 1 \leq k \leq n\}$ such that $i < j$, and $y \in {}_IN^+$ **do**
      ${}_OR = {}_OR \cup \{A_i \rightarrow zy | \ A_j \rightarrow z \in {}_OR, z \in {}_I\Delta_IN^*\}$
  for $i = 1, 2, \ldots, m$ **do**
    for each $B_i \rightarrow Cw \in {}_IR$ with $C \in \{A_k | \ 1 \leq k \leq n\} \cup \{B_l | \ 1 \leq l \leq i - 1\}$ and $w \in {}_IN^*$ **do**
      ${}_OR = {}_OR \cup \{B_i \rightarrow zw | \ C \rightarrow z \in {}_OR, z \in {}_I\Delta_IN^*\}$
end.

Based on the basic idea preceding Algorithm 6.44, prove Theorem 6.45.

Theorem 6.45 Algorithm 6.44 is correct. Therefore, for every $L \in {}_{CFG}\Phi$, there exists $G \in {}_{CFG}\Psi$ in Greibach normal form satisfying $L(G) = L - \{\varepsilon\}$. ■

Example 6.13 Consider the non-left-recursive CFG

I. $A_1 \rightarrow i, A_1 \rightarrow iB_1, A_5 \rightarrow (A_5A_6, A_5 \rightarrow (A_5B_1A_6, A_5 \rightarrow iA_6, A_5 \rightarrow iB_1A_6, A_3 \rightarrow o, A_4 \rightarrow (, A_6 \rightarrow)$
II. $A_1 \rightarrow A_4A_5, A_1 \rightarrow A_4A_5B_1, A_2 \rightarrow A_3A_1$
III. $B_1 \rightarrow A_2B_1, B_1 \rightarrow A_2$

obtained in Example 6.12. Let this CFG be I in Algorithm 6.44. Notice that it satisfies all the input requirements stated in this algorithm.

Consider I. All these rules are in Greibach normal form. Thus, initialize ${}_OR$ with them.

Consider II. Notice that the first **for** loop works with these rules. For $i = 2$, as $A_2 \rightarrow A_3A_1$ is in II and ${}_OR$ contains $A_3 \rightarrow o$, this loop adds $A_2 \rightarrow oA_1$ to ${}_OR$. For $i = 1$, since $A_1 \rightarrow A_4A_5$ and $A_1 \rightarrow A_4A_5B_1$ are in II and $A_4 \rightarrow ($ is in ${}_OR$, this loop also adds $A_1 \rightarrow (A_5$ and $A_1 \rightarrow (A_5B_1$ to ${}_OR$.

Consider III. The second **for** loop works with the two B_1-rules listed in III. As $B_1 \rightarrow A_2B_1$ and $B_1 \rightarrow A_2$ are in III and $A_2 \rightarrow oA_1$ is in ${}_OR$, the second **for** loop includes $B_1 \rightarrow oA_1B_1$ and $B_1 \rightarrow oA_1$ into ${}_OR$.

Consequently, as O, Algorithm 6.44 produces this CFG in Greibach normal form:

$$A_1 \to i, A_1 \to iB_1, A_5 \to (A_5A_6, A_5 \to (A_5B_1A_6, A_5 \to iA_6, A_5 \to iB_1A_6, A_3 \to o,$$
$$A_4 \to (, A_6 \to), A_2 \to oA_1, A_1 \to (A_5, A_1 \to (A_5B_1, B_1 \to oA_1B_1, B_1 \to oA_1$$

As an exercise, verify that $L(I) = L(O)$.

If a Greibach normal form CFG has n or fewer nonterminals on the right-hand side of every rule, where $n \in {}_0\mathbb{N}$, then we say that it is in n-standard Greibach normal form.

Definition 6.46 Let $G = (\Sigma, R)$ be a CFG in Greibach normal form. G is in *n-standard Greibach normal form* if every rule $A \to ax \in R$ satisfies $a \in \Delta$, $x \in N^*$, and $|x| \leq n$. ■

In the rest of this section, we take a closer look at CFGs in n-standard Greibach normal form with $n \leq 2$. As obvious, any zero-standard Greibach normal form CFG generates $\varnothing$ or a language that, in fact, represents an alphabet—that is, a finite language in which every string is of length one.

Theorem 6.47 A language L is generated by a CFG in zero-standard Greibach normal form iff L represents a finite set of symbols. ■

In one-standard Greibach normal form CFGs, every rule is of the form $A \to aB$ or $A \to a$. These CFGs are usually referred to as *regular CFGs* because of the next result concerning their generative power.

Theorem 6.48 A language L is generated by a CFG in one-standard Greibach normal form iff $L - \{\varepsilon\}$ is regular.

Proof. Leaving a fully detailed version of this proof as an exercise, we give only its sketch. First, convert any CFG in one-standard Greibach normal form to an equivalent FA (see Definition 3.1). Then, turn any DFA M (see Definition 3.9) to a one-standard Greibach normal form CFG that generates $L(M) - \{\varepsilon\}$. By Theorem 3.38, Theorem 6.48 holds true. ■

Consider two-standard Greibach normal form CFGs. For instance, return to the CFG discussed in Example 6.2—that is,

$$S \to aB, S \to bA, A \to a, A \to aS, A \to bAA, B \to b, B \to bS, B \to aBB$$

This CFG represents a CFG that satisfies two-standard Greibach normal form. Interestingly enough, for every CFL L, there is a two-standard Greibach normal form CFG that generates $L - \{\varepsilon\}$ as Theorem 6.49 says.

Theorem 6.49 For every CFL L, there exists a CFG G in two-standard Greibach normal form satisfying $L(G) = L - \{\varepsilon\}$. Consequently, let $n \geq 2$, and let K be a CFL; then, $K - \{\varepsilon\}$ is generated by a CFG in n-standard Greibach normal form.

Proof. By Theorem 6.45, for every CFL L, there exists a CFG H in Greibach normal form that generates $L - \{\varepsilon\}$. Consider the basic idea underlying the transformation to the Chomsky normal form (see Algorithm 6.35). As an exercise, modify this idea to convert H to an equivalent CFG G that satisfies two-standard Greibach normal form. ■

6.3 Pushdown Automata

In essence, a pushdown automaton is an FA extended by a potentially infinite stack, commonly referred to as a pushdown list or, briefly, a pushdown. The present section demonstrates that a language is context-free iff it is accepted by a pushdown automaton. It is divided into Sections 6.3.1 through 6.3.4. Section 6.3.1 defines pushdown automata. Section 6.3.2 establishes the equivalence between them and CFGs. Section 6.3.3 introduces three ways of accepting languages by these automata and shows that they all are equally powerful. Finally, Section 6.3.4 narrows its attention to the deterministic versions of pushdown automata and demonstrates that they are less powerful than their nondeterministic versions.

6.3.1 Pushdown Automata and Their Languages

Definition 6.50 A *pushdown automaton* (*PDA*) is a rewriting system, $M = (\Sigma, R)$, where

- Σ is divided into subalphabets Q, Γ, Δ such that $Q \cap (\Gamma \cup \Delta) = \emptyset$.
- R is a finite *set of rules* of the form $x \rightarrow y$, where $x \in \Gamma^* Q(\Delta \cup \{\varepsilon\})$ and $y \in \Gamma^* Q$.

Q, Γ, and Δ are referred to as the *set of states*, the *alphabet of pushdown symbols*, and the *alphabet of input symbols*, respectively. Q contains the *start state*, denoted by s, and a *set of final states*, denoted by F. Γ contains the *start symbol*, S. If $Ssw \Rightarrow^* f$ in M with $f \in F$, *M accepts w*. The set of all strings that M accepts is the *language accepted by M*, denoted by $L(M)$—that is,

$$L(M) = \{w \mid w \in \Delta^*, Ssw \Rightarrow^* f, f \in F\}$$

■

Thus, according to Definition 6.50, PDAs represent special cases of rewriting systems, introduced in Section 2.2. We frequently make use of the terminology concerning rewriting systems introduced in Section 2.2.1 when discussing PDAs.

Convention 6.51 We denote the set of all PDAs by ${}_{PDA}\Psi$, and we set ${}_{PDA}\Phi = \{L(M) \mid M \in {}_{PDA}\Psi\}$. For every $M \in {}_{PDA}\Psi$, a *configuration* of M is a string of the form wqv, where $w \in \Gamma^*$, $q \in Q$, and $v \in \Delta^*$. Unless $w = \varepsilon$, the rightmost symbol of w represents the *pushdown top* symbol. ${}_{M}X$ denotes the set of all configurations of M. If $\beta \Rightarrow \chi$ in M, where $\beta, \chi \in {}_{M}X$, M makes a *move* from β to χ. M makes a *sequence of moves* or, more briefly, a *computation* from β to χ if $\beta \Rightarrow^* \chi$ in M, where $\beta, \chi \in {}_{M}X$. Furthermore, we automatically assume that Σ, Γ, Δ, Q, s, S, F, and R denote the total alphabet, the alphabet of pushdown symbols, the alphabet of input symbols, the set of states, the start state, the start pushdown symbol, the set of final states, and the set of rules of M, respectively. If there exists any danger of confusion, we mark Σ, Γ, Δ, Q, s, F, and R with M as ${}_{M}\Sigma$, ${}_{M}\Gamma$, ${}_{M}\Delta$, ${}_{M}Q$, ${}_{M}s$, ${}_{M}F$, and ${}_{M}R$, respectively, to explicitly relate these components to M.

For brevity, M is often defined by simply listing its rules together with specifying the members of ${}_{M}\Gamma$, ${}_{M}\Delta$, ${}_{M}Q$, and ${}_{M}F$. ■

Example 6.14 Reconsider the language $L = \{a^k b^k \mid k \geq 1\}$ from Example 6.1, in which we constructed a CFG that generates L. In the present example, we construct $M \in {}_{PDA}\Psi$ that accepts L.

Informally, M works in the following two-phase way. First, it pushes down *a*s. Then, when the first occurrence of b appears, M pops up *a*s and pairs them off with *b*s. If the number of *a*s and *b*s coincides, M accepts the input string; otherwise, it rejects. Formally, $M = (\Sigma, R)$, where $\Sigma = \Gamma \cup \Delta \cup Q$, $\Gamma = \{S, a\}$, $\Delta = \{a, b\}$, $Q = \{s, f\}$, $F = \{f\}$, and

$$R = \{Ssa \to as,\ asa \to aas,\ asb \to f,\ afb \to f\}$$

Under Convention 6.51, we can succinctly specify M by listing its four rules, labeled by 1 through 4, as

$$1\text{: } Ssa \to as,\ 2\text{: } asa \to aas,\ 3\text{: } asb \to f,\ 4\text{: } afb \to f$$

For instance, on $aaabbb$, M performs this sequence of moves

$$\begin{aligned} Ssaaabbb &\Rightarrow asaabbb && [1] \\ &\Rightarrow aasabbb && [2] \\ &\Rightarrow aaasbbb && [2] \\ &\Rightarrow aafbb && [3] \\ &\Rightarrow afb && [4] \\ &\Rightarrow f && [4] \end{aligned}$$

As f is final, M accepts $aaabbb$.

In general, observe that M makes every acceptance according to a sequence of rules 12^n34^n, for some $n \geq 0$; more specifically, by 12^n34^n, M accepts $a^{n+1}b^{n+1}$. Consequently, $L(M) = \{a^kb^k \mid k \geq 1\}$; a rigorous proof of this identity is left as an exercise.

Example 6.15 Consider

$$L = \{vw \mid v, w \in \{a, b\}^*, v = reversal(w)\}$$

Next, we construct a PDA M such that $L(M) = L$. In many respects, M works similarly to the PDA designed in Example 6.14. Indeed, $z \in \{a, b\}^*$ be an input string. M first pushes down a prefix of z. Whenever, however, it can take a guess that it has pushed down precisely $|z|/2$ initial symbols of z, so it starts to pop up the symbols from the pushdown and pair them off with the remaining symbols of w. When and if M simultaneously empties the pushdown and completes reading z, it accepts; otherwise, it rejects.

Formally, $M = (\Sigma, R)$, where $\Sigma = \Gamma \cup \Delta \cup Q$, $\Gamma = \{S, a, b\}$, $\Delta = \{a, b\}$, $Q = \{s, q, f\}$, $F = \{f\}$, and

$$\begin{aligned} R &= \{Ssc \to Scs \mid c \in \{a, b\}\} \\ &\cup \{dsc \to dcs \mid c, d \in \{a, b\}\} \\ &\cup \{s \to q\} \\ &\cup \{cqc \to q \mid c \in \{a, b\}\} \\ &\cup \{Sq \to f\} \end{aligned}$$

A proof that $L(M) = L$ is left as an exercise.

6.3.2 Equivalence with Context-Free Grammars

In this section, we demonstrate the equivalence between CFGs and PDAs.

6.3.2.1 From Context-Free Grammars to Pushdown Automata

We begin by explaining how to turn any $I \in {}_{CFG}\Psi$ to $O \in {}_{PDA}\Psi$ so $L(I) = L(O)$.

Basic Idea. O uses its pushdown to simulate every leftmost derivation in I. In a greater detail, this simulation is performed in the following way. If a terminal a occurs as the pushdown top symbol, O removes a from the pushdown and, simultaneously, reads a as the input symbol; in this way, it verifies their coincidence with each other. If a nonterminal A occurs as the pushdown top symbol, O simulates a leftmost derivation step made by a rule $A \to X_1X_2 \ldots X_n \in {}_IR$, where each $X_i \in {}_G\Sigma$, $1 \le i \le n$, for some $n \in {}_0\mathbb{N}$ ($n = 0$ means $X_1X_2\ldots X_n = \varepsilon$), so that it replaces the pushdown top A with $X_n\ldots X_1$. In somewhat greater detail, consider ${}_IS\ {}_{lm}\Rightarrow^* w$ in I, where $w \in {}_G\Delta^*$, expressed as

$$\begin{aligned} S\ & {}_{lm}\Rightarrow^*\ vAy && [\rho] \\ & {}_{lm}\Rightarrow\ vX_1X_2\ldots X_ny && [A \to X_1X_2\ldots X_n] \\ & {}_{lm}\Rightarrow^*\ vu && \end{aligned}$$

where $w = vu$, so $v, u \in {}_G\Delta^*$. Suppose that I has just simulated the first portion of this derivation, $S\ {}_{lm}\Rightarrow^* vAy$; at this point, the pushdown contains Ay in reverse while having u as the remaining input to read. In symbols, O occurs in the configuration $reversal(y)Asu$, from which it simulates $vAy\ {}_{lm}\Rightarrow vX_1X_2\ldots X_ny\ [A \to X_1X_2\ldots X_n]$ as

$$reversal(y)Asu \Rightarrow reversal(y)X_n\ldots X_1su$$

by using $As \to X_n\ldots X_1s$ from ${}_OR$; notice that $reversal(y)X_n\ldots X_1 = reversal(X_1\ldots X_ny)$. In this step-by-step way, O simulates $S\ {}_{lm}\Rightarrow^* w$ in G. Next, we give Algorithm 6.52, which describes the construction of O from I in a rigorous way.

Algorithm 6.52 CFG to PDA Conversion.

Input. A CFG, $I = ({}_I\Sigma, {}_IR)$.

Output. A PDA, $O = ({}_O\Sigma, {}_OR)$, such that $L(O) = L(I)$.

Method.

begin

set ${}_O\Sigma = {}_I\Sigma \cup \{s\}$, where ${}_OQ = {}_OF = \{s\}$, s is a new state ($s \notin {}_I\Sigma$), ${}_O\Gamma = {}_IN \cup {}_I\Delta$, ${}_O\Delta = {}_I\Delta$, and ${}_OS = {}_IS$;

set ${}_OR = \{As \to reversal(x)s \mid A \to x \in {}_IR\} \cup \{asa \to s \mid a \in {}_I\Delta\}$

end.

As an exercise, give a fully detailed proof of Theorem 6.53.

Theorem 6.53 Algorithm 6.52 is correct. Therefore, ${}_{CFG}\Phi \subseteq {}_{PDA}\Phi$. ■

Notice that Algorithm 6.52 produces its output PDA so that by using each of its rules, the PDA changes precisely one symbol on the pushdown top. In other words, we have proved Corollary 6.54, which fulfills an important role later in this section (see Theorem 6.58).

Corollary 6.54 For every $L \in {}_{CFG}\Phi$, there exists a PDA, $M = ({}_M\Sigma, {}_MR)$, such that $L(M) = L$ and every rule $r \in {}_MR$ is of the form $r: Aqa \to yp$, where $q, p \in {}_MQ$, $a \in {}_M\Delta \cup \{\varepsilon\}$, $y \in {}_M\Gamma^*$, and, most importantly, $A \in {}_M\Gamma$. ■

6.3.2.2 From Pushdown Automata to Context-Free Grammars

First, we show that every $L \in {}_{PDA}\Phi$ is accepted by a PDA that satisfies the properties stated in Corollary 6.54.

Theorem 6.55 $L \in {}_{PDA}\Phi$ iff there exists a PDA, $M = ({}_M\Sigma, {}_MR)$, such that $L(M) = L$ and every rule $r \in {}_MR$ is of the form r: $Aqa \rightarrow yp$, where $q, p \in {}_MQ$, $a \in {}_M\Delta \cup \{\varepsilon\}$, $y \in {}_M\Gamma^*$, $A \in {}_M\Gamma$.

Proof. The *if* part of this theorem is clearly true. Indeed, if $L(M) = L$, where M is a PDA that satisfies the required properties, then it obviously holds that $L(M) \in {}_{PDA}\Phi$.

To prove the *only-if* part of the equivalence in Theorem 6.55, consider any $L \in {}_{PDA}\Phi$. Let $N = ({}_N\Sigma, {}_NR)$ be a PDA such that $L(N) = L$. From N, we construct a PDA, $M = ({}_M\Sigma, {}_MR)$, satisfying the required properties so M simulates every move in N by several moves during which it records top pushdown symbols of N in its states. More precisely, suppose that N makes a move according to a rule of the form $xqa \rightarrow yp \in {}_NR$, where $q, p \in {}_NQ$, $a \in {}_N\Delta \cup \{\varepsilon\}$, $x, y \in {}_N\Gamma^*$. Assume that $|x| \geq 1$, so $x = Xz$, for some $X \in {}_N\Gamma$ and $z \in {}_N\Gamma^*$. M simulates this move in the following two-phase way.

1. Starting from q, M makes $|z|$ moves during which in a symbol-by-symbol way, it stores the string u consisting of the top $|z|$ pushdown symbols into its state of the form $\langle uq\rangle$.
2. From $\langle uq\rangle$, by applying a rule of the form $X\langle zq\rangle a \rightarrow yp \in {}_MR$, M verifies that $z = u$, reads a, pushes y onto its pushdown, and moves to state p. In other words, M completes the simulation of this move in N, and it is ready to simulate another move of N.

As an exercise, explain how to make this simulation under the assumption that $|x| = 0$. Then, rephrase all this proof in a fully rigorous way. ■

Next, we explain how to turn any PDA that satisfies the properties stated in Theorem 6.55 to an equivalent CFG.

Basic Idea. Suppose that $I = ({}_I\Sigma, {}_IR)$ is a PDA in which every rule has the form $Aqa \rightarrow yp \in {}_IR$ where $q, p \in {}_IQ$, $a \in {}_I\Delta \cup \{\varepsilon\}$, $y \in {}_I\Gamma^*$, and $A \in {}_I\Gamma$. To transform I to an equivalent $O \in {}_{CFG}\Psi$, the following algorithm constructs O so a leftmost derivation of $w \in {}_O\Delta^*$ in O simulates a sequence of moves made by I on w. O performs this simulation by using nonterminals of the form $\langle qAp\rangle$, where $q, p \in {}_IQ$, and $A \in {}_I\Gamma$. More precisely, $\langle qAp\rangle \;{}_{lm}\Rightarrow^* w$ in O iff $Aqw \Rightarrow^* p$ in I. In addition, we introduce a new symbol, ${}_OS$, as the start symbol of O and define all ${}_OS$-rules as $\{{}_OS \rightarrow \langle {}_Is\,{}_ISf\rangle |\ f \in {}_IF\}$. Thus, ${}_OS \Rightarrow \langle {}_Is\,{}_ISf\rangle \;{}_{lm}\Rightarrow^* w$ in O iff ${}_IS\,{}_Isw \Rightarrow^* f$ in I with $f \in {}_IF$. As a result, $L(O) = L(I)$.

Algorithm 6.56 PDA to CFG Conversion.

Input. A PDA, $I = ({}_I\Sigma, {}_IR)$, in which every rule is of the form $Aqa \rightarrow yp \in {}_IR$ where q, $p \in {}_IQ$, $a \in {}_I\Delta \cup \{\varepsilon\}$, $y \in {}_I\Gamma^*$, and $A \in {}_I\Gamma$.

Output. A CFG, $O = ({}_O\Sigma, {}_OR)$, such that $L(O) = L(I)$.

Method.

begin

set ${}_O\Sigma = {}_I\Delta \cup {}_ON \cup \{{}_OS\}$, where ${}_ON = \{\langle pAq\rangle |\ p, q \in {}_IQ, A \in {}_I\Gamma\}$ and ${}_OS$ is a newly introduced symbol, used as the start symbol of O

set ${}_O\Delta = {}_I\Delta$

set ${}_OR = \{{}_OS \rightarrow \langle {}_Is\,{}_ISf\rangle |\ f \in {}_IF$ (${}_Is$ and ${}_IS$ are the start state and the start pushdown symbol of I, respectively)$\}$

add $\langle q_0 A q_{n+1}\rangle \to a\langle q_1 X_1 q_2\rangle\langle q_2 X_2 q_3\rangle\ldots\langle q_n X_n q_{n+1}\rangle$ to ${}_OR$ for all $Aq_0a \to X_n\ldots X_1 q_1 \in {}_IR$,
where $q_0, q_{n+1} \in {}_IQ$, $a \in {}_I\Delta \cup \{\varepsilon\}$, $A \in {}_I\Gamma$, and
$q_j \in {}_IQ$, $X_j \in {}_I\Gamma$, $\langle q_j X_j q_{j+1}\rangle \in {}_ON$, $1 \leq j \leq n$, for some $n \in {}_0\mathbb{N}$
($n = 0$ means $X_n\ldots X_1 = \langle q_1 X_1 q_2\rangle\ldots\langle q_n X_n q_{n+1}\rangle = \varepsilon$)

end.

Lemma 6.57 Algorithm 6.56 is correct.

Proof. We open this proof by establishing the next claim concerning I and O from Algorithm 6.56.

Claim. For all $w \in {}_I\Delta^*$, $A \in {}_I\Gamma$, and $p, q \in {}_IQ$,

$$\langle qAp\rangle \ {}_{lm}\Rightarrow^* w \text{ in } O \text{ iff } Aqw \Rightarrow^* p \text{ in } I.$$

Proof of the Claim. First, we establish the *only-if* part of this equivalence. That is, by induction on $i \geq 0$, we prove that $\langle qAp\rangle \ {}_{lm}\Rightarrow^i w$ in O implies $Aqw \Rightarrow^* p$ in I.

Basis. For $i = 0$, $\langle qAp\rangle \ {}_{lm}\Rightarrow^0 w$ never occurs in O for any $w \in {}_I\Delta^*$, so the basis holds true.

Induction Hypothesis. Assume that the implication holds for all derivations consisting of no more than j steps, for some $j \in {}_0\mathbb{N}$.

Induction Step. Consider any derivation of the form $\langle qAp\rangle \ {}_{lm}\Rightarrow^{j+1} w$ in O $[p\pi]$, where $|\pi| = j$. Let this derivation start by the application of a rule of the form

$$\langle q_0 A q_{n+1}\rangle \to a\langle q_1 X_1 q_2\rangle\langle q_2 X_2 q_3\rangle\ldots\langle q_n X_n q_{n+1}\rangle$$

from ${}_OR$, where $a \in {}_I\Delta \cup \{\varepsilon\}$, $A \in {}_I\Gamma$, $X_k \in {}_I\Gamma$, $1 \leq k \leq n$, $q = q_0$, $p = q_{n+1}$, and $q_l \in {}_IQ$, $0 \leq l \leq n + 1$, for some $n \in {}_0\mathbb{N}$. Thus, we can express $\langle qAp\rangle \ {}_{lm}\Rightarrow^{j+1} w$ as

$$\begin{aligned}\langle q_0 A q_{n+1}\rangle \ &{}_{lm}\Rightarrow a\langle q_1 X_1 q_2\rangle\langle q_2 X_2 q_3\rangle\ldots\langle q_n X_n q_{n+1}\rangle \\ &{}_{lm}\Rightarrow^j aw_1w_2\ldots w_n\end{aligned}$$

where for all $1 \leq l \leq n$, $\langle q_l X_l q_{l+1}\rangle \Rightarrow^* w_l$, and each of these n derivations consists of j or fewer steps. Thus, by the induction hypothesis, $X_l q_l w_l \Rightarrow^* q_{l+1}$ in I, $1 \leq l \leq n$. Algorithm 6.56 constructs $\langle q_0 A q_{n+1}\rangle \to a\langle q_1 X_1 q_2\rangle\langle q_2 X_2 q_3\rangle\ldots\langle q_n X_n q_{n+1}\rangle \in {}_OR$ from $Aq_0a \to X_n\ldots X_2 X_1 q_1 \in {}_IR$, so

$$\begin{aligned}Aq_0w &\Rightarrow^* X_n\ldots X_2X_1q_1w_1w_2\ldots w_n \\ &\Rightarrow^* X_n\ldots X_2q_2w_2\ldots w_n \\ &\Rightarrow^* X_n\ldots q_3\ldots w_n \\ &\ \vdots \\ &\Rightarrow^* X_nq_nw_n \\ &\Rightarrow^* q_{n+1}\end{aligned}$$

in I. Because $q = q_0$ and $p = q_{n+1}$, $Aqw \Rightarrow^* p$ in I, and the inductive step is completed.

Next, we establish the *if* part of the equivalence stated in the claim so we show that $Aqw \Rightarrow^i p$ in I implies $\langle qAp\rangle \ {}_{lm}\Rightarrow w$ in O by induction on $i \geq 0$.

Basis. The basis holds vacuously because $Aqw \Rightarrow^0 p$ in I is false for all $w \in {}_I\Delta^*$; indeed, I cannot remove A from the pushdown top by making zero moves.

Induction Hypothesis. Assume that the implication holds for all sequences consisting of no more than j moves, for some $j \in {}_0\mathbb{N}$.

Induction Step. Let $Aqw \Rightarrow^{j+1} p$ in I $[r\rho]$, where $|\rho| = j$. Let r be a rule of the form $Aq_0a \rightarrow X_n\ldots X_2X_1q_1 \in {}_IR$, where $a \in {}_I\Delta \cup \{\varepsilon\}$, $A \in {}_I\Gamma$, $X_l \in {}_I\Gamma$, $1 \leq l \leq n$, for some $n \in {}_0\mathbb{N}$. Express $Aqw \Rightarrow^{j+1} p$ as

$$\begin{aligned} Aq_0a &\Rightarrow X_n\ldots X_2X_1q_1w_1w_2\ldots w_n \\ &\Rightarrow^* X_n\ldots X_2q_2w_2\ldots w_n \\ &\Rightarrow^* X_n\ldots q_3\ldots w_n \\ &\vdots \\ &\Rightarrow^* X_nq_nw_n \\ &\Rightarrow^* q_{n+1} \end{aligned}$$

in I, where $q = q_0$, $p = q_{n+1}$, and $w = aw_1w_2\ldots w_n$. Clearly, for all $1 \leq k \leq n$, $X_n\ldots X_{k+1}X_kq_kw_kw_{k+1}\ldots w_n \Rightarrow^* X_n\ldots X_{k+1}q_{k+1}w_{k+1}\ldots w_n$ consists of no more than j steps, so by the induction hypothesis, $\langle q_lX_lq_{l+1}\rangle \Rightarrow^* w_l$, for $1 \leq l \leq n$. From $Aq_0a \rightarrow X_n\ldots X_2X_1q_1 \in {}_IR$, Algorithm 6.56 constructs $\langle q_0Aq_{n+1}\rangle \rightarrow a\langle q_1X_1q_2\rangle\langle q_2X_2q_3\rangle\ldots\langle q_nX_nq_{n+1}\rangle \in {}_OR$. Thus, O makes

$$\begin{aligned} \langle q_0Aq_{n+1}\rangle &{}_{lm}\Rightarrow a\langle q_1X_1q_2\rangle\langle q_2X_2q_3\rangle\ldots\langle q_nX_nq_{n+1}\rangle \\ &{}_{lm}\Rightarrow^* aw_1w_2\ldots w_n \end{aligned}$$

with $w = aw_1w_2\ldots w_n$, and the induction step is completed. Thus, the claim holds.

Considering the claim for ${}_IS = A$ and ${}_Is = q$, we have for all $w \in {}_I\Delta^*$ and $p \in {}_IQ$, $\langle {}_Is_ISp\rangle\ {}_{lm}\Rightarrow^* w$ in O iff ${}_IS_Isw \Rightarrow^* p$ in I. As follows from the algorithm, O starts every derivation by applying a rule of the form ${}_OS \rightarrow \langle {}_Is_ISf\rangle$ with $f \in {}_IF$. Consequently, ${}_OS\ {}_{lm}\Rightarrow \langle {}_Is_ISf\rangle\ {}_{lm}\Rightarrow^* w$ in O iff ${}_IS_Isw \Rightarrow^* f$ in I, so $L(I) = L(O)$.

Thus, the algorithm is correct. As a result, every language in ${}_{PDA}\Phi$ also belongs to ${}_{CFG}\Phi$, so ${}_{PDA}\Phi \subseteq {}_{CFG}\Phi$. ■

Example 6.16 Reconsider $M \in {}_{PDA}\Psi$ from Example 6.14. Recall that M is defined as

$$Ssa \rightarrow as,\ asa \rightarrow aas,\ asb \rightarrow f,\ afb \rightarrow f$$

where f is a final state. Recall that $L(M) = \{a^nb^n \mid n \geq 1\}$. With $I = M$, Algorithm 6.56 constructs $O \in {}_{CFG}\Psi$ satisfying $L(O) = L(I)$ in the following way. Denote the new start symbol of O by Z. Initially, set

$${}_ON = \{\langle pAq\rangle \mid p, q \in \{s, f\}, A \in \{S, a\}\} \cup \{Z\}, \text{ and}$$
$${}_OR = \{Z \rightarrow \langle sSf\rangle\}$$

From $Ssa \rightarrow as$, Algorithm 6.56 produces these two rules

$$\langle sSs\rangle \rightarrow a\langle sas\rangle \text{ and } \langle sSf\rangle \rightarrow a\langle saf\rangle$$

From $asa \rightarrow aas$, it produces

$$\langle sas\rangle \rightarrow a\langle sas\rangle\langle sas\rangle,\ \langle sas\rangle \rightarrow a\langle saf\rangle\langle fas\rangle,\ \langle saf\rangle \rightarrow a\langle sas\rangle\langle saf\rangle,\ \langle saf\rangle \rightarrow a\langle saf\rangle\langle faf\rangle$$

From $asb \rightarrow f$, the algorithm makes

$$\langle sas\rangle \rightarrow b,\ \langle saf\rangle \rightarrow b$$

Construct the rest of the output grammar as an exercise. In addition, by using Algorithm 6.20, remove from the grammar all useless symbols to obtain the resulting grammar O defined as

$$Z \rightarrow \langle sSf \rangle,\ \langle sSf \rangle \rightarrow a\langle saf \rangle,\ \langle saf \rangle \rightarrow a\langle saf \rangle\langle fbf \rangle,\ \langle saf \rangle \rightarrow b,\ \langle fbf \rangle \rightarrow b$$

For instance, I accepts $aabb$ as

$$Ssaabb \Rightarrow asabb \Rightarrow aasbb \Rightarrow afb \Rightarrow f$$

O generates this string by this leftmost derivation

$$Z\ {}_{lm}\!\Rightarrow \langle sSf \rangle\ {}_{lm}\!\Rightarrow a\langle saf \rangle\ {}_{lm}\!\Rightarrow aa\langle saf \rangle\langle fbf \rangle\ {}_{lm}\!\Rightarrow aab\langle fbf \rangle\ {}_{lm}\!\Rightarrow aabb$$

As a simple exercise, give a rigorous proof that $L(O) = \{a^n b^n \mid n \geq 1\}$.

The crucial Theorem 6.58, which says that PDAs and CFGs are equivalent, follows from Theorem 6.53, Corollary 6.54, Theorem 6.55, Algorithm 6.56, and Lemma 6.57.

Theorem 6.58 ${}_{CFG}\Phi = {}_{PDA}\Phi$. ■

6.3.3 Equivalent Types of Acceptance

Consider any M in ${}_{PDA}\Psi$. According to Definition 6.50, $L(M) = \{w \mid w \in \Delta^*, Ssw \Rightarrow^* f, f \in F\}$. In other words, M accepts w *by empty pushdown and final state* because after reading w, M has to (i) empty its pushdown and (ii) end up in a final state to accept $w \in {}_M\Delta^*$. Next, we relax this way of acceptance by requiring that only one of conditions (i) or (ii) is satisfied.

Definition 6.59 Let $M = ({}_M\Sigma, {}_MR)$ be a PDA.

I. If $Ssw \Rightarrow^* q$ in M with $q \in Q$, *M accepts w by empty pushdown*. The set of all strings that M accepts in this way is the *language accepted by M by empty pushdown*, denoted by ${}_\varepsilon L(M)$.
II. If $Ssw \Rightarrow^* vf$ in M with $v \in \Gamma^*$ and $f \in F$, *M accepts w by final state*. The set of all strings that M accepts in this way is the *language accepted by M by final state*, denoted by ${}_f L(M)$. ■

Example 6.17 Consider a PDA M defined by its five rules

$$1{:}\ Ssa \rightarrow Sas,\ 2{:}\ asa \rightarrow aas,\ 3{:}\ asb \rightarrow q,\ 4{:}\ aqb \rightarrow q,\ 5{:}\ Sq \rightarrow f$$

where ${}_M\Gamma = \{S, a\}$, ${}_M\Delta = \{a, b\}$, ${}_MQ = \{s, q, f\}$, and ${}_MF = \{s, f\}$. To describe how M works, observe that M reads a and pushes down Sa by using rule 1. Then, M pushes down as by using rule 2 while remaining in the final state s. When and if the first occurrence of b appears, M begins to pop up as and pair them off with bs while remaining in the only nonfinal state q.

For instance, on aa, M works as

$Ssaa$	$\Rightarrow$	$Sasa$	[1]
	$\Rightarrow$	$Saas$	[2]

On $aabb$, M works in the following way

$Ssaabb$	$\Rightarrow$	$Sasabb$	[1]
	$\Rightarrow$	$Saasbb$	[2]
	$\Rightarrow$	$Saqb$	[3]
	$\Rightarrow$	Sq	[4]
	$\Rightarrow$	f	[5]

As s and f are final, M accepts aa and $aabb$ by final state.

Consider the three types of acceptance and corresponding three languages that M accepts—${}_fL(M)$, ${}_\varepsilon L(M)$, and $L(M)$—in terms of Definitions 6.50 and 6.59. Observe that

$$ {}_fL(M) = \{a^k b^k \mid k \geq 1\} \cup \{a\}^+ \text{ and } {}_\varepsilon L(M) = L(M) = \{a^k b^k \mid k \geq 1\} $$

Convention 6.60 Set ${}_{PDA}\Phi_\varepsilon = \{{}_\varepsilon L(M) \mid M \in {}_{PDA}\Psi\}$ and ${}_{PDA}\Phi_f = \{{}_fL(M) \mid M \in {}_{PDA}\Psi\}$. ■

We next establish Lemmas 6.61 through 6.64, whose proofs describe how to convert the three types of acceptance to each other. As a consequence, these lemmas imply ${}_{PDA}\Phi = {}_{PDA}\Phi_\varepsilon = {}_{PDA}\Phi_f$ (see Convention 6.51 for ${}_{PDA}\Phi$).

Lemma 6.61 For any $I \in {}_{PDA}\Psi$, there is $O \in {}_{PDA}\Psi$ such that ${}_fL(I) = {}_\varepsilon L(O)$. Therefore, ${}_{PDA}\Phi_f \subseteq {}_{PDA}\Phi_\varepsilon$.

Proof. Let $I \in {}_{PDA}\Psi$. O keeps its start symbol ${}_OS$ on the pushdown bottom; otherwise, it simulates I move by move. If I enters a final state and accepts, O completely empties its pushdown list, including ${}_OS$, and accepts, too. If I empties its pushdown while occurring in a nonfinal state and, therefore, does not accept its input by final state, then the pushdown of O contains ${}_OS$, so O does not accept its input either. A fully rigorous proof is left as an exercise. ■

Lemma 6.62 For any $I \in {}_{PDA}\Psi$, there is $O \in {}_{PDA}\Psi$ such that $L(I) = {}_fL(O)$. Therefore, ${}_{PDA}\Phi \subseteq {}_{PDA}\Phi_f$.

Proof. Let $I \in {}_{PDA}\Psi$. Construct $O \in {}_{PDA}\Psi$ with ${}_OF = \{f\}$, where f is a new final state, by analogy with the proof of Lemma 6.61. That is, O keeps ${}_OS$ on the pushdown bottom while simulating I. If I empties its pushdown, enters a final state, and accepts, then after simulating this computation in I, O occurs in the same state with the pushdown containing ${}_OS$; from this configuration, O enters f to accept the input by final state. ■

Lemma 6.63 For any $I \in {}_{PDA}\Psi$, there is $O \in {}_{PDA}\Psi$ such that ${}_\varepsilon L(I) = {}_fL(O) = L(O)$. Therefore, ${}_{PDA}\Phi_\varepsilon \subseteq {}_{PDA}\Phi_f$ and ${}_{PDA}\Phi_\varepsilon \subseteq {}_{PDA}\Phi$.

Proof. Let $I \in {}_{PDA}\Psi$ with ${}_IF \neq \emptyset$. Construct $O \in {}_{PDA}\Psi$ so it has the same final states like I. O keeps its start symbol ${}_OS$ on the pushdown bottom while simulating I. If I empties its pushdown and accepts its input, then O has its pushdown containing only ${}_OS$, and from this configuration, it enters a final state while removing ${}_OS$ from the pushdown. Observe that O constructed in this way satisfies ${}_\varepsilon L(I) = {}_fL(O) = L(O)$. As an exercise, prove this lemma for $I \in {}_{PDA}\Psi$ with ${}_IF = \emptyset$. ■

Lemma 6.64 For any $I \in {}_{PDA}\Psi$, there is $O \in {}_{PDA}\Psi$ such that $L(I) = {}_\varepsilon L(O)$. Therefore, ${}_{PDA}\Phi \subseteq {}_{PDA}\Phi_\varepsilon$.

Proof. Let $I \in {}_{PDA}\Psi$. Construct $O \in {}_{PDA}\Psi$ so it keeps its start symbol ${}_OS$ on the pushdown bottom; otherwise, it simulates I move by move. If I empties its pushdown and enters a final state, then O has its pushdown containing only ${}_OS$, so it removes ${}_OS$ from the pushdown to accept the input by empty pushdown. ■

Lemmas 6.61 through 6.63 imply that ${}_{PDA}\Phi_f \subseteq {}_{PDA}\Phi_\varepsilon \subseteq {}_{PDA}\Phi \subseteq {}_{PDA}\Phi_f$, so ${}_{PDA}\Phi = {}_{PDA}\Phi_\varepsilon = {}_{PDA}\Phi_f$. By Theorem 6.58, we, thus, obtain Theorem 6.65, which concludes this section.

Theorem 6.65 ${}_{CFG}\Phi = {}_{PDA}\Phi = {}_{PDA}\Phi_\varepsilon = {}_{PDA}\Phi_f$. ■

6.3.4 Deterministic Pushdown Automata

In general, PDAs work in a nondeterministic way—that is, they can make many different sequences of moves on the same input. Since this nondeterminism obviously complicates their implementation and application in practice, we study their deterministic versions in this section. First, we demonstrate that the equivalence of the three types of acceptance discussed in Section 6.3.3 does not hold in terms of these deterministic versions although it holds in terms of PDAs. Then, we show that the deterministic versions of PDAs are less powerful than PDAs although they are stronger than FAs.

Definition 6.66 Let $M \in {}_{PDA}\Psi$. M is a *deterministic PDA* (*DPDA*) if for every $xqa \rightarrow yp \in {}_{M}R$, where $x, y \in \Gamma^*$, $q, p \in Q$, and $a \in \Delta \cup \{\varepsilon\}$, it holds that $\boldsymbol{lhs}(r) \notin \Gamma^*\{xq\}\{a, \varepsilon\}$, for all $r \in {}_{M}R - \{xqa \rightarrow yp\}$. ■

For instance, observe that M discussed in Example 6.16 is a DPDA.

In Convention 6.67, we introduce three language families—${}_{DPDA}\Phi$, ${}_{DPDA}\Phi_\varepsilon$, and ${}_{DPDA}\Phi_f$—corresponding to the three types of acceptance discussed in Section 6.3.3 in terms of PDAs.

Convention 6.67 We denote the set of DPDAs by ${}_{DPDA}\Psi$ and set ${}_{DPDA}\Phi = \{L(M) \mid M \in {}_{DPDA}\Psi\}$, ${}_{DPDA}\Phi_\varepsilon = \{{}_{\varepsilon}L(M) \mid M \in {}_{DPDA}\Psi\}$, and ${}_{DPDA}\Phi_f = \{{}_{f}L(M) \mid M \in {}_{DPDA}\Psi\}$ (see Definition 6.59 for ${}_{\varepsilon}L(M)$ and ${}_{f}L(M)$). ■

Recall that ${}_{PDA}\Phi = {}_{PDA}\Phi_\varepsilon = {}_{PDA}\Phi_f$ (see Theorem 6.65). Surprisingly, this identity cannot be reformulated in terms of ${}_{DPDA}\Phi$, ${}_{DPDA}\Phi_\varepsilon$, and ${}_{DPDA}\Phi_f$. Indeed, ${}_{DPDA}\Phi_\varepsilon = {}_{DPDA}\Phi \subset {}_{DPDA}\Phi_f$ as demonstrated by Theorems 6.68 and 6.70.

Theorem 6.68 ${}_{DPDA}\Phi_\varepsilon = {}_{DPDA}\Phi$.

Proof. Establish this identity by analogy with the proofs of Lemmas 6.63 and 6.64. ■

Lemma 6.69 $\{a^kb^k \mid k \geq 1\} \cup \{a\}^+ \notin {}_{DPDA}\Phi$.

Proof. Let $L = \{a^kb^k \mid k \geq 1\} \cup \{a\}^+$. We prove $L \notin {}_{DPDA}\Phi$ by contradiction. Suppose that $L = L(M)$ for some $M \in {}_{DPDA}\Psi$. As ${}_{M}F$ is finite and M accepts any string in $\{a\}^+$, there surely exist $i, j \in \mathbb{N}$ such that $1 \leq i < j$, and M accepts both a^i and a^j so that after reading both a^i and a^j, M empties its pushdown and enters the same final state, $f \in {}_{M}F$. Consider $a^jb^j \in L(M)$. Since M is deterministic, during the acceptance of a^jb^j, M empties its pushdown and enters f after reading both the prefix a^i and the prefix a^j. Thus, M also accepts a^ib^j, which is out of L. Hence, $L \notin {}_{DPDA}\Phi$, and Lemma 6.69 holds. ■

Theorem 6.70 ${}_{DPDA}\Phi \subset {}_{DPDA}\Phi_f$.

Proof. Consider the conversion of any PDA I to a PDA O so $L(I) = {}_fL(O)$ described in the proof of Lemma 6.62. Observe that if I is a DPDA, then O is a DPDA, too. Thus, ${}_{DPDA}\Phi \subseteq {}_{DPDA}\Phi_f$. Return to the PDA M in Example 6.17. Recall that ${}_fL(M) = \{a^kb^k \mid k \geq 1\} \cup \{a\}^+$. Observe that M is deterministic. Thus, by Lemma 6.69, ${}_{DPDA}\Phi_f - {}_{DPDA}\Phi \neq \emptyset$, so ${}_{DPDA}\Phi \subset {}_{DPDA}\Phi_f$. ■

According to Definition 6.66, any $M \in {}_{DPDA}\Psi$ makes no more than one move from any configuration, so it makes a unique sequence of moves on any input—a property highly appreciated in practice when M is implemented. Unfortunately, DPDAs have also their disadvantage: they are less powerful than their nondeterministic versions as demonstrated by Lemma 6.71.

Lemma 6.71 Let $L = \{vw \mid v, w \in \{a, b\}^*, v = reversal(w)\}$. $L \notin {}_{DPDA}\Phi_f$.

Proof. We only give a gist underlying this proof, whose rigorous version is beyond the scope of this introductory text. Any PDA M such that ${}_fL(M) = L$ necessarily works on its input $u \in \{a, b\}^*$ by performing these four computational phases:

1. M pushes down a prefix of u.
2. M takes a guess that it is right in the middle of u, which means that the length of its current pushdown equals the length of the suffix that remains to be read.
3. M pops up the symbols from the pushdown and pairs them off with the same input symbols.
4. When and if M completes reading u, it accepts.

Notice, however, that M ends (1) and begins (2) based on its guess, so M makes necessarily more than one move from the same configuration at this point. As a result, M cannot be deterministic, so $L \notin {}_{DPDA}\Phi_f$. ■

Theorem 6.72 ${}_{DPDA}\Phi_f \subset {}_{PDA}\Phi$.

Proof. By Definitions 6.50 and 6.66, DPDAs are special cases of PDAs, so ${}_{DPDA}\Phi_f \subseteq {}_{PDA}\Phi_f$. By Theorem 6.65, ${}_{PDA}\Phi_f = {}_{PDA}\Phi$. Let $L = \{vw \mid v, w \in \{a, b\}^*, v = reversal(w)\}$. By Example 6.15 and Lemma 6.71, $L \in {}_{PDA}\Phi - {}_{DPDA}\Phi_f$, so ${}_{PDA}\Phi - {}_{DPDA}\Phi_f \neq \emptyset$. Thus, Theorem 6.72 holds true. ■

Clearly, DPDAs are stronger than FAs.

Theorem 6.73 ${}_{FA}\Phi \subset {}_{DPDA}\Phi$.

Proof. By Definitions 3.9 and 6.66, any DFA can be seen as a DPDA that keeps its pushdown empty during any computation. As ${}_{FA}\Phi = {}_{DFA}\Phi$ (see Corollary 3.22), ${}_{FA}\Phi \subseteq {}_{DPDA}\Phi$. In Example 6.14, M is a DPDA such that $L(M) = \{a^kb^k \mid k \geq 1\}$. By analogy with Example 5.4, prove that $\{a^kb^k \mid k \geq 1\} \notin {}_{reg}\Phi$. Since ${}_{reg}\Phi = {}_{FA}\Phi$ (see Theorem 3.38), ${}_{FA}\Phi \subset {}_{DPDA}\Phi$. ■

Putting together Theorems 6.65, 6.68, 6.70, 6.72, and 6.73, we obtain Corollary 6.74 of a fundamental importance.

Corollary 6.74 ${}_{FA}\Phi \subset {}_{DPDA}\Phi_\varepsilon = {}_{DPDA}\Phi \subset {}_{DPDA}\Phi_f \subset {}_{PDA}\Phi = {}_{PDA}\Phi_\varepsilon = {}_{PDA}\Phi_f = {}_{CFG}\Phi$. ■

DPDAs fulfill a crucial role in applications of PDAs in practice. Perhaps most significantly, they are central to syntax analysis—the subject of Chapter 7.

Exercises

1 S. Consider the following three CFLs, described in an informal way.

i. Let L be the language of all balanced strings of two types of parentheses, () and [], ended by #. For instance, ([([])])[]# and ()# belong to L, but (([])# and ([]) do not.

ii. Let L be the language of all arithmetic expressions in the Polish prefix notation with an operand i and operators +, −, *, and / (see Section 1.1). For instance, +**iii* is in L, but *iii*+ is not.

iii. A *palindrome* is a string that is identical to itself written backward. Let L be the language of all palindromes over {0, 1}. For instance, 001100 belongs to L, but 110 does not.

For each of them, perform (a) and (b), given next.

a. Construct a CFG that generates L and explain this construction.

b. Construct a PDA that accepts L and explain this construction. If possible, construct this PDA deterministic. If this is impossible, explain why there exists no DPDA that accepts the language.

2 S. Consider the following CFLs over $\{a, b, c\}$.

i. $\{a^i bc^j ba^i \mid i, j \geq 1\}$

ii. $\{a^i ba^i \mid i \geq 0\}$

iii. $\{a^{2i} b^i \mid i \geq 0\}$

iv. $\{a^i b^j c^i \mid i \geq 0 \text{ and } j \geq 1\}$

v. $\{b^i a^i b^j c^j \mid i, j \geq 0\}$

vi. $\{b^i a^j b^k \mid i, j, k \geq 0, i = j, \text{ or } j = k\}$

vii. $\{xc \mid x \in \{a, b\}^*, occur(x, a) > occur(x, b)\}$

viii. $\{x \mid x \in \{a, b, c\}^*, occur(x, a) = occur(x, b) \text{ or } occur(x, b) = occur(x, c)\}$

ix. $\{cxc \mid x \in \{a, b\}^*, occur(x, a) = 2occur(x, b)\}$

x. $\{xy \mid x \in \{a, b\}^*, x = reversal(y)\}$

For each of these languages, perform (a) and (b), given next.

a. Construct a CFG that generates the language and verify this construction by a rigorous proof.

b. Construct a PDA that accepts it and verify this construction by a proof. If possible, make the PDA deterministic. If this is impossible, prove that the language is in $_{PDA}\Phi - {}_{DPDA}\Phi$ (see Section 6.3.4).

3. Consider the following CFGs.

i. $S \rightarrow aSbS, S \rightarrow bSaS, S \rightarrow \varepsilon$

ii. $S \rightarrow SS, S \rightarrow (S), S \rightarrow \varepsilon$

iii. $S \rightarrow abSba, S \rightarrow A, S \rightarrow cAc, A \rightarrow cc$

iv. $S \rightarrow aSbSa, S \rightarrow \varepsilon$

v. $S \rightarrow ASB, S \rightarrow \varepsilon, A \rightarrow aSb, A \rightarrow \varepsilon, B \rightarrow aBb, B \rightarrow ba$

vi. $S \rightarrow SS, S \rightarrow aSb, S \rightarrow bSa, S \rightarrow \varepsilon$

vii. $S \rightarrow aS, S \rightarrow Sa, S \rightarrow b$

viii. $S \rightarrow SaSa, S \rightarrow b$

ix. $S \rightarrow Sb, S \rightarrow aSb, S \rightarrow Sa, S \rightarrow a$

x. $S \rightarrow aaSb, S \rightarrow aaaSb, S \rightarrow ab$

xi. $S \rightarrow A, S \rightarrow aSb, S \rightarrow bS, A \rightarrow Aa, A \rightarrow a$

xii. $S \rightarrow AA, A \rightarrow AAA, A \rightarrow bA, A \rightarrow Ab, A \rightarrow a$

xiii. $S \rightarrow ABB, A \rightarrow CAC, A \rightarrow a, B \rightarrow Bc, B \rightarrow c, B \rightarrow ABB, C \rightarrow bB, C \rightarrow b, C \rightarrow a$

xiv. $S \rightarrow aSASb, S \rightarrow Saa, S \rightarrow AA, A \rightarrow caA, A \rightarrow Ac, A \rightarrow bca, A \rightarrow \varepsilon$

xv. $S \rightarrow AB, S \rightarrow CA, A \rightarrow a, B \rightarrow BC, B \rightarrow AB, C \rightarrow aB, C \rightarrow b$

xvi. $S \rightarrow AB, S \rightarrow \varepsilon, A \rightarrow aASb, A \rightarrow a, B \rightarrow bS$

xvii. $S \rightarrow ABA, A \rightarrow aA, A \rightarrow \varepsilon, B \rightarrow bB, B \rightarrow \varepsilon$

xviii. $S \rightarrow aSa, S \rightarrow bSb, S \rightarrow A, A \rightarrow aBb, A \rightarrow bBa, B \rightarrow aB, B \rightarrow bB, B \rightarrow \varepsilon$

xix. $S \rightarrow aA, S \rightarrow abB, A \rightarrow bc, B \rightarrow c$

xx. $S \rightarrow cBA, S \rightarrow B, A \rightarrow cB, A \rightarrow AbbS, B \rightarrow aaa$

For each of these CFG, perform (a) through (f), as follows:

a. Determine the generated language and verify it by a rigorous proof.
b. Give an equivalent PDA and verify the equivalence by a rigorous proof. If possible, construct this PDA deterministic. If this is impossible, explain why there exists no equivalent DPDA.
c. Prove or disprove that the CFG is ambiguous. If it is ambiguous, then either give an equivalent unambiguous CFG or explain that the generated language is inherently unambiguous. In either case, prove the answer rigorously.
d. Construct an equivalent proper CFG.
e. Construct an equivalent CFG in Chomsky normal form.
f. Construct an equivalent CFG in Greibach normal form.

4 S. Consider this CFG G in Chomsky normal form

$$1: S \rightarrow CB,\ 2: S \rightarrow EA,\ 3: C \rightarrow BS,\ 4: E \rightarrow SD,$$
$$5: A \rightarrow a,\ 6: B \rightarrow b,\ 7: C \rightarrow c,\ 8: D \rightarrow d$$

Show that G is left-recursive although it is not directly left-recursive. Determine its language. By using Algorithm 6.38, turn G to an equivalent non-left-recursive CFG.

5. Define the following PDAs, (i) through (v), by their lists of rules, in which s, q, f are states; s is the start state, and f is the only final state.

i. $Ssa \rightarrow Sas$, $asa \rightarrow aas$, $asb \rightarrow q$, $aqb \rightarrow q$, $Sq \rightarrow Ss$, $Sq \rightarrow f$
ii. $Ss \rightarrow SSs$, $Ssa \rightarrow Sas$, $asa \rightarrow aas$, $asb \rightarrow q$, $aqb \rightarrow q$, $Sq \rightarrow f$
iii. $Ssa \rightarrow As$, $Asa \rightarrow AAs$, $Asc \rightarrow q$, $Sqb \rightarrow As$, $Aqb \rightarrow AAq$, $Aqc \rightarrow f$
iv. $Ssa \rightarrow cas$, $asa \rightarrow aas$, $bsb \rightarrow s$, $asb \rightarrow s$, $bsa \rightarrow s$, $csc \rightarrow f$
v. $Ssa \rightarrow As$, $Asa \rightarrow AAAs$, $Asb \rightarrow q$, $Aqb \rightarrow q$, $Aqc \rightarrow f$

Consider each of these PDAs. For brevity, let M denote the PDA under consideration. Perform (a) through (e), as follows:

a. Determine $L(M)$ and verify it by a rigorous proof.
b. Determine $_fL(M)$ and $_\varepsilon L(M)$ in a rigorous way (see Section 6.3.3).
c. Construct an equivalent CFG and verify the equivalence by a rigorous proof.
d. By using Algorithm 6.56 PDA to CFG Conversion, convert M to a CFG G satisfying $L(G) = L(M)$.
e. Prove or disprove that M is deterministic. If it is not, then either give an equivalent DPDA or explain why the accepted language is in $_{PDA}\Phi - {}_{DPDA}\Phi$. In either case, prove the answer rigorously.

6. Let $G = (\Sigma, R)$ be a CFG in Chomsky normal form (see Definition 6.34), and let $S \Rightarrow^i w$ in G, where $i \in \mathbb{N}$ and $w \in \Delta^+$ (according to Convention 6.2, S is the start symbol of G). Does i imply $|w|$? Does $|w|$ imply i? Answers these questions and verify the answers by proofs. Reformulate and answer these questions in terms of two-standard Greibach normal form (see Definition 6.46).

7. Let $G = ({}_G\Sigma, {}_GR)$ be a proper CFG. A nonterminal $A \in {}_GN$ is *recursive* iff $A \Rightarrow^* uAv$, for some $uv \in {}_G\Delta^+$. Prove that $L(G)$ is infinite iff $_GN$ contains a recursive nonterminal.

8. Prove that for every CFL L, there exists a CFG, $G = (\Sigma, R)$, satisfying these four conditions:

a. $L(G) = L - \{\varepsilon\}$;
b. G is in Chomsky normal form;
c. $A \rightarrow BC \in R$ implies $B \neq C$, where $A, B, C \in N$;
d. if $A \rightarrow BC$ and $D \rightarrow CE$ are two different rules in R, where $A, B, C, D, E \in N$, then $A \neq D$.

9. Prove that for every $L \in {}_{CFG}\Phi$ (see Convention 6.2), there exists a CFG, $G = (\Sigma, R)$, such that $L(G) = L - \{\varepsilon\}$, and every $A \rightarrow x \in R$ satisfies $x \in \Delta \cup \Delta\Sigma^*\Delta$.

10 S. *E0S systems* are CFGs generalized so they can rewrite terminals. Define E0S systems rigorously. Prove that they are as powerful as CFGs.

11 S. *Pure CFGs* are CFGs modified so they have only terminals. Perform (a) through (c), as follows:

a. Define the notion of a pure CFG formally.
b. Compare the language family generated by pure CFGs with the families of finite, regular, and CFLs.

c. Prove that for every CFG G, there exists a pure CFG H such that $F(G) = L(H)$ (see Definition 6.1 for $F(G)$).

12. An *operator CFG* represents an ε-free CFG such that no rule has two consecutive nonterminals on its right-hand side. Define the notion of an operator CFG formally. Prove that for every CFG G, there exists an operator CFG O satisfying $L(G) = L(O)$.
13. Let $I = ({}_I\Sigma, {}_IR)$ be a CFG. Let k be the length of the longest right-hand side of a rule in ${}_IR$. Convert I to a proper CFG, $O = ({}_O\Sigma, {}_OR)$, such that $L(O) = L(I) - \{\varepsilon\}$ by the method described in the proof of Theorem 6.33. What is the maximum number of rules in ${}_OR$? Demonstrate the answer by a rigorous proof.
14. Design a tabular and graphical PDA representation by analogy with the FA state tables and the FA state diagrams (see Section 3.1).

15 S. Modify Algorithm 6.56 PDA to CFG Conversion so it converts any PDA M to a CFG that generates ${}_\varepsilon L(M)$. Verify the resulting modified algorithm by a rigorous proof. Illustrate the modified algorithm by using

$$Ssa \rightarrow Sas,\ asa \rightarrow aas,\ asb \rightarrow q,\ aqb \rightarrow q,\ Sq \rightarrow q$$

as its input PDA M, where s is the start state.

16. As their name indicates, *two-PDA* have two pushdowns. Define them rigorously. Prove that they are more powerful than ordinary PDAs (see Definition 6.50). Note that the Exercises of Chapter 9 reconsider these automata in a greater detail.
17. Let $M = (\Sigma, R)$ be a PDA; then, $\{w \mid Ssw \Rightarrow^* wq, w \in \Delta^*, q \in F\}$ represents a regular language. Prove this result rigorously.

18 S. Consider the standard definition of a PDA (see Definition 6.50). Generalize it so the PDA can read an entire string during a single move to obtain the definition of a *long-reading PDA* (${}_{long}$*PDA*). Formalize this generalization. Are ${}_{long}$PDAs and standard PDAs equivalent? If so, design an algorithm that turns any ${}_{long}$PDA to an equivalent PDA and verify this algorithm by a rigorous proof. If not, give a ${}_{long}$PDA such that there is no PDA equivalent with the ${}_{long}$PDA and, in addition, a rigorous proof that demonstrates this non-equivalence.

19. A *pushdown transducer* M is a PDA modified so it emits an output string during every move. Consider $a_1 \ldots a_n$, where each a_i is an input symbol or ε, and suppose that M emits a string x_i during a move on a_i. If M accepts $a_1 \ldots a_n$ by analogy with the standard PDA way of acceptance (see Definition 6.50), then it translates $a_1 \ldots a_n$ to $x_1 \ldots x_n$. The *translation of* M is the relation consisting of all pairs (x, y) such that M translates x to y. Formalize this gist. That is, define the notion of a pushdown transducer and its translation rigorously. Design a tabular and graphical representation of these transducers.
20. A *two-way PDA* moves either way on its input. Formalize this generalization. Prove that two-way PDAs are stronger than PDAs.

21 S. Let $M = (\Sigma, R)$ be a PDA. M is a *counter* if $card(\Gamma - \Delta) = 1$. Reconsider Section 6.3.3 in terms of counters. Compare the power of PDAs with the power of counters.

22. An *atomic* PDA is a PDA such that during any move, it changes the current state and, in addition, performs one of these three actions
    i. Popping a symbol from the pushdown.
    ii. Pushing a symbol onto the pushdown.
    iii. Reading the current input symbol.

    Define the notion of an *atomic* PDA rigorously. Prove that PDAs and atomic PDAs are equally powerful.
23. Let $M = ({}_M\Sigma, {}_MR)$ be a DPDA, and let # be a symbol such that $\# \notin {}_M\Sigma$; then, there exists a DPDA O such that ${}_fL(M)\{\#\} = {}_\varepsilon L(O)$. Prove this result.
24. This chapter contains results whose proofs were only sketched or even completely omitted. These results include Algorithms 6.16, 6.18, 6.24, and 6.28; Examples 6.13, 6.14, 6.15, and 6.16; Lemmas 6.61, 6.69; and Theorems 6.7, 6.21, 6.26, 6.27, 6.31, 6.36, 6.39, 6.42, 6.45, 6.47, 6.48, 6.49, 6.53, 6.55, 6.58, 6.65, 6.68, and 6.73. Prove them rigorously.

Solutions to Selected Exercises

1. Consider language (i). As obvious, the following CFG generates this language.

$$S \to A\#,\ A \to AA,\ A \to [A],\ A \to (A),\ A \to \varepsilon$$

Construct a DPDA M that accepts language (i) as follows. M has two states—s and q, where s is the start state and the only final state. During any computation, M uses its start symbol S as a pushdown-bottom marker. If the first input symbol is a left parenthesis, it pushes it onto the pushdown and, simultaneously, moves to q. In q, it pushes left parentheses of either type onto its pushdown. Whenever a right parenthesis appears as an input symbol, M matches it with a left parenthesis of the same type on the pushdown top. If this match is successful, M pops the pushdown-top symbol. Whenever S occurs as the pushdown top, M returns to s, and if there are more parentheses on the input, the machine proceeds as if from the beginning. If M reads # in s, it accepts. Formally, M is defined by its rules

$$Ss(\to S(q,\ Ss[\to S[q,\ (q(\to ((q,\ [q(\to [(q,\ (q[\to ([q,$$
$$[q[\to [[q,\ (q) \to q,\ [q] \to q,\ Sq \to Ss,\ Ss\# \to s$$

2. We only solve (b) with respect to (vii). That is, we next construct a DPDA M that accepts language (vii). First, we give a gist of this construction. During any computation, M uses its start symbol S solely as a pushdown-bottom marker. Apart from S used in this way, M pushes a or b onto the pushdown so a temporary excess of one symbol over the other is saved on the pushdown. Whenever M reads an input symbol of the opposite type, it simultaneously pops the pushdown-top symbol. Accordingly, based on the pushdown-top symbol, M can make these three implications. If the pushdown-top symbol is S, M has read an equal number of both symbols. An occurrence of a as the pushdown-top symbol implies a surplus of as. Finally, an occurrence of b as the pushdown-top symbol implies that M has read more bs than as. Consequently, when M reads c with a occurring as the pushdown-top symbol, it accepts; otherwise, it rejects. Formally, M is defined by the following rules:

$$Ssa \to as,\ Ssb \to bs,\ asa \to aas,\ bsb \to bbs,$$
$$asb \to s,\ bsa \to s,\ asc \to q,\ aq \to q,\ Sq \to f$$

where s, q, f are states, s is the start state, and f is the only final state.

4. As obvious, G is not directly left-recursive. However, it is left-recursive because, for instance, $S \Rightarrow^+ SDA$. By analogy with the proof technique demonstrated in Example 6.2 prove that $L(G) = \{b^n cx \mid n \geq 0,\ x \in (\{b\}\{da\}^*)^{n+1}\}$. Use Algorithm 6.38 to turn G to an equivalent non-left-recursive CFG.

10. We only formalize the notion of an E0S system.

Definition An *E0S system* is a rewriting system $G = (\Sigma, R)$, where

- Σ is divided into two disjoint subalphabets, denoted by N and Δ.
- R is a finite *set of rules* of the form $A \to x$, where $A \in \Sigma$ and $x \in \Sigma^*$.

N and Δ are referred to as the *alphabet of nonterminal symbols* and the *alphabet of terminal symbols*, respectively. N contains a special *start symbol*, denoted by S.

If $S \Rightarrow^* w$, where $w \in \Sigma^*$, G *derives* w, and w is a *sentential form*. $F(G)$ denotes the set of all sentential forms derived by G. The *language generated by* G, symbolically denoted by $L(G)$, is defined as $L(G) = F(G) \cap \Delta^*$. ■

11. We perform (a) through (c) as follows:

a. **Definition** A *pure CFG* is a rewriting system $G = (\Sigma, R)$, where

- Σ is an alphabet.
- R is a finite *set of rules* of the form $A \to x$, where $A \in \Sigma$ and $x \in \Sigma^*$.

In addition, a special *start string*, $S \in \Sigma^+$, is specified. The *language generated by G*, symbolically denoted by $L(G)$, is defined as $L(G) = \{w \mid S \Rightarrow^* w\}$. ■

Notice that by this definition, S is always in $L(G)$. By ${}_{pure\text{-}CFG}\Phi$, denote the language family generated by pure CFGs. Recall that the families of finite, regular, and CFLs are denoted by ${}_{fin}\Phi$, ${}_{reg}\Phi$, and ${}_{CFG}\Phi$, respectively (see Sections 1.2, 3.1, and 6.1).

b. First, prove that $\{a, aa\}$ is not in ${}_{pure\text{-}CFG}\Phi$ by contradiction. Suppose that there is a pure CFG, $G = (\Sigma, R)$, that generates $\{a, aa\}$. Its start string S is in $\{a, aa\}$. If $S = a$, then $a \rightarrow aa \in R$, so $L(G) = \{a\}^+$, which differs from $\{a, aa\}$. If $S = aa$, then $a \rightarrow \varepsilon \in R$, so $\varepsilon \in L(G)$, but $\varepsilon \notin \{a, aa\}$. Thus, there is no pure CFG that generates $\{a, aa\}$. Hence, ${}_{fin}\Phi - {}_{pure\text{-}CFG}\Phi \neq \emptyset$. Clearly, ${}_{pure\text{-}CFG}\Phi - {}_{fin}\Phi \neq \emptyset$; for instance, $\{a\}^+$ belongs to ${}_{pure\text{-}CFG}\Phi - {}_{fin}\Phi$. Furthermore, ${}_{fin}\Phi \cap {}_{pure\text{-}CFG}\Phi \neq \emptyset$; for example, $\{a\} \in {}_{fin}\Phi \cap {}_{pure\text{-}CFG}\Phi$. Thus, ${}_{fin}\Phi$ and ${}_{pure\text{-}CFG}\Phi$ are incomparable (two sets X and Y are *incomparable* if $X - Y$, $Y - X$, and $X \cap Y$ are all nonempty).

By analogy with the above, prove that ${}_{reg}\Phi \cap {}_{pure\text{-}CFG}\Phi \neq \emptyset$ and ${}_{reg}\Phi - {}_{pure\text{-}CFG}\Phi \neq \emptyset$. Consider the pure CFG, $G = (\Sigma, R)$, where $\Sigma = \{a, b\}$, $R = \{b \rightarrow aba\}$, and b is the start string. Clearly, $L(G) = \{a^iba^i \mid i \geq 0\}$. By using the pumping lemma for regular languages (Lemma 5.1), prove that $\{a^iba^i \mid i \geq 0\} \notin {}_{reg}\Phi$, so ${}_{pure\text{-}CFG}\Phi - {}_{reg}\Phi \neq \emptyset$. Thus, ${}_{reg}\Phi$ and ${}_{pure\text{-}CFG}\Phi$ are incomparable, too.

As obvious, ${}_{CFG}\Phi - {}_{pure\text{-}CFG}\Phi \neq \emptyset$ and ${}_{pure\text{-}CFG}\Phi \subseteq {}_{CFG}\Phi$, so ${}_{pure\text{-}CFG}\Phi \subset {}_{CFG}\Phi$.

c. Recall that for any CFG, $G = (\Sigma, R)$, $F(G) = \{w \in \Sigma^* \mid S \Rightarrow^* w\}$. Consider the pure CFG defined as $H = (\Sigma, R)$, where S is the start string. Clearly, $F(G) = L(H)$.

15. Given a PDA, $M = ({}_M\Sigma, {}_MR)$, the next algorithm constructs a CFG, $G = ({}_G\Sigma, {}_GR)$, so $L(G) = {}_\varepsilon L(M)$. For all states $p, q \in {}_MQ$, and all pushdown symbols $A \in {}_M\Gamma$, it introduces a nonterminal $\langle pAq \rangle$ into ${}_GN$. It constructs G so $\langle pAq \rangle$ ${}_{lm}\Rightarrow^*$ w in G iff $Apw \Rightarrow^* q$ in M, where $w \in {}_M\Delta^*$. In addition, it adds ${}_GS \rightarrow \langle {}_Ms_MSo \rangle$ to ${}_GR$, for all $o \in {}_GQ$. Thus, ${}_GS \Rightarrow \langle {}_Ms_MSo \rangle$ ${}_{lm}\Rightarrow^*$ w in G iff ${}_MS_Msw \Rightarrow^* o$ in M, so $L(G) = {}_\varepsilon L(M)$.

Algorithm PDA to CFG Conversion: ε-Variant.

Input. A PDA, $M = ({}_M\Sigma, {}_MR)$.

Output. A CFG, $G = ({}_G\Sigma, {}_GR)$, such that ${}_\varepsilon L(M) = L(G)$.

Method.

begin

initialize ${}_GR = \{{}_GS \rightarrow \langle {}_Ms_MSo \rangle \mid o \in {}_MQ\}$, ${}_G\Sigma = {}_GN \cup {}_G\Delta$ with ${}_G\Delta = {}_M\Delta$,
and ${}_GN = \{\langle pAq \rangle \mid A \in {}_M\Gamma, p, q \in {}_MQ\} \cup \{{}_GS\}$

repeat
if $Aq_0a \rightarrow B_nB_{n-1}\ldots B_1q_1 \in {}_MR$, where $A \in {}_M\Gamma$, $B_i \in {}_M\Gamma$, $1 \leq i \leq n$, $a \in {}_M\Delta \cup \{\varepsilon\}$, $q_0, q_1 \in {}_MQ$, for some $n \geq 1$ **then**
include $\{\langle q_0Aq_{n+1} \rangle \rightarrow a\langle q_1B_1q_2 \rangle\langle q_2B_2q_3 \rangle\ldots\langle q_{n-1}B_{n-1}q_n \rangle\langle q_nB_nq_{n+1} \rangle \mid q_j \in {}_MQ, 2 \leq j \leq n+1\}$ into ${}_GR$
until no change

repeat
if $Aq_0a \rightarrow q_1 \in {}_MR$, where $q_0, q_1 \in {}_MQ$, $A \in {}_M\Gamma$, $a \in {}_M\Delta \cup \{\varepsilon\}$ **then**
add $\langle q_0Aq_1 \rangle \rightarrow a$ to ${}_GR$
until no change

end.

Lemma. Let M be a pushdown automaton. With M as its input, Algorithm PDA to CFG Conversion: ε-Variant correctly constructs a CFG G such that $L(G) = {}_{\varepsilon}L(M)$.

Proof. To establish $L(G) = {}_{\varepsilon}L(M)$, this proof first demonstrates the following claim.

Claim. For all $w \in {}_M\Delta^*$, $A \in {}_M\Gamma$, and $q, q' \in Q$, $\langle qAq'\rangle \;{}_{lm}\Rightarrow^* w$ in G iff $Aqw \Rightarrow^* q$ in M.

Only if. For all $i \geq 0$, $\langle qAq'\rangle \;{}_{lm}\Rightarrow^i w$ in G implies $Aqw \Rightarrow^* q'$ in M, where $w \in {}_M\Delta^*$, $A \in {}_M\Gamma$, and $q, q' \in Q$.

Basis. For $i = 0$, G cannot make $\langle qAq'\rangle \;{}_{lm}\Rightarrow^i w$. Thus, this implication holds vacuously, and the basis is true.

Induction hypothesis. Assume that the implication holds for all j-step derivations, where $j = 1, \ldots, i$, for some $i > 0$.

Induction step. Consider $\langle qAq'\rangle \;{}_{lm}\Rightarrow^* w\ [p\pi]$ in G, where π consists of i rules, and $p \in {}_GR$. Thus, $\langle qAq'\rangle \;{}_{lm}\Rightarrow^* w\ [p\pi]$ is a derivation that has $i + 1$ steps. Examine the algorithm to see that p has the form p: $\langle qAq'\rangle \rightarrow a\langle q_1B_1q_2\rangle\langle q_2B_2q_3\rangle\ldots\langle q_nB_nq_{n+1}\rangle$, where $q' = q_{n+1}$. Express $\langle qAq'\rangle \;{}_{lm}\Rightarrow^* w\ [p\pi]$ as

$$\langle qAq'\rangle \;{}_{lm}\Rightarrow a\langle q_1B_1q_2\rangle\langle q_2B_2q_3\rangle\ldots\langle q_nB_nq_{n+1}\rangle \;{}_{lm}\Rightarrow^* w$$

In more detail, $\langle qAq'\rangle \;{}_{lm}\Rightarrow a\langle q_1B_1q_2\rangle\langle q_2B_2q_3\rangle\ldots\langle q_nB_nq_{n+1}\rangle \;{}_{lm}\Rightarrow^* w$, where $w = aw_1w_2\ldots w_n$ and $\langle q_lB_lq_{l+1}\rangle \;{}_{lm}\Rightarrow^* w_l$ in G, for all $l = 1, \ldots, n$. As π consists of no more than i rules, the induction hypothesis implies $B_lq_lw_l \Rightarrow^* q_{l+1}$ in M, so $B_n\ldots B_{l+1}B_lq_lw_l \Rightarrow^* B_n\ldots B_{l+1}q_{l+1}$ in M. As p: $\langle qAq'\rangle \rightarrow a\langle q_1B_1q_2\rangle\langle q_2B_2q_3\rangle\ldots\langle q_nB_nq_{n+1}\rangle \in {}_GR$, ${}_MR$ contains r: $Aqa \rightarrow B_n\ldots B_1q_1$. Thus, $Aqw \Rightarrow B_n\ldots B_1q_1w_1w_2\ldots w_n$ [r] in M. Consequently,

$$Aqw \Rightarrow B_n\ldots B_1q_1w_1w_2\ldots w_n \Rightarrow^* B_n\ldots B_2q_2w_2\ldots w_n \Rightarrow^* B_nq_nw_n \Rightarrow^* q_{n+1}$$

in M. Because $q' = q_{n+1}$, $Aqw \Rightarrow^* q'$ in M, and the inductive step is completed.

If. For $i \geq 0$, $Aqw \Rightarrow^i q'$ in M implies $\langle qAq'\rangle \;{}_{lm}\Rightarrow^* w$ in G, where $w \in {}_M\Delta^*$, $A \in {}_M\Gamma$, and $q, q' \in Q$.

Basis. For $i = 0$, $Aqw \Rightarrow^i q'$ in M is ruled out, so this implication holds vacuously, and the basis is true.

Induction hypothesis. Assume that the above implication holds for every computation consisting of i or fewer moves, for some $i > 0$.

Induction step. Consider $Aqw \Rightarrow^* q'$ [$r\rho$] in M, where ρ represents a rule string consisting of i rules, and $r \in {}_MR$. Thus, $Aqw \Rightarrow^{i+1} q'$ [$r\rho$] in M. Examine the algorithm to see that r has the form r: $Aqa \rightarrow B_n\ldots B_1q_1$. Now express $Aqw \Rightarrow^* q'$ [$r\rho$] as

$$Aqav_1v_2\ldots v_n \Rightarrow B_n\ldots B_1q_1v_1v_2\ldots v_n\ [r] \Rightarrow^* B_n\ldots B_2q_2v_2\ldots v_n\ [\rho_1] \Rightarrow^* \ldots \Rightarrow^* B_nq_nv_n\ [\rho_{n-1}] \Rightarrow^* q_{n+1}\ [\rho_n]$$

where $q' = q_{n+1}$, $w = av_1v_2\ldots v_n$, and $\rho = \rho_1\ldots\rho_{n-1}\rho_n$. As ρ_j consists of no more than i rules, the induction hypothesis implies $\langle q_jB_jq_{j+1}\rangle \;{}_{lm}\Rightarrow^* v_j\ [\pi_j]$ in G, for all $j = 1, \ldots, n$. Since r: $Aqa \rightarrow B_n\ldots B_1q_1 \in {}_MR$ and $q_2, \ldots, q_{n+1} \in {}_MQ$, ${}_GR$ contains p: $\langle qAq_{n+1}\rangle \rightarrow a\langle q_1B_1q_2\rangle\langle q_2B_2q_3\rangle\ldots\langle q_nB_nq_{n+1}\rangle$ as follows from the algorithm. Thus,

$$\langle qAq_{n+1}\rangle \ {}_{lm}\Rightarrow a\langle q_1B_1q_2\rangle\langle q_2B_2q_3\rangle\ldots\langle q_nB_nq_{n+1}\rangle \ [p] \ {}_{lm}\Rightarrow^* av_1v_2\ldots v_n \ [\pi]$$

where $\pi = \pi_1\pi_2\ldots\pi_n$. As $q' = q_{n+1}$ and $w = av_1v_2\ldots v_n$, G makes this derivation $\langle qAq'\rangle \ {}_{lm}\Rightarrow^* w$. That is, the inductive step is completed. Consequently, the *if* part of this claim is true as well, so the claim holds.

Consider the above claim for $A = {}_MS$ and $q = {}_Ms$. At this point, for all $w \in {}_M\Delta^*$, $\langle {}_Ms{}_MSq'\rangle \ {}_{lm}\Rightarrow^* w$ in G iff ${}_MS{}_Msw \Rightarrow^* q'$ in M. Therefore,

$${}_GS \ {}_{lm}\Rightarrow \langle {}_Ms{}_MSq'\rangle \ {}_{lm}\Rightarrow^* w \text{ in } G \text{ iff } {}_MS{}_Msw \Rightarrow^* q' \text{ in } M$$

In other words, $L(G) = {}_\varepsilon L(M)$. Thus, this lemma holds. ■

Let

$$Ssa \rightarrow Sas, \ asa \rightarrow aas, \ asb \rightarrow q, \ aqb \rightarrow q, \ Sq \rightarrow q$$

be the input PDA of Algorithm PDA to CFG Conversion: ε-Variant, given above. Initially, this algorithm sets

$$N = \{\langle sSs\rangle, \langle qSq\rangle, \langle sSq\rangle, \langle qSs\rangle, \langle sas\rangle, \langle qaq\rangle, \langle saq\rangle, \langle qas\rangle, S\}$$

and $\Delta = \{a, b\}$. Then, the algorithm enters its first **repeat** loop. From $Ssa \rightarrow Sas$, this loop produces $\langle sSs\rangle \rightarrow a\langle sas\rangle\langle sSs\rangle$, $\langle sSs\rangle \rightarrow a\langle saq\rangle\langle qSs\rangle$, $\langle sSq\rangle \rightarrow a\langle sas\rangle\langle sSq\rangle$, $\langle sSq\rangle \rightarrow a\langle saq\rangle\langle qSq\rangle$ and adds these four rules to ${}_GR$. Analogously, from $asa \rightarrow aas$, the loop constructs $\langle sas\rangle \rightarrow a\langle sas\rangle\langle sas\rangle$, $\langle sas\rangle \rightarrow a\langle saq\rangle\langle qas\rangle$, $\langle saq\rangle \rightarrow a\langle sas\rangle\langle saq\rangle$, $\langle saq\rangle \rightarrow a\langle saq\rangle\langle qaq\rangle$ and adds these four rules to ${}_GR$. From $asb \rightarrow q$, the second **repeat** loop adds $\langle saq\rangle \rightarrow b$ to ${}_GR$. From $aqb \rightarrow q$, it constructs $\langle qaq\rangle \rightarrow b$ and includes this rule in ${}_GR$. Finally, from $Sq \rightarrow q$, this loop produces $\langle qSq\rangle \rightarrow \varepsilon$ and adds it to ${}_GR$. As a result, ${}_GR$ consists of the following rules

$$\begin{gathered}
S \rightarrow \langle sSs\rangle, \ S \rightarrow \langle sSq\rangle, \\
\langle sSs\rangle \rightarrow a\langle sas\rangle\langle sSs\rangle, \ \langle sSs\rangle \rightarrow a\langle saq\rangle\langle qSs\rangle, \\
\langle sSq\rangle \rightarrow a\langle sas\rangle\langle sSq\rangle, \ \langle sSq\rangle \rightarrow a\langle saq\rangle\langle qSq\rangle, \\
\langle sas\rangle \rightarrow a\langle sas\rangle\langle sas\rangle, \ \langle sas\rangle \rightarrow a\langle saq\rangle\langle qas\rangle, \\
\langle saq\rangle \rightarrow a\langle sas\rangle\langle saq\rangle, \ \langle saq\rangle \rightarrow a\langle saq\rangle\langle qaq\rangle, \\
\langle saq\rangle \rightarrow b, \ \langle qaq\rangle \rightarrow b, \\
\langle qSq\rangle \rightarrow \varepsilon
\end{gathered}$$

For simplicity, by using Algorithm 6.20 Useful Symbols, turn this CFG to the following equivalent CFG containing only useful symbols

$$\begin{gathered}
S \rightarrow \langle sSq\rangle, \ \langle sSq\rangle \rightarrow a\langle saq\rangle\langle qSq\rangle, \ \langle saq\rangle \rightarrow a\langle saq\rangle\langle qaq\rangle, \\
\langle saq\rangle \rightarrow b, \ \langle qaq\rangle \rightarrow b, \ \langle qSq\rangle \rightarrow \varepsilon
\end{gathered}$$

Observe that this CFG generates $\{a^nb^n \mid n \geq 1\}$.

18. First, we define the notion of a long-reading PDA.

Definition A *long-reading PDA* (${}_{long}$*PDA*) is a rewriting system, $M = (\Sigma, R)$, where

- Σ is divided into subalphabets Q, Γ, Δ such that $Q \cap (\Gamma \cup \Delta) = \emptyset$.
- R is a finite *set of rules* of the form $x \rightarrow y$, where $x \in \Gamma^*Q\Delta^*$ and $y \in \Gamma^*Q$.

Q, Γ, and Δ are referred to as the *set of states*, the *alphabet of pushdown symbols*, and the *alphabet of input symbols*, respectively. Q contains the *start state*, denoted by s, and a *set of final states*, denoted by F. Γ contains the *start symbol*, S. If $Ssw \Rightarrow^* f$ in M with $f \in F$, *M accepts w*. The set of all strings that M accepts is the *language accepted by M*, denoted by $L(M)$—that is,

$$L(M) = \{w \mid w \in \Delta^*, Ssw \Rightarrow^* f, f \in F\}$$ ■

We only sketch a proof that PDAs are as powerful as ${}_{long}$PDAs. Clearly, every PDA is a special case of a ${}_{long}$PDA. On the other hand, we sketch how to turn any ${}_{long}$PDA M to an equivalent PDA N so N simulates every computation in M move by move. That is, if M reads zero or one input symbol during a move, N simulates this move analogically. If M reads n input symbols during a move, where $n \geq 2$, then N simulates this move by n consecutive moves during which it reads these n symbols one by one. Otherwise, N works just like M, so they both accept the same language. Consequently, PDAs and ${}_{long}$PDAs are equally powerful. Prove this result rigorously.

21. We only give a hint regarding the reconsideration of Section 6.3.3 in terms of counters that accept by empty pushdown and counters that accept by final state and empty pushdown. Demonstrate that every counter I can be converted to a counter O such that ${}_{\varepsilon}L(I) = L(O)$. Consider $L = \{a^i b^j c \mid i \geq j \geq 1\}$. By contradiction, prove that there is no counter that accepts L by empty pushdown. Construct a counter M such that $L(M) = L$. Thus, the family of languages accepted by counters by empty pushdown represents a proper subfamily of the language family accepted by counters by final state and empty pushdown. Prove the above results rigorously; then, complete the rest of this solution.

Chapter 7

Applications of Models for Context-Free Languages: Syntax Analysis

In this chapter, we demonstrate the use of context-free grammars (CFGs) and pushdown automata (PDAs) in practice. More specifically, we apply them to the syntax analysis of programming languages because this analysis is literally unthinkable without these models. First, we explain how to specify the programming language syntax by using CFGs. Then, we construct syntax analyzers based on PDAs.

Today, CFGs are recognized as the most widely used specification tool for the syntactic structures of programming languages. Accordingly, PDAs, which represent the basic automaton-based counterpart to CFGs (see Theorem 6.64), usually underlie syntax analyzers, whose fundamental task is to decide whether the syntactic structures are correctly specified according to the grammatical rules. If they are not, the syntax analyzers detect and specify all the errors in them. If the structures are syntactically correct, the syntax analyzers produce *parses*—that is, the sequences of rules according to which the syntactic structures are generated because these parses are usually important to engineering techniques for language processing within which the syntax analyzer is applied. For instance, compilers make use of parses obtained in this way to direct the translation of programs written in high-level programming languages to functionally equivalent machine-language programs, which perform the computation specified by the input high-level programs.

This chapter consists of three sections. By using the terminology and results obtained in the theoretically oriented discussion in Chapter 6, Section 7.1 conceptualizes two fundamental approaches to syntax analysis—*top-down parsing* and *bottom-up parsing*. Then, Section 7.2 explains the former approach while Section 7.3 explores the latter. The style of presentation in Sections 7.2 and 7.3 slightly differs from that used in Section 7.1, which is more theoretically oriented and, therefore, gives all results and concepts in the form of mathematical statements and formulas. Instead of this theoretical approach, Sections 7.2 and 7.3 approach parsing less formally because they are primarily application-oriented. Indeed, they describe parsing in terms of easy-to-implement tables and algorithms based on them.

7.1 Introduction to Syntax Analysis

This section gives the basics of syntax analysis in terms of CFGs and PDAs, introduced in Chapter 6. Its purpose is threefold. First, it gives a quite general insight into the syntax analysis of programming languages. Second, it explains how CFGs and PDAs conceptually underlie syntax analyzers. Finally, it introduces important conventions that make syntax analyzers simple to describe and easy to implement in Sections 7.2 and 7.3.

The syntax of a programming language L is almost always specified by a CFG, $G = (\Sigma, R)$, satisfying $L = L(G)$. In essence, a syntax analyzer for G is a PDA M that decides whether a string $w \in L(G)$. M makes this decision by accepting w exactly when G generates w; consequently, $L(M) = L(G)$. In greater detail, to demonstrate that $w \in L(G)$, M simulates the construction of ${}_GS \Rightarrow^* w$ [ρ], where ρ represents a *parse* of w—that is, a sequence of rules from ${}_GR$ by which G derives w in G. If M successfully completes this construction, it usually produces the parse ρ as its output, hence it is customarily referred to as a *G-based parser*. Typically, M is designed so it constructs ${}_GS \Rightarrow^* w$ either in a leftmost way or in a rightmost way. Accordingly, there exist two different approaches to parsing, customarily referred to as *top-down parsing* and *bottom-up parsing*, which produce *left parses* and *right parses*, respectively. Both the approaches together with the two notions of parses are described as follows:

I. M simulates ${}_GS\ {}_{lm}\Rightarrow^* w$ [ρ] so it starts from ${}_GS$ and proceeds toward w by simulating leftmost derivation steps according to rules from ${}_GR$. If and when it completes ${}_GS\ {}_{lm}\Rightarrow^* w$ [ρ], it usually also produces ρ as the *left parse of w corresponding to* ${}_GS\ {}_{lm}\Rightarrow^* w$ [ρ]—the sequence of rules according to which G makes this leftmost derivation. In terms of the corresponding derivation tree ♣(${}_GS\ {}_{lm}\Rightarrow^* w$), this approach can be naturally rephrased as the construction of ♣(${}_GS\ {}_{lm}\Rightarrow^* w$) so it starts from the root and proceeds down toward the frontier, hence a parser that works in this top-down way is called a *G-based top-down parser.*

II. If M simulates ${}_GS\ {}_{rm}\Rightarrow^* w$ [ρ], it makes this simulation in reverse. That is, it starts from w and proceeds toward ${}_GS$ by making rightmost derivation steps, each of which is performed in reverse by reducing the right-hand side of a rule to its left-hand side. If and when it completes this reverse construction of ${}_GS\ {}_{rm}\Rightarrow^* w$ [ρ], it produces *reversal*(ρ) as the *right parse of w corresponding to* ${}_GS\ {}_{rm}\Rightarrow^* w$ [ρ]—the reverse sequence of rules according to which G makes this rightmost derivation. To express this construction in terms of ♣(${}_GS\ {}_{rm}\Rightarrow^* w$), a parser like this constructs this tree so it starts from its frontier w and proceeds up toward the root, hence a parser that works in this way is referred to as a *G-based bottom-up parser.*

Whichever way a parser is designed, it is always based on a PDA. Convention 7.1 simplifies the upcoming discussion of parsers by considering only one-state PDAs, which are equivalent with ordinary PDAs as follows from Algorithm 6.52, and Theorems 6.53 and 6.58. In addition, some pragmatically motivated conventions concerning configurations are introduced too.

Convention 7.1 Throughout this chapter, we assume that every PDA M has a single state denoted by ◇, so ${}_MQ = {}_MF = \{◇\}$. Instead of a configuration of the form $x◇y$ from ${}_MX$ (see Convention 6.51), we write $▷x◇y◁$, where ▷ and ◁ are two special symbols such that $\{▷, ◁\} \cap {}_M\Sigma = \emptyset$. By *pd*, we refer to the pushdown $▷x$, whose rightmost symbol represents the *pd* top symbol and ▷ is called the *pd bottom*. We consider *pd* empty if $x = \varepsilon$ and, therefore, ▷ occurs on the pushdown top. By *ins*, we refer to the *in*put *s*ymbol defined as the leftmost symbol of $y\triangleleft$. When $ins = \triangleleft$, referred to as the *input end*, all the input string has been read. As a result, M always accepts in a configuration of the form $\triangleright\diamond\triangleleft$. ■

7.1.1 Syntax Specified by Context-Free Grammars

Of course, parsers can verify the syntax of a programming language only if it is precisely specified. Today, CFGs are almost exclusively used for this purpose. The following example illustrates how to specify the syntax of common syntactical structures, such as logical expressions, by using CFGs.

Example 7.1 We want to describe logical expression of the form

$$\iota_0 o_1 \iota_1 o_2 \iota_2 \ldots \iota_{n-1} o_n \iota_n$$

where $o_j \in \{\vee, \wedge\}$, and ι_k is a logical variable, symbolically denoted by i (intuitively, i stands for an *i*dentifier) or another logical expression enclosed in parentheses, for all $1 \leq j \leq n$ and $0 \leq k \leq n$, for some $n \in {}_0\mathbb{N}$. For instance, $(i \vee i) \wedge i$ is an expression like this. A logical variable can be simply derived by this rule

$$S \rightarrow i$$

We also introduce

$$S \rightarrow (S)$$

to derive a parenthesized expression—that is, any valid expression enclosed by parentheses. To derive logical operators $\vee$ and $\wedge$, we add these two rules

$$S \rightarrow S \vee S \text{ and } S \rightarrow S \wedge S$$

As a result, we define the expressions by the four-rule CFG defined as

$$1\colon S \rightarrow S \vee S,\ 2\colon S \rightarrow S \wedge S,\ 3\colon S \rightarrow (S),\ 4\colon S \rightarrow i$$

This CFG is obviously ambiguous (see Definition 6.13); for instance, $S\ {}_{lm}\Rightarrow^* i \vee i \wedge i$ [14244] as well as $S\ {}_{lm}\Rightarrow^* i \vee i \wedge i$ [21444]. Observe, however, that the same language that the four-rule CFG generates is also generated by the unambiguous six-rule CFG defined as

$$1\colon S \rightarrow S \vee A,\ 2\colon S \rightarrow A,\ 3\colon A \rightarrow A \wedge B,\ 4\colon A \rightarrow B,\ 5\colon B \rightarrow (S),\ 6\colon B \rightarrow i$$

Both previous CFGs are left-recursive (see Definition 6.37). However, some important methods of syntax analysis work only with non-left-recursive CFGs; in fact, all the methods described in Section 7.2 are of this kind. Therefore, we give one more equivalent non-left-recursive unambiguous CFG, obtained from the previous CFG by Algorithm 6.38:

$$1\colon S \rightarrow AC,\ 2\colon C \rightarrow \vee AC,\ 3\colon C \rightarrow \varepsilon,\ 4\colon A \rightarrow BD,\ 5\colon D \rightarrow \wedge BD,\ 6\colon D \rightarrow \varepsilon,\ 7\colon B \rightarrow (S),\ 8\colon B \rightarrow i$$

Compare the three equivalent CFGs introduced in this example. Intuitively, we obviously see that in the syntax analysis, any grammatical ambiguity may represent an undesirable phenomenon, and if it does, we prefer the second CFG to the first CFG. On the other hand, the definition of the former is more succinct than the definition of the latter because the former contains a single nonterminal and four rules while the latter has three nonterminals and six rules. As already noted, some methods of syntax analysis necessitate using non-left-recursive CFGs, in which case we obviously use the third CFG, which has more nonterminals and rules than the other two CFGs in this example. Simply put, all three CFGs have their pros and cons.

Consequently, from a broader perspective, the previous example illustrates a typical process of designing an appropriate grammatical specification for a programming language in practice. Indeed, we often design several equivalent CFGs that generate the language, carefully consider their advantages and disadvantages, and based on this consideration, we choose the CFG that is optimal under given circumstances.

In what follows, we make use of the CFGs from the previous example so often that we introduce Convention 7.2 for the sake of brevity.

Convention 7.2 Consider the CFGs defined in Example 7.1. Throughout the rest of this chapter, E, H, and J denote its first, second, and third CFG, respectively. That is,

I. E denotes 1: $S \rightarrow S \vee S$, 2: $S \rightarrow S \wedge S$, 3: $S \rightarrow (S)$, 4: $S \rightarrow i$;

II. H denotes 1: $S \rightarrow S \vee A$, 2: $S \rightarrow A$, 3: $A \rightarrow A \wedge B$, 4: $A \rightarrow B$, 5: $B \rightarrow (S)$, 6: $B \rightarrow i$;

III. J denotes 1: $S \rightarrow AC$, 2: $C \rightarrow \vee AC$, 3: $C \rightarrow \varepsilon$, 4: $A \rightarrow BD$, 5: $D \rightarrow \wedge BD$, 6: $D \rightarrow \varepsilon$, 7: $B \rightarrow (S)$, 8: $B \rightarrow i$. ■

7.1.2 Top-Down Parsing

Let $I \in {}_{CFG}\Psi$. Given $w \in \Delta^*$, an I-based top-down parser works on w so it simulates a leftmost derivation of w in I. If there is no leftmost derivation of w in I, the parser rejects w because $w \notin L(I)$. On the other hand, if the parser successfully completes the simulation of $S \,{}_{lm}\!\Rightarrow^* w\ [\rho]$ in I, which means that $w \in L(I)$, the parser accepts w to express that I generates w; in addition, it often produces the left parse ρ as output too.

Algorithm 7.3 transforms any CFG I to an equivalent PDA O that acts as an I-based top-down parser. In many respects, this transformation resembles Algorithm 6.52, reformulated in terms of Convention 7.1. Notice that O performs only the following two pushdown operations—*popping* and *expanding*.

I. If a terminal a occurs as the pushdown top symbol, O *pops* a off the pushdown by a rule of the form $a\diamond a \rightarrow \diamond$, by which O removes a from the pushdown top and, simultaneously, reads the input symbol a, so it actually verifies their identity.
II. If a nonterminal A occurs as the pushdown top symbol, O simulates a leftmost derivation step made by a rule r: $A \rightarrow X_1X_2\ldots X_n \in {}_IR$, where each $X_i \in {}_I\Sigma$, $1 \leq i \leq n$, for some $n \in {}_0\mathbb{N}$ ($n = 0$ means $X_1X_2\ldots X_n = \varepsilon$). O performs this simulation so it *expands* its pushdown by using

$A\diamond \to reversal(X_1X_2\ldots X_n)\diamond$ so it replaces the pushdown top A with $X_n\ldots X_1$. To describe an expansion like this more formally, consider ${}_IS\ {}_{lm}\Rightarrow^* w\ [\rho]$ in I, where $w \in {}_I\Delta^*$, expressed as

$$\begin{aligned} {}_IS\ {}_{lm}&\Rightarrow^* vAy \\ {}_{lm}&\Rightarrow vX_1X_2\ldots X_ny \\ {}_{lm}&\Rightarrow^* vu \end{aligned}$$

where $w = vu$, so $v, u \in {}_I\Delta^*$. Suppose that I has just simulated the first portion of this derivation, $S\ {}_{lm}\Rightarrow^* vAy$; at this point, the pushdown of O contains Ay in reverse, and u is the remaining input to be read. In symbols, the PDA O occurs in the configuration $\triangleright reversal(y)A\diamond u\triangleleft$, from which it simulates $vAy\ {}_{lm}\Rightarrow vX_1X_2\ldots X_ny\ [r]$ by performing

$$\triangleright reversal(y)A\diamond u\triangleleft \Rightarrow \triangleright reversal(y)X_n\ldots X_1\diamond u\triangleleft$$

according to the rule $A\diamond \to X_n\ldots X_1\diamond$ from the set of rules in O; notice that $reversal(y)X_n\ldots X_1 = reversal(X_1\ldots X_ny)$.

Algorithm 7.3 Top-Down Parser.

Input. $I \in {}_{CFG}\Psi$.

Output. $O \in {}_{PDA}\Psi$ such that O works as an I-based top-down parser.

Method.

begin

set ${}_O\Sigma = {}_I\Sigma$ with ${}_O\Gamma = {}_IN \cup {}_I\Delta$, ${}_O\Delta = {}_I\Delta$, ${}_OS = {}_IS$
set ${}_OR = \emptyset$
for each $A \to x \in {}_IR$, where $A \in {}_IN$ and $x \in {}_I\Sigma^*$ **do**
  add $A\diamond \to reversal(x)\diamond$ to ${}_OR$ {expansion rules}
for each $a \in {}_I\Delta$ **do**
  add $a\diamond a \to \diamond$ to ${}_OR$ {popping rules}

end.

Prove Lemma 7.4 as an exercise.

Lemma 7.4 Algorithm 7.3 is correct. ■

Left Parses. Consider the top-down parser O produced by Algorithm 7.3 from $I \in {}_{CFG}\Psi$. Observe that the expansion rules in O correspond to the grammatical rules in I according to the equivalence

$$A \to x \in {}_IR \text{ iff } A\diamond \to reversal(x)\diamond \in {}_OR$$

Suppose that O simulates $S\ {}_{lm}\Rightarrow^* w\ [\rho]$ in I. To obtain ρ as the left parse of w corresponding to this derivation, record the grammatical rules corresponding to the expansion rules applied by O during this simulation. Specifically, if O makes an expansion by $A\diamond \to reversal(x)\diamond$ to simulate

Derivation in I	Left Parse	Computation in O
$\underline{S}$		$\triangleright S\diamond i \vee i \wedge i \triangleleft$
$_{lm}\Rightarrow \underline{S} \vee S$	1	$\Rightarrow \triangleright S \vee S\diamond i \vee i \wedge i \triangleleft$
$_{lm}\Rightarrow i \vee \underline{S}$	4	$\Rightarrow \triangleright S \vee i\diamond i \vee i \wedge i \triangleleft$
		$\Rightarrow \triangleright S \vee \diamond \vee i \wedge i \triangleleft$
		$\Rightarrow \triangleright S\diamond i \wedge i \triangleleft$
$_{lm}\Rightarrow i \vee \underline{S} \wedge S$	2	$\Rightarrow \triangleright S \wedge S\diamond i \wedge i \triangleleft$
$_{lm}\Rightarrow i \vee i \wedge \underline{S}$	4	$\Rightarrow \triangleright S \wedge i\diamond i \wedge i \triangleleft$
		$\Rightarrow \triangleright S \wedge \diamond \wedge i \triangleleft$
		$\Rightarrow \triangleright S\diamond i \triangleleft$
$_{lm}\Rightarrow i \vee i \wedge i$	4	$\Rightarrow \triangleright i\diamond i \triangleleft$
		$\Rightarrow \triangleright \diamond \triangleleft$

Figure 7.1 Top-down parsing of $i \vee i \wedge i$.

the application of r: $A \to x \in {}_IR$ in I, write r. After the simulation of $S\ {}_{lm}\Rightarrow^*\ w$ is completed, the sequence of all rules recorded in this way is the left parse ρ. Example 7.2 describes O that produces left parses in this way.

Example 7.2 Take the grammar E (see Convention 7.2), defined as

$$1: S \to S \vee S,\ 2: S \to S \wedge S,\ 3: S \to (S),\ 4: S \to i$$

Consider E as the input grammar I of Algorithm 7.3. This algorithm turns I to a top-down parser for I, O, which has these expansion rules

$$S\diamond \to S \vee S\diamond,\ S\diamond \to S \wedge S\diamond,\ S\diamond \to)S(\diamond,\ S\diamond \to i\diamond$$

Apart from these rules, the second **for** loop of the algorithm introduces the popping rules $a\diamond a \to \diamond$, for all $a \in \{\vee, \wedge, (,), i\}$.

For instance, consider S $_{lm}\Rightarrow^*\ i \vee i \wedge i$ [14244] in I. O parses $i \vee i \wedge i$ as described in the table given in Figure 7.1, whose columns contain the following information.

Column 1: $S\ {}_{lm}\Rightarrow^*\ i \vee i \wedge i$ [14244] in I;
Column 2: the production of the left parse 14244;
Column 3: $\triangleright S\diamond i \vee i \wedge i\triangleleft \Rightarrow^* \triangleright\diamond\triangleleft$ in O.

7.1.3 Bottom-Up Parsing

Let $G \in {}_{CFG}\Psi$. Given $w \in \Delta^*$, a G-based bottom-up parser works on w so it reversely simulates a rightmost derivation of w in G. If there is no rightmost derivation of w in G, the parser rejects w because $w \notin L(G)$. However, if the parser successfully completes the reverse simulation of $S\ {}_{rm}\Rightarrow^*\ w$ [ρ] in G, the parser accepts w to express that $w \in L(G)$, and in addition, it usually produces the right parse *reversal*(ρ) as output.

Next, we give Algorithm 7.5 that turns any CFG I to a PDA O so O acts as an I-based bottom-up parser. To give an insight into this algorithm, consider any rightmost derivation ${}_IS\ {}_{rm}\Rightarrow^*\ w$ in I, where $w \in \Delta^*$. In essence, O simulates this derivation in reverse, proceeding from w toward ${}_IS$, and during all this simulation it keeps its start symbol ${}_OS$ as the deepest symbol, occurring right behind $\triangleright$. When it reaches the configuration $\triangleright {}_OS_IS\diamond\triangleleft$, it moves to $\triangleright\diamond\triangleleft$ and, thereby, successfully completes the parsing of w. More specifically, express ${}_IS\ {}_{rm}\Rightarrow^*\ w$ in I as ${}_IS\ {}_{rm}\Rightarrow^*\ zv\ {}_{rm}\Rightarrow^*\ tv$, where $t, v \in \Delta^*$, $w = tv$, and $z \in \Sigma^*$. After reading t and making a sequence of moves corresponding to

$zv \ {}_{rm}\Rightarrow^* tv$, O uses its pushdown to record z and contains v as the remaining input to read. In brief, it occurs in the configuration $\triangleright_O Sz\diamond v\triangleleft$. To explain the next move of O that simulates the rightmost derivation step in I, express ${}_I S \ {}_{rm}\Rightarrow^* zv \ {}_{rm}\Rightarrow^* tv$ in greater detail as

$$\begin{aligned} {}_I S \ {}_{rm}\Rightarrow^* & \ yAv \\ {}_{rm}\Rightarrow & \ yxv \ [A \rightarrow x] \\ {}_{rm}\Rightarrow^* & \ tv \end{aligned}$$

where $yx = z$ and $A \rightarrow x \in {}_I R$. From $\triangleright_O Syx\diamond v\triangleleft$, which equals $\triangleright_O Sz\diamond v\triangleleft$, M simulates $yAv \ {}_{rm}\Rightarrow yxv \ [A \rightarrow x]$ in reverse as

$$\triangleright_O Syx\diamond v\triangleleft \Rightarrow \triangleright_O SyA\diamond v\triangleleft$$

In addition, whenever needed, O can shift the first symbol of the remaining input onto the pushdown. In this way, step by step, O simulates ${}_I S \ {}_{rm}\Rightarrow^* zv \ {}_{rm}\Rightarrow^* tv$ in I until it reaches the configuration $\triangleright_O S_I S\diamond\triangleleft$. To reach $\triangleright\diamond\triangleleft$ and complete the acceptance of w, we add ${}_O S_I S\diamond \rightarrow \diamond$ to ${}_O R$.

Algorithm 7.5 Bottom-Up Parser.

Input. $I \in {}_{CFG}\Psi$.

Output. $O \in {}_{PDA}\Psi$ such that O works as an I-based bottom-up parser.

Method.

begin

set ${}_O\Sigma = {}_I\Sigma \cup \{{}_O S\}$ with ${}_O\Delta = {}_I\Delta$ and ${}_O\Gamma = {}_I N \cup {}_I\Delta \cup \{{}_O S\}$, where ${}_O S \notin {}_I\Sigma$
set ${}_O R = \{{}_O S_I S\diamond \rightarrow \diamond\}$
for each $r: A \rightarrow x \in {}_I R$ **do** {reducing rules}
  add $x\diamond \rightarrow A\diamond$ to ${}_O R$
for each $a \in {}_I\Delta$ **do**
  add $\diamond a \rightarrow a\diamond$ to ${}_O R$ {shifting rules}

end.

Next we prove that $L(O) = L(I)$. In addition, in this proof, we demonstrate that O works as an I-based bottom-up parser in the sense that O simulates the construction of rightmost derivations in I in reverse.

Lemma 7.6 Algorithm 7.5 is correct—that is, $L(O) = L(I)$ and O acts as an I-based bottom-up parser.

Proof. To prove $L(I) = L(O)$, we first establish Claims A and B.

Claim A. Let

$$\begin{aligned} {}_I S \ {}_{rm}\Rightarrow^* & \ xv \\ {}_{rm}\Rightarrow^* & \ uv \quad [\pi] \end{aligned}$$

in I, where $v, u \in {}_I\Delta^*$, $x \in {}_I\Sigma^*$, and $\pi \in {}_IR^*$. Then, O computes

$$\triangleright_O S\diamond uv\triangleleft \Rightarrow^* \triangleright_O Sx\diamond v\triangleleft$$

Proof of Claim A by induction on $|\pi| \geq 0$.

Basis. Let $|\pi| = 0$. That is, $S\ {}_{rm}\Rightarrow^* xv\ {}_{rm}\Rightarrow^0 uv$ in I, so $u = x$. Observe that O computes $\triangleright_O S\diamond uv\triangleleft \Rightarrow^{|u|} \triangleright_O Su\diamond v\triangleleft$ by shifting u onto the pushdown by $|u|$ consecutive applications of shifting rules of the form $\diamond a \rightarrow a\diamond$, where $a \in {}_I\Delta$ (see Algorithm 7.5). Thus, the basis holds true.

Induction hypothesis. Suppose that the claim holds for each $\pi \in {}_IR^*$ with $|\pi| \leq i$, for some $i \in {}_0\mathbb{N}$.

Induction step. Consider

$$\begin{aligned} S\ &{}_{rm}\Rightarrow^* xv \\ &{}_{rm}\Rightarrow^* uv \quad [p\pi] \end{aligned}$$

in I, where $\pi \in {}_IR^*$, $|\pi| = i$, and $p \in {}_IR$, so $|p\pi| = i + 1$. Express $xv\ {}_{rm}\Rightarrow^* uv\ [p\pi]$ as

$$\begin{aligned} xv\ &{}_{rm}\Rightarrow y\textbf{\textit{rhs}}(p)v \quad [p] \\ &{}_{rm}\Rightarrow^* uv \quad [\pi] \end{aligned}$$

where $x = y\textbf{\textit{lhs}}(p)$ (see Convention 2.3 for ***lhs*** and ***rhs***). By inspecting Algorithm 7.5, we see that $p \in {}_IR$ implies $\textbf{\textit{rhs}}(p)\diamond \rightarrow \textbf{\textit{lhs}}(p)\diamond \in {}_OR$. In the rest of this proof, we distinguish these two cases—(1) $y\textbf{\textit{rhs}}(p) \in {}_I\Delta^*$ and (2) $y\textbf{\textit{rhs}}(p) \notin {}_I\Delta^*$.

1. Let $y\textbf{\textit{rhs}}(p) \in {}_I\Delta^*$. Then, $y\textbf{\textit{rhs}}(p) = u$. Construct $\triangleright_O S\diamond uv\triangleleft \Rightarrow^{|u|} \triangleright_O Sy\textbf{\textit{rhs}}(p)\diamond v\triangleleft$ in O by shifting u onto the pushdown, so

$$\begin{aligned} \triangleright_O S\diamond uv\triangleleft &\Rightarrow^{|u|} \triangleright_O Sy\textbf{\textit{rhs}}(p)\diamond v\triangleleft \\ &\Rightarrow \triangleright_O Sy\textbf{\textit{lhs}}(p)\diamond v\triangleleft \quad [\textbf{\textit{rhs}}(p)\diamond \rightarrow \textbf{\textit{lhs}}(p)\diamond] \end{aligned}$$

   As $x = y\textbf{\textit{lhs}}(p)$, we have just proved $\triangleright_O S\diamond uv\triangleleft \Rightarrow^* \triangleright_O Sx\diamond v\triangleleft$ in O.

2. Let $y\textbf{\textit{rhs}}(p) \notin {}_I\Delta^*$. Express $y\textbf{\textit{rhs}}(p)$ as $y\textbf{\textit{rhs}}(p) = zBt$, where $t \in {}_I\Delta^*$, $z \in {}_I\Sigma^*$, and $B \in {}_IN$, so B is the rightmost nonterminal appearing in $y\textbf{\textit{rhs}}(p)$. Consider

$$\begin{aligned} S\ &{}_{rm}\Rightarrow^* xv \\ &{}_{rm}\Rightarrow zBtv \quad [p] \\ &{}_{rm}\Rightarrow^* uv \quad [\pi] \end{aligned}$$

   Since $|\pi| = i$, $\triangleright_O S\diamond uv\triangleleft \Rightarrow^* \triangleright_O SzB\diamond tv\triangleleft$ by the inductive hypothesis. By shifting t onto the pushdown, we obtain $\triangleright_O SzB\diamond tv\triangleleft \Rightarrow^* \triangleright_O SzBt\diamond v\triangleleft$. As $y\textbf{\textit{rhs}}(p) = zBt$, we have

$$\begin{aligned} \triangleright_O S\diamond uv\triangleleft &\Rightarrow^* \triangleright_O Sy\textbf{\textit{rhs}}(p)\diamond v\triangleleft \\ &\Rightarrow \triangleright_O Sy\textbf{\textit{lhs}}(p)\diamond v\triangleleft \quad [\textbf{\textit{rhs}}(p)\diamond \rightarrow \textbf{\textit{lhs}}(p)\diamond] \end{aligned}$$

Therefore, $\triangleright_O S\Diamond uv\triangleleft \Rightarrow^* \triangleright_O Sx\Diamond v\triangleleft$ in O because $x = \textit{\textbf{ylhs}}(p)$, which completes (2).

Consequently, Claim A holds true.

Claim B. Let $\triangleright_O S\Diamond uv\triangleleft \Rightarrow^* \triangleright_O Sx\Diamond v\triangleleft$ [ρ] in O, where $u, v \in {}_O\Delta^*$, $x \in {}_I\Sigma^*$, and $\rho \in ({}_OR - \{{}_OS_IS\Diamond \rightarrow \Diamond\})^*$. Then, $xv\ {}_{rm}\Rightarrow^*\ uv$ in I.

Proof of Claim B by induction on $|\rho| \geq 0$.

Basis. Let $|\rho| = 0$, so $u = x = \varepsilon$ and $\triangleright_O S\Diamond v\triangleleft \Rightarrow^0 \triangleright_O S\Diamond v\triangleleft$ in O. Clearly, $v\ {}_{rm}\Rightarrow^0\ v$ in I.

Induction hypothesis. Suppose that the claim holds for each $\rho \in ({}_OR - \{{}_OS_IS\Diamond \rightarrow \Diamond\})^*$ with $|\rho| \leq i$, for some $i \geq 0$.

Induction step. Consider any sequence of $i + 1$ moves of the form $\triangleright_O S\Diamond uv\triangleleft \Rightarrow^* \triangleright_O Sx\Diamond v\triangleleft$ [ρr] in O, where $u, v \in {}_O\Delta^*$, $x \in {}_I\Sigma^*$, $\rho \in ({}_OR - \{{}_OS_IS\Diamond \rightarrow \Diamond\})^*$, $|\rho| = i$, and $r \in {}_OR - \{{}_OS_IS\Diamond \rightarrow \Diamond\}$. Express $\triangleright_O S\Diamond uv\triangleleft \Rightarrow^* \triangleright_O Sx\Diamond v\triangleleft$ [ρr] as

$$\begin{array}{llll} \triangleright_O S\Diamond uv\triangleleft & \Rightarrow^* & \triangleright_O Sy\Diamond t\triangleleft & [\rho] \\ & \Rightarrow & \triangleright_O Sx\Diamond v\triangleleft & [r] \end{array}$$

where $y \in {}_I\Sigma^*$ and $t \in {}_O\Delta^*$. As $r \neq {}_OS_IS\Diamond \rightarrow \Diamond$, either $\textit{\textbf{rhs}}(r) = A\Diamond$ with $A \in {}_IN$ or $\textit{\textbf{rhs}}(r) = a\Diamond$ with $a \in {}_O\Delta$. Next, we distinguish these two cases—(1) $\textit{\textbf{rhs}}(r) = A\Diamond$ with $A \in {}_IN$ and (2) $\textit{\textbf{rhs}}(r) = a\Diamond$ with $a \in {}_O\Delta$.

1. Let $\textit{\textbf{rhs}}(r) = A\Diamond$ with $A \in {}_IN$, so $t = v$, r is of the form $z\Diamond \rightarrow A\Diamond$, $x = hA$, and $y = hz$, for some $A \rightarrow z \in {}_IR$ and $h \in {}_I\Sigma^*$. By using $A \rightarrow z \in {}_IR$, I makes $hAv\ {}_{rm}\Rightarrow\ hzv$. By the induction hypothesis, $yv\ {}_{rm}\Rightarrow^*\ uv$ in I. Thus, $xv\ {}_{rm}\Rightarrow^*\ uv$ in I.
2. Let $\textit{\textbf{rhs}}(r) = a\Diamond$ with $a \in {}_O\Delta$, so $t = av$, r is of the form $\Diamond a \rightarrow a\Diamond$, $x = ya$. Thus, $xv = yt$. Recall that $\triangleright_O S\Diamond uv\triangleleft \Rightarrow^* \triangleright_O Sy\Diamond t\triangleleft$ [ρ] with $|\rho| = i$. By the induction hypothesis, $yt\ {}_{rm}\Rightarrow^*\ uv$ in I. Since $xv = yt$, $xv\ {}_{rm}\Rightarrow^*\ uv$ in I.

Thus, Claim B holds true.

Consider Claim A for $v = \varepsilon$ and $x = {}_IS$. At this point, for all $u \in {}_I\Delta^*$, ${}_IS\ {}_{rm}\Rightarrow^*\ u$ in I implies $\triangleright_O S\Diamond u\triangleleft \Rightarrow^* \triangleright_O S_IS\Diamond\triangleleft$ in O. By using ${}_OS_IS\Diamond \rightarrow \Diamond$, O makes $\triangleright_O S_IS\Diamond\triangleleft \Rightarrow \triangleright\Diamond\triangleleft$ in O. Hence, $L(I) \subseteq L(O)$.

Consider Claim B for $v = \varepsilon$ and $x = {}_IS$. Under this consideration, if $\triangleright_O S\Diamond u\triangleleft \Rightarrow^* \triangleright_O S_IS\Diamond\triangleleft$ [ρ] in O, then ${}_IS\ {}_{rm}\Rightarrow^*\ u$ in I, for all $u \in {}_I\Delta^*$. During any acceptance of a string, $u \in {}_I\Delta^*$, O applies ${}_OS_IS\Diamond \rightarrow \Diamond$ precisely once, and this application occurs during the very last step to remove ${}_OS_IS$ and reach the configuration $\triangleright\Diamond\triangleleft$. Indeed, observe that any earlier application of this rule implies that subsequently O can never completely read u and, simultaneously, empty the pushdown; the details of this observation are left as an exercise. Thus, $\triangleright_O S\Diamond u\triangleleft \Rightarrow^* \triangleright\Diamond\triangleleft$ [ρ] in O implies ${}_IS\ {}_{rm}\Rightarrow^*\ u$ in I, so $L(O) \subseteq L(I)$.

Consequently, $L(I) = L(O)$ because $L(I) \subseteq L(O)$ and $L(O) \subseteq L(I)$. As an exercise, examine the proof of Claim A to see that O works so it simulates rightmost derivations in I in reverse. Thus, O works as an I-based bottom-up parser, and Lemma 7.6 holds true. ■

Right Parses. Consider the I-based top-down parser O produced by Algorithm 7.5 from $I \in {}_{CFG}\Psi$. Observe that the reducing rules in O correspond to the grammatical rules in I according to the equivalence

$$A \rightarrow x \in {}_IR \text{ iff } x\diamond \rightarrow A\diamond \in {}_OR$$

Suppose that O reversely simulates ${}_IS\ {}_{rm}\Rightarrow^* w\ [\rho]$ in I. To obtain *reversal*(ρ) as the right parse of w corresponding to ${}_IS\ {}_{rm}\Rightarrow^* w\ [\rho]$, record the reducing rules applied by O during this simulation. That is, if O makes a reduction by $x\diamond \rightarrow A\diamond$ to simulate the application of r: $A \rightarrow x \in {}_IR$ in I, write out r. When the simulation of ${}_IS\ {}_{rm}\Rightarrow^* w\ [\rho]$ is completed, the corresponding right parse is obtained in this way. Example 7.3 illustrates O extended in this way.

We have described O in terms of reverse simulation of rightmost derivations in I. As noted in the beginning of this section, instead of this description, the way O works can be also described in terms of derivation trees constructed in a bottom-up way so this construction starts from their frontiers and proceeds up toward the roots. Leaving a general version of this alternative description as an exercise, we include such a bottom-up construction of a derivation tree within Example 7.3.

Example 7.3 Consider the CFG H (see Convention 7.2), defined as

$$1: S \rightarrow S \vee A,\ 2: S \rightarrow A,\ 3: A \rightarrow A \wedge B,\ 4: A \rightarrow B,\ 5: B \rightarrow (S),\ 6: B \rightarrow i$$

Consider H as the input grammar I of Algorithm 7.5. This algorithm turns it to the H-based bottom-up parser O, which has these reducing rules

$$1: S \vee A\diamond \rightarrow S\diamond,\ 2: A\diamond \rightarrow S\diamond,\ 3: A \wedge B\diamond \rightarrow A\diamond,\ 4: B\diamond \rightarrow A\diamond,\ 5: (S)\diamond \rightarrow B\diamond,\ 6: i\diamond \rightarrow B\diamond$$

We have labeled these rules by the labels that denote the grammatical rules from which they are constructed; for instance, 1: $S \vee A\diamond \rightarrow S\diamond$ is constructed from 1: $S \rightarrow S \vee A$. Apart from these six rules, the algorithm adds the shifting rules $\diamond a \rightarrow a\diamond$, for all $a \in \{\vee, \wedge, (,), i\}$. It also introduces $ZS\diamond \rightarrow \diamond$, where Z is declared as the start pushdown symbol of O.

For instance, take $i \vee i \wedge i$ as the input string. Consider the table in Figure 7.2. This table explains how O parses $i \vee i \wedge i$ by using its three columns, whose contents are described next.

Derivation Tree in I	Right Parse	Computation in O
$i\vee i\wedge i$		$\triangleright Z\diamond i\vee i\wedge i\triangleleft$
		$\Rightarrow \triangleright Zi\diamond \vee i\wedge i\triangleleft$
$B\langle i\rangle\vee i\wedge i$	6	$\Rightarrow \triangleright ZB\diamond \vee i\wedge i\triangleleft$
$A\langle B\langle i\rangle\rangle\vee i\wedge i$	4	$\Rightarrow \triangleright ZA\diamond \vee i\wedge i\triangleleft$
$S\langle A\langle B\langle i\rangle\rangle\rangle\vee i\wedge i$	2	$\Rightarrow \triangleright ZS\diamond \vee i\wedge i\triangleleft$
		$\Rightarrow \triangleright ZS\vee\diamond i\wedge i\triangleleft$
		$\Rightarrow \triangleright ZS\vee i\diamond \wedge i\triangleleft$
$S\langle A\langle B\langle i\rangle\rangle\rangle\vee B\langle i\rangle\wedge i$	6	$\Rightarrow \triangleright ZS\vee B\diamond \wedge i\triangleleft$
$S\langle A\langle B\langle i\rangle\rangle\rangle\vee A\langle B\langle i\rangle\rangle\wedge i$	4	$\Rightarrow \triangleright ZS\vee A\diamond \wedge i\triangleleft$
		$\Rightarrow \triangleright ZS\vee A\wedge\diamond i\triangleleft$
		$\Rightarrow \triangleright ZS\vee A\wedge i\diamond\triangleleft$
$S\langle A\langle B\langle i\rangle\rangle\rangle\vee A\langle B\langle i\rangle\rangle\wedge B\langle i\rangle$	6	$\Rightarrow \triangleright ZS\vee A\wedge B\diamond\triangleleft$
$S\langle A\langle B\langle i\rangle\rangle\rangle\vee A\langle A\langle B\langle i\rangle\rangle\wedge B\langle i\rangle\rangle$	3	$\Rightarrow \triangleright ZS\vee A\diamond\triangleleft$
$S\langle S\langle A\langle B\langle i\rangle\rangle\rangle\vee A\langle A\langle B\langle i\rangle\rangle\wedge B\langle i\rangle\rangle\rangle$	1	$\Rightarrow \triangleright ZS\diamond\triangleleft$
		$\Rightarrow \triangleright\diamond\triangleleft$

Figure 7.2 Bottom-up parsing of $i \vee i \wedge i$.

Column 1: the bottom-up construction of ♣($S\ {}_{rm}\Rightarrow^{*}\ i \vee i \wedge i$) in I
Column 2: the construction of 64264631 as the right parse
Column 3: $\triangleright Z\diamond i \vee i \wedge i\triangleleft \Rightarrow^{*} \triangleright\diamond\triangleleft$ in O

Take the resulting right parse 64264631. Reverse it to obtain 13646246, according to which I makes the following rightmost derivation

$$
\begin{aligned}
S &\ {}_{rm}\Rightarrow S \vee A & [1]\\
&\ {}_{rm}\Rightarrow S \vee A \wedge B & [3]\\
&\ {}_{rm}\Rightarrow S \vee A \wedge i & [6]\\
&\ {}_{rm}\Rightarrow S \vee B \wedge i & [4]\\
&\ {}_{rm}\Rightarrow S \vee i \wedge i & [6]\\
&\ {}_{rm}\Rightarrow A \vee i \wedge i & [2]\\
&\ {}_{rm}\Rightarrow B \vee i \wedge i & [4]\\
&\ {}_{rm}\Rightarrow i \vee i \wedge i & [6]
\end{aligned}
$$

In brief, $S\ {}_{rm}\Rightarrow^{*}\ i \vee i \wedge i$ [13646246].

The algorithms and lemmas achieved earlier in this section have their important theoretical consequences. Indeed, in Section 6.3.2, we have left a proof that ${}_{CFG}\Phi \subseteq {}_{PDA}\Phi$ as an exercise (see Theorem 6.53). Observe that this inclusion follows from Algorithm 7.3 and Lemma 7.4. Alternatively, Algorithm 7.5 and Lemma 7.6 imply ${}_{CFG}\Phi \subseteq {}_{PDA}\Phi$, too.

Corollary 7.7 For every $I \in {}_{CFG}\Psi$, there exists an equivalent $O \in {}_{PDA}\Psi$, so ${}_{CFG}\Phi \subseteq {}_{PDA}\Phi$. ■

The parsers constructed in Algorithms 7.3 and 7.5 represent a framework of most top-down and bottom-up parsers, respectively. In general, however, they work in a nondeterministic way, and as such, they are difficult to implement and apply. Therefore, throughout the upcoming two application-oriented sections, we concentrate our attention solely on their deterministic versions, which are central to parsing in practice. Furthermore, up to now, this chapter has still maintained the mathematical terminology used in Chapter 6. The following convention relaxes this strict formalism to make the upcoming parsers easy to implement.

Convention 7.8 Every parser discussed throughout Sections 7.2 and 7.3 is deterministic. Rather than its strictly mathematical rule-based specification, we describe it as a *parsing algorithm* based on its *parsing table*. Although every parsing table always depends on the parser in question, its general format represents a two-dimensional array with rows and columns denoted by top pushdown symbols and input symbols, respectively. If A occurs on the pushdown top and *ins* is the current input symbol, the entry corresponding to A and *ins* specifies the proper parsing action to be performed in this configuration.

Consider the two special symbols, $\triangleright$ and $\triangleleft$, which always denote the pushdown bottom and the input end, respectively (see Convention 7.1). The parser finds out that the pushdown is empty when $\triangleright$ appears on the pushdown top. Similarly, when $\triangleleft$ occurs as the input symbol, all the input string has been read. Of course, O can never remove $\triangleright$ or $\triangleleft$. ■

7.2 Top-Down Parsing

Compared to Section 7.1, Sections 7.2 and 7.3 become less theoretical and more practical. Regarding top-down parsing, although Section 7.1 has sketched its basic methodology in general, this section gives a more realistic insight into this approach to parsing because it restricts its attention to deterministic top-down parsers, which fulfill a central role in practice.

Take a CFG G and a G-based top-down parser working on an input string w (see Section 7.1). Recall that a top-down parser verifies that w is syntactically correct so it simulates the construction of a derivation tree for w in a top-down way. That is, reading w from left to the right, the parser starts from the tree root and proceeds down toward the frontier denoted by w. To put it in derivation terms, it builds up the leftmost derivation of w so it starts from ${}_GS$ and proceeds toward w. If the parser works deterministically, the parser makes a completely deterministic selection of an applied rule during every single computational step.

Section 7.2, which consists of two subsections, concentrates its attention on *predictive parsing*, which is the most frequently used deterministic top-down parsing method in practice. Section 7.2.1 defines and discusses predictive sets and LL grammars, where the first L stands for the *l*eft-to-right scan of the input string w while the second L means that the parser simulates the *l*eftmost derivation of w. By using the predictive sets, the parser makes the simulation of leftmost derivations in a completely deterministic way. Section 7.2.2 describes two fundamental versions of predictive parsing. First, it explains *recursive descent parsing*, which frees us from explicitly implementing a pushdown list. Then, it uses the LL grammars and predictive sets to construct predictive tables used by *predictive table-driven parsing*, which explicitly implements a pushdown list. In this version of predictive parsing, any grammatical change leads only to a modification of the table while its control procedure remains unchanged, which is obviously its great advantage. We also explain how predictive parsers handle the syntax errors to recover from them.

Throughout this section, we make frequent use of the terminology introduced in Section 2.1, such as *suffixes*, *prefixes*, and *symbol*. In the examples, we illustrate the material under discussion in terms of the CFG J from Convention 7.2.

7.2.1 Predictive Sets and LL Grammars

Consider a CFG, $G = ({}_G\Sigma, {}_GR)$ and an input string w. Let M be a G-based top-down parser constructed by Algorithm 7.3. Suppose that M has already found the beginning of the leftmost derivation for w, $S \;{}_{lm}\!\Rightarrow^* tAv$, where t is a prefix of w. More precisely, let $w = taz$, where a is the current input symbol, which follows t in w, and z is the suffix of w, which follows a. In tAv, A is the leftmost nonterminal to be rewritten in the next step. Suppose that there exist several different A-rules. Under the assumption that M works deterministically (see Convention 7.8), M has to select one of the A-rules to continue the parsing process, and it cannot revise this selection later on. If M represents a *predictive parser*, it selects the right rule by predicting whether its application gives rise to a leftmost derivation of a string starting with a. To make this prediction, every rule $r \in {}_GR$ is accompanied with its *predictive set* containing all terminals that can begin a string resulting from a derivation whose first step is made by r. If the A-rules have their predictive sets pairwise disjoint, M deterministically selects the rule whose predictive set contains a. To construct the predictive sets, we first need the *first* and *follow* sets, described next.

The predictive set corresponding to $r \in {}_GR$ obviously contains the terminals that occur as the first symbol in a string derived from ***rhs***(r), and this observation gives rise to Definition 7.9.

Definition 7.9 Let $G = ({}_G\Sigma, {}_GR)$ be a CFG. For every string $x \in {}_G\Sigma^*$,

$$first(x) = \{a \mid x \Rightarrow^* w, \text{ where either } w \in {}_G\Delta^+ \text{ with } a = symbol(w, 1) \text{ or } w = \varepsilon = a\}$$

where *symbol*$(w, 1)$ denotes the leftmost symbol of w (see Section 2.1). ■

In general, *first* is defined in terms of $\Rightarrow$, but we could rephrase this definition in terms of the leftmost derivations, which play a crucial role in top-down parsing, because for every $w \in {}_G\Delta^*$, $x \Rightarrow^* w$ iff $x \,_{lm}\!\Rightarrow^* w$ (see Theorem 6.5). That is,

$$first(x) = \{a \mid x \,_{lm}\!\Rightarrow^* w, \text{ where either } w \in {}_G\Delta^+ \text{ with } a = symbol(w, 1) \text{ or } w = \varepsilon = a\}$$

It is worth noticing that if $x \Rightarrow^* \varepsilon$, where $x \in \Sigma^*$, then ε is in *first*(x); as a special case, for $x = \varepsilon$, *first*$(\varepsilon) = \{\varepsilon\}$.

Next, we will construct the *first* sets for all strings contained in ${}_G\Delta \cup \{\mathbf{lhs}(r) \mid r \in {}_GR\} \cup \{y \mid y \in suffixes(\mathbf{rhs}(r))$ with $r \in {}_GR\}$. We make use of some subsets of these *first* sets in this section (see Algorithm 7.12 and Definition 7.13).

Basic Idea. To construct *first*(x) for every $x \in {}_G\Delta \cup \{\mathbf{lhs}(r) \mid r \in {}_GR\} \cup \{y \mid y \in suffixes(\mathbf{rhs}(r))$ with $r \in {}_GR\}$, we initially set *first*(a) to $\{a\}$ for every $a \in {}_G\Delta \cup \{\varepsilon\}$ because $a \,_{lm}\!\Rightarrow^0 a$ for these as. If $A \rightarrow uw \in {}_GR$ with $u \Rightarrow^* \varepsilon$, then $A \Rightarrow^* w$, so we add the symbols of *first*(w) to *first*(A) (by Algorithm 6.24, we can determine whether u is a string consisting of ε-nonterminals, in which case $u \,_{lm}\!\Rightarrow^* \varepsilon$). Keep extending all the *first* sets in this way until no more symbols can be added to any of the *first* sets.

Algorithm 7.10 *first.*

Input. A CFG, $G = ({}_G\Sigma, {}_GR)$.

Output. Set *first*(u) for every $u \in {}_G\Delta \cup \{\varepsilon\} \cup \{\mathbf{lhs}(r) \mid r \in {}_GR\} \cup \{y \mid y \in suffixes(\mathbf{rhs}(r))$ with $r \in {}_GR\}$.

Method.

```
begin
   set first(a) = {a} for every a ∈ GΔ ∪ {ε}, and
   set all the other constructed first sets to ∅
   repeat
      if r ∈ GR, u ∈ prefixes(rhs(r)) and u lm⇒* ε then
      begin
         extend first(suffix(rhs(r), |rhs(r)| − |u|)) by first(symbol(rhs(r), |u| + 1)) and
         extend first(lhs(r)) by first(suffix(rhs(r), |rhs(r)| − |u|))
      end {of the if statement}
   until no change
end.
```

The ε-rules deserve our special attention because they may give rise to derivations that erase substrings of sentential forms, and this possible erasure complicates the selection of the next applied rule. Indeed, consider a CFG, $G = ({}_G\Sigma, {}_GR)$, and suppose that $A \rightarrow x \in {}_GR$ with $x \,_{lm}\!\Rightarrow^* \varepsilon$. At this point, the parser needs to decide whether from A, it should make either $A \,_{lm}\!\Rightarrow x \,_{lm}\!\Rightarrow^* \varepsilon$ or a derivation that produces a nonempty string. To make this decision, we need to determine the set *follow*(A)

containing all terminals that can follow A in any sentential form; if this set contains the current input symbol that is out of *first*(x), the parser simulates $A\ _{lm}\Rightarrow x\ _{lm}\Rightarrow^* \varepsilon$. In addition, to express that a sentential form ends with A, we include $\triangleleft$ into *follow*(A) (see Convention 7.1 for $\triangleleft$).

Definition 7.11 Let $G = ({}_G\Sigma, {}_GR)$ be a CFG. For every $A \in {}_GN$,

$$follow(A) = \{a \in {}_G\Delta \cup \{\triangleleft\} \mid Aa \in substrings(F(G)\{\triangleleft\})\}$$

where $F(G)$ denotes the set of sentential forms of G (see Definition 6.1). ■

Basic Idea. We next construct *follow*(A) for every $A \in N$. As the start symbol S represents a sentential form, we start by initializing *follow*(S) with $\{\triangleleft\}$. Consider any $B \rightarrow uAv \in {}_GR$. If a is a terminal in *first*(v), then $Aa \in substrings(F(G))$, so we add a to *follow*(A). In addition, if ε is in *first*(v), then $v\ _{lm}\Rightarrow^* \varepsilon$ and, consequently, $follow(B) \subseteq follow(A)$, so we add all symbols from *follow*(B) to *follow*(A). Keep extending all the *follow* sets in this way until no symbol can be added to any of them.

Algorithm 7.12 *follow*.

Input. A CFG, $G = ({}_G\Sigma, {}_GR)$, and
first(u) for every $u \in \{y \mid y \in suffixes(\boldsymbol{rhs}(r))$ with $r \in {}_GR\}$ (see Algorithm 7.10).

Output. Sets *follow*(A) for all $A \in {}_GN$.

Method.

begin
  set *follow*(S) = $\{\triangleleft\}$, and
  set all the other constructed *follow* sets to $\emptyset$
  repeat
    if $r \in {}_GR$ **and** $Au \in suffixes(\boldsymbol{rhs}(r))$, where $A \in {}_GN$, $u \in {}_G\Sigma^*$ **then**
    begin
      add the symbols in $(first(u) - \{\varepsilon\})$ to *follow*(A)
      if $\varepsilon \in first(u)$ **then**
        add the symbols in *follow*($\boldsymbol{lhs}(r)$) to *follow*(A)
    end
  until no change
end.

Based on the *first* and *follow* sets, we define the predictive sets as in Definition 7.13.

Definition 7.13 For each $r \in {}_GR$, its *predictive set* is denoted by *predictive-set*(r) and defined as follows:

i. if $\varepsilon \notin first(\boldsymbol{rhs}(r))$, $predictive\text{-}set(r) = first(\boldsymbol{rhs}(r))$, and
ii. if $\varepsilon \in first(\boldsymbol{rhs}(r))$, $predictive\text{-}set(r) = (first(\boldsymbol{rhs}(r)) - \{\varepsilon\}) \cup follow(\boldsymbol{lhs}(r))$. ■

7.2.1.1 LL Grammars

Reconsider the discussion in the very beginning of this section. Recall that G, M, and w denote a CFG, a G-based top-down parser, and an input string w, respectively. Suppose that M has already simulated the beginning of the leftmost derivation $S\ {}_{lm}\Rightarrow^* tAv$ for an input string taz, where a is the current input symbol and $taz = w$, and it needs to select one of several different A-rules to rewrite A in tAv and, thereby, make another step. If for an A-rule r, $a \in$ *predictive-set*(r) and for any other A-rule p, $a \notin$ *predictive-set*(p), M deterministically selects r. This idea leads to Definition 7.14 of LL grammars.

Definition 7.14 A CFG $G = ({}_G\Sigma, {}_GR)$ is an *LL grammar* if for each $A \in N$, any two different A-rules, $p, q \in {}_GR$ and $p \neq q$, satisfy *predictive-set*$(p) \cap$ *predictive-set*$(q) = \emptyset$. ■

As already noted, in *LL grammars*, the first L stands for a *l*eft-to-right scan of symbols and the other L stands for a *l*eftmost derivation. Sometimes, in greater detail, the literature refers to the LL grammars as *LL*(1) *grammars* to point out that the top-down parsers based on these grammars always look at one input symbol during each step of the parsing process. Indeed, these grammars represent a special case of *LL*(k) *grammars*, where $k \geq 1$, which underlie parsers that make a k-symbol lookahead. In this introductory book, however, we discuss only LL(1) grammars and simply refer to them as LL grammars for brevity.

Example 7.4 Consider the CFG J (see Convention 7.2), defined as

$$1: S \rightarrow AC,\ 2: C \rightarrow \vee AC,\ 3: C \rightarrow \varepsilon,\ 4: A \rightarrow BD,\ 5: D \rightarrow \wedge BD,\ 6: D \rightarrow \varepsilon,\ 7: B \rightarrow (S),\ 8: B \rightarrow i$$

Algorithm 7.10 *first*. For each rule in J, we construct *first*(u) for every $u \in \Delta \cup \{\varepsilon\} \cup \{$***lhs***$(r))|\ r \in {}_JR\} \cup \{y|\ y \in$ *suffixes*(***rhs***(r)) with $r \in {}_JR\}$ by Algorithm 7.10. First, we set *first*$(a) = \{a\}$ for every $a \in \{i, (,), \vee, \wedge\} \cup \{\varepsilon\}$. Consider $B \rightarrow i$. By the **repeat** loop of Algorithm 7.10, as *first*$(i) = \{i\}$, we include i into *first*(B). As $i \in$ *first*(B) and $A \rightarrow BD \in {}_JR$, we add i to *first*(BD) as well. Complete this construction as an exercise. However, to construct *predictive-set*(r) for each $r \in {}_JR$, we need only $\{$*first*(***rhs***(r))$|\ r \in {}_JR\}$, which represents a subset of all the *first* sets constructed by Algorithm 7.10. The members of $\{$*first*(***rhs***(r))$|\ r \in {}_JR\}$ are listed in the second column of the table given in Figure 7.3.

Algorithm 7.12 *follow*. Consider *first*(u) for each $u \in \{y|\ y \in$ *suffixes*(***rhs***(r)) with $r \in {}_JR\}$. We construct *follow*(X), for every $X \in {}_JN$ by Algorithm 7.12 as follow. We initially have *follow*$(S) = \{\lhd\}$. As $B \rightarrow (S) \in {}_JR$ and $) \in$ *first*$())$, we add) to *follow*(S). Since (i) $S \rightarrow AC \in {}_JR$, (ii) $\varepsilon \in$ *first*(C), and (iii) *follow*(S) contains) and $\lhd$, we add) and $\lhd$ to *follow*(A). As $\vee \in$ *first*(C), we add $\vee$ to

Rule r	*first*(***rhs***(r))	*follow*(***lhs***(r))	*predictive-set*(r)
$S \rightarrow AC$	i, (	), $\lhd$	i, (
$C \rightarrow \vee AC$	$\vee$	), $\lhd$	$\vee$
$C \rightarrow \varepsilon$	ε	), $\lhd$	), $\lhd$
$A \rightarrow BD$	i, (	$\vee$,), $\lhd$	i, (
$D \rightarrow \wedge BD$	$\wedge$	$\vee$,), $\lhd$	$\wedge$
$D \rightarrow \varepsilon$	ε	$\vee$,), $\lhd$	$\vee$,), $\lhd$
$B \rightarrow (S)$	(	$\wedge$, $\vee$,), $\lhd$	(
$B \rightarrow i$	i	$\wedge$, $\vee$,), $\lhd$	i

Figure 7.3 Predictive sets for rules in $_JR$.

follow(A), too. Complete this construction as an exercise. The third column of the table given in Figure 7.3 contains *follow*(**lhs**(r)) for each $r \in {}_JR$.

Predictive sets (see Definition 7.13). The fourth column of the table in Figure 7.3 contains *predictive-set*(r) for each $r \in {}_JR$. Notice that *follow*(**lhs**(r)) is needed to determine *predictive-set*(r) if $\varepsilon \in$ *first*(**rhs**(r)) because at this point *predictive-set*(r) = (*first*(**rhs**(r)) − {ε}) ∪ *follow*(**lhs**(r)); if $\varepsilon \notin$ *first*(**rhs**(r)), it is not needed because *predictive-set*(r) = *first*(**rhs**(r)) (see Definition 7.13). Take, for instance, $S \rightarrow AC \in {}_JR$ with *first*(AC)) = {i, (}. As $\varepsilon \notin$ *first*(**rhs**(r)), *predictive-set*($S \rightarrow AC$) = *first*(AC) = {i, (}. Consider $C \rightarrow \varepsilon \in {}_JR$ with *first*(ε) = {ε} and *follow*(C) = {), ⊲}. As $\varepsilon \in$ *first*(**rhs**($C \rightarrow \varepsilon$)), *predictive-set*($C \rightarrow \varepsilon$) = (*first*(ε) − {ε}) ∪ *follow*(C) = ∅ ∪ {), ⊲} = {), ⊲}. Complete this construction as an exercise.

LL grammar. Observe that *predictive-set*($C \rightarrow \vee AC$) ∩ *predictive-set*($C \rightarrow \varepsilon$) = {∨} ∩ {), ⊲} = ∅. Analogously, *predictive-set*($D \rightarrow \wedge BD$) ∩ *predictive-set*($D \rightarrow \varepsilon$) = ∅ and *predictive-set*($B \rightarrow (S)$) ∩ *predictive-set*($B \rightarrow i$) = ∅. Thus, J is an LL CFG. ■

7.2.2 Predictive Parsing

In this section, we first describe the recursive-descent parsing method. Then we use the LL grammars and their predictive sets to create predictive tables and deterministic top-down parsers driven by these tables. Finally, we explain how to handle errors in predictive parsing.

7.2.2.1 Predictive Recursive-Descent Parsing

Given an LL grammar, $G = ({}_G\Sigma, {}_GR)$, we next explain how to construct a *G-based predictive recursive-descent parser*, which makes use of programming routines **SUCCESS** and **ERROR**, described in the next convention.

Convention 7.15 SUCCESS announces a successful completion of the parsing process while **ERROR** announces a syntax error in the parsed program. ■

It is worth noting that the following parser moves back to the symbol preceding the current input symbol. As demonstrated shortly, it performs this return when a rule selection is made by using a symbol from the *follow* set; at this point, this symbol is not actually used up, so the parser needs to move back to the symbol preceding *ins*.

Reconsider Algorithm 7.3, which turns a CFG G to a G-based top-down parser M as a PDA, which requires, strictly speaking, an implementation of a pushdown list. As a crucial advantage, *recursive descent*—that is, a top-down parsing method discussed next—frees us from this implementation. Indeed, the pushdown list is invisible in this method because it is actually realized by the pushdown used to support recursion in the programming language in which we write the recursive-descent parser. As this method does not require an explicit manipulation with the pushdown list, it comes as no surprise that it is extremely popular in practice. Therefore, in its next description, we pay a special attention to its implementation.

Basic Idea. Consider a programming language defined by an LL grammar G. Let $w = t_1 \ldots t_j t_{j+1} \ldots t_m$ be an input string, so each t_j is a terminal in terms of G. Like any top-down parser, a G-based recursive-descent parser simulates the construction of a derivation tree with its frontier equal to w by using the grammatical rules so it starts from the root and works down to the leaves, reading w in a left-to-right way. In terms of derivations, the parser looks for the leftmost derivation of w. To find it, for each nonterminal Y, the parser has a Boolean function, *rd-function* Y, which simulates rewriting the leftmost nonterminal Y. More specifically, with the right-hand side of a Y-rule, $Y \rightarrow X_1 \ldots X_i X_{i+1} \ldots X_n$, *rd-function* Y proceeds from X_1 to X_n. Assume that *rd-function* Y currently works with X_i and that t_j is the input symbol. At this point, depending on whether X_i is a terminal or a nonterminal, this function works as follows:

- If X_i is a terminal, *rd-function* Y matches X_i against t_j. If $X_i = t_j$, it reads t_j and proceeds to X_{i+1} and t_{j+1}. If $X_i \neq t_j$, a syntax error occurs, which the parser has to handle.
- If X_i is a nonterminal, the parser finds out whether there is an X_i-rule r satisfying $t_j \in$ *predictive-set*(r). If so, the parser calls *rd-function* X_i, which simulates rewriting X_i according to r. If not, a syntax error occurs, and the parser has to handle it.

The parser starts the parsing process from *rd-function* S, which corresponds to the start symbol of G and ends when it eventually returns to this function after completely reading w. If during this entire process no syntax error occurs, G-based recursive-descent parser has found the leftmost derivation of w, which thus represents a syntactically well-formed program; otherwise, w is syntactically incorrect.

As this method does not require explicitly manipulating a pushdown list, it is very popular in practice; in particular, it is suitable for parsing declarations and general program flow as Example 7.5 illustrates. This example describes every *rd-function* Y as a Boolean Pascal-like function

```
function Y: Boolean;
begin
  ⋮
end
```

Just like any Boolean function in Pascal, a function like this returns a result by setting a true-false value to the function name Y within the function body.

Example 7.5 Reconsider the LL grammar J (see Convention 7.2 and Example 7.4). Figure 7.4 repeats its rules together with the corresponding predictive sets.

Next, we construct a J-based recursive-descent parser as a collection of Boolean *rd-functions* corresponding to nonterminals S, A, B, C, and D. By using the predictive sets, we make this construction so the parser always selects the next applied rule deterministically.

Rule r	*predictive-set*(r)
$S \rightarrow AC$	i, (
$C \rightarrow \vee AC$	$\vee$
$C \rightarrow \varepsilon$	), $\triangleleft$
$A \rightarrow BD$	i, (
$D \rightarrow \wedge BD$	$\wedge$
$D \rightarrow \varepsilon$	$\vee$,), $\triangleleft$
$B \rightarrow (S)$	(
$B \rightarrow i$	i

Figure 7.4 Rules in $_JR$ together with their predictive sets.

Consider the start symbol S and the only S-rule $S \to AC$ with *predictive-set*($S \to AC$) = {*i*, (}. As a result, *rd-function S* has the following form:

```
function S: Boolean;
begin
  set S to false
  if ins ∈ {i, (} then
    if A then
      if C then
        set S to true
end
```

Consider the two C-rules that include $C \to \vee AC$ with *predictive-set*($C \to \vee AC$) = {∨} and $C \to \varepsilon$ with *predictive-set*($C \to \varepsilon$) = {), ◁}. Therefore, *rd-function C* selects $C \to \vee AC$ if the input symbol is ∨ and this function selects $C \to \varepsilon$ if this symbol is in {), ◁}. If the input symbol differs from ∨,), or ◁, the syntax error occurs. Thus, *rd-function C* has the following form:

```
function C: Boolean;
begin
  set C to false
  case ins of
    ∨:
    begin   {C → ∨AC}
      set ins to the next input symbol; {advance to the next input symbol}
      if A then
        if C then
          set C to true
    end
    ), ◁:   set C to true {C → ε}   {) and ◁ are in follow(C)}
  end {of the case statement}
end
```

There exists a single A-rule of the form $A \to BD$ in J with *predictive-set*($A \to BD$) = {*i*, (}. Its *rd-function A*, given next, is similar to *rd-function S*.

```
function A: Boolean;
begin
  set A to false
  if ins ∈ {i, (} then
    if B then
      if D then
        set A to true
end
```

Consider the two D-rules $D \to \wedge BD$ with *predictive-set*($D \to \wedge BD$) = {∧} and $D \to \varepsilon$ with *predictive-set*($D \to \varepsilon$) = {∨,), ◁}. Therefore, *rd-function D* selects $D \to \wedge BD$ if the input symbol is ∧, and it selects $D \to \varepsilon$ if this symbol is in {∨,), ◁}. The *rd-function D* has thus the following form:

```
function D: Boolean;
begin
  set D to false
  case ins of
    ∧:
    begin {D → ∧BD}
      set ins to the next input symbol; {advance to the next input symbol}
      if B then
        if D then
          set D to true
    end
```

```
      ∨, ), ◁:  set D to true {D → ε}   {∨, ), ◁ are in follow(D)}
   end {of the case statement}
end
```

Finally, consider the B-rules $B \rightarrow (S)$ with *predictive-set*$(B \rightarrow (S)) = \{(\}$ and $B \rightarrow i$ with *predictive-set*$(B \rightarrow i) = \{i\}$. Therefore, *rd-function B* selects $B \rightarrow (S)$ if the input symbol is (and this function selects $B \rightarrow i$ if the input symbol is i. If the input symbol differs from (or i, the syntax error occurs. Thus, *rd-function B* has the following form:

```
function B: Boolean;
begin
   set B to false
   case ins of
      (:
      begin
         set ins to the next input symbol; {advance to the next input symbol}
         if S then {B → (S)}
            if ins = ) then
            begin
               set ins to the next input symbol; {advance to the next input symbol}
               set B to true
            end
      end
      i:
      begin
         set ins to the next input symbol; {advance to the next input symbol}
         set B to true
      end
   end {of the case statement}
end
```

Having these functions in the parser, its main body is based on the following simple **if** statement, which decides whether the source program is syntactically correct by the final Boolean value of *rd-function S*:

```
if S then
   SUCCESS
else
   ERROR
```

In the above functions, we frequently need to make an advance within the string of input symbols. As an exercise, explain how to implement this advancement.

7.2.2.2 Predictive Table-Driven Parsing

In the predictive recursive-descent parsing, for every nonterminal A and the corresponding A-rules, there exists a specific Boolean function, so any grammatical change usually necessitates reprogramming several of these functions. Therefore, unless a change of this kind is ruled out, we often prefer an alternative *predictive table-driven parsing* based on a single general control procedure that is completely based on a predictive table. At this point, a change of the grammar only implies an adequate modification of the table while the control procedure remains unchanged. As opposed to the predictive recursive-descent parsing, however, this parsing method maintains a pushdown explicitly, not implicitly via recursive calls like in predictive recursive-descent parsing.

Consider an LL CFG G. Like a general top-down parser (see Algorithm 7.3), a *G-based predictive table-driven parser* is underlain by a PDA, $M = ({}_M\Sigma, {}_MR)$ (see Definition 6.50). However, a strictly mathematical specification of M, including all its rules in ${}_MR$, would be somewhat tedious and lengthy from a practical point of view. Therefore, to make the parser easy to implement, we describe the parser in the way announced in Convention 7.8—that is, M is specified as an algorithm together with a *G-based predictive table*, denoted by ${}_GPT$, by which the parser determines a move from every configuration. The rows and columns of ${}_GPT$ are denoted by the members of ${}_GN \cup \{\triangleright\}$ and ${}_G\Delta \cup \{\triangleleft\}$, respectively. Each of its entry contains a member of ${}_GR$, or it is blank. More precisely, for each $A \in {}_GN$ and each $t \in {}_G\Delta$, if there exists $r \in {}_GR$ such that ***lhs***$(r) = A$ and $t \in$ *predictive-set*(r), ${}_GPT[A, t] = r$; otherwise, ${}_GPT[A, t]$ is blank, which signalizes a syntax error. Making use of ${}_GPT$, M works with the input string as described next. Before giving this description, we want to point out once again that G represents an LL CFG. Indeed, unless G is an LL CFG, we might place more than one rule into a single ${}_GPT$ entry and, thereby, make M nondeterministic.

Let X be the *pd* top symbol. Initially, set *pd* to $\triangleright S$. Perform one of the actions I through V.

I. If $X \in {}_G\Delta$ and $X =$ *ins*, the *pd* top symbol is a terminal coinciding with *ins*, so M *pops* the pushdown by removing X from its top and, simultaneously, advances to the next input symbol.
II. If $X \in {}_G\Delta$ and $X \neq$ *ins*, the pushdown top symbol is a terminal that differs from *ins*, so the parser announces an error by **ERROR**.
III. If $X \in {}_GN$ and ${}_GPT[X, ins] = r$ with $r \in {}_GR$, where ***lhs***$(r) = X$, M *expands* the pushdown by replacing X with *reversal*(***rhs***(r)).
IV. If $X \in {}_GN$ and ${}_GPT[X, ins]$ is blank, M announces an error by **ERROR**.
V. If $\triangleright = X$ and $ins = \triangleleft$, the pushdown is empty and the input string is completely read, so M halts and announces a successful completion of parsing by **SUCCESS**.

Throughout the rest of this section, we also often make use of operations **EXPAND** and **POP**. We next define them in terms of the general version of a top-down parser constructed by Algorithm 7.3.

Definition 7.16 Let $G = ({}_G\Sigma, {}_GR)$ be a CFG. Let $M = ({}_M\Sigma, {}_MR)$ be a PDA that represents a G-based top-down parser produced by Algorithm 7.3.

I. Let $r: A \rightarrow x \in {}_GR$. **EXPAND**$(r)$ applies $A\diamond \rightarrow$ *reversal*$(x)\diamond$ in M.
II. **POP** applies $a\diamond a \rightarrow \diamond$ in M. ■

Less formally, **EXPAND**$(A \rightarrow x)$ replaces the *pd* top with the reversal of x. If *ins* coincides with the *pd* top, **POP** removes the *pd* top and, simultaneously, advances to the next input symbol.

Algorithm 7.17 Predictive Table-Driven Parser.

Input. An LL grammar G, its predictive table ${}_GPT$, and an input string, $w\triangleleft$, where $w \in {}_G\Delta^*$.

Output. **SUCCESS** if $w \in L(G)$, and **ERROR** if $w \notin L(G)$.

Method.

begin

set pd to $\triangleright S$; {initially $pd = \triangleright S$}
repeat
let X denote the current pd top symbol
case X **of**
in ${}_G\Delta$: **if** $X = ins$ **then** {the pd top is a terminal}
POP {pop pd}
else
ERROR {the pd top symbol differs from ins}
in ${}_GN$: **if** ${}_GPT[X, ins] = r$ with $r \in {}_GR$ **then**
EXPAND(r)
else
ERROR {the table entry is blank}
$\triangleright$: **if** $ins = \triangleleft$ **then**
SUCCESS
else
ERROR {the pushdown is empty, but the input string is not completely read}
end {of the **case** statement}
until SUCCESS or **ERROR**

end.

As explained in Section 7.1, apart from deciding whether $w \in L(G)$, a G-based top-down parser frequently produces the left parse of w—that is, the sequence of rules according to which the leftmost derivation of w is made in G provided that $w \in L(G)$. Consider the parser represented by Algorithm 7.17. To obtain left parses, extend this parser by writing out r whenever this algorithm performs **EXPAND**(r), where $r \in {}_GR$. In this way, we produce the left parse of an input string in the conclusion of Example 7.6.

Example 7.6 Reconsider the LL grammar J (see Example 7.4). Figure 7.5 recalls its rules with the corresponding predictive sets.

By using the predictive sets corresponding to these rules, we construct the predictive table ${}_JPT$ (see Figure 7.6).

Take $i \wedge i \vee i$. Algorithm 7.17 parses this string as described in the table given in Figure 7.7. The first column gives the configurations of the parser. The second column states the corresponding ${}_JPT$ entries together with the rules they contain. The third column gives the action made by the parser. The fourth column gives the sentential forms derived in the leftmost derivation.

Suppose that the parser should produce the left parse of $i \wedge i \vee i$—that is, the sequence of rules according to which the leftmost derivation of $i \wedge i \vee i$ is made in J (see I in the beginning of Section 7.1). The parser can easily obtain this parse by writing out the applied rules according to which the expansions are performed during the parsing process. Specifically, take the sequence of rules in the second column of Figure 7.7 to obtain 14858624863 as the left parse of $i \wedge i \vee i$ in J. Indeed, $S \;{}_{lm}\!\Rightarrow^* i \wedge i \vee i$ [14858624863] in J.

Before closing this example, let us point out that from Algorithm 7.17 and ${}_JPT$, we could obtain a strictly mathematical specification of the parser as a PDA M. In essence, M has the form of the parser constructed in Algorithm 7.3 in Section 7.1. That is, M makes **SUCCESS** by $\triangleright\diamond\triangleleft \rightarrow \diamond$.

Rule r	*predictive-set*(r)
1: $S \to AC$	i, (
2: $C \to \vee AC$	$\vee$
3: $C \to \varepsilon$	), $\lhd$
4: $A \to BD$	i, (
5: $D \to \wedge BD$	$\wedge$
6: $D \to \varepsilon$	$\vee$,), $\lhd$
7: $B \to (S)$	(
8: $B \to i$	i

Figure 7.5 Rules of $_JR$ together with their predictive sets.

	$\vee$	$\wedge$	(	)	i	$\lhd$
S			1		1	
C	2			3		3
A			4		4	
D	6	5		6		6
B			7		8	
$\rhd$						☺

Figure 7.6 $_JPT$.

Configuration	Table Entry and Rule	Action	Sentential Form
			$\underline{S}$
$\rhd S\diamond i \wedge i \vee i\lhd$	$[S, i] = 1: S \to AC$	**EXPAND**(1)	$_{lm}\Rightarrow \underline{A}C$ [1]
$\rhd CA\diamond i \wedge i \vee i\lhd$	$[A, i] = 4: A \to BD$	**EXPAND**(4)	$_{lm}\Rightarrow \underline{B}DC$ [4]
$\rhd CDB\diamond i \wedge i \vee i\lhd$	$[B, i] = 8: B \to i$	**EXPAND**(8)	$_{lm}\Rightarrow i\underline{D}C$ [8]
$\rhd CDi\diamond i \wedge i \vee i\lhd$		**POP**	
$\rhd CD\diamond \wedge i \vee i\lhd$	$[D, \wedge] = 5: D \to \wedge BD$	**EXPAND**(5)	$_{lm}\Rightarrow i \wedge \underline{B}DC$ [5]
$\rhd CDB\wedge\diamond \wedge i \vee i\lhd$		**POP**	
$\rhd CDB\diamond i \vee i\lhd$	$[B, i] = 8: B \to i$	**EXPAND**(8)	$_{lm}\Rightarrow i \wedge i\underline{D}C$ [8]
$\rhd CDi\diamond i \vee i\lhd$		**POP**	
$\rhd CD\diamond \vee i\lhd$	$[D, \vee] = 6: D \to \varepsilon$	**EXPAND**(6)	$_{lm}\Rightarrow i \wedge i\underline{C}$ [6]
$\rhd C\diamond \vee i\lhd$	$[C, \vee] = 2: C \to \vee AC$	**EXPAND**(2)	$_{lm}\Rightarrow i \wedge i \vee \underline{A}C$ [2]
$\rhd CA\vee\diamond \vee i\lhd$		**POP**	
$\rhd CA\diamond i\lhd$	$[A, i] = 4: A \to BD$	**EXPAND**(4)	$_{lm}\Rightarrow i \wedge i \vee \underline{B}DC$ [4]
$\rhd CDB\diamond i\lhd$	$[B, i] = 8: B \to i$	**EXPAND**(8)	$_{lm}\Rightarrow i \wedge i \vee i\underline{D}C$ [8]
$\rhd CDi\diamond i\lhd$		**POP**	
$\rhd CD\diamond\lhd$	$[D, \lhd] = 6: D \to \varepsilon$	**EXPAND**(6)	$_{lm}\Rightarrow i \wedge i \vee i\underline{C}$ [6]
$\rhd C\diamond\lhd$	$[C, \lhd] = 3: C \to \varepsilon$	**EXPAND**(3)	$_{lm}\Rightarrow i \wedge i \vee i$ [3]
$\rhd\diamond\lhd$	$[\rhd, \lhd] =$ ☺	**SUCCESS**	

Figure 7.7 Predictive table-driven parsing.

If a pair of the *pd* top X and the current input symbol b leads to **ERROR**, $_MR$ has no rule with $X\diamond b$ on its left-hand side. It performs **POP** by rules of the form $a\diamond a \to \diamond$ for each $a \in {_J\Delta}$. Finally, if a pair of the *pd* top and the current input symbol leads to **EXPAND**(r), where r is a rule from $_JR$, M makes this expansion according to r by $A\diamond \to$ *reversal*(x)$\diamond$. For instance, as $_JPT[S, i] = 1$ and $1\text{: } S \to AC \in {_JR}$, $_MR$ has $S\diamond \to CA\diamond$ to make an expansion according to 1. A completion of this mathematical specification of M is left as an exercise. However, not only is this completion a tedious task but also the resulting parser M specified in this way is difficult to understand what it actually does with its incredibly many rules. That is why, as already pointed out (see Convention 7.8), we always prefer the description of a parser as an algorithm together with a parsing table throughout the rest of this book.

7.2.2.3 Handling Errors

Of course, a predictive parser struggles to handle each syntax error occurrence as best as it can. It carefully diagnoses the error and issues an appropriate error message. Then, it recovers from the error by slightly modifying *pd* or skipping some input symbols. After the recovery, the parser resumes its analysis of the syntactically erroneous program, possibly discovering further syntax errors. Most importantly, no matter what it does, the parser has to avoid any endless loop during the error recovery so that all the input symbols are read eventually. Throughout the rest of this section, we sketch two simple and popular error recovery methods in terms of predictive table-driven parsing while leaving their straightforward adaptation for recursive descent parsing as an exercise.

Panic-mode error recovery. Let $G = ({}_G\Sigma, {}_GR)$ be an LL grammar, and let M be a predictive table-driven parser. For every nonterminal $A \in {}_GN$, we define a set of synchronizing input symbols as *synchronizing-set*(A) = *first*$(A) \cup$ *follow*(A). Suppose that M occurs in a configuration with X as the *pd* top and *ins* as the input symbol when a syntax error occurs. At this point, this error recovery method handles the error as follows.

- If $X \in {}_GN$ and ${}_GPT[X, ins]$ is blank, skip the input symbols until the first occurrence of t that belongs to *synchronizing-set*(X). If $t \in$ *first*(X), resume parsing according to the rule in ${}_GPT[X, t]$ without any further change. If $t \in$ *follow*(X), pop the *pd* top and resume parsing.
- If $X \in {}_G\Delta$ and $X \neq ins$, pop the *pd* top, X, and resume parsing.

As an exercise, discuss further variants of this method. Base these variants on alternative definitions of the synchronizing sets.

Ad-hoc recovery. Let $G = ({}_G\Sigma, {}_GR)$ be an LL grammar, and let M be a predictive table-driven parser. In this method, we design a specific recovery routine, **RECOVER**$[X, t]$, for every error-implying pair of a top *pd* symbol X and an input symbol t. That is, if X and t are two different input symbols, we call **RECOVER**$[X, t]$. We also design **RECOVER**$[X, t]$ if $X \in N \cup \{\triangleright\}$ and ${}_GPT[X, t]$ is blank. **RECOVER**$[X, t]$ figures out the most probable mistake that leads to the given syntax error occurrence, issues an error message, and decides on a recovery procedure that takes a plausible action to resume parsing. Typically, **RECOVER**$[X, t]$ skips a tiny portion of the input string or modifies *pd* by changing, inserting, or deleting some symbols; whatever it does, however, the recovery procedure needs to guarantee that this modification surely avoids any infinite loop so that the parser eventually proceeds its normal process. Otherwise, the parser with this type of error recovery works just like Algorithm 7.17 except that if the error occurs in a configuration such that its *pd* top and the input symbol t represent an error-implying pair, then it performs the **RECOVER** routine corresponding to this pair. In this way, the parser detects and recovers from the syntax error, after which it resumes the parsing process. Of course, once the parser detects a syntax error and recovers from it, it can never proclaim that the program is syntactically correct later during the resumed parsing process. That is, even if the parser eventually reaches ${}_GPT[\triangleright,\triangleleft]$ = ☺ after a recovery from a syntax error, it performs **ERROR**, not **SUCCESS**.

Configuration	Table Entry
$\triangleright S \diamond)\, i \triangleleft$	$[S,)]$ is blank, so **RECOVER**$[S,)]$
$\triangleright S \diamond i \triangleleft$	$[S, i] = 1\text{: } S \to AC$
$\triangleright CA \diamond i \triangleleft$	$[A, i] = 4\text{: } A \to BD$
$\triangleright CDB \diamond i \triangleleft$	$[B, i] = 8\text{: } B \to i$
$\triangleright CDi \diamond i \triangleleft$	
$\triangleright CD \diamond \triangleleft$	$[D, \triangleleft] = 6\text{: } D \to \varepsilon$
$\triangleright C \diamond \triangleleft$	$[C, \triangleleft] = 3\text{: } C \to \varepsilon$
$\triangleright \diamond \triangleleft$	**ERROR**

Figure 7.8 Predictive table-driven parsing with error recovery.

Example 7.7 Return to the LL grammar J (see Examples 7.4), defined as

$$1\text{: } S \to AC,\ 2\text{: } C \to \vee AC,\ 3\text{: } C \to \varepsilon,\ 4\text{: } A \to BD,\ 5\text{: } D \to \wedge BD,\ 6\text{: } D \to \varepsilon,\ 7\text{: } B \to (S),\ 8\text{: } B \to i$$

Consider the J-based predictive table-driven parser discussed in Example 7.6. Take input $)i$. As obvious, $)i \notin L(J)$. With $)i$, the parser immediately interrupts its parsing because ${}_J PT[S,)]$ is blank (see Figure 7.6). Reconsidering this interruption in detail, we see that if S occurs as the *pd* top and) is the input symbol, then the following error-recovery routine is appropriate. Design the other error-recovery routines as an exercise.

name:	**RECOVER**$[S,)]$
diagnostic:	improperly used parentheses: a. either there is no expression in between (and), or b.) is the first symbol of the input string
recovery:	Case (a) is detected by an occurrence of) as the second topmost *pd* symbol; otherwise, case (b) takes place. To recover from (a), insert i in front of *ins*. To recover from (b), skip) as *ins*. Resume parsing.

With $)i$, the parser works as described in Figure 7.8, in which the error-recovery information is pointed up.

7.2.2.4 Exclusion of Left Recursion

Deterministic top-down parsing places some nontrivial restrictions on the CFGs it is based on. Perhaps most importantly, no deterministic top-down parser can be based on a left-recursive CFG (see Section 6.2.6). Indeed, suppose that to simulate a leftmost derivation step, a deterministic top-down parser would select a directly left-recursive rule of the form $A \to Ax$, where A is a nonterminal and x is a string (see Definition 6.37). Since the right-hand side starts with A, the parser would necessarily simulate the next leftmost derivation step according to the same rule, and it would loop in this way endlessly. Of course, general left recursion would also lead to an infinite loop like this. Therefore, deterministic top-down parsing is always underlain by non-left-recursive CFGs.

As demonstrated in Example 7.1, however, left-recursive CFGs specify some common programming-language syntactical constructions, such as conditions and expressions, in a very elegant and succinct way, so we want deterministic parsers based on them, too. Fortunately, deterministic bottom-up parsers work with left-recursive CFGs perfectly well, which brings us to the topic of Section 7.3.

7.3 Bottom-Up Parsing

Given an input string, w, a standard bottom-up parser constructs a derivation tree with frontier w in a bottom-up way. That is, reading w from left to right, the parser starts from frontier w and proceeds up toward the root. To put it in terms of derivations, it builds up the rightmost derivation of w in reverse so it starts from w and proceeds toward the start symbol. Each action during this parsing process represents a *shift* or a *reduction*. The former consists in shifting the current input symbol onto the pushdown. During a reduction, the parser selects a *handle*—that is, an occurrence of the right-hand side of a rule in the current sentential form—and after this selection, it reduces the handle to the left-hand side of the rule so that this reduction, seen in reverse, represents a rightmost derivation step.

As already pointed out in Section 7.1, in practice, we are primarily interested in deterministic bottom-up parsing, which always precisely determines how to make every single step during the parsing process. That is why we narrow our attention to fundamental deterministic bottom-up parsing methods in this section. We describe two of them. First, we describe *precedence parsing*, which is a popular deterministic bottom-up parsing method for expressions whose operators and their priorities actually control the parsing process (see Section 7.3.1). Then, we describe *LR parsing*, where *L* stands for a *l*eft-to-right scan of the input string and *R* stands for a *r*ightmost derivation constructed by the parser (see Section 7.3.2). LR parsers are as powerful as deterministic PDAs, so they represent the strongest possible parsers that work in a deterministic way. That is probably why they are so often implemented in practice, and we discuss them in detail later in this section.

Both sections have a similar structure. First, they describe fundamental parsing algorithms together with parsing tables the algorithms are based on. Then, they explain how to construct these tables. Finally, they sketch how to handle syntax errors.

Throughout the section, we use the same notions and conventions as in Section 7.2, including **SUCCESS** and **ERROR** (see Convention 7.15).

7.3.1 Operator-Precedence Parsing

In practice, we almost always apply an operator-precedence parser to expressions, such as the logical expressions defined by the CFG E (see Convention 7.2), and we explain how to make this parser based on this CFG rather than give a general explanation. First, we explain how an operator-precedence parser based on E works, describe the construction of its parsing table, and sketch how to handle syntax errors. Then, we base this parser on other expression-generating grammars. Finally, we outline advantages and disadvantages of operator-precedence parsing from a general viewpoint.

Recall that $E = ({}_E\Sigma, {}_ER)$ is defined as

$$1: S \rightarrow S \vee S,\ 2: S \rightarrow S \wedge S,\ 3: S \rightarrow (S),\ 4: S \rightarrow i$$

where ${}_E\Delta = \{\vee, \wedge, (,), i\}$ and ${}_EN = \{S\}$. The *operator-precedence parsing table* of E, ${}_EOP$, has a relatively simple format. Indeed, this table has its rows and columns denoted by the members of ${}_E\Delta \cup \{\triangleright\}$ and ${}_E\Delta \cup \{\triangleleft\}$, respectively. Each ${}_EOP$ entry is a member of $\{\lfloor, \rfloor, \square, ☺\}$, where $\square$ denotes a blank entry. Figure 7.9 presents ${}_EOP$, whose construction is explained later in this section.

	$\wedge$	$\vee$	i	(	)	$\triangleleft$
$\wedge$	$\rfloor$	$\rfloor$	$\lfloor$	$\lfloor$	$\rfloor$	$\rfloor$
$\vee$	$\lfloor$	$\rfloor$	$\lfloor$	$\lfloor$	$\rfloor$	$\rfloor$
i	$\rfloor$	$\rfloor$			$\rfloor$	$\rfloor$
(	$\lfloor$	$\lfloor$	$\lfloor$	$\lfloor$		
)	$\rfloor$	$\rfloor$			$\rfloor$	$\rfloor$
$\triangleright$	$\lfloor$	$\lfloor$	$\lfloor$	$\lfloor$		☺

Figure 7.9 $_E OP$.

7.3.1.1 Operator-Precedence Parser

An E-based operator-precedence parser makes shifts and reductions by operations **OP-SHIFT** and **OP-REDUCE**, respectively. We define both operations next, making use of the *pd* and *ins* notation introduced in Convention 7.1.

Definition 7.18 Let $E = ({}_E\Sigma, {}_ER)$ and $_E OP$ have the same meaning as above. Operations **OP-REDUCE** and **OP-SHIFT** are defined in the following way.

I. **OP-REDUCE** performs (1) through (3) given next.
   1. Let $pd = y$, where $y \in \{\triangleright\}{}_E\Sigma^*$, and let a be the topmost *pd* symbol such that $a \in \{\triangleright\} \cup {}_E\Delta$ and $y = xaubv$ with $_E OP[a, b] = \lfloor$, where $x \in \{\triangleright\}{}_E\Sigma^* \cup \{\varepsilon\}$ ($a = \triangleright$ iff $x = \varepsilon$), $b \in {}_E\Delta$, $u \in {}_EN^*$, $v \in {}_E\Sigma^*$. Then, the current *handle* is ubv.
   2. Select $r \in {}_ER$ with $\boldsymbol{rhs}(r) = ubv$.
   3. Change ubv to $\boldsymbol{lhs}(r)$ on the *pd* top.

   To express, in a greater detail, that **OP-REDUCE** is performed according to $r \in {}_ER$, write **OP-REDUCE**(r).

II. **OP-SHIFT** pushes *ins* onto the *pd* top and advances to the next input symbol. ■

To illustrate **OP-REDUCE**, suppose that the current configuration of the parser is of the form $\triangleright(S)\diamond\triangleleft$. In terms of (1) in Definition 7.18, $y = \triangleright(S)$, and the topmost *pd* terminal a satisfying (1) is $\triangleright$; to be quite precise, $x = \varepsilon$, $a = \triangleright$, $u = \varepsilon$, $b =$ (, and $v = S$). Thus, (S) is the handle. In (2), select 3: $S \rightarrow (S)$. In (3), reduce (S) to S and, thereby, change $\triangleright(S)\diamond\triangleleft$ to $\triangleright S\diamond\triangleleft$; in symbols, perform **OP-REDUCE**(3). It is worth noting that the case when $a = \triangleright$ is not ruled out as illustrated by this example as well. To give another example, briefly, apply **OP-REDUCE** to the configuration $\triangleright(S \vee S\diamond) \wedge S\triangleleft$. This application actually performs **OP-REDUCE**(1) and changes $\triangleright(S \vee S\diamond) \wedge S\triangleleft$ to $\triangleright(S\diamond) \wedge S\triangleleft$. Observe that **OP-REDUCE** is not applicable to any configuration. Indeed, consider $\triangleright()\diamond\triangleleft$. As E contains no rule with the right-hand side equal to (), **OP-REDUCE** is inapplicable to $\triangleright()\diamond\triangleleft$.

To illustrate the other operation, **OP-SHIFT**, take, for instance, $\triangleright S \vee\diamond i\triangleleft$. Notice that **OP-SHIFT** changes $\triangleright S \vee\diamond i\triangleleft$ to $\triangleright S \vee i\diamond\triangleleft$.

Basic idea. Let X be the *pd* topmost terminal. The parser determines each parsing step based on the entry $_E OP[X, ins]$. According to this entry, the parser performs one of the following actions I through IV.

I. If ${}_EOP[X, ins]$ contains ⌊, the parser performs **OP-SHIFT**.
II. If ${}_EOP[X, ins]$ is ⌋, the parser performs **OP-REDUCE**.
III. Let ${}_EOP[X, ins]$ = ▫. If X = (and ins =), the parser performs **OP-SHIFT** onto pd to prepare the performance of **OP-REDUCE** according to 3: $S \rightarrow (S)$ right after this shift; otherwise—that is, $X \neq$ (or $ins \neq$)—the blank entry signalizes a syntax error, so the parser performs **ERROR**.
IV. If ${}_EOP[X, ins]$ = ☺, the parser performs **SUCCESS** and successfully completes the parsing process.

Algorithm 7.19 Operator-Precedence Parser.

Input. E, ${}_EOP$, and $w\lhd$, where $w \in {}_E\Delta^*$, where E and ${}_EOP$ have the same meaning as above.

Output. If $w \in L(E)$, **SUCCESS**, and if $w \notin L(E)$, **ERROR**.

Method.

```
begin
    set pd to ▷

    repeat
        let X be the pd topmost terminal
        case EOP[X, ins] of
            ⌊  :  OP-SHIFT
            ⌋  :  OP-REDUCE
            ▫  :  if X = ( and ins = ) then    {▫ denotes a blank}
                      OP-SHIFT
                  else
                      ERROR
            ☺  :  SUCCESS
        end {of the case statement}
    until SUCCESS or ERROR

end.
```

As already explained in Section 7.1, apart from deciding whether $w \in L(E)$, we may want Algorithm 7.19 to produce the right parse of w, defined as the reverse sequence of rules according to which E makes this rightmost derivation (see II in the beginning of Section 7.1), if w belongs to $L(E)$. To obtain this parse, we extend the parser by writing out r whenever this algorithm performs **OP-REDUCE**(r), where $r \in {}_ER$. In this way, we produce the right parse of an input string in the conclusion of Example 7.8.

Example 7.8 Let us take, for instance, $w = i \wedge (i \vee i)$ in Algorithm 7.19, which represents the E-based operator-precedence parser, whose parsing table ${}_EOP$ is in Figure 7.9. In Figure 7.10, we describe the parse of $i \wedge (i \vee i)$ by Algorithm 7.19. In the first column, we give the ${}_EOP$ entries, and in the second, we present the actions taken by the parser according to these entries. In the third

Table Entry	Action	Configuration
		$\underline{\triangleright}\diamond i\wedge(i\vee i)\triangleleft$
$[\triangleright, i] = \lfloor$	**OP-SHIFT**	$\triangleright\underline{i}\diamond\wedge(i\vee i)\triangleleft$
$[i, \wedge] = \rfloor$	**OP-REDUCE(4)**	$\underline{\triangleright}S\diamond\wedge(i\vee i)\triangleleft$
$[\triangleright, \wedge] = \lfloor$	**OP-SHIFT**	$\triangleright S\,\underline{\wedge}\diamond(i\vee i)\triangleleft$
$[\wedge, (] = \lfloor$	**OP-SHIFT**	$\triangleright S\wedge\underline{(}\diamond i\vee i)\triangleleft$
$[(, i] = \lfloor$	**OP-SHIFT**	$\triangleright S\wedge(\underline{i}\diamond\vee i)\triangleleft$
$[i, \vee] = \rfloor$	**OP-REDUCE(4)**	$\triangleright S\wedge\underline{(}S\diamond\vee i)\triangleleft$
$[(, \vee] = \lfloor$	**OP-SHIFT**	$\triangleright S\wedge(S\underline{\vee}\diamond i)\triangleleft$
$[\vee, i] = \lfloor$	**OP-SHIFT**	$\triangleright S\wedge(S\vee\underline{i}\diamond)\triangleleft$
$[i,)] = \rfloor$	**OP-REDUCE(4)**	$\triangleright S\wedge(S\underline{\vee}S\diamond)\triangleleft$
$[\vee,)] = \rfloor$	**OP-REDUCE(1)**	$\triangleright S\wedge\underline{(}S\diamond)\triangleleft$
$[(,)] = \square$	**OP-SHIFT**	$\triangleright S\wedge(S\underline{)}\diamond\triangleleft$
$[), \triangleleft] = \rfloor$	**OP-REDUCE(3)**	$\triangleright S\,\underline{\wedge}\,S\diamond\triangleleft$
$[\wedge, \triangleleft] = \rfloor$	**OP-REDUCE(2)**	$\underline{\triangleright}S\diamond\triangleleft$
$[\triangleright, \triangleleft] =$ ☺	**SUCCESS**	

Figure 7.10 Operator-precedence parsing.

column, we give the parser configurations, which have the form $\triangleright x\diamond y\triangleleft$, where $\triangleright x$ is the current *pd*, and $y\triangleleft$ is the input suffix that remains to be parsed; the leftmost symbol of $y\triangleleft$ represents *ins*. We underline the topmost *pd* terminals in these configurations.

Suppose that the parser should produce the right parse of $i \wedge (i \vee i)$. The parser can easily obtain this parse by writing out the applied rules according to which the reductions are performed during the parsing process. Specifically, take the sequence of rules in the second column of Figure 7.10 to obtain 444132 as the right parse of $i \wedge (i \vee i)$ in E.

7.3.1.2 Construction of Operator-Precedence Parsing Table

The parsing table $_{E}OP$ (see Figure 7.9) can be easily constructed by using common sense and elementary mathematical rules concerning precedence and associativity of operators occurring in the expressions generated by E. This construction thus assumes that for every pair of two operators, their mutual precedence is stated, and in addition, for every operator, it is specified whether it is left-associative or right-associative.

Basic idea. Mathematically, $\lfloor$ and $\rfloor$ can be viewed as two binary relations over Δ, defined as follows. For any pair of operators a and b, $a\lfloor b$ means that a has a lower precedence than b, so a handle containing a is reduced after a handle containing b. Regarding the other relation, $a\rfloor b$ says that a has a precedence before b, meaning that a handle containing a is reduced before a handle containing b. To obtain the complete definition of $\lfloor$ and $\rfloor$, perform I through IV, in which $a \in {}_{E}\Delta \cup \{\triangleright\}$ and $b \in {}_{E}\Delta \cup \{\triangleleft\}$.

I. If a and b are operators such that a has a higher mathematical precedence than b, then $a\rfloor b$ and $b\lfloor a$.
II. If a and b are left-associative operators of the same precedence, then $a\rfloor b$ and $b\rfloor a$. If a and b are right-associative operators of the same precedence, then $a\lfloor b$ and $b\lfloor a$.
III. In $_{E}\Delta$, consider i, which represents an identifier and occurs on the right-hand side of rule 4: $S \rightarrow i$ in $_{E}R$. If a is a terminal that can legally precede operand i, then $a\lfloor i$, and if a can legally follow i, then $i\rfloor a$.
IV. If a is a terminal that can legally precede (, then $a\lfloor($. If a can legally follow (, then $(\lfloor a$. Similarly, if a can legally precede), then $a\rfloor)$, and if a can legally follow), then $)\rfloor a$.

Following I through IV, we now construct ${}_EOP$ by using these two equivalences

$$ {}_EOP[a, b] = \lfloor \text{ iff } a\lfloor b, \text{ and } {}_EOP[a, b] = \rfloor \text{ iff } a\rfloor b $$

for all $a \in {}_E\Delta \cup \{\triangleright\}$ and all $b \in {}_E\Delta \cup \{\triangleleft\}$. In addition, set ${}_EOP[\triangleright, \triangleleft] =$ ☺. The other entries are blank. All these blank entries signalize syntax errors except ${}_EOP[(,)]$; if the parser occurs in ${}_EOP[(,)]$, it shifts) onto *pd* to perform **OP-REDUCE** according to 3: $S \rightarrow (S)$ right after this shift.

Example 7.9 In E, suppose that $\vee$ and $\wedge$ satisfy the standard mathematical precedence and associative rules. That is, $\wedge$ has a precedence before $\vee$, and both operators are left-associative. From I above, as $\wedge$ has a precedence before $\vee$, $\wedge\rfloor\vee$ and $\vee\lfloor\wedge$. From II, since $\wedge$ is left-associative, define $\wedge\rfloor\wedge$. Regarding i, as $\vee$ can legally precede i, define $\vee\lfloor i$ according to III. Considering the parentheses, IV implies $\wedge\lfloor($. Complete the definitions of $\lfloor$ and $\rfloor$ and use them to construct ${}_EOP$ (see Figure 7.9).

7.3.1.3 Handling Errors

In practice, after detecting the first error, a well-written bottom-up parser does not stop. Instead, it somehow deals with that error so it eventually resumes the parsing process and allows further possible errors to be detected. Next, we sketch how to handle errors in this pragmatically sophisticated way in terms of operator-precedence parsing, in which we distinguish two basic kinds of errors:

I. Table-detected errors
II. Reduction errors

Let X be the *pd* topmost terminal.

Table-Detected Errors. If ${}_EOP[X, ins]$ is blank, an error is detected by the table (an exception represents ${}_EOP[(,)]$ as already explained above). To handle it, the parser modifies its pushdown or the input by changing, inserting, or deleting some symbols. Whatever the parser does, it has to guarantee a recovery from the error. After the recovery, it resumes the parsing process so that all the input string is eventually processed. The precise modification depends on the type of an error that the table detects, and the exact recovery action chosen always requires some ingeniousness from the compiler author to select the best possible action. When the parser reaches a blank entry, the error-recovery routine corresponding to this entry is performed.

Reduction Errors. If ${}_EOP[X, ins] = \rfloor$, the parser should perform a reduction. If there is no rule by which the parser can make this reduction, a reduction error occurs. More precisely, this error occurs when no grammatical rule has the right-hand side equal to the string y delimited by $\lfloor$ and $\rfloor$ on the *pd* top. After issuing a diagnostic of this error, the parser selects a *recovery rule* $A \rightarrow x$ such that x can be obtained from y by a slight modification, such as the deletion of a single symbol. To recover, it changes y to A on the *pd* top, then resumes the parsing process.

In practice, operator-precedence parsers frequently handle errors more sophisticatedly and effectively. Indeed, they detect most errors described earlier during the parsing process by some additional checks. Indeed, they usually make the *length-of-handle check* to verify that a handle always occurs within the pushdown top consisting of no more than *j* symbols, where *j* is the length of the longest right-hand side of a rule in *E*. At this point, they can narrow its attention to finitely many illegal strings of length *j* or less and associate a recovery rule with each of them in advance. Furthermore, a reduction error can be frequently detected earlier by a *valid handle-prefix check*, which verifies that there is a rule *r* whose prefix occurs on the pushdown top; if there is none, a reduction error is inescapable.

When a recovery action leads to skipping some input symbols, then it represents a rather straightforward task. Consider, for instance, $_EOP[\triangleright,)] = \square$, which detects an error. To recover, the parser skips) by advancing to the input symbol behind this), issues an error diagnostic stating that an unbalanced right parenthesis has occurred, and continues with the parsing process. A recovery action that modifies *pd* is usually more difficult. Consider $_EOP[i, (] = \square$. To recover, the parser first changes the *pd* top symbol, $X = i$, to S, then pushes $\wedge$ onto the pushdown top. As a result, after this modification of the pushdown, $\wedge$ is the topmost pushdown symbol under which S occurs. To complete this recovery, the parser issues an error diagnostic that an operator is missing and resumes the parsing process. Unfortunately, we can hardly determine whether the source program's author left out $\wedge$ or $\vee$ in front of (. We can only speculate that the input left parenthesis might indicate that the author left out $\wedge$ because the parentheses are normally used to change the common priorities of operators in the expressions; for instance, the parentheses are necessary in $i \wedge (i \vee i)$, but they are superfluous in $i \vee (i \wedge i)$. Therefore, we have chosen $\wedge$ as the operator inserted onto the pushdown in this recovery action although we can never be absolutely sure that this is what the source program's author improperly left out. In Figure 7.11, we give $_EOP$ with the error entries filled with the names of the error-recovery routines, ① through ⑥, schematically described next.

① $_EOP$ **entry**: $[i, i]$
diagnostic: missing operator between two *i*s
recovery: *X* equals *i*; replace it with $S \wedge$

② $_EOP$ **entry**: $[i, (]$
diagnostic: missing operator between *i* and (
recovery: *X* equals *i*; replace it with $S \wedge$

③ $_EOP$ **entry**: $[(, \triangleleft]$
diagnostic: missing right parenthesis
recovery: *ins* equals $\triangleleft$; insert) in front of it, and after this insertion, set *ins* to the newly inserted)

④ $_EOP$ **entry**: $[), i]$
diagnostic: missing operator between) and *i*

	$\wedge$	$\vee$	i	(	)	$\triangleleft$
$\wedge$	⌋	⌋	⌊	⌊	⌋	⌋
$\vee$	⌊	⌋	⌊	⌊	⌋	⌋
i	⌋	⌋	①	②	⌋	⌋
(	⌊	⌊	⌊	⌊		③
)	⌋	⌋	④	⑤	⌋	⌋
$\triangleright$	⌊	⌊	⌊	⌊	⑥	☺

Figure 7.11 $_EOP$ **with error-recovery routines.**

recovery: *ins* equals *i*; insert ∧ in front of it, and after this insertion, set *ins* to the newly inserted ∧

⑤ $_EOP$ **entry:** [), (]
diagnostic: missing operator between) and (
recovery: *ins* equals *i*; insert ∧ in front of it, and after this insertion, set *ins* to the newly inserted ∧

⑥ $_EOP$ **entry:** [▷,)]
diagnostic: unbalanced)
recovery: ignore *ins* and advance to the next input symbol

To illustrate the reduction errors, consider ( )◁. By $_EOP$, the parser detects no table-detected error in this obviously incorrect expression. However, when ( ) occurs as the two-symbol pushdown top, a reduction error is reported because ( ) does not coincide with the right-hand side of any rule. To recover, the parser replaces ( ) with (*S*) on the pushdown top and resumes the parsing process as usual. Observe that this reduction error is detectable earlier provided that the parser makes a valid handle-prefix check. Indeed, when (is on the pushdown top and the parser is about to shift) onto the pushdown, it checks whether there is a rule whose right-hand side begins with ( ). As there is none, the parser detects and reports a reduction error even before shifting) onto the pushdown. To recover, it pushes *S* onto the pushdown, then resumes the parsing process. Next, we describe three kinds of reduction errors, ❶ through ❸, from each of which the parser recovers by pushing *S* onto the pushdown top before it makes a shift.

❶ **configuration:** *X* = (and *ins* =)
diagnostic: no expression between parentheses
recovery: push *S* onto the *pd* top

❷ **configuration:** *X* ∈ {∧, ∨} and *ins* ∉ {*i*, (}
diagnostic: missing right operand
recovery: push *S* onto the *pd* top

❸ **configuration:** *X* ∈ {(, ▷} is the *pd* top symbol and *ins* ∈ {∧, ∨}
diagnostic: missing left operand
recovery: push *S* onto the *pd* top

Example 7.10 Consider *i* (*i* ∨)◁. As obvious, this expression is ill-formed. Working on *i* (*i* ∨)◁, Algorithm 7.19 interrupts its parsing process after making only the first two steps described in Figure 7.12 because it reaches a blank entry in $_EOP$, which means a syntax error.

The parser that handles syntax errors by the routines described earlier works with this expression as described in Figure 7.13, which points up information related to handling errors. In the third column, apart from giving the parser configurations presented in the same way as above, we point out the parts related to error recovery. Observe that the parser recovers from both errors occurring in the expressions. As a result, the parser completes the parsing of this expression. The parsing process obviously ends by **ERROR** for the previously detected errors.

In the second step, the parser detects that an operator is missing between *i* and (, and recovery routine ② handles this error by replacing *i* with *S* and, then, pushing ∧ on the *pd* top. In the seventh step, the parser detects a reduction error because ∨ occurs on the *pd* top and the next input symbol equals). Indeed, at this point, *S* ∨ forms the handle but there is no rule with the right-hand

OPPT entry	Action	Configuration
		$\triangleright \diamond i\,(i \vee)\triangleleft$
$[\triangleright, i] = \lfloor$	**OP-SHIFT**	$\triangleright i \diamond (i \vee)\triangleleft$
$[i, (] = \Box$	**ERROR**	

Figure 7.12 Operator-precedence parser working on $\triangleright \diamond i\,(i \vee)\triangleleft$.

Entry	Action	Configuration
		$\underline{\triangleright} \diamond i\,(i \vee)\triangleleft$
$[\triangleright, i] = \lfloor$	**OP-SHIFT**	$\triangleright \underline{i} \diamond (i \vee)\triangleleft$
$[i, (] = ②$	recovery ②	$\triangleright S \underline{\wedge} \diamond (i \vee)\triangleleft$
$[\wedge, (] = \lfloor$	**OP-SHIFT**	$\triangleright S \wedge \underline{(} \diamond i \vee)\triangleleft$
$[(, i] = \lfloor$	**OP-SHIFT**	$\triangleright S \wedge (\underline{i} \diamond \vee)\triangleleft$
$[i, \vee] = \rfloor$	**OP-REDUCE**(4)	$\triangleright S \wedge \underline{(} S \diamond \vee)\triangleleft$
$[(, \vee] = \rfloor$	recovery ❷	$\triangleright S \wedge (S \underline{\vee} S \diamond)\triangleleft$
$[\vee,)] = \rfloor$	**OP-REDUCE** (1)	$\triangleright S \wedge \underline{(} S \diamond)\triangleleft$
$[(,)] = \Box$	**OP-SHIFT**	$\triangleright S \wedge (S\underline{)} \diamond \triangleleft$
$[), \triangleleft] = \rfloor$	**OP-REDUCE**(3)	$\triangleright S \underline{\wedge} S \diamond \triangleleft$
$[\wedge, \triangleleft] = \rfloor$	**OP-REDUCE**(2)	$\underline{\triangleright} S \diamond \triangleleft$
$[\triangleright, \triangleleft]$	**ERROR**	errors in ② and ❷

Figure 7.13 Operator-precedence parser that recovers from errors in $\triangleright \diamond i\,(i \vee)\triangleleft$.

side equals to $S \vee$. To recover, recovery routine ❷ pushes S onto the *pd* top. As a result, the parser completes the parsing of $i\,(i \vee)$ rather than gets stuck inside of this expression as in Figure 7.12.

7.3.1.4 Operator-Precedence Parsers for Other Expressions

Up until now, we have based the explanation of operator-precedence parsing strictly on E. Of course, apart from the logical expressions generated by E, this parsing method elegantly handles other expressions. Next, we explain how this method handles unary operators. Then, we sketch how to adapt it for arithmetic expressions. Finally, we point out that it works well with both ambiguous and unambiguous grammars.

Unary Operators. Consider $\neg$ as a unary operator that denotes a logical negation. To incorporate this operator, we extend the CFG E by adding a rule of the form $S \rightarrow \neg S$ to obtain the CFG defined as

$$S \rightarrow \neg S,\ S \rightarrow S \vee S,\ S \rightarrow S \wedge S,\ S \rightarrow (S),\ S \rightarrow i$$

Assume that $\neg$ satisfies the standard precedence and associative rules used in logic. That is, $\neg$ is a right-associative operator having a higher precedence than $\wedge$ and $\vee$. Return to rules I through IV, preceding Example 7.9 in this section. By using these rules, we easily obtain the table that includes this unary operator (see Figure 7.14).

Arithmetic Expressions with Right-Associative Operators. Consider this CFG

$$S \rightarrow S + S,\ S \rightarrow S - S,\ S \rightarrow S * S,\ S \rightarrow S / S,\ S \rightarrow S \uparrow S,\ S \rightarrow (S),\ S \rightarrow i$$

in which the operators have the standard meaning and satisfy the common arithmetic precedence and associative rules ($\uparrow$ denotes the operator of exponentiation). That is, $\uparrow$ has a precedence before $*$ and $/$, which have a precedence before $+$ and $-$. The exponentiation operator $\uparrow$ is right-associative while the others are left-associative. The precedence table for this grammar is straightforwardly made by construction rules I through IV (see Figure 7.15).

	$\neg$	$\wedge$	$\vee$	i	(	)	$\lhd$
$\neg$	$\lfloor$	$\rfloor$	$\rfloor$	$\lfloor$	$\lfloor$	$\rfloor$	$\rfloor$
$\wedge$	$\lfloor$	$\rfloor$	$\rfloor$	$\lfloor$	$\lfloor$	$\rfloor$	$\rfloor$
$\vee$	$\lfloor$	$\lfloor$	$\rfloor$	$\lfloor$	$\lfloor$	$\rfloor$	$\rfloor$
i	$\rfloor$	$\rfloor$	$\rfloor$			$\rfloor$	$\rfloor$
(	$\lfloor$	$\lfloor$	$\lfloor$	$\lfloor$	$\lfloor$		
)		$\rfloor$	$\rfloor$			$\rfloor$	$\rfloor$
$\rhd$	$\lfloor$	$\lfloor$	$\lfloor$	$\lfloor$	$\lfloor$		☺

Figure 7.14 Operator precedence table with unary operator ¬.

	$\uparrow$	$*$	/	+	−	i	(	)	$\lhd$
$\uparrow$	$\lfloor$	$\rfloor$	$\rfloor$	$\rfloor$	$\rfloor$	$\lfloor$	$\lfloor$	$\rfloor$	$\rfloor$
$*$	$\lfloor$	$\rfloor$	$\rfloor$	$\rfloor$	$\rfloor$	$\lfloor$	$\lfloor$	$\rfloor$	$\rfloor$
/	$\lfloor$	$\rfloor$	$\rfloor$	$\rfloor$	$\rfloor$	$\lfloor$	$\lfloor$	$\rfloor$	$\rfloor$
+	$\lfloor$	$\lfloor$	$\lfloor$	$\rfloor$	$\rfloor$	$\lfloor$	$\lfloor$	$\rfloor$	$\rfloor$
−	$\lfloor$	$\lfloor$	$\lfloor$	$\rfloor$	$\rfloor$	$\lfloor$	$\lfloor$	$\rfloor$	$\rfloor$
i	$\rfloor$	$\rfloor$	$\rfloor$	$\rfloor$	$\rfloor$			$\rfloor$	$\rfloor$
(	$\lfloor$	$\lfloor$	$\lfloor$	$\lfloor$	$\lfloor$	$\lfloor$	$\lfloor$		
)	$\rfloor$	$\rfloor$	$\rfloor$	$\rfloor$	$\rfloor$			$\rfloor$	$\rfloor$
$\rhd$	$\lfloor$	$\lfloor$	$\lfloor$	$\lfloor$	$\lfloor$	$\lfloor$	$\lfloor$		☺

Figure 7.15 Arithmetic-operator precedence table.

Expressions involving relational operators are handled analogously, so we leave their discussion as an exercise.

Ambiguity. As opposed to most top-down parsers, such as the predictive parsers (see Section 7.2), the precedence parsers work with ambiguous grammars without any problems. In fact, all the previous precedence parsers discussed in this section are based on ambiguous grammars, such as E. As obvious, these parsers can be based on unambiguous grammars, too. To illustrate, consider the unambiguous grammar H (see Convention 7.2), defined as

$$S \rightarrow S \vee A,\ S \rightarrow A,\ A \rightarrow A \wedge B,\ A \rightarrow B,\ B \rightarrow (S),\ B \rightarrow i$$

Suppose that all the operators satisfy the same precedence and associative rules as in the equivalent ambiguous grammar above. As an exercise, by rules I through IV, construct ${}_{H}OP$ and observe that this table coincides with the table given in Figure 7.9.

On the one hand, as demonstrated earlier in this section, operator-precedence parsers work nicely for the CFGs that generate expressions even if these grammars are ambiguous. On the other hand, they place several strict restrictions on the CFGs they are based on; perhaps most significantly, they exclude any involvement of ε-rules or rules having the same right-hand side but different left-hand sides. As a result, in practice, these parsers are frequently used in a combination with predictive parsers discussed in Section 7.2. Combined in this way, the precedence parsers handle the syntax of expressions while the other parsers handle the rest. Alternatively, bottom-up parsers are designed as LR parsers, discussed in Section 7.3.2.

7.3.2 LR Parsing

This section discusses the *LR parsers* (*L* stands for the *l*eft-to-right scan of symbols, and *R* is for the *r*ightmost derivation, which the bottom-up parsers construct in reverse as already explained in Section 7.1). LR parsers are based on *LR tables* constructed from *LR CFGs*—that is, the CFGs for which LR tables can be constructed; let us point out that there are non-LR CFGs, for which these tables cannot be built up.

In practice, LR parsers belong to the most popular parsers for their several indisputable advantages. First, they work fast. Furthermore, they easily and elegantly handle syntax errors because they never shift an erroneous input symbol onto the pushdown, and this property obviously simplifies the error recovery process. Most importantly, out of all deterministic parsers, they are ultimately powerful because LR CFGs generate the language family coinciding with $_{DPDA}\Phi_f$—that is, the language family accepted by deterministic pushdown automata by final state (see Definition 6.66 and Corollary 6.74).

In this section, we first describe the fundamental LR parsing algorithm. Then, we explain how to construct the LR tables, which the algorithm makes use of. Finally, we discuss how this parsing method handles errors.

7.3.2.1 LR Parsing Algorithm

Consider an LR grammar, $G = ({}_G\Sigma, {}_GR)$. Its *G-based LR table* consists of the *G-based action part* and the *G-based goto part*, denoted by $_G$*action* and $_G$*goto*, respectively. Both parts have their rows denoted by members of the set $_G\Theta = \{\theta_1, \ldots, \theta_m\}$, whose construction is described later in this section. The columns of $_G$*action* and $_G$*goto* are denoted by the symbols of $_G\Delta$ and $_GN$, respectively; recall that $_G\Delta$ and $_GN$ denote G's alphabets of terminals and nonterminals, respectively. For each $\theta_j \in {}_G\Theta$ and $t_i \in {}_G\Delta \cup \{\lhd\}$, $_G$*action*$[\theta_j, t_i]$ entry is either a member of $_G\Theta \cup {}_GR \cup \{☺\}$ or a blank entry (see Figure 7.16). Frequently, the rules of $_GR$ are labeled throughout this section, and instead of the rules themselves, only their labels are written in $_G$*action* for brevity. For each $\theta_j \in {}_G\Theta$ and $A_i \in {}_GN$, $_G$*goto*$[\theta_j, A_i]$ is either a member of $_G\Theta$ or a blank entry (see Figure 7.17).

Convention 7.20 As usual, whenever there is no danger of confusion, we omit G in the denotation above, so we simplify $_G\Theta$, $_G$*action*, $_G$*goto*, $_G\Delta$, and $_GN$ to Θ, *action*, *goto*, Δ, and N, respectively. ■

Basic Idea. Like an operator-precedence parser (see Algorithm 7.19), an LR parser scans w from left to right, and during this scan, it makes shifts and reductions. If $w \in L(G)$, it accepts w; otherwise,

	t_1	…	t_i	…	t_n
θ_1					
⋮					
θ_j			$action[\theta_j, t_i]$		
⋮					
θ_m					

Figure 7.16 $_G$***action*****.**

	A_1	…	A_i	…	A_k
θ_1					
⋮					
θ_j			$goto[\theta_j, A_i]$		
⋮					
θ_m					

Figure 7.17 $_G$***goto*****.**

it rejects w. During the parsing process, every configuration of the parser is of the form $\triangleright q_0Y_1q_1\ldots Y_{m-1}q_{m-1}Y_mq_m\diamond v\triangleleft$, where the qs and the Ys are in ${}_G\Theta$ and ${}_G\Sigma$, respectively, and $v \in$ *suffixes*(w). Recall that according to Definition 6.50 and Convention 6.51, the pushdown is written in the right-to-left way, so q_m is the topmost *pd* symbol, Y_m occurs as the second *pd* symbol, and so on up to the *pd* bottom, $\triangleright$. As a result, a member of ${}_G\Theta$ always appears as the topmost *pd* symbol. The LR parser makes shifts and reductions in a specific LR way, though. Next, we describe operations **LR-REDUCE** and **LR-SHIFT** that denote the actions by which the LR parser makes its reductions and shifts, respectively (as usual, in the definition of **LR-REDUCE** and **LR-SHIFT**, we make use of the *pd* and *ins* notation introduced in Convention 7.1).

Definition 7.21 *Operations* **LR-REDUCE** *and* **LR-SHIFT**. Let $G = ({}_G\Sigma, {}_GR)$, ${}_G\Theta$, ${}_Gaction$, and ${}_Ggoto$ have the same meaning as above. In a G-based LR parser, we use operations **LR-REDUCE** and **LR-SHIFT** defined as follows:

LR-REDUCE. If p: $A \rightarrow X_1X_2\ldots X_n \in {}_GR$, $X_j \in {}_G\Sigma$, $1 \leq j \leq n$, for some $n \geq 0$ ($n = 0$ means $X_1X_2\ldots X_n = \varepsilon$), $o_0X_1o_1X_2o_2\ldots o_{n-1}X_no_n$ occurs as the $(2n+1)$-symbol *pd* top—that is, the current configuration of the parser is of the form $\triangleright\ldots o_0X_1o_1X_2o_2\ldots o_{n-1}X_no_n\diamond\ldots\triangleleft$ with o_n as the topmost *pd* symbol, where $o_k \in {}_G\Theta$, $0 \leq k \leq n$, then **LR-REDUCE**(p) replaces $X_1o_1X_2o_2\ldots o_{n-1}X_no_n$ with Ah on the pushdown top, where $h \in {}_G\Theta$ is defined as $h = {}_Ggoto[o_0, A]$; otherwise, **ERROR**.

LR-SHIFT. Let t and q denote *ins* and the *pd* top symbol, respectively. Let $action[q, t] = o$, where $o \in {}_G\Theta$. At this point, **LR-SHIFT**(t) extends *pd* by to, so o is the topmost pushdown symbol after this extension. In addition, it sets *ins* to the input symbol that follows t and, thereby, advances to the next input symbol. ■

Notice that the following LR parser has always its *pd* top symbol from ${}_G\Theta$ as follows from Definition 7.21.

Algorithm 7.22 LR Parser.

Input. An LR grammar, $G = ({}_G\Sigma, {}_GR)$,
an input string, w, with $w \in {}_G\Delta^*$, and
a G-based LR table consisting of *action* and *goto*.

Output. **SUCCESS** if $w \in L(G)$, or
ERROR if $w \notin L(G)$.

Method.

begin

set $pd = \triangleright\theta_1$ {θ_1 denotes the first row of *action* and *goto*}

repeat

let q denote the *pd* topmost symbol

case *action*[*q*, *ins*] **of**
  in ${}_G\Theta$: **LR-SHIFT**(*ins*)
  in ${}_GR$: **LR-REDUCE**(*r*) with $r = action[q, ins]$
  □: **ERROR** {□ denotes a blank}
  ☺: **SUCCESS**
end {of the **case** statement}

until SUCCESS or **ERROR**

end.

To obtain the right parse of *w*, extend Algorithm 7.22 by writing out *r* whenever **LR-REDUCE**(*r*) occurs, where $r \in {}_GR$. This straightforward extension is left as an exercise.

Example 7.11 Consider the CFG *H* (see Convention 7.2), whose rules are

$$1: S \rightarrow S \vee A,\ 2: S \rightarrow A,\ 3: A \rightarrow A \wedge B,\ 4: A \rightarrow B,\ 5: B \rightarrow (S),\ 6: B \rightarrow i$$

where *S* is the start symbol. This grammar has its two-part LR table, consisting of *action* and *goto*, depicted in Figures 7.18 and 7.19, respectively. Both *action* and *goto* have their rows denoted by the members of ${}_H\Theta = \{\theta_1, \theta_2, \ldots, \theta_{12}\}$. The columns of *action* are denoted by terminals ∧, ∨, *i*, (,), and ◁. The columns of *goto* are denoted by nonterminals *S*, *A*, and *B*.

	∧	∨	*i*	(	)	◁
θ_1			θ_6	θ_5		
θ_2		θ_7				☺
θ_3	θ_8	2			2	2
θ_4	4	4			4	4
θ_5			θ_6	θ_5		
θ_6	6	6			6	6
θ_7			θ_6	θ_5		
θ_8			θ_6	θ_5		
θ_9		θ_7			θ_{12}	
θ_{10}	θ_8	1			1	1
θ_{11}	3	3			3	3
θ_{12}	5	5			5	5

Figure 7.18 ${}_H$***action*****.**

	S	*A*	*B*
θ_1	θ_2	θ_3	θ_4
θ_2			
θ_3			
θ_4			
θ_5	θ_9	θ_3	θ_4
θ_6			
θ_7		θ_{10}	θ_4
θ_8			θ_{11}
θ_9			
θ_{10}			
θ_{11}			
θ_{12}			

Figure 7.19 ${}_H$***goto*****.**

Configuration	*Table Entry*	*Parsing Action*
$\triangleright\theta_1\diamond i \wedge i \vee i\triangleleft$	*action*$[\theta_1, i] = \theta_6$	**LR-SHIFT(*i*)**
$\triangleright\theta_1 i\,\theta_6\diamond\wedge i \vee i\triangleleft$	*action*$[\theta_6, \wedge] = 6$, goto$[\theta_1, B] = \theta_4$	**LR-REDUCE(6)**
$\triangleright\theta_1 B\,\theta_4\diamond\wedge i \vee i\triangleleft$	*action*$[\theta_4, \wedge] = 4$, goto$[\theta_1, A] = \theta_3$	**LR-REDUCE(4)**
$\triangleright\theta_1 A\,\theta_3\diamond\wedge i \vee i\triangleleft$	*action*$[\theta_3, \wedge] = \theta_8$	**LR-SHIFT (∧)**
$\triangleright\theta_1 A\,\theta_3\wedge\theta_8\diamond i \vee i\triangleleft$	*action*$[\theta_8, i] = \theta_6$	**LR-SHIFT(*i*)**
$\triangleright\theta_1 A\,\theta_3\wedge\theta_8\; i\,\theta_6\diamond\vee i\triangleleft$	*action*$[\theta_6, \vee] = 6$, goto$[\theta_8, B] = \theta_{11}$	**LR-REDUCE(6)**
$\triangleright\theta_1 A\,\theta_3\wedge\theta_8\; B\,\theta_{11}\diamond\vee i\triangleleft$	*action*$[\theta_{11}, \vee] = 3$, goto$[\theta_1, A] = \theta_3$	**LR-REDUCE(3)**
$\triangleright\theta_1 A\,\theta_3\diamond\vee i\triangleleft$	*action*$[\theta_3, \vee] = 2$, goto$[\theta_1, S] = \theta_2$	**LR-REDUCE(2)**
$\triangleright\theta_1 S\,\theta_2\diamond\vee i\triangleleft$	*action*$[\theta_2, \vee] = \theta_7$	**LR-SHIFT(∨)**
$\triangleright\theta_1 S\,\theta_2\vee\theta_7\diamond i\triangleleft$	*action*$[\theta_7, i] = \theta_6$	**LR-SHIFT(*i*)**
$\triangleright\theta_1 S\,\theta_2\vee\theta_7\, i\,\theta_6\diamond\triangleleft$	*action*$[\theta_6, \triangleleft] = 6$, goto $[\theta_7, B] = \theta_4$	**LR-REDUCE(6)**
$\triangleright\theta_1 S\,\theta_2\vee\theta_7\, B\,\theta_4\diamond\triangleleft$	*action*$[\theta_4, \triangleleft] = 4$, goto $[\theta_7, A] = \theta_{10}$	**LR-REDUCE(4)**
$\triangleright\theta_1 S\,\theta_2\vee\theta_7\, A\,\theta_{10}\diamond\triangleleft$	*action*$[\theta_{10}, \triangleleft] = 1$, goto $[\theta_1, S] = \theta_2$	**LR-REDUCE(1)**
$\triangleright\theta_1 S\,\theta_2\diamond\triangleleft$	*action*$[\theta_2, \triangleleft] =$ ☺	**SUCCESS**

Figure 7.20 LR parsing.

With $i \wedge i \vee i \in L(H)$ as the expression, Algorithm 7.22 works as described in Figure 7.20. The algorithm makes the successful parsing of $i \wedge i \vee i$ by the sequence of configurations given in the first column of this figure. The second column gives the relevant entries of *action* and *goto*, and the third column specifies the actions made by the algorithm. Notice that *goto* is relevant only when a reduction is performed; regarding a shift, it is not needed at all.

By writing out the rules according to which the LR parser makes each reduction, we obtain 64632641 as the right parse of $i \wedge i \vee i$ in H.

7.3.2.2 Construction of LR Table

The parsing theory has developed many sophisticated methods of constructing the LR tables. Most of them are too complicated to include them into this introductory text, however. Therefore, we just restrict our explanation of this construction to the fundamental ideas underlying a *simple LR table construction*. As its name indicates, it is simpler than the other constructions of LR tables, and this aspect represents its principle advantage. On the other hand, there exist LR CFGs for which this construction does not work. In other words, the LR parsers based on tables constructed in this way are slightly less powerful than LR parsers based on tables produced by more complicated methods, which are equivalent with LR CFGs and, therefore, characterize ${}_{DPDA}\Phi_f$ as already pointed out in the beginning of Section 7.3.2. However, these complicated LR-table constructions are too complex to be included in this introductory text.

As a matter of fact, even if we restrict our attention to the simple LR-table construction, this construction still belongs to the most complicated topics of this introductory book. Therefore, we give only its gist while reducing the formalism concerning this construction as much as possible.

Items. Let G be an LR CFG. In every configuration, the *pd* top contains a handle prefix, which the G-based LR parser tries to extend so a complete handle occurs on the *pd* top. As soon as the *pd* top contains a complete handle, the parser can make a reduction according to a rule $r \in {}_MR$ with ***rhs***(r) equal to the handle. To express that a handle prefix appears as the *pd* top, we introduce an *item* of the form

$$A \rightarrow x|y$$

for each rule $A \rightarrow z \in {}_GR$ and any two strings x and y such that $z = xy$. Intuitively, $A \rightarrow x|y$ means that if x occurs as the *pd* top and the parser makes a sequence of moves resulting in producing

y right behind x on the *pd* top, then the parser gets z as the handle on the *pd* top, which can be reduced to A according to $A \to z$. An item of the form $A \to |z$ is called a *start item* while an item of the form $A \to z|$ is called an *end item*.

Example 7.12 Reconsider the six-rule CFG H (see Convention 7.2), defined as

$$S \to S \vee A,\ S \to A,\ A \to A \wedge B,\ A \to B,\ B \to (S),\ B \to i$$

From $S \to S \vee A$, we obtain these four items

$$S \to |S \vee A,\ S \to S|\vee A,\ S \to S \vee|A, \text{ and } S \to S \vee A|$$

in which $S \to |S \vee A$ and $S \to S \vee A|$ represent a start item and an end item, respectively. Consider $S \to S|\vee A$. In essence, this item says that if S currently appears as the *pd* top and a prefix of the input is reduced to $\vee A$, the parser obtains $S \vee A$ as the handle, which can be reduced to S by using $S \to S \vee A$.

Before going any further, notice that several different items may be relevant to the same *pd* top string. To illustrate, take $S \to S \vee A|$ and $A \to A|\wedge B$. Notice that both items have to be taken into account whenever the LR parser occurs in a configuration with the three-symbol string $S \vee A$ as the *pd* top. Consider, for instance, $\triangleright S \vee A\diamond\triangleleft$ and $\triangleright S \vee A\diamond\wedge\, i\triangleleft$. From $\triangleright S \vee A\diamond\triangleleft$, the H-based LR parser makes a reduction according to $S \to S \vee A$ and, thereby, successfully completes the parsing process. More formally, the parser performs

$$\triangleright S \vee A\diamond\triangleleft \Rightarrow \triangleright S\diamond\triangleleft$$

In $\triangleright S \vee A\diamond\wedge\, i\triangleleft$, the parser has actually A as a prefix of the handle $A \wedge B$ on the pushdown. As a result, from $\triangleright S \vee A\diamond\wedge\, i\triangleleft$, it first makes several shifts and reductions before it obtains $A \wedge B$ as the handle on the pushdown top. Then, it reduces $A \wedge B$ to A according to $A \to A \wedge B$, after which it obtains $S \vee A$ as the handle, makes a reduction according to $S \to S \vee A$ and, thereby, completes the parsing process. To summarize this part of parsing process formally, from $\triangleright S \vee A\diamond\wedge\, i\triangleleft$, the H-based LR parser computes

$$\begin{aligned}
\triangleright S \vee A\diamond\wedge\, i\triangleleft \quad & \Rightarrow \triangleright S \vee A \wedge\diamond i\triangleleft \\
& \Rightarrow \triangleright S \vee A \wedge i\diamond\triangleleft \\
& \Rightarrow \triangleright S \vee A \wedge B\diamond\triangleleft \\
& \Rightarrow \triangleright S \vee A\diamond\triangleleft \\
& \Rightarrow \triangleright S\diamond\triangleleft
\end{aligned}$$

Convention 7.23 Throughout the rest of this chapter, for an LR CFG G, ${}_GI$, ${}_GI_{start}$, and ${}_GI_{end}$ denote the set of all its items, the set of start items, and the set of end items, respectively, so ${}_GI_{start} \subseteq {}_GI$ as well as ${}_GI_{end} \subseteq {}_GI$. Furthermore, ${}_G\Omega = power({}_GI)$—that is, ${}_G\Omega$ denotes the power set of ${}_GI$, defined as the set of all subsets of ${}_GI$ (see Section 1.2). As usual, we omit the subscript G in this notation if no confusion exists; for instance, we often write I instead of ${}_GI$ if G is understood. ■

As sketched in the conclusion of Example 7.12, several items are usually related to a single prefix of the right-hand side of some rules when the prefix occurs on the *pd* top to determine the next LR parsing step. Next, we construct the item sets corresponding to all prefixes of the right-hand sides of rules in ${}_GR$, and these sets are then used as members of ${}_G\Theta$, so ${}_G\Theta \subseteq {}_G\Omega$. By using the members of ${}_G\Theta$, we then construct the G-based LR table.

Construction of ${}_G\Theta$. Initially, we change the start symbol S to a new start symbol Z in G, and add a dummy rule of the form $Z \to S$. As a result, we can be sure that in G, every derivation that generates a sentence in $L(G)$ starts by applying $Z \rightarrow S$. Apart from ${}_G\Theta$, we introduce an auxiliary item set ${}_GW$. Initially, we set ${}_G\Theta$ and ${}_GW$ to $\varnothing$ and $\{\{Z \rightarrow |S\}\}$, respectively. We repeat extensions I and II, until no new item set can be included into ${}_GW$ to obtain all item sets in ${}_G\Theta$. Let us note that during the computation of I and II, ${}_G\Theta$ and ${}_GW$ always represent subsets of ${}_G\Omega$.

I. Let $I \in {}_GW$. Suppose that u appears on the *pd* top, and let $A \rightarrow uBv \in {}_GR$, where $A, B \in {}_GN$, and $u, v \in {}_G\Sigma^*$. Observe that if $A \rightarrow u|Bv \in I$ and $B \rightarrow |y \in {}_GI_{start}$, then by using $B \rightarrow y$, the G-based LR parser can reduce y to B, and this reduction does not affect u appearing on the *pd* top at all because $B \rightarrow |y$ is a start item. Thus, extend I by adding $B \rightarrow |y$ into it. Repeat this extension until I can no longer be extended in this way. Take the resulting I and add it to ${}_G\Theta$ (if I was already there, ${}_G\Theta$ remains unchanged). To summarize this extension as a Pascal-like procedure, for $I \in {}_GW$, perform

repeat
  if $A \rightarrow u|Bv \in I$ **and** $B \rightarrow z \in {}_GR$ **then**
    include $B \rightarrow |z$ into I
until no change
include I into ${}_G\Theta$

II. This extension is based on a relation ${}_G\circlearrowright$ from ${}_G\Omega \times {}_G\Sigma$ to ${}_G\Omega$, defined next. Intuitively, for $I \in {}_G\Omega$ and $X \in {}_G\Sigma$, ${}_G\circlearrowright(I, X)$ specifies the set of items related to the configuration that M enters from I by pushing X on the *pd* top. Formally, for all $I \in {}_G\Omega$ and all $X \in {}_G\Sigma$,

$$ {}_G\circlearrowright(I, X) = \{A \rightarrow uX|v| \; A \rightarrow u|Xv \in I, A \in {}_GN, u, v \in {}_G\Sigma^*\} $$

Let $I \in {}_GW$ and $A \rightarrow uX|v \in I$, where $A \in {}_GN$, $u, v \in {}_G\Sigma^*$, and $X \in {}_G\Sigma$. Consider a part of a rightmost derivation in G in reverse during which a portion of the input string is reduced to X. Simulating this derivation part, the G-based LR parser actually obtains X on the *pd*. As a result, for every $I \in {}_GW$ and $X \in {}_G\Sigma$, the following **for** loop extends ${}_GW$ by ${}_G\circlearrowright(I, X)$ unless ${}_G\circlearrowright(I, X)$ is empty.

for each $X \in {}_G\Sigma$ with ${}_G\circlearrowright(I, X) \neq \varnothing$ **do**
  include ${}_G\circlearrowright(I, X)$ into ${}_GW$

Based on repeat extensions I and II, we next construct ${}_G\Theta$.

Algorithm 7.24 Construction of ${}_G\Theta$.

Input. An LR grammar, $G = ({}_G\Sigma, {}_GR)$, extended by the dummy rule $Z \rightarrow S$, where Z is the new start symbol.

Output. ${}_G\Theta$.

Note. Apart from ${}_G\Theta$, an auxiliary set ${}_GW \subseteq {}_G\Omega$ is used.

Method.

begin

set ${}_GW = \{\{Z \rightarrow |S\}\}$
set ${}_G\Theta = \varnothing$

```
repeat
  for each I ∈ _G W do
  begin

    repeat                                         {start of extension I}
      if A → u|Bv ∈ I and B → z ∈ _G R then
        include B → |z into I
    until no change
    include I into _G Θ                            {end of extension I}

    for each X ∈ _G Σ with _G ↻(I, X) ≠ ∅ do       {start of extension II}
      include _G ↻(I, X) into _G W                 {end of extension II}

  end {of the for loop}

until no change
end.
```

Example 7.13 Consider again H (see Convention 7.2). Add a dummy rule of the form $Z \rightarrow S$ to its rules, and define Z as the start symbol. The resulting LR CFG is defined as

$$Z \rightarrow S,\ S \rightarrow S \vee A,\ S \rightarrow A,\ A \rightarrow A \wedge B,\ A \rightarrow B,\ B \rightarrow (S),\ B \rightarrow i$$

Next, apply Algorithm 7.24 with H as its input. At the beginning, set ${}_H\Theta = \emptyset$ and $W = \{\{Z \rightarrow |S\}\}$. By extension I, the algorithm extends $\{Z \rightarrow |S\} \in {}_HW$ to

$$\{Z \rightarrow |S,\ S \rightarrow |S \vee A,\ S \rightarrow |A,\ A \rightarrow |A \wedge B,\ A \rightarrow |B,\ B \rightarrow |(S),\ B \rightarrow |i\}$$

Include this item set into ${}_H\Theta$. Notice that this new item set I contains $Z \rightarrow |S$, $S \rightarrow |S \vee A$, and for $I = \{Z \rightarrow |S, S \rightarrow |S \vee A, S \rightarrow |A, A \rightarrow |A \wedge B, A \rightarrow |B, B \rightarrow |(S), B \rightarrow |i\}$, we have ${}_H\circlearrowleft(I, S) = \{Z \rightarrow S|, S \rightarrow S|\vee A\}$. Thus, by permitting extension II, the algorithm includes $\{Z \rightarrow S|, S \rightarrow S|\vee A\}$ into ${}_HW$, after which it performs the second iteration of I and II, and so on. Continuing in this way, this algorithm eventually produces the 12-item sets listed in the second column of Figure 7.21. For brevity, these 12-item sets are referred to as θ_1 through θ_{12} according to the first column of Figure 7.21.

${}_H\Theta$	Item Sets
θ_1	$\{Z \rightarrow |S, S \rightarrow |S \vee A, S \rightarrow |A, A \rightarrow |A \wedge B, A \rightarrow |B, B \rightarrow |(S), B \rightarrow |i\}$
θ_2	$\{Z \rightarrow S|, S \rightarrow S|\vee A\}$
θ_3	$\{S \rightarrow A|, A \rightarrow A|\wedge B\}$
θ_4	$\{A \rightarrow B|\}$
θ_5	$\{B \rightarrow (|S), S \rightarrow |S \vee A, S \rightarrow |A, A \rightarrow |A \wedge B, A \rightarrow |B, B \rightarrow |(S), B \rightarrow |i\}$
θ_6	$\{B \rightarrow i|\}$
θ_7	$\{S \rightarrow S \vee |A, A \rightarrow |A \wedge B, A \rightarrow |B, B \rightarrow |(S), B \rightarrow |i\}$
θ_8	$\{A \rightarrow A \wedge |B, B \rightarrow |(S), B \rightarrow |i\}$
θ_9	$\{B \rightarrow (S|), S \rightarrow S|\vee A\}$
θ_{10}	$\{S \rightarrow S \vee A|, A \rightarrow A|\wedge B\}$
θ_{11}	$\{A \rightarrow A \wedge B|\}$
θ_{12}	$\{B \rightarrow (S)|\}$

Figure 7.21 ${}_H\Theta$.

Construction of LR Table. Making use of ${}_G\Theta$, we construct the *action* and *goto* parts of LR table by performing I through III, given next, in which we automatically suppose that θ_i and θ_j belong to ${}_G\Theta$. Concerning I and II, it is important to realize that for all $\theta_i \in {}_G\Omega$ and all $X \in {}_G\Sigma$, ${}_G\circlearrowright(\theta_i, X)$ and ${}_GI_{start}$ (see Convention 7.23) are necessarily disjoint.

I. To explain the construction of *goto*, consider item $A \to u|Bv \in I$, where $I \in {}_G\Theta$, $A, B \in {}_GN$ and $u, v \in {}_G\Sigma^*$. At this point, after reducing a portion of the input string to B, M actually extends the prefix u of the handle by B, so uB occurs on the *pd* top, which leads to this extension:

if ${}_G\circlearrowright(\theta_i, B) = \theta_j - {}_GI_{start}$, where $B \in {}_GN$ **then**
  $goto[\theta_i, B] = \theta_j$

II. By analogy with the construction of the *goto* entries in I, we obtain the *action* shift entries in this way

if ${}_G\circlearrowright(\theta_i, b) = \theta_j - {}_GI_{start}$, where $b \in {}_G\Delta$ **then**
  $action[\theta_i, b] = \theta_j$

III. To explain the construction of the reduction entries in *action*, consider a rule $r: A \to u \in {}_GR$ and $A \to u| \in {}_GI_{end}$ (see Convention 7.23), which means that a complete handle u occurs on the pushdown top. At this point, the parser reduces u to A according to this rule provided that after this reduction, A is followed by a terminal a that may legally occur after A in a sentential form. As a result, we obtain

if $A \to u| \in \theta_i$, $a \in follow(A)$, $r: A \to u \in {}_GR$ **then**
  $action[\theta_i, a] = r$

(see Definition 7.11 and Algorithm 7.12 for the definition and construction of *follow*, respectively).

Recall that G starts every derivation by applying $0: Z \to S$, and the LR parser works so it simulates rightmost derivations in G in reverse. Furthermore, notice that when the input symbol equals $\triangleleft$, all the input has been read by the parser. Consequently, if $Z \to S| \in \theta_i$, we set $action[\theta_i, \triangleleft] =$ ☺ to signalize that the parsing process has been successfully completed.

Therefore,

if $Z \to S| \in \theta_i$ **then**
  $action[\theta_i, \triangleleft] =$ ☺

Algorithm 7.25 LR Table.

Input. An LR CFG, $G = ({}_G\Sigma, {}_GR)$, in which Z and $0: Z \to S$ have the same meaning as in Algorithm 7.24, and ${}_G\Theta$, which is constructed by Algorithm 7.24.

Output. A G-based LR table, consisting of the *action* and *goto* parts.

Note. We suppose that $A, B \in {}_GN$, $b \in {}_G\Delta$, and $u, v \in {}_G\Sigma^*$ in this algorithm.

Method.

begin

denote the rows of *action* and *goto* with the members of $_G\Theta$
denote the columns of *action* and *goto* with the members of $_G\Delta \cup \{\triangleleft\}$ and $_GN$, respectively

repeat
for all $\theta_i, \theta_j \in {_G\Theta}$ **do**
begin
if $_G\circlearrowleft(\theta_i, B) = \theta_j - {_GI_{start}}$, where $B \in {_GN}$ **then**
$goto[\theta_i, B] = \theta_j$ {*goto* entries; see I}
if $_G\circlearrowleft(\theta_i, b) = \theta_j - {_GI_{start}}$, where $b \in {_G\Delta}$ **then**
$action[\theta_i, b] = \theta_j$ {*action* shift entries; see II}
if $A \to u| \in \theta_i \cap {_GI_{end}}$, $a \in follow(A)$, j: $A \to u \in {_GR}$ **then**
$action[\theta_i, a] = j$ {*action* reduction entries; see III}
end
until no change

if $Z \to S| \in \theta_i$ **then**
$action[\theta_i, \triangleleft] =$ ☺ {success}
{all the other entries remain blank and, thereby, signalizes a syntax error}

end.

Example 7.14 Consider the same grammar as in Example 7.13. Number its rules to obtain

$$0: Z \to S,\ 1: S \to S \vee A,\ 2: S \to A,\ 3: A \to A \wedge B,\ 4: A \to B,\ 5: B \to (S),\ 6: B \to i$$

Consider $_H\Theta = \{\theta_1, \theta_2, \ldots, \theta_{12}\}$, obtained in Example 7.13 (see Figure 7.21). Denote the rows of *action* and *goto* with the members of $_H\Theta$. Denote the columns of *action* and *goto* with the members of $\{\vee, \wedge, (,), i, \triangleleft\}$ and $\{S, A, B\}$, respectively.

According to the first **if** statement in Algorithm 7.25, $goto[\theta_1, S] = \theta_2$ because $S \to |S \vee A \in \theta_1$ and $S \to S|\vee A \in \theta_2$. By the second **if** statement, $action[\theta_2, \vee] = \theta_7$ because $S \to S|\vee A \in \theta_2$ and $S \to S \vee|A \in \theta_7$. By the third **if** statement, $action[\theta_3, \vee] = 2$ because 2: $S \to A| \in \theta_3$ and $\vee \in follow(A)$. As an exercise, perform a complete execution of the **repeat** loop, containing the three **if** statements. After this, according to the conclusion of Algorithm 7.25, set $action[\theta_2, \triangleleft] =$ ☺ because θ_2 contains $Z \to S|$. The resulting table produced by this algorithm is given in Figures 7.18 and 7.19.

Out of existing constructions of LR tables, the construction described in this section belongs to the simplest methods of obtaining LR tables. Unfortunately, there exist LR grammars for which this construction does not work. In fact, it breaks down even when some quite common grammatical phenomenon occurs. Specifically, it cannot handle *reduction-shift conflict*, whose decision requires to figure out whether the parser should perform a shift or a reduction when both actions are possible. Furthermore, if two or more different reductions can be made in the given configuration, it cannot decide which of them it should select. To give an insight into this latter *reduction-reduction conflict*, suppose that the same set in $_H\Theta$ contains two end items, $A \to u|$ and $B \to v|$, but $follow(A) \cap follow(B) \neq \emptyset$. At this point, Algorithm 7.25 would illegally place both rules, $A \to u$ and $B \to v$, into the same entry in the action part of the LR table. There exists a number of complicated constructions that resolve these conflicts. However, these constructions are too complex to be included into this introductory text as already pointed out.

7.3.2.3 Handling Errors in LR Parsing

Compared to handling errors in precedence parsing, LR parsing handles syntax errors more exactly and elegantly. Indeed, LR parsing detects an error as soon as there is no valid continuation for the portion of the input thus far scanned. As a result, it detects all possible errors by using only the action part of the table; as a side effect, this property allows us to significantly reduce the size of the *goto* part by removing its unneeded blank entries. Next, we sketch two frequently used methods of LR error recovery. As before, we suppose that $G = ({}_G\Sigma, {}_GR)$ is an LR grammar, and M is a G-based LR parser, which uses LR table, consisting of *action* and *goto*.

A *panic-mode error recovery* represents a method that tries to isolate the shortest possible erroneous substring derivable from a selected nonterminal, skips this substring, and resumes the parsing process. This method has a selected set of nonterminals, ${}_GO$, which usually represents major program pieces, such as expressions or statements. In principle, this method finds the shortest string uv such that $u \in {}_G\Sigma^*$ is a string obtained from a current pushdown top $x \in ({}_G\Sigma_G\Theta)^*$ by deleting all symbols from ${}_G\Theta$, and v is the shortest input prefix followed by an input symbol a from *follow*(A), where $A \in O$ and $A \;{}_{rm}\!\Rightarrow^* uv$. Let x be preceded by $o \in {}_G\Theta$ and *goto*[o, A] $= \theta$. To recover, this method replaces x with $A\theta$ on the *pd* top and skips the input prefix v. In this way, it pretends that the parser has reduced a portion of the input string that ends with v to A. After this, it resumes the parsing process from *action*[θ, a]. As an exercise, discuss this method in detail.

Ad-hoc recovery. This method resembles the way the precedence parser handles the table-detected errors. That is, this method considers each blank *action* entry, which signalizes only an error without any diagnostic specification. Based on a typical language usage, it decides the most probable mistake that led to the particular error in question, and in accord with this decision, it designs an ingenious recovery procedure that takes an appropriate recovery action. This design always requires some ingeniousness from the compiler's author, who is encouraged to consult some other computer-science areas, ranging from computational psychology through artificial intelligence to the formal language theory, to design the best possible error recovery routine. Typically, this routine handles an error of this kind so that it modifies the pushdown or the input by changing, inserting, or deleting some symbols; whatever modification it performs, however, it has to guarantee that this modification surely avoids any infinite loop so that the parser eventually proceeds its normal process. Finally, each blank entry is filled with the reference to the corresponding recovery routine. In practice, this method is very popular, and we illustrate its application in Example 7.15.

Example 7.15 To demonstrate how LR parsing handles syntax errors by using the ad-hoc recovery method, consider the grammar H (see Convention 7.2), defined as

$$1: S \rightarrow S \vee A,\ 2: S \rightarrow A,\ 3: A \rightarrow A \wedge B,\ 4: A \rightarrow B,\ 5: B \rightarrow (S),\ 6: B \rightarrow i$$

and its LR table consisting of *action* and *goto* given in Figures 7.18 and 7.19, respectively. Consider the ill-formed expression $i \vee$). With $i \vee$), the H-based LR parser interrupts its parsing process after making the six steps described in Figure 7.22 because it reaches a blank entry in *action*, so the error recovery is in order.

Next, we schematically describe four diagnoses together with the corresponding recovery procedures—① through ④, whose straightforward incorporation into Algorithm 7.25 is left as an exercise. Figure 7.23 presents a new version of *action* with the appropriate error-recovery routine

Configuration	*Table Entry*	*Parsing Action*
$\triangleright\theta_1\diamond i\vee)\triangleleft$	$action[\theta_1, i] = \theta_6$	LR-SHIFT(i)
$\triangleright\theta_1 i\theta_6\diamond\vee)\triangleleft$	$action[\theta_6, \vee] = 6$, $goto[\theta_1, B] = \theta_4$	LR-REDUCE(6)
$\triangleright\theta_1 B\theta_4\diamond\vee)\triangleleft$	$action[\theta_4, \vee] = 4$, $goto[\theta_1, A] = \theta_3$	LR-REDUCE(4)
$\triangleright\theta_1 A\theta_3\diamond\vee)\triangleleft$	$action[\theta_3, \vee] = 2$, $goto[\theta_1, S] = \theta_2$	LR-REDUCE(2)
$\triangleright\theta_1 S\theta_2\diamond\vee)\triangleleft$	$action[\theta_2, \vee] = \theta_7$	LR-SHIFT($\vee$)
$\triangleright\theta_1 S\theta_2\vee\theta_7\diamond)\triangleleft$	$action[\theta_7,)] = \square$	ERROR

Figure 7.22 *H*-based LR parser working on *i* ∨) without error recovery.

	$\wedge$	$\vee$	i	(	)	$\triangleleft$
θ_1	①	①	θ_6	θ_5	②	①
θ_2		θ_7			②	☺
θ_3	θ_8	2			2	2
θ_4	4	4			4	4
θ_5	①	①	θ_6	θ_5	②	①
θ_6	6	6	③	③	6	6
θ_7	①	①	θ_6	θ_5	②	①
θ_8	①	①	θ_6	θ_5	②	①
θ_9		θ_7			θ_{12}	④
θ_{10}	θ_8	1			1	1
θ_{11}	3	3			3	3
θ_{12}	5	5	③	③	5	5

Figure 7.23 $_H$*action* with error-recovery routines.

Configuration	*Table Entries*	*Parsing Action*
$\triangleright\theta_1\diamond i\vee)\triangleleft$	$action[\theta_1, i] = \theta_6$	LR-SHIFT(i)
$\triangleright\theta_1 i\theta_6\diamond\vee)\triangleleft$	$action[\theta_6, \vee] = 6$, $goto[\theta_1, B] = \theta_4$	LR-REDUCE(6)
$\triangleright\theta_1 B\theta_4\diamond\vee)\triangleleft$	$action[\theta_4, \vee] = 4$, $goto[\theta_1, A] = \theta_3$	LR-REDUCE(4)
$\triangleright\theta_1 A\theta_3\diamond\vee)\triangleleft$	$action[\theta_3, \vee] = 2$, $goto[\theta_1, S] = \theta_2$	LR-REDUCE(2)
$\triangleright\theta_1 S\theta_2\diamond\vee)\triangleleft$	$action[\theta_2, \vee] = \theta_7$	LR-SHIFT($\vee$)
$\triangleright\theta_1 S\theta_2\vee\theta_7\diamond)\triangleleft$	$action[\theta_7,)] =$ ②	②—skip)
$\triangleright\theta_1 S\theta_2\vee\theta_7\diamond\triangleleft$	$action[\theta_7, \triangleleft] =$ ①	①—push $i\,\theta_6$ onto *pd*
$\triangleright\theta_1 S\theta_2\vee\theta_7 i\theta_6\diamond\triangleleft$	$action[\theta_6, \triangleleft] = 6$, $goto[\theta_7, B] = \theta_4$	LR-REDUCE(6)
$\triangleright\theta_1 S\theta_2\vee\theta_7 B\theta_4\diamond\triangleleft$	$action[\theta_4, \triangleleft] = 4$, $goto[\theta_7, A] = \theta_{10}$	LR-REDUCE(4)
$\triangleright\theta_1 S\theta_2\vee\theta_7 A\theta_{10}\diamond\triangleleft$	$action[\theta_{10}, \triangleleft] = 1$, $goto[\theta_1, S] = \theta_2$	LR-REDUCE(1)
$\triangleright\theta_1 S\theta_2\diamond\triangleleft$	$action[\theta_2, \triangleleft] =$ ☺	error reports

Figure 7.24 *H*-based LR parser working on *i* ∨) with ad-hoc error recovery.

placed in each blank entry. With *i* ∨) as its input, the *H*-based LR parser makes the error recovery described in Figure 7.24. As an exercise, prove that the parser can never detect an error in the blank entries of the table. Indeed, the parser cannot detect an error in any entry of the *goto* part, which thus contains no recovery routines (Figure 7.25). However, for the same reason, the *action* part in Figure 7.23 contains some blank entries, too.

① **diagnostic:** missing *i* or (
recovery: insert $i\,\theta_6$ onto the pushdown

② **diagnostic:** unbalanced)
recovery: delete the input symbol) and, thereby, advance to the next input symbol

	S	A	B
θ_1	θ_2	θ_3	θ_4
θ_2			
θ_3			
θ_4			
θ_5	θ_9	θ_3	θ_4
θ_6			
θ_7		θ_{10}	θ_4
θ_8			θ_{11}
θ_9			
θ_{10}			
θ_{11}			
θ_{12}			

Figure 7.25 ${}_{H}$*goto*

③ **diagnostic:** missing operator
recovery: insert ∨ in front of the current input symbol *ins*, and after this insertion, set *ins* to the newly inserted ∨

④ **diagnostic:** missing)
recovery: insert) θ_{12} onto the pushdown

Exercises

1. Chapter 7 contains results whose proofs are only sketched or even completely omitted. These results include Lemmas 7.4 and 7.6 and Examples 7.4, 7.6, 7.7, and 7.15. Prove them rigorously.
2. Consider each of Algorithms 7.10, 7.12, 7.17, 7.19, 7.22, 7.24, and 7.25. Write a program to implement them.
3. Consider the following CFGs (i) through (iv), which describe the **if-then-else** statement. In these CFGs, the nonterminals have the form ⟨*x*⟩, where *x* intuitively indicates the syntax construct generated from ⟨*x*⟩. The start symbol is denoted by ⟨start⟩. The other symbols are terminals.

   Are these CFGs all equivalent? Which of them define this statement ambiguously? Which of them make this definition easy to understand? Discuss other syntax-analysis-related advantages and disadvantages of these CFGs, such as their succinctness with respect to the number of nonterminals and rules.

   i. ⟨start⟩ → ⟨if-statement⟩
   ⟨if-statement⟩ → **if** ⟨expression⟩ **then** ⟨statement⟩ **else** ⟨if-statement⟩
   ⟨if-statement⟩ → **if** ⟨expression⟩ **then** ⟨if-statement⟩
   ⟨if-statement⟩ → ⟨ statement⟩
   ⟨statement⟩ → *s*
   ⟨expression⟩ → *e*

   ii. ⟨start⟩ → ⟨statement⟩
   ⟨statement⟩ → **if** ⟨expression⟩ **then** ⟨statement⟩ **else** ⟨statement⟩
   ⟨statement⟩ → **if** ⟨expression⟩ **then** ⟨statement⟩
   ⟨statement⟩ → *s*
   ⟨expression⟩ → *e*

   iii. ⟨start⟩ → ⟨if-statement⟩
   ⟨if-statement⟩ → **if** ⟨expression⟩ **then** ⟨statement⟩ **else** ⟨if-statement⟩
   ⟨if-statement⟩ → **if** ⟨expression⟩ **then** ⟨statement⟩
   ⟨if-statement⟩ → *s*
   ⟨expression⟩ → *e*

iv. ⟨start⟩ → ⟨if-statement⟩
⟨if-statement⟩ → **if** ⟨expression⟩ **then** ⟨if-statement⟩ **else** ⟨statement⟩
⟨if-statement⟩ → **if** ⟨expression⟩ **then** ⟨if-statement⟩
⟨if-statement⟩ → ⟨statement⟩
⟨statement⟩ → *s*
⟨expression⟩ → *e*

4 S. Consider the next CFG *G*, in which the nonterminals have the form ⟨*x*⟩, where *x* intuitively indicates the syntax construct generated from ⟨*x*⟩; for instance, from ⟨variable list⟩, *G* generates a well-formed list of variables. The start symbol is denoted by ⟨program⟩.

As obvious, *G* defines the syntax of a programming language. Examine the rules in *G* one by one to describe the syntax constructs defined by them. Justify this description soundly, but informally—that is, omit a strictly rigorous proof verifying the description. Illustrate the programming language defined by *G* by a syntactically correct program.

⟨program⟩ → ***program*** ⟨declaration part⟩ ⟨execution part⟩ ***end***
⟨declaration part⟩ → ***declaration*** ⟨declaration list⟩
⟨declaration list⟩ → ⟨declaration⟩ ; ⟨declaration list⟩
⟨declaration list⟩ → ⟨declaration⟩
⟨declaration⟩ → ***integer*** ⟨variable list⟩
⟨declaration⟩ → ***real*** ⟨variable list⟩
⟨declaration⟩ → ***label*** ⟨label list⟩
⟨variable list⟩ → *i* , ⟨variable list⟩
⟨variable list⟩ → *i*
⟨label list⟩ → *l* , ⟨label list⟩
⟨label list⟩ → *l*
⟨execution part⟩ → ***execution*** ⟨statement list⟩
⟨statement list⟩ → ⟨statement⟩ ; ⟨statement list⟩
⟨statement list⟩ → ⟨statement⟩
⟨statement⟩ → *i* = ⟨expression⟩
⟨statement⟩ → *l* ⟨statement⟩
⟨statement⟩ → ***goto*** *l*
⟨statement⟩ → ***read***(⟨input list⟩)
⟨statement⟩ → ***write***(⟨output list⟩)
⟨statement⟩ → ***if*** ⟨condition⟩ ***then*** ⟨statement⟩
⟨statement⟩ → ***if*** ⟨condition⟩ ***then*** ⟨statement⟩ ***else*** ⟨statement⟩
⟨statement⟩ → ***provided*** ⟨condition⟩ ***iterate*** ⟨statement⟩
⟨statement⟩ → ***for*** *i* = ⟨expression⟩ ***through*** ⟨expression⟩ ***iterate*** ⟨statement⟩
⟨statement⟩ → ***begin*** ⟨statement list⟩ ***end***
⟨input list⟩ → *i* , ⟨input list⟩
⟨input list⟩ → *i*
⟨output list⟩ → ⟨write member⟩ , ⟨output list⟩
⟨write member⟩ → ⟨expression⟩
⟨write member⟩ → *t*
⟨condition⟩ → ⟨condition⟩ ∧ ⟨condition⟩
⟨condition⟩ → ⟨condition⟩ ∨ ⟨condition⟩
⟨condition⟩ → ¬ ⟨condition⟩
⟨condition⟩ → (⟨condition⟩)
⟨condition⟩ → ⟨expression⟩
⟨expression⟩ → ⟨expression⟩ + ⟨term⟩
⟨expression⟩ → ⟨expression⟩ − ⟨term⟩
⟨expression⟩ → ⟨term⟩
⟨term⟩ → ⟨term⟩ * ⟨factor⟩
⟨term⟩ → ⟨term⟩ / ⟨factor⟩
⟨term⟩ → ⟨factor⟩
⟨factor⟩ → (⟨expression⟩)

⟨factor⟩ → i
⟨factor⟩ → #
⟨factor⟩ → ¢

5 S. The following three-rule CFG G represents the well-known ambiguous specification of the **if-then-else** statement that occurred in the original description of the programming language ALGOL 60, which represented an important ancestor of Pascal.

1: $S \rightarrow$ **if** b **then** S **else** S
2: $S \rightarrow$ **if** b **then** S
3: $S \rightarrow a$

Perform (a) through (d).

a. Prove that G is ambiguous.
b. Turn G to an equivalent unambiguous CFG H. Give a rigorous proof that H is unambiguous. Then, prove the equivalence rigorously.
c. Select a suitable deterministic parsing method discussed in Chapter 7, and based on this method, construct an H-based deterministic parser.
d. Write a program to implement the parser constructed in (c).

6 S. Consider the language consisting of all well-formed arithmetic expressions. Erase everything but parentheses from this language. The language resulting from this reduction thus contains all correctly balanced strings of (s and)s; for instance, ((()(())) is in this language, but ()) is not. To avoid any confusion, replace each (and each) with a and b, respectively, and denote the resulting language by L.

Perform (a) through (c).

a. Introduce a CFG G such that $L(G) = L$.
b. Based on Algorithm 7.3, turn G to a G-based top-down parser.
c. Consider *abaabb*. Parse it by the parser obtained in (b).

7 S. Algorithm 7.5 transforms any CFG to an equivalent G-based bottom-up parser represented by a PDA, which simulates the rightmost derivations in G in reverse. The parsing theory has also developed algorithms that act as parsers, but they are not based on PDAs simulating canonical derivations in G. One of them, called the *Cocke–Younger–Kasami parsing algorithm* after its authors, works with CFGs in Chomsky normal form, in which every rule has one terminal or two nonterminals on its right-hand side. Its gist follows next.

Given a CFG, $G = (\Sigma, R)$, in the Chomsky normal form and a string, $x = a_1a_2\ldots a_n$ with $a_i \in {}_G\Delta$, $1 \leq i \leq n$, for some $n \geq 1$, the Cocke–Younger–Kasami parsing algorithm decides whether $x \in L(G)$. In essence, it makes a decision of whether $x \in L(G)$ in a bottom-up way. It works so it constructs sets of nonterminals, $CYK[i, j]$, where $1 \leq i \leq j \leq n$, satisfying $A \in CYK[i, j]$ iff $A \Rightarrow^* a_i\ldots a_j$; therefore, as a special case, $L(G)$ contains x iff $CYK[1, n]$ contains G's start symbol, S. To construct the sets of nonterminals, this algorithm initially includes A into $CYK[i, i]$ iff $A \rightarrow a_i$ is in R because $A \Rightarrow a_i$ in G by using $A \rightarrow a_i$. Then, whenever $B \in CYK[i, j]$, $C \in CYK[j + 1, k]$, and $A \rightarrow BC \in {}_GR$, we add A to $CYK[i, k]$ because $B \in CYK[i, j]$ and $C \in CYK[j + 1, k]$ imply $B \Rightarrow^* a_i\ldots a_j$, and $C \Rightarrow^* a_{j+1}\ldots a_k$, respectively, so

$$\begin{aligned} A &\Rightarrow BC \quad [A \rightarrow BC] \\ &\Rightarrow^* a_i\ldots a_jC \\ &\Rightarrow^* a_i\ldots a_ja_{j+1}\ldots a_k \end{aligned}$$

When this construction cannot extend any set, we examine whether $S \in CYK[1, n]$. If so, $S \Rightarrow^* a_1\ldots a_n$ and $x = a_1\ldots a_n \in L(G)$, so this algorithm announces **SUCCESS** (see Convention 7.15); otherwise, $x \notin L(G)$ and the algorithm announces **ERROR**.

Describe this algorithm formally.

8 S. Consider each of CFGs (i) through (iv). Prove that the CFG is not an LL CFG. Determine its language. Construct a proper LL CFG that generates the same language.

i. 1: ⟨program⟩ → **begin** ⟨statement list⟩ **end**
2: ⟨statement list⟩ → ⟨statement⟩ ; ⟨statement list⟩
3: ⟨statement list⟩ → ⟨statement⟩

4: ⟨statement⟩ → **read** *i*
5: ⟨statement⟩ → **write** *i*
6: ⟨statement⟩ → *i* = **sum** (⟨item list⟩)
7: ⟨item list⟩ → *i* , ⟨item list⟩
8: ⟨item list⟩ → *i*

ii. 1: ⟨program⟩ → **begin** ⟨statement list⟩ **end**
2: ⟨statement list⟩ → ⟨statement⟩ ; ⟨statement list⟩
3: ⟨statement list⟩ → ⟨statement⟩
4: ⟨statement⟩ → **read** ⟨item list⟩
5: ⟨statement⟩ → **write** ⟨item list⟩
6: ⟨statement⟩ → *i* = ⟨expression⟩
7: ⟨item list⟩ → *i* , ⟨item list⟩
8: ⟨item list⟩ → *i*
9: ⟨expression⟩ → *i* + ⟨expression⟩
10: ⟨expression⟩ → *i* – ⟨expression⟩
11: ⟨expression⟩ → *i*

iii. 1: ⟨program⟩ → ⟨function⟩ ; ⟨function list⟩
2: ⟨function list⟩ → ⟨function⟩
3: ⟨function⟩ → ⟨head⟩⟨body⟩
4: ⟨head⟩ → **function** *i* ( ) : ⟨type⟩
5: ⟨head⟩ → **function** *i* (⟨parameter list⟩) : ⟨type⟩
6: ⟨parameter list⟩ → ⟨parameter⟩ , ⟨parameter list⟩
7: ⟨parameter list⟩ → ⟨parameter⟩
8: ⟨parameter⟩ → *i* : ⟨type⟩
9: ⟨type⟩ → **integer**
10: ⟨type⟩ → **real**
11: ⟨type⟩ → **string**
12: ⟨body⟩ → **begin** ⟨statement list⟩ **end**
13: ⟨statement list⟩ → ⟨statement⟩ ; ⟨statement list⟩
14: ⟨statement list⟩ → ⟨statement⟩
15: ⟨statement⟩ → s
16: ⟨statement⟩ → ⟨program⟩

iv. 1: ⟨block⟩ → **begin** ⟨declaration list⟩⟨execution part⟩ **end**
2: ⟨declaration list⟩ → ⟨declaration list⟩ ; ⟨declaration⟩
3: ⟨declaration list⟩ → ⟨declaration⟩
4: ⟨declaration⟩ → **integer** ⟨variable list⟩
5: ⟨declaration⟩ → **real** ⟨variable list⟩
6: ⟨variable list⟩ → *i* , ⟨variable list⟩
7: ⟨variable list⟩ → *i*
8: ⟨execution part⟩ → **compute** ⟨statement list⟩
9: ⟨statement list⟩ → ⟨statement list⟩ ; ⟨statement⟩
10: ⟨statement list⟩ → ⟨statement⟩
11: ⟨statement⟩ → *s*
12: ⟨statement⟩ → ⟨block⟩

9 S. Consider this five-rule CFG

1: ⟨if-statement⟩ → **if** ⟨condition⟩ **then** ⟨if-statement⟩⟨else-part⟩
2: ⟨if-statement⟩ → *a*
3: ⟨condition⟩ → *c*
4: ⟨else-part⟩ → **else** ⟨if-statement⟩
5: ⟨else-part⟩ → ε

Construct *predictive-set*(*r*) for each rule $r = 1, \ldots, 5$. Demonstrate that both *predictive-set*(4) and *predictive-set*(5) contain **else**, so this grammar is no LL CFG.

Introduce the notion of a *generalized predictive table* for any CFG so its entries may simultaneously contain several rules. Specifically, as far as the above CFG is concerned, entry [⟨else-part⟩, **else**] simultaneously contains 4 and 5 in this table. Remove 5 from this multiple entry. Demonstrate that after this removal, Algorithm 7.17 *Predictive Table-Driven Parsing* works with the resulting table quite deterministically so it associates an **else** with the most recent unmatched **then**, which is exactly what most real high-level programming languages do.

10 S. Consider the next two CFGs grammars. Determine the languages they generate. Construct their predictive tables.

i. 1: ⟨program⟩ → ⟨statement⟩⟨statement list⟩ .
2: ⟨statement list⟩ → ; ⟨statement⟩⟨statement list⟩
3: ⟨statement list⟩ → ε
4: ⟨statement⟩ → *i* = ⟨expression⟩
5: ⟨statement⟩ → **read** *i*
6: ⟨statement⟩ → **write** ⟨expression⟩
7: ⟨statement⟩ → **for** *i* = ⟨expression⟩ **to** ⟨expression⟩ **perform** ⟨statement⟩
8: ⟨statement⟩ → **begin** ⟨statement⟩⟨statement list⟩ **end**
9: ⟨expression⟩ → ⟨operand⟩⟨continuation⟩
10: ⟨continuation⟩ → ⟨operator⟩⟨expression⟩
11: ⟨continuation⟩ → ε
12: ⟨operand⟩ → (⟨expression⟩)
13: ⟨operand⟩ → *i*
14: ⟨operator⟩ → +
15: ⟨operator⟩ → –

ii. 1: ⟨program⟩ → **begin** ⟨statement⟩⟨statement list⟩ **end**
2: ⟨statement list⟩ → ; ⟨statement⟩⟨statement list⟩
3: ⟨statement list⟩ → ε
4: ⟨statement⟩ → *i* = ⟨boolean expression⟩
5: ⟨statement⟩ → **read** *i*
6: ⟨statement⟩ → **write** ⟨boolean expression⟩
7: ⟨statement⟩ → **if** ⟨boolean expression⟩ **then** ⟨statement⟩ **else** ⟨statement⟩
8: ⟨statement⟩ → **while** ⟨boolean expression⟩ **do** ⟨statement⟩
9: ⟨statement⟩ → **repeat** ⟨statement⟩⟨statement list⟩ **until** ⟨boolean expression⟩
10: ⟨statement⟩ → **begin** ⟨statement⟩⟨statement list⟩ **end**
11: ⟨boolean expression⟩ → ⟨operand⟩⟨continuation⟩
12: ⟨continuation⟩ → ⟨operator⟩⟨boolean expression⟩
13: ⟨continuation⟩ → ε
14: ⟨operand⟩ → (⟨boolean expression⟩)
15: ⟨operand⟩ → *i*
16: ⟨operand⟩ → **not** ⟨boolean expression⟩
17: ⟨operator⟩ → **and**
18: ⟨operator⟩ → **or**

11 S. Demonstrate that the following CFG generates the expressions in Polish postfix notation with operand and operators + and *. Prove that it is not an LL CFG. Construct an equivalent LL CFG and its predictive table.

1: ⟨expression⟩ → ⟨expression⟩⟨expression⟩ +
2: ⟨expression⟩ → ⟨expression⟩⟨expression⟩ *
3: ⟨expression⟩ → *i*

12. Consider languages (i) and (ii), given next; prove that no LL grammar generates either of them.

i. $\{a^ib^i \mid i \geq 1\} \cup \{a^jb^{2j} \mid j \geq 1\}$
ii. $\{a^ib^jc^k \mid i, j, k \geq 1, \text{ and } i = j \text{ or } j = k\}$

13. Prove that every LL grammar is unambiguous. Based on this result, demonstrate that no LL grammar can generate any inherently ambiguous language.

14. Consider the next CFG *G*. The start symbol is denoted by ⟨declaration part⟩.

⟨declaration part⟩ → ***declaration*** ⟨declaration list⟩
⟨declaration list⟩ → ⟨declaration⟩ ; ⟨declaration list⟩
⟨declaration list⟩ → ⟨declaration⟩

⟨declaration⟩ → ***integer*** ⟨variable list⟩
⟨declaration⟩ → ***real*** ⟨variable list⟩
⟨declaration⟩ → ***label*** ⟨label list⟩
⟨variable list⟩ → i , ⟨variable list⟩
⟨variable list⟩ → i

Construct a G-based predictive recursive-descent parser. Write a program to implement it.

15. Consider operators o_1, o_2, o_3, o_4 in the following precedence table. Determine the precedence and associativity of these operators from the table.

	o_1	o_2	o_3	o_4
o_1	$\lfloor$	$\lfloor$	$\lfloor$	$\lfloor$
o_2	$\rfloor$	$\lfloor$	$\rfloor$	$\lfloor$
o_3	$\lfloor$	$\lfloor$	$\lfloor$	$\lfloor$
o_4	$\rfloor$	$\rfloor$	$\rfloor$	$\rfloor$

16. Consider the language consisting of all well-formed expressions in your favorite programming language, such as C. Write a CFG G that generates the language. Construct a G-based operator-precedence parser, which also handles errors. Write a program to implement the parser.

17 S. Give a two-rule LR CFG G such that (a) $L(G)$ is infinite and (b) G is not an LL CFG.

18 S. Consider LR CFGs (i) through (iii).

i. 1: $E \rightarrow \vee EE$
   2: $E \rightarrow \wedge EE$
   3: $E \rightarrow i$

ii. 1: $E \rightarrow E + T$
   2: $E \rightarrow T$
   3: $T \rightarrow T * i$
   4: $T \rightarrow i$

iii. 1: ⟨declaration list⟩ → ⟨declaration list⟩ ; ⟨type⟩⟨identifiers⟩
   2: ⟨declaration list⟩ → ⟨type⟩⟨identifiers⟩
   3: ⟨type⟩ → **int**
   4: ⟨type⟩ → **real**
   5: ⟨identifiers⟩ → ⟨identifiers⟩ , i
   6: ⟨identifiers⟩ → i

For each of these LR CFGs, perform (a) through (c).

a. Construct its LR table.
b. Construct an LR parser based on the table obtained in (a).
c. Describe how the parser obtained in (b) works on a sentence generated by the CFG.

Solution to Selected Exercises

4. Consider the start symbol ⟨program⟩ and its only ⟨program⟩-rule (recall that according to Convention 6.2, a ⟨program⟩-rule means a rule whose left-hand side is ⟨program⟩)

⟨program⟩ → ***program*** ⟨declaration part⟩ ⟨execution part⟩ ***end***

According to this rule, every program starts and ends with keywords ***program*** and ***end***, respectively. Like in most programming languages, it consists of two essential parts—a declaration part and an execution part.

Consider

$$\langle\text{declaration part}\rangle \to \textbf{\textit{declaration}}\ \langle\text{declaration list}\rangle$$

According to this rule, the declaration part starts with keyword ***declaration*** followed by a declaration list of program variables. More precisely, G makes

$$\langle\text{declaration part}\rangle \Rightarrow^* \textbf{\textit{declaration}}\ x$$

where x represents a list of declarations, derived by using these two rules

$\langle\text{declaration list}\rangle \to \langle\text{declaration}\rangle\ ;\ \langle\text{declaration list}\rangle$
$\langle\text{declaration list}\rangle \to \langle\text{declaration}\rangle$

Indeed, these two rules derive a string that consists of some substrings separated by semicolons so that each of these substrings represents a declaration; formally,

$$\langle\text{declaration list}\rangle \Rightarrow^* y_1; \ldots; y_n$$

where $\langle\text{declaration}\rangle \Rightarrow^* y_i$, $1 \leq i \leq n$, for some $n \geq 1$ ($n = 1$ means $\langle\text{declaration list}\rangle \Rightarrow^* y_1$), and each y_i represents a declaration, which starts with ***integer***, ***real***, or ***label*** as follows from these three rules

$\langle\text{declaration}\rangle \to \textbf{\textit{integer}}\ \langle\text{variable list}\rangle$
$\langle\text{declaration}\rangle \to \textbf{\textit{real}}\ \langle\text{variable list}\rangle$
$\langle\text{declaration}\rangle \to \textbf{\textit{label}}\ \langle\text{label list}\rangle$

Consider the first two rules together with

$\langle\text{variable list}\rangle \to i\ ,\ \langle\text{variable list}\rangle$
$\langle\text{variable list}\rangle \to i$

Thus, by using these rules, G makes

$\langle\text{declaration}\rangle \Rightarrow a\langle\text{variable list}\rangle \Rightarrow^* ay$

in which $a \in \{\textbf{\textit{integer}}, \textbf{\textit{real}}\}$ and $y = i, \ldots, i$. As a result, if a declaration starts with ***integer*** or ***real***, this keyword follows by a list of the form $i, \ldots, i$; intuitively, i stands for an *i*dentifier in this list.

Consider $\langle\text{declaration}\rangle \to \textbf{\textit{label}}\ \langle\text{label list}\rangle$ together with

$\langle\text{label list}\rangle \to l\ ,\ \langle\text{label list}\rangle$
$\langle\text{label list}\rangle \to l$

Thus, if a declaration starts with ***label***, this keyword is followed by a list of the form $l, \ldots, l$, where l stands for a *l*abel.

The execution part of a program starts with ***execution*** followed by a list of statements as follows from this rule

$$\langle\text{execution part}\rangle \to \textbf{\textit{execution}}\ \langle\text{statement list}\rangle$$

Consider

$\langle\text{statement list}\rangle \to \langle\text{statement}\rangle\ ;\ \langle\text{statement list}\rangle$
$\langle\text{statement list}\rangle \to \langle\text{statement}\rangle$

By these rules, the statement list that follows ***execution*** consists of a sequence of statements separated by semicolons; more formally,

$$\langle \text{statement list} \rangle \Rightarrow^* y_1; \ldots; y_n$$

where $\langle \text{statement} \rangle \Rightarrow^* y_i$, $1 \leq i \leq n$, for some $n \geq 1$ ($n = 1$ means $\langle \text{statement list} \rangle \Rightarrow^* y_1$), and each y_i represents a statement. Complete the description of the programming language syntax.

The next program is syntactically correct according to the definition by *G*.

```
program
declaration
        integer i
execution
        begin
           read(i);
           i = i * i;
           write(i)
        end
```

5. We only solve (a) and (b).
   a. For instance, *G* generates **if** *b* **then if** *b* **then** *a* **else** *a* by these two different leftmost derivations

   $$S\ {}_{lm}\Rightarrow^* \textbf{if } b \textbf{ then if } b \textbf{ then } a \textbf{ else } a\ [1233] \text{ and}$$
   $$S\ {}_{lm}\Rightarrow^* \textbf{if } b \textbf{ then if } b \textbf{ then } a \textbf{ else } a\ [2133]$$

   Thus, it is ambiguous. As a consequence of this ambiguity, there exist two different interpretations of **if** *b* **then if** *b* **then** *a* **else** *a*. The first interpretation associates the **else** part of this statement with the first **then** while the other interpretation makes this association with the second **then**.
   b. Define the **if-then-else** statement by the following equivalent unambiguous two-nonterminal five-rule grammar *H*. This grammar always attaches each **else** to the last proceeded unmatched **then**, which is what most real programming languages do.

   $S \rightarrow$ **if** b **then** S
   $S \rightarrow$ **if** b **then** A **else** S
   $S \rightarrow a$
   $A \rightarrow$ **if** b **then** A **else** A
   $A \rightarrow a$
6. Solutions to (a) through (c) are as follows.
   a. The following CFG *G* generates *L*.
   1: $S \rightarrow SS$
   2: $S \rightarrow aSb$
   3: $S \rightarrow \varepsilon$
   b. Algorithm 7.3 turns *G* to this *G*-based top-down parser:
   $S\diamond \rightarrow SS\diamond$
   $S\diamond \rightarrow bSa\diamond$
   $S\diamond \rightarrow \diamond$
   $a\diamond a \rightarrow \diamond$
   $b\diamond b \rightarrow \diamond$
   c. On *abaabb*, the parser works as follows

$\triangleright S\diamond abaabb\triangleleft$	$\Rightarrow$	$\triangleright SS\diamond abaabb\triangleleft$	$[S\diamond \rightarrow SS\diamond]$
	$\Rightarrow$	$\triangleright SbSa\diamond abaabb\triangleleft$	$[S\diamond \rightarrow bSa\diamond]$
	$\Rightarrow$	$\triangleright SbS\diamond baabb\triangleleft$	$[a\diamond a \rightarrow \diamond]$
	$\Rightarrow$	$\triangleright Sb\diamond baabb\triangleleft$	$[S\diamond \rightarrow \diamond]$
	$\Rightarrow$	$\triangleright S\diamond aabb\triangleleft$	$[b\diamond b \rightarrow \diamond]$
	$\Rightarrow$	$\triangleright bSa\diamond aabb\triangleleft$	$[S\diamond \rightarrow bSa\diamond]$

$\Rightarrow$	$\triangleright bS\diamond abb\triangleleft$	$[a\diamond a \to \diamond]$
$\Rightarrow$	$\triangleright bbSa\diamond abb\triangleleft$	$[S\diamond \to bSa\diamond]$
$\Rightarrow$	$\triangleright bbS\diamond bb\triangleleft$	$[a\diamond a \to \diamond]$
$\Rightarrow$	$\triangleright bb\diamond bb\triangleleft$	$[S\diamond \to \diamond]$
$\Rightarrow$	$\triangleright b\diamond b\triangleleft$	$[b\diamond b \to \diamond]$
$\Rightarrow$	$\triangleright\diamond\triangleleft$	$[b\diamond b \to \diamond]$

7. The Cocke–Younger–Kasami algorithm is formalized next.

Algorithm Cocke–Younger–Kasami Parsing Algorithm.

Input. A CFG, $G = ({}_G\Sigma, {}_GR)$, in Chomsky normal form, and $w = a_1a_2\ldots a_n$ with $a_i \in {}_G\Delta$, $1 \leq i \leq n$, for some $n \geq 1$.

Output. **SUCCESS** if $w \in L(G)$, and **ERROR** if $w \notin L(G)$.

Method.

begin

introduce sets $CYK[i, j] = \emptyset$ for $1 \leq i \leq j \leq n$
for $i = 1, \ldots, n$ **do**
  if $A \to a_i \in R$ **then**
    add A to $CYK[i, i]$
repeat
  if $B \in CYK[i, j]$, $C \in CYK[j + 1, k]$, $A \to BC \in R$ for some $A, B, C \in {}_GN$ **then**
    add A to $CYK[i, k]$
until no change
if $S \in CYK[1, n]$ **then**
  SUCCESS
else
  ERROR

end.

8. We only give a partial solution to (i). An equivalent proper LL grammar to this CFG follows next.
   1: ⟨program⟩ → **begin** ⟨statement⟩ ⟨statement list⟩
   2: ⟨statement list⟩ → ; ⟨statement⟩ ⟨statement list⟩
   3: ⟨statement list⟩ → **end**
   4: ⟨statement⟩ → **read** *i*
   5: ⟨statement⟩ → **write** *i*
   6: ⟨statement⟩ → *i* = **sum** (*i* ⟨item list⟩
   7: ⟨item list⟩ → , *i* ⟨item list⟩
   8: ⟨item list⟩ →)
9. We only give the generalized predictive table below. Its first row is denoted by ⟨if-statement⟩.

	if	**then**	**else**	*c*	*a*	◁
⟨if-statement⟩	1				2	
⟨condition⟩				3		
⟨else-part⟩			4, 5			5
▷						

10. We only give the predictive table of (i) below. Its first row is denoted by ⟨program⟩.

	.	;	i	=	**read**	**write**	**for**	**to**	**perform**	**begin**	**end**	(	)	+	−	◁
⟨program⟩			1		1	1	1			1						
⟨statement⟩			4		5	6	7			8						
⟨statement list⟩	3	2									3					
⟨expression⟩			9									9				
⟨operand⟩			13									12				
⟨continuation⟩	11	11						11	11		11		11	10	10	
⟨operator⟩														14	15	
▷																

11. Give a trivial proof that the CFG considered in this exercise is no LL CFG. An equivalent LL CFG follows next. Its predictive table is given below. The first row is denoted by ⟨expression⟩.
    1: ⟨expression⟩ → i ⟨continuous⟩
    2: ⟨continuous⟩ → ⟨expression⟩ ⟨operator⟩ ⟨continuous⟩
    3: ⟨continuous⟩ → ε
    4: ⟨operator⟩ → +
    5: ⟨operator⟩ → *

	+	*	i	◁
⟨expression⟩			1	
⟨continuous⟩	3	3	2	3
⟨operator⟩	4	5		
▷				

17. Define G as $S \rightarrow Sa$ and $S \rightarrow a$.
18. We only consider (i) and solve (a). The LR table, including its *action* and *goto* parts, follows next.

	i	$\vee$	$\wedge$	$\triangleleft$
θ_1	θ_5	θ_3	θ_4	
θ_2				☺
θ_3	θ_5	θ_3	θ_4	
θ_4	θ_5	θ_3	θ_4	
θ_5	3	3	3	3
θ_6	θ_5	θ_3	θ_4	
θ_7	θ_5	θ_3	θ_4	
θ_8	1	1	1	1
θ_9	2	2	2	2

	E
θ_1	θ_2
θ_2	
θ_3	θ_6
θ_4	θ_7
θ_5	
θ_6	θ_8
θ_7	θ_9
θ_8	
θ_9	

Chapter 8

Properties of Context-Free Languages

By analogy with the presentation of properties concerning regular languages (see Chapter 5), this chapter establishes fundamental properties of context-free languages (CFLs). First, similarly to giving a pumping lemma for regular languages, Section 8.1 establishes a pumping lemma for CFLs and explains how to use it to prove that some languages are out of ${}_{CFG}\Phi$. Then, Section 8.2 establishes fundamental closure properties concerning ${}_{CFG}\Phi$.

8.1 Pumping Lemma for Context-Free Languages

The pumping lemma established in this section is frequently used to disprove that a language K is context-free. The lemma says that for every CFL, L, there is a constant $k \geq 1$ such that every $z \in L$ with $|z| \geq k$ can be expressed as $z = uvwxy$ with $vx \neq \varepsilon$ so that L also contains $uv^m wx^m y$, for every $m \geq 0$. Consequently, to show the noncontext-freedom of a language, K, by contradiction, assume that K is a CFL, and k is its pumping lemma constant. Select a string $z \in K$ with $|z| \geq k$, consider all possible decompositions of z into $uvwxy$, and for each of these decompositions, prove that $uv^m wx^m y$ is out of K, for some $m \geq 0$, which contradicts the pumping lemma. Thus, K is not a CFL.

Without any loss of generality, we prove the pumping lemma based on context-free grammars (CFGs) satisfying Chomsky normal form (see Section 6.2.5). We also make use of some notions introduced earlier in this chapter, such as the derivation tree $\clubsuit(A \Rightarrow^* x)$ corresponding to a derivation $A \Rightarrow^* x$ in a CFG G, where $A \in N$ and $x \in \Delta^*$ (see Convention 6.9). In addition, we use some related graph-theory notions introduced in Chapter 1, such as $depth(\clubsuit(A \Rightarrow^* x))$, which denotes the depth of $\clubsuit(A \Rightarrow^* x)$.

Lemma 8.1 Let G be a CFG in Chomsky normal form. For every derivation $A \Rightarrow^* x$ in G, where $A \in N$ and $x \in \Delta^*$, its corresponding derivation tree $\clubsuit(A \Rightarrow^* x)$ satisfies $|x| \leq 2^{depth(\clubsuit(A \Rightarrow^* x))-1}$.

Proof (by induction on $depth(♣(A \Rightarrow^* x)) \geq 1$).

Basis. Let $depth(♣(A \Rightarrow^* x)) = 1$, where $A \in N$ and $x \in \Delta^*$. Because G is in Chomsky normal form, $A \Rightarrow^* x$ $[A \rightarrow x]$ in G, where $x \in \Delta$, so $|x| = 1$. For $depth(♣(A \Rightarrow^* x)) = 1$, $2^{depth(♣(A \Rightarrow^* x))-1} = 2^0$. As $2^0 = 1$, $|x| \leq 2^{depth(♣(A \Rightarrow^* x))-1}$ in this case, so the basis holds true.

Induction Hypothesis. Suppose that this lemma holds for all derivation trees of depth n or less, for some $n \in {}_0\mathbb{N}$.

Induction Step. Let $A \Rightarrow^* x$ in G with $depth(♣(A \Rightarrow^* x)) = n + 1$, where $A \in N$ and $x \in \Delta^*$. Let $A \Rightarrow^* x$ $[r\rho]$ in G, where $r \in R$ and $\rho \in R^*$. As G is in Chomsky normal form, $r: A \rightarrow BC \in R$, where $B, C \in N$. Let $B \Rightarrow^* u$ $[\pi]$, $C \Rightarrow^* v$ $[\theta]$, $\pi, \theta \in R^*$, $x = uv$, $\rho = \pi\theta$ so that $A \Rightarrow^* x$ can be expressed in greater detail as $A \Rightarrow \underline{B}C$ $[r] \Rightarrow^* u\underline{C}$ $[\pi] \Rightarrow^* uv$ $[\theta]$. Observe that $depth(♣(B \Rightarrow^* u\ [\pi])) \leq depth(♣(A \Rightarrow^* x)) - 1 = n$, so $|u| \leq 2^{depth(♣(B \Rightarrow^* u))-1}$ by the induction hypothesis. Analogously, as $depth(♣(C \Rightarrow^* v\ [\theta])) \leq depth(♣(A \Rightarrow^* x)) - 1 = n$, $|v| \leq 2^{depth(♣(C \Rightarrow^* v))-1}$. Thus, $|x| = |u| + |v| \leq 2^{depth(♣(B \Rightarrow^* u))-1} + 2^{depth(♣(C \Rightarrow^* v))-1} \leq 2^{n-1} + 2^{n-1} = 2^n = 2^{depth(♣(A \Rightarrow^* x))-1}$. ■

Corollary 8.2 Let G be a CFG in Chomsky normal form. For every derivation $A \Rightarrow^* x$ in G, where $A \in N$ and $x \in \Delta^*$ with $|x| \geq 2^m$ for some $m \geq 0$, its corresponding derivation tree $♣(A \Rightarrow^* x)$ satisfies $depth(♣(A \Rightarrow^* x)) \geq m + 1$.

Proof. This corollary follows from Lemma 8.1 and the contrapositive law (see Section 1.1). ■

Lemma 8.3 Pumping Lemma for CFLs. Let L be an infinite CFL. Then, there exists $k \in \mathbb{N}$ such that every string $z \in L$ satisfying $|z| \geq k$ can be expressed as $z = uvwxy$, where $0 < |vx| < |vwx| \leq k$, and $uv^mwx^my \in L$, for all $m \geq 0$.

Proof. Let $L \in {}_{CFG}\Phi$, and $L = L(G)$, where $G = (\Sigma, R)$ be a CFG in Chomsky normal form. Let G have n nonterminals, for $n \in \mathbb{N}$; in symbols, $card({}_GN) = n$. Set $k = 2^n$. Let $z \in L(G)$ satisfying $|z| \geq k$. As $z \in L(G)$, $S \Rightarrow^* z$, and by Corollary 8.2, $depth(♣(S \Rightarrow^* z)) \geq card({}_GN) + 1$, so $♣(S \Rightarrow^* z)$ contains some subtrees in which there is a path with two or more nodes labeled by the same nonterminal. Express $S \Rightarrow^* z$ as $S \Rightarrow^* uAy \Rightarrow^+ uvAxy \Rightarrow^+ uvwxy$ with $uvwxy = z$ so that the derivation tree corresponding to $A \Rightarrow^+ vAx \Rightarrow^+ vwx$ contains no proper subtree with a path containing two or more different nodes labeled with the same nonterminal.

To prove that $0 < |vx| < |vwx| \leq k$, recall that every rule in R has on its right-hand side either a terminal or two nonterminals because G is in Chomsky normal form. Thus, $A \Rightarrow^+ vAx$ implies $0 < |vx|$, and $vAx \Rightarrow^+ vwx$ implies $|vx| < |vwx|$. As the derivation tree corresponding to $A \Rightarrow^+ vAx \Rightarrow^+ vwx$ contains no subtree with a path containing two different nodes labeled with the same nonterminal, $depth(♣(A \Rightarrow^* vwx)) \leq card({}_GN) + 1$, so by Lemma 8.1, $|vx| < |vwx| \leq 2^n = k$.

Finally, we show that for all $m \geq 0$, $uv^mwx^my \in L$. As $S \Rightarrow^* uAy \Rightarrow^+ uvAxy \Rightarrow^+ uvwxy$, $S \Rightarrow^* uAy \Rightarrow^+ uwy$, so $uv^0wx^0y = uwy \in L$. Similarly, since $S \Rightarrow^* uAy \Rightarrow^+ uvAxy \Rightarrow^+ uvwxy$, $S \Rightarrow^* uAy \Rightarrow^+ uvAxy \Rightarrow^+ uvvAxxy \Rightarrow^+ \ldots \Rightarrow^+ uv^mAx^my \Rightarrow^+ uv^mwx^my$, so $uv^mwx^my \in L$, for all $m \geq 1$.

Thus, Lemma 8.3 holds true. ■

8.1.1 Applications of the Pumping Lemma

We usually use the pumping lemma in a proof by contradiction to show that a given language L is not context-free. Typically, we make a proof of this kind in the following way.

1. Assume that L is context-free.
2. Select a string $z \in L$ whose length depends on the pumping lemma constant k so that $|z| \geq k$ is necessarily true.
3. For all possible decompositions of z into $uvwxy$ satisfying the pumping lemma conditions, find $m \in {}_0\mathbb{N}$ such that $uv^mwx^my \notin L$, which contradicts Lemma 8.3.
4. The contradiction obtained in (3) means that the assumption in (1) is incorrect; therefore, L is not context-free.

Example 8.1 Consider $L = \{a^nb^nc^n \mid n \geq 1\}$. Next, under the guidance of the recommended proof structure preceding this example, we show that $L \notin {}_{CFG}\Phi$.

1. Assume that $L \in {}_{CFG}\Phi$.
2. In L, select $z = a^kb^kc^k$ with $|z| = 3k \geq k$, where k is the pumping lemma constant.
3. By Lemma 8.3, z can be written as $z = uvwxy$ so that this decomposition satisfies the pumping lemma conditions. As $0 < |vx| < |vwx| \leq k$, either $vwx \in \{a\}^*\{b\}^*$ or $vwx \in \{b\}^*\{c\}^*$. If $vwx \in \{a\}^*\{b\}^*$, uv^0wx^0y has k *cs* but fewer than k *as* or *bs*, so $uv^0wx^0y \notin L$, but by the pumping lemma, $uv^0wx^0y \in L$. If $vwx \in \{b\}^*\{c\}^*$, uv^0wx^0y has k *as* but fewer than k *bs* or *cs*, so $uv^0wx^0y \notin L$, but by the pumping lemma, $uv^0wx^0y \in L$. In either case, we obtain the contradiction that $uv^0wx^0y \notin L$ and, simultaneously, $uv^0wx^0y \in L$.
4. By the contradiction obtained in (3), $L \notin {}_{CFG}\Phi$.

Omitting some obvious details, we usually proceed in a briefer way than above when proving the noncontext-freedom of a language by using Lemma 8.3.

Example 8.2 Let $L = \{a^nb^ma^nb^m \mid n, m \geq 1\}$. Assume that L is context-free. Set $z = a^kb^ka^kb^k$ with $|a^kb^ka^kb^k| = 4k \geq k$. By Lemma 8.3, express $z = uvwxy$. Observe that $0 < |vx| < |vwx| \leq k$ implies $uwy \notin L$ in all possible occurrences of vwx in $a^kb^ka^kb^k$; however, by Lemma 8.3, $uwy \in L$—a contradiction. Thus, $L \notin {}_{CFG}\Phi$.

Even some seemingly trivial unary languages are not context-free as shown next.

Example 8.3 Consider $L = \{a^{n^2} \mid \text{for some } n \geq 0\}$. To show $L \notin {}_{CFG}\Phi$, assume that $L \in {}_{CFG}\Phi$ and select $z = a^{k^2} \in L$ where k is the pumping lemma constant. As a result, $|z| = k^2 \geq k$, so $z = uvwxy$, which satisfies the pumping lemma conditions. As $k^2 < |uv^2wx^2y| \leq k^2 + k < k^2 + 2k + 1 = (k + 1)^2$, we have $uv^2wx^2y \notin L$, but by Lemma 8.3, $uv^2wx^2y \in L$—a contradiction. Thus, $L \notin {}_{CFG}\Phi$.

8.2 Closure Properties

In this section, we discuss whether ${}_{CFG}\Phi$ is closed under these operations:

- Union
- Concatenation
- Closure

- Intersection
- Complement
- Homomorphism

8.2.1 Union, Concatenation, and Closure

Basic Idea. To prove that ${}_{CFG}\Phi$ is closed under union, we transform any pair of CFGs to a single CFG that generates the union of the languages generated by the two CFGs. That is, we convert any two CFGs, $H = ({}_H\Sigma, {}_HR)$ and $K = ({}_K\Sigma, {}_KR)$, to a CFG, $G = ({}_G\Sigma, {}_GR)$, so $L(G) = L(H) \cup L(K)$. Without any loss of generality, we suppose that ${}_HN \cap {}_KN = \emptyset$ (if ${}_HN \cap {}_KN \neq \emptyset$, we can always rename the nonterminals in either H or K so that ${}_HN \cap {}_KN = \emptyset$ and the generated language remains unchanged). Initially, we set ${}_GR = {}_HR \cup {}_KR$. In addition, we include ${}_GS \to {}_HS$ and ${}_GS \to {}_KS$ into ${}_GR$, where ${}_GS$ is the start symbol of G such that ${}_GS \notin {}_HN \cup {}_KN$. If G generates $x \in L(G)$ by a derivation that starts by applying ${}_GS \to {}_HS$, then $x \in L(H)$. Analogically, if G generates $x \in L(G)$ by a derivation that starts by applying ${}_GS \to {}_KS$, then $x \in L(K)$. Thus, $L(G) = L(H) \cup L(K)$.

Algorithm 8.4 Union of Context-Free Languages.

Input. Two CFGs, $H = ({}_H\Sigma, {}_HR)$ and $K = ({}_K\Sigma, {}_KR)$, such that ${}_HN \cap {}_KN = \emptyset$.

Output. A CFG, $G = ({}_G\Sigma, {}_GR)$, such that $L(G) = L(H) \cup L(K)$.

Method.

begin

construct $G = ({}_G\Sigma, {}_GR)$ with ${}_G\Sigma = {}_H\Sigma \cup {}_K\Sigma \cup \{{}_GS\}$, where ${}_GS \notin {}_HN \cup {}_KN$, and
${}_GR = {}_HR \cup {}_KR \cup \{{}_GS \to {}_HS, {}_GS \to {}_KS\}$

end.

As an exercise, we leave proofs of Theorems 8.5 and 8.6.

Theorem 8.5 Algorithm 8.4 is correct. Therefore, ${}_{CFG}\Phi$ is closed under union. ■

Theorem 8.6 ${}_{CFG}\Phi$ is closed under concatenation and closure. ■

8.2.2 Intersection and Complement

Recall that ${}_{reg}\Phi$ is closed under intersection (see Theorem 5.4). However, ${}_{CFG}\Phi$ is not.

Theorem 8.7 ${}_{CFG}\Phi$ is not closed under intersection.

Proof. Consider these two languages

$$A = \{a^ib^jc^k \mid i, j, k \geq 1 \text{ and } i = j\} \text{ and } B = \{a^ib^jc^k \mid i, j, k \geq 1 \text{ and } j = k\}$$

Clearly, A and B are ${}_{CFG}\Phi$. However, by Example 8.1, $A \cap B = \{a^ib^ic^i \mid i \geq 1\}$ is out of ${}_{CFG}\Phi$. ■

Set $\Gamma = \{L|\ L = J \cap K, J \in {}_{CFG}\Phi, K \in {}_{reg}\Phi\}$. Considering Theorem 8.7, it comes as a surprise that $\Gamma = {}_{CFG}\Phi$ as proved next.

Basic Idea. Every CFL is accepted by a one-state PDA (see Convention 7.1), and every regular language is accepted by a deterministic finite automaton (DFA) (see Theorem 3.38). Next, we explain how to convert any DFA, $X = ({}_X\Sigma, {}_XR)$, and any one-state pushdown automaton (PDA), $Y = ({}_Y\Sigma, {}_YR)$, to a PDA, M, such that $L(M) = L(X) \cap L(Y)$. Thus, every language in Γ is context-free.

Let $\Diamond$ be the only state of Y just like in Convention 7.1. Let the states, final states, and start state of M coincide with the states, final states, and start state of X, respectively. For every $qa \rightarrow o \in {}_XR$ and every $A\Diamond a \rightarrow x\Diamond \in {}_YR$, add $Aqa \rightarrow xo$ to the rules of M so M can simulate a move by $qa \rightarrow o$ in X and, simultaneously, a move by $A\Diamond a \rightarrow x\Diamond$ in Y. For every $q \in {}_XQ$ and every $A\Diamond \rightarrow x\Diamond \in {}_YR$, add $Aq \rightarrow xq$ to the rules of M so M can make the pushdown change by analogy with X and, simultaneously, keep its current state q unchanged. In this way, M simultaneously simulates the sequences of moves made by X and Y. As a result, X and Y accept an input w iff M accepts w. Thus, $L(M) = L(X) \cap L(Y)$.

Algorithm 8.8 PDA for the intersection of context-free and regular languages.

Input. A DFA X and a one-state PDA Y.

Output. A PDA M such that $L(M) = L(X) \cap L(Y)$.

Method.

begin

set ${}_M\Sigma = {}_MQ \cup {}_M\Gamma \cup {}_M\Delta$ with
${}_MQ = {}_XQ, {}_Ms = {}_Xs, {}_MF = {}_XF, {}_M\Gamma = {}_Y\Gamma, {}_MS = {}_YS, {}_M\Delta = {}_X\Delta \cap {}_Y\Delta$
set ${}_MR = \{Aqa \rightarrow xo|\ qa \rightarrow o \in {}_XR, q, o \in {}_XQ, a \in {}_X\Delta, A\Diamond a \rightarrow x\Diamond \in {}_YR, A, x \in {}_Y\Gamma^*\}$
$\cup \{Aq \rightarrow xq|\ q \in {}_XQ, A\Diamond \rightarrow x\Diamond \in {}_YR, A, x \in {}_Y\Gamma^*\}$

end.

We leave a rigorous verification of Algorithm 8.8 as an exercise. By this algorithm, $\Gamma \subseteq {}_{CFG}\Phi$. Consider any $L \in {}_{CFG}\Phi$. Let $L \subseteq \Delta^*$, for an alphabet Δ. Clearly, $L = L \cap \Delta^*$. Since $\Delta^* \in {}_{reg}\Phi$, ${}_{CFG}\Phi \subseteq \Gamma$ holds true. Because $\Gamma \subseteq {}_{CFG}\Phi$ and ${}_{CFG}\Phi \subseteq \Gamma$, we have proved that $\Gamma = {}_{CFG}\Phi$ as stated in Theorem 8.9.

Theorem 8.9 Algorithm 8.8 is correct. Therefore, $\Gamma = {}_{CFG}\Phi$, where $\Gamma = \{L|\ L = J \cap K, J \in {}_{CFG}\Phi, K \in {}_{reg}\Phi\}$. ■

Making use of Theorem 8.9, we can easily prove that ${}_{CFG}\Phi$ is not closed under complement.

Theorem 8.10 ${}_{CFG}\Phi$ is not closed under complement.

Proof (by contradiction). Assume that ${}_{CFG}\Phi$ is closed under complement. Consider $A = \{a^ib^jc^k|\ i, j, k \geq 1 \text{ and } i = j\}$ and $B = \{a^ib^jc^k|\ i, j, k \geq 1 \text{ and } j = k\}$. Clearly, $A \in {}_{CFG}\Phi$ and $B \in {}_{CFG}\Phi$. By Theorem 8.5, ${}_{CFG}\Phi$ is closed under union. Thus, under the assumption that ${}_{CFG}\Phi$ is closed under complement, $\sim(\sim A \cup \sim B) \in {}_{CFG}\Phi$. However, by DeMorgan's laws (see Section 1.2), $\sim(\sim A \cup \sim B) = A \cap B = \{a^i b^i c^i \mid i \geq 1\}$, which is out of ${}_{CFG}\Phi$ (see Example 8.1)—a contradiction. ■

8.2.3 Homomorphism

Basic Idea. We prove that ${}_{CFG}\Phi$ is closed under homomorphism. More precisely, we show that for every CFG G in Chomsky normal form, every alphabet Ξ, and every homomorphism h from ${}_G\Delta^*$ to Ξ^*, there is a CFG H such that $L(H) = h(L(G))$. As a result, ${}_{CFG}\Phi$ is closed under homomorphism because every CFL is generated by a CFG in Chomsky normal form (see Theorem 6.36).

Without any loss of generality, assume that ${}_GN \cap \Xi = \emptyset$. Set ${}_H\Sigma$ to ${}_GN \cup \Xi$. As G satisfies Chomsky normal form, every rule in ${}_GR$ has on its right-hand side either a terminal or a two-nonterminal string. Construct H as follows. Move every rule that has two nonterminals on its right-hand side from ${}_GR$ to ${}_HR$. For every rule $A \rightarrow a \in {}_GR$, add $A \rightarrow h(a)$ to ${}_HR$. As a result, $a_1a_2\ldots a_n \in L(G)$ iff $h(a_1)h(a_2)\ldots h(a_n) \in L(H)$, so $L(H) = h(L(G))$.

Algorithm 8.11 Construction of a context-free grammar for homomorphism.

Input. A CFG G in Chomsky normal form, and
a homomorphism h from ${}_G\Delta^*$ to Ξ^*, where Ξ is an alphabet, ${}_GN \cap \Xi = \emptyset$.

Output. A CFG H such that $L(H) = h(L(G))$.

Method.

begin

set ${}_H\Sigma = {}_GN \cup \Xi$
set ${}_HR = \{A \rightarrow h(a) \mid A \rightarrow a \in {}_GR, A \in {}_GN, a \in {}_G\Delta\}$
$\cup \{A \rightarrow BC \mid A \rightarrow BC \in {}_GR, A, B, C \in {}_GN\}$

end.

As an exercise, prove Theorem 8.12.

Theorem 8.12 Algorithm 8.11 is correct. Therefore, ${}_{CFG}\Phi$ is closed under homomorphism. ■

8.2.4 Applications of the Closure Properties

Making use of closure properties concerning ${}_{CFG}\Phi$, we frequently prove or disprove that a language L is a CFL in a rather simple way. To show that $L \notin {}_{CFG}\Phi$, we usually follow the next schema of a proof by contradiction, in which we combine closure properties with the pumping lemma for CFLs (see Lemma 8.3).

1. Assume that $L \in {}_{CFG}\Phi$.
2. From L and some CFLs, construct a new language K by using operations under which ${}_{CFG}\Phi$ is closed, so under the assumption that $L \in {}_{CFG}\Phi$, K should be in ${}_{CFG}\Phi$, too.

3. By the pumping lemma, prove that K is not context-free, which contradicts (2); therefore, $L \notin {}_{CFG}\Phi$.

Example 8.4 Let $L = \{ww \mid w \in \{a, b\}^+\}$. Assume that L is context-free. As $\{a\}^+\{b\}^+\{a\}^+\{b\}^+$ is regular, $L \cap \{a\}^+\{b\}^+\{a\}^+\{b\}^+ = \{a^n b^m a^n b^m \mid n, m \geq 1\}$ represents a CFL by Theorem 8.9. However, $\{a^n b^m a^n b^m \mid n, m \geq 1\} \notin {}_{CFG}\Phi$ (see Example 8.2), so neither is L.

Similarly, we can often show that some common high-level programming languages, such as Pascal, are not in ${}_{CFG}\Phi$ either.

Example 8.5 Let L denote the language consisting of all well-formed Pascal programs. Assume that L is context-free. Let K denote this regular language.

{**program**}{□}{p}{□}{(}{**input**}{)}{;}{**var**}{□}{X,Y}$^+${:**integer**}{;}{**begin**}{}{X,Y}$^+${:=0}{□}{end}{.}

where □ represents a blank. Let h be the homomorphism defined as $h(\text{X}) = \text{X}$, $h(\text{Y}) = \text{Y}$, and $h(Z) = \varepsilon$, where Z denotes any symbol from the Pascal alphabet but X or Y. Pascal requires that all identifiers are declared, but it places no limit on their length. As a result, $h(L \cap K) = \{ww \mid w \in \{\text{X}, \text{Y}\}^+\}$. Introduce the homomorphism g from $\{\text{X}, \text{Y}\}^*$ to $\{a, b\}^*$ defined as $g(\text{X}) = a$ and $g(\text{Y}) = b$. By Theorem 8.12, $g(\{ww \mid w \in \{\text{X}, \text{Y}\}^+\}) = \{ww \mid w \in \{a, b\}^+\}$ is a CFL. However, Example 8.4 shows that $\{ww \mid w \in \{a, b\}^+\}$ is not a CFL—a contradiction. Thus, $L \notin {}_{CFG}\Phi$; in words, the language consisting of all well-formed Pascal programs is not context-free.

As already pointed out, the closure properties are also frequently used to simplify proofs that some languages are in ${}_{CFG}\Phi$. Indeed, given a language L, a direct proof that $L \in {}_{CFG}\Phi$ consists in designing a CFG and giving a rigorous verification that the grammar generates L, which might represent a tedious and difficult task. Instead, we can frequently simplify this task by introducing several simple CFLs and combine them by operations under which ${}_{CFG}\Phi$ is closed in such a way that the language resulting from this combination coincides with L, which means that $L \in {}_{CFG}\Phi$.

Example 8.6 Consider $L = \{a^n b^n c^n \mid n \geq 1\}$, which is out of ${}_{CFG}\Phi$ (see Example 8.1). To show that its complement $\sim L$ is a CFL, express $\sim L = A \cup B \cup C$, where $A = \{a, b, c\}^* - \{a\}^+\{b\}^+\{c\}^+$, $B = \{a^i b^j c^k \mid i, j, k \geq 1, i \neq j\}$, and $C = \{a^i b^j c^k \mid i, j, k \geq 1, j \neq k\}$. As an exercise, prove that A, B, and C are CFLs. Thus, $\sim L \in {}_{CFG}\Phi$ by Theorem 8.5.

Exercises

1. This chapter contains results whose proofs are only sketched or even completely omitted. These results include Example 8.6 and Theorems 8.5, 8.6, 8.9, and 8.12. Prove them rigorously.
2. Consider the following languages. Use the pumping lemma for CFLs (Lemma 8.3) and closure properties to show that none of them is context-free.
   i. $\{a^i b^j c^k \mid i, j, k \geq 0 \text{ and } i < j < k\}$
   ii. $\{a^i b^j a^i \mid i, j \geq 0 \text{ and } j = i^2\}$
   iii. $\{a^i \mid i \text{ is a prime}\}$
   iv. $\{w \mid w \in \{a, b, c\}^* \text{ and } occur(w, a) = occur(w, b) = occur(w, c)\}$
   v. $\{a^i b^i a^j \mid i, j \geq 0 \text{ and } j \neq i\}$
   vi. $\{a^i b^i c^j \mid i, j \geq 0 \text{ and } i \neq j \neq 2i\}$
   vii. $\{a^i b^j c^k \mid i, j, k \geq 0, i \neq j, k \neq i, \text{ and } j \neq k\}$
   viii. $\{a^i b^j c^j d^i \mid i, j \geq 0 \text{ and } j \neq i\}$

ix. $\{a^i b^{2i} c^i \mid i \geq 0\}$
x. $\{waw \mid w \in \{a, b\}^*\}$
xi. $\{0^i 1 0^i 1 0^i 1 0^i \mid i \geq 1\}$
xii. $\{wcv \mid v, w \in \{a, b\}^*$ and $w = vv\}$

3 S. Consider languages (i) through (x) over $\{a, b, c\}$.
i. $\{a^i b^j a^i \mid i, j \geq 1\}$
ii. $\{a^i b^j \mid i \geq 0$ and $j \geq 1\}$
iii. $\{a^i b^j c^k \mid i, j, k \geq 0$ and $i = j$ or $j = k\}$
iv. $\{a^i b^j c^i b^j \mid i \geq 0$ and $j \geq 1\}$
v. $\{a^j cab^i a^j \mid i, j \geq 0\}$
vi. $\{x \mid x \in \{a, b\}^*, aa \in substrings(x), occur(x, a) = occur(x, b)\}$
vii. $\{x \mid x \in \{a, b, c\}^*, occur(x, a) \geq occur(x, b) \geq occur(x, c)\}$
viii. $\{x \mid x \in \{a, b\}^*, occur(x, a) = 2^{occur(x, b)}\}$
ix. $\{x \mid x \in \{a, b\}^*, occur(x, b) \geq occur(x, a), |x|$ is divisible by 3$\}$
x. $\{x \mid x \in \{a, b, c\}^*, occur(x, a) \geq occur(x, b)$ iff $occur(x, c) < occur(x, a)\}$

Consider each of these languages; for brevity, denote it by L. Prove or disprove that $L \in {}_{CFG}\Phi$. If $L \in {}_{CFG}\Phi$, find two non-CFLs, H and K, such that $H \subset L \subset K$. If $L \notin {}_{CFG}\Phi$, find two CFLs, I and J, such that $I \subset L \subset J$.

4. Consider the proof of the pumping lemma for CFLs given in Section 8.1 (see the proof of Lemma 8.3). Rephrase this proof so it is based on (a) CFGs in Greibach normal form, (b) CFGs in general, and (c) PDAs.
5. State and prove a pumping lemma for the family of languages accepted by counters (see Exercise 21 in Chapter 6).
6. Prove the following lemma.

Lemma *The Ogden's Lemma.* Let L be a CFL over an alphabet, Δ. Then, there exists a natural number, k, such that if for some $n \geq k$, $z_0 a_1 z_1 a_2 z_2 \ldots a_n z_n \in L$, where $z_i \in \Delta^*$ for all $i = 0, \ldots, n$, and $a_j \in \Delta$ for all $j = 0, \ldots, n$, then $z_0 a_1 z_1 a_2 z_2 \ldots a_n z_n$ can be written as $z_0 a_1 z_1 a_2 z_2 \ldots a_n z_n = uvwxy$ where

I. For some $t = 1, \ldots, n$, a_t appears in vx.
II. If vwx contains $a_r, \ldots, a_s$, for some $r = 1, \ldots, n$, and $s = r, \ldots, n$, then $s - r \leq k - 1$.
III. $uv^m wx^m y \in L$, for all $m \geq 0$. ■

Consider languages (a) and (b). Prove that they are not context-free by using the Ogden's lemma.

a. $\{a^i b^j c^k d^l \mid i, j, k, l \geq 0$, and either $i = 0$ or $j = k = l\}$
b. $\{a^i b^j c^k \mid i, j, k \geq 0, i \neq j, k \neq i$, and $j \neq k\}$

7. Recall that ${}_{LG}\Phi$ denotes the family of linear languages—that is, the language family defined by linear grammars (LGs) (see Section 2.2). Consider

Lemma *Pumping lemma for linear languages.* Let $L \in {}_{LG}\Phi$. Then, there exists $k \in \mathbb{N}$ such that every string $z \in L$ satisfying $|z| \geq k$ can be expressed as $z = uvwxy$, where $1 \leq |vx| \leq |uvxy| \leq k$, and $uv^m wx^m y \in L$, for all $m \geq 0$. ■

a. Prove this lemma.
b. Let $L = \{a^i b^i \mid i \geq 0\}$. Prove that $L^2 \notin {}_{LG}\Phi$ by using this lemma.

8 S. Consider

Definition Let $k \in \mathbb{N}$. Let $G = (\Sigma, R)$ be a CFG. G is a *k-linear CFG* if each rule $A \rightarrow y \in R$ satisfies (i) or (ii):
i. $A = S$, and precisely k nonterminals occur in y.
ii. $A \neq S$, and no more than one nonterminal occurs in y.

In addition, in either case, S does not occur in y.

Let $_{k\text{-}LG}\Phi = \{L(G) | G \text{ is a } k\text{-linear CFG}\}$. A language L is *metalinear* if there exists $k \in \mathbb{N}$ such that $L \in {_{k\text{-}LG}\Phi}$. Let $_{meta\text{-}LG}\Phi$ denote the family of all metalinear languages. ■

a. Prove that $_{k\text{-}LG}\Phi \subset {_{k+1\text{-}LG}\Phi}$, for all $k \geq 1$.
b. Establish the relations between $_{CFG}\Phi$, $_{DPDA}\Phi$, $_{meta\text{-}LG}\Phi$, $_{LG}\Phi$, and $_{reg}\Phi$.

9 S. Let L be a language over an alphabet Σ. Recall the following language operations, introduced in the Exercises of Chapter 5.
   i. $min(L) = \{w | w \in L \text{ and} (prefix(w) - \{w\}) \cap L = \emptyset\}$
   ii. $max(L) = \{w | w \in L \text{ and } \{w\}\Sigma^+ \cap L = \emptyset\}$
   iii. $sqrt(L) = \{x | xy \in L \text{ for some } y \in \Sigma^*, \text{ and } |y| = |x|^2\}$
   iv. $log(L) = \{x | xy \in L \text{ for some } y \in \Sigma^*, \text{ and } |y| = 2^{|x|}\}$
   v. $cycle(L) = \{vw | wv \in L \text{ for some } v, w \in \Sigma^*\}$
   vi. $half(L) = \{w | wv \in L \text{ for some } v \in \Sigma^*, \text{ and } |w| = |v|\}$
   vii. $inv(L) = \{xwy | xzy \in L \text{ for some } x, y, w, z \in \Sigma^*, z = reversal(w)\}$

   For each of these operations and for each of the families $_{CFG}\Phi$, $_{DPDA}\Phi$, $_{meta\text{-}LG}\Phi$, and $_{LG}\Phi$, prove or disprove that the family is closed under the operation in question.

10 S. For a language L over an alphabet Δ and a symbol $a \in \Delta$, $_aEraser(L)$ is the language obtained by deleting all *a*s in the strings from L. Formalize $_aEraser(L)$. For each of the language families $_{CFG}\Phi$, $_{DPDA}\Phi$, $_{meta\text{-}LG}\Phi$, and $_{LG}\Phi$, prove or disprove that the family is closed under this operation.

11 S. Consider each of the language operations introduced in Section 2.1. For each of the language families $_{CFG}\Phi$, $_{DPDA}\Phi$, $_{meta\text{-}LG}\Phi$, and $_{LG}\Phi$, prove or disprove that the family is closed under the operation.

12. Consider the language consisting of all well-written programs in your favorite programming language, such as Java. Prove or disprove that the language under consideration is context-free.

13. Select a subset of a natural language, such as English. For instance, take the subset of all well-formed English sentences whose last word is *respectively*, such as

    She and he ate a cake and a steak, respectively.

    Prove or disprove that the selected language is context-free.

14. Let L and K be two languages over an alphabet, Σ. Let 0 and 1 be two special symbols such that $\{0, 1\} \cap \Sigma = \emptyset$. Then,
   i. $\{0\}L \cup \{1\}K$ is the *marked union* of L and K.
   ii. $\{0\}L\{1\}K$ is the *marked concatenation* of L and K.
   iii. $(\{0\}L)^*$ is the *marked closure* of L.

   Prove that $_{DPDA}\Phi$ is closed under these operations.

15. Let T and U be two alphabets. Let τ be a substitution from T^* to U^* (see Section 2.1) such that for all $x \in T^*$, $\tau(x)$ is linear. Then, τ is a *linear substitution*.

    Prove that $_{LG}\Phi$ is not closed under linear substitution.

Solution to Selected Exercises

3. We only consider (iii). That is, set $L = \{a^ib^jc^k | i, j, k \geq 0 \text{ and } i = j \text{ or } j = k\}$. Prove that $L \in {_{CFG}\Phi}$. Set $H = \{a^nb^nc^n | n \geq 0\}$ and $K = HL$. Observe that H and K are non-CFLs. Clearly, $H \subset L \subset K$.

8. We only sketch the solution to (a). By the definition given in Exercise 8, $_{k\text{-}LG}\Phi \subseteq {_{k+1\text{-}LG}\Phi}$, for all $k \geq 1$. Take $L = \{a^ib^i | i \geq 0\}$ (see Exercise 7). Consider L^{k+1}. Observe that the CFG

$$S \to A^{k+1}, A \to aAb, A \to \varepsilon$$

generates L^{k+1}. By analogy with the pumping lemma established in Exercise 7, show a pumping lemma for $_{k\text{-}LG}\Phi$ and make use of it to prove that $L^{k+1} \notin {_{k\text{-}LG}\Phi}$ (in fact, for $k = 1$, Exercise 7 shows that $L^2 \notin {_{1\text{-}LG}\Phi}$). Therefore, $L^{k+1} \in {_{k+1\text{-}LG}\Phi} - {_{k\text{-}LG}\Phi}$, so $_{k\text{-}LG}\Phi \subset {_{k+1\text{-}LG}\Phi}$.

9. We only point out that under *min* and *max*, $_{DPDA}\Phi$ is closed, but $_{CFG}\Phi$ is not.

10. We only formalize ${}_{a}Eraser(L)$. For a language, L, over an alphabet, Δ, and a symbol, $a \in \Delta$, define

    ${}_{a}Eraser(L) = \{b_1 \ldots b_n |\ \{a\}^*\{b_1\}\{a\}^* \ldots \{a\}^*\{b_n\}\{a\}^* \cap L \neq \emptyset, b_i \in (\Delta - \{a\}), 1 \leq i \leq n$, for some $n \geq 0$ $(b_1 \ldots b_n = \varepsilon$ if $n = 0)\}$.

11. We only consider union, concatenation, and closure. ${}_{DPDA}\Phi$ is not closed under any of them. ${}_{CFG}\Phi$ is closed under all of them. ${}_{meta\text{-}LG}\Phi$ is closed under union and concatenation, but it is not closed under closure.

TURING MACHINES AND COMPUTATION

IV

The Church–Turing Thesis. The intuitive notion of a procedure is functionally identical with the formal notion of a Turing machine.

This crucially important declaration, originated by Alonzo Church in 1936, brings us to the very heart of the theoretical foundations of computation and, thereby, makes the Turing machine exceptionally significant. Indeed, as the intuitive notion of an effective procedure is central to computation as a whole, we really do need to formalize it by an adequate formal model to explore these foundations quite clearly and validly, and the Church–Turing thesis assures us that the Turing machine fulfills this role properly.

Named after its inventor Alan Turing, the Turing machine represents a relatively simple language-defining model, and as follows from its description given shortly, it obviously constitutes a procedure. Much more surprisingly, the Church–Turing thesis also asserts that every procedure in the intuitive sense can be completely formalized by this strictly mathematical notion of a Turing machine. Observe that it is really a thesis, not a theorem because it cannot be proved. Indeed, any proof of this kind would necessitate a formalization of our intuitive notion of a procedure, so it could be rigorously compared with the notion of a Turing machine. At this point, however, there would be a problem whether this newly formalized notion is equivalent to the intuitive notion of a procedure, which would give rise to another thesis similar to the Church–Turing thesis. Therefore, any attempt to prove this thesis inescapably ends up with an infinite regression. However, the evidence supporting the Church–Turing thesis is hardly disputable because throughout its history, computer science has formalized the notion of a procedure in the intuitive sense by other mathematical models; including Post systems, μ-recursive functions, and λ-calculus; all of them have eventually turned out to be equivalent with Turing machines. Even more importantly, nobody has ever come with a procedure in the intuitive sense and demonstrated that no Turing machine can formalize it. Thus, the strictly mathematical notion of a Turing machine has become the universally accepted formalization of the intuitive notion of a procedure. In other words, it is a general-enough mathematical model for the notion of a procedure in the intuitive sense, so any possible procedure can be realized as a Turing machine. Playing such a significant role, the Turing machine model underlies most fundamental ideas behind computation as demonstrated in Section IV, consisting of Chapters 9 through 11.

Chapter 9 gives the basic definition of a Turing machine. In many respects, it resembles the notion of a finite automaton discussed in Section II. Indeed, it is based on, finitely, many states and symbols, and it operates by making moves that depend on a state and a symbol. In addition, however, it can not only read its tape but also write on it. Furthermore, its read-write head can move both to the right and to the left on the tape. Finally, and most importantly, the tape can be limitlessly extended to the right. Several restricted and universal versions of the basic model of a Turing machine are covered in Chapter 9 too.

Based on Turing machines, Chapter 10 develops the fundamental theory of computation. This chapter first studies the general limits of computation based on the statement that every procedure can be formalized by a Turing machine, so any computation beyond their power is also beyond the computer power in general. More specifically, the chapter performs this study in terms of two key areas of the computation theory—computability and decidability. Regarding computability, it considers Turing machines as computers of functions over non-negative integers and demonstrates the existence of functions whose computation cannot be specified by any procedure. As far as decidability is concerned, it formalizes problem-deciding algorithms by Turing machines that halt on every input. It formulates several important problems concerning the language models discussed earlier in this book and constructs algorithms that decide them. On the other hand, it describes several problems that are algorithmically undecidable. Apart from giving specific undecidable problems, it builds us a general theory of undecidability. Finally, it reconsiders algorithms that decide problems in terms of their computational complexity measured according to time and space requirements. Perhaps most importantly, it shows that although some problems are decidable in principle, they are intractable for unreasonably high computational requirements of the algorithms that decide them.

Chapter 11 returns to formal language theory—that is, the principal subject of this book—and reconsiders Turing machines within this theory. It generalizes context-free grammars to grammars that represent a grammatical counterpart to Turing machines in the sense that they are equally powerful. In addition, it covers several special cases of Turing machines and the grammars, including their normal forms.

Throughout Chapters 10 and 11, Section IV also demonstrates many properties of the language family resulting from Turing machines. More specifically, it establishes a relation between various subfamilies of this family. It also gives some results related to closure and non-closure properties of this family; perhaps most significantly, Chapter 10 shows that this family is not closed under complement, from which it demonstrates the existence of important undecidable problems. Consequently, as properties of languages resulting from Turing machines are covered within Chapters 10 and 11, Section IV contains no separate chapter about them as opposed to Sections II and III, which demonstrate the properties of regular and context-free languages in Chapters 5 and 8, respectively.

Chapter 9

Turing Machines and Their Variants

This three-section chapter introduces Turing machines (TMs) and their variants. Section 9.1 gives their basic definition. Then, Section 9.2 covers several special variants of these machines while Section 9.3 presents their universal versions, which fulfill an important role in Chapter 10.

9.1 Turing Machines and Their Languages

Return to the notion of a finite automaton (FA) (see Section 3.1). TM generalizes the FA in three essential ways. First, it can read and write on its tape. Second, its read-write head can move both to the right and to the left on the tape. Finally, the tape can be limitlessly extended to the right.

Definition 9.1 A *Turing machine* (TM) is a rewriting system $M = (\Sigma, R)$, where

- Σ contains subalphabets $Q, F, \Gamma, \Delta, \{\rhd, \lhd\}$ such that $\Sigma = Q \cup \Gamma \cup \{\rhd, \lhd\}$, $F \subseteq Q$, $\Delta \subset \Gamma$, $\Gamma - \Delta$ always contains $\square$—the *blank* symbol (see Convention 4.6), and $\{\rhd, \lhd\}$, Q, Γ are pairwise disjoint
- R is a finite *set of rules* of the form $x \to y$ satisfying
  - i. $\{x, y\} \subseteq \{\rhd\}Q$, or
  - ii. $\{x, y\} \subseteq \Gamma Q \cup Q\Gamma$, or
  - iii. $x \in Q\{\lhd\}$ and $y \in Q\{\square\lhd, \lhd\}$

Q, F, Γ, and Δ are referred to as the *set of states*, the *set of final states*, the *alphabet of tape symbols*, and the *alphabet of input symbols*, respectively. Q contains the *start state*, denoted by $\blacktriangleright$. Relations $\Rightarrow$ and $\Rightarrow^*$ are defined like in any rewriting system (see Definition 2.2 and Convention 2.3). *M accepts* $w \in \Delta^*$ if $\rhd\blacktriangleright w\lhd \Rightarrow^* \rhd ufv\lhd$ in M, where $u, v \in \Gamma^*, f \in F$. The *language* *accepted by M* or, briefly, the *language of M* is denoted by $L(M)$ and defined as the set of all strings that M accepts; formally,

$$L(M) = \{w \mid w \in \Delta^*, \rhd\blacktriangleright w\lhd \Rightarrow^* \rhd ufv\lhd, u, v \in \Gamma^*, f \in F\}$$ ■

A *configuration* of M is a string of the form $\rhd uqv\lhd$, $u, v \in \Gamma^*$, $q \in Q$, and let $_M\mathrm{X}$ denote the set of all configurations of M. We say that uv is on the *tape* of M, which is always delimited by $\rhd$ and $\lhd$, referred to as the *left* and *right bounders*, respectively. In essence, $\rhd uqv\lhd$ captures the current situation M occurs in. That is, in $\rhd uqv\lhd$, q is the current state of M, whose read-write *head* occurs over the current *input symbol* defined as the leftmost symbol of $v\lhd$. If $\beta \Rightarrow \chi$ in M, where $\beta, \chi \in {_M\mathrm{X}}$, we say that M makes a *move* or a *computational step* from β to χ. A move made by an *extending rule* of the form $q\lhd \rightarrow p\Box\lhd \in R$, where $q, p \in Q$, deserves our special attention because it actually extends the current tape by inserting a new occurrence of $\Box$ in front of $\lhd$; more formally and briefly, $\rhd uq\lhd \Rightarrow \rhd up\Box\lhd$, where $u \in \Gamma^*$. As follows from Definition 9.1, $\rhd\blacktriangleright w\lhd \Rightarrow^* \chi$ implies $\chi \in {_M\mathrm{X}}$. We say that M makes a *sequence of moves* or a *computation* from β to χ if $\beta \Rightarrow^* \chi$ in M, where $\beta, \chi \in {_M\mathrm{X}}$.

Convention 9.2 For any TM M, we automatically assume that Q, F, Γ, Δ, and R have the same meaning as in Definition 9.1. If there exists any danger of confusion, we mark Q, F, Γ, Δ, and R with M as $_MQ$, $_MF$, $_M\Gamma$, $_M\Delta$, and $_MR$, respectively, to emphasize that they represent the components of M (in particular, we use these marks when several TMs are simultaneously discussed). ■

Example 9.1 Consider $L = \{x \mid x \in \{a, b, c\}^*, occur(x, a) = occur(x, b) = occur(x, c)\}$. Less formally, x is in L iff x has an equal number of *a*s, *b*s, and *c*s; for instance, $babcca \in L$, but $babcc \notin L$. In this example, we construct a TM M such that $L(M) = L$.

Gist. M records symbols it has read by using its states from $power(\{a, b, c\})$ (see Section 1.2). That is, M moves on the tape in any direction. Whenever it reads an input symbol that is not already recorded in the current state, M can add this symbol into its current state while simultaneously changing it to $\Box$ on the tape. M can anytime change the state that records all three symbols to the state that records no symbol at all. By using a special state, $\hookleftarrow$, M can scan the entire tape so it starts from $\lhd$ and moves left toward $\rhd$ to find out whether the tape is completely blank, and if this is the case, M accepts.

Definition. Define $M = (\Sigma, R)$, where $\Sigma = Q \cup \Gamma \cup \{\rhd, \lhd\}$, $\Gamma = \Delta \cup \{\Box\}$, $\Delta = \{a, b, c\}$, $Q = \{\blacktriangleright, \hookleftarrow, \blacksquare\} \cup W$ with $W = \{\langle O\rangle \mid O \subseteq \{a, b, c\}\}$ and $F = \{\blacksquare\}$. Construct the rules of R by performing (1) through (5). (As stated in Section 1.2, $\{\}$ denotes the empty set just like $\emptyset$ does. In this example, we use $\{\}$ for this purpose.)

1. Add $\rhd\blacktriangleright \rightarrow \rhd\langle\{\}\rangle$ to R.
2. For every $\langle O\rangle \in W$ and every $d \in \Delta \cup \{\Box\}$, add $\langle O\rangle d \rightarrow d\langle O\rangle$ and $d\langle O\rangle \rightarrow \langle O\rangle d$ to R.
3. For every $\langle O\rangle \in W$ such that $O \subset \{a, b, c\}$ and every $d \in \Delta - O$, add $\langle O\rangle d \rightarrow \langle O \cup \{d\}\rangle\Box$ to R.
4. Add $\langle\{a, b, c\}\rangle d \rightarrow \langle\{\}\rangle d$ to R, where $d \in \Delta \cup \{\Box, \lhd\}$.
5. Add $\langle\{\}\rangle\lhd \rightarrow \hookleftarrow\lhd$, $\Box\hookleftarrow \rightarrow \hookleftarrow\Box$, and $\rhd\hookleftarrow \rightarrow \rhd\blacksquare$ to R.

Computation. Consider both the informal and formal description of M. Observe that by (1), M starts every computation. By (2), M moves on its tape. By (3), M adds the input symbol into its current state from $power(\Delta)$ and, simultaneously, changes the input symbol to $\Box$ on the tape. By (4), M empties $\{a, b, c\}$ so it changes this state to the state equal to the empty set. By (5), M makes a final scan of the tape, starting from $\triangleleft$ and moving left toward $\triangleright$, to make sure that the tape is completely blank, and if it is, M accepts.

For instance, in this way, M accepts $babcca$ as follows:

$$\begin{aligned}
\triangleright\blacktriangleright babcca\triangleleft &\Rightarrow \triangleright\langle\{\}\rangle babcca\triangleleft \\
&\Rightarrow^* \triangleright babc\langle\{\}\rangle ca\triangleleft \\
&\Rightarrow \triangleright babc\langle\{c\}\rangle\square a\triangleleft \\
&\Rightarrow^* \triangleright ba\langle\{c\}\rangle bc\square a\triangleleft \\
&\Rightarrow \triangleright ba\langle\{b, c\}\rangle\square c\square a\triangleleft \\
&\Rightarrow^* \triangleright ba\square c\square\langle\{b, c\}\rangle a\triangleleft \\
&\Rightarrow \triangleright ba\square c\square\langle\{a, b, c\}\rangle\square\triangleleft \\
&\Rightarrow^* \triangleright b\langle\{a, b, c\}\rangle a\square c\square\square\triangleleft \\
&\Rightarrow \triangleright b\langle\{\}\rangle a\square c\square\square\triangleleft \\
&\Rightarrow^* \triangleright\square\square\square\square\square\square\langle\{\}\rangle\triangleleft \\
&\Rightarrow \triangleright\square\square\square\square\square\square\hookleftarrow\triangleleft \\
&\Rightarrow \triangleright\square\square\square\square\square\hookleftarrow\square\triangleleft \\
&\Rightarrow^* \triangleright\hookleftarrow\square\square\square\square\square\square\triangleleft \\
&\Rightarrow \triangleright\blacksquare\square\square\square\square\square\square\triangleleft
\end{aligned}$$

Notice, however, M accepts the same string in many other ways, including

$$\begin{aligned}
\triangleright\blacktriangleright babcca\triangleleft &\Rightarrow \triangleright\langle\{\}\rangle babcca\triangleleft \\
&\Rightarrow \triangleright\langle\{b\}\rangle\square abcca\triangleleft \\
&\Rightarrow \triangleright\square\langle\{b\}\rangle abcca\triangleleft \\
&\Rightarrow \triangleright\square\langle\{a, b\}\rangle\square bcca\triangleleft \\
&\Rightarrow^* \triangleright\square\square b\langle\{a, b\}\rangle cca\triangleleft \\
&\Rightarrow \triangleright\square\square b\langle\{a, b, c\}\rangle\square ca\triangleleft \\
&\Rightarrow \triangleright\square\square b\langle\{\}\rangle\square ca\triangleleft \\
&\Rightarrow \triangleright\square\square\langle\{\}\rangle b\square ca\triangleleft \\
&\Rightarrow \triangleright\square\square\langle\{b\}\rangle\square\square ca\triangleleft \\
&\Rightarrow^* \triangleright\square\square\square\square\square\square\hookleftarrow\triangleleft \\
&\Rightarrow^* \triangleright\hookleftarrow\square\square\square\square\square\square\triangleleft \\
&\Rightarrow \triangleright\blacksquare\square\square\square\square\square\square\triangleleft
\end{aligned}$$

Working on the same string in several different ways, M represents a nondeterministic rewriting system (see Section 2.2.3). In Chapter 10, we construct another TM that accepts L in a deterministic way (see Example 9.2). From a more general viewpoint, we explain how to turn any TM to an equivalent TM that works deterministically later in this chapter (see Theorem 9.5).

As illustrated in Example 9.1, the strictly *formal description* of a TM spells out the states, symbols, and rules of the TM under discussion. It is the most detailed and, thereby, rigorous description. At the same time, this level of description tends to be tremendously lengthy and tedious. Thus, paradoxically, this fully detailed description frequently obscures what the TM actually is designed for. For instance, without any intuitive comments included in Example 9.1, we would found somewhat difficult to figure out the way the TM accepts its language. Therefore, in the sequel, we prefer an *informal description* of TMs. That is, we describe them as procedures, omitting various details concerning their components. Crucially, the Church–Turing thesis makes both ways of description perfectly legitimate because it assures us that every procedure is identifiable with a TM defined in a rigorously mathematical way. As a matter of fact, whenever describing TMs in an informal way, we always make sure that the translation from this informal description to the corresponding formal description represents a straightforward task; unfortunately, this task is usually unbearably time-consuming, too. To illustrate an informal description of TMs, we give the following example that informally describes a TM as a Pascal-like procedure, which explains the changes of the tape but omits the specification of states or rules.

Convention 9.3 By analogy with Convention 4.1, when informally describing a TM as a Pascal-like procedure, we express that the machine accepts or rejects its input by **ACCEPT** or **REJECT**, respectively. ■

Example 9.2 Consider $L = \{a^i \mid i \text{ is a prime number}\}$. This example constructs a TM M satisfying $L(M) = L$. Therefore, from a more general viewpoint, TMs are able to recognize the primes as opposed to pushdown automata (PDAs) (see Theorem 6.65 and Exercise 2 in Chapter 8). M is defined as a Pascal-like procedure in the following way:

Let a^i be the input string on the tape, where $i \in \mathbb{N}$;

if $i \leq 1$ **then**
  REJECT

change a^i to AAa^{i-2} on the tape
while $A^k a^h$ occurs on the tape with $k \leq h$ and $i = k + h$ **do**
begin
  on the tape, change $A^k a^h$ to the unique string y satisfying $i = |y|$ and $y \in A^k\{a^k A^k\}^* z$ with $z \in prefix(a^k A^{k-1})$;
  if $|z| = 0$ **or** $|z| = k$ **then**
   REJECT
  else
   change y to $A^{k+1} a^{h-1}$ on the tape
end {of the **while** loop}
ACCEPT.

Observe that i is no prime iff an iteration of the **while** loop obtains $y = A^k a^k A^k \ldots a^k A^k$. Indeed, at this point, i is divisible by k, so M rejects a^i. On the other hand, if during every iteration, $y = A^k a^k A^k \ldots a^k A^k z$ such that $z \in prefix(a^k A^{k-1}) - \{\varepsilon, a^k\}$, then after exiting from this loop, M accepts the input string because i is a prime.

In the **while** loop, consider the entrance test whether $A^k a^h$ occurs on the tape with $k \leq h$ and $i = k + h$. By using several states, tape symbols, and rules, we can easily reformulate this test to its strictly formal description in a straightforward way. However, a warning is in order: this reformulation also represents a painfully tedious task. As obvious, a strictly mathematical definition of the other parts of M is lengthy as well.

Even more frequently and informally, we just use English prose to describe procedures representing TMs under consideration. As a matter of fact, this *highly informal description* of TMs is used in most proofs of theorems given in the sequel.

9.2 Restricted Turing Machines

In this section, we restrict TMs so that compared to their general versions (see Definition 9.1), the resulting restricted TMs are easier to deal with, and yet, they are equally powerful. In essence, we classify all the restrictions into (i) restrictions placed on the way TMs perform their computation and (ii) restrictions placed on the size of TMs.

9.2.1 Computational Restrictions

Perhaps most importantly, we want TMs to work deterministically—that is, from any configuration, they can make no more than one move. As TMs are defined based on rewriting systems (see Definition 9.1), we make use of these systems and simply define deterministic TMs in the following way.

Definition 9.4 A TM is *deterministic* if it represents a rewriting system that is deterministic over ${}_{M}\mathrm{X}$ (see Definition 2.6). ■

In the proof of Theorem 9.5, we demonstrate how to turn any TM to an equivalent deterministic TM (of course, just like any rewriting systems, TMs are *equivalent* if they define the same language). As an exercise, give this proof in greater detail.

Theorem 9.5 From every TM I, we can construct equivalent deterministic TM O.

Proof. Let I be any TM. From I, we obtain an equivalent deterministic TM O so on every input string $x \in {}_{M}\Delta^{*}$, O works as follows. First, O saves x somewhere on the tape so this string is available whenever needed. Then, O systematically produces the sequences of the rules from ${}_{I}R$ on its tape, for instance, in the lexicographical order. Always after producing a sequence of the rules from ${}_{I}R$ in this way, O simulates the moves that I performs on x according to this sequence. If the sequence causes I to accept, O accepts as well; otherwise, it proceeds to the simulation according to the next sequence of rules. If there exists a sequence of moves according to which I accepts x, O eventually produces this sequence and accepts x, too. ■

Next, without affecting the power of TMs, we place further reasonable restrictions on the way deterministic TMs work.

Definition 9.6 Let M be a TM. If from $\chi \in {}_{M}\mathrm{X}$, M can make no move, then χ is a *halting configuration* of M. ■

Theorem 9.7 From every deterministic TM I, we can construct an equivalent deterministic TM $O = ({}_{O}\Sigma, {}_{O}R)$ such that ${}_{O}Q$ contains two new states, ♦ and ■, which do not occur on the left-hand side of any rule in ${}_{O}R$, ${}_{O}F = \{■\}$, and

I. Every halting configuration $\chi \in {}_{O}\mathrm{X}$ has the form $\chi = \rhd qu\lhd$ with $q \in \{♦, ■\}$ and $u \in {}_{O}\Gamma^{*}$, and every non-halting configuration $\nu \in {}_{O}\mathrm{X}$ satisfies $\{♦, ■\} \cap symbols(\nu) = \varnothing$.
II. On every input string $x \in {}_{O}\Delta^{*}$, O performs one of these three kinds of computation:
    i. $\rhd▸x\lhd \Rightarrow^{*} \rhd■u\lhd$, where $u \in {}_{O}\Gamma^{*}$.
    ii. $\rhd▸x\lhd \Rightarrow^{*} \rhd♦v\lhd$, where $v \in {}_{O}\Gamma^{*}$.
    iii. Never enters any halting configuration.

Proof. Let I be a deterministic TM. From I, construct O satisfying the properties of Theorem 9.7 as follows. In both I and O, ▶ is the start state. Introduce ♦ and ■ as two new states into ${}_OQ$. Define ■ as the only final state in O; formally, set ${}_OF = \{■\}$. On every input string x, O works as

1. Runs I on x.
2. If I halts in $\triangleright yqv \triangleleft$, where $y, v \in {}_I\Gamma^*$ and $q \in {}_IQ$, O continues from $\triangleright yqv \triangleleft$ and computes $\triangleright yqv \triangleleft \Rightarrow^* \triangleright qyv \triangleleft$.
3. If $q \in {}_IF$, O computes $\triangleright qyv \triangleleft \Rightarrow \triangleright ■yv \triangleleft$ and halts, and if $q \in {}_IQ - {}_IF$, O computes $\triangleright qyv \triangleleft \Rightarrow \triangleright ♦yv \triangleleft$ and halts.

As obvious, O satisfies the properties stated in Theorem 9.7. ■

We use Convention 9.8 in almost all proofs throughout the discussion concerning TMs in this book, so pay special attention to it.

Convention 9.8 In what follows, we automatically assume that every TM has the properties satisfied by O stated in Theorems 9.5 and 9.7. We denote the set of all these TMs by ${}_{TM}\Psi$. We set ${}_{TM}\Phi = \{L(M) | M \in {}_{TM}\Psi\}$ and refer to ${}_{TM}\Phi$ as the *family of Turing languages*.

Consider the three ways of computation described in part II of Theorem 9.7—(i), (ii), and (iii). Let $M \in {}_{TM}\Psi$ and $x \in {}_M\Delta^*$. We say that *M accepts x* iff on x, M makes a computation of the form (i). *M rejects x* iff on x, M makes a computation of the form (ii). *M halts* on x iff it accepts or rejects x; otherwise, *M loops* on x—in other words, M loops on x iff it performs a computation of the form (iii). States ■ and ♦ are referred to as the *accepting* and *rejecting states*, respectively; accordingly, configurations of the form $\triangleright ■u \triangleleft$ and $\triangleright ♦u \triangleleft$, where $u \in {}_M\Gamma^*$, are referred to as *accepting* and *rejecting configurations*, respectively.

We assume that Δ denotes the input alphabet of all TMs in what follows. Under this assumption, for brevity, we usually simply state that $M \in {}_{TM}\Psi$ works on an input string x instead of stating that M works on an input string x, where $x \in \Delta^*$. ■

According to Convention 9.8, we restrict our attention strictly to ${}_{TM}\Psi$ and ${}_{TM}\Phi$ in the sequel (a single exception is made in Section 10.2.5). Observe that this restriction is without any loss of generality because ${}_{TM}\Phi$ is also characterized by the general versions of TMs (see Definition 9.1) as follows from Theorems 9.5 and 9.7.

Next, we prove that every $L \in {}_{TM}\Phi$ is accepted by $O \in {}_{TM}\Psi$ that never rejects any input x—that is, either O accepts x or O loops on x. It is worth noting that we cannot reformulate this result so O never loops on any input. In other words, ${}_{TM}\Phi$ contains languages accepted only by TMs that loop on some inputs; we prove this important result and explain its crucial consequences in computer science as a whole in Section 10.2.3 of Chapter 10 (see Theorem 10.42).

Theorem 9.9 From any $I \in {}_{TM}\Psi$, we can construct $O \in {}_{TM}\Psi$ such that $L(I) = L(O)$ and O never rejects any input.

Proof. Consider any $I \in {}_{TM}\Psi$. In I, replace every rule with ♦ on its right-hand side with a set of rules that cause the machine to keep looping in the same configuration. Let O be the TM resulting from this simple modification. Clearly, $L(I) = L(O)$ and O never rejects any input. A fully rigorous proof of this theorem is left to the reader. ■

9.2.2 Size Restrictions

By Theorem 9.10 and Corollary 9.11, we can always place a limit on the number of tape symbols in TMs.

Theorem 9.10 From any $I \in {}_{TM}\Psi$ with $card({}_I\Delta) \geq 2$, we can construct $O \in {}_{TM}\Psi$ with ${}_O\Gamma = {}_I\Delta \cup \{\square\}$.

Proof. Let $I = ({}_I\Sigma, {}_IR)$ be a TM in ${}_{TM}\Psi$ such that $a, b \in {}_I\Delta$. Let $2^{k-1} \leq card({}_I\Gamma) \leq 2^k$, for some $k \in \mathbb{N}$. We encode every symbol in ${}_I\Gamma - \{\square\}$ as a unique string of length k over $\{a, b\}$ by a function f from ${}_I\Gamma - \{\square\}$ to $\{a, b\}^k$. Based on f, define the homomorphism g from ${}_I\Sigma^*$ to $({}_IQ \cup \{\triangleright, \triangleleft, \square, a, b\})^*$ so that for all $Z \in {}_I\Gamma - \{\square\}$, $g(Z) = f(Z)$, and for all $Z \in ({}_IQ \cup \{\triangleright, \triangleleft, \square\})$, $g(Z) = Z$ (see Section 2.1 of Chapter 2 for the definition of homomorphism). Next, we construct a TM O that simulates I over the configurations encoded by g in the following way.

1. *Initialization.* Let $w = c_1c_2\ldots c_n$ be an input string, where $c_1, \ldots, c_n$ are input symbols from ${}_I\Delta$. O starts its computation on w by changing w to $g(w)$; in greater detail, it changes $\triangleright\blacktriangleright c_1c_2\ldots c_n\triangleleft$ to $g(\triangleright\blacktriangleright c_1c_2\ldots c_n\triangleleft)$, which equals $\triangleright\blacktriangleright f(c_1)f(c_2)\ldots f(c_n)\triangleleft$.
2. *Simulation of a Move.* If $\triangleright d_1d_2\ldots d_{i-1}qd_i\ldots d_m\triangleleft \in {}_IX$ is the current configuration of I, where $q \in {}_IQ$ and $d_i \in {}_I\Gamma$, $1 \leq i \leq m$, then the corresponding configuration in ${}_OX$ encoded by g is $g(\triangleright d_1d_2\ldots d_{i-1}qd_i\ldots d_m\triangleleft) = \triangleright f(d_1d_2\ldots d_{i-1})qf(d_i\ldots d_m)\triangleleft$. Let $\chi, \kappa \in {}_IX$, and let I compute $\chi \Rightarrow \kappa$ by using $r \in {}_IR$. Then, O simulates $\chi \Rightarrow \kappa$ so it computes $g(\chi) \Rightarrow g(\kappa)$, during which it changes $g(\boldsymbol{lhs}(r))$ to $g(\boldsymbol{rhs}(r))$ by performing several moves.
3. *Simulation of a Computation.* O continues the simulation of moves in I one by one. If I makes a move by which it accepts, O also accepts; otherwise, O continues the simulation. ■

Notice that we can apply the encoding technique used in the proof of Theorem 9.10 even if a or b are not in ${}_I\Delta$, which gives rise to Corollary 9.11.

Corollary 9.11 Let $I \in {}_{TM}\Psi$. Then, there exists $O \in {}_{TM}\Psi$ with ${}_O\Gamma = \{a, b, \square\} \cup {}_I\Delta$. ■

Theorem 9.12, whose proof is left as an exercise, says we can also place a limit on the number of states in TMs without affecting their power.

Theorem 9.12 Let $I \in {}_{TM}\Psi$. Then, there exists $O \in {}_{TM}\Psi$ with $card({}_OQ) \leq 3$. ■

The bottom line of all the restricted versions of TMs discussed in this section is that they are as powerful as the general versions of TMs according to Definition 9.1. Of course, there also exist restrictions placed on TMs that decrease their power. As a matter of fact, whenever we simultaneously place a limit on both the number of noninput tape symbols and the number of states, we decrease the power of TMs (a proof of this result is omitted because it is beyond the scope of this introductory text). Furthermore, in Chapters 10 and 11, we introduce some more restricted versions of TMs, such as Turing deciders in Section 10.2.1 and linear-bounded automata in Section 11.2.2, which are less powerful than TMs.

9.3 Universal Turing Machines

A formally described TM in ${}_{TM}\Psi$ resembles the machine code of a program executed by a computer, which thus acts as a universal device that executes all possible programs of this kind. Considering the subject of this chapter, we obviously want to know whether there also exists a TM acting as such a universal device, which simulates all machines in ${}_{TM}\Psi$. The answer is yes, and in this section, we construct a *universal TM* $U \in {}_{TM}\Psi$ that does the job—that is, U simulates every $M \in {}_{TM}\Psi$ working on any input w. However, because the input of any TM, including U, is always a string, we first show how to encode every $M \in {}_{TM}\Psi$ as a string, symbolically denoted by $\langle M \rangle$, from which U interprets M before it simulates its computation. To be quite precise, as its input, U has the code of M followed by the code of w, denoted by $\langle M, w \rangle$, from which U decodes M and w to simulate M working on w so U accepts $\langle M, w \rangle$ iff M accepts w. As a result, before the construction of U, we explain how to obtain $\langle M \rangle$ and $\langle M, w \rangle$ for every $M \in {}_{TM}\Psi$ and every input w.

9.3.1 *Turing Machine Codes*

Any reasonable encoding for TMs over a fixed alphabet $\vartheta \subseteq \Delta$ is acceptable provided that for every $M \in {}_{TM}\Psi$, U can mechanically and uniquely interpret $\langle M \rangle$ as M. Mathematically speaking, this encoding should represent a total function *code* from ${}_{TM}\Psi$ to ϑ^* such that $code(M) = \langle M \rangle$ for all $M \in {}_{TM}\Psi$. In addition, we select an arbitrary but fixed $Z \in {}_{TM}\Psi$ and define the decoding of TMs, *decode*, so for every $x \in range(code)$, $decode(x) = inverse(code(M))$ and for every $y \in \vartheta^* - range(code)$, $decode(y) = Z$ so $range(decode) = {}_{TM}\Psi$. As a result, *decode* is a total surjection because it maps every string in ϑ^*, including the strings that *code* maps to no machine in ${}_{TM}\Psi$, to a machine in ${}_{TM}\Psi$. Notice, on the other hand, that several strings in ϑ^* may be decoded to the same machine in ${}_{TM}\Psi$; mathematically, *decode* may not be an injection. From a more practical viewpoint, we just require that the mechanical interpretation of both *code* and *decode* is relatively easily performable. Apart from encoding and decoding all machines in ${}_{TM}\Psi$, we also use *code* and *decode* to encode and decode the pairs consisting of TMs and input strings. Next, we illustrate *code* and *decode* in binary.

A Binary Code for TMs. Consider any $M \in {}_{TM}\Psi$. Recall that we automatically apply Convention 9.2 to M, including the meaning of Q, F, Γ, Δ, and R. Consider Q as the set of states of M. Rename these states to $q_1, q_2, q_3, q_4, \ldots, q_m$ so $q_1 = \blacktriangleright$, $q_2 = \blacksquare$, $q_3 = \blacklozenge$, where $m = card(Q)$. Rename the symbols of $\{\triangleright, \triangleleft\} \cup \Gamma$ to $a_1, a_2, \ldots, a_n$ so $a_1 = \triangleright$, $a_2 = \triangleleft$, $a_3 = \square$, where $n = card(\Gamma) + 2$. Introduce the homomorphism h from $Q \cup \{\triangleright, \triangleleft\} \cup \Gamma$ to $\{0, 1\}^*$ as $h(q_i) = 10^i$, $1 \leq i \leq m$, and $h(a_j) = 110^j$, $1 \leq j \leq n$ (homomorphism is defined in Section 2.1). Extend h so it is defined from $(\{\triangleright, \triangleleft\} \cup \Gamma \cup Q)^*$ to $\{0, 1\}^*$ in the standard way—that is, $h(\varepsilon) = \varepsilon$, and $h(X_1 \ldots X_k) = h(X_1) h(X_2) \ldots h(X_k)$, where $k \geq 1$, and $X_l \in \{\triangleright, \triangleleft\} \cup \Gamma \cup Q$, $1 \leq l \leq k$ (see Section 2.1). Based on h, we now define the function *code* from R to $\{0, 1\}^*$ so that for each rule $r: x \rightarrow y \in R$, $code(r) = h(xy)$. Then, write the rules of R one after the other in an order as $r_1, r_2, \ldots, r_o$ with $o = card(R)$; for instance, order them lexicographically. Set $code(R) = code(r_1)111code(r_2)111\ldots code(r_o)111$. Finally, from $code(R)$, we obtain the desired $code(M)$ by setting $code(M) = 0^m10^n1code(R)1$. Taking a closer look at $code(M) = 0^m10^n1code(R)1$, 0^m1 and 0^n1 state that $m = card(Q)$ and $n = card(\Gamma) + 2$, respectively, and $code(R)$ encodes the rules of R. Seen as a function from ${}_{TM}\Psi$ to $\{0, 1\}^*$, *code* obviously represents a total function ${}_{TM}\Psi$ to ϑ^*. On the other hand, there are binary strings that represent no legal code of any machine in ${}_{TM}\Psi$; mathematically, *inverse*(*code*) is a partial function, not a total function. For example, ε, any string in $\{0\}^* \cup \{1\}^*$, or any string that starts with 1 are illegal codes, so their inverses are undefined. Select an arbitrary but fixed $Z \in {}_{TM}\Psi$; for instance, take Z as a TM that immediately rejects every input after it starts its computation. Extend *inverse*(*code*) to the total function *decode* from $\{0, 1\}^*$ to ${}_{TM}\Psi$ so that *decode* maps all binary strings that represent no code of any TM in ${}_{TM}\Psi$ to Z. More precisely, for every $x \in \{0, 1\}^*$, if x is a legal code of a TM K in ${}_{TM}\Psi$, *decode* maps x to K, but if it is not, *decode* maps x to Z; equivalently and briefly, if x encodes $K \in {}_{TM}\Psi$ and, therefore, $x \in range(code)$, $decode(x) = K$, and if $x \in \{0, 1\}^* - range(code)$, $decode(x) = Z$ (notice that *decode* represents a surjection).

To encode every $w \in \Delta^*$, we simply set $code(w) = h(w)$, where h is the homomorphism defined above. Select an arbitrary but fixed $y \in \Delta^*$; for instance, take $y = \varepsilon$. Define the total surjection *decode* from $\{0, 1\}^*$ to Δ^* so for every $x \in \{0, 1\}^*$, if $x \in range(code)$, $decode(x) = inverse(code(w))$; otherwise, $decode(x) = y$.

For every $(M, w) \in {}_{TM}\Psi \times \Delta^*$, define $code(M, w) = code(M)code(w)$. Viewed as a function from ${}_{TM}\Psi \times \Delta^*$ to $\{0, 1\}^*$, *code* obviously represents a total function from ${}_{TM}\Psi \times \Delta^*$ to ϑ^*. Define the total surjection *decode* from $\{0, 1\}^*$ to ${}_{TM}\Psi \times \Delta^*$ so $decode(xy) = decode(x)decode(y)$, where $decode(x) \in {}_{TM}\Psi$ and $decode(y) \in \Delta^*$.

Example 9.3 Consider this trivial TM $M \in {}_{TM}\Psi$, where $M = (\Sigma, R)$, $\Sigma = Q \cup \Gamma \cup \{\rhd, \lhd\}$, $Q = \{\blacktriangleright, \blacksquare, \blacklozenge, A, B, C, D\}$, $\Gamma = \Delta \cup \{\square\}$, $\Delta = \{b\}$, and R contains these rules

$$\blacktriangleright\lhd \rightarrow \blacksquare\lhd,\ \blacktriangleright b \rightarrow bA,\ Ab \rightarrow bB,\ Bb \rightarrow bA,\ A\lhd \rightarrow C\lhd,\ B\lhd \rightarrow D\lhd,$$
$$bD \rightarrow D\square,\ bC \rightarrow C\square,\ \rhd C \rightarrow \rhd\blacklozenge,\ \rhd D \rightarrow \rhd\blacksquare$$

Leaving a simple proof that $L(M) = \{b^i \mid i \geq 0,\ i \text{ is even}\}$ as an exercise, we next obtain the binary code of M by applying the encoding method described above. Introduce the homomorphism h from $Q \cup \{\rhd, \lhd\} \cup \Gamma$ to $\{0, 1\}^*$ as $h(q_i) = 10^i$, $1 \leq i \leq 7$, where $q_1, q_2, q_3, q_4, q_5, q_6$, and q_7 coincide with $\blacktriangleright, \blacksquare, \blacklozenge, A, B, C$, and D, respectively, and $h(a_j) = 110^j$, $1 \leq j \leq 4$, where a_1, a_2, a_3, and a_4 coincide with $\rhd, \lhd, \square$, and b, respectively. Extend h so it is defined from $(Q \cup \{\rhd, \lhd\} \cup \Gamma)^*$ to $\{0, 1\}^*$ in the standard way. Based on h, define the function *code* from R to $\{0, 1\}^*$ so for each rule $x \rightarrow y \in R$, $code(x \rightarrow y) = h(xy)$. For example, $code(\blacktriangleright b \rightarrow bA) = 1011000011000010000$. Take, for instance, the above order of the rules from R, and set

$$\begin{aligned} code(R) = {} & code(\blacktriangleright\lhd \rightarrow \blacksquare\lhd)\ 111\ code(\blacktriangleright b \rightarrow bA)\ 111 \\ & code(Ab \rightarrow bB)\ 111\ code(Bb \rightarrow bA)\ 111 \\ & code(A\lhd \rightarrow C\lhd)\ 111\ code(B\lhd \rightarrow D\lhd)\ 111 \\ & code(bD \rightarrow D\square)\ 111\ code(bC \rightarrow C\square)\ 111 \\ & code(\rhd C \rightarrow \rhd\blacklozenge)\ 111\ code(\rhd D \rightarrow \rhd\blacksquare)\ 111 \end{aligned}$$

$$\begin{aligned} = {} & 10110010011001111011000011000010000111 \\ & 10000110000110000100000011110000011000011000010000111 \\ & 1000011001000000110011110000011001000000001100111 \\ & 11000010000000010000000011000111110000100000001000000011000111 \\ & 1101000000110100011111010000000110100111 \end{aligned}$$

To encode M as a whole, set

$$
\begin{aligned}
code(M) &= 0^7 10^4 1 code(R) 1 \\
&= 0000000100001 \\
&\quad 10110010011001111011000011000010000111 \\
&\quad 1000011000011000010000011110000011000011000010000111 \\
&\quad 10000110010000000110011110000011001000000001100111 \\
&\quad 11000010000000010000000110001111100001000000010000000011000111 \\
&\quad 1101000000110100011111010000000110100111 \\
&\quad 1
\end{aligned}
$$

Take $w = bb$, whose $code(bb) = 110000110000$. As a result, the binary string denoted by $code(M, bb)$ is

0000000100001101100100110011110110000110000100001111000011000011000010000 0111
1000001100001100001000011110000110010000000110011110000011001000000001100111110
000100000000100000000110001111100001000000010000000011000111110100000001101000 11111
01000000011010011111110000110000

Convention 9.13 In what follows, we suppose there exist a fixed encoding and a fixed decoding of all TMs in $_{TM}\Psi$. We just require that both are uniquely and mechanically interpretable; otherwise, they may differ from *code* and *decode* (in fact, they may not even be in binary). As already stated in the beginning of this section, we denote the code of $M \in {}_{TM}\Psi$ by $\langle M \rangle$. Similarly, we suppose there exist an analogical encoding and decoding of the members of Δ^*, $_{TM}\Psi \times \Delta^*$, $_{TM}\Psi \times {}_{TM}\Psi$, and $_{TM}\Psi \times {}_0\mathbb{N}$. Again, for brevity, we denote the codes of $w \in \Delta^*$, $(M, w) \in {}_{TM}\Psi \times \Delta^*$, $(M, N) \in {}_{TM}\Psi \times {}_{TM}\Psi$, and $(M, i) \in {}_{TM}\Psi \times {}_0\mathbb{N}$ by $\langle w \rangle$, $\langle M, w \rangle$, $\langle M, N \rangle$, and $\langle M, i \rangle$, respectively (as an exercise, encode and decode the members of $_0\mathbb{N}$ similarly to encoding the machine in $_{TM}\Psi$). Even more generally, for any automaton or grammar, X, discussed in Chapters 2 through 8, $\langle X \rangle$ represents its code analogical to $\langle M \rangle$. ■

Out of all the terminology introduced in Convention 9.13, we just need $\langle M \rangle$ and $\langle M, w \rangle$ in the rest of Chapter 9.

9.3.2 Construction of Universal Turing Machines

We are now ready to construct U—that is, a universal TM (see Section 9.3). As a matter of fact, we construct two versions of U. The first version, denoted by $_{TM\text{-}Acceptance}U$, simulates every $M \in {}_{TM}\Psi$ on $w \in \Delta^*$ so $_{TM\text{-}Acceptance}U$ accepts $\langle M, w \rangle$ iff M accepts w. In other words, $L(_{TM\text{-}Acceptance}U) = {}_{TM\text{-}Acceptance}L$ with

$$_{TM\text{-}Acceptance}L = \{\langle M, w \rangle \mid M \in {}_{TM}\Psi, w \in \Delta^*, M \text{ accepts } w\}$$

The other version, denoted by $_{TM\text{-}Halting}U$, simulates every $M \in {}_{TM}\Psi$ on $w \in \Delta^*$ in such a way that $_{TM\text{-}Halting}U$ accepts $\langle M, w \rangle$ iff M halts on w (see Convention 9.8). To rephrase this in terms of formal languages, $L(_{TM\text{-}Halting}U) = {}_{TM\text{-}Halting}L$ with

$$_{TM\text{-}Halting}L = \{\langle M, w \rangle \mid M \in {}_{TM}\Psi, w \in \Delta^*, M \text{ halts on } w\}$$

Convention 9.14 Strictly speaking, in the proof of Theorem 9.15, we should state that ${}_{TM\text{-}Acceptance}U$ works on $\langle M, w\rangle$ so it first interprets $\langle M, w\rangle$ as M and w; then, it simulates the moves of M on w. However, instead of a long and obvious statement like this, we just state that ${}_{TM\text{-}Acceptance}U$ runs M on w. In a similar manner, we shorten the other proofs of results concerning TMs in the sequel whenever no confusion exists. ■

Theorem 9.15 There exists ${}_{TM\text{-}Acceptance}U \in {}_{TM}\Psi$ such that $L({}_{TM\text{-}Acceptance}U) = {}_{TM\text{-}Acceptance}L$.

Proof. On every input $\langle M, w\rangle$, ${}_{TM\text{-}Acceptance}U$ works so it runs M on w. ${}_{TM\text{-}Acceptance}U$ accepts $\langle M, w\rangle$ if and when it finds out that M accepts w; otherwise, ${}_{TM\text{-}Acceptance}U$ keeps simulating the moves of M in this way. ■

Observe that ${}_{TM\text{-}Acceptance}U$ represents a procedure, not an algorithm because if M loops on w, so does ${}_{TM\text{-}Acceptance}U$ on $\langle M, w\rangle$. As a matter of fact, in Section 10.2.3 of Chapter 10, we demonstrate that no TM can halt on every input and, simultaneously, act as a universal TM (see Theorem 10.43). To reformulate this in terms of formal languages, no TM accepts ${}_{TM\text{-}Acceptance}L$ in such a way that it halts on all strings. Indeed, for all $X \in {}_{TM}\Psi$ satisfying ${}_{TM\text{-}Acceptance}L = L(X)$, $\Delta^* - {}_{TM\text{-}Acceptance}L$ necessarily contains a string on which X loops.

By analogy with the proof of Theorem 9.15, we next obtain ${}_{TM\text{-}Halting}U$ that accepts ${}_{TM\text{-}Halting}L$, defined earlier.

Theorem 9.16 There exists ${}_{TM\text{-}Halting}U \in {}_{TM}\Psi$ such that $L({}_{TM\text{-}Halting}U) = {}_{TM\text{-}Halting}L$.

Proof. On every $\langle M, w\rangle$, ${}_{TM\text{-}Halting}U$ works so it runs M on w. ${}_{TM\text{-}Halting}U$ accepts $\langle M, w\rangle$ iff M halts w, which means that M either accepts w or rejects w (see Convention 9.8). Thus, ${}_{TM\text{-}Halting}U$ loops on $\langle M, w\rangle$ iff M loops on w, which means that $\langle M, w\rangle \notin {}_{TM\text{-}Halting}L$. Observe that $L({}_{TM\text{-}Halting}U) = {}_{TM\text{-}Halting}L$. ■

Exercises

1. This chapter contains results whose proofs are only sketched or even completely omitted. These results include Theorems 9.5 and 9.12, Example 9.2, and Convention 9.13. Complete them.
2. Construct three equivalent TMs; A, B, and C; so A accepts every input string by infinitely many sequences of moves, B accepts every input string by exactly two sequences of moves, and C is deterministic. Give a rigorous proof that A, B, and C are equivalent.
3. Consider the TM M from Example 9.1. Construct an equivalent TM that has fewer rules than M has. Give a proof that both TMs are equivalent.
4. Consider each of languages (i) through (xxiii). Construct a TM that accepts it. Define the constructed TM strictly formally. Give a rigorous proof that verifies the construction.
   i. $\{a^i b^j c^k \mid i, j, k \geq 0 \text{ and } i < j < k\}$
   ii. $\{a^i b^j a^i \mid i, j \geq 0 \text{ and } j = i^2\}$
   iii. $\{a^i \mid i \text{ is not a prime}\}$
   iv. $\{w \mid w \in \{a, b, c\}^* \text{ and } (occur(w, a) \neq occur(w, b) \text{ or } occur(w, b) \neq occur(w, c))\}$
   v. $\{a^i b^i a^j \mid i, j \geq 0 \text{ and } j \neq i\}$
   vi. $\{a^i b^i c^j \mid i, j \geq 0 \text{ and } i \neq j \neq 2i\}$
   vii. $\{a^i b^j c^k \mid i, j, k \geq 0,\ i \neq j,\ k \neq i, \text{ and } j \neq k\}$
   viii. $\{a^i b^j c^j d^i \mid i, j \geq 0 \text{ and } j \neq i\}$

ix. $\{a^i b^{2i} c^i \mid i \geq 0\}$
x. $\{ww \mid w \in \{a, b\}^*\}$
xi. $\{wvw \mid v, w \in \{a, b\}^*, reversal(v) = w\}$
xii. $\{0^i 10^i 10^i 10^i \mid i \geq 1\}$
xiii. $\{wcv \mid v, w \in \{a, b\}^*$ and $w = vv\}$
xiv. $\{a^i b^i a^i \mid i, j \geq 1\}$
xv. $\{a^i b^j \mid i \geq 0$ and $j \geq 1\}$
xvi. $\{a^i b^j c^k \mid i, j, k \geq 0$ and $i = j$ or $j = k\}$
xvii. $\{a^i b^j c^i b^j \mid i \geq 0$ and $j \geq 1\}$
xviii. $\{a^j cab^i a^j \mid i, j \geq 0\}$
xix. $\{x \mid x \in \{a, b\}^*, aa \in substring(x), occur(x, a) = occur(x, b)\}$
xx. $\{x \mid x \in \{a, b, c\}^*, occur(x, a) \geq occur(x, b) \geq occur(x, c)\}$
xxi. $\{x \mid x \in \{a, b\}^*, occur(x, a) = 2^{occur(x, b)}\}$
xxii. $\{x \mid x \in \{a, b\}^*, occur(x, b) \geq occur(x, a), |x|$ is divisible by $3\}$
xxiii. $\{x \mid x \in \{a, b, c\}^*, occur(x, a) \geq occur(x, b)$ iff $occur(x, c) < occur(x, a)\}$

5 S. Introduce a graph-based representation for TMs. Then, by using this representation, describe the TMs constructed in Exercise 4.

6. Consider the TM binary code in Section 9.3. Introduce an alternative binary code for TMs and rephrase all the discussion given in Section 9.3 in terms of this alternative code. Then, introduce a ternary code for this purpose and reformulate Section 9.3 in terms of this ternary code.

7. Consider the basic definition of a TM, M (see Definition 9.1). Restrict this definition so M changes the position of its tape head to the left or to the right during every single move; in other words, it never keeps its head stationary during any move. Define this restriction rigorously. Construct an algorithm that turns any TM to an equivalent TM restricted in this way. Verify this algorithm formally.

8. Generalize the definition of a TM by allowing a set of start states. Formalize this generalization. Construct an algorithm that turns any TM generalized in this way to an equivalent one-start-state TM, which satisfies Definition 9.1.

9. During every move, a *simple TM* cannot simultaneously change its state, the tape symbol, and the position of its head; otherwise, it works just like any TM. Formalize the notion of a simple TM. Construct an algorithm that converts any TM to an equivalent simple TM. Verify this algorithm by a rigorous proof.

10. During a single move, a *long-reading TM* can read a string, consisting of several tape symbols. Formalize this generalization. Construct an algorithm that turns any TM generalized in this way to an equivalent TM, defined according to Definition 9.1. Verify this algorithm by a rigorous proof.

11 S. A *two-way TM M* has its tape infinite both to the right and to the left. Initially, M occurs in its start state with an input string w placed on the tape. The tape head occurs over the leftmost symbol of w. Starting from this initial configuration, M works by analogy with the basic model of a TM (see Definition 9.1). As opposed to this basic model, however, M can always make a left move because its tape is infinite to both directions.

Formalize the notion of a two-way TM. Construct an algorithm that turns any two-way TM M to an equivalent TM, defined according to Definition 9.1. Verify this algorithm by a rigorous proof.

12 S. Let $k \in \mathbb{N}$. A *k-head TM M* is a TM with k tape heads over a single tape. A move made by M depends on the current state and the k symbols scanned by the tape heads. During a move, M changes its state and rewrites the k scanned symbols; in addition, M can change the position of any of its heads to the left or to the right. Consider the special case when n tape heads occur at the same tape position, for some $n \in \{2, \ldots, k\}$; at this point, M makes the next move only if all these n tape heads rewrite the scanned tape symbol to the same symbol. Initially, the tape contains the input string, each of the k heads scans its leftmost symbol, and M is in its start state. If from this initial configuration, M can make a sequence of moves that ends in a final state, then M accepts the input string. The language accepted by M consists of all strings that M accepts in this way.

Formalize the notion of a k-head TM. Construct an algorithm that turns any k-head TM M to an equivalent one-head TM (see Definition 9.1). Verify this algorithm by a rigorous proof.

13. Let $k \in \mathbb{N}$. A *k-tape TM M* represents a TM with k tapes, each of which has its read-write tape head. A move made by M depends on the current state and on the k symbols scanned by the k tape heads. During a move, M can change the current state and rewrite any of the k scanned symbols; in addition, it can change the position of any of its k heads. Initially, the first tape contains the input string, the other tapes are blank, each read-write head scans the leftmost symbol, and M occurs in its start state. If from this initial configuration, M can make a sequence of moves that ends in a final state, then M accepts the input string. The set of all strings that M accepts represents the language accepted by M.

    Formalize the notion of a k-tape TM. Construct an algorithm that turns any k-tape TM M to an equivalent one-tape TM, defined according to Definition 9.1.
14. We often accept a language whose strings satisfy a certain condition by a k-head TM because its multiple heads usually simplify verifying that a given input string w satisfies the condition in question. Typically, a verification of this kind is carried out so some of the k heads keep a finger on particular symbols on the tape while the other heads synchronously read some other symbols and, thereby, verify the condition. Consider each of the one-tape TMs constructed in Exercise 4. Denote the TM by I. Construct an equivalent k-head TM O (see Exercise 12) so O has fewer states, tape symbols, or rules than I has.
15. Reformulate and solve Exercise 14 in terms of two-way and k-tape TMs, introduced in Exercises 11 and 13, respectively.
16. Write a program that decides whether a given TM is deterministic.
17. Write a program that simulates any deterministic TM, M. Observe that in a general case, a program like this may enter an infinite loop because M may loop endlessly.
18. Write a program that simulates a universal TM (see Section 9.3). Just like in Exercise 17, a program like this may loop endlessly on some inputs.
19. Consider PDAs (see Section 6.3). Extend them to *two-PDAs* by adding another pushdown to them. Formalize this extension. Introduce table- and graph-based representations for them.

20 S. Construct an algorithm that turns any TM to an equivalent two-PDA (see Exercise 19).

21 S. As any two-PDA can be seen as a procedure, by the Church–Turing thesis, there exists an equivalent TM to it. This exercise, however, asks to demonstrate this result effectively by constructing an algorithm that converts any two-PDA to an equivalent TM.

Solutions to Selected Exercises

5. Let $M = (\Sigma, R)$ be any TM. In a pictorial way, M can be specified by its *state diagram*, which represents a labeled directed graph such that each node is labeled with a state $q \in Q$. To symbolically state that a state s is the start state, we point to it with an arrow. Final states are doubly circled. For two nodes $q, p \in Q$, there is an edge (q, p) if there is a rule $r \in R$ with q and p on its left-hand side and its right-hand side, respectively. If r is of the form $qX \rightarrow Yp \in R$, where $X, Y \in \Gamma$, then it is labeled by $\langle X/Y, right\rangle$, which says that M moves from q to p, rewrites X as Y on the tape, and moves its head to the right. Represent all other possible forms of rules analogically. Complete this solution by yourself.
11. Before giving the solution to this exercise, we intuitively sketch what we mean by the notion of a *k-tract tape* of a TM, where $k \in \mathbb{N}$, because the rest of Section IV, including this solution, makes use of it in what follows. Loosely speaking, at each position of a k-tract tape, there occurs a symbol X represented by a k-tuple $(X_1, \ldots, X_k)$. On a k-tract tape organized like this, the ith track contains the string consisting of the ith components of these k-tuples, where $1 \leq i \leq k$. We can realize X recorded so its k elements, X_1 through X_k, are vertically written above each other at this tape position; pictorially, a k-tract tape, organized in this way, can be sketched as in the figure below.

    Regarding Exercise 11, we only sketch an algorithm that converts any two-way TM I to an equivalent TM O, which satisfies Definition 9.1. Let $a_1 \ldots a_n$ be the input string of M with each a_i being an input symbol. By S, we denote the tape position at which a_1 initially occurs. O uses a two-track tape, so at each tape position, there occur two symbols above each

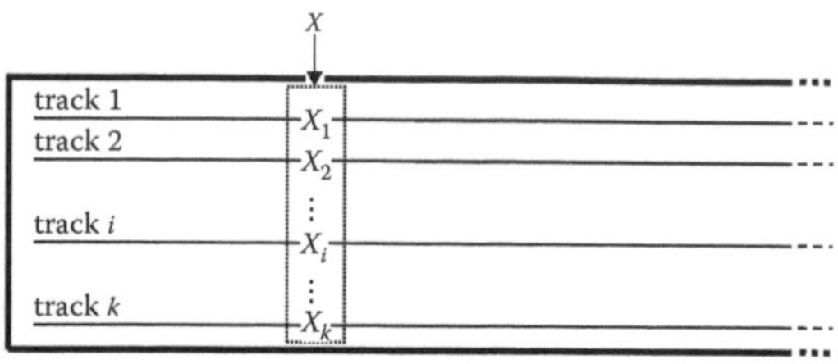

other—an upper symbol and a lower symbol. First, O places $a_1...a_n$ as the n upper symbols on the first tape track while setting all the n corresponding lower symbols to blanks on the second track. If I makes a move at S or to the right of S, O straightforwardly simulates this move within the first track. If M makes a move with its tape head to the left of S, O simulates this move by using the lower symbols placed on the second track (in the direction opposite to the direction in which I moves). Moves I and II deserve our special attention:

I. When I makes a move from S to the left, O first leaves the leftmost upper symbol on the first tape track for the leftmost lower symbol on the second tape track, after which it simulates the move. Analogically, when I makes a move during which it enters S from the left, O first leaves the first lower symbol for the first upper symbol, after which it performs the move simulation.

II. If I extends its tape at either end of the tape, O extends its tape by two blanks placed above each other on both tracks.

Naturally, O accepts $a_1...a_n$ when and if I accepts it.

12. We only sketch how to convert any k-head TM I to an equivalent one-head TM O, satisfying Definition 9.1. O uses a (k+1)-tract tape (see the solution to Exercise 11). Denote the tracks $t_0, t_1, \ldots, t_k$. Track t_0 corresponds to the original tape of I. The other tracks correspond to the k heads. That is, t_j is completely blank except for a single occurrence of a state placed at the tape position corresponding to the symbol scanned by the jth head of I, where $j = 1, \ldots, k$. Consequently, the entire tape holds k state occurrences, all of which specify the same state, which coincides with the current state of the simulated TM I. To simulate a move in I, O sweeps right t_1 through t_k on its tape to find out whether I has a rule applicable in the current configuration. If not, O rejects. If it has a rule r, O simulates the move according to r on t_0 and updates $t_1, \ldots, t_k$ accordingly. O accepts its input when and if I does.

20. We give only a gist of an algorithm that turns any TM to an equivalent two-PDA (see Exercise 19). Let I be a TM. From I, construct a two-PDA O that simulates I by using its two pushdowns as follows. O stores the symbols to the left of the tape head onto one pushdown so that symbols closer to the tape head appear closer to the pushdown top than symbols further from the tape head. Analogously, O stores the symbols to the right of the tape head onto the other pushdown. By using these two pushdowns, O simulates moves made by I. O accepts its input if and when I accepts it.

21. We only sketch an algorithm that turns any two-PDA to an equivalent TM. Let I be a two-PDA. From I, construct a three-tape TM O (see Exercise 13), which uses its tapes as follows. The first tape contains the input string of I. The second tape simulates one pushdown of I while the third tape simulates the other pushdown of I. By using its tapes in this way, O simulates I move by move. O accepts its input if and when I does. Convert O to an equivalent one-tape TM (see Exercise 13). The resulting TM is equivalent to I.

Chapter 10

Applications of Turing Machines: Theory of Computation

In Chapter 9, we have considered Turing machines (TMs) as language acceptors by analogy with other language acceptors, such as finite and pushdown automata, discussed earlier in this book. In this chapter, we make use of TMs to show the fundamentals of *theory of computation*, which is primarily oriented toward determining the theoretical limits of computation in general. This orientation comes as no surprise: by the Church–Turing thesis, which opened Section IV of this book, every procedure can be formalized by a TM, so any computation beyond the power of TMs is also beyond the computer power in general.

This two-section chapter gives an introduction to two key areas of the theory of computation—computability and decidability. In Section 10.1, regarding computability, we view TMs as computers of functions over nonnegative integers and show the existence of functions whose computation cannot be specified by any procedure. Then, regarding decidability, we formalize algorithms that decide problems by using TMs that halt on every input in Section 10.2, which is divided into five subsections. In Section 10.2.1, we conceptualize this approach to decidability. In Section 10.2.2, we formulate several important problems concerning the language models discussed in Chapters 3 and 6, such as finite automata (FAs) and context-free grammars (CFGs), and construct algorithms that decide them. In Section 10.2.3, more surprisingly, we present problems that are algorithmically undecidable, and in Section 10.2.4, we approach undecidability from a more general viewpoint. Finally, in Section 10.2.5, we reconsider algorithms that decide problems in terms of their computational complexity measured according to time and space requirements. Perhaps most importantly, we point out that although some problems are decidable in principle, they are intractable for unreasonably high computational requirements of the algorithms that decide them.

10.1 Computability

Considering the TM model as the formalization of an effective procedure, we show the existence of functions whose computation cannot be specified by any procedure, so they can never be computed by any computer. As a matter of fact, the existence of these uncomputable functions immediately follows from the following counting argument. Consider the set of all functions that map $\mathbb{N}$ onto {0, 1} and the set of all procedures. Whereas the former is uncountable, the latter is countable under our assumption that every procedure has a finite description (see Section 9.1). Thus, there necessarily exist functions with no procedures to compute them. In this section, based on the following TM-based formalization, we take a more specific look at functions whose computation can or, in contrast, cannot be specified by any procedure.

Definition 10.1 Let $M \in {}_{TM}\Psi$. The *function computed by M*, symbolically denoted by M-f, is defined over Δ^* as $M\text{-}f = \{(x, y) |\ x, y \in \Delta^*, \rhd\blacktriangleright x\lhd \Rightarrow^* \rhd\blacksquare yu\lhd \text{ in } M, u \in \{\square\}^*\}$. ■

Consider M-f, where $M \in {}_{TM}\Psi$, and an argument $x \in \Delta^*$. In a general case, M-f is partial, so M-$f(x)$ may or may not be defined. Clearly, if $M\text{-}f(x) = y$ is defined, M computes $\rhd\blacktriangleright x\lhd \Rightarrow^* \rhd\blacksquare yu\lhd$, where $u \in \{\square\}^*$. However, if M-$f(x)$ is undefined, M, starting from $\rhd\blacktriangleright x\lhd$, never reaches a configuration of the form $\rhd\blacksquare vu\lhd$, where $v \in \Delta^*$ and $u \in \{\square\}^*$, so it either rejects x or loops on x (see Convention 9.8).

Definition 10.2 A function f is a *computable function* if there exists $M \in {}_{TM}\Psi$ such that $f = M$-f; otherwise, f is an *uncomputable function.* ■

10.1.1 Integer Functions Computed by Turing Machines

By Definition 10.1, for every $M \in {}_{TM}\Psi$, M-f is defined over Δ^*, where Δ is an alphabet. However, in mathematics, we usually study numeric functions defined over sets of infinitely many numbers. To use TMs to compute functions like these, we first need to represent these numbers by strings over Δ. In this introductory book, we restrict our attention only to integer functions over ${}_0\mathbb{N}$, so we need to represent every nonnegative integer $i \in {}_0\mathbb{N}$ as a string over Δ. Traditionally, we represent i in unary as *unary*(i) for all $i \in {}_0\mathbb{N}$, where *unary* is defined in Example 2.4. That is, *unary*(j) $= a^j$ for all $j \geq 0$; for instance, *unary*(0), *unary*(2), and *unary*(999) are equal to ε, aa, and a^{999}, respectively. Under this representation, used in the sequel, we obviously automatically assume that $\Delta = \{a\}$ simply because a is the only input symbol needed. Next, we formalize the computation of integer functions by TMs based on *unary*.

Definition 10.3

I. Let g be a function over ${}_0\mathbb{N}$ and $M \in {}_{TM}\Psi$. *M computes g in unary* or, more briefly, *M computes g* iff *unary*(g) $= M$-f.
II. A function h over ${}_0\mathbb{N}$ is a *computable function* if there exists $M \in {}_{TM}\Psi$ such that M computes h; otherwise, h is an *uncomputable function*. ■

In greater detail, part I of Definition 10.3 says that M computes an integer function g over ${}_0\mathbb{N}$ if this equivalence holds:

$$g(x) = y \text{ iff } (unary(x), unary(y)) \in M\text{-}f, \text{ for all } x, y \in {}_0\mathbb{N}$$

Convention 10.4 Whenever $M \in {}_{TM}\Psi$ works on an integer $x \in {}_0\mathbb{N}$, x is expressed as *unary*(x). For brevity, whenever no confusion exists, instead of stating that M *works on* x *represented as unary*(x), we just state that M *works on* x in what follows. ■

Example 10.1 Let g be the *successor function* defined as $g(i) = i + 1$, for all $i \geq 0$. Construct a TM M that computes $\triangleright\blacktriangleright a^i\triangleleft \Rightarrow^* \triangleright\blacksquare a^{i+1}\triangleleft$ so it moves across a^i to the right bounder $\triangleleft$, replaces it with $a\triangleleft$, and returns to the left to finish its accepting computation in $\triangleright\blacksquare a^{i+1}\triangleleft$. As a result, M increases the number of as by one on the tape. Thus, by Definition 10.3, M computes g.

Example 10.2 Let g be the total function defined as $g(i) = j$, for all $i \geq 0$, where j is the smallest prime satisfying $i \leq j$. Construct a TM M that tests whether i, represented by a^i, is a prime in the way described in Example 9.2. If i is prime, M accepts in the configuration $\triangleright\blacksquare a^i\triangleleft$. If not, M continues its computation from $\triangleright\blacktriangleright a^{i+1}\triangleleft$ and tests whether $i + 1$ is prime; if it is, it accepts in $\triangleright\blacksquare a^{i+1}\triangleleft$. In this way, it continues increasing the number of as by one and testing whether the number is prime until it reaches a^j such that j is prime. As this prime j is obviously the smallest prime satisfying $i \leq j$, M accepts in $\triangleright\blacksquare a^j\triangleleft$. Thus, M computes g.

Both functions discussed in Examples 10.1 and 10.2 are total. However, there also exist partial integer functions, which may be undefined for some arguments. Suppose that g is a function over ${}_0\mathbb{N}$, which is undefined for some arguments. Let $M \in {}_{TM}\Psi$ compute g. According to Definition 10.3, for any $x \in {}_0\mathbb{N}$, $g(x)$ is undefined iff (*unary*(x), *unary*(y)) $\notin$ M-f for all $y \in {}_0\mathbb{N}$. Example 10.3 illustrates a partial integer function computed in this way.

Convention 10.5 As opposed to Examples 10.1 and 10.2, the next function as well as all other functions discussed throughout the rest of this section is defined over the set of positive integers, $\mathbb{N}$, which excludes 0. ■

Example 10.3 In this example, we consider a partial function g over $\mathbb{N}$ that is defined for 1, 2, 4, 8, 16, …, but it is undefined for the other positive integers. More precisely, $g(x) = 2x$ if $x = 2^n$, for some $n \in \mathbb{N}$; otherwise, $g(x)$ is undefined (see Figure 10.1).

We construct $M \in {}_{TM}\Psi$ that computes g as follows. Starting from $\triangleright\blacktriangleright a^i\triangleleft$, M computes $\triangleright\blacktriangleright a^i\triangleleft \Rightarrow^* \triangleright\blacktriangleright a^iA^j\triangleleft$ with j being the smallest natural number simultaneously satisfying $i \leq j$ and $j = 2^n$ with $n \in \mathbb{N}$. If $i = j$, then $i = 2^n$ and $g(i) = 2i = 2^{n+1}$, so M computes $\triangleright\blacktriangleright a^iA^j\triangleleft \Rightarrow^* \triangleright\blacksquare a^ia^j\triangleleft$ and, thereby, defines $g(i) = 2^{n+1}$. If $i < j$, then $2^{n-1} < i < 2^n$ and $g(i)$ is undefined, so M rejects a^i by $\triangleright\blacktriangleright a^iA^j\triangleleft \Rightarrow^* \triangleright\blacklozenge a^i\square^j\triangleleft$.

In somewhat greater detail, we describe M by the following Pascal-like algorithm that explains how M changes its configurations.

x	$g(x)$
1	2
2	4
3	undefined
4	8
5	undefined
6	undefined
7	undefined
8	16
⋮	⋮

Figure 10.1 Partial function g discussed in Example 10.3.

Let $\triangleright\blacktriangleright a^i\triangleleft$ be the input, for some $i \in \mathbb{N}$;
change $\triangleright\blacktriangleright a^i\triangleleft$ to $\triangleright\blacktriangleright a^iA\triangleleft$;
while the current configuration $\triangleright\blacktriangleright a^iA^j\triangleleft$ satisfies $j \leq i$ **do**
begin
  if $i = j$ **then**
    ACCEPT by computing $\triangleright\blacktriangleright a^iA^j\triangleleft \Rightarrow^* \triangleright\blacksquare a^ia^i\triangleleft$ {because $i = j = 2^m$ for some $m \in \mathbb{N}$}
  else
    compute $\triangleright\blacktriangleright a^iA^j\triangleleft \Rightarrow^* \triangleright\blacktriangleright a^iA^{2j}\triangleleft$ by changing each A to AA
end {of the **while** loop}
REJECT by computing $\triangleright\blacktriangleright a^iA^j\triangleleft \Rightarrow^* \triangleright\blacklozenge a^i\square^j\triangleleft$ {because $j > i$, so $i \neq 2^m$ for any $m \in \mathbb{N}$}.

As explained in the conclusion of Section 2.2.3, the set of all rewriting systems is countable because every definition of a rewriting system is finite, so this set can be put into a bijection with $\mathbb{N}$. For the same reason, the set of all TMs, which are defined as rewriting systems, is countable. However, the set of all functions is uncountable (see Example 1.3). From this observation, it straightforwardly follows the existence of uncomputable functions: there are just more functions than TMs. More surprisingly, however, even some simple total well-defined functions over $\mathbb{N}$ are uncomputable as Example 10.4 illustrates.

Example 10.4 For every $k \in \mathbb{N}$, set

$$_kX = \{M \in {}_{TM}\Psi \mid card(_MQ) = k + 1,\ _M\Delta = \{a\}\}$$

Informally, $_kX$ denotes the set of all TMs in $_{TM}\Psi$ with $k + 1$ states such that their languages are over $\{a\}$. Without any loss of generality, suppose that $_MQ = \{q_0, q_1, \ldots, q_k\}$ with $\blacktriangleright = q_0$ and $\blacksquare = q_k$. Let g be the total function over $\mathbb{N}$ defined for every $i \in \mathbb{N}$ so $g(i)$ equals the greatest integer $j \in \mathbb{N}$ satisfying $\triangleright q_0a\triangleleft \Rightarrow^* \triangleright q_ia^ju\triangleleft$ in M with $M \in {}_iX$, where $u \in \{\square\}^*$. In other words, $g(i) = j$ iff j is the greatest positive integer satisfying $M\text{-}f(a) = a^j$, where $M \in {}_iX$. Consequently, for every TM $K \in {}_iX$, either $|K\text{-}f(a)| \leq g(i)$ or $K\text{-}f(a)$ is undefined.

Observe that for every $i \in \mathbb{N}$, $_iX$ is finite. Furthermore, $_iX$ always contains $M \in {}_{TM}\Psi$ such that $\triangleright q_0a\triangleleft \Rightarrow^* \triangleright q_ia^ju\triangleleft$ in M with $j \in \mathbb{N}$, so g is total. Finally, $g(i)$ is defined quite rigorously because each TM in $_iX$ is deterministic (see Convention 9.8). At first glance, these favorable mathematical properties might suggest that g is computable, yet we next show that g is uncomputable by a proof based on diagonalization (see Example 1.3).

Gist. To show that g is uncomputable, we proceed, in essence, as follows. We assume that g is computable. Under this assumption, $_{TM}\Psi$ contains a TM M that computes g. We convert M to a TM N, which we subsequently transform to a TM O and show that O performs a computation that contradicts the definition of g, so our assumption that g is computable is incorrect. Thus, g is uncomputable.

In greater detail, let $M \in {}_{TM}\Psi$ be a TM that computes g. We can easily modify M to another TM $N \in {}_{TM}\Psi$ such that N computes $h(x) = g(2x) + 1$ for every $x \in \mathbb{N}$. Let $N \in {}_mX$, where $m \in \mathbb{N}$, so $_NQ = \{q_0, q_1, \ldots, q_m\}$ with $\blacktriangleright = q_0$ and $\blacksquare = q_m$. Modify N to the TM $O = (_O\Sigma, {}_OR)$, $O \in {}_{TM}\Psi$, in the following way. Define q_m as a nonfinal state. Set $_OQ = \{q_0, q_1, \ldots, q_m, q_{m+1}, \ldots, q_{2m}\}$ with $\blacktriangleright = q_0$ and $\blacksquare = q_{2m}$, so $O \in {}_{2m}X$. Initialize $_OR$ with the rules of $_NR$. Then, extend $_OR$ by the following new rules:

- $q_ma \rightarrow aq_m$ and $q_m\square \rightarrow aq_m$
- $q_h\triangleleft \rightarrow q_{h+1}\square\triangleleft$ and $q_{h+1}\square \rightarrow aq_{h+1}$, for all $m \leq h \leq 2m - 1$
- $aq_{2m} \rightarrow q_{2m}a$

Starting from $\triangleright q_0a\triangleleft$, O first computes $\triangleright q_0a\triangleleft \Rightarrow^* \triangleright q_ma^{h(m)}u\triangleleft$ with $u \in \{\square\}^*$ just like N does. Then, by the newly introduced rules, O computes $\triangleright q_ma^{h(m)}u\triangleleft \Rightarrow^* \triangleright q_{2m}a^{h(m)}a^{|u|}a^m\triangleleft$ with $q_{2m} = \blacksquare$. In brief, $\triangleright q_0a\triangleleft \Rightarrow^* \triangleright q_{2m}a^{h(m)}a^{|u|}a^m\triangleleft$ in O, which is impossible, however. Indeed, $|a^{h(m)}a^{|u|}a^m| = |a^{g(2m)+1}a^{|u|}a^m| > g(2m)$, so $O\text{-}f(1) > g(2m)$, which contradicts $K\text{-}f(1) \leq g(2m)$ for all $K \in {}_{2m}X$ because $O \in {}_{2m}X$. From this contradiction, we conclude that g is uncomputable.

In what follows, we often consider an enumeration of ${}_{TM}\Psi$. In essence, to enumerate ${}_{TM}\Psi$ means to list all TMs in ${}_{TM}\Psi$. We can easily obtain a list like this, for instance, by enumerating their codes according to length and alphabetic order (see Convention 10.6). If the code of $M \in {}_{TM}\Psi$ is the ith string in this lexicographic enumeration, we let M be the ith TM in the list.

Convention 10.6 In the sequel, ζ denotes some fixed enumeration of all possible TMs,

$$\zeta = {}_1M, {}_2M, \ldots$$

Regarding ζ, we just require the existence of two algorithms—(1) an algorithm that translates every $i \in \mathbb{N}$ to ${}_iM$ and (2) an algorithm that translates every $M \in {}_{TM}\Psi$ to i so $M = {}_iM$, where $i \in \mathbb{N}$. Let

$$\xi = {}_1M\text{-}f, {}_2M\text{-}f, \ldots$$

That is, ξ corresponds to ζ so ξ denotes the enumeration of the functions computed by the TMs listed in ζ. The positive integer i of ${}_iM\text{-}f$ is referred to as the *index of* ${}_iM\text{-}f$; in terms of ζ, i is referred to as the *index of* ${}_iM$. ■

Throughout the rest of this chapter, we frequently discuss TMs that construct other TMs, represented by their codes, and the TMs constructed in this way may subsequently create some other machines, and so on. Let us note that a construction like this commonly occurs in real-world computer science practice; for instance, a compiler produces a program that itself transforms the codes of some other programs, and so forth. Crucially, by means of universal TMs described in Section 9.3, we always know how to run any TM on any string, including a string that encodes another TM.

10.1.2 Recursion Theorem

Consider any total computable function γ over $\mathbb{N}$ and apply γ to the indices of TMs in ζ (see Convention 10.6). Theorem 10.7 says that there necessarily exists $n \in \mathbb{N}$, customarily referred to as a *fixed point* of γ, such that ${}_nM$ and ${}_{\gamma(n)}M$ compute the same function—that is, in terms of ξ, ${}_nM\text{-}f = {}_{\gamma(n)}M\text{-}f$. As a result, this important theorem rules out the existence of a total computable function that would map each index i to another index j so ${}_iM\text{-}f \neq {}_jM\text{-}f$.

Theorem 10.7 *Recursion Theorem*. For every total computable function γ over $\mathbb{N}$, there is $n \in \mathbb{N}$ such that ${}_nM\text{-}f = {}_{\gamma(n)}M\text{-}f$ in ξ.

Proof. Let γ be any total computable function over $\mathbb{N}$, and let $X \in {}_{TM}\Psi$ computes γ—that is, $X\text{-}f = \gamma$. First, for each $i \in \mathbb{N}$, introduce a TM $N_i \in {}_{TM}\Psi$ that works on every input $x \in \mathbb{N}$ as follows:

1. N_i saves x
2. N_i runs ${}_iM$ on i (according to Convention 10.6, ${}_iM$ denotes the TM of index i in ζ)
3. If ${}_iM\text{-}f(i)$ is defined and, therefore, ${}_iM$ actually computes ${}_iM\text{-}f(i)$, then N_i runs X on ${}_iM\text{-}f(i)$ to compute $X\text{-}f({}_iM\text{-}f(i))$
4. N_i runs ${}_{X\text{-}f({}_iM\text{-}f(i))}M$ on x to compute ${}_{X\text{-}f({}_iM\text{-}f(i))}M\text{-}f(x)$

Let O be a TM in ζ that computes the function $O\text{-}f$ over $\mathbb{N}$ such that for each $i \in \mathbb{N}$, $O\text{-}f(i)$ is equal to the index of N_i in ζ, constructed earlier. Note that although ${}_iM\text{-}f(i)$ may be undefined in (3), $O\text{-}f$ is total because N_i is defined for all $i \in \mathbb{N}$. Furthermore, ${}_{O\text{-}f(i)}M\text{-}f = {}_{X\text{-}f({}_iM\text{-}f(i))}M\text{-}f$ because

$O\text{-}f(i)$ is the index of N_i in ζ, and N_i computes ${}_{X\text{-}f(_iM\text{-}f(i))}M\text{-}f$. As $X\text{-}f = \gamma$, we have ${}_{X\text{-}f(_iM\text{-}f(i))}M\text{-}f = {}_{\gamma(_iM\text{-}f(i))}M\text{-}f$. Let $O = {}_kM$ in ζ, where $k \in \mathbb{N}$; in other words, k is the index of O. Set $n = O\text{-}f(k)$ to obtain ${}_nM\text{-}f = {}_{O\text{-}f(k)}M\text{-}f = {}_{X\text{-}f(_kM\text{-}f(k))}M\text{-}f = {}_{\gamma(_kM\text{-}f(k))}M\text{-}f = {}_{\gamma(O\text{-}f(k))}M\text{-}f = {}_{\gamma(n)}M\text{-}f$. Thus, n is a fixed point of γ, and Theorem 10.7 holds true. ■

The recursion theorem is a powerful tool frequently applied in the theory of computation as illustrated next.

Example 10.5 Consider the enumeration $\zeta = {}_1M, {}_2M, \ldots$ (see Convention 10.6). Observe that Theorem 10.7 implies the existence of $n \in \mathbb{N}$ such that ${}_nM\text{-}f = {}_{n+1}M\text{-}f$, meaning that ${}_nM$ and ${}_{n+1}M$ compute the same function. Indeed, define the total computable function γ for each $i \in \mathbb{N}$ as $\gamma(i) = i + 1$. By Theorem 10.7, there is $n \in \mathbb{N}$ such that ${}_nM\text{-}f = {}_{\gamma(n)}M\text{-}f$ in ξ, and by the definition of γ, $\gamma(n) = n + 1$. Thus, ${}_nM\text{-}f = {}_{n+1}M\text{-}f$.

From a broader perspective, this result holds in terms of any enumeration of ${}_{TM}\Psi$, which may differ from ζ, provided that it satisfies the simple requirements stated in Convention 10.6. That is, the enumeration can be based on any representation whatsoever provided that there exists an algorithm that translates each representation to the corresponding machine in ${}_{TM}\Psi$ and vice versa. As an exercise, consider an alternative enumeration of this kind and prove that it necessarily contains two consecutive TMs that compute the same function. To rephrase this generalized result in terms of the Church–Turing thesis, any enumeration of procedures contains two consecutive procedures that compute the same function.

Before closing this section, we generalize functions so they map multiple arguments to a set, and we briefly discuss their computation by TMs. For k elements, $a_1, \ldots, a_k$, where $k \in \mathbb{N}$, $(a_1, \ldots, a_k)$ denotes the *ordered k-tuple* consisting of a_1 through a_k in this order. Let $A_1, \ldots, A_k$ be k sets. The *Cartesian product of* $A_1, \ldots, A_k$ is denoted by $A_1 \times \ldots \times A_k$ and defined as

$$A_1 \times \ldots \times A_k = \{(a_1, \ldots, a_k) |\ a_i \in A_i,\ 1 \le i \le k\}$$

Let $m \in \mathbb{N}$ and B be a set. Loosely speaking, an *m-argument function* from $A_1 \times \ldots \times A_m$ to B maps each $(a_1, \ldots, a_m) \in A_1 \times \ldots \times A_m$ to no more than one $b \in B$. To express that a function f represents an m-argument function, we write $f^{\underline{m}}$ (carefully distinguish $f^{\underline{m}}$ from f^m, which denotes the m-fold product of f, defined in the conclusion of Section 1.3). If $f^{\underline{m}}$ maps $(a_1, \ldots, a_m) \in A_1 \times \ldots \times A_m$ to $b \in B$, then $f^{\underline{m}}(a_1, \ldots, a_m)$ is defined as b, written as $f^{\underline{m}}(a_1, \ldots, a_m) = b$, where b is the *value* of $f^{\underline{m}}$ for arguments $a_1, \ldots, a_m$. If $f^{\underline{m}}$ maps $(a_1, \ldots, a_m)$ to no member of B, $f^{\underline{m}}(a_1, \ldots, a_m)$ is *undefined*. If $f^{\underline{m}}(a_1, \ldots, a_m)$ is defined for all $(a_1, \ldots, a_m) \in A_1 \times \ldots \times A_m$, $f^{\underline{m}}$ is *total*. If we want to emphasize that $f^{\underline{m}}$ may not be total, we say that $f^{\underline{m}}$ is *partial*.

Next, we generalize Definition 10.1 to the m-argument function $M\text{-}f^{\underline{m}}$ computed by $M \in {}_{TM}\Psi$. For the sake of this generalization, we assume that Δ contains #, used in the following definition to separate the m arguments of $M\text{-}f^{\underline{m}}$.

Definition 10.8 Let $M \in {}_{TM}\Psi$. The *m-argument function computed by M* is denoted by $M\text{-}f^{\underline{m}}$ and defined as

$$M\text{-}f^{\underline{m}} = \{(x, y) |\ x \in \Delta^*, occur(x, \#) = m - 1, y \in (\Delta - \{\#\})^*, \triangleright\blacktriangleright x\triangleleft \Rightarrow^* \triangleright\blacksquare yu\triangleleft \text{ in } M, u \in \{\square\}^*\}$$

■

That is, $f^{\underline{m}}(x_1, x_2, \ldots, x_m) = y$ iff $\triangleright\blacktriangleright x_1\#x_2\#\ldots\#x_m\triangleleft \Rightarrow^* \triangleright\blacksquare yu\triangleleft$ in M with $u \in \{\square\}^*$, and $f^{\underline{m}}(x_1, x_2, \ldots, x_m)$ is undefined iff M loops on $x_1\#x_2\#\ldots\#x_m$ or rejects $x_1\#x_2\#\ldots\#x_m$. Notice that $M\text{-}f^{\underline{1}}$ coincides with $M\text{-}f$ (see Definition 10.1).

According to Definition 10.8, for every $M \in {}_{TM}\Psi$ and every $m \in \mathbb{N}$, there exists $M\text{-}f^{\underline{m}}$. At a glance, it is hardly credible that every $M \in {}_{TM}\Psi$ defines $M\text{-}f^{\underline{m}}$ because ${}_{TM}\Psi$ obviously contains TMs that never perform a computation that define any member of $M\text{-}f^{\underline{m}}$. However, if we realize that we might have $M\text{-}f^{\underline{m}}$ completely undefined—that is, $M\text{-}f^{\underline{m}} = \emptyset$, which is perfectly legal from a mathematical point of view, then the existence of $M\text{-}f^{\underline{m}}$ corresponding to every $M \in {}_{TM}\Psi$ comes as no surprise.

Definition 10.9 Let $m \in \mathbb{N}$. A function $f^{\underline{m}}$ is a *computable function* if there exists $M \in {}_{TM}\Psi$ such that $f^{\underline{m}} = M\text{-}f^{\underline{m}}$; otherwise, $f^{\underline{m}}$ is *uncomputable.* ■

To use TMs as computers of m-argument integer functions, we automatically assume that TMs work with the *unary*-based representation of integers by analogy with one-argument integer functions computed by TMs (see Definition 10.3 and Convention 10.4).

Definition 10.10 Let $M \in {}_{TM}\Psi$, $m \in \mathbb{N}$, and $f^{\underline{m}}$ be an m-argument function from $A_1 \times \ldots \times A_m$ to $\mathbb{N}$, where $A_i = \mathbb{N}$, for all $1 \leq i \leq m$. *M computes* $f^{\underline{m}}$ iff this equivalence holds

$$f^{\underline{m}}(x_1, \ldots, x_m) = y \text{ iff } (unary(x_1)\#\ldots\#unary(x_m), unary(y)) \in M\text{-}f^{\underline{m}}$$ ■

10.1.3 Kleene's s-m-n Theorem

Theorem 10.12 says that for all $m, n \in \mathbb{N}$, there is a total computable function s of $m + 1$ arguments such that ${}_iM\text{-}f^{\underline{m+n}}(x_1, \ldots, x_m, y_1, \ldots, y_n) = {}_{s(i, x_1, \ldots, x_m)}M\text{-}f^{\underline{n}}(y_1, \ldots, y_n)$ for all $i, x_1, \ldots, x_m, y_1, \ldots, y_n$. In other words, considering the Church–Turing thesis, there is an algorithm such that from ${}_iM$ and $x_1, \ldots, x_m$, it determines another TM that computes ${}_iM\text{-}f^{\underline{m+n}}(x_1, \ldots, x_m, y_1, \ldots, y_n)$ with only n arguments $y_1, \ldots, y_n$. In this way, the number of arguments is lowered, yet the same function is computed.

Convention 10.11 In this chapter, we often construct $M \in {}_{TM}\Psi$ from a finite sequence of strings, $z_1, \ldots, z_n$ (see, for instance, Theorem 10.12 and Example 10.6), and to express this clearly and explicitly, we denote M constructed in this way by $M_{[z_1, \ldots, z_n]}$. Specifically, in the proof of Theorem 10.12, $M_{[i, x_1, \ldots, x_m]}$ is constructed from $i, x_1, \ldots, x_m$, which are unary strings representing integers (see Convention 10.4). ■

Theorem 10.12 *Kleene's s-m-n Theorem*. For all $i, m, n \in \mathbb{N}$, there is a total computable $(m+1)$-argument function $s^{\underline{m+1}}$ such that ${}_iM\text{-}f^{\underline{m+n}}(x_1, \ldots, x_m, y_1, \ldots, y_n) = {}_{s^{\underline{m+1}}(i, x_1, \ldots, x_m)}M\text{-}f^{\underline{n}}(y_1, \ldots, y_n)$.

Proof. We first construct a TM $S \in {}_{TM}\Psi$. Then, we show that $S\text{-}f^{\underline{m+1}}$ satisfies the properties of $s^{\underline{m+1}}$ stated in Theorem 10.12, so we just take $s^{\underline{m+1}} = S\text{-}f^{\underline{m+1}}$ to complete the proof.

Construction of S. Let $m, n \in \mathbb{N}$. We construct a TM $S \in {}_{TM}\Psi$ so S itself constructs another machine in ${}_{TM}\Psi$ and produces its index in ζ as the resulting output value. More precisely, given input $i\#x_1\#\ldots\#x_m$, S constructs a TM, denoted by $M_{[i, x_1, \ldots, x_m]}$, for $i = 1, 2, \ldots$, and produces the index of $M_{[i, x_1, \ldots, x_m]}$—that is, j satisfying $M_{[i, x_1, \ldots, x_m]} = {}_jM$ in ζ—as the resulting output value. $M_{[i, x_1, \ldots, x_m]}$ constructed by S works as follows:

1. When given input $y_1\#\ldots\#y_n$, $M_{[i, x_1, \ldots, x_m]}$ shifts $y_1\#\ldots\#y_n$ to the right, writes $x_1\#\ldots\#x_m\#$ to its left, so it actually changes $y_1\#\ldots\#y_n$ to $x_1\#\ldots\#x_m\#y_1\#\ldots\#y_n$
2. $M_{[i, x_1, \ldots, x_m]}$ runs ${}_iM$ on $x_1\#\ldots\#x_m\#y_1\#\ldots\#y_n$

Properties of $S\text{-}f^{\underline{m+1}}$. Consider the $(m+1)$-argument function $S\text{-}f^{\underline{m+1}}$ computed by S constructed earlier. Recall that $S\text{-}f^{\underline{m+1}}$ maps $(i, x_1, \ldots, x_m)$ to the resulting output value equal to the index of $M_{[i, x_1, \ldots, x_m]}$ in ζ. More briefly, $S\text{-}f^{\underline{m+1}}(i, x_1, \ldots, x_m) = j$ with j satisfying $M_{[i, x_1, \ldots, x_m]} = {}_jM$ in ζ. Observe that $M_{[i, x_1, \ldots, x_m]}$ computes ${}_iM\text{-}f^{\underline{m+n}}(x_1, \ldots, x_m, y_1, \ldots, y_n)$ on every input $(y_1, \ldots, y_n)$, where ${}_iM\text{-}f^{\underline{m+n}}$ denotes the $(m+n)$-argument computable function. By these properties,

$$ {}_iM\text{-}f^{\underline{m+n}}(x_1, \ldots, x_m, y_1, \ldots, y_n) = {}_jM\text{-}f^{\underline{n}}(y_1, \ldots, y_n) = {}_{S\text{-}f^{\underline{m+1}}(i, x_1, \ldots, x_m)}M\text{-}f^{\underline{n}}(y_1, \ldots, y_n) $$

Therefore, to obtain the total computable $(m+1)$-argument function $s^{\underline{m+1}}$ satisfying Theorem 10.12, set $s^{\underline{m+1}} = S\text{-}f^{\underline{m+1}}$. ■

Theorem 10.12 represents a powerful tool for demonstrating closure properties concerning computable functions. To illustrate, by using this theorem, we prove that the set of computable one-argument functions is closed with respect to composition in Example 10.6.

Example 10.6 There is a total computable 2-argument function $g^{\underline{2}}$ such that ${}_iM\text{-}f({}_jM\text{-}f(x)) = {}_{g^{\underline{2}}(i, j)}M\text{-}f(x)$ for all $i, j, x \in \mathbb{N}$. We define the 3-argument function $h^{\underline{3}}$ as $h^{\underline{3}}(i, j, x) = {}_iM\text{-}f({}_jM\text{-}f(x))$ for all $i, j, x \in \mathbb{N}$. First, we show that $h^{\underline{3}}$ is computable. Given $i, j, x \in \mathbb{N}$, we introduce a TM H that computes $h^{\underline{3}}$ so it works on every input x as follows:

1. H runs ${}_jM$ on x
2. If ${}_jM\text{-}f(x)$ is defined and, therefore, produced by H in (1), H runs ${}_iM$ on ${}_jM\text{-}f(x)$
3. If ${}_iM\text{-}f({}_jM\text{-}f(x))$ is defined, H produces ${}_iM\text{-}f({}_jM\text{-}f(x))$, so H computes ${}_iM\text{-}f({}_jM\text{-}f(x))$

Thus, $h^{\underline{3}}$ is computable. Let $h^{\underline{3}}$ be computed by ${}_kM$ in ζ. That is, ${}_kM\text{-}f^{\underline{3}} = h^{\underline{3}}$. By Theorem 10.12, there is a total computable function s such that ${}_{s^{\underline{3}}(k, i, j)}M\text{-}f(x) = {}_kM\text{-}f^{\underline{3}}(i, j, x)$ for all $i, j, x \in \mathbb{N}$. Set $g^{\underline{2}}(i, j) = s^{\underline{3}}(k, i, j)$ for all $i, j \in \mathbb{N}$. Thus, ${}_iM\text{-}f({}_jM\text{-}f(x)) = {}_{s^{\underline{3}}(k, i, j)}M\text{-}f(x) = {}_{g^{\underline{2}}(i, j)}M\text{-}f(x)$, for all $i, j, x \in \mathbb{N}$.

As already noted, from a broader perspective, we have actually proved that the composition of two computable functions is again computable, so the set of computable one-argument functions is closed with respect to composition. Establishing more closure properties concerning other common operations, such as addition and product, is left as an exercise.

Most topics concerning the computability of multi-argument functions are far beyond this introductory text. Therefore, we narrow our attention to one-argument functions. In fact, we just consider total functions from Δ^* to $\{\varepsilon\}$, on which we base Section 10.2, which discusses another crucially important topic of the computation theory—decidability.

10.2 Decidability

In this section, we formally explore the power of algorithms that decide problems. Because problem-deciding algorithms are used in most computer science areas, it is unfeasible to examine them all. Therefore, we consider only the algorithmic decidability concerning problems related to the language models, such as automata and grammars, discussed in Chapters 3, 6, and 9.

10.2.1 *Turing Deciders*

In essence, we express every problem by a language in this book. More specifically, a problem P is associated with the set of all its instances $\prod$ and with a property π that each instance either satisfies or, in contrast, does not satisfy. Given a particular instance $i \in \prod$, P asks whether i satisfies π. To decide

P by means of Turing deciders, which work on strings like any TMs, we represent P by an encoding language as

$${}_{P}L = \{\langle i\rangle \mid i \in \prod, i \text{ satisfies } \pi\}$$

where $\langle i\rangle$ is a string representing instance i (see Convention 9.13). A Turing decider M, which halts on all inputs, decides P if (1) M rejects every input that represents no instance from $\prod$ and (2) for every $\langle i\rangle$ with $i \in \prod$, M accepts $\langle i\rangle$ iff i satisfies π, so M rejects $\langle i\rangle$ iff i does not satisfy π. More formally, $L(M) = {}_{P}L$, and $\Delta^* - L(M) = (\Delta^* - \{\langle i\rangle \mid i \in \prod\}) \cup \{\langle i\rangle \mid i \in \prod, i \text{ does not satisfy } \pi\}$.

In brief, we state P as

Problem 10.13 *P.*
Question: a formulation of *P*.
Language: ${}_{P}L$.

To illustrate our approach to decidability, we consider the problem referred to as *FA-Emptiness*. For any FA M, *FA-Emptiness* asks whether the language accepted by M is empty. ${}_{FA}\Psi$ is thus the set of its instances. The language encoding *FA-Emptiness* is defined as

$${}_{FA\text{-}Emptiness}L = \{\langle M\rangle \mid M \in {}_{FA}\Psi, L(M) = \varnothing\}$$

Formally, *FA-Emptiness* is specified as

Problem 10.14 *FA-Emptiness.*
Question: Let $M \in {}_{FA}\Psi$. Is $L(M)$ empty?
Language: ${}_{FA\text{-}Emptiness}L = \{\langle M\rangle \mid M \in {}_{FA}\Psi, L(M) = \varnothing\}$.

We can construct a Turing decider for ${}_{FA\text{-}Emptiness}L$ in a trivial way as demonstrated shortly (see Theorem 10.20).

In general, a problem that can be decided by a Turing decider is referred to as a *decidable problem* while an *undecidable problem* cannot be decided by any Turing decider. For instance, Problem 10.14 of emptiness reformulated in terms of TMs, symbolically referred to as *TM-Emptiness*, is undecidable as we demonstrate in Section 10.2.3.2 (see Problem 10.56 and Theorem 10.57). That is, we encode this important undecidable problem by its encoding language

$${}_{TM\text{-}Emptiness}L = \{\langle M\rangle \mid M \in {}_{TM}\Psi, L(M) = \varnothing\}$$

and prove that no Turing decider accepts ${}_{TM\text{-}Emptiness}L$ (see Theorem 10.57).

Next, we define Turing deciders rigorously. As already pointed out, any Turing decider M halts on every input string. In addition, we require that M always halts with its tape completely blank. The following definition makes use of *M-f* (see Definition 10.1) and the domain of a function (see Section 1.3), so recall both notions before reading it.

Definition 10.15

I. Let $M \in {}_{TM}\Psi$. If M always halts and *M-f* is a function from Δ^* to $\{\varepsilon\}$, then M is a *Turing decider* (a *TD* for short).
II. Let L be a language and M be a TD. M is a *TD for L* if *domain*(*M-f*) $= L$.
III. A language is *decidable* if there is a TD for it; otherwise, the language is *undecidable*. ■

By part I in Definition 10.15, $M \in {}_{TM}\Psi$ is a TD if it never loops, and for every $x \in \Delta^*$, $\rhd\blacktriangleright x\lhd \Rightarrow^* \rhd iu\lhd$ in M with $i \in \{\blacksquare, \blacklozenge\}$ and $u \in \{\Box\}^*$. By part II, a TD M for a language L satisfies $\rhd\blacktriangleright x\lhd \Rightarrow^* \rhd\blacksquare u\lhd$ in M for every $x \in L$ and $\rhd\blacktriangleright y\lhd \Rightarrow^* \rhd\blacklozenge v\lhd$ in M for every $y \in {}_{M}\Delta^* - L$, where $u, v \in \{\Box\}^*$.

Convention 10.16 ${}_{TD}\Psi$ denotes the set of all TDs, and ${}_{TD}\Phi = \{L(M)|\ M \in {}_{TD}\Psi\}$; in other words, ${}_{TD}\Phi$ denotes the family of all decidable languages. ■

We close this section strictly in terms of formal languages—the principal subject of this book. First, we give a specific decidable formal language in Example 10.7. Then, we state a relation between the language families ${}_{FA}\Phi$, ${}_{CF}\Phi$, and ${}_{TD}\Phi$.

Example 10.7 Return to Example 9.1, in which we have designed a TM that accepts $L = \{x|\ x \in \{a, b, c\}^*, occur(x, a) = occur(x, b) = occur(x, c)\}$. As obvious, the TM does not satisfy Convention 9.8; in fact, it is not even deterministic. As a result, it is out of ${}_{TM}\Psi$, so it is definitely out of ${}_{TD}\Psi$ as well.

In this example, we design another TM D such that $D \in {}_{TD}\Psi$ and D accepts L. D repeatedly scans across the tape in a left-to-right way, erasing the leftmost occurrence of a, b, and c during every single scan. When it reaches $\lhd$ after erasing all these three occurrences, it moves left to $\rhd$ and makes another scan like this. However, when D reaches $\lhd$ while some of the three symbols are missing on the tape, it can decide whether the input string is accepted. Indeed, if all three symbols are missing, D accepts; otherwise, it rejects. Therefore, D performs its final return to $\rhd$ in either of the following two ways.

1. If the tape is completely blank and, therefore, all *a*s, *b*s, and *c*s have been erased during the previous scans, D moves its head left to $\rhd$ and accepts in a configuration of the form $\rhd\blacksquare\Box\ldots\Box\lhd$.
2. If the tape is not blank and, therefore, contains some occurrences of symbols from X, where $\emptyset \subset X \subset \{a, b, c\}$, then during its return to $\rhd$, D changes all these occurrences to $\Box$ and rejects in a configuration of the form $\rhd\blacklozenge\Box\ldots\Box\lhd$.

Omitting the state specification, Figure 10.2 schematically describes the acceptance of *babcca* by D.

Clearly, D is a TD for L, so L is a decidable language. Symbolically and briefly, $D \in {}_{TD}\Psi$ and $L \in {}_{TD}\Phi$.

We close this section by establishing the relations between ${}_{FA}\Phi$, ${}_{CF}\Phi$, and ${}_{TD}\Phi$, which are used in Section 11.3.

Theorem 10.17 ${}_{FA}\Phi \subset {}_{CF}\Phi \subset {}_{TD}\Phi$.

Proof. By Corollary 6.74, ${}_{FA}\Phi \subset {}_{CF}\Phi$. As an exercise, prove ${}_{CF}\Phi \subseteq {}_{TD}\Phi$. Consider L in Example 10.7. By the pumping lemma for ${}_{CF}\Phi$ (see Lemma 8.3), prove that $L \notin {}_{CF}\Phi$. Since $L \in {}_{TD}\Phi$ (see Example 10.7), ${}_{CF}\Phi \subset {}_{TD}\Phi$. Thus, Theorem 10.17 holds. ■

Scan	Tape
0	*babcca*
1	$\Box\Box b\Box ca$
2	$\Box\Box\Box\Box\Box\Box$
ACCEPT	

Figure 10.2 Acceptance of *babcca*.

10.2.2 Decidable Problems

In this section, we present several decidable problems for FAs and CFGs. However, we also point out that there exist problems that are decidable for FAs but undecidable for CFGs.

10.2.2.1 Decidable Problems for Finite Automata

Let M be any FA (see Definition 3.1). We give algorithms for deciding the following three problems.

- Is the language accepted by M empty?
- Is the language accepted by M finite?
- Is the language accepted by M infinite?

In addition, for any input string w, we decide the next problem.

- Is w a member of the language accepted by M?

Strictly speaking, we decide all these four problems for $_{cs}$DFAs (as stated in Section 3.2.2, a $_{cs}$DFA stands for a *c*ompletely *s*pecified *d*eterministic *f*inite *a*utomaton) because deciding them in this way is somewhat simpler than deciding these problems for the general versions of FAs, contained in $_{FA}\Psi$ (see Definitions 3.1 and 3.17, and Convention 3.2). However, because any FA can be algorithmically converted to an equivalent $_{cs}$DFA, all four problems are decidable for the general versions of FAs in $_{FA}\Psi$, too.

Convention 10.18 $_{_{cs}DFA}\Psi$ denotes the set of all $_{cs}$DFA. We suppose there exist a fixed encoding and decoding of automata in $_{_{cs}DFA}\Psi$ by analogy with the encoding and decoding of TMs (see Convention 9.13). That is, $\langle M \rangle$ represents the code of $M \in {_{_{cs}DFA}\Psi}$. Similarly, we suppose there exist an analogical encoding and decoding of the members of $_{_{cs}DFA}\Psi \times \Delta^*$ and $_{_{cs}DFA}\Psi \times {_{_{cs}DFA}\Psi}$. For brevity, we denote the codes of $(M, w) \in {_{_{cs}DFA}\Psi} \times \Delta^*$ and $(M, N) \in {_{_{cs}DFA}\Psi} \times {_{_{cs}DFA}\Psi}$ by $\langle M, w \rangle$ and $\langle M, N \rangle$, respectively. ■

As already stated in Section 10.2.1, the *FA-Emptiness* problem asks whether the language accepted by an FA is empty. Next, we prove that *FA-Emptiness* is decidable by demonstrating that its encoding language $_{FA\text{-}Emptiness}L$ belongs to $_{TD}\Phi$.

Problem 10.19 *FA-Emptiness.*
Question: Let $M \in {_{_{cs}DFA}\Psi}$. Is $L(M)$ empty?
Language: $_{FA\text{-}Emptiness}L = \{\langle M \rangle \mid M \in {_{_{cs}DFA}\Psi}, L(M) = \emptyset\}$.

Theorem 10.20 $_{FA\text{-}Emptiness}L \in {_{TD}\Phi}$.

Proof. As M is a $_{cs}$DFA, each of its states is reachable (see Definition 3.17). Thus, $L(M) = \emptyset$ iff $_MF = \emptyset$, which says that M has no final state. Design a TD D that works on every $\langle M \rangle$, where $M \in {_{_{cs}DFA}\Psi}$, so D accepts $\langle M \rangle$ iff $_MF = \emptyset$, and D rejects $\langle M \rangle$ iff $_MF \neq \emptyset$. ■

The *FA-Membership* problem asks whether a string $w \in {_M\Delta^*}$ is a member of the language accepted by $M \in {_{_{cs}DFA}\Psi}$. Like *FA-Emptiness*, *FA-Membership* is decidable.

Problem 10.21 *FA-Membership.*
Question: Let $M \in {}_{\alpha DFA}\Psi$ and $w \in {}_{M}\Delta^{*}$. Is w a member of $L(M)$?
Language: ${}_{FA\text{-}Membership}L = \{\langle M, w\rangle \mid M \in {}_{\alpha DFA}\Psi, w \in {}_{M}\Delta^{*}, w \in L(M)\}$.

Theorem 10.22 ${}_{FA\text{-}Membership}L \in {}_{TD}\Phi$.

Proof. Recall that any $M \in {}_{\alpha DFA}\Psi$ reads an input symbol during every move. Thus, after making precisely $|w|$ moves on $w \in \Delta^{*}$, M either accepts or rejects w. Therefore, construct a TD D that works on every $\langle M, w\rangle$ as follows:

1. D runs M on w until M accepts or rejects w (after $|w|$ moves)
2. D accepts $\langle M, w\rangle$ iff M accepts w, and D rejects $\langle M, w\rangle$ iff M rejects w ■

FA-Infiniteness is a problem that asks whether the language accepted by $M \in {}_{\alpha DFA}\Psi$ is infinite. To show that the decidability of the same problem can be often proved in several different ways, we next give two alternative proofs that *FA-Infiniteness* is decidable. We only sketch the first proof while describing the other in detail.

Problem 10.23 *FA-Infiniteness.*
Question: Let $M \in {}_{\alpha DFA}\Psi$. Is $L(M)$ infinite?
Language: ${}_{FA\text{-}Infiniteness}L = \{\langle M\rangle \mid M \in {}_{\alpha DFA}\Psi, L(M) \text{ is infinite}\}$.

Under our assumption that M is from ${}_{\alpha DFA}\Psi$, we obviously see that $L(M)$ is infinite iff its state diagram contains a cycle, so we can easily reformulate and decide this problem in terms of the graph theory in this way. Alternatively, we can prove this by using the pumping lemma for regular languages (see Lemma 5.1) in the following way. For every $M \in {}_{\alpha DFA}\Psi$, let ${}_{\infty?}L(M)$ denote this finite language

$$ {}_{\infty?}L(M) = \{x \mid x \in L(M), card({}_{M}Q) \leq |x| < 2card({}_{M}Q)\} \subseteq L(M) $$

Lemma 10.24 For every $M \in {}_{\alpha DFA}\Psi$, $L(M)$ is infinite iff ${}_{\infty?}L(M) \neq \emptyset$.

Proof. To prove the *if* part of the equivalence, suppose that ${}_{\infty?}L(M) \neq \emptyset$. Take any $z \in {}_{\infty?}L(M)$. Recall that the pumping lemma constant k equals $card({}_{M}Q)$ in the proof of Lemma 5.1. As $card({}_{M}Q) \leq |z|$ by the definition of ${}_{\infty?}L(M)$, Lemma 5.1 implies that $z = uvw$, where $0 < |v| \leq |uv| \leq card({}_{M}Q)$, and most importantly, $uv^{m}w \in L$, for all $m \geq 0$. Hence, $L(M)$ is infinite.

To prove the *only-if* part, assume that L is infinite. Let z be the shortest string such that $z \in L(M)$ and $|z| \geq 2card({}_{M}Q)$. As $|z| \geq 2card({}_{M}Q) \geq card({}_{M}Q)$, Lemma 5.1 implies that $z = uvw$, where $0 < |v| \leq |uv| \leq card({}_{M}Q)$, and $uv^{m}w \in L$, for all $m \geq 0$. Take $uv^{0}w = uw \in L(M)$. Observe that $uw \in L(M)$ and $0 < |v|$ imply $2card({}_{M}Q) > |uw|$; indeed, if $2card({}_{M}Q) \leq |uw| < |z|$, then z would not be the shortest string satisfying $z \in L(M)$ and $|z| \geq 2card({}_{M}Q)$—a contradiction. As $0 < |v| \leq card({}_{M}Q)$, $card({}_{M}Q) \leq |uw| < 2card({}_{M}Q) \leq |z|$, so $uw \in {}_{\infty?}L(M)$ and, therefore, ${}_{\infty?}L(M) \neq \emptyset$. ■

Theorem 10.25 ${}_{FA\text{-}Infiniteness}L \in {}_{TD}\Phi$.

Proof. Construct a TD D that works on every $\langle M\rangle \in {}_{FA\text{-}Infiniteness}L$ so it first constructs ${}_{\infty?}L(M)$. After the construction of this finite language, D accepts $\langle M\rangle$ iff ${}_{\infty?}L(M) \neq \emptyset$, and D rejects $\langle M\rangle$ iff ${}_{\infty?}L(M) = \emptyset$. ■

Consequently, Problem 10.26 is decidable as well.

Problem 10.26 *FA-Finiteness.*
Question: Let $M \in {}_{{}_{\alpha}DFA}\Psi$. Is $L(M)$ finite?
Language: ${}_{FA\text{-}Finiteness}L = \{\langle M\rangle \mid M \in {}_{{}_{\alpha}DFA}\Psi, L(M) \text{ is finite}\}$.

Corollary 10.27 ${}_{FA\text{-}Finiteness}L \in {}_{TD}\Phi$. ■

The *FA-Equivalence* problem asks whether two ${}_{cs}$DFAs are equivalent; in other words, it asks whether both automata accept the same language. We decide this problem by using some elementary results of the set theory.

Problem 10.28 *FA-Equivalence.*
Question: Let $M, N \in {}_{{}_{\alpha}DFA}\Psi$. Are M and N equivalent?
Language: ${}_{FA\text{-}Equivalence}L = \{\langle M, N\rangle \mid M, N \in {}_{{}_{\alpha}DFA}\Psi, L(M) = L(N)\}$.

Theorem 10.29 ${}_{FA\text{-}Equivalence}L \in {}_{TD}\Phi$.

Proof. Let M and N be in ${}_{{}_{\alpha}DFA}\Psi$. As an exercise, prove that $L(M) = L(N)$ iff $\varnothing = (L(M) \cap {\sim}L(N)) \cup (L(N) \cap {\sim}L(M))$. Construct a TD D that works on every $\langle M, N\rangle \in {}_{FA\text{-}Equivalence}L$ as follows:

1. From M and N, D constructs an FA O such that $L(O) = (L(M) \cap {\sim}L(N)) \cup (L(N) \cap {\sim}L(M))$
2. From O, D constructs an equivalent ${}_{cs}$DFA P
3. D decides whether $L(P) = \varnothing$ (see Theorem 10.20 and its proof)
4. If $L(P) = \varnothing$, $L(M) = L(N)$ and D accepts $\langle M, N\rangle$ while if $L(P) \neq \varnothing$, D rejects $\langle M, N\rangle$

Consider the constructions in (1) and (2); as an exercise, describe them in detail. ■

10.2.2.2 Decidable Problems for Context-Free Grammars

Let G be any CFG (see Definition 6.1). We give algorithms for deciding the following three problems.

- Is the language generated by G finite?
- Is the language accepted by G infinite?

In addition, for any input string w, we decide the next problem.

- Is w a member of the language generated by G?

Rather than discuss these problems in general terms of CFGs in ${}_{CFG}\Psi$, we decide them for CFGs in the Chomsky normal form, in which every rule has either a single terminal or two nonterminals on its right-hand side (see Definition 6.34). Making use of this form, we find easier to decide two of them—*CFG-Membership* and *CFG-Infiniteness.* As any grammar in ${}_{CFG}\Psi$ can be turned to an equivalent grammar in the Chomsky normal form by algorithms given in Section 6.2, deciding these problems for grammars satisfying the Chomsky normal form obviously implies their decidability for grammars in ${}_{CFG}\Psi$ as well.

Convention 10.30 ${}_{CNF\text{-}CFG}\Psi$ denotes the set of all CFGs in Chomsky normal form. We suppose there exist a fixed encoding and decoding of the grammars in ${}_{CNF\text{-}CFG}\Psi$. Similarly to TMs and FAs (see Conventions 9.13 and 10.18), $\langle G \rangle$ represents the code of $G \in {}_{CNF\text{-}CFG}\Psi$. Similarly, we suppose there exist an analogical encoding and decoding of the members of ${}_{CNF\text{-}CFG}\Psi \times \Delta^*$ and ${}_{CNF\text{-}CFG}\Psi \times {}_{CNF\text{-}CFG}\Psi$. Again, for brevity, we denote the codes of $(G, w) \in {}_{CNF\text{-}CFG}\Psi \times \Delta^*$ and $(G, H) \in {}_{CNF\text{-}CFG}\Psi \times {}_{CNF\text{-}CFG}\Psi$ by $\langle G, w \rangle$ and $\langle G, H \rangle$, respectively. ■

Problem 10.31 *CFG-Emptiness.*
Question: Let $G \in {}_{CNF\text{-}CFG}\Psi$. Is $L(G)$ empty?
Language: ${}_{CFG\text{-}Emptiness}L = \{\langle G \rangle \mid G \in {}_{CNF\text{-}CFG}\Psi, L(G) = \emptyset\}$.

Theorem 10.32 ${}_{CFG\text{-}Emptiness}L \in {}_{TD}\Phi$.

Proof. Let $G \in {}_{CNF\text{-}CFG}\Psi$. Recall that a symbol in G is terminating if it derives a string of terminals (see Definition 6.15). As a result, $L(G)$ is nonempty iff ${}_GS$ is terminating, where ${}_GS$ denotes the start symbol of G (see Convention 6.2). Therefore, construct a TD D that works on $\langle G \rangle$ as follows:

1. D decides whether ${}_GS$ is terminating by Algorithm 6.16
2. D rejects $\langle G \rangle$ if ${}_GS$ is terminating; otherwise, D accepts $\langle G \rangle$ ■

Notice that the decision of *CFG-Emptiness* described in the proof of Theorem 10.32 is straightforwardly applicable to any CFG in ${}_{CFG}\Psi$ because this decision does not actually make use of the Chomsky normal form. During the decision of the next two problems, however, we make use of this form significantly.

Given a string w in Δ^* and a grammar G in ${}_{CNF\text{-}CFG}\Psi$, the *CFG-Membership* problem asks whether w is a member of $L(G)$. Of course, we can easily decide this problem by any of the general parsing algorithms discussed in Chapter 7 (see Algorithms 7.3 and 7.5). Next, we add yet another algorithm that decides this problem based on the Chomsky normal form.

Problem 10.33 *CFG-Membership.*
Question: Let $G \in {}_{CNF\text{-}CFG}\Psi$ and $w \in \Delta^*$. Is w a member of $L(G)$?
Language: ${}_{CFG\text{-}Membership}L = \{\langle G, w \rangle \mid G \in {}_{CNF\text{-}CFG}\Psi, w \in \Delta^*, w \in L(G)\}$.

The proof of Lemma 10.34 is simple and left as an exercise.

Lemma 10.34 Let $G \in {}_{CNF\text{-}CFG}\Psi$. Then, G generates every $w \in L(G)$ by making no more than $2|w| - 1$ derivation steps. ■

Theorem 10.35 ${}_{CFG\text{-}Membership}L \in {}_{TD}\Phi$.

Proof. As follows from the Chomsky normal form, ${}_{CNF\text{-}CFG}\Psi$ contains no grammar that generates ε. Therefore, we construct the following TD D that works on every $\langle G, w \rangle$ in either of the following two ways (A) and (B), depending on whether $w = \varepsilon$ or not.

A. Let $w = \varepsilon$. Clearly, $\varepsilon \in L(G)$ iff ${}_GS$ is an ε-nonterminal—that is, ${}_GS$ derives ε (see Definition 6.23). Thus, D decides whether ${}_GS$ is an ε-nonterminal by Algorithm 6.24, and if so, D accepts $\langle G, w \rangle$; otherwise, D rejects $\langle G, w \rangle$.

B. Let $w \neq \varepsilon$. Then, D works on $\langle G, w\rangle$ as follows:
   1. D constructs the set of all sentences that G generates by making no more than $2|w| - 1$ derivation steps
   2. If this set contains w, D accepts $\langle G, w\rangle$; otherwise, it rejects $\langle G, w\rangle$ ■

The *CFG-Infiniteness* problem asks whether the language generated by a CFG is infinite.

Problem 10.36 *CFG-Infiniteness.*
Question: Let $G \in {}_{CNF\text{-}CFG}\Psi$. Is $L(G)$ infinite?
Language: ${}_{CFG\text{-}Infiniteness}L = \{\langle G\rangle |\ G \in {}_{CNF\text{-}CFG}\Psi, L(G) \text{ is infinite}\}$.

As an exercise, prove Lemma 10.37.

Lemma 10.37 Let $G \in {}_{CNF\text{-}CFG}\Psi$. $L(G)$ is infinite iff $L(G)$ contains a sentence x such that $k \leq |x| < 2k$ with $k = 2^{card({}_GN)}$. ■

Theorem 10.38 ${}_{CFG\text{-}Infiniteness}L \in {}_{TD}\Phi$.

Proof. Construct a TD D that works on every $G \in {}_{CNF\text{-}CFG}\Psi$ as follows:

1. D constructs the set of all sentences x in $L(G)$ satisfying $k \leq |x| < 2k$ with $k = 2^{card({}_GN)}$
2. If this set is empty, D rejects $\langle G\rangle$; otherwise, D accepts $\langle G\rangle$ ■

Theorem 10.38 implies that we can also decide the following problem.

Problem 10.39 *CFG-Finiteness.*
Question: Let $G \in {}_{CNF\text{-}CFG}\Psi$. Is $L(G)$ finite?
Language: ${}_{CFG\text{-}Finiteness}L = \{\langle G\rangle |\ G \in {}_{CNF\text{-}CFG}\Psi, L(G) \text{ is finite}\}$.

Corollary 10.40 ${}_{CFG\text{-}Finiteness}L \in {}_{TD}\Phi$. ■

Recall that for FAs, we have formulated the problem *FA-Equivalence* and proved that it is decidable for them (see Theorem 10.29). However, we have not reformulated this problem for CFGs in this section. The reason is that this problem is undecidable for these grammars, which brings us to the topic of Section 10.2.3.

10.2.3 Undecidable Problems

As the central topic of this section, we consider several problems concerning TMs and show that they are undecidable. In addition, without any rigorous proofs, we briefly describe some undecidable problems not concerning TMs in the conclusion of this section.

Let P be a problem concerning TMs, and let P be encoded by a language ${}_PL$. Demonstrating that P is undecidable consists in proving that ${}_PL$ is an undecidable language. Like every rigorous proof in mathematics, a proof like this requires some ingenuity. Nevertheless, it is usually achieved by contradiction based on either of these two proof techniques—*diagonalization* and *reduction*.

10.2.3.1 Diagonalization

As a rule, a diagonalization-based proof is schematically performed in the following way.

1. Assume that ${}_{P}L$ is decidable, and consider a TD D such that $L(D) = {}_{P}L$.
2. From D, construct another TD O; then, by using the diagonalization technique (see Example 1.3), apply O on its own description $\langle O \rangle$ so this application results into a contradiction.
3. The contradiction obtained in (2) implies that the assumption in (1) is incorrect, so ${}_{P}L$ is undecidable.

Following this proof scheme almost literally, we next show the undecidability of the famous *halting problem* that asks whether $M \in {}_{TM}\Psi$ halts on input x. Observe that the following formulation of the *TM-Halting* problem makes use of the encoding language ${}_{TM\text{-}Halting}L$, introduced in the conclusion of Section 9.3.

Problem 10.41 *TM-Halting.*
Question: Let $M \in {}_{TM}\Psi$ and $w \in \Delta^*$. Does M halt on w?
Language: ${}_{TM\text{-}Halting}L = \{\langle M, w \rangle | \ M \in {}_{TM}\Psi, w \in \Delta^*, M \text{ halts on } w\}$.

Theorem 10.42 ${}_{TM\text{-}Halting}L \notin {}_{TD}\Phi$.

Proof. Assume that ${}_{TM\text{-}Halting}L$ is decidable. Then, there exists a TD D such that $L(D) = {}_{TM\text{-}Halting}L$. That is, for any $\langle M, w \rangle \in {}_{TM\text{-}Halting}L$, D accepts $\langle M, w \rangle$ iff M halts on w, and D rejects $\langle M, w \rangle$ iff M loops on w. From D, construct another TD O that works on every input w, where $w = \langle M \rangle$ with $M \in {}_{TM}\Psi$ (recall that according to Convention 9.13, every input string encodes a TM in ${}_{TM}\Psi$, so the case when w encodes no TM is ruled out), as follows:

1. O replaces w with $\langle M, M \rangle$, where $w = \langle M \rangle$
2. O runs D on $\langle M, M \rangle$
3. O accepts iff D rejects, and O rejects iff D accepts

That is, for every $w = \langle M \rangle$, O accepts $\langle M \rangle$ iff D rejects $\langle M, M \rangle$, and since $L(D) = {}_{TM\text{-}Halting}L$, D rejects $\langle M, M \rangle$ iff M loops on $\langle M \rangle$. Thus, O accepts $\langle M \rangle$ iff M loops on $\langle M \rangle$. Now, we apply the diagonalization technique in this proof: as O works on every input w, it also works on $w = \langle O \rangle$. Consider this case. Since O accepts $\langle M \rangle$ iff M loops on $\langle M \rangle$ for every $w = \langle M \rangle$, this equivalence holds for $w = \langle O \rangle$ as well, so O accepts $\langle O \rangle$ iff O loops on $\langle O \rangle$. Thus, $\langle O \rangle \in L(O)$ iff $\langle O \rangle \notin L(O)$—a contradiction. Therefore, ${}_{TM\text{-}Halting}L$ is undecidable; in symbols, ${}_{TM\text{-}Halting}L \notin {}_{TD}\Phi$. ■

Observe that Theorem 10.42 has its crucial consequences in practice as well as in theory. Indeed, considering the Church–Turing thesis, it rules out the existence of a universal algorithm that would decide, for any procedure, whether the procedure is an algorithm, which halts on all inputs (see Section 9.1). As a result, although we would obviously appreciate an algorithm like this in practice very much, we have to give up its existence once and for all. In terms of the formal language theory—the subject of this book—this theorem straightforwardly implies the following relation between the language families ${}_{TD}\Phi$ and ${}_{TM}\Phi$.

Theorem 10.43 ${}_{TD}\Phi \subset {}_{TM}\Phi$.

Proof. Clearly, ${}_{TD}\Phi \subseteq {}_{TM}\Phi$. By Theorems 9.16 and 10.42, ${}_{TM\text{-}Halting}L \in {}_{TM}\Phi - {}_{TD}\Phi$, so ${}_{TD}\Phi \subset {}_{TM}\Phi$. ■

As *TM-Halting* is undecidable, it comes as no surprise that the problem whether $M \in {}_{TM}\Psi$ loops on $w \in \Delta^*$ is not decidable either.

Problem 10.44 *TM-Looping.*
Question: Let $M \in {}_{TM}\Psi$ and $w \in \Delta^*$. Does M loop on x?
Language: ${}_{TM\text{-}Looping}L = \{\langle M, w\rangle |\ M \in {}_{TM}\Psi, x \in \Delta^*, M \text{ loops on } w\}$.

To prove the undecidability of *TM-Looping*, we establish Theorems 10.45 and 10.46. The first of them is obvious.

Theorem 10.45 ${}_{TM\text{-}Looping}L$ is the complement of ${}_{TM\text{-}Halting}L$. ■

Next, we prove that a language L is decidable iff ${}_{TM}\Phi$ contains both L and its complement $\sim L$.

Theorem 10.46 Let $L \subseteq \Delta^*$. $L \in {}_{TD}\Phi$ iff both L and $\sim L$ are in ${}_{TM}\Phi$.

Proof. To prove the *only-if* part of the equivalence, suppose that L is any decidable language, symbolically written $L \in {}_{TD}\Phi$. By Theorem 10.43, $L \in {}_{TM}\Phi$. By Definition 10.15, there is $M \in {}_{TD}\Psi$ such that $L = L(M)$. Change M to a TM $N \in {}_{TM}\Psi$ so that N enters a nonfinal state in which it keeps looping exactly when M enters the final state ■ (see Convention 9.8). As a result, $L(N) = \sim L(M) = \sim L$, so $\sim L \in {}_{TM}\Phi$. Thus, L and $\sim L$ are in ${}_{TM}\Phi$.

To prove the *if* part of the equivalence, suppose that $L \in {}_{TM}\Phi$ and $\sim L \in {}_{TM}\Phi$. That is, there exist $N \in {}_{TM}\Psi$ and $O \in {}_{TM}\Psi$ such that $L(N) = L$ and $L(O) = \sim L$. Observe that N and O cannot accept the same string because $L \cap \sim L = \emptyset$. On the other hand, every input w is accepted by either N or O because $L \cup \sim L = \Delta^*$. These properties underlie the next construction of a TD M for L from N and O. M works on every input w in the following way.

1. M simultaneously runs N and O on w so M executes by turns one move in N and O—that is, step by step, M computes the first move in N, the first move in O, the second move in N, the second move in O, and so forth.
2. M continues the simulation described in (1) until a move that would take N or O to an accepting configuration, and in this way, M finds out whether $w \in L(N)$ or $w \in L(O)$.
3. Instead of entering the accepting configuration in N or O, M halts and either accepts if $w \in L(N)$ or rejects if $w \in L(O)$—in greater detail, M changes the current configuration to a halting configuration of the form $\triangleright iu \triangleleft$, where $u \in \{\square\}^*$, $i \in \{■, ♦\}$, $i =$ ■ iff $w \in L(N)$, and $i =$ ♦ iff $w \in L(O)$.

Observe that $L(M) = L$. Furthermore, M always halts, so $M \in {}_{TD}\Psi$ and $L \in {}_{TD}\Phi$. ■

Making use of Theorems 9.16 and 10.46, we easily show *TM-Looping* as an undecidable problem. In fact, we prove a much stronger result stating that ${}_{TM\text{-}Looping}L$ is not even in ${}_{TM}\Phi$.

Theorem 10.47 ${}_{TM\text{-}Looping}L \notin {}_{TM}\Phi$.

Proof. Assume ${}_{TM\text{-}Looping}L \in {}_{TM}\Phi$. Recall that ${}_{TM\text{-}Looping}L$ is the complement of ${}_{TM\text{-}Halting}L$ (see Theorem 10.45). Furthermore, ${}_{TM\text{-}Halting}L \in {}_{TM}\Phi$ (see Theorem 9.16). Thus, by Theorem 10.46, ${}_{TM\text{-}Halting}L$ would be decidable, which contradicts Theorem 10.42. Thus, ${}_{TM\text{-}Looping}L \notin {}_{TM}\Phi$. ■

Theorems 10.45 and 10.47 imply Corollary 10.48, which says that *TM-Looping* is undecidable.

Corollary 10.48 ${}_{TM\text{-}Looping}L \notin {}_{TD}\Phi$. ■

10.2.3.2 Reduction

Apart from diagonalization, we often establish the undecidability of a problem P so the decidability of P would imply the decidability of a well-known undecidable problem U, and from this contradiction, we conclude that P is undecidable. In other words, from the well-known undecidability of U, we actually derive the undecidability of P; hence, we usually say that we *reduce U to P* when demonstrating that P is undecidable in this way. In terms of the problem-encoding languages, to prove that a language ${}_{P}L$, encoding P, is undecidable, we usually follow the proof scheme given next.

1. Assume that ${}_{P}L$ is decidable, and consider a TD D such that $L(D) = {}_{P}L$.
2. Modify D to another TD that would decide a well-known undecidable language ${}_{U}L$—a contradiction.
3. The contradiction obtained in (2) implies that the assumption in (1) is incorrect, so ${}_{P}L$ is undecidable.

On the basis of this reduction-proof scheme, we next show the undecidability of the *TM-Membership* problem that asks whether input w is a member of $L(M)$, where $M \in {}_{TM}\Psi$ and $w \in \Delta^*$. It is worth noting that the following formulation of this problem makes use of the encoding language ${}_{TM\text{-}Membership}L$ that coincides with ${}_{TM\text{-}Acceptance}L$ defined in Section 9.3.

Problem 10.49 *TM-Membership.*
Question: Let $M \in {}_{TM}\Psi$ and $w \in \Delta^*$. Is w a member of $L(M)$?
Language: ${}_{TM\text{-}Membership}L = \{\langle M, w\rangle \mid M \in {}_{TM}\Psi, w \in \Delta^*, w \in L(M)\}$.

We prove the undecidability of this problem by reducing Problem 10.41 *TM-Halting* to it. That is, we show that if there were a way of deciding the *TM-Membership* problem, we could decide Problem 10.41 *TM-Halting*, which contradicts Theorem 10.42.

Theorem 10.50 ${}_{TM\text{-}Membership}L \notin {}_{TD}\Phi$.

Proof. Given $\langle M, x\rangle$, construct a TM N that coincides with M except that N accepts x iff M halts on x (recall that M halts on x iff M either accepts or rejects x according to Convention 9.3). In other words, $x \in L(N)$ iff M halts on x. If there were a TD D for ${}_{TM\text{-}Membership}L$, we could use D and this equivalence to decide ${}_{TM\text{-}Halting}L$. Indeed, we could decide ${}_{TM\text{-}Halting}L$ by transforming M to N as described earlier and asking whether $x \in L(N)$; from $x \in L(N)$, we would conclude that M halts on x while from $x \notin L(N)$, we would conclude that M loops on x. However, Problem 10.41 *TM-Halting* is undecidable (see Theorem 10.42), which rules out the existence of D. Thus, there is no TD for ${}_{TM\text{-}Membership}L$, so ${}_{TM\text{-}Membership}L \notin {}_{TD}\Phi$. ■

Next, we formulate the *Non-TM-Membership* problem, and based on Theorems 9.15 and 10.50, we prove that it is not decidable either.

Problem 10.51 *Non-TM-Membership.*
Question: Let $M \in {}_{TM}\Psi$ and $w \in \Delta^*$. Is w out of $L(M)$?
Language: ${}_{Non\text{-}TM\text{-}Membership}L = \{\langle M, w\rangle \mid M \in {}_{TM}\Psi, w \in \Delta^*, w \notin L(M)\}$.

By analogy with the proof of Theorem 10.50, we prove that ${}_{Non\text{-}TM\text{-}Membership}L$ is even out of ${}_{TM}\Phi$.

Theorem 10.52 ${}_{Non\text{-}TM\text{-}Membership}L \notin {}_{TM}\Phi$.

Proof. For the sake of obtaining a contradiction, suppose that ${}_{Non\text{-}TM\text{-}Membership}L \in {}_{TM}\Phi$. As already pointed out, ${}_{TM\text{-}Membership}L = {}_{TM\text{-}Acceptance}L$, so ${}_{TM\text{-}Membership}L \in {}_{TM}\Phi$ (see Theorem 9.15). As obvious, ${}_{Non\text{-}TM\text{-}Membership}L$ is the complement of ${}_{TM\text{-}Membership}L$. Thus, by Theorem 10.46, ${}_{TM\text{-}Membership}L$ would belong to ${}_{TD}\Phi$, which contradicts Theorem 10.50. Thus, ${}_{Non\text{-}TM\text{-}Membership}L \notin {}_{TM}\Phi$. ■

From Theorems 10.43 and 10.52, we obtain Corollary 10.53, saying that *Non-TM-Membership* is an undecidable problem.

Corollary 10.53 ${}_{Non\text{-}TM\text{-}Membership}L \notin {}_{TD}\Phi$. ■

Problem 10.54 asks whether $L(M)$ is regular, where $M \in {}_{TM}\Psi$. By reducing *TM-Halting* to it, we prove its undecidability.

Problem 10.54 *TM-Regularness.*
Question: Let $M \in {}_{TM}\Psi$. Is $L(M)$ regular?
Language: ${}_{TM\text{-}Regularness}L = \{\langle M\rangle \mid M \in {}_{TM}\Psi, L(M) \in {}_{reg}\Phi\}$.

Theorem 10.55 ${}_{TM\text{-}Regularness}L \notin {}_{TD}\Phi$.

Proof. Consider ${}_{TM\text{-}Halting}L = \{\langle M, w\rangle \mid M \in {}_{TM}\Psi, w \in \Delta^*, M$ halts on $w\}$. Recall that ${}_{TM\text{-}Halting}L \in {}_{TM}\Phi - {}_{TD}\Phi$ (see Theorems 10.42 and 10.43). Take any TM O such that $L(O) = {}_{TM\text{-}Halting}L$; for instance, in the proof of Theorem 9.16, ${}_{TM\text{-}Halting}U$ satisfies this requirement because $L({}_{TM\text{-}Halting}U) = {}_{TM\text{-}Halting}L$. Next, we construct a TM $W \in {}_{TM}\Psi$ so that W converts every input $\langle M, w\rangle$, where $M \in {}_{TM}\Psi$ and $w \in \Delta^*$, to a new TM, denoted by $N_{[M, w]}$. Next, we describe this conversion in a greater detail. Given $\langle M, w\rangle$, W constructs a TM $N_{[M, w]}$ that works on every input $y \in \Delta^*$ as follows:

1. $N_{[M, w]}$ places w somewhere behind y on its tape
2. $N_{[M, w]}$ runs M on w
3. If M halts on w, $N_{[M, w]}$ runs O on y and accepts if and when O accepts

If M loops on w, $N_{[M, w]}$ never gets behind (2), so the language accepted by $N_{[M, w]}$ equals $\varnothing$ in this case. If M halts on w, $N_{[M, w]}$ accepts y in (3) if and when O accepts y, so the language accepted by $N_{[M, w]}$ coincides with $L(O)$ in this case. Thus, the language accepted by $N_{[M, w]}$ equals $L(O)$ iff M halts on w, and the language accepted by $N_{[M, w]}$ equals $\varnothing$ iff M loops on w. By Theorems 10.17 and 10.43, $L(O)$ is not regular because $L(O) \in {}_{TM}\Phi - {}_{TD}\Phi$ and ${}_{reg}\Phi \subset {}_{TD}\Phi$. By Definition 3.23, $\varnothing$ is regular. Thus, the language accepted by $N_{[M, w]}$ is regular iff M loops on w, and the language accepted by $N_{[M, w]}$ is nonregular iff M halts on w. Hence, if ${}_{TM\text{-}Regularness}L$ were decidable by a TD $V \in {}_{TD}\Psi$, W could make use of V and these equivalences to decide ${}_{TM\text{-}Halting}L$. Simply put, W would represent a TD for ${}_{TM\text{-}Halting}L$, which contradicts Theorem 10.42. Thus, ${}_{TM\text{-}Regularness}L$ is undecidable. ■

As an exercise, show the undecidability of the following three problems by analogy with the proof of Theorem 10.55.

Problem 10.56 *TM-Emptiness.*
Question: Let $M \in {}_{TM}\Psi$. Is $L(M)$ empty?
Language: ${}_{TM\text{-}Emptiness}L = \{\langle M\rangle \mid M \in {}_{TM}\Psi, L(M) = \varnothing\}$.

Theorem 10.57 ${}_{TM\text{-}Emptiness}L \notin {}_{TD}\Phi$. ■

Problem 10.58 *TM-Finiteness.*
Question: Let $M \in {}_{TM}\Psi$. Is $L(M)$ finite?
Language: ${}_{TM\text{-}Finiteness}L = \{\langle M\rangle \mid M \in {}_{TM}\Psi, L(M)$ is finite$\}$.

Theorem 10.59 ${}_{TM\text{-}Finiteness}L \notin {}_{TD}\Phi$. ■

Problem 10.60 *TM-Context-freeness.*
Question: Let $M \in {}_{TM}\Psi$. Is $L(M)$ context-free?
Language: ${}_{TM\text{-}Context\text{-}freeness}L = \{\langle M\rangle \mid M \in {}_{TM}\Psi, L(M) \in {}_{CF}\Phi\}$.

Theorem 10.61 ${}_{TM\text{-}Context\text{-}freeness}L \notin {}_{TD}\Phi$. ■

Consider Problem 10.62 that asks whether $L(M) = \Delta^*$, where $M \in {}_{TM}\Psi$. We again prove its undecidability by reducing Problem 10.41 *TM-Halting* to it.

Problem 10.62 *TM-Universality.*
Question: Let $M \in {}_{TM}\Psi$. Is $L(M)$ equal to Δ^*?
Language: ${}_{TM\text{-}Universality}L = \{\langle M\rangle \mid M \in {}_{TM}\Psi, L(M) = \Delta^*\}$.

Theorem 10.63 ${}_{TM\text{-}Universality}L \notin {}_{TD}\Phi$.

Proof. We reduce Problem 10.41 *TM-Halting* to Problem 10.62 *TM-Universality.* Once again, recall that ${}_{TM\text{-}Halting}L = \{\langle M, w\rangle \mid M \in {}_{TM}\Psi, w \in \Delta^*, M$ halts on $w\}$. We introduce a TM $W \in {}_{TM}\Psi$ so that W constructs the following TM $N_{[M, w]}$ from every input $\langle M, w\rangle$, where $M \in {}_{TM}\Psi$ and $w \in \Delta^*$. That is, given $\langle M, w\rangle$, W makes $N_{[M, w]}$ that works on every input $y \in \Delta^*$ as follows:

1. $N_{[M, w]}$ replaces y with w
2. $N_{[M, w]}$ runs M on w and halts if and when M halts

As $N_{[M, w]}$ works on every y in this way, its language equals Δ^* iff M halts on w while its language is empty iff M loops on w. Assume that ${}_{TM\text{-}Universality}L \in {}_{TD}\Phi$, so there is a TD V for ${}_{TM\text{-}Universality}L$. Thus, W could use V and these equivalences to decide ${}_{TM\text{-}Halting}L$, which contradicts Theorem 10.42. Hence, ${}_{TM\text{-}Universality}L \notin {}_{TD}\Phi$. ■

10.2.3.3 Undecidable Problems Not Concerning Turing Machines

We have concentrated our attention on the undecidability concerning TMs and their languages so far. However, undecidable problems arise in a large variety of areas in the formal language theory as well as out of this theory. Therefore, before concluding this section, we present some of them, but we completely omit proofs that rigorously show their undecidability.

Take CFGs, which are central to Section III of this book. For these grammars, the following problems are undecidable.

Problem 10.64 *CFG-Equivalence.*
Question: Let $G, H \in {}_{CFG}\Psi$. Are G and H equivalent?
Language: ${}_{CFG\text{-}Equivalence}L = \{\langle G, H\rangle |\ G, H \in {}_{CFG}\Psi, L(G) = L(H)\}$.

Problem 10.65 *CFG-Containment.*
Question: Let $G, H \in {}_{CFG}\Psi$. Does $L(G)$ contain $L(H)$?
Language: ${}_{CFG\text{-}Containment}L = \{\langle G, H\rangle |\ G, H \in {}_{CFG}\Psi, L(H) \subseteq L(G)\}$.

Problem 10.66 *CFG-Intersection.*
Question: Let $G, H \in {}_{CFG}\Psi$. Is the intersection of $L(G)$ and $L(H)$ empty?
Language: ${}_{CFG\text{-}Intersection}L = \{\langle G, H\rangle |\ G, H \in {}_{CFG}\Psi, L(H) \cap L(G) = \emptyset\}$.

Problem 10.67 *CFG-Universality.*
Question: Let $G \in {}_{CFG}\Psi$. Is $L(G)$ equal to ${}_{G}\Delta^{*}$?
Language: ${}_{CFG\text{-}Universality}L = \{\langle G\rangle |\ G \in {}_{CFG}\Psi, L(G) = {}_{G}\Delta^{*}\}$.

Problem 10.68 *CFG-Ambiguity.*
Question: Let $G \in {}_{CFG}\Psi$. Is G ambiguous?
Language: ${}_{CFG\text{-}Ambiguity}L = \{\langle G\rangle |\ G \in {}_{CFG}\Psi, G \text{ is ambiguous}\}$.

Within the formal language theory, however, there exist many undecidable problems concerning languages without involving their models, and some of them were introduced long time ago. To illustrate, in 1946, Post introduced a famous problem, which we here formulate in terms of ε-free homomorphisms, defined in Section 2.1. Let X, Y be two alphabets and g, h be two ε-free homomorphisms from X^{*} to Y^{*}; *Post's Correspondence Problem* is to determine whether there is $w \in X^{+}$ such that $g(w) = h(w)$. For example, consider $X = \{1, 2, 3\}$, $Y = \{a, b, c\}$, $g(1) = abbb$, $g(2) = a$, $g(3) = ba$, $h(1) = b$, $h(2) = aab$, and $h(3) = b$ and observe that $2231 \in X^{+}$ satisfies $g(2231) = h(2231)$. Consider a procedure that systematically produces all possible $w \in X^{+}$, makes $g(w)$ and $h(w)$, and tests whether $g(w) = h(w)$. If and when the procedure finds out that $g(w) = h(w)$, it halts and answers yes; otherwise, it continues to operate endlessly. Although there is a procedure like this, there is no algorithm, which halts on every input, to decide this problem. Simply put, Post's Correspondence Problem is undecidable.

Of course, out of the formal language theory, there exist many undecidable problems as well. To illustrate, mathematics will never have a general algorithm that decides whether statements in number theory with the plus and times are true or false. Although these results are obviously more than significant from a purely mathematical point of view, they are somewhat out of the scope of this book, which primarily concentrates its attention on formal languages and their models; therefore, we leave their discussion as an exercise.

10.2.4 General Approach to Undecidability

As showed in Section 10.2.3.2, many reduction-based proofs of undecidability are very similar. This similarity has inspired the theory of computation to undertake a more general approach to reduction, based on Definition 10.69, which makes use of the notion of a computable function (see Definition 10.2).

Definition 10.69 Let K, $L \subseteq \Delta^*$ be two languages. A total computable function f over Δ^* is a *reduction of K to L*, symbolically written as $K\ {}_f\!\angle\ L$, if for all $w \in \Delta^*$, $w \in K$ iff $f(w) \in L$. ■

Convention 10.70 Let K, $L \subseteq \Delta^*$. We write $K \angle L$ to express that there exists a reduction of K to L. Let us note that instead of $\angle$, $\leq$ is also used in the literature. ■

First, we establish a general theorem concerning $\angle$ in terms of ${}_{TM}\Phi$.

Theorem 10.71 Let K, $L \subseteq \Delta^*$. If $K \angle L$ and $L \in {}_{TM}\Phi$, then $K \in {}_{TM}\Phi$.

Proof. Let K, $L \subseteq \Delta^*$, $K \angle L$, and $L \in {}_{TM}\Phi$. Recall that $K \angle L$ means that there exists a reduction f of K to L, written as $K\ {}_f\!\angle\ L$ (see Definition 10.69 and Convention 10.70). As $L \in {}_{TM}\Phi$, there is a TM M satisfying $L = L(M)$. Construct a new TM N that works on every input $w \in \Delta^*$ as follows:

1. N computes $f(w)$ (according to Definition 10.2, f is computable)
2. N runs M on $f(w)$
3. If M accepts, then N accepts, and if M rejects, then N rejects

Notice that N accepts w iff M accepts $f(w)$. As $L = L(M)$, M accepts $f(w)$ iff $f(w) \in L$. As $K \angle L$ (see Definition 10.69), $w \in K$ iff $f(w) \in L$. Thus, $K = L(N)$, so $K \in {}_{TM}\Phi$. ■

Corollary 10.72 Let K, $L \subseteq \Delta^*$. If $K \angle L$ and $K \notin {}_{TM}\Phi$, then $L \notin {}_{TM}\Phi$. ■

By Theorem 10.71, we can easily prove that a language K belongs to ${}_{TM}\Phi$. Indeed, we take a language $L \in {}_{TM}\Phi$ and construct a TM M that computes a reduction of K to L, so $K \angle L$. Then, by Theorem 10.71, $K \in {}_{TM}\Phi$. For instance, from Theorem 9.15 (recall that ${}_{TM\text{-}Membership}L = {}_{TM\text{-}Acceptance}L$), it follows that ${}_{TM\text{-}Membership}L \in {}_{TM}\Phi$. Take this language. Demonstrate that ${}_{TM\text{-}Halting}L \angle {}_{TM\text{-}Membership}L$ to prove ${}_{TM\text{-}Halting}L \in {}_{TM}\Phi$. As a result, we have obtained an alternative proof that ${}_{TM\text{-}Halting}L \in {}_{TM}\Phi$, which also follows from Theorem 9.16.

Perhaps even more importantly, Corollary 10.72 saves us much work to prove that a language L is out of ${}_{TM}\Phi$. Typically, a proof like this is made in one of the following two ways.

I. Take a well-known language $K \notin {}_{TM}\Phi$ and construct a TM M that computes a reduction of K to L, $K \angle L$. As a result, Corollary 10.72 implies $L \notin {}_{TM}\Phi$.
II. By Definition 10.69, if f is a reduction of K to L, then f is a reduction of $\sim K$ to $\sim L$ as well. Therefore, to prove that $L \notin {}_{TM}\Phi$, take a language K with its complement $\sim K \notin {}_{TM}\Phi$ and construct a TM that computes a reduction of K to $\sim L$. As $K \angle \sim L$, we have $\sim K \angle \sim\sim L$. That is, $\sim K \angle L$, and by Corollary 10.72, $L \notin {}_{TM}\Phi$.

In fact, by a clever use of Corollary 10.72, we can sometimes show that both $L \notin {}_{TM}\Phi$ and $\sim L \notin {}_{TM}\Phi$, and both proofs, frequently resemble each other very much. To illustrate, in this way, we next prove that ${}_{TM\text{-}Equivalence}L \notin {}_{TM}\Phi$ and its complement ${}_{Non\text{-}TM\text{-}Equivalence}L \notin {}_{TM}\Phi$, where

$$_{TM\text{-}Equivalence}L = \{\langle M, N\rangle \mid M, N \in {}_{TM}\Psi, L(M) = L(N)\}, \text{ and}$$

$$_{Non\text{-}TM\text{-}Equivalence}L = \{\langle M, N\rangle \mid M, N \in {}_{TM}\Psi, L(M) \neq L(N)\}$$

Theorem 10.73 $_{TM\text{-}Equivalence}L \notin {}_{TM}\Phi$.

Proof. To show $_{TM\text{-}Equivalence}L \notin {}_{TM}\Phi$, we follow proof method II listed earlier. More specifically, we prove that $_{TM\text{-}Membership}L \angle {}_{Non\text{-}TM\text{-}Equivalence}L$ (see Problem 10.49 *TM-Membership* for $_{TM\text{-}Membership}L$); therefore, $_{TM\text{-}Equivalence}L \notin {}_{TM}\Phi$ because $_{Non\text{-}TM\text{-}Membership}L \notin {}_{TM}\Phi$ (see method II listed earlier and Theorem 10.52). To establish $_{TM\text{-}Membership}L \angle {}_{Non\text{-}TM\text{-}Equivalence}L$, we construct a TM X that computes a reduction of $_{TM\text{-}Membership}L$ to $_{Non\text{-}TM\text{-}Equivalence}L$. Specifically, X transforms every $\langle O, w\rangle$, where $O \in {}_{TM}\Psi$ and $w \in \Delta^*$, to the following two TMs, M and $N_{[O, w]}$, and produces $\langle M, N_{[O, w]}\rangle$ as output (we denote M without any information concerning $\langle O, w\rangle$ because its construction is completely independent of it—that is, X produces the same M for every $\langle O, w\rangle$). M and $N_{[O, w]}$ work as follows:

1. M rejects every input
2. On every input $x \in \Delta^*$, $N_{[O, w]}$ works so it runs O on w and accepts x if and when O accepts w

As obvious, $L(M) = \emptyset$. Because $N_{[O, w]}$ works on every input $x \in \Delta^*$ in the way described earlier, these two implications hold:

- If $w \in L(O)$, then $L(N_{[O, w]}) = \Delta^*$, which implies $L(M) \neq L(N_{[O, w]})$
- If $w \notin L(O)$, then $L(N_{[O, w]}) = \emptyset$, which means $L(M) = L(N_{[O, w]})$

Thus, X computes a reduction of $_{TM\text{-}Membership}L$ to $_{Non\text{-}TM\text{-}Equivalence}L$, so $_{TM\text{-}Equivalence}L \notin {}_{TM}\Phi$. ■

Observe that the proof of Theorem 10.74, which says that the complement of $_{TM\text{-}Equivalence}L$ is out of $_{TM}\Phi$ as well, parallels the proof of Theorem 10.73 significantly. As a matter of fact, while in the proof of Theorem 10.74, M always rejects, in the following proof, M always accepts; otherwise, both proofs coincide with each other.

Theorem 10.74 $_{Non\text{-}TM\text{-}Equivalence}L \notin {}_{TM}\Phi$.

Proof. To show that $_{Non\text{-}TM\text{-}Equivalence}L \notin {}_{TM}\Phi$, we prove that $_{TM\text{-}Membership}L \angle {}_{TM\text{-}Equivalence}L$. We define a reduction of $_{TM\text{-}Membership}L$ to $_{TM\text{-}Equivalence}L$ by a TM X that transforms every $\langle O, w\rangle$, where $O \in {}_{TM}\Psi$ and $w \in \Delta^*$, to the following two TMs $M, N_{[O, w]} \in {}_{TM}\Psi$ and produces $\langle M, N_{[O, w]}\rangle$ as output. M and $N_{[O, w]}$ are defined as follows:

1. M accepts every input string
2. On every input string x, $N_{[O, w]}$ runs O on w and accepts x if and when O accepts w

As obvious, $L(M) = \Delta^*$. If $w \in L(O)$, $L(N_{[O, w]}) = \Delta^*$ and $L(M) = L(N_{[O, w]})$; otherwise, $L(M) \neq L(N_{[O, w]})$. Hence, $_{TM\text{-}Membership}L \angle {}_{TM\text{-}Equivalence}L$. Therefore, by using proof method II, we obtain $_{Non\text{-}TM\text{-}Equivalence}L \notin {}_{TM}\Phi$. ■

Returning to the key topic of this section, we see that such results as Theorem 10.71 and Corollary 10.72 have often significant consequences in terms of undecidability. Indeed, if $L \notin {}_{TM}\Phi$, then a problem encoded by L is undecidable because $_{TD}\Phi \subset {}_{TM}\Phi$ (see Theorem 10.43).

Specifically, in this way, Theorems 10.73 and 10.74 imply the undecidability of the next two problems encoded by languages ${}_{TM\text{-}Equivalence}L$ and ${}_{Non\text{-}TM\text{-}Equivalence}L$, introduced earlier; for convenience, we repeat the definition of ${}_{TM\text{-}Equivalence}L$ and ${}_{Non\text{-}TM\text{-}Equivalence}L$ in the following problems again.

Problem 10.75 *TM-Equivalence.*
Question: Are M and N equivalent, where $M, N \in {}_{TM}\Psi$?
Language: ${}_{TM\text{-}Equivalence}L = \{\langle M, N\rangle \mid M, N \in {}_{TM}\Psi, L(M) = L(N)\}$.

Problem 10.76 *Non-TM-Equivalence.*
Question: Are M and N nonequivalent, where $M, N \in {}_{TM}\Psi$?
Language: ${}_{Non\text{-}TM\text{-}Equivalence}L = \{\langle M, N\rangle \mid M, N \in {}_{TM}\Psi, L(M) \neq L(N)\}$.

Corollary 10.77 ${}_{TM\text{-}Equivalence}L \notin {}_{TD}\Phi$ and ${}_{Non\text{-}TM\text{-}Equivalence}L \notin {}_{TD}\Phi$. ■

Next, we state results analogical to Theorem 10.71 and Corollary 10.72 in terms of ${}_{TD}\Phi$.

Theorem 10.78 Let $K, L \subseteq \Delta^*$. If $K \angle L$ and $L \in {}_{TD}\Phi$, then $K \in {}_{TD}\Phi$.

Proof. Let $K, L \subseteq \Delta^*$, $K \angle L$, and $L \in {}_{TD}\Phi$. Let f be a reduction of K to L. As already pointed out, by Definition 10.69, f is a reduction of $\sim K$ to $\sim L$, too. By Theorem 10.46, $L \in {}_{TD}\Phi$ iff $L \in {}_{TM}\Phi$ and $\sim L \in {}_{TM}\Phi$. By Theorem 10.71, $K \in {}_{TM}\Phi$ and $\sim K \in {}_{TM}\Phi$. Thus, $K \in {}_{TD}\Phi$ by Theorem 10.46. ■

Corollary 10.79 Let $K, L \subseteq \Delta^*$. If $K \angle L$ and $K \notin {}_{TD}\Phi$, then $L \notin {}_{TD}\Phi$. ■

Theorem 10.78 and Corollary 10.79 often save us much work when we show undecidability. In Examples 10.8 and 10.9, we revisit some of our earlier results concerning undecidability to see how they follow from Corollary 10.79.

Example 10.8 Reconsider Problem 10.56 *TM-Emptiness* and Theorem 10.57, stating that this problem is undecidable. In essence, this undecidability is established so that from any TM M and any string x, we algorithmically construct a TM N such that $L(N) = \emptyset$ iff M halts on x. To rephrase this in terms of languages, we define a reduction of ${}_{TM\text{-}Halting}L$ to ${}_{TM\text{-}Emptiness}L$, so ${}_{TM\text{-}Halting}L \angle {}_{TM\text{-}Emptiness}L$. As ${}_{TM\text{-}Halting}L \notin {}_{TD}\Phi$ (see Theorem 10.41), ${}_{TM\text{-}Emptiness}L \notin {}_{TD}\Phi$ by Corollary 10.79, so Problem 10.56 *TM-Emptiness* is undecidable.

Example 10.9 Earlier in this section, by using diagonalization, we proved that Problem 10.41 *TM-Halting* is undecidable, after which we showed that Problem 10.49 *TM-Membership* is undecidable so we reduced *TM-Halting* to *TM-Membership*. As this example shows, we could proceed the other way around. That is, first, by using diagonalization, we could prove that Problem 10.49 *TM-Membership* is undecidable; a proof like this is similar to the proof of Theorem 10.42 and, therefore, left as an exercise. Next, we show ${}_{TM\text{-}Membership}L \angle {}_{TM\text{-}Halting}L$, so the undecidability of *TM-Membership* implies the undecidability of *TM-Halting* by Corollary 10.79.

We construct a TM O that computes a total function f over Δ^* that maps every $\langle M, w\rangle$ to $\langle N, v\rangle$ so

$$\langle M, w\rangle \in {}_{TM\text{-}Membership}L \text{ iff } \langle N, v\rangle \in {}_{TM\text{-}Halting}L$$

Therefore, ${}_{TM\text{-}Membership}L \ {}_{f}\angle \ {}_{TM\text{-}Halting}L$. O is defined as follows:

1. On every input $\langle M, w\rangle$, O constructs a TM $W_{[M]}$ that works on every input in this way:
   a. $W_{[M]}$ runs M on the input
   b. $W_{[M]}$ accepts if M accepts, and $W_{[M]}$ loops if M rejects
2. Write $\langle W_{[M]}, w\rangle$ as output

Observe that $W_{[M]}$ loops on w iff M rejects w or loops on w; thus, in terms of the above equivalence, $W_{[M]}$ fulfills the role of N with v equal to w. Clearly, ${}_{TM\text{-}Membership}L \angle {}_{TM\text{-}Halting}L$. As ${}_{TM\text{-}Membership}L \notin {}_{TD}\Phi$, ${}_{TM\text{-}Halting}L \notin {}_{TD}\Phi$ by Corollary 10.79.

10.2.4.1 Rice's Theorem

Next, we discuss the undecidability concerning properties of Turing languages in ${}_{TM}\Phi$ rather than TMs in ${}_{TM}\Psi$. More specifically, we identify a property of Turing languages, π, with the subfamily of ${}_{TM}\Phi$ defined by this property—that is, this subfamily contains precisely the Turing languages that satisfy π. For instance, the property of being finite equals $\{L \in {}_{TM}\Phi \mid L \text{ is finite}\}$. In this way, we consider π as a decidable property if there exists a TD $D \in {}_{TD}\Psi$ such that $L(D)$ consists of all descriptions of TMs whose languages are in the subfamily defined by π.

Definition 10.80 Let $\pi \subseteq {}_{TM}\Phi$. Then, π is said to be a *property of Turing languages.*

I. A language $L \in {}_{TM}\Phi$ *satisfies* π if $L \in \pi$.
II. Set ${}_{\pi}L = \{\langle M\rangle \mid M \in {}_{TM}\Psi, L(M) \in \pi\}$. We say that π is *decidable* if ${}_{\pi}L \in {}_{TD}\Phi$; otherwise, π is *undecidable.*
III. We say that π is *trivial* if $\pi = {}_{TM}\Phi$ or $\pi = \emptyset$; otherwise, π is *nontrivial.* ■

For instance, the property of being finite is nontrivial because $\{L \in {}_{TM}\Phi \mid L \text{ is finite}\}$ is a nonempty proper subfamily of ${}_{TM}\Phi$. As a matter of fact, there are only two trivial properties—${}_{TM}\Phi$ and $\emptyset$—and both are trivially decidable because they are true either for all members of ${}_{TM}\Phi$ or for no member of ${}_{TM}\Phi$. As a result, we concentrate our attention on the nontrivial properties in what follows. Surprisingly, Rice's theorem, Theorem 10.81, states that all nontrivial properties are undecidable.

Theorem 10.81 *Rice's theorem.* Every nontrivial property is undecidable.

Proof. Let π be a nontrivial property. Without any loss of generality, suppose that $\emptyset \notin \pi$ (as an exercise, reformulate this proof in terms of $\sim\pi$ if $\emptyset \in \pi$). As π is nontrivial, π is nonempty, so there exists a Turing language $K \in \pi$. Let $N \in {}_{TM}\Psi$ be a TM such that $K = L(N)$.

For the sake of obtaining a contradiction, assume that π is decidable. In other words, there exists a TD $D \in {}_{TD}\Psi$ that decides ${}_{\pi}L$. Next, we demonstrate that under this assumption, ${}_{TM\text{-}Halting}L$ would belong to ${}_{TD}\Phi$, which contradicts Theorem 10.42. Indeed, we construct an algorithm that takes any $\langle M, x\rangle$, where $M \in {}_{TM}\Psi$ and $x \in \Delta^*$, and produces $\langle O\rangle$ as output, where $O \in {}_{TM}\Psi$, so $\langle M, x\rangle \in {}_{TM\text{-}Halting}L$ iff $\langle O\rangle \in {}_{\pi}L$, and by using this equivalence and D, we would decide ${}_{TM\text{-}Halting}L$. O is designed so that it works on every input string y as follows:

1. Saves y and runs M on x
2. If M halts on x, O runs N on y and accepts iff N accepts y

If M loops on x, so does O. As O works on every y in this way, $L(O) = \varnothing$ iff M loops on x. If M halts on x, O runs N on y, and O accepts y iff N accepts y, so $L(O) = L(N) = K$ in this case (recall that the case when $K = \varnothing$ is ruled out because $\varnothing \notin \pi$). Thus, $\langle M, x\rangle \in {}_{TM\text{-}Halting}L$ iff $\langle O\rangle \in {}_{\pi}L$. Apply D to decide whether $\langle O\rangle \in {}_{\pi}L$. If so, $\langle M, x\rangle \in {}_{TM\text{-}Halting}L$, and if not, $\langle M, x\rangle \notin {}_{TM\text{-}Halting}L$, so ${}_{TM\text{-}Halting}L$ would be in ${}_{TD}\Phi$, which contradicts ${}_{TM\text{-}Halting}L \notin {}_{TD}\Phi$ (see Theorem 10.42). Therefore, ${}_{\pi}L$ is undecidable. ■

Rice's theorem is a powerful result that has a great variety of consequences. For instance, consider the properties of being finite, regular, and context-free as properties of Turing languages. Rice's theorem straightforwardly implies that all these properties are undecidable.

10.2.5 Computational Complexity

This section takes a finer look at TDs by discussing their *computational complexity*. This complexity is measured according to their time and space computational requirements. The *time complexity* equals the number of moves they need to make a decision while the *space complexity* is defined as the number of visited tape symbols. Perhaps most importantly, this section points out that some problems are *tractable* for their reasonable computational requirements while others are *intractable* for their unmanageably high computational requirements to decide them. Simply put, there exist problems that are decidable in theory, but their decision is intractable in practice.

As most topics concerning complexity are too complicated to be discussed in this introductory text, this section differs from Sections 10.1.2 through 10.2.4, which have discussed their material in the form of mathematical formulas and proofs. Rather than give a fully rigorous presentation of computational complexity, this section explains only the basic ideas underlying it. Indeed, it restricts its attention to the very fundamental concepts and results, which are usually described informally. This section omits mathematically precise proofs. On the other hand, it points out some important open problems concerning the computational complexity.

We begin with the explanation of time complexity, after which we briefly conceptualize space complexity.

10.2.5.1 Time Complexity

Observe that the following definition that formalizes the time complexity of a TD considers the worst-case scenario concerning this complexity.

Definition 10.82 Let $M = ({}_{M}\Sigma, {}_{M}R)$ be a TD. The *time-complexity function of M*, denoted by ${}_{M}time$, is defined over ${}_{0}\mathbb{N}$ so for all $n \in {}_{0}\mathbb{N}$, ${}_{M}time(n)$ is the maximal number of moves M makes on an input string of length n before halting. ■

Example 10.10 Return to the TD D in Example 10.7 such that $L(D) = \{x \mid x \in \{a, b, c\}^*, occur(x, a) = occur(x, b) = occur(x, c)\}$. Recall that D scans across the tape in a left-to-right way while erasing the leftmost occurrence of a, b, and c. When it reaches $\lhd$ after erasing all three occurrences, it moves left to $\rhd$ and makes another scan of this kind. However, when D reaches $\lhd$ while some of the three symbols are missing on the tape, D makes its final return to $\rhd$ and halts by making one more move during which it accepts or rejects as described in Example 10.7. Let g be the integer function over ${}_{0}\mathbb{N}$ defined for all ${}_{0}\mathbb{N}$, so that if $n \in {}_{0}\mathbb{N}$ is divisible by 3, $g(n) = n(2(n/3)) + 1$, and if $n \in \mathbb{N}$ is indivisible by 3, $g(n) = g(m) + 2n$, where m is the smallest $m \in {}_{0}\mathbb{N}$ such that $m \leq n$ and m is divisible by 3. Observe that ${}_{D}time(n) = g(n)$. As an exercise, design another TD E such that $L(D) = L(E)$ and ${}_{E}time(n) < {}_{D}time(n)$, for all $n \in \mathbb{N}$.

As a general rule, for $M \in {}_{TD}\Phi$, ${}_{M}time$ is a complicated polynomial, whose determination represents a tedious and difficult task. Besides this difficulty, we are usually interested in the time complexity of M only when it is run on large inputs. As a result, rather than determine ${}_{M}time$ rigorously, we often consider the highest order term of ${}_{M}time$; on the other hand, we disregard the coefficient of this term as well as any lower terms. The elegant *big-*O *notation*, defined next, is customarily used for this purpose.

Definition 10.83

I. Let f and g be two functions over ${}_{0}\mathbb{N}$. If there exist $c, d \in \mathbb{N}$ such that for every $n \geq d$, $f(n)$ and $g(n)$ are defined and $f(n) \leq cg(n)$, then g is an *upper bound* for f, written as $f = \mathrm{O}(g)$.
II. If $f = \mathrm{O}(g)$ and g is of the form n^m, where $m \in \mathbb{N}$, then g is a *polynomial bound* for f.
III. Let $M \in {}_{TD}\Psi$. M is *polynomially bounded* if there is a polynomial bound for ${}_{M}time$. ■

Let f and g be two polynomials. In essence, according to points I and II of Definition 10.83, $f = \mathrm{O}(g)$ says that f is less than or equal to g if we disregard differences regarding multiplicative constants and lower-order terms. Indeed, $f = \mathrm{O}(g)$ implies $kf = \mathrm{O}(g)$ for any $k \in \mathbb{N}$, so the multiplication constants are ignored. As $f(n) = cg(n)$ holds for all $n \geq d$, the values of any $n \leq d$ are also completely ignored as well. In practice, to obtain $g = n^m$ as described in point II, we simply take n^m as the highest-order term of f without its coefficient; for instance, if $f(n) = 918273645n^5 + 999n^4 + 1111n^3 + 71178n^2 + 98765431n + 1298726$, then $f = \mathrm{O}(n^5)$. On the other hand, if $f \neq \mathrm{O}(g)$, then there exist infinitely many values of n satisfying $f(n) > cg(n)$.

Based on point III of Definition 10.83, from a more practical point of view, we next distinguish the decidable problems that are possible to compute from those that are not.

Definition 10.84 Let P be a decidable problem. If P is decided by a polynomially bounded TD, P is *tractable*; otherwise, P is *intractable.* ■

Informally, this definition says that although intractable problems are decidable in principle, they can hardly be decided in reality as no decision maker can decide them in polynomial time. On the other hand, tractable problems can be decided in polynomial time, so they are central to practically oriented computer science. Besides their practical significance, however, tractable problems lead to some crucial topics of theoretical computer science as demonstrated next.

According to Convention 9.8, up until now, we have automatically assumed that the TMs work deterministically. We also know that deterministic TMs are as powerful as their nondeterministic versions (see Definition 9.4 and Theorem 9.5). In terms of their time complexity, however, their relationship remains open as pointed out shortly. Before this, we reformulate some of the previous notions in terms of nondeterministic TMs.

Definition 10.85

I. Let M be a TM according to Definition 9.1 (thus, M may not be deterministic). M is a *nondeterministic TD* if M always halts on every input string.
II. Let M be a nondeterministic TD. The *time complexity of* M, ${}_{M}time$, is defined by analogy with Definition 10.82—that is, for all $n \in {}_{0}\mathbb{N}$, ${}_{M}time(n)$ is the maximal number of moves M makes on an input string of length n before halting.
III. Like in Definition 10.83, a nondeterministic TD M is *polynomially bounded* if there is a polynomial bound for ${}_{M}time$. ■

Convention 10.86 $_P\Phi$ denotes the family of languages accepted by polynomially bounded (deterministic) TDs, and $_{NP}\Phi$ denotes the family of languages accepted by polynomially bounded nondeterministic TDs. ■

Notice that any TD represents a special case of a nondeterministic TD, so $_P\Phi \subseteq {}_{NP}\Phi$. However, it is a long-standing open problem whether $_P\Phi = {}_{NP}\Phi$, referred to as the *P* = *NP problem*. By using various methods, theoretical computer science has intensively attempted to decide this problem. One of the most important approaches to this problem is based on ordering the languages in $_{NP}\Phi$. The equivalence classes defined by this ordering consist of languages coding equally difficult problems. Considering the class corresponding to the most difficult problems, any problem coded by a language from this family is as difficult as any other problem coded by a language from $_{NP}\Phi$. Consequently, if we prove that this class contains a language that also belongs to $_P\Phi$, then $_P\Phi = {}_{NP}\Phi$; on the other hand, if we demonstrate that this class contains a language that does not belong to $_P\Phi$, then $_P\Phi \subset {}_{NP}\Phi$. Next, we describe this approach to the *P* = *NP* problem in somewhat greater detail.

Let $M \in {}_{TM}\Psi$. *M* is a *nonerasing TD* if it halts on every input string; consequently, as opposed to the basic definition of a TD (see Definition 10.15), *M* may halt with a non-blank tape. Definition 10.87, given next, makes use of the notion of a nonerasing TD.

Definition 10.87 Let Δ and ς be two alphabets, $J \subseteq \Delta^*$, and $K \subseteq \varsigma^*$. Then, *J* is *polynomially transformable* into *K*, symbolically written as $J \propto K$, if there is a polynomially bounded nonerasing TD *M* such that *M-f* (see Definition 10.1) is a total function from Δ^* to ς^* satisfying $x \in J$ iff $M\text{-}f(x) \in K$. ■

In other words, $J \propto K$ means that the difficulty of deciding *J* is no greater than the difficulty of deciding *K*, so the problem encoded by *J* is no more difficult than the problem encoded by *K*.

Definition 10.88 Let $L \in {}_{NP}\Phi$. If $J \propto L$ for every $J \in {}_{NP}\Phi$, then *L* is *NP-complete*. ■

A decision problem coded by an *NP*-complete language is an *NP-complete problem*. There exist a number of well-known *NP*-complete problems, such as Problem 10.89.

Problem 10.89 *Time-Bounded Acceptance.*
Question: Let *M* be a nondeterministic TM, $w \in {}_M\Delta^*$, and $i \in \mathbb{N}$. Does *M* accept *w* by computing no more than *i* moves?
Language: $_{TBA}L = \{\langle M, w, i\rangle |\ M$ is a nondeterministic TM, $w \in {}_M\Delta^*$, $i \in \mathbb{N}$, M accepts w by computing i or fewer moves$\}$.

Once again, by finding an *NP*-complete language *L* and proving either $L \in {}_P\Phi$ or $L \notin {}_P\Phi$, we would decide the *P* = *NP* problem. Indeed, if $L \in {}_P\Phi$, then $_P\Phi = {}_{NP}\Phi$, and if $L \notin {}_P\Phi$, then $_P\Phi \subset {}_{NP}\Phi$. So far, however, a proof like this has not been achieved yet, and the *P* = *NP* problem remains open.

10.2.5.2 Space Complexity

We close this section by a remark about the space complexity of TDs.

Definition 10.90 Let $M = ({}_M\Sigma, {}_MR)$ be a TD. A function over $_0\mathbb{N}$ represents the *space complexity of M*, denoted by $_Mspace$, if $_Mspace(i)$ equals the minimal number $j \in {}_0\mathbb{N}$ such that for all $x \in {}_M\Delta^i$, $y, v \in \Gamma^*$, $\triangleright_M sx\triangleleft \Rightarrow^* \triangleright yqv\triangleleft$ in *M* implies $|yv| \leq j$. ■

Thus, starting with an input string of length i, M always occurs in a configuration with no more than ${}_{M}space(i)$ symbols, including blanks, on the tape. As an exercise, define *polynomially space-bounded (deterministic) TDs* and *polynomially space-bounded nondeterministic TDs* by analogy with the corresponding deciders in terms of time complexity (see Definitions 10.83 and 10.85).

Convention 10.91 ${}_{PS}\Phi$ denotes the family of languages accepted by polynomially space-bounded (deterministic) TDs, and ${}_{NPS}\Phi$ denotes the family of languages accepted polynomially space-bounded nondeterministic TDs. ■

As opposed to the unknown relationship between ${}_{P}\Phi$ and ${}_{NP}\Phi$, we know more about ${}_{PS}\Phi$ and ${}_{NPS}\Phi$. Indeed, it holds that ${}_{PS}\Phi = {}_{NPS}\Phi \subset {}_{TD}\Phi$. It is also well-known that ${}_{NP}\Phi \subseteq {}_{PS}\Phi$, but it is not known whether this inclusion is proper—another important long-standing open problem in the theory of computation.

Exercises

1. This chapter contains results whose proofs are only sketched or even omitted. These results include Examples 10.5, 10.6, 10.9, and 10.10; Lemmas 10.34 and 10.37; and Theorems 10.17, 10.29, 10.57, 10.59, 10.61, and 10.81. Prove them rigorously.
2. Define the *constant function* f as $f(x) = 0$, for all $x \in {}_{0}\mathbb{N}$. Construct a TM that computes f (see Definition 10.3). Verify the construction by a rigorous proof.
3. Consider each of the following functions defined for all $x \in {}_{0}\mathbb{N}$. Construct a TM that computes it (see Definition 10.3). Verify the construction by a rigorous proof.
   i. $f(x) = 3x$
   ii. $f(x) = x + 3$
   iii. $f(x) = 3x + 3$
   iv. $f(x) = x^2$
   v. $f(x) = 2^x$
4 S. Consider each of the following total two-argument functions defined for all $x, y \in {}_{0}\mathbb{N}$. Construct a TM that computes it (Definition 10.10). Verify the construction by a rigorous proof.
   i. $f(x, y) = x + y$
   ii. $f(x, y) = xy$
   iii. $f(x, y) = x^y$
   iv. $f(x, y) = 1$ if $x = 0$; otherwise, $f(x, y) = x^y$
   v. $f(x, y) = 0$ if $x < y$; otherwise, $f(x, y) = x - y$
   vi. $f(x, y) = x^y$ if $x \geq y$; otherwise, $f(x, y) = y^x$
5. Let $\xi = {}_{1}M\text{-}f, {}_{2}M\text{-}f, \ldots$ have the same meaning as in Convention 10.6. Let $c \in \mathbb{N}$ be a constant. By analogy with Example 10.5, prove that there necessarily exists $i \in \mathbb{N}$ satisfying ${}_{i}M\text{-}f = {}_{i+c}M\text{-}f$.
6. For all $i, m \in \mathbb{N}$ satisfying $1 \leq i \leq m$, the *i-m-projection function*, ${}_{i\text{-}m}f$, is defined by

$${}_{i\text{-}m}f(n_1, \ldots, n_i, \ldots, n_m) = n_i$$

   for all $n_1, \ldots, n_i, \ldots, n_m \in {}_{0}\mathbb{N}$. Construct a TM that computes it (see Definition 10.10). Verify the construction by a rigorous proof.
7. Let g be a function of i variables, and let h_1 through h_i be i functions of j variables, where $i, j \in \mathbb{N}$. Then, the function f defined by $f = g(h_1(n_1, \ldots, n_j), \ldots, h_i(n_1, \ldots, n_j))$, where $n_1, \ldots, n_j \in {}_{0}\mathbb{N}$, represents the *composition of g and h_1 through h_i*. Construct a TM that computes it (see Definition 10.10). Verify the construction by a rigorous proof.

8. Let $m \in \mathbb{N}$. Let h be an m-argument function, g be an $(m+2)$-argument function of $m + 2$ variables, and f be the $(m+1)$-argument function defined by

$$f(n_1, \ldots, n_{m+1}) = h(n_1, \ldots, n_m) \text{ if } n_{m+1} = 0; \text{ otherwise,}$$

$$f(n_1, \ldots, n_{m+1}) = g(n_{m+1} - 1, f(n_1, \ldots, n_{m+1} - 1), n_1, \ldots, n_m) \text{ if } n_{m+1} \neq 0$$

for all $n_1, \ldots, n_{m+1} \in {}_0\mathbb{N}$. Then, f is the *recursion of h and g*. Design a TM that computes f. Verify the construction by a rigorous proof.

9. Let i be the constant function (see Exercise 2), a projection function (see Exercise 6), or the successor function (see Example 10.1); then, i is called an *initial function*.

   Any initial function is a *primitive recursive function*. Furthermore, the composition of primitive recursive functions is a primitive recursive function, and the recursion of primitive recursive functions is a primitive recursive function (see Exercises 7 and 8).

   Formalize the notion of a primitive recursive function strictly rigorously by a recursive definition. Prove that all primitive recursive functions are computable, but some computable functions are not primitive recursive functions.

10. Consider the function f over ${}_0\mathbb{N}$ defined for $n = 0, f(n) = 1$, and for $n > 0, f(n) = g(h(n - 1, f(n - 1)))$, where g is the constant function and h is a 1-2-projection function. Explain why f is a primitive recursive function. Simplify the definition of f. Design a TM that computes f. Verify the construction by a rigorous proof.

11. Let $j \in \mathbb{N}$. Let f be a total function of $j + 1$ variables and g be a partial function of j variables such that $g(n_1, \ldots, n_j)$ is the smallest k satisfying $f(n_1, \ldots, n_j, k) = 0$, and $g(n_1, \ldots, n_j)$ is undefined if for any $k, f(n_1, \ldots, n_j, k) \neq 0$, where $n_1, \ldots, n_j, k \in {}_0\mathbb{N}$. Then, g is the *minimization of f*.

    Design a TM that computes g. Verify the construction by a rigorous proof.

12. Any primitive recursive function is a *recursive function* (see Exercise 9). Furthermore, the composition of recursive functions is a recursive function, the recursion of recursive functions is a recursive function, and the minimization of a recursive function is a recursive function, too (see Exercises 7, 8, and 11).

    Formalize the notion of a recursive function strictly rigorously by a recursive definition. Prove statements (a) through (c).
    a. Every primitive recursive function is recursive.
    b. Some recursive functions are not primitive recursive functions.
    c. A function is recursive iff it is computable.

13. *Ackermann's function* f is the two-argument function over ${}_0\mathbb{N}$ defined by (i) through (iii) as follows:
    i. For $m \geq 0, f(0, m) = m + 1$
    ii. For $n \geq 1, f(n, 0) = f(n - 1, 1)$
    iii. For $n, m \geq 1, f(n, m) = f(n - 1, f(n, m - 1))$

    Demonstrate that f is a recursive function (see Exercise 12). Then, prove or disprove that f is a primitive recursive function (see Exercise 9).

14 S. Formalize the following problems by analogy with the formalization used throughout Section 10.2. Prove that all the following problems are decidable.
    i. Let $M \in {}_{FA}\Psi$. Is $L(M) = {}_M\Delta^*$?
    ii. Let $M, N \in {}_{FA}\Psi$. Is $L(M)$ contained in $L(N)$?
    iii. Let $M, N \in {}_{FA}\Psi$. Is $L(M) \cap L(N)$ empty?

15. Consider each of problems (i) through (v). Formalize it by analogy with the formalization used throughout Section 10.2. Prove or disprove that it is decidable.
    i. Let $G \in {}_{LG}\Psi$ (see Example 2.7). Is $L(G)$ regular?
    ii. Let $G \in {}_{LG}\Psi$. Is $\sim L(G)$ linear?
    iii. Let $G \in {}_{LG}\Psi$. Is $\sim L(G)$ context-free?
    iv. Let $G \in {}_{CFG}\Psi$. Is $L(G)$ linear?
    v. Let $G \in {}_{CFG}\Psi$. Is $\sim L(G)$ context-free?

16 S. Formalize the following problems by analogy with the formalization used throughout Section 10.2. Prove that they all are undecidable.

i. Let $G, H \in {}_{CFG}\Psi$. Is $L(G)$ contained in $L(H)$?
ii. Let $G, H \in {}_{CFG}\Psi$. Is $L(G) \cap L(H)$ empty?
iii. Let $M \in {}_{TM}\Psi$. Does $L(M)$ contain ε?
iv. Let $M, N \in {}_{TM}\Psi$. Is $L(M)$ contained in $L(N)$?
v. Let $M, N \in {}_{TM}\Psi$. Is $L(M) \cap L(N)$ empty?

17. A *Post Tag System* G is a triple $G = (\Delta, R, S)$, where Σ is an alphabet, R is a finite *set of rules* of the form $x \to y$, where $x, y \in \Delta^*$, and $S \in \Delta^+$ is the start string. Define relation $\Rightarrow$ over Δ^* so $xz \Rightarrow zy$ for all $x \to y \in R$ and $z \in \Delta^*$. As usual, $\Rightarrow^*$ is the transitive and reflexive closure of $\Rightarrow$. The *language of* G is denoted by $L(G)$ and defined as $L(G) = \{w \mid w \in \Delta^*, S \Rightarrow^* w\}$.

    Consider the following problem. Formalize it by analogy with the formalization used throughout Section 10.2. Prove that it is undecidable.

    Let $G = (\Delta, R, S)$ be any Post Tag system and $w \in \Delta^*$. Is w a member of $L(G)$?

18. Reconsider Post's correspondence problem described in the conclusion of Section 10.2.3.3; pay a special attention to X therein. Assume that X contains a single symbol. Prove that under this assumption, this problem is decidable.
19. To demonstrate some very practical consequences implied by the results of undecidability covered in Section 10.2.3, consider an ordinary programming language, such as Java. Let L be the set of all well-written programs in this language. Demonstrate that the following problems are undecidable. In other words, computer science will never have software tools to answer these natural yes-no questions.

    i. Let $p \in L$. Can p enter an infinite loop?
    ii. Let $p \in L$. Can p produce any output?
    iii. Let $p, q \in L$. Do p and q produce the same output on all inputs?

20. Formalize the notion of a nondeterministic TM-based decision maker.
21. Let γ, η, θ be three functions over $\mathbb{N}$ such that $\gamma = O(\theta)$ and $\eta = O(\theta)$. Prove that $\gamma + \eta = O(\theta)$.
22. Let γ and θ be two functions such that θ is polynomial, and $\gamma = O(\theta)$. Prove that there exists a polynomial function η such that $\gamma(n) \leq \eta(n)$ for all $n \geq 1$.
23. Prove the following three results.

    a. The family of polynomial-space-bounded languages contains the family of nondeterministic polynomial-time-bounded languages.
    b. ${}_{TD}\Phi$ properly contains the family of nondeterministic polynomial-space-bounded languages.
    c. The family of polynomial-space-bounded languages coincides with the family of nondeterministic polynomial-space-bounded languages.

24. Prove that Problem 10.89 *Time-Bounded Acceptance* is NP-complete.

Solutions to Selected Exercises

4. Only (i) and (ii) are considered here.

    Consider (i). That is, $f(x, y) = x + y$ for all $x, y \in {}_0\mathbb{N}$. Construct a TM M so $(unary(x)\#unary(y), unary(x + y)) \in M\text{-}f^2$ (see Definition 10.10). Starting from $\triangleright\blacktriangleright a^x\#a^y\triangleleft$, M works as follows:

    a. Replaces # with a
    b. Changes the rightmost occurrence of a to □

    Thus, M computes $\triangleright\blacktriangleright a^x\#a^y\triangleleft \Rightarrow^* \triangleright\blacksquare a^{xy}\square\triangleleft$ and, therefore, $f(x, y) = x + y$. It is noteworthy that this construction takes care of the case when $x = 0$ or $y = 0$, too.

    Consider (ii). That is, $f(x, y) = xy$ for all $x, y \in {}_0\mathbb{N}$. Construct a TM M that computes this function as follows. Starting from $\triangleright\blacktriangleright a^x\#a^y\triangleleft$, M first finds out whether $x = 0$ or $y = 0$; if so, it computes $\triangleright\blacktriangleright a^x\#a^y\triangleleft \Rightarrow^* \triangleright\blacksquare\square^{x+y+1}\triangleleft$ and halts because $f(x, y) = 0$ in this case. Suppose that $x \geq 1$ and $y \geq 1$. M changes the current ordinary tape to a three-track tape, which has an analogical meaning to a two-track tape in Exercise 11 in Chapter 9. It places a^x and a^y on the second and third tracks, respectively, while having the first track completely blank. Then, it performs this loop

i. Makes one new copy of a^x on the first track from the second track
ii. Changes one a to □ on the third track
iii. If an a occurs on the third track, continues from (1), and if no a occurs on the third track, M leaves this loop

When the third track contains no a, the first track contains xy occurrences of as. M changes the current three-track tape back to an ordinary one-track tape that contains a^{xy}. As a result, M computes $\triangleright\blacktriangleright a^x\#a^y\triangleleft \Rightarrow^* \triangleright\blacksquare a^{xy}\triangleleft$, so it computes $f(x, y) = xy$.

14. Consider (i). Formalize this problem in the following way.

Problem *FA-Universality.*
Question: Let $M \in {}_{{}_{cs}DFA}\Psi$. Is $L(M) = {}_M\Delta^*$?
Language: ${}_{FA\text{-}Universality}L = \{\langle M\rangle |\ M \in {}_{{}_{cs}DFA}\Psi, L(M) = {}_M\Delta^*\}$.

Theorem ${}_{FA\text{-}Universality}L \in {}_{TD}\Phi$.

Proof. From M, construct another $N \in {}_{{}_{cs}DFA}\Psi$ so N coincides with M except that ${}_NF = {}_MQ - {}_MF$. As M and N are completely specified, all their states are reachable (see Definition 3.13). Consequently, $L(M) = {}_M\Delta^*$ iff $L(N) = \emptyset$. Recall that ${}_{FA\text{-}Emptiness}L \in {}_{TD}\Phi$ (see Theorem 10.20); therefore, ${}_{FA\text{-}Universality}L \in {}_{TD}\Phi$. ■

This proof makes use of Theorem 10.20 to demonstrate ${}_{FA\text{-}Universality}L \in {}_{TD}\Phi$. However, in a simpler way, this result can be proved without any involvement of Theorem 10.20. An alternative proof like this is left as an exercise.

16. Consider (iii). Formalize the problem in the following way.

Problem ε-*TM-Membership.*
Question: Let $M \in {}_{TM}\Psi$. Does M accepts ε?
Language: ${}_{\varepsilon\text{-}TM\text{-}Membership}L = \{\langle M\rangle |\ M \in {}_{TM}\Psi, \varepsilon \in L(M)\}$.

To prove that this problem is undecidable, recall Problem 10.41 *TM-Halting* and Theorem 10.42.

Next, prove that the ε-*TM-Membership* problem is undecidable by contradiction. That is, assume that this problem is decidable. Under this assumption, show that Problem 10.41 *TM-Halting* would be decidable, which contradicts Theorem 10.42. Thus, the ε-*TM-Membership* problem is undecidable.

Theorem ${}_{\varepsilon\text{-}TM\text{-}Membership}L \notin {}_{TD}\Phi$.

Proof. Let M be any TM, and let $x \in \Delta^*$ be any input string. Without any loss of generality, suppose that either M accepts x or M loops on it (see Theorem 9.9). From M and x, construct a new TM $N_{[M,x]}$ that works on every input string $y \in \Delta^*$ as follows:

1. Replaces y with x on the tape
2. Runs M on x
3. Accepts if M accepts x

Observe that for all $y \in \Delta^*$, M accepts x iff $N_{[M,x]}$ accepts y, and M loops on x iff $N_{[M,x]}$ loops on y. Thus, $L(N_{[M,x]}) = \Delta^*$ iff $x \in L(M)$, and $L(N_{[M,x]}) = \emptyset$ iff $x \notin L(M)$.

Suppose that ${}_{\varepsilon\text{-}TM\text{-}Membership}L \in {}_{TD}\Phi$, so there exists a TD D such that $L(D) = {}_{\varepsilon\text{-}TM\text{-}Membership}L$. Of course, $\varepsilon \in \Delta^*$. Thus, $N_{[M,x]}$ accepts ε iff M halts on x while accepting x, and $N_{[M,x]}$ rejects ε iff M loops on $x \in L(M)$. Consequently, Problem 10.41 *TM-Halting* would be decidable, which contradicts Theorem 10.42. Thus, ${}_{\varepsilon\text{-}TM\text{-}Membership}L \notin {}_{TD}\Phi$, so the ε-*TM-Membership* problem is undecidable. ■

Chapter 11

Turing Machines and General Grammars

In this chapter, we show the equivalence of Turing machines (TMs) and *general grammars* (GGs), which represent a straightforward generalization of context-free grammars (CFGs). Indeed, in GGs, we permit rules with left-hand sides consisting of strings rather than single nonterminals; otherwise, their definition coincides with the definition of CFGs.

In Section 11.1, we define GGs, establish their normal forms and, most importantly, prove the equivalence between them and TMs. In Section 11.2, we introduce special cases of TMs, called *linear-bounded automata* (LBAs), and special cases of GGs, called *context-sensitive grammars* (CSGs); we show they are equally powerful. We also prove that the language family defined by them is properly included in the family of decidable languages. Finally, in Section 11.3, we summarize the relations between major language families discussed in this book.

11.1 General Grammars and Their Equivalence with Turing Machines

GGs represent grammatical counterparts to TMs just like CFGs are counterparts to PDAs. In this section, we define these grammars (Section 11.1.1), establish their normal forms (Section 11.1.2), and prove their equivalence with TMs (Section 11.1.3).

11.1.1 General Grammars

Consider CFGs (see Definition 6.1). Generalize them so that their rules are of the form $u \rightarrow v$, where u and v are any strings with $u \neq \varepsilon$, to obtain GGs, defined in Definition 11.1.

Definition 11.1 A *general grammar* (a *GG* for short) is a rewriting system $G = (\Sigma, R)$, where

- Σ is divided into two disjoint subalphabets.
- R is a finite *set of rules* of the form $u \to v$, where $u \in \Sigma^+$ and $v \in \Sigma^*$.

As an exercise, define N, Δ, S, $\Rightarrow$, $\Rightarrow^*$, $F(G)$, and $L(G)$ for G just like for CFGs (see Section 6.1). ■

Consider Convention 6.2 introduced for CFGs in Section 6.1. We apply these conventions to GGs throughout, too.

Example 11.1 Consider a GG G defined by the following seven rules:

$$1: S \to CAaD,\ 2: Aa \to aaA,\ 3: AD \to BD,\ 4: aB \to Ba,\ 5: CB \to CA,\ 6: CA \to A,\ 7: AD \to \varepsilon$$

In G, a is the only terminal while all the other symbols are nonterminals.

For instance, from $CAaD$, G derives $CAaaD$ by carrying out these five derivation steps

$$\begin{aligned} CAaD &\Rightarrow CaaAD\ [2] \\ &\Rightarrow CaaBD\ [3] \\ &\Rightarrow CaBaD\ [4] \\ &\Rightarrow CBaaD\ [4] \\ &\Rightarrow CAaaD\ [5] \end{aligned}$$

Thus, $CAaD \Rightarrow^5 CAaaD$ [23445] or, briefly, $CAaD \Rightarrow^5 CAaaD$. Therefore, $CAaD \Rightarrow^+ CAaaD$ and $CAaD \Rightarrow^* CAaaD$. From a more general viewpoint, observe that every generation of a sentence in $L(G)$ has this form

$$S \Rightarrow CAaD \Rightarrow^* CAa^2D \Rightarrow^* CAa^4D \Rightarrow^* \ldots \Rightarrow^* CAa^{2^j}D \Rightarrow^* CAa^{2^{j+1}}D \Rightarrow^* \ldots \Rightarrow^* CAa^{2^{k-1}}D \Rightarrow^* a^{2^k}$$

for some $j \in {}_0\mathbb{N}$ and $k \in \mathbb{N}$ such that $j \leq k$. Consequently,

$$L(G) = \{a^{2^i} : i \geq 1\}$$

11.1.2 Normal Forms

Just like we often make use of CFGs transformed into normal forms, such as Chomsky normal form (see Section 6.2.5), we frequently transform GGs to some normal forms, in which their rules have a prescribed form. In this section, we convert GGs to Kuroda normal form and its special case—Pentonnen normal form.

Definition 11.2 A GG, $G = (\Sigma, R)$, is in *Kuroda normal form* if every rule $r \in R$ has one of these four forms

$$AB \to DC,\ A \to BC,\ A \to a, \text{ or } A \to \varepsilon$$

where $A, B, C, D \in N$ and $a \in \Delta$. ■

Basic idea. Next, we sketch how to turn any GG $I = ({}_I\Sigma, {}_IR)$ to an equivalent GG $O = ({}_O\Sigma, {}_OR)$ in Kuroda normal form.

Initially, set ${}_ON$ to ${}_IN$. Move all rules satisfying Kuroda normal form from ${}_IR$ to ${}_OR$. Carry out the following five steps, (1) through (5). Notice that after performing (1) and (2), every $x \rightarrow y \in {}_IR$ satisfies $x, y \in {}_ON^*$ and $|x| \leq |y|$.

1. Consider every $a \in {}_I\Delta$ and every $r \in {}_IR$. For every occurrence of a in r, introduce a special new nonterminal, X, into ${}_ON$. In ${}_IR$, change this occurrence with X, and if after this change, the rule satisfies Kuroda normal form, move it to ${}_OR$. Add $X \rightarrow a$ into ${}_OR$.
2. For every $u \rightarrow v \in {}_IR$ with $|u| > |v|$ with $n = |u| - |v|$, introduce a special new nonterminal X into ${}_ON$. In ${}_IR$, change this rule to $u \rightarrow vX^n$, and if after this change, the rule satisfies Kuroda normal form ($|u| = 2$, $|v| = 1$, and $n = 1$), move it to ${}_OR$. Add $X \rightarrow \varepsilon$ into ${}_OR$.
3. For every $A \rightarrow B \in {}_IR$ with $A, B \in {}_ON$, introduce a special new nonterminal, X, into ${}_ON$. Add $A \rightarrow BX$ and $X \rightarrow \varepsilon$ into ${}_OR$. Remove $A \rightarrow B$ from ${}_IR$.

Repeat (4) and (5), given next, until ${}_IR = \emptyset$.

4. Turn every $A \rightarrow X_1X_2X_3\ldots X_{n-1}X_n \in {}_IR$, where $X_i \in {}_ON$, $1 \leq i \leq n$, for some $n \geq 3$, into a set of $n - 1$ rules with two-nonterminal right-hand sides exactly like in Algorithm 6.35 *Chomsky Normal Form*. That is, introduce new nonterminals $\langle X_2\ldots X_n\rangle$, $\langle X_3\ldots X_n\rangle$, …, $\langle X_{n-2}X_{n-1}X_n\rangle$, $\langle X_{n-1}X_n\rangle$ into ${}_ON$ and add the following rules:

$$
\begin{aligned}
&A \rightarrow X_1\langle X_2\ldots X_n\rangle,\\
&\langle X_2\ldots X_n\rangle \rightarrow X_2\langle X_3\ldots X_n\rangle,\\
&\vdots\\
&\langle X_{n-2}X_{n-1}X_n\rangle \rightarrow X_{n-2}\langle X_{n-1}X_n\rangle,\\
&\langle X_{n-1}X_n\rangle \rightarrow X_{n-1}X_n
\end{aligned}
$$

   to ${}_OR$. Remove $A \rightarrow X_1X_2X_3\ldots X_{n-1}X_n$ from ${}_IR$.
5. For every $A_1A_2A_3\ldots A_{n-1}A_n \rightarrow B_1B_2\ldots B_{m-1}B_m \in {}_IR$, where $A_i \in {}_ON$, $1 \leq i \leq n$, $B_j \in {}_ON$, $1 \leq j \leq m$, for some $n \geq 2$ and $m \geq 3$, introduce a special new nonterminal, X, into ${}_ON$. Add $A_1A_2 \rightarrow B_1X$ into ${}_OR$. If $|A_3\ldots A_{n-1}A_n| = 0$ and $|B_2\ldots B_{m-1}B_m| = 2$, add $X \rightarrow B_2B_3$ into ${}_OR$; otherwise, add $XA_3\ldots A_{n-1}A_n \rightarrow B_2\ldots B_{m-1}B_m$ into ${}_IR$. Remove $A_1A_2A_3\ldots A_{n-1}A_n \rightarrow B_1B_2\ldots B_{m-1}B_m$ from ${}_IR$.

As an exercise, express the basic idea above as an algorithm, verify the algorithm formally and prove Theorem 11.3.

Theorem 11.3 For every $I \in {}_{GG}\Psi$, there exists $O \in {}_{GG}\Psi$ such that O is in Kuroda normal form and $L(O) = L(I)$. ■

Although GGs in Kuroda normal form allow only four forms of rules:

$$AB \rightarrow DC,\ A \rightarrow BC,\ A \rightarrow a,\ \text{or}\ A \rightarrow \varepsilon$$

where A, B, C, and D are nonterminals and a is a terminal, they are as powerful as ordinary GGs as follows from Theorem 11.3. Notice that an exclusion of any of these forms results in a decrease of their generative power, however. Indeed, without rules of the form $AB \rightarrow DC$, GGs in Kuroda normal form become CFGs, which are less powerful than GGs as stated later (see Theorems 11.9 and 11.24). Without rules of the form $A \rightarrow BC$, these grammars cannot actually expand the start symbol, so they can generate only terminal symbols or ε. Without rules of the form $A \rightarrow a$, they obviously generate only ε. Finally, without rules of the form $A \rightarrow \varepsilon$, GGs also decrease their power as shown in Section 11.2.1.

We close this section by introducing Pentonnen normal form, which represents a more restrictive version of Kuroda normal form.

Definition 11.4 Let $G = (\Sigma, R)$ be a GG in Kuroda normal form. If every rule of the form $AB \rightarrow DC \in R$, where $A, B, C, D \in N$, satisfies $A = D$, G is in *Pentonnen normal form.* ■

Prove Theorem 11.5 as an exercise.

Theorem 11.5 For every $I \in {}_{GG}\Psi$, there exists $O \in {}_{GG}\Psi$ such that O is in Pentonnen normal form and $L(O) = L(I)$. ■

11.1.3 Equivalence of General Grammars and Turing Machines

First, this section explains how to transform any GG to an equivalent TM. Then, it shows how to convert any TM to an equivalent GG. As a result, it establishes the equivalence of GGs and TMs; in symbols, ${}_{GG}\Phi = {}_{TM}\Phi$.

11.1.3.1 From General Grammars to Turing Machines

Any GG obviously represents a procedure, so the Church–Turing thesis immediately implies.

Lemma 11.6 ${}_{GG}\Phi \subseteq {}_{TM}\Phi$. ■

Nevertheless, one might ask for an effective proof of this result. Therefore, we next sketch how to turn any $G \in {}_{GG}\Psi$ to an equivalent $M \in {}_{TM}\Psi$ algorithmically. In fact, we give two alternative methods of this conversion:

I. Given $G \in {}_{GG}\Psi$, the first method constructs a TM M that explores all possible derivations in G. More precisely, M has three tracks on its tape (see the solution to Exercise 11 in Chapter 9). On the first track, M places any $w \in {}_{G}\Delta^*$. On the second track, it systematically generates sequences of rules from ${}_{G}R$, according to which it simulates the derivations in G on the third track. If $w \in L(G)$, M eventually simulates the generation of w in G, accepts w and halts. If $w \notin L(G)$, M never simulates the generation of w in G, so it runs endlessly, never accepting w. Hence, $L(G) = L(M)$.
II. Construct M with a tape having three tracks. Initially, M writes any $w \in {}_{G}\Delta^*$ on the first track. Then, it lists the rules of ${}_{G}R$ on the second track. Finally, it writes ${}_{G}S$ on the third track, which M uses to record the current sentential form of G during the upcoming simulation of

a derivation in G. After this initialization phase, M works as follows (recall that for any rule $r \in {}_GR$, $\boldsymbol{lhs}(r)$ and $\boldsymbol{rhs}(r)$ denote its left-hand side and right-hand side, respectively):

1. M nondeterministically selects any $r \in {}_GR$ on the second track.
2. If there is no occurrence of $\boldsymbol{lhs}(r)$ on the third track, M rejects; otherwise, it nondeterministically selects any occurrence of $\boldsymbol{lhs}(r)$ and replaces it with $\boldsymbol{rhs}(r)$.
3. If the first and third tracks coincide, accept; otherwise, go to (1).

As an exercise, describe methods I and II more formally.

11.1.3.2 From Turing Machines to General Grammars

The next algorithm converts any $I \in {}_{TM}\Psi$ to an equivalent $O \in {}_{GG}\Psi$. In essence, G simulates every accepting computation $\triangleright\blacktriangleright w\triangleleft \Rightarrow^* \triangleright\blacksquare u\triangleleft$ in M in reverse (see Convention 9.8) by a derivation of the form $S \Rightarrow^* \triangleright\blacksquare u\triangleleft \Rightarrow^* \triangleright\blacktriangleright w\triangleleft \Rightarrow^* w$.

Algorithm 11.7 TM to GG Conversion.

Input. A TM, $I = ({}_I\Sigma, {}_IR)$.

Output. A GG, $O = ({}_O\Sigma, {}_OR)$, such that $L(O) = L(I)$.

Method.

begin

set ${}_O\Sigma = {}_I\Sigma \cup \{S, 1, 2\}$, where S, 1 and 2 are new symbols, $\{S, 1, 2\} \cap {}_I\Sigma = \emptyset$, ${}_O\Delta = {}_I\Delta$, ${}_ON = {}_O\Sigma - {}_I\Delta$, and ${}_OR = \{S \rightarrow \triangleright 1\triangleleft, 1 \rightarrow \blacksquare, \triangleright\blacktriangleright \rightarrow 2, 2\triangleleft \rightarrow \varepsilon\}$;
for every $a \in {}_I\Gamma$, add $1 \rightarrow 1a$ to ${}_OR$;
for every $y \rightarrow x \in {}_IR$, add $x \rightarrow y$ to ${}_OR$;
for every $a \in {}_I\Delta$, add $2a \rightarrow a2$ to ${}_OR$

end.

O always makes its first derivation step by using $S \rightarrow \triangleright 1\triangleleft$, so $S \Rightarrow^* \triangleright 1\triangleleft$. Then, by using rules of the form $1 \rightarrow 1a$, where $a \in {}_I\Gamma$, O performs $\triangleright 1\triangleleft \Rightarrow^* \triangleright 1u\triangleleft$, after which it makes $\triangleright 1u\triangleleft \Rightarrow \triangleright\blacksquare u\triangleleft$ by using $1 \rightarrow \blacksquare$, where $u \in {}_I\Gamma^*$. In sum, O starts every derivation as $S \Rightarrow^* \triangleright\blacksquare u\triangleleft$, for any $u \in {}_I\Gamma^*$. Since $y \rightarrow x \in {}_IR$ iff $x \rightarrow y \in {}_OR$, $\triangleright\blacktriangleright w\triangleleft \Rightarrow^* \triangleright\blacksquare u\triangleleft$ in I iff $\triangleright\blacksquare u\triangleleft \Rightarrow^* \triangleright\blacktriangleright w\triangleleft$ in O, where $u \in {}_I\Gamma^*$, $w \in {}_I\Delta^*$. By using $\triangleright\blacktriangleright \rightarrow 2$, $2a \rightarrow a2$, and $2\triangleleft \rightarrow \varepsilon$, where $a \in {}_I\Delta$, O completes the generation of w so it crosses $\triangleright\blacktriangleright w\triangleleft$ from left to right and, simultaneously, removes $\triangleright$, $\blacktriangleright$, and $\triangleleft$. Thus, $L(O) = L(I)$. Based on these observations, give a formal proof of Lemma 11.8 as an exercise.

Lemma 11.8 Algorithm 11.7 is correct. Therefore, ${}_{TM}\Phi \subseteq {}_{GG}\Phi$. ■

Lemmas 11.6 and 11.8 imply Theorem 11.9.

Theorem 11.9 ${}_{TM}\Phi = {}_{GG}\Phi$. ■

11.2 Context-Sensitive Grammars and Linear-Bounded Automata

CSGs represent special cases of GGs in which each rule has its right-hand side at least as long as its left-hand side. LBAs are special cases of TMs that cannot extend its tape. In this section, we show that these grammars and automata have the same power.

First, we define CSGs in Section 11.2.1. In this section, we also present their normal forms. In Section 11.2.2, we define LBAs and show that they are as powerful as CSGs. Finally, in Section 11.2.3, we prove that every language generated by a CSG is decidable; on the other hand, there exist decidable languages that cannot be generated by any CSG.

Throughout this section, we express only basic ideas underlying the key results while leaving their rigorous verification as an exercise.

11.2.1 Context-Sensitive Grammars and Their Normal Forms

Definition 11.10 Let $G = (\Sigma, R)$ be a GG. G is a *CSG* if every $u \to v \in R$ satisfies $|u| \leq |v|$. Otherwise, N, Δ, S, $\Rightarrow$, $\Rightarrow^*$, $F(G)$, and $L(G)$ are defined just like for CFGs (see Section 6.1). ■

The name *context-sensitive* comes from their special variants, in which every rule is of the form $uAv \to uwv$, where A is a nonterminal and u, v, w are strings with $w \neq \varepsilon$. In essence, a rule like this permits replacement of A with w provided that the replaced A occurs in the context of u and v. These special variants are equivalent with CSGs according to Definition 11.10; as a matter of fact, CSGs in Pentonnen normal form, given later in this section, satisfy this context-sensitive form even in a more restrictive way.

In the literature, CSGs are also referred to as *length-increasing* grammars, which reflect the property that in every CSG, $G = (\Sigma, R)$, $x \Rightarrow^* y$ implies $|x| \leq |y|$ because each $u \to v \in R$ satisfies $|u| \leq |v|$. Consequently, if $S \Rightarrow^* w$ with $w \in L(G)$, then $1 \leq |w|$, so ε is necessarily out of $L(G)$.

Example 11.2 Consider a CSG G defined by the following 11 rules:

$$1: S \to ASc,\ 2: S \to Z,\ 3: Z \to BZ,\ 4: Z \to X,\ 5: BX \to XB,\ 6: AX \to XA,\ 7: AX \to aY,$$
$$8: YA \to AY,\ 9: YB \to BY,\ 10: YB \to Xb,\ 11: Yb \to bb$$

In G, a, b, and c are terminals while all the other symbols are nonterminals. In every derivation that generates a sentence from $L(G)$, G first applies rules 1 through 3 to produce $A^nB^mZc^n$, for some m, $n \in \mathbb{N}$. By using the other rules, G verifies that $n = m + 1$ and, simultaneously, changes As and Bs to as and bs, respectively. As a result, the generated sentence is of the form $a^nb^nc^n$. For instance, from S, G derives $aabbcc$ as follows:

$$S \Rightarrow ASc \Rightarrow AAScc \Rightarrow AAZcc \Rightarrow AABZcc \Rightarrow AABXcc \Rightarrow AAXBcc \Rightarrow$$
$$AXABcc \Rightarrow aYABcc \Rightarrow aAYBcc \Rightarrow aAXbcc \Rightarrow aaYbcc \Rightarrow aabbcc$$

Consequently,

$$L(G) = \{a^nb^nc^n \mid n \geq 2\}$$

As an exercise, prove that $L(G)$ is not a CFL (see Example 8.1).

11.2.1.1 Normal Forms

In Section 11.1.2, we introduced Kuroda and Pentonnen normal forms for GGs (see Definitions 11.2 and 11.4). We conclude this section by adapting these forms for CSGs.

Definition 11.11 A CSG, $G = (\Sigma, R)$, is in *Kuroda normal form* if every rule $r \in R$ has one of the following three forms:

$$AB \rightarrow DC, A \rightarrow BC, \text{ or } A \rightarrow a$$

where $A, B, C, D \in N$ and $a \in \Delta$. ■

Definition 11.12 Let $G = (\Sigma, R)$ be a CSG in Kuroda normal form. If every $AB \rightarrow DC \in R$, where $A, B, C, D \in N$, satisfies $A = D$, then G is in *Pentonnen normal form*. ■

Of course, CSGs in Pentonnen normal form are special cases of CSGs in Kuroda normal form. As an exercise, prove Theorem 11.13 by analogy with the proof of Theorem 11.3.

Theorem 11.13 For every $I \in {}_{CSG}\Psi$, there exists an equivalent CSG O in Pentonnen normal form; thus, O is in Kuroda normal form, too. ■

11.2.2 Linear-Bounded Automata and Their Equivalence with Context-Sensitive Grammars

In this section, we introduce LBAs as special cases of TMs that cannot extend the tape. In other words, they contain no extending rule of the form $q\lhd \rightarrow p\square\lhd \in R$, where q and p are states (see Definition 11.14).

Definition 11.14 Let $M = (\Sigma, R)$ be a TM (see Definition 9.1). M is an *LBA* if $q\lhd \rightarrow p\square\lhd \notin R$, for any $q, p \in Q$. ■

We show that LBAs are as powerful as CSGs except that LBAs can accept ε while CSGs cannot generate ε as already noted. In other words, LBAs characterize ${}_{CSG}\Phi$, defined next.

Convention 11.15 ${}_{LBA}\Psi$ and ${}_{CSG}\Psi$ denote the set of all LBAs and CSGs, respectively. Set ${}_{LBA}\Phi = \{L(M) |\ M \in {}_{LBA}\Psi\}$ and ${}_{CSG}\Phi = \{L |\ L - \{\varepsilon\} = L(G) \text{ with } G \in {}_{CSG}\Psi\}$. ■

11.2.2.1 From Context-Sensitive Grammars to Linear-Bounded Automata

Next, we show how to turn any $I \in {}_{CSG}\Psi$ to $O \in {}_{LBA}\Psi$ so $L(I) = L(O)$.

Basic idea. Let $I = ({}_I\Sigma, {}_IR)$ be any CSG. By analogy with II in the proof of Lemma 11.6, turn I to an equivalent LBA, $O = ({}_O\Sigma, {}_OR)$. O is constructed so it has a three-track tape (see the solution to Exercise 11 in Chapter 9). Initially, O writes w on the first track. Then, it writes the rules of R on the second track (since R is finite, it can always place them all there possibly in a condense way). Finally, O writes ${}_OS$ on the third track. Having initialized the three tracks in this way, O performs (1) through (3), described next (recall that for any rule $r \in {}_IR$, ***lhs***(r) and ***rhs***(r) denote its left-hand side and right-hand side, respectively):

1. O nondeterministically selects $r \in {}_IR$ on the second track.
2. O rejects and halts if there is no occurrence of ***lhs***(r) on the third track; otherwise, it nondeterministically selects any occurrence of ***lhs***(r) and replaces it with ***rhs***(r).
3. If the first track and third track coincide, O accepts and halts; otherwise, O goes to (1) and continues.

As an exercise, based on the idea sketched previously, give an algorithm that transforms any $I \in {}_{CSG}\Psi$ to $O \in {}_{LBA}\Psi$ such that $L(I) = L(O)$. Then, prove Lemma 11.16.

Lemma 11.16 For every $I \in {}_{CSG}\Psi$, there is $O \in {}_{LBA}\Psi$ such that $L(I) = L(O)$. Therefore, ${}_{CSG}\Phi \subseteq {}_{LBA}\Phi$. ■

11.2.2.2 From Linear-Bounded Automata to Context-Sensitive Grammars

Basic idea. To convert any $I \in {}_{LBA}\Psi$ to $O \in {}_{CSG}\Psi$ so $L(I) - \{\varepsilon\} = L(O)$, modify Algorithm 11.7 TM to GG Conversion so that it performs this conversion. That is, from $I \in {}_{LBA}\Psi$, construct $O \in {}_{CSG}\Psi$ so that it simulates every accepting computation $\rhd\blacktriangleright w\lhd \Rightarrow^* \rhd\blacksquare u\lhd$ in I in reverse, where $w \in {}_I\Delta^*$ and $u \in {}_I\Gamma^*$. However, as opposed to the GG produced by Algorithm 11.7, O cannot erase any symbols. Therefore, in the string on the tape during the simulation of $\rhd\blacktriangleright w\lhd \Rightarrow^* \rhd\blacksquare u\lhd$, O incorporates $\rhd$ and $\lhd$ into the leftmost symbol and the rightmost symbol, respectively, to detect that it performs rewriting at the very left or right tape end. Furthermore, O incorporates the current state of the simulated computation into the symbol that is rewritten. Otherwise, O works just like the GG constructed by Algorithm 11.7.

As an exercise, formulate the basic idea sketched previously as an algorithm and prove Lemma 11.17.

Lemma 11.17 For every $I \in {}_{LBA}\Psi$, there is $O \in {}_{CSG}\Psi$ such that $L(I) - \{\varepsilon\} = L(O)$. Therefore, ${}_{LBA}\Phi \subseteq {}_{CSG}\Phi$. ■

Lemmas 11.16 and 11.17 imply

Theorem 11.18 ${}_{LBA}\Phi = {}_{CSG}\Phi$. ■

11.2.3 Context-Sensitive Languages and Decidable Languages

In this section, we prove that every language in ${}_{CSG}\Phi$ is decidable, so ${}_{CSG}\Phi \subseteq {}_{TD}\Phi$, where ${}_{TD}\Phi$ denotes the family of decidable languages according to Convention 10.16. However, we also show that ${}_{TD}\Phi - {}_{CSG}\Phi \neq \emptyset$; consequently, ${}_{CSG}\Phi \subset {}_{TD}\Phi$.

To prove that every language in ${}_{CSG}\Phi$ belongs to ${}_{TD}\Phi$, we give an algorithm that decides whether $w \in L(G)$, for every $G \in {}_{CSG}\Psi$, so ${}_{CSG}\Phi \subseteq {}_{TD}\Phi$.

Convention 11.19 We suppose there exist a fixed encoding and decoding of CSGs obtained by analogy with obtaining the encoding and decoding of the members of ${}_{TM}\Psi \times \Delta^*$ (see Convention 9.13). We denote the codes of $(G, w) \in {}_{CSG}\Psi \times \Delta^*$ by $\langle G, w\rangle$. ■

Problem 11.20 *CSG-Membership.*
Question: Let $G = (\Sigma, R)$ be a CSG and $w \in {}_G\Delta^*$. Is w a member of $L(G)$?
Language: ${}_{CSG\text{-}Membership}L = \{\langle G, w\rangle |\ G \in {}_{CSG}\Psi, w \in {}_G\Delta^*, w \in L(G)\}$.

Basic idea. We sketch an algorithm that decides Problem 11.20 *CSG-Membership* based on the property that any CSG generates every sentence by a derivation that contains no sentential form longer than the sentence. That is, given $\langle G, w\rangle$, where $G = (\Sigma, R)$ be a CSG and $w \in {}_G\Delta^*$, we consider the set of all derivations of the form $S \Rightarrow^* x$, where $x \in {}_G\Sigma^*$, such that $|x| \leq |w|$ and $S \Rightarrow^* x$ does not contain two identical sentential forms. As the length of any string cannot decrease at any step of the derivations satisfying the properties stated above, we can obviously design a TM, D that constructs this set of derivations in such a way that it does not loop forever. If during this construction, D produces a derivation that generates w, it accepts $\langle G, w\rangle$ and halts. If D completes this construction without ever producing a derivation that generates w, it rejects $\langle G, w\rangle$ and halts (notice that $\langle G, \varepsilon\rangle$ is always rejected). Therefore, D represents a Turing decider (TD), so ${}_{CSG\text{-}Membership}L \in {}_{TD}\Phi$.

As an exercise, formalize the design of D and prove Theorem 11.21.

Theorem 11.21 ${}_{CSG\text{-}Membership}L \in {}_{TD}\Phi$. Therefore, ${}_{CSG}\Phi \subseteq {}_{TD}\Phi$. ■

Some decidable languages, however, are out of ${}_{CSG}\Phi$ as shown by using diagonalization (see Example 1.3).

Lemma 11.22 ${}_{TD}\Phi - {}_{CSG}\Phi \neq \emptyset$.

Proof. Consider a fixed enumeration of all possible CSGs,

$$ {}_1G, {}_2G, \ldots $$

(this enumeration can be obtained similarly to obtaining the enumeration of all TMs, ζ, in Convention 10.6). Let

$$ {}_1x, {}_2x, \ldots $$

be all the strings in $\{0, 1\}^+$ listed in a canonical order, such as the lexicographic order—that is, 0, 1, 00, 01, ... Consider this binary language

$$ L = \{{}_ix \mid {}_ix \notin L({}_iG), i \in \mathbb{N}\} $$

Given $x \in \{0, 1\}^+$, we can obviously find the ${}_ix$ satisfying ${}_ix = x$ in ${}_1x$, ${}_2x$, ..., and by Theorem 11.21, we can decide whether $x \in L({}_iG)$, so $L \in {}_{TD}\Phi$.

By contradiction, we prove that $L \notin {}_{CSG}\Phi$. Suppose that $L \in {}_{CSG}\Phi$. Thus, there is ${}_jG$ in ${}_1G$, ${}_2G$, ... such that $L = L({}_jG)$. Consider ${}_jx$. If ${}_jx \in L$, then the definition of L implies ${}_jx \notin L({}_jG)$, and if ${}_jx \notin L$, then ${}_jx \in L({}_jG)$. This statement contradicts $L = L({}_jG)$, so $L \notin {}_{CSG}\Phi$.

Therefore, $L \in {}_{TD}\Phi - {}_{CSG}\Phi$, and Lemma 11.22 holds true. ■

Theorem 11.23 ${}_{CFG}\Phi \subset {}_{CSG}\Phi \subset {}_{TD}\Phi$.

Proof. For every $L \in {}_{CFG}\Phi$, there exists $G \in {}_{CFG}\Psi$ such that G is a proper CFG and $L(G) = L - \{\varepsilon\}$ (see Theorem 6.33). Every proper CFG is a special case of a CSG, so ${}_{CFG}\Phi \subseteq {}_{CSG}\Phi$. Consider the CSG G in Example 11.2. Recall that $L(G) \notin {}_{CFG}\Phi$; therefore, ${}_{CFG}\Phi \subset {}_{CSG}\Phi$. By Theorem 11.21 and Lemma 11.22, ${}_{CSG}\Phi \subset {}_{TD}\Phi$. ■

From a practical standpoint, let us close this section by pointing out that ${}_{CSG}\Phi$ contains, in essence, all real-world languages. Indeed, the only known languages out of ${}_{CSG}\Phi$ are the languages defined based on diagonalization, such as L in the proof of Lemma 11.22.

11.3 Relations between Language Families

Throughout this book, we have introduced several types of language models and studied the language families that they define. We have also established fundamental relations between these language families. In this section, we summarize these relations. Specifically, Corollary 6.74, Theorem 10.43, and Theorem 11.23 imply Theorem 11.24.

Theorem 11.24 ${}_{fin}\Phi \subset {}_{FA}\Phi \subset {}_{DPDA}\Phi \subset {}_{CFG}\Phi \subset {}_{CSG}\Phi \subset {}_{TD}\Phi \subset {}_{TM}\Phi \subset {}_{all}\Phi$. ■

Concerning language families, this theorem represents the most important and comprehensive result of this book, which deserves rephrasing its mathematical terminology in words. Recall that ${}_{fin}\Phi$ and ${}_{infin}\Phi$ denote the families of finite and infinite languages, respectively, and ${}_{all}\Phi$ denotes the family of all languages (see Convention 2.1). As obvious, every finite language is regular, but there are infinite regular languages. ${}_{FA}\Phi$ denotes the family of regular languages characterized by finite automata and regular expressions (see Chapter 3). CFGs and pushdown automata characterize the family of context-free languages, ${}_{CFG}\Phi$ (see Chapter 6); deterministic pushdown automata define an important proper subfamily of ${}_{CFG}\Phi$, namely, ${}_{DPDA}\Phi$ (see Section 6.3.4). As shown in Section 11.2.2, ${}_{CSG}\Phi$ is generated by CSGs, which are as powerful as LBAs except for the fact that the automata can accept ε while the grammars cannot generate ε. TDs define the family of decidable languages, ${}_{TD}\Phi$ (see Section 10.2). Finally, TMs and GGs characterize ${}_{TM}\Phi$ (see Chapter 9). Finally, there exist languages that are not even in ${}_{TM}\Phi$; in fact, Section 10.2 presents several specific infinite languages that are out of ${}_{TM}\Phi$ (see Theorems 10.47, 10.52, 10.73, 10.74). Therefore, ${}_{TM}\Phi \subset {}_{all}\Phi$, where ${}_{all}\Phi$ denotes the family of all formal languages (see Convention 2.1). Clearly, ${}_{all}\Phi - {}_{TM}\Phi \subset {}_{infin}\Phi$.

Exercises

1. Complete Definition 11.1.
2. This chapter contains results whose proofs are only sketched or even completely omitted. These results include Example 11.2; Lemmas 11.6, 11.8, 11.16, and 11.17; Theorems 11.3, 11.5, and 11.21; and statements I and II, which follow Lemma 11.6. Prove them rigorously.
3. Consider each of GGs, (i) through (iv). *A*, *B*, *C*, and *S* are nonterminals, where *S* is the start symbol. Give a rigorous proof that shows the language generated by the GG under consideration.
   i. $S \rightarrow aAbc$, $S \rightarrow \varepsilon$, $A \rightarrow aAbC$, $A \rightarrow \varepsilon$, $Cb \rightarrow bC$, $Cc \rightarrow cc$
   ii. $S \rightarrow CAaDS$, $Aa \rightarrow aA$, $AD \rightarrow BD$, $aB \rightarrow Baaa$, $CB \rightarrow CA$, $CA \rightarrow A$, $AD \rightarrow \varepsilon$
   iii. $S \rightarrow CAaSD$, $S \rightarrow \varepsilon$, $Aa \rightarrow aaA$, $AD \rightarrow BD$, $aB \rightarrow Ba$, $CB \rightarrow CA$, $CA \rightarrow A$, $AD \rightarrow \varepsilon$
   iv. $S \rightarrow AaB$, $A \rightarrow AC$, $Ca \rightarrow aaC$, $CB \rightarrow B$, $A \rightarrow \varepsilon$, $B \rightarrow \varepsilon$
4. Introduce an infinite language, *L*. Construct three equivalent GGs; *A*, *B*, and *C*; which generate *L* in the following ways. *A* generates every string from *L* by infinitely many derivations. *B* generates every string from *L* by two different derivations. Finally, *C* generates every string from *L* by one derivation.
5. Consider the GG *G* from Example 11.1. Construct an equivalent GG that has fewer rules than *G* has. Give a rigorous proof that both GGs are equivalent.
6. Define languages (i) through (xvii) as follows:
   i. $\{a^ib^jc^k \mid i, j, k \geq 0 \text{ and } i < j < k\}$
   ii. $\{a^i \mid i \text{ is a prime}\}$
   iii. $\{w \mid w \in \{a, b, c\}^* \text{ and } occur(w, a) = occur(w, b) = occur(w, c)\}$
   iv. $\{a^ib^ia^j \mid i, j \geq 0 \text{ and } j \neq i\}$
   v. $\{a^ib^ic^j \mid i, j \geq 0 \text{ and } i \neq j \neq 2i\}$
   vi. $\{a^ib^jc^k \mid i, j, k \geq 0, i \neq j, k \neq i, \text{ and } j \neq k\}$
   vii. $\{0^i10^i10^i10^i \mid i \geq 1\}$
   viii. $\{a^ib^ia^i \mid i \geq 1\}$
   ix. $\{a^ib^j \mid i \geq 0 \text{ and } j \geq 1\}$
   x. $\{a^ib^jc^k \mid i, j, k \geq 0 \text{ and } i = j \text{ or } j = k\}$
   xi. $\{a^ib^jc^ib^j \mid i \geq 0 \text{ and } j \geq 1\}$
   xii. $\{a^icab^ia^j \mid i, j \geq 0\}$
   xiii. $\{waw \mid w \in \{a, b\}^*\}$
   xiv. $\{0, 1\}^* - \{0^i10^i10^i \mid i \geq 1\}$
   xv. $\{a^ib^jc^k \mid i, j, k \geq 0 \text{ and } j = i + k\}$
   xvi. $\{a, b\}^* - \{a^ib^ja^i \mid j \geq i \geq 1\}$
   xvii. $\{x \mid x \in \{a, b, c\}^*, occur(x, a) \geq occur(x, b) \text{ iff } occur(x, c) < occur(x, a)\}$

   Consider each of these languages. Perform (a) through (d).
   a. Construct a GG that generates the language under consideration.
   b. Give a rigorous proof that verifies the construction.

c. Convert the GG to an equivalent GG in Kuroda normal form.
d. Convert the GG to an equivalent GG in Pentonnen normal form.

7. Consider the general notion of a GG (see Definition 11.1). Restrict it so that the left-hand side of every rule contains only nonterminals. Formalize this restriction. Prove that the original notion and the restricted notion of a GG are equivalent.
8. Let G be a CSG in Pentonnen normal form and $w \in L(G)$. Based on $|w|$, determine the greatest integer $n \in \mathbb{N}$ such that if ${}_GS \Rightarrow^m w$ in G, then $m \geq n$, for all $m \in \mathbb{N}$.
9 S. Consider the notion of a GG (see Definition 11.1). Generalize it so that any string, including ε, may represent the left-hand side of a rule. Formalize this generalization. Prove that the original notion of a GG and this generalized notion are equivalent.
10 S. Consider the general notion of a GG, G (see Definition 11.1). A *pure GG* is obtained by modifying G so that G has only terminals, and instead of a start symbol, it has a start string. Formalize the notion of a pure GG. Determine the relation between the language family defined by pure GGs, the family of finite languages, ${}_{FA}\Phi$, ${}_{CFG}\Phi$, and ${}_{CSG}\Phi$.
11. Consider the general notion of a GG, G (see Definition 11.1). Assume that there exists a constant $k \in \mathbb{N}$ such that for every derivation of the form ${}_GS \Rightarrow^* v \Rightarrow^* w$ in G with $w \in L(G)$, $|v| \leq k|w|$. Prove that $L(G) \in {}_{CSG}\Phi$ under this assumption.
12. Restrict the definition of a TM so that it shifts its head to the left or right during every move. Formalize this restriction. Show how to turn every TM to an equivalent TM restricted in this way.

Consider the basic language operations, such as union, concatenation, closure, intersection, and complement. For each of these operations and for each of the families ${}_{CSG}\Phi$, ${}_{TD}\Phi$, and ${}_{TM}\Phi$, prove or disprove that the family is closed under the operation in question.

13. Let L be a language over an alphabet Σ. Consider the next language operations.
    i. $min(L) = \{w |\ w \in L \text{ and } (prefix(w) - \{w\}) \cap L = \emptyset\}$
    ii. $max(L) = \{w |\ w \in L \text{ and } \{w\}\Sigma^+ \cap L = \emptyset\}$
    iii. $sqrt(L) = \{x |\ xy \in L \text{ for some } y \in \Sigma^*, \text{ and } |y| = |x|^2\}$
    iv. $log(L) = \{x |\ xy \in L \text{ for some } y \in \Sigma^*, \text{ and } |y| = 2^{|x|}\}$
    v. $cycle(L) = \{vw |\ wv \in L \text{ for some } v, w \in \Sigma^*\}$
    vi. $half(L) = \{w |\ wv \in L \text{ for some } v \in \Sigma^*, \text{ and } |w| = |v|\}$
    vii. $inv(L) = \{xwy |\ xzy \in L \text{ for some } x, y, w, z \in \Sigma^*, z = reversal(w)\}$

    For each of these operations and for each of the families ${}_{CSG}\Phi$, ${}_{TD}\Phi$, and ${}_{TM}\Phi$, prove or disprove that the family is closed under the operation in question.
14. Select a noncontext-free subset of a natural language, such as English. Construct a GG that generates the subset. Verify the construction by a rigorous proof.
15 S. Consider each of the languages in Exercise 6. Prove or disprove that the language belongs to ${}_{CSG}\Phi$. If the language belongs to ${}_{CSG}\Phi$, construct a CSG that generates it and verify the construction by a rigorous proof.
16 S. Consider Definition 11.10. Extend the notion of a CSG so that it can generate ε. Prove that any language L is accepted by an LBA iff it is generated by a CSG extended in this way.

Solutions to Selected Exercises

9. To formalize this generalization, consider the original notion of a GG, $G = (\Sigma, R)$ (see Definition 11.1). Modify it so R is a finite set of rules of the form $u \rightarrow v$, where $u, v \in \Sigma^*$; otherwise, the definition remains unchanged. Specifically, N, Δ, S, $\Rightarrow$, $\Rightarrow^*$, $F(G)$, and $L(G)$ have the same meaning as for any GG. In this way, the desired generalization is obtained.

   Clearly, any GG represents a special case of the above-generalized version of a GG. Therefore, we only sketch how to transform any generalized version of a GG, $I = ({}_I\Sigma, {}_IR)$, to an equivalent GG, $O = ({}_O\Sigma, {}_OR)$, which satisfies Definition 11.1. Set ${}_O\Sigma = {}_I\Sigma \cup \{{}_OS, E\}$, where ${}_OS$ and E are two new nonterminals (${}_OS$ is the start symbol of O). Initialize ${}_OR$ as ${}_OR = \{{}_OS \rightarrow {}_ISE, E \rightarrow \varepsilon\}$. For every $X \in {}_I\Sigma$, introduce $XE \rightarrow EX$ and $EX \rightarrow XE$ into ${}_OR$. Finally, for every $x \rightarrow y \in {}_IR$, where $u, v \in \Sigma^*$, introduce $xE \rightarrow yE$ into ${}_OR$. Explain this transformation informally. Then, verify it by a rigorous proof.

10. A *pure grammar* is defined just like the notion of a rewriting system $G = (\Sigma, R)$, where Σ is an alphabet, and R is a finite *set of rules* of the form $u \rightarrow v$, where $u \in \Sigma^+$ and $v \in \Sigma^*$ (see Definition 2.2). Consequently, all the notions, such as $\Rightarrow$ and $\Rightarrow^*$, introduced for rewriting systems are applicable to G as well. The *language generated by* G is denoted by $L(G)$ and defined as $L(G) = \{x | \; s \Rightarrow^* x\}$, where s is a special *start string* over Σ.

    By contradiction, prove that no pure grammar generates $\{a\}^*\{b\} \cup \{b\}\{a\}^*$. Base this proof on considering all possible forms of the start string. Make use of this result to complete this solution.
15. All the languages belong to ${}_{CSG}\Phi$. Complete this solution by constructing CSGs for them.
16. We next extend the notion of a CSG to the notion of an ${}_\varepsilon$CSG in the following way.

    Definition Let $G = (\Sigma, R)$ be a GG such that its start symbol S does not occur on the right-hand side of any rule in R. If $G = (\Sigma, R - \{S \rightarrow \varepsilon\})$ satisfy Definition 11.10, G is an ${}_\varepsilon$*CSG*.

    As obvious, an ${}_\varepsilon$CSG can generate ε by using $S \rightarrow \varepsilon$. By analogy with the proof technique described in Section 11.2.2, prove that any language L is accepted by an LBA iff it is generated by an ${}_\varepsilon$CSG. ■

CONCLUSION V

The purpose of this final one-chapter section is threefold. First, it sums up all the material covered in this book. Then, it gives an overview of selected current trends in formal language theory and its applications. Finally, it places the subject of this book into a historical and bibliographical context, and it also suggests further reading on this subject.

Chapter 12

Concluding and Bibliographical Remarks

This concluding chapter consists of three sections. Section 12.1 summarizes this book. Section 12.2 outlines selected modern trends, which were omitted in this book. Section 12.3 places all its material into a historical and bibliographical context; in addition, it recommends further reading to the serious student.

12.1 Summary

This book gives an introduction to the theory of formal languages and its applications in computer science. It is meant as the basis of a one-term undergraduate-level course on this subject. The text maintains a balance between a theoretical and practical approach to this subject. From a theoretical viewpoint, it covers all rudimental topics concerning formal languages and their models, especially grammars and automata. The book shows basic properties of languages defined by these models. Concerning applications, it explains how these models underlie computer science engineering techniques for language processing, such as lexical and syntax analysis. From a more theoretical viewpoint, this book applies these models to computation in general and, thereby, shows the basic ideas underlying the theory of computation, including computability, decidability, and computational complexity.

This book is divided into five sections.

Section I, consisting of Chapters 1 and 2, gives an introduction to this book. Chapter 1 reviews basic mathematical notions needed to follow the rest of this book. Chapter 2 first defines formal languages and rewriting systems, and based on these systems, it conceptualizes (i) language-defining models and (ii) models of computation.

Section II, consisting of Chapters 3 through 5, discusses regular languages and their models. Chapter 3 introduces finite automata (FAs) and regular expressions (REs) as fundamental language models that characterize the family of regular languages, denoted by ${}_{reg}\Phi$ (see Theorem 3.38). In fact, regarding FAs, this chapter defines a broad variety of these automata and shows their equivalence (see Corollary 3.22). Chapter 4 describes applications of REs and FAs in lexical analysis. Chapter 5 establishes important properties of regular languages. It concentrates its attention on establishing properties that allow us to prove or, in contrast, disprove that a given language is regular.

Section III, consisting of Chapters 6 through 8, covers context-free languages and their models. Chapter 6 introduces context-free grammars (CFGs) and pushdown automata (PDAs) as language-generating models and language-accepting models, respectively, and it shows that both characterize the family of context-free languages, ${}_{CFG}\Phi$ (see Theorem 6.57). Chapter 6 also shows that deterministic versions of PDAs are less powerful than their nondeterministic counterparts (see Theorem 6.71). Chapter 7 applies CFGs and PDAs to the syntax analysis of programming languages. Both top-down and bottom-up parsers are covered in this chapter in detail. In many respects, Chapter 8 parallels Chapter 5; however, Chapter 8 obviously studies language properties in terms of ${}_{CFG}\Phi$. That is, it shows several properties concerning ${}_{CFG}\Phi$ and explains how to use them to answer whether or not certain languages are in ${}_{CFG}\Phi$.

Section IV, consisting of Chapters 9 through 11, defines important language-accepting rewriting systems referred to as Turing machines (TMs) and uses them primarily as models of computation. Chapter 9 defines them. Based on TMs, Chapter 10 outlines the theory of computation, including computability, decidability, and computational complexity. To link TMs to the theory of formal languages, Chapter 11 defines their grammatical counterparts (see Section 11.1). It also considers ${}_{TM}\Phi$ as the family of languages defined by TMs and establishes

$${}_{fin}\Phi \subset {}_{reg}\Phi \subset {}_{CFG}\Phi \subset {}_{TM}\Phi \subset {}_{all}\Phi$$

where ${}_{fin}\Phi$ and ${}_{all}\Phi$ denote the family of finite languages and the entire family of all languages, respectively (see Convention 2.1 and Theorem 11.24).

Section V, consisting of this chapter, closes this book by summarizing its material, outlining selected modern topics and placing its subject into a historical and bibliographical context.

This book has paid special attention to closure properties. Most of them were proved in Sections 5.2, 8.2, and 10.2; some of them were established as exercises (see Exercise 12 in Chapter 11). In Figure 12.1, which closes this section, we summarize the closure properties of ${}_{reg}\Phi$, ${}_{CFG}\Phi$, and ${}_{TM}\Phi$ under operations union (∪), concatenation (.), closure (*), intersection (∩), and complement (~).

	∪	·	*	∩	~
${}_{reg}\Phi$	yes	yes	yes	yes	yes
${}_{CFG}\Phi$	yes	yes	yes	no	no
${}_{TM}\Phi$	yes	yes	yes	yes	no

Figure 12.1 Summary of closure properties.

12.2 Modern Trends

This section describes modern directions of formal language theory and its applications in an informal way. By no means is this chapter intended to be exhaustive in any way, however. As a matter of fact, it selects only four CFG-based grammatical models and their applications. Specifically, these models include conditional grammars, regulated grammars, scattered context grammars, and grammar systems. Rather than defining them mathematically, we quite intuitively sketch their concept and purpose in words. We also include key references concerning them.

For a survey that covers most important trends that emerged up to 1997 in formal language theory, consult the three-volume handbook by Rozenberg and Salomaa (1997). We also add some remarks on this subject in Section 12.3, including very recent references concerning advanced directions and latest developments of formal languages and their models.

12.2.1 Conditional Grammars

Conditional CFG-based grammars restrict their derivations by context conditions, which can be classified into these three categories: (i) context conditions placed on derivation domains, (ii) context conditions placed on the use of productions, and (iii) context conditions placed on the neighborhood of the rewritten symbols. These grammars are more powerful than ordinary CFGs even if the number of their components, such as the number of nonterminals or the number of rules, is significantly reduced. By using their context conditions, these grammars can elegantly and flexibly control their derivations and, thereby, perform them deterministically. Regarding conditional grammars, consult Meduna and Švec (2005) and its references. In its conclusion, this monograph also describes many biologically oriented applications of these grammars. In fact, Chapter 7 of Meduna and Švec (2005) develops a new programming language for applications of this kind.

12.2.2 Regulated Grammars

Regulated CFG-based grammars restrict their derivations by auxiliary mathematical mechanisms, which regulate the use of rules during derivations. These grammars are stronger than CFGs, and they work in a more deterministic way than CFGs. In formal language theory, there exist many types of these grammars. Up to 1989, all the principal results concerning these grammars have been summarized in Dassow and Paun (1989). Apart from this monograph, these grammars have been investigated in many more important studies, including Abraham (1972), Aho (1968), Bar-Hillel et al. (1961), Csuhaj-Varju (1992), Dassow et al. (1993), Ehrenfeucht et al. (1985), Ehrenfeucht et al. (1994), Fris (1968), Greibach and Hopcroft (1969), Habel (1992), Kelemen (1984, 1989), Kral (1973), Meduna (1986, 1987a, b, 1990a, b, 1991, 1992, 1993a, b, 1994, 1995a, b, 1996, 1997a–c, 1998a–c, 1999a, b, 2000b, c, 2001, 2002, 2003a, b, 2004), Meduna and Csuhaj-Varju (1993), Meduna and Fernau (2003a, b), Meduna and Gopalaratnam (1994), Meduna and Horvath (1988), Meduna and Kolář (2000a, b, 2002a, b), Meduna and Švec (2002, 2003a, b), Meduna and Vurm (2001), Meduna et al. (1994), Navratil (1970), Paun (1979, 1985), Rosenkrantz (1967, 1969), Rosenkrantz and Stearns (1970), Rozenberg (1977), Thatcher (1967), and Urbanek (1983).

12.2.3 Scattered Context Grammars

Many modern information technologies cope with processing broadly scattered pieces of mutually related information throughout various computer systems. As a result, a mathematical exploration of scattered information processing based on adequate formal models represents an important investigation area of today's informatics. In formal language theory, which traditionally provides informatics with formal models, information processing of this kind is formalized by *scattered context grammars*. As these grammars formalize scattered information processing in a very natural and rigorous way, it comes as no surprise that formal language theory has devoted to their investigation a great number of studies since their introduction more than four decades ago in Greibach and Hopcroft (1969). Consult Meduna and Techet (2010), which systematically and compactly summarizes all the knowledge obtained in these studies. In addition, from a practical point of view, this monograph also describes several applications of these grammars in linguistics.

12.2.4 Grammar Systems

As computational cooperation, distribution, concurrence, and parallelism have recently fulfilled a crucial role in computer science, the current software components tend to make use of these computational modes as much as possible. To illustrate, consider parsers. Compared to their traditional construction (see Chapter 7), today's parsers are designed in a more complicated and sophisticated way. Indeed, they integrate the highly effective computational modes mentioned earlier so the parsing process works in an optimal way. As a result, some parts of modern parsers are further divided into various subparts, which are performed in parallel. Indeed, a typical current parser is usually divided into two parts, which work concurrently. One part works as a precedence parser that analyzes expressions and conditions (see Section 7.3.1). The other part represents a predictive parser that processes the general program flow (see Section 7.2). In fact, both parts are sometimes further divided into several subprocesses; for instance, several expressions may be parsed in parallel rather than parse them one by one. Of course, this massively parallel and cooperating design of today's parsers necessitates a careful control over all the subprocesses running in parallel. Frequently, this design is based upon *grammar systems*, which combine together various cooperating and distributing versions of CFGs. As a result, they can act as appropriate grammatical models that adequately formalize the control and coordination over all involved computational processes and subprocesses, many of which work in mutually cooperating way. Therefore, they are often used to conceptualize modern parser design, sketched earlier. Meduna (2004) and its references may be consulted about grammar systems. Allen (2002), Almasi (1989), Cooper (2004), Grune et al. (2000), Haghighat (1995), Lee and Yew (2001), Srikant (2003), Tseng (1990), and Zima (1991) cover modern trends in parser design very well.

12.3 Bibliographical and Historical Remarks

This book has covered formal language theory in a constant relation to its two important application areas in computer science. First, by means of formal languages and their models, particularly TMs, it has outlined the theory of computation, including computability, decidability, and complexity. Second, from a more practical viewpoint, by using language-defining models, it has described computer science engineering techniques for language processing, such as the lexical and syntax analysis of programming languages. This section sketches the development of this theory in view of these two application areas from a historical and bibliographical perspective. In its conclusion, it recommends further reading to the serious student.

From a historical point of view, concerning the theory of computation underlain by formal languages and their models, Turing (1936) opened this scientific area by proving that the *TM-Halting* problem is undecidable (see Problem 10.41). Moore (1956) proved the decidability of all the problems concerning FAs covered in Section 10.2.2, and Rabin and Scott (1959) continue with this subject by investigating many more decision problems for FAs. Bar-Hillel et al. (1961) establish several results concerning the decidability and undecidability for CFGs. Cantor (1962), Floyd (1962), and Chomsky and Schutzenberger (1963) proved that the *CF-Ambiguity* problem is undecidable (see Problem 10.68). Davis (1965) summarized all the basic articles on decidability and computability published before 1965. Hoare and Allison (1972) provided a very readable introduction to computability at that time. For a throughout coverage of the theory of computation expressed in terms of formal languages and their models, consult Beigel and Floyd (1994), Berstel (1979), Book (1980), Bucher and Maurer (1984), Cleaveland and Uzgalis (1977), Davis and Weyuker (1983), Eilenberg (1974, 1976), Ginsburg (1966), Harrison (1978), Hopcroft et al. (2006), Kelley (1995), Kozen (2007), Linz (1990), Martin (2010), McNaughton (1982), Meduna (2000a), Revesz (1983), Rozenberg and Salomaa (1997), Salomaa (1969, 1973, 1985), Shyr (1991), Sipser (2005), Sudkamp (2005), and Wood (1987).

Concerning formal language theory applied to programming language processing, the earliest works on this subject appeared in the 1960s when the first high-level programming languages, such as FORTRAN and ALGOL 60, were developed. The crucial studies published at that time include Aho and Ullman (1969a, b), Barnett and Futrelle (1962), Conway (1963), de Bakker (1969), Evey (1963), Ginsburg and Rice (1962), Hartmanis et al. (1965), Irons (1961), Johnson et al. (1968), Kasami (1965), Knuth (1967a, b), Korenjak and Hopcroft (1966), Kurki-Suonio (1964), Landin (1965), Lewis and Stearns (1968), McCarthy (1960), McCarthy and Painter (1967), Naur (1960), Oettinger (1961), and van Wijngaarden (1969). During the past three decades of the twentieth century, the basic knowledge concerning engineering techniques for programming language processing was summarized in the books by Aho and Ullman (1972, 1973, 1977), Aho et al. (2007), Alblas (1996), Appel (1998), Bergmann (1994), Elder (1994), Fischer (1991, 1999), Fraser (1995), Gries (1971), Haghighat (1995), Hendrix (1990), Holmes (1995), Holub (1990), Hunter (1999), Kiong (1997), Lemone (1992a, b), Lewis et al. (1976), Louden (1997), Mak (1996), Morgan (1998), Muchnick (1997), Parsons (1992), Pittman (1992), Sampaio (1997), Sorenson and Tremblay (1985), Waite (1993), Wilhelm (1995), and Wirth (1996). Most of them are still useful and readable today. Recently, programming language processors have been well explained in Allen (2002), Cooper (2004), Grune et al. (2000), Lee and Yew (2001), Meduna (2008), and Srikant (2003).

This book was designed so that all its material can be comfortably covered during a one-term undergraduate term. As a result, more complicated topics were partially or even entirely omitted in the text. These topics are comprehensively covered in several books, including Beigel and Floyd (1994), Berstel (1979), Book (1980), Bucher and Maurer (1984), Cleaveland and Uzgalis (1977), Davis and Weyuker (1983), Eilenberg (1974, 1976), Ginsburg (1966), Harrison (1978), Hopcroft et al. (2006), Kelley (1995), Kozen (2007), Linz (1990), Martin (2010), McNaughton (1982), Meduna (2000a), Revesz (1983), Rozenberg and Salomaa (1997), Salomaa (1969, 1973, 1985), Shyr (1991), Sipser (2005), Sudkamp (2005), and Wood (1987).

We close this chapter and, in fact, the entire book by recommending the following five books, as further reading to the serious student.

I. Hopcroft, J. E., Motwani, R., and Ullman, J. D. (2006)
Authors: John E. Hopcroft, Rajeev Motwani, and Jeffrey D. Ullman
Title: Introduction to Automata Theory, Languages, and Computation
Publisher: Pearson Education; Third Edition, Addison-Wesley, 2006
ISBN: 0321486811

This famous book is a revised and updated version of its 1979 version, whose predecessor was published in 1969 under the title *Formal Languages and Their Relation to Automata*. It covers all the major topics in the theory of formal languages, automata, and computation, and it is a splendid reference for research in these areas. It is primarily a textbook for graduate students in theoretical computer science. This textbook is too complicated for ordinary undergraduate students. This book contains hardly any applications.

II. Sipser, M. (2005)
Author: Michael Sipser
Title: Introduction to the Theory of Computation
Publisher: Course Technology Inc.; International Edition, 2005
ISBN: 0619217642

This book contains all the material needed for an advanced course on theory of computation and complexity. Its author is a talented writer, and thanks to his writing style, it nicely presents all the knowledge concerning this theory in an effective way. Proofs on theorems are given almost always in the following two-phase way: first, the book gives the idea that lies behind the proof, and second, it gives the proof itself in a rigorous way. Regarding formal languages and their models, the book restricts its attention to the models needed in the theory of computation. Just like Hopcroft, J. E., Motwani, R., and Ullman, J. D. (2006), however, this book lacks any applications.

III. Kozen, D. C. (2007)
Author: Dexter C. Kozen
Title: Automata and Computability
Publisher: Springer; 2007
ISBN: 9780387949079

As its title indicates, this book provides an introduction to the theory of automata and computability. It contains a reasonable selection of essential material concerning the theory of formal languages, automata, and computation. The presentation is somewhat unusual because it consists of lectures rather than chapters. Apart from the basic lectures, the text adds 11 supplementary lectures that cover special and advanced topics on the subject. Frequently, this book makes seemingly difficult-to-understand topics easy to grasp. Regarding applications, it contains a single lecture about parsing, explained in a rather theoretical way.

IV. Martin, J. C. (2010)
Author: John Martin
Title: Introduction to Languages and the Theory of Computation
Publisher: McGraw-Hill Higher Education; Fourth Edition, 2010
ISBN: 0071289429

This book is a mathematically oriented survey of some important fundamental concepts in the theory of languages and computation, which covers a wider range of topics than most other introductory books on the subject. It contains worked-out proofs of every major theorem, but the reader needs a fairly high level of mathematical sophistication to fully grasp these proofs. It is strictly theoretically oriented. As a result, it is not designed for undergraduate students. Although it contains some algorithms and examples, their presentation is theoretical, too.

V. Sudkamp, T. A. (2005)
Author: Thomas A. Sudkamp
Title: Languages and Machines: An Introduction to the Theory of Computer Science
Publisher: Pearson Education; Third Edition, 2005
ISBN: 0321315340

This book provides the reader with a mathematically sound presentation of the theory of formal languages and computation at a level corresponding to senior-level computer science majors. The theoretical concepts are presented so that they are preceded by an intuitive understanding of the concepts through numerous examples and illustrations. It contains a good selection of topics concerning computational complexity. It provides a flexible format giving professors the ability to design their courses that concentrate on specific areas within automata theory, computability, or computational complexity. Parsing based on LL and LR grammars is included to provide the groundwork for the study of compiler design, but its presentation is so theoretical that ordinary students can hardly see how to implement parsers on the basis of these grammars.

Appendix I: Index to Special Symbols

Symbol	*Meaning*	*Page*
$\neg$	Logical connective *not*	3
$\wedge$	Logical connective *and*	3
$\vee$	Logical connective *or*	3
$\mathbf{0}$	Falsity	3
$\mathbf{1}$	Truth	3
$\in$	Membership	4
$\notin$	Nonmembership	4
$\varnothing$	Empty set	5
$\mathbb{N}$	Natural numbers	5
${}_0\mathbb{N}$	Natural numbers with 0	5
$\cup$	Union	5
$\cap$	Intersection	5
$\subseteq$	Subset	5
$\subset$	Proper subset	5
$\sim$	Complement	5
$-$	Difference	5
$\lvert x \rvert$	Length of a finite sequence x	6
$\times$	Cartesian product	6
ε	The empty string	13

(*Continued*)

Symbol	*Meaning*	*Page*
⇒	Direct rewriting	16
→	Rule	16
◁	Input end	62
□	Blank symbol	67
♣	Derivation tree	93
◇	The only state of parsers in Chapter 7	132
▷	Pushdown bottom	133
☺	**SUCCESS**	152
⌊	**OP-SHIFT**	156
⌋	**OP-REDUCE**	156
|	Separator of rule items	167
↺	Set of items	169
▶	Start state	199
■	Accepting state	204
♦	Rejecting state	204
ζ	Enumeration of all Turing machines	217
ξ	Enumeration of all computable functions	217
Π	Set of all problem instances	220
∠	Reduction	234
O	Big-O notation	239
$\propto$	Polynomially transformable	240

Appendix II: Index to Language Models

Based on rewriting systems, this book introduces many language models. The alphabetical index lists their abbreviated and full names. According to Convention 2.4, if *LM* abbreviates the notion of a language model, then ${}_{LM}\Psi$ denotes all its instances and ${}_{LM}\Phi$ denotes the language family defined by them. For example, CFG abbreviates the notion of a context-free grammar, ${}_{CFG}\Psi$ denotes all possible instances of these grammars, and ${}_{CFG}\Phi$ denotes the language family defined by them.

Apart from the aforementioned families, this book often refers to four more important language families: ${}_{all}\Phi$, ${}_{fin}\Phi$, ${}_{infin}\Phi$, and ${}_{reg}\Phi$ (see Convention 2.1 and Definition 3.23). ${}_{all}\Phi$ denotes the entire family of all formal languages. ${}_{fin}\Phi$, ${}_{infin}\Phi$, and ${}_{reg}\Phi$ denote the families of finite, infinite, and regular languages, respectively.

Abbreviation	*Name*	*Page*
CFG	Context-free grammar	86
CSG	Context-sensitive grammar	250
DFA	Deterministic finite automaton	38
${}_{cs}$DFA	Completely specified DFA	42
${}_{min}$DFA	Minimum-state DFA	43
DPDA	Deterministic pushdown automaton	121
FA	Finite automaton	31
${}_{\varepsilon\text{-}free}$FA	ε-Free FA	34
GG	General grammar	246
LBA	Linear-bounded automaton	251
LG	Linear grammar	87
PDA	Pushdown automaton	113
TD	Turing decider	221
TM	Turing machine	199

References

This reference list contains all the publications referenced in Section V.

Abraham, S. (1972). "Compound and Serial Grammars," *Information and Control* 20, 432–438.
Aho, A. V. (1968). "Indexed Grammars—An Extension of Context-free Grammars," *Journal of the ACM* 15, 647–671.
Aho, A. V. and Ullman, J. D. (1969a). "Syntax Directed Translations and the Pushdown Assembler," *Journal of Computer and System Sciences* 3, 37–56.
Aho, A. V. and Ullman, J. D. (1969b). "Properties of Syntax Directed Relations," *Journal of Computer and System Sciences* 3, 319–334.
Aho, A. V. and Ullman, J. D. (1972). *The Theory of Parsing, Translation and Compiling, Volume I: Parsing*, Prentice Hall, Englewood Cliffs, NJ.
Aho, A. V. and Ullman, J. D. (1973). *The Theory of Parsing, Translation and Compiling, Volume II: Compiling*, Prentice Hall, Englewood Cliffs, NJ.
Aho, A. V. and Ullman, J. D. (1977). *Principles of Compiler Design*, Addison-Wesley, Reading, MA.
Aho, A. V., Lam, M. S., Sethi, R., and Ullman, J. D. (2007). *Compilers: Principles, Techniques, and Tools*, Second Edition, Pearson Education, Boston, MA.
Alblas, H. (1996). *Practice and Principles of Compiler Building with C*, Prentice Hall, London.
Allen, R. (2002). *Optimizing Compilers for Modern Architectures: A Dependence-Based Approach*, Morgan Kaufmann, London.
Almasi, G. S. (1989). *Highly Parallel Computing*, Benjamin/Cummings, Redwood City, CA.
Appel, A. W. (1998). *Modern Compiler Implementation in ML*, Cambridge University Press, Cambridge, UK.
Bar-Hillel, Y., Perles, M., and Shamir, E. (1961). "On Formal Properties of Simple Phrase Structure Grammars," *Zeitschrift fur Phonetik Sprachwissenschaft und Kommunikations-Forschung* 14, 143–172.
Barnett, M. P. and Futrelle, R. P. (1962). "Syntactic Analysis by Digital Computer," *Communications of the ACM* 5, 515–526.
Beigel, R. and Floyd, R. W. (1994). *The Language of Machines*, Freeman, New York.
Bergmann, S. (1994). *Compiler Design: Theory, Tools, and Examples*, W.C. Brown, Oxford, UK.
Berstel, J. (1979). *Transductions and Context-Free Languages*, Teubner, Stuttgart, West Germany.
Book, R. V. (ed.) (1980). *Formal Language Theory: Perspectives and Open Problems*, Academic Press, New York.
Bucher, W. and Maurer, H. A. (1984). *Teoretische Grundlagen der Programmiersprachen: Automatem und Sprachen* [*Theoretical Foundation of Programming Languages: Automata and Languages*], Bibliographisches Institut, Zurich, Switzerland.
Cantor, D. C. (1962). "On the Ambiguity Problem of Backus Systems," *Journal of the ACM* 9, 477–479.
Chomsky, N. and Schutzenberger, M. P. (1963). "The Algebraic Theory of Context Free Languages," in Braffort, P. and Hirschberg, D. (eds.), *Computer Programming and Formal Systems*, North-Holland, Amsterdam, 118–161.
Cleaveland, J. C. and Uzgalis, R. (1977). *Grammars for Programming Languages*, Elsevier, North-Holland, Amsterdam.

Conway, M. E. (1963). "Design of a Separable Transition-Diagram Compiler," *Communications of the ACM* 6, 396–408.
Cooper, K. D. (2004). *Engineering a Compiler*, Morgan Kaufmann, London.
Csuhaj-Varju, E. (1992). "On Grammars with Local and Global Context Conditions," *International Journal of Computer Mathematics* 47, 17–27.
Dassow, J. and Paun, G. (1989). *Regulated Rewriting in Formal Language Theory*, Springer, Berlin.
Dassow, J., Paun, G., and Salomaa, A. (1993). "Grammars Based on Patterns," *International Journal of Foundations of Computer Science* 4(1), 41640.
Davis, M. (ed.) (1965). *The Undecidable: Basic Papers on Undecidable Propositions, Unsolvable Problems, and Computable Functions*, Raven Press, Hewlett, NY.
Davis, M. D. and Weyuker, E. J. (1983). *Computability, Complexity, and Languages*, Academic Press, New York.
de Bakker, J. W. (1969). "Semantics of Programming Languages," in Tou, J.T.(ed.), *Advances in Information Systems and Sciences*, Vol. 2, Plenum Press, New York, 173–227.
Ehrenfeucht, A., Kleijn, J., and Rozenberg, G. (1985). "Adding Global Forbidding Context to Context-Free Grammars," *Theoretical Computer Science* 37, 337–360.
Ehrenfeucht, A., Pas ten, P., and Rozenberg, G. (1994). "Context-Free Text Grammars," *Acta Informatica* 31, 161–206.
Eilenberg, S. (1974). *Automata, Languages, and Machines*, Volume A, Academic Press, New York.
Eilenberg, S. (1976). *Automata, Languages, and Machines*, Volume B, Academic Press, New York.
Elder, J. (1994). *Compiler Construction: A Recursive Descent Model*, Prentice Hall, London.
Evey, J. (1963). "Application of Pushdown Store Machines," *Proceedings 1963 Fall Joint Computer Conference*, AFIPS Press, Montvale, NJ, 215–227.
Fischer, C. N. (1991). *Crafting a Compiler with C*, Benjamin/Cummings, Redwood City, CA.
Fischer, C. N. (1999). *Crafting a Compiler Featuring Java*, Addison-Wesley, Harlow, UK.
Floyd, R. W. (1962). "On Ambiguity in Phrase Structure Languages," *Communications of the ACM* 5, 526–534.
Fraser, C. W. (1995). *A Retargetable C Compiler: Design and Implementation*, Addison-Wesley, Wokingham, UK.
Fris, I. (1968). "Grammars with Partial Ordering of the Rules," *Information and Control* 12, 415–425.
Ginsburg, S. (1966). *The Mathematical Theory of Context-Free Languages*, McGraw-Hill, New York.
Ginsburg, S. and Rice, H. G. (1962). "Two Families of Languages Related to ALGOL," *Journal of the ACM* 9, 350–371.
Greibach, S. and Hopcroft, J. (1969). "Scattered Context Grammars," *Journal of Computer and Systems Sciences* 3, 233–247.
Grune, D., Bal, H., Jacobs, C., and Langendoen, K. (2000). *Modern Compiler Design*, John Wiley & Sons, Hoboken, NY.
Habel, A. (1992). *Hyperedge Replacement: Grammars and Languages*, LNCS 643, Springer, Berlin.
Haghighat, M. R. (1995). *Symbolic Analysis for Parallelizing Compilers*, Kluwer Academic Publishers, Boston, MA.
Harrison, M. A. (1978). *Introduction to Formal Language Theory*, Addison-Wesley, Reading, MA.
Hartmanis, J., Lewis, P. M., II., and Stearns, R. E. (1965). "Hierarchies of Memory Limited Computations," *Proceedings of the Sixth Annual Symposium on Switching Circuit Theory and Logical Design*, Princeton, NJ, 179–190.
Hendrix, J. E. (1990). *A Small C Compiler*, Prentice Hall, London.
Hoare, C. A. R. and Allison, D. C. S. (1972). "Incomputability," *Computing Surveys* 4, 169–178.
Holmes, J. (1995). *Building Your Own Compiler with C++*, Prentice Hall, London.
Holub, A. I. (1990). *Compiler Design in C*, Prentice Hall, London.
Hopcroft, J. E., Motwani, R., and Ullman, J. D. (2006). *Introduction to Automata Theory, Languages, and Computation*, Third Edition, Addison-Wesley, Boston, MA.
Hunter, R. (1999). *The Essence of Compilers*, Prentice Hall, London.
Irons, E. T. (1961). "A Syntax Directed Compiler for ALGOL 60," *Communications of the ACM* 4, 51–55.
Johnson, W. L., Porter, J. H., Ackley, S. I., and Ross, D. T. (1968). "Automatic Generation of Efficient Lexical Analyzers Using Finite-State Techniques," *Communications of the ACM* 11, 805–813.
Kasami, T. (1965). "An Efficient Recognition and Syntax Algorithm for Context-Free Languages," *Scientific Report AFCRL-65-758*, Air Force Cambridge Research Laboratory, Bedford, MA.

Kelemen, J. (1984). "Conditional Grammars: Motivations, Definition, and Some Properties," in Peak, I. and Szep, J. (eds.), *Proceedings on Automata, Languages and Mathematical Systems*, K. Marx University of Economics, Budapest, 110–123.

Kelemen, J. (1989). "Measuring Cognitive Resources Use (A Grammatical Approach)," *Computers and Artificial Intelligence* 8(1), 29–42.

Kelley, D. (1995). *Automata and Formal Languages*, Prentice Hall, Englewood Cliffs, NJ.

Kiong, D. B. K. (1997). *Compiler Technology: Tools, Translators, and Language Implementation*, Kluwer Academic Publishers, London.

Knuth, D. E. (1967a). "On the Translation of Languages from Left to Right," *Information and Control* 8, 611–618.

Knuth, D. E. (1967b). "The Remaining Trouble Spots in ALGOL 60," *Communications of the ACM* 10, 611–618.

Korenjak, A. J. and Hopcroft, J. E. (1966). "Simple Deterministic Languages," *Proceedings of the Seventh Annual IEEE Symposium on Switching and Automata Theory*, MIT, Boston, MA, 36–46.

Kozen, D. C. (2007). *Automata and Computability*, Springer-Verlag, New York.

Kral, J. (1973). "A Note on Grammars with Regular Restrictions," *Kybernetika* 9(3), 159–161.

Kurki-Suonio, R. (1964). "Note on Top-Down Languages," *Information and Control* 7, 207–223.

Landin, P. J. (1965). "A Correspondence between Algol 60 and Church 's Lambda Notation," *Communications of the ACM* 8, 89–101 and 158–165.

Lee, G. and Yew, P. (2001). *Interaction between Compilers and Computer Architectures*, Kluwer Academic Publishers, London.

Lemone, K. A. (1992a). *Design of Compilers: Techniques of Programming Language Translation*, CRC Press, Boca Raton, FL.

Lemone, K. A. (1992b). *Fundamentals of Compilers: An Introduction to Computer Language Translation*, CRC Press, Boca Raton, FL.

Lewis, P. M., II. and Stearns, R. E. (1968). "Syntax-Directed Transduction," *Journal of the ACM* 15, 465–488.

Lewis, P. M., II., Rosenkrantz, D. J., and Stearns, R. E. (1976). *Compiler Design Theory*, Addison-Wesley, Reading, MA.

Linz, P. (1990). *An Introduction to Formal Languages and Automata*, D.C. Heath, Lexington, MA.

Louden, K. C. (1997). *Compiler Construction: Principles and Practice*, PWS Publishing, London.

Mak, R. (1996). *Writing Compilers and Interpreters*, John Wiley & Sons, NY.

Martin, J. C. (2010). *Introduction to Languages and the Theory of Computation*, Fourth Edition, McGraw-Hill, New York.

McCarthy, J. (1960). "Recursive Functions of Symbolic Expressions and Their Computation by Machine, Part I," *Communications of the ACM* 3, 184–195.

McCarthy, J. and Painter, J. (1967). "Correctness of a Compiler for Arithmetic Expressions," in Schwartz, J. T. (ed.), *Mathematical Aspects of Computer Science*, American Mathematical Society, Providence, RI, 33–41.

McNaughton, R. (1982). *Elementary Computability, Formal Languages, and Automata*, Prentice Hall, Englewood Cliffs, NJ.

Meduna, A. (1986). "A Note on Exponential Density of ET0L Languages," *Kybernetika* 22, 514–518.

Meduna, A. (1987a). "Characterization of the Chomsky Hierarchy through Sequential-Parallel Grammars," *Rostocker Mathematische Kolloquium* 32, 4–14.

Meduna, A. (1987b). "Evaluated Grammars," *Acta Cybernetica* 8, 169–176.

Meduna, A. (1990a). "Context Free Derivations on Word Monoids," *Acta Informatica* 27, 781–786.

Meduna, A. (1990b). "Generalized Forbidding Grammars," *International Journal of Computer Mathematics* 36, 31–38.

Meduna, A. (1991). "Global Context Conditional Grammars," *Journal of Information Processing and Cybernetics* 27, 159–165.

Meduna, A. (1992). "Symbiotic E0L Systems," *Acta Cybernetica* 12, 164–172.

Meduna, A. (1993a). "A Formalization of Sequential, Parallel, and Continuous Rewriting," *International Journal of Computer Mathematics* 39, 24–32.

Meduna, A. (1993b). "Canonical Scattered Rewriting," *International Journal of Computer Mathematics* 51, 122–129.

Meduna, A. (1994). "Matrix Grammars under Leftmost and Rightmost Restrictions," in Paun, G. (ed.), *Mathematical Linguistics and Related Topics*, The Publishing House of the Romanian Academy, Bucharest, Romania, 243–257.

Meduna, A. (1995a). "A Trivial Method of Characterizing the Family of Recursively Enumerable Languages by Scattered Context Grammars," *EATCS Bulletin* 56, 104–106.

Meduna, A. (1995b). "Syntactic Complexity of Scattered Context Grammars," *Acta Informatica* 32, 285–298.

Meduna, A. (1996). "Syntactic Complexity of Context-Free Grammars over Word Monoids," *Acta Informatica* 33, 457–462.

Meduna, A. (1997a). "Four-Nonterminal Scattered Context Grammars Characterize the Family of Recursively Enumerable Languages," *International Journal of Computer Mathematics* 63, 67–83.

Meduna, A. (1997b). "On the Number of Nonterminals in Matrix Grammars with Leftmost Derivations," *LNCS* 1217, 27–38.

Meduna, A. (1997c). "Six-Nonterminal Multi-Sequential Grammars Characterize the Family of Recursively Enumerable Languages," *International Journal of Computer Mathematics* 65, 179–189.

Meduna, A. (1998a). "Descriptional Complexity of Multi-Continues Grammars," *Acta Cybernetica* 13, 375–384.

Meduna, A. (1998b). "Economical Transformation of Phrase-Structure Grammars to Scattered Context Grammars," *Acta Cybernetica* 13, 225–242.

Meduna, A. (1998c). "Uniform Rewriting Based on Permutations," *International Journal of Computer Mathematics* 69, 57–74.

Meduna, A. (1999a). "Prefix Pushdown Automata," *International Journal of Computer Mathematics* 71, 215–228.

Meduna, A. (1999b). "Terminating Left-Hand Sides of Scattered Context Productions," *Theoretical Computer Science* 237, 567–601.

Meduna, A. (2000a). *Automata and Languages: Theory and Applications*, Springer, London.

Meduna, A. (2000b). "Generative Power of Three-Nonterminal Scattered Context Grammars," *Theoretical Computer Science* 246, 276–284.

Meduna, A. (2000c). "Terminating Left-Hand Sides of Scattered Context Grammars," *Theoretical Computer Science* 248, 423–427.

Meduna, A. (2001). "Uniform Generation of Languages by Scattered Context Grammars," *Fundamenta Informaticae* 44, 231–235.

Meduna, A. (2002). "Descriptional Complexity of Scattered Rewriting and Multirewriting: An Overview," *Journal of Automata, Languages and Combinatorics* 7, 571–577.

Meduna, A. (2003a). "Coincidental Extension of Scattered Context Languages," *Acta Informatica* 39, 307–314.

Meduna, A. (2003b). "Simultaneously One-Turn Two-Pushdown Automata," *International Journal of Computer Mathematics* 80, 679–687.

Meduna, A. (2004). "Two-Way Metalinear PC Grammar Systems and Their Descriptional Complexity," *Acta Cybernetica* 92, 126–137.

Meduna, A. (2008). *Elements of Compiler Design*, Taylor & Francis, New York.

Meduna, A. and Csuhaj-Varju, E. (1993). "Grammars with Context Conditions," *EATCS Bulletin* 32, 112–124.

Meduna, A. and Fernau, H. (2003a). "A Simultaneous Reduction of Several Measures of Descriptional Complexity in Scattered Context Grammars," *Information Processing Letters* 86, 235–240.

Meduna, A. and Fernau, H. (2003b). "On the Degree of Scattered Context-Sensitivity," *Theoretical Computer Science* 290, 2121–2124.

Meduna, A. and Gopalaratnam, M. (1994). "On Semi-Conditional Grammars with Productions Having Either Forbidding or Permitting Conditions," *Acta Cybernetica* 11, 309–323.

Meduna, A. and Horvath, G. (1988). "On State Grammars," *Acta Cybernetica* 8, 237–245.

Meduna, A. and Kolář, D. (2000a). "Descriptional Complexity of Multi-Parallel Grammars with Respect to the Number of Nonterminals," in *Grammars and Automata for String Processing from Mathematics and Computer Science to Biology, and Back*, Taylor & Francis, Tarragona, Spain, 724–732.

Meduna, A. and Kolář, D. (2000b). "Regulated Pushdown Automata," *Acta Cybernetica* 18, 653–664.

Meduna, A. and Kolář, D. (2002a). "Homogenous Grammars with a Reduced Number of Non-Context-Free Productions," *Information Processing Letters* 81, 253–257.
Meduna, A. and Kolář, D. (2002b). "One-Turn Regulated Pushdown Automata and Their Reduction," *Fundamenta Informaticae*, 2002(16), 399–405. Amsterdam.
Meduna, A. and Švec, M. (2002). "Reduction of Simple Semi-Conditional Grammars with Respect to the Number of Conditional Productions," *Acta Cybernetica* 15, 353–360.
Meduna, A. and Švec, M. (2003a). "Descriptional Complexity of Generalized Forbidding Grammars," *International Journal of Computer Mathematics* 80, 11–17.
Meduna, A. and Švec, M. (2003b). "Forbidding E0L Systems," *Theoretical Computer Science* 54, 256–276.
Meduna, A. and Švec, M. (2005). *Grammars with Context Conditions and Their Applications*, Wiley & Sons, Hoboken, NJ.
Meduna, A. and Techet, J. (2010). *Scattered Context Grammars and their Applications*, WIT Press, Southampton, UK.
Meduna, A. and Vurm, P. (2001). "Multisequential Grammars with Homogeneous Selectors," *Fundamenta Informaticae* 34, 1–7.
Meduna, A., Crooks, C., and Sarek, M. (1994). "Syntactic Complexity of Regulated Rewriting," *Kybernetika* 30, 177–186.
Moore, E. F. (1956). "Gedanken Experiments on Sequential Machines," in Shannon, C. E. and McCarthy, J. (eds.), *Automata Studies*, Princeton University Press, Princeton, NJ, 129–153.
Morgan, R. C. (1998). *Building an Optimizing Compiler*, Butterworth-Heinemann, Oxford, UK.
Muchnick, S. S. (1997). *Advanced Compiler Design and Implementation*, Morgan Kaufmann Publishers, London.
Naur, P. (ed.) (1960). "Report on the Algorithmic Language ALGOL 60," *Communications of the ACM* 3, 299–314, revised in *Communications of the ACM* 6(1963), 1–17.
Navratil, E. (1970). "Context-Free Grammars with Regular Conditions," *Kybernetika* 6(2), 118–125.
Oettinger, A. G. (1961). "Automatic Syntactic Analysis and Pushdown Store," *Proceedings of the Symposia in Applied Mathematics* 12, American Mathematical Society, Providence, RI, 104–109.
Parsons, T. W. (1992). *Introduction to Compiler Construction*, Computer Science, Oxford, UK.
Paun, G. (1979). "On the Generative Capacity of Conditional Grammars," *Information and Control* 43, 178–186.
Paun, G. (1985). "A Variant of Random Context Grammars: Semi-Conditional Grammars," *Theoretical Computer Science* 41, 42736.
Pittman, T. (1992). *The Art of Compiler Design: Theory and Practice*, Prentice Hall, Englewood Cliffs, NJ.
Rabin, M. O. and Scott, D. (1959). "Finite Automata and Their Decision Problems," *IBM Journal of Research and Development* 3, 115–125.
Revesz, G. E. (1983). *Introduction to Formal Language Theory*, McGraw-Hill, New York.
Rosenkrantz, D. J. (1967). "Matrix Equations and Normal Forms for Context-Free Grammars," *Journal of the ACM* 14, 501–507.
Rosenkrantz, D. J. (1969). "Programmed Grammars and Classes of Formal Languages," *Journal of the ACM* 16, 107–131.
Rosenkrantz, D. J. and Stearns, R. E. (1970). "Properties of Deterministic Top-Down Grammars," *Information and Control* 17, 226–256.
Rozenberg, G. (1977). "Selective Substitution Grammars (Towards a Framework for Rewriting Systems), Part I: Definitions and Examples," *Journal of Information Processing and Cybernetics* 13, 455–463.
Rozenberg, G. and Salomaa, A. (eds.) (1997). *Handbook of Formal Languages*, Volume 1 through 3, Springer, Berlin.
Salomaa, A. (1969). *Theory of Automata*, Pergamon Press, London.
Salomaa, A. (1973). *Formal Languages*, Academic Press, New York.
Salomaa, A. (1985). *Computation and Automata*, Cambridge University Press, Cambridge, UK.
Sampaio, A. (1997). *An Algebraic Approach to Compiler Design*, World Scientific, London.
Shyr, H. J. (1991). *Free Monoids and Languages*, Hon Min Book, Taichung, Taiwan.
Sipser, M. (2005). *Introduction to the Theory of Computation*. International Edition, Thomson Course Technology, Boston, MA.
Sorenson, P. G. and Tremblay, J. P. (1985). *The Theory and Practice of Compiler Writing*, McGraw-Hill, New York.

Srikant, Y. N. (2003). *The Compiler Design Handbook: Optimizations and Machine Code Generation*, CRC Press, London.
Sudkamp, T. A. (2005). *Languages and Machines: An Introduction to the Theory of Computer Science*, Third Edition, Pearson Education, Reading, MA.
Thatcher, J. W. (1967). "Characterizing Derivation Trees of a Context-Free Grammar through a Generalization of Finite-Automata Theory," *Journal of Computer and System Sciences* 1, 317–322.
Tseng, P. (1990). *A Systolic Array Parallelizing Compiler*, Kluwer Academic Publishers, London.
Turing, A. M. (1936). "On Computable Numbers with an Application to the Entscheidungs-Problem," *Proceedings of the London Mathematical Society* 2, 230–265.
Urbanek, F. J. (1983). "A Note on Conditional Grammars," *Revue Roumaine de Mathématique Pures et Appliquées* 28, 341–342.
van Wijngaarden, A. (ed.) (1969). "Report on the Algorithmic Language ALGOL 68," *Numerische Mathematik* 14, 79–218.
Waite, W. (1993). *An Introduction to Compiler Construction*, HarperCollins, New York.
Wilhelm, R. (1995). *Compiler Design*, Addison-Wesley, Wokingham, UK.
Wirth, N. (1996). *Compiler Construction*, Addison-Wesley, Harlow, UK.
Wood, D. (1987). *Theory of Computation*, Harper & Row, New York.
Zima, H. (1991). *Supercompilers for Parallel and Vector Computers*, ACM Press, New York.

Bibliography

Aho, A. V. (1980). "Pattern Matching in Strings," in Book, R.V. (ed.), *Formal Language Theory: Perspectives and Open Problems*, Academic Press, New York, 325–247.

Aho, A. V. (ed.) (1973). *Currents in the Theory of Computing*, Prentice Hall, Englewood Cliffs, NJ.

Appel, A. W. (2002). *Modern Compiler Implementation in Java*, Cambridge University Press, Cambridge, UK.

Arbib, M. A., Kfoury, A. J., and Moll, R. N. (1981). *A Basis for Theoretical Computer Science*, Springer-Verlag, New York.

Ashcroft, E. A. and Wadge, W. W. (1976). "LUCID A Formal System for Writing and Proving Programs," *SIAM Journal on Computing* 5, 336–354.

Backus, J. W. (1959). "The Syntax and Semantics of the Proposed International Algebraic Language of the Zurich ACM-GAMM Conference," *Proceedings of the International Conference on Information Processing*, UNESCO, Zurich, 125–132.

Banerji, R. B. (1963). "Phrase Structure Languages, Finite Machines, and Channel Capacity," *Information and Control* 6, 153–162.

Bar-Hillel, Y. (1964). *Language and Information*, Addison-Wesley, Reading, MA.

Barnes, B. H. (1970). "A Programmer's View of Automata," *Computing Surveys* 4, 221–239.

Becker, C. B. (1983). *Software Testing Techniques*, Van Nastrand Reinhold, New York.

Beckmann, F. S. (1980). *Mathematical Foundations of Programming*, Addison-Wesley, Reading, MA.

Bellmann, R. E. and Dreyfus, S. E. (1962). *Applied Dynamic Programming*, Princeton University Press, Princeton, NJ.

Bennett, J. P. (1990). *Introduction to Compiling Techniques: A First Course Using ANSI C, LEX and YACC*, McGraw-Hill, London.

Bentley, J. L. and Ottmann, T. (1981). "The Complexity of Manipulating Hierarchically Defined Sets of Rectangles," Mathematical Foundations of Computer Science 1981, *Springer-Verlag Lecture Notes in Computer Science* 118, 126–142.

Bentley, J. L., Ottmann, T., and Widmayer, P. (1983). "The Complexity of Manipulating Hierarchically Defined Sets of Rectangles," in Preparata, F.P. (ed.), *Advances in Computing Research* 1, JAI Press, Greenwich, CT, 127–158.

Berger, R. (1966). "The Undecidability of the Domino Problem," *Memoirs of the American Mathematical Society* 66, 238–249.

Berlekamp, E. R., Conway, J. H., and Guy, R. K. (1982). *Winning Ways for Your Mathematical Plays, Volume 2: Games in Particular*, Academic Press, NY.

Bobrow, L. S. and Arbib, M. A. (1974). *Discrete Mathematics: Applied Algebra for Computer and Information Science*, W. B. Saunders, Philadelphia, PA.

Bourne, S. R. (1983). *The UNIX System*, Addison-Wesley, Reading, MA.

Braffort, P. and Hirschberg, D. (eds.) (1963). *Computer Programming and Formal Systems*, North-Holland, Amsterdam.

Brainerd, W. S. and Landweber, L. H. (1974). *Theory of Computation*, John Wiley & Sons, Hoboken, NY.

Brookshear, J. G. (1989). *Theory of Computation: Formal Languages, Automata and Complexity*, Benjamin/Cummings, Redwood City, CA.

Brzozowski, J. A. (1962). "A Survey of Regular Expressions and Their Applications," *IEEE Transactions on Electronic Computers* 11, 324–335.

Brzozowski, J. A. (1964). "Derivates of Regular Expressions," *Journal of the ACM* 11, 481–494.

Brzozowski, J. A. (1980). "Open Problems about Regular Languages," in Book, R.V. (ed.), *Formal Language Theory: Perspectives and Open Problems*, Academic Press, New York, 23–47.

Brzozowski, J. A. and McCluskey, E. J., Jr. (1963). "Signal Flow Graph Techniques for Sequential Circuit State Diagrams," *IEEE Transactions on Electronic Computers* EC-12, 67–76.

Brzozowski, J. A. and Yoeli, M. (1976). *Digital Networks*, Prentice Hall, Englewood Cliffs, NJ.

Buchi, J. R. (1962). "Turing-Machines and the Entscheidungsproblem," *Mathematische Annalen* 148, 201–213.

Burge, W. H. (1975). *Recursive Programming Techniques*, Addison-Wesley, Reading, MA.

Burks, A. W. (ed.) (1970). *Essays in Cellular Automata*, University of Illinois Press, Champaign, IL.

Burks, A. W., Warren, D. W., and Wright, J. B. (1954). "An Analysis of a Logical Machine Using Parenthesis-Free Notation," *Mathematical Tables and Other Aids to Computation* 8, 55–57.

Carroll, J. and Long, D. (1989). *Theory of Finite Automata*, Prentice Hall, Englewood Cliffs, NJ.

Choffrut, C. and Culik, K., II. (1983). "Properties of Finite and Pushdown Transducers," *SIAM Journal on Computing* 12, 300–315.

Chomsky, N. (1956). "Three Models for the Description of Language," *IRE Transactions on Information Theory* 2, 113–124.

Chomsky, N. (1957). *Syntactic Structures*, The Hague, Mouton.

Chomsky, N. (1959). "On Certain Formal Properties of Grammars," *Information and Control* 2, 137–167.

Chomsky, N. (1962). "Context-Free Grammars and Pushdown Storage," *Quarterly Progress Report* No. 65, MIT Research Laboratory of Electronics, Cambridge, MA, 187–194.

Chomsky, N. (1963). *Formal Properties of Grammars, Handbook of Mathematical Psychology*, Vol. 2, John Wiley & Sons, Hoboken, NY, 323–418.

Chomsky, N. and Miller, G. A. (1958). "Finite-State Languages," *Information and Control* 1, 91–112.

Christofides, N. (1976). *Worst-Case Analysis of a New Heuristic for the Traveling Salesman Problem, Technical Report*, Graduate School of Industrial Administration, Carnegie-Mellon University, Pittsburgh, PA.

Church, A. (1936). "An Unsolvable Problem of Elementary Number Theory," *American Journal of Mathematics* 58, 345–363.

Church, A. (1941). *The Calculi of Lambda-Conversion, Annals of Mathematics Studies* 6, Princeton University Press, Princeton, NJ.

Clocksin, W. F. and Mullish, C. S. (1981). *Programming in PROLOG*, Springer-Verlag, Heidelberg, Germany.

Cobham, A. (1964). "The Intrinsic Computational Difficulty of Functions," *Proceedings of the 1964 Congress for Logic, Mathematics, and Philosophy of Science*, North-Holland, Amsterdam, 24–30.

Cohen, D. J. and Gotlieb, C. C. (1970). "A List Structure Form of Grammars for Syntactic Analysis," *Computing Surveys* 2, 62–83.

Cohen, J. (1979). "Nondeterministic Algorithms," *Computing Surveys* 11, 79–94.

Comer, D. (1979). "Heuristic for Trie Index Minimization," *ACM Transactions on Data Base Systems* 4, 383–395.

Cook, S. A. (1971a). "The Complexity of Theorem-Proving Procedures," *Proceedings of the Third Annual ACM Symposium on the Theory of Computing*, Princeton, NJ, 151–158.

Cook, S. A. (1971b). "Linear-Time Simulation of Deterministic Two-Way Pushdown Automata," *Proceeding of the 1971 IFIP Congress*, North-Holland, Amsterdam, 75–80.

Dantzig, G. B. (1960). "On the Significance of Solving Linear Programming Problems with Integer Variables," *Econometrica* 28, 30–44.

Davis, M. (1958). *Computability and Unsolvability*, McGraw-Hill, NY.

Davis, M. (1973). "Hilbert's Tenth Problem is Unsolvable," *American Mathematical Monthly* 80, 233–269.

Dawes, J., Pickett, M. J., and Wearing, A. (1990). *Selecting an Ada Compilation System*, Cambridge University Press, Cambridge, UK.

Dekker, J. C. E. (ed.) (1962). "Recursive Function Theory," *Proceedings of Symposia in Pure Mathematics* 5, American Mathematical Society, Providence, RI.

DeMillo, R. A., Dobkin, D. P., Jones, A. K., and Lipton, R. J. (eds.) (1978). *Foundations of Secure Computation*, Academic Press, New York.

DeMillo, R. A., Lipton, R. J., and Perlis, A. J. (1979). "Social Processes and Proofs of Theorems and Programs," *Communications of the ACM* 22, 271–280.

Denning, P. J., Dennis, J. B., and Qualitz, J. E. (1978). *Machines, Languages, and Computation*, Prentice Hall, Englewood Cliffs, NJ.

Dewdney, A. K. (1984). "Computer Recreations: A Computer Trap for the Busy Beaver, the Hardest-Working Turing Machine," *Scientific American* 251, 19–23.

Dijkstra, E. W. (1976). *A Discipline of Programming*, Prentice Hall, Englewood Cliffs, NJ.

Edmonds, J. (1962). "Covers and Packings in a Family of Sets," *Bulletin of the American Mathematical Society* 68, 494–499.

Edmonds, J. (1965). "Paths, Trees and Flowers," *Canadian Journal of Mathematics* 17, 499–467.

Ehrenfeucht, A., Karhumaki, J., and Rozenberg, G. (1982). "The (Generalized) Post Correspondence Problem with Lists Consisting of Two Words is Decidable," *Theoretical Computer Science* 21, 119–144.

Ehrenfeucht, A., Parikh, R., and Rozenberg, G. (1981). "Pumping Lemmas for Regular Sets," *SIAM Journal on Computing* 10, 536–541.

Elgot, C. C. and Mezei, J. E. (1965). "On Relations Defined by Generalized Finite Automata," *IBM Journal of Research and Development* 9, 47–68.

Elspas, B., Levitt, K., Waldinger, R., and Waksman, A. (1972). "An Assessment of Techniques for Proving Program Correctness," *Computing Surveys* 4, 97–147.

Engelfriet, J. (1980). "Some Open Questions and Recent Results on Tree Transducers and Tree Languages," in Book, R. V. (ed.), *Formal Language Theory: Perspectives and Open Problems*, Academic Press, New York, 241–286.

Engelfriet, J., Schmidt, E. M., and van Leeuwen, J. (1980). "Stack Machines and Classes of Nonnested Macro Languages," *Journal of the ACM* 27, 6–17.

Fischer, M. J. (1968). "Grammars with Macro-Like Productions," *Proceedings of the Ninth Annual IEEE Symposium on Switching and Automata Theory*, Chicago, IL, 131–142.

Fisher, J. A. (2005). *Embedded Computing: A VLIW Approach to Architecture, Compilers and Tools*, Elsevier, London.

Floyd, R. W. (1964a). *New Proofs and Old Theorems in Logic and Formal Linguistics*, Computer Associates, Wakefield, MA.

Floyd, R. W. (1964b). "The Syntax of Programming Languages—a Survey," *IEEE Transactions on Electronic Computers* EC-13, 346–353. Reprinted in Rosen, S. (ed.), *Programming Systems and Languages*, McGraw-Hill, New York, 1967 and Pollack, B. W., *Compiler Techniques*, Auerbach Press, Philadelphia, PA, 1972.

Floyd, R. W. (1967a). "Assigning Meaning to Programs," in Schwartz, J. T. (ed.), *Mathematical Aspects of Computer Science*, American Mathematical Society, Providence, RI, 19–32.

Floyd, R. W. (1967b). "Nondeterministic Algorithms," *Journal of the ACM* 14, 636–644.

Floyd, R. W. and Ullman, J. D. (1984). "The Compilation of Regular Expressions into Integrated Circuits," *Journal of the ACM* 29, 603–622.

Fosdick, L. D. and Osterweil, L. J. (1976). "Data Flow Analysis in Software Reliability," *Computing Surveys* 8, 305–330.

Foster, J. M. (1968). "A Syntax-Improving Program," *Computer Journal* 11, 31–34.

Foster, J. M. (1970). *Automatic Syntactic Analysis*, American Elsevier, New York.

Galler, B. A. and Perlis, A. J. (1970). *A View of Programming Languages*, Addison-Wesley, Reading, MA.

Gardner, M. (1983). *Wheels, Life and Other Mathematical Amusements*, W.H. Freeman, San Francisco, CA.

Gardner, M. (1985). "The Traveling Salesman's Travail," *Discover* 6, 87–90.

Garey, M. R. and Johnson, D. S. (1979). *Computers and Intractability: A Guide to the Theory of NP-Completeness*, W. H. Freeman, San Francisco, CA.

Gesceg, F. and Steinby, M. (1984). *Tree Automata*, Akademia Kiado, Budapest.

Ginsburg, S. and Greibach, S. A. (1966). "Deterministic Context-Free Languages," *Information and Control* 9, 563–582.

Ginsburg, S. and Greibach, S. A. (1969). "Studies in Abstract Families of Languages," in Ginsburg, S., Greibach, S. A., and Hopcroft, J. E. (eds.), 1–32. *Memoirs of the American Mathematical Society* 87, Princeton University Press, Princeton, NJ, 1–32.

Ginsburg, S. and Rose, G. F. (1963). "Operations Which Preserve Definability in Languages," *Journal of the ACM* 10, 175–195.

Ginsburg, S. and Spanier, E. H. (1963). "Quotients of Context-Free Languages," *Journal of the ACM* 10, 487–492.

Goldstine, J. (1980). "A Simplified Proof of Parikh's Theorem," unpublished manuscript.

Gonnet, G. H. (1984). *Handbook of Algorithms and Data Structures*, Addison-Wesley, Reading, MA.

Gonnet, G. H. and Tompa, F. W. (1983). "A Constructive Approach to the Design of Algorithms and Data Structures," *Communications of the ACM* 26, 912–920.

Gouda, M. G. and Rosier, L. E. (1985). "Priority Networks of Communicating Finite State Machines," *SIAM Journal on Computing* 14, 569–584.

Gough, B. (2004). *An Introduction to GCC: For the GNU Compilers gcc and g++*, Network Theory, Bristol, CT.

Graham, R. L. (1978). "The Combinatorial Mathematics of Scheduling," *Scientific American* 238(3), 124–132.

Gray, J. N. and Harison, M. A. (1966). "The Theory of Sequential Relations," *Information and Control* 9, 435–468.

Greibach, S. A. (1963). "The Undecidability of the Ambiguity Problem for Minimal Linear Grammars," *Information and Control* 6, 117–125.

Greibach, S. A. (1965). "A New Normal Form Theorem for Context-Free Phrase Structure Grammars," *Journal of the ACM* 12, 42–52.

Greibach, S. A. (1970). "Chains of Full AFLs," *Mathematical Systems Theory* 4, 231–242.

Greibach, S. A. (1972). "A Generalization of Parikh's Theorem," *Discrete Mathematics* 2, 347–355.

Greibach, S. A. (1973). "The Hardest Context-Free Language," *SIAM Journal on Computing* 2, 304–310.

Gries, D. (1971). *Compiler Construction for Digital Computers*, John Wiley & Sons, Hoboken, NY.

Gries, D. (1981). *The Science of Programming*, Springer-Verlag, New York.

Grune, D. and Jacobs, C. (1988). "A Programmer-friendly LL(1) Parser Generator," *Software—Practice and Experience* 18, 29–38.

Gruska, J. (1971). "A Characterization of Context-Free Languages," *Journal of Computer and System Sciences* 5, 353–364.

Hantler, S. L. and King, J. C. (1976). "An Introduction to Proving the Correctness of Programs," *Computing Surveys* 8, 331–353.

Harrison, M. A. (1965). *Introduction to Switching and Automata Theory*, McGraw-Hill, New York.

Harrison, M. A., Ruzzo, W. L., and Ullman, J. D. (1976). "Protection in Operating Systems," *Communications of the ACM* 19, 461–471.

Hartmanis, J. (1967). "Context-Free Languages and Turing Machine Computations," in Schwartz, J. T. (ed.), *Mathematical Aspects of Computer Science*, American Mathematical Society, Providence, RI, 42–51.

Hartmanis, J. and Hopcroft, J. E. (1971). "An Overview of the Theory of Computational Complexity," *Journal of the ACM* 18, 444–475.

Hartmanis, J. and Stearns, R. E. (1965). "On the Computational Complexity of Algorithms," *Transactions of the AMS* 117, 285–306.

Hayes, B. (1983). "Computer Recreations," *Scientific American* 249, 19–28.

Hayes, B. (1984). "Computer Recreations," *Scientific American* 250, 10–16.

Hays, D. G. (1967). *Introduction to Computational Linguistics*, American Elsevier, New York.

Hein, J. L. (1995). *Discrete Structures, Logic, and Computability*, Jones & Bartlett, London.

Heman, G. T. (1973). "A Biologically Motivated Extension of ALGOL-Like Languages," *Information and Control* 22, 487–502.

Henderson, P. (1980). *Functional Programming: Application and Implementation*, Prentice Hall, Englewood Cliffs, NJ.

Hennie, F. C. (1977). *Introduction to Computability*, Addison-Wesley, Reading, MA.

Hennie, F. C. and Stearns, R. E. (1966). "Two-Tape Simulation of Multitape Turing Machines," *Journal of the ACM* 13, 533–546.

Herman, G. T. and Rozenberg, G. (1975). *Developmental Systems and Languages*, American Elsevier, New York.

Hermes, H. (1969). *Enumerability, Decidability, Computability*, Springer-Verlag, New York.

Hoare, C. A. R. and Lauer, P. (1974). "Consistent and Complementary Formal Theories of the Semantics of Programming Languages," *Acta Informatica* 3, 135–153.

Hoare, C. A. R. and Wirth, N. (1973). "An Axiomatic Definition of the Programming Language PASCAL," *Acta Informatica* 2, 335–355.

Hopcroft, J. E. (1971). "An *n* log *n* Algorithm for Minimizing the States in a Finite Automaton," in Kohavi, Z. and Paz, A. (eds.), *Theory of Machines and Computations*, Academic Press, New York, 189–196.

Horowitz, E. and Sahni, S. (1978). *Fundamentals of Computer Algorithms*, Computer Science Press, Potomac, MD.

Ito, M. (ed.) (1992). *Words, Languages, and Combinatorics*, World Scientific, Singapore.

Johnson, J. H. (1983). *Formal Models for String Similarity*, PhD Dissertation, Department of Computer Science, University of Waterloo.

Johnson, S. C. (1974). "YACC—Yet Another Compiler Compiler," *Computer Science Technical Report* 32, Bell Laboratories, Murray Hill, NJ.

Kaplan, R. M. (1955). *Constructing Language Processors for Little Languages*, John Wiley & Sons, Hoboken, NY.

Kernighan, B. W. and Plauger, P. J. (1976). *Software Tools*, Addison-Wesley, Reading, MA.

Kfoury, A. J., Moll, R. N., and Arbib, M. A. (1982). *A Programming Approach to Computability*, Springer-Verlag, New York.

Kleene, S. C. (1936). "General Recursive Functions of Natural Numbers," *Mathematische Annalen* 112, 727–742.

Kleene, S. C. (1943). "Recursive Predicates and Quantifiers," *Transactions of the American Mathematical Society* 53, 41–73.

Kleene, S. C. (1952). *Introduction to Metamathematics*, D. Van Nostrand, Princeton, NJ.

Kleene, S. C. (1956). "Representation of Events in Nerve Nets and Finite Automata," in Shannon, C. E. and McCarthy, J. (eds.), *Automata Studies*, Princeton University Press, Princeton, NJ, 15401.

Kleijn, H. C. M. and Rozenberg, G. (1981). "Context-Free-Like Restrictions on Selective Rewriting," *Theoretical Computer Science* 16, 237–239.

Knoop, J. (1998). *Optimal Interprocedural Program Optimization: A New Framework and Its Application*, Springer-Verlag, London.

Knuth, D. E. (1971). "Top-Down Syntax Analysis," *Acta Informatica* 1, 79–110.

Knuth, D. E. (1973). *The Art of Computer Programming, Vol.3: Sorting and Searching*, Addison-Wesley, Reading, MA.

Knuth, D. E., Morris, J. H., Jr., and Pratt, V. R. (1977). "Fast Pattern Matching in Strings," *SIAM Journal on Computing* 6, 323–350.

Kuich, W. and Salomaa, A. (1985). *Semirings, Automata, Languages*, Springer-Verlag, New York.

Kuroda, S. Y. (1969). "Classes of Languages and Linear Bounded Automata," *BIT* 9, 225–238.

Larson, L. C. (1983). *Problem-Solving through Problems*, Springer-Verlag, New York.

Lauer, P. E., Torrigiani, P. R., and Shields, M. W. (1979). "COSY: A System Specification Language Based on Paths and Processes," *Acta Informatica* 12, 109–158.

Leupers, L. and Marwedel, P. (2001). *Retargetable Compiler Technology for Embedded Systems: Tools and Applications*, Kluwer Academic Publishers, London.

Levine, J. R. (1992). *Lex & Yacc*, O'Reilly & Associates, Sebastopol, CA.

Lewis, H. R. and Papadimitriou, C. (1981). *Elements of the Theory of Computation*, Prentice Hall, Englewood Cliffs, NJ.

Lewis, P. M., II., Stearns, R. E., and Hartmanis, J. (1965). "Memory Bounds for Recognition of Context-Free and Context-Sensitive Languages," *Proceedings of the Sixth Annual IEEE Symposium on Switching Circuit Theory and Logical Design*, Princeton, NJ, 191–202.

Lindenmayer, A. (1971). "Mathematical Models for Cellular Interactions in Development, Parts I and II," *Journal of Theoretical Biology* 30, 455–484.

Linger, R. C., Mills, H. D., and Witt, B. I. (1979). *Structured Programming: Theory and Practice*, Addison-Wesley, Reading, MA.

Mallozi, J. S. and De Lillo, N. J. (1984). *Computability with PASCAL*, Prentice Hall, Englewood Cliffs, NJ.

Marcotty, M., Ledgard, H.F., and Bochmann, G. V. (1976). "A Sampler of Formal Definitions," *Computing Surveys* 8, 191–276.

Markov, A. A. (1960). *The Theory of Algorithms* (translated from Russian by J. J. Schorrkon), U.S. Dept. of Commerce, Office of Technical Services, No. OTS 60–5108.

Maurer, D. and Wilhelm, R. (1995). *Compiler Design*, Addison-Wesley, Reading, MA.

McCarthy, J. (1963). "A Basis for a Mathematical Theory of Computation," in Braffort, P. and Hirschberg, D. (eds.), *Programming and Formal Systems*, North-Holland, Amsterdam, 33–70.

McCulloch, W. S. and Pitts, W. (1943). "A Logical Calculus of the Ideas Immanent in Nervous Activity," *Bulletin of Mathematical Biophysics* 5, 115–133.

McGuire, T. M. (2005). *The Austin Protocol Compiler*, Springer-Verlag, New York.

McNaughton, R. and Papert, S. (1971). *Counter-Free Automata*, MIT Press, Cambridge, MA.

McNaughton, R. and Yamada, H. (1960). "Regular Expressions and State Graphs for Automata," *IEEE Transactions on Electronic Computers* 9, 39–47.

McWhirter, I. P. (1971). "Substitution Expressions," *Journal of Computer and System Sciences* 5, 629–637.

Mead, C. A. and Conway, L. A. (1980). *Introduction to VLSI Systems*, Addison-Wesley, Reading, MA.

Meduna, A. (2006). "Deep Pushdown Automata," *Acta Informatica* 98, 114–124.

Meduna, A. and Kopeček, T. (2004). "Simple-Semi-Conditional Versions of Matrix Grammars with a Reduced Regulating Mechanism," *Computing and Informatics* 23, 287–302.

Meduna, A. and Koutný, J. (2012). "Tree-controlled Grammars with Restrictions Placed upon Cuts and Paths," *Kybernetika* 48, 165–175.

Meduna, A. and Leupold, P. (2010). "Finitely Expandable Deep PDAs," in *Automata, Formal Languages and Algebraic Systems*, World Scientific Publishing, Kyoto University, Kyoto, Japan, 113–123.

Meduna, A. and Lorenc, L. (2005). "Self-Reproducing Pushdown Transducers," *Kybernetika* 4, 533–539.

Meduna, A. and Lukáš, R. (2010). "Multigenerative Grammar Systems and Matrix Grammars," *Kybernetika* 46, 68–82.

Meduna, A. and Masopust, T. (2007). "Descriptional Complexity of Semi-Conditional Grammars," *Information Processing Letters* 104, 29–31.

Meduna, A. and Masopust, T. (2008). "On Descriptional Complexity of Partially Parallel Grammars," *Fundamenta Informaticae* 87, 407–415.

Meduna, A. and Masopust, T. (2009). "On context-free rewriting with a simple restriction and its computational completeness," *RAIRO—Theoretical Informatics and Applications* 43, 365–378.

Meduna, A. and Techet, J. (2007). "Canonical Scattered Context Generators of Sentences with Their Parses," *Theoretical Computer Science* 389, 73–81.

Meduna, A. and Techet, J. (2008). "Scattered Context Grammars that Erase Nonterminals in a Generalized *k*-Limited Way," *Acta Informatica* 45, 593–608.

Meduna, A. and Techet, J. (2009). "An Infinite Hierarchy of Language Families Generated by Scattered Context Grammars with *n*-Limited Derivations," *Theoretical Computer Science* 410, 1961–1969.

Meduna, A. and Zemek, P. (2011a). "One-Sided Random Context Grammars," *Acta Informatica* 48, 149–163.

Meduna, A. and Zemek, P. (2011b). "Workspace Theorems for Regular-Controlled Grammars," *Theoretical Computer Science* 412, 4604–4612.

Meduna, A. and Zemek, P. (2012a). "Controlled Pure Grammar Systems," *Journal of Universal Computer Science* 18, 2024–2040.

Meduna, A. and Zemek, P. (2012b). "Jumping Finite Automata," *International Journal of Foundations of Computer Science* 23, 1555–1578.

Meduna, A. and Zemek, P. (2012c). "Nonterminal Complexity of One-Sided Random Context Grammars," *Acta Informatica* 49, 55–68.

Meduna, A. and Zemek, P. (2012d). "One-Sided Forbidding Grammars and Selective Substitution Grammars," *International Journal of Computer Mathematics* 89, 586–596.

Meduna, A. and Zemek, P. (2013). "Generalized One-Sided Forbidding Grammars," *International Journal of Computer Mathematics* 90, 172–182.

Meduna, A., Bidlo, R., and Blatný, P. (2007). Automata with Two-Sided Pushdowns Defined over Free Groups Generated by Reduced Alphabets. *Kybernetika* 43, 265–278.

Meduna, A., Goldefus, F., and Masopust, T. (2010). "Left-Forbidding Cooperating Distributed Grammar Systems," *Theoretical Computer Science* 411, 3661–3667.

Meduna, A., Kopeček, T., and Švec, M. (2007). "Equivalent language models that closely simulate one another and their illustration in terms of L systems," *International Journal of Computer Mathematics* 84, 1555–1566.

Meduna, A., Křivka, Z., and Schönecker, R. (2006). "Generation of Languages by Rewriting Systems That Resemble Automata," *International Journal of Foundations of Computer Science* 17, 1223–1229.

Meyer, A. R. and Stockmeyer, L. J. (1972). "The Equivalence Problem for Regular Expressions with Squaring Requires Exponential Time," *Proceedings of the Thirteenth Annual IEEE Symposium on Switching and Automata Theory*, Boston, MA, 125–129.

Minsky, M. L. (1960). "A 6-Symbol, 7-State Universal Turing Machine," *MIT Laboratory Group Report* 54G-OO27, MIT, Boston, MA.

Minsky, M. L. (1962). *Size and Structure of Universal Turing Machines Using Tag Systems*, Marcel Dekker, Hoboken, NJ, 229–238.

Minsky, M. L. (1967). *Computation: Finite and Infinite Machines*, Prentice Hall, Englewood Cliffs, NJ.

Myhill, J. (1957). "Finite Automata and the Representation of Events," *WADD* TR-57-624, Wright Patterson AFB, OH, 112–137.

Newman, W. and Sproul, R. (1979). *Principles of Interactive Computer Graphics*, Second Edition, McGraw-Hill, New York.

Ogden, W. (1968). "A Helpful Result for Proving Inherent Ambiguity," *Mathematical Systems Theory* 2, 191–194.

Pagan, F. G. (1981). *Formal Specification of Programming Languages L: A Panoramic Primer*, Prentice Hall, Englewood Cliffs, NJ.

Pansiot, J. J. (1981). "A Note on Post's Correspondence Problem," *Information Processing Letters* 12, 233.

Papadimitriou, C. H. and Steiglitz, K. (1982). *Combinatorial Optimization: Algorithms and Complexity*, Prentice Hall, Englewood Cliffs, NJ.

Parikh, R. J. (1966). "On Context-Free Languages," *Journal of the ACM* 13, 570–581.

Paun, G. (ed.) (1995a). *Artificial Life: Grammatical Models*, Black Sea University Press, Bucharest, Romania.

Paun, G. (ed.) (1995b). *Mathematical Linguistics and Related Topics*, The Publishing House of the Romanian Academy, Bucharest, Romania.

Pavlenko, V. A. (1981). "Post Combinatorial Problem with Two Pairs of Words," *Dokladi AN Ukr. SSR* 33, 9–11.

Pilling, D. L. (1973). "Commutative Regular Equations and Parikh's Theorem," *Journal of the London Mathematical Society II* 6, 663–666.

Pippenger, N. (1978). "Complexity Theory," *Scientific American* 238(6), 114–124.

Post, E. L. (1936). "Finite Combinatory Processes-Formulation I," *Journal of Symbolic Logic* 1, 103–105.

Post, E. L. (1947). "Recursive Unsolvability of a Problem of Thue," *Journal of Symbolic Logic* 12, 39022.

Prather, R. E. (1976). *Discrete Mathematical Structures for Computer Science*, Houghton Mifflin, Boston, MA.

Pratt, T. W. (1982). "The Formal Analysis of Computer Programs," in Pollack, S. V. (ed.), *Studies in Mathematics*, Mathematical Association of America, Princeton, NJ, 169–195.

Priese, L. (1979). "Towards a Precise Characterization of the Complexity of Universal and Nonuniversal Turing Machines," *SIAM Journal on Computing* 8, 508–523.

Pugsley, D. (2000). *Justinian's Digest and the Compilers*, Faculty of Law, University of Exeter, Exeter, UK.

Rado, T. (1962). "On Noncomputable Functions," *Bell System Technical Journal* 41, 877–884.

Reynolds, J. C. (1981). *The Craft of Programming*, Prentice Hall, Englewood Cliffs, NJ.

Rice, H. G. (1953). "Classes of Recursively Enumerable Sets and Their Decision Problems," *Transactions of AMS* 74, 358–366.

Rogers, H., Jr. (1967). *The Theory of Recursive Functions and Effective Computability*, McGraw-Hill, New York.

Rosenkrantz, D. J., Stearns, R. E., and Lewis, P. M. (1977). "An Analysis of Several Heuristic for the Travelling Salesman Problem," *SIAM Journal on Computing* 6, 563–581.

Rozenberg, G. (1973). "Extension of Tabled 0L Systems and Languages," *International Journal of Computer and Information Sciences* 2, 311–334.

Rozenberg, G. and Salomaa, A. (1980). *The Mathematical Theory of L Systems*, Academic Press, New York.

Rozenberg, G. and Solms, von S. H. (1978). "Priorities on Context Conditions in Rewriting Systems," *Information Sciences* 14, 15–50.

Rustin, R. (ed.) (1972). *Formal Semantics of Programming Languages*, Prentice Hall, Englewood Cliffs, NJ.
Savitch, W. J. (1970). "Relationships between Nondeterministic and Deterministic Tape Complexities," *Journal of Computer and System Sciences* 4, 177–192.
Savitch, W. J. (1982). *Abstract Machines and Grammars*, Little, Brown, Boston, MA.
Scheinberg, S. (1963). "Note on the Boolean Properties of Context-Free Languages," *Information and Control* 6, 246–264.
Schutzenberger, M. P. (1963). "On Context-Free Languages and Pushdown Automata," *Information and Control* 6, 246–264.
Scott, D. (1967). "Some Definitional Suggestions for Automata Theory," *Journal of Computer and System Sciences* 1, 187–212.
Shannon, C. E. (1956). "A Universal Turing Machine with Two Internal States," in Shannon, C. E. and McCarthy, J. (eds.), *Automata Studies*, Princeton University Press, Princeton, NJ, 129–153.
Shannon, C. E. and McCarthy, J. (eds.) (1956). *Automata Studies*, Princeton University Press, Princeton, NJ.
Sharp, R. (2004). *Higher Level Hardware Synthesis*, Springer-Verlag, London.
Shepherdson, J. C. and Sturgis, H. E. (1963). "Computability of Recursive Functions," *Journal of the ACM* 10, 217–255.
Sippu, S. and Soisalon-Soininen, E. (1987). *Parsing Theory*, Springer-Verlag, New York.
Sippu, S., Soisalon-Soininen, E., and Ukkonen, E. (1983). "The Complexity of LALR(*k*) Testing," *Journal of the ACM* 30, 259–270.
Smith, A. R. (1984). "Plants, Fractals, and Formal Languages," *Computer Graphics* 18, 1–10.
Solow, D. (1982). *How to Read and Do Proofs*, John Wiley & Sons, Hoboken, NY.
Stepherdson, J. C. (1959). "The Reduction of Two-Way Automata to One-Way Automata," *IBM Journal of Research and Development* 3, 198–200.
Stepney, S. (1992). *High Integrity Compilation: A Case Study*, Prentice Hall, London.
Stockmeyer, L. J. and Chandra, A. K. (1979). "Intrinsically Difficult Problems," *Scientific American* 240(5), 140–159.
Stone, H. S. (1973). *Discrete Mathematical Structures and Their Applications*, SRA, Chicago, IL.
Tarjan, R. E. (1981). "A Unified Approach to Path Problems," *Journal of the ACM* 28, 577–593.
Tennet, R. D. (1981). *The Denotational Semantics of Programming Languages*, Prentice Hall, Englewood Cliffs, NJ.
Thatcher, J. W. (1973). "Tree Automata: An Informal Survey," in Aho, A. V. (ed.), *Currents in the Theory of Computing*, Prentice Hall, Englewood Cliffs, NJ, 143–172.
Thompson, K. (1968). "Regular Expression Search Algorithm," *Communications of the ACM* 11, 419–422.
Ullman, J. D. (1984). *Computational Aspects of VLSI*, Computer Science Press, Rockville, MD.
Valiant, L. G. (1975). "General Context-Free Recognition in Less than Cubic Time," *Journal of Computer and Systems Sciences* 10, 308–315.
van Leewen, J. (1974a). "A Generalization of Parikh's Theorem in Formal Language Theory," *Proceedings of ICALP '74, Springer-Verlag Lecture Notes in Computer Science* 14, 17–26.
van Leewen, J. (1974b). "Notes on Pre-Set Pushdown Automata," *Springer-Verlag Lecture Notes in Computer Science* 15, 177–188.
van Wijngaarden, A., Mailloux, B. J., Peck, J. E. L., Koster, C. H. A., Sintzoff, M., Lindsey, C. H., Meertens, L. G., Fisker, R. G. (eds.) (1974). "Revised Report on the Algorithmic Language ALGOL 68," *Acta Informatica* 5, 1–236.
Vere, S. (1970). "Translation Equations," *Communications of the ACM* 13, 83–89.
Walt, van der A. P. J. (1972). "Random Context Languages," *Information Processing* 71, 66–68.
Watanabe, S. (1960). "On a Minimal Universal Turing Machine," *MCB Report*, Tokyo.
Watanabe, S. (1961). "5-Symbol 8-State and 5-Symbol 6-State Universal Turing Machines," *Journal of the ACM* 8, 476–483.
Wegner, P. (1972a). "Programming Language," *Computing Surveys* 4, 5–63.
Wegner, P. (1972b). "Programming Language Semantics," in Rustin, R. (ed.), *Formal Semantics of Programming Languages*, Prentice Hall, Englewood Cliffs, NJ, 149–248.
Wirth, N. (1973). *Systematic Programming: An Introduction*, Prentice Hall, Englewood Cliffs, NJ.
Wirth, N. (1984). "Data Structures and Algorithms," *Scientific American* 251, 60–69.

Wise, D. S. (1976). "A Strong Pumping Lemma for Context-Free Languages," *Theoretical Computer Science* 3, 359–370.

Wolfram, S., Farmer, J. D., and Toffoli, T. (eds.) (1984). "Cellular Automata," *Proceedings of an Inter-Disciplinary Workshop*, Physica 10D, Nos. 1 and 2, Vienna, Austria.

Wood, D. (1969a). "The Normal Form Theorem—Another Proof," *Computer Journal* 12, 139–147.

Wood, D. (1969b). "The Theory of Left-Factored Languages," *Computer Journal* 12, 349–356.

Wood, D. (1984). *Paradigms and Programming with PASCAL*, Computer Science Press, Rockville, MD.

Yentema, M. K. (1971). "Cap Expressions for Context-Free Languages," *Information and Control* 8, 311–318.

Younger, D. H. (1976). "Recognition and Parsing of Context-Free Languages in Time *n* 3," *Information and Control* 10, 189–208.

Index

A

Acceptance, 17
  by a finite automaton, 31
  by a pushdown automaton, 119–121
    by empty pushdown, 119
    by empty pushdown and final state, 119
    by final state, 119
  by a Turing machine, 199
Ackermann's function, 242
Acyclic graph, 8
Algorithm, 21
Alphabet, 13, 14
  of input symbols, 113, 119
  of pushdown symbols, 113
  of tape symbols, 199
Ambiguity, 19, 94–96
Ancestor, 8
and, 3
Antisymmetric relation, 10
Arithmetic expression, 4, 162
A-rule, 86
Associativity, 9
Automaton, 21
  finite, 31, 199
    completely specified, 42
    deterministic, 38
    minimum-state, 43
  pushdown, 113
    deterministic, 121–122
  two-pushdown, 125, 211, 212
Axioms, 3

B

Balanced strings of parentheses, 123
Basis of an inductive proof, 5
Big-O notation, 239
Bijection, 6
Binary code for TMs, 206–208
Binary relation, 6
Blank, 67, 199
Boolean
  algebra, 9–10
  function, 146–149
Bottom-up parsing, 132, 136–139
  LR parsing, *See* LR parsing
  operator-precedence parsing, *See* operator-precedence parsing
  right parses, 140–141

C

Call graph, 7
Canonical derivations, 90
  ambiguity, 94–96
  leftmost derivations, 90–91
  rightmost derivations, 92
Cardinality, 5, 6
Cartesian product, 6
Case-statement implementation, 64–65
CFG, *See* Context-free grammars
CFLs, *See* Context-free languages
Characteristic function, 10
Child, 8
Chomsky normal form, 104–106, 187–188
Church–Turing thesis, 201, 248
Closed under an operation, 20–21
Closure
  of language, 14
  properties, 20–21
    applications of, 80–81, 192–193
    of CFLs, 189–193
    homomorphism, 192
    intersection and complement, 190–192
    of regular languages, 77–80
    union, concatenation and closure, 190
  reflexive-transitive, 7
  transitive, 7

Codes, Turing machine, 206–208
Commutativity, 9
Complement
  of CFLs, 190–192
  of decidable language, 229
  of regular languages, 77
  of sets, 5
  of Turing language, 234–235
Complete specification, 42
Computability, 214
  integer functions computed by TM, 214–217
  Kleene's s-m-n theorem, 219–220
  recursion theorem, 218–219
  theory of, 24
Computable function, 214, 219
Computational complexity
  space complexity, 240–241
  time complexity, 238–240
Computational model, 15
  rewriting systems as, 21–25
Computational restrictions of Turing machines, 203–205
Concatenation, 14
  of CFLs, 190
  FA for, 51–52
  of languages, 13
  of regular languages, 77
  of Turing languages, 253–254
  of strings, 14
Configuration
  of a finite automaton, 32
  of a parser, 132
  of a pushdown automaton, 113
  of a Turing machine, 200
Context-free
  closure properties, 189–193
  inherent ambiguity, 94
  languages, 85, 86
Context-free grammars (CFGs), 19, 85–89, 187, 190, 193, 245
  in Chomsky normal form, 104–106, 188
  decidable problems for, 225–227
  restrictions
    canonical derivations and derivation trees, 90–96
    erasing rules, removal of, 99–102
    Greibach normal form, 110–112
    left recursion elimination, 106–110
    single rules, removal of, 103–104
    useless symbols, removal of, 96–99
  syntax analysis, 133–134
Context-free languages (CFLs), 19, 85
  CFGs, *See* Context-free grammars (CFGs)
  closure properties, 189–193
  PDA, *See* Pushdown automaton
  pumping lemma for, 187–189
Context-sensitive
  decidability, 250
  grammar, 250
    equivalence with, 251–252
  languages, 253–254
Contradiction, 5–7
Contrapositive law, 4
Countable set, 6

D

Decidability, 24, 25, 220
Decidable languages, 221–222, 253–254
Decision
  algorithm, 223, 225
  problems
    concerning context-free languages, 223, 225–227
    concerning regular languages, 223–225
    concerning Turning machines, 227
    decidable, 223–227
    undecidable, 227
Decoding, 206–208
DeMorgan laws, 5, 27
Derivation, 19–20, 86
  canonical, 90
  leftmost, 90–91
  rightmost, 90, 92
  successful, 86
  trees, 90, 92–96
Descendant, 8
Deterministic
  parsing, 141
  pushdown automaton, 121–122
  Turing machines (TMs), 203
Deterministic finite automata (DFA), 38, 61–63, 65, 191
  complete specification, 42
  $_{\varepsilon\text{-}free}$FA, 34
  equivalent RE, 47
  state diagram of, 40, 41
  state table of, 39, 40
Deterministic PDA (DPDA), 121–122
DFA, *See* Deterministic finite automata
Diagonalization, 6–7, 24, 228–230
Difference, 5
Directed graph, 7
  acyclic, 8
  labeled, 7–8
Direct left recursion, 106–107
Disjoint set, 5
Distinguishable states, 43
Distributivity, 9
Domain, 6
DPDA, *See* Deterministic PDA

E

Edges, 7
Effective procedure, 22
Elementary subtree, 8
Emptiness problem, 223, 226
Empty
  pushdown, 119
  sequence, 6
  set, 5
  string, 13
English, 13, 15, 46, 195, 202
Enumerability, 217
ε-free context-free grammar, 125
ε-move, 34
ε-rules, 34, 99
  removal of, 34–38
Equivalence
  classes, 10
  from finite automata to regular expressions, 47–48
  from GG to TM, 248–249
  problem, 225, 233, 236
  from regular expressions to finite automata, 49–56
  relation, 10
  from TM to GG, 249

F

FA, *See* Finite automaton
Families of languages, 13
Families of sets, 5
Final language, 17
Final state, 22, 33, 199
Finite
  language, 13
  relation, 6
  set, 5, 6
  substitution, 80
Finite automaton (FA), 31–32, 61, 199
  closure properties, 77–80
  completely specified, 42
  decidable problems for, 223–225
  deterministic, 38
  equivalence, *See* Equivalence
  implementation, 62–64
    algorithm, 62–64
    case-statement, 64–65
    table-based, 62–64
  minimum-state, 43
  regular expressions, 45–47
  representations, 32–34
  restriction
    determinism, 38–42
    ε-rules, removal of, 34–38
    minimization, 43–45
  scanners and, 66–67
Formal language, 13–15
Formal mathematical system, 3
Formation rules, 3
Fully parenthesized regular expression, 46
Function, 6
  computable, 214, 219
  partial, 6
  polynomially bounded, 239
  primitive recursive, 242
  uncomputable, 214, 219

G

Grammar, 18
  context-free, 19, 85–89
  context-sensitive, 250–252
  general, 245–246
  linear, 20
  pure, 256, 257
Graphs, 7–11
Graph-theory notions, 187
Greibach normal form, 110–112

H

Halting
  configuration, 203
  problem, 228
Homomorphism, 15, 80
  context-free grammar for, 192

I

iff, 4
Inaccessible symbol, 97–98
In-degree, 7, 8
Index
  of a computable function, 217–219
  of a Turing machine, 217
Indistinguishable states, 43
Induction, 4, 5
Inductive hypothesis, 4, 5
Inductive proof, 5
Inductive step, 4, 5
Inference rules, 3
Infinite
  relation, 6
  set, 5
Infiniteness problem, 224, 227
Inherent ambiguity, 94
Injection, 6
Input
  alphabet, 31, 32, 199
  end marker, 62
  symbols, 31, 32, 199, 200
Integer functions, computing, 214–217
Interior node, 8

Intersection, 5
  of context-free languages, 233
    and regular languages, 190–192
  of languages, 14
  of regular languages, 78
  of sets, 5
Intractable problem, 25
Inverse relation, 6
Iteration, FA for, 52–53

K

Kleene's s-m-n theorem, 219–220
Kuroda normal form
  context-sensitive grammars, 251
  general grammar, 246–248

L

Labeled graph, 7–8
Language, 13
  accepted by
    finite automaton, 31
    pushdown automaton, 113
    Turing machine, 199–200
  context-free, 85, 86
  context-sensitive, 253–254
  decidable, 221–222, 253–254
  families, relations between, 254–255
  finite, 13, 254–255
  generated by
    context-free grammar, 19, 85–86
    general grammar, 245–246
    linear grammar, 20
  infinite, 13, 254–255
  models, rewriting systems as, 17–21
  regular, 45
  Turing, 204
Language-accepting model, 17
Language-defining models, 15
Language-generating models, 17–18
LBAs, *See* Linear-bounded automata
Leftmost derivation, 19–20, 90–91
Left recursion, 106–110
Length
  of a finite sequence, 6
  of a string, 13
Length-increasing grammars, 250
Lexical analysis, 61, 67
  implementation of, 64
  lexical units and REs, 66
  scanners
    and finite automata, 66–67
    implementation of, 67–71
Lexical units, 66, 67
LG, *See* Linear grammar
Linear-bounded automata (LBAs), 245, 251–252
Linear grammar (LG), 20, 87
Linear order, 10
Logic, 3–4
Logical
  connectives, 3
  statement, 3
LR parsing, bottom-up parsing
  ad-hoc recovery, 173–175
  algorithm, 164–167
  handling errors in, 173–175
  LR table construction, 167–172

M

Machines, 21
Membership problem, 223, 226, 230
Metaphysics of computation, 24
Minimization, 43–45
Minimum-state finite automaton, 43
Model of computation, 21–25
Morse code, 15, 16
Move, 32, 113, 200

N

Natural
  language, 13
  number, 5
Nodes, 7
Noncontext-freedom of a language, 187, 189
Nondeterministic
  finite automaton, 38
  pushdown automaton, 121, 122
  Turing decider, 239–240
  Turing machine, 239
Nondeterministic polynomial time, 239
Nondeterministic space complexity, 241
Nondeterministic time complexity, 239
Nonregular language, 77
Nonterminal, 18–19, 86
  accessible, 97
  symbols, 19
  terminating, 96, 97
  useful, 99
  useless, 99
Normal form
  for context-free grammars
    Chomsky, 104–106
    Greibach, 110–112
  for context-sensitive grammars, 250
    Kuroda, 251
    Pentonnen, 251
  for general grammars
    Kuroda, 246–248
    Pentonnen, 248
not, 3
NP-complete problem, 240

O

Ogdenn's lemma, 194
only if, 3
Operations, 14
Operator-precedence parsing, bottom-up parsing
  ambiguity, 163
  OP-SHIFT and OP-REDUCE, 156
  parsing table $_EOP$, 158–159
  reduction errors, 159–161
  right-associative operators, arithmetic expressions with, 162–163
  table-detected errors, 159
Ordered pair, 6, 7
Ordered tree, 8
Out-degree graphs, 7

P

Pairwise disjoint set, 5
PALM, *See* Parenthesis-accepting language model
Panic-mode error recovery, 173
Parent-children portion, 8
Parenthesis-accepting language model (PALM), 18
Parenthesis-generating language model (PGLM), 17–18
Parsing
  bottom-up, *See* Bottom-up parsing
  top-down, *See* Top-down parsing
Partial
  function, 6
  order, 10
Pascal implementation of scanner, 69–71
Pascal-like pseudo-code, 67
Path, 7
PDA, *See* Pushdown automaton
Pentonnen normal form
  context-sensitive grammars, 251
  general grammar, 248
PGLM, *See* Parenthesis-generating language model
$P = NP$ problem, 240
Polish notation
  postfix, 4
  prefix, 4
Polynomial
  bound, 239
  space-bounded non-deterministic Turing decider, 241
  space-bounded Turing decider, 241
  time-bounded non-deterministic Turing decider, 239
  time-bounded Turing decider, 239
Polynomial-space-bounded language, 243
Polynomial-time-bounded language, 243
Positive closure, 14
Postfix notation, 4
Post's Correspondence Problem, 233
Power set, 5
Predictive parsing, top-down parsing
  ad-hoc recovery, 153–154
  handling errors, 153–154
  left recursion, exclusion of, 154
  panic-mode error recovery, 153
Predictive recursive-descent parsing, 146–149
Predictive table-driven parsing, 149–153
Prefix, 14
  notation, 4
Problem(s)
  decidable, 223–227
  equivalence, 225, 233
  halting, 228
  infiniteness, 224, 227
  membership, 223–224, 226, 230
  undecidable, *See* Undecidable problems
Procedure, 22
Programming language, 61, 66, 132
Proof
  by contradiction, 4, 5
  contrapositive law, 4
  by induction, 4, 5
Proper
  context-free grammar, 104
  prefix, 14
  subset, 5
  suffix, 14
Properties
  associativity, 9
  closure, 20–21, 77–80, 189–193
  commutativity, 9
  distributivity, 9
Pumping lemma, 73
  applications, 75–77, 189
  for CFLs, 187–188
  for regular languages, 73–75
Pure grammar, 256, 257
Pushdown, 113
  transducer, 125
Pushdown automaton (PDA), 85, 113, 191, *See also* Context-free grammars (CFGs)
  acceptance, equivalent types of, 119–121
  configuration, 113
  deterministic, 121–122
  equivalence, 114–119
    CFGs to PDA, 114–115
    PDA to CFGs, 115–119
  and languages, 113–114
  syntax analysis, 132–133
    popping and expanding, 134–135

Q

Question, 221

R

Range, 6
Reachable state, 39
Recursion
  left, 106–110
  theorem, 217–219
Recursive
  definition, 7, 14
  function, 242
Reduction, undecidable problem, 230–232
Redundant symbols, 89
Reflexive and transitive closure, 7
Regular
  languages, 46
    closure properties, 77–80
    pumping lemma for, 73–75
  substitution, 78–80
Regular expressions (REs), 45–47, 61
  lexical units, definition of, 66, 67
Regular languages, context-free languages and, 190–192
Relations, 6–7
Restricted finite automata, 34
  determinism, 38–42
  ε-rules, removal of, 34–38
  minimization, 43–45
Restricted Turing machines, 202
  computational, 203–205
  size, 205–206
Reversal, 14
  of a language, 14
  of a string, 14
Rewriting relation, 16
Rewriting systems, 15
  as computational models, 21–25
  in general, 16–17
  as language models, 17–21
Rice's theorem, 237–238
Rightmost derivation, 90, 92
Root, 8
Rule, 3
  in a context-free grammar, 19, 86
  in a general grammar, 246
  in a linear grammar, 20
  in a mathematical system, 3
  in a rewriting system, 21
  trees, 92–95

S

Scanners, 66
  application of, 68
  and finite automata, 66–67
  for identifiers, 67
  implementation of, 67–71
  for integers and real numbers, 67
Sentences, 86
Sentential form, 86
Sequence
  empty, 6
  of rules, 16
  sets and, 4–6
Sets
  cardinality, 5, 6
  complement, 5
  countable, 6
  difference, 5
  empty, 5
  finite, 5, 6
  infinite, 5, 6
  intersection, 5
  natural number, 5
  and sequences, 4–6
  uncountable, 6
  union, 5
Single rule, 103–104
Size restrictions of Turing machines, 205–206
s-m-n theorem, 219–220
Space complexity, 25, 240–241
Start language, 17
Start state, 22
  in a finite automaton, 31
  in a pushdown automaton, 113
  in Turing machine, 199
Start symbol, 19, 86, 113
State diagram, 32–33, 41
State table, 32–33
String, 13
  empty, 13
Subrelation, 6
Subset, 5
Substitution, 15
  finite, 80
  regular, 78–80
Substring, 14
Subtree, 8–9
Successor function, 22
Suffix, 14
Surjection, 6
Symbol, 3, 13, 14
Symmetric relation, 10
Syntax analysis, 132–133
  bottom-up parsing, 136–141
  context-free grammars, 133–134
  top-down parsing, 134–136

T

Table-based implementation, 62–64
Tabular method, 62
Tape, 199
  alphabet, 199
  head, 199

symbol, 199
two-way infiniteness, 210
Tautology, 9
TD, *See* Turing decider
Terminal, 18–19
symbols, 18
Theorem, 3
Theory of computation
computability, 213
integer functions computed by TM, 214–217
Kleene's s-m-n theorem, 219–220
recursion theorem, 217–219
decidability, 220
Theory of decidability, 24
Time complexity, 25, 238–240
TM, *See* Turing machine
Top-down parsing, 134–136
handling errors, 153–154
left parses, 135–136
left recursion, exclusion of, 154
LL grammars, 145–146
predictive recursive-descent parsing, 146–149
predictive sets, 142–144
predictive table-driven parsing, 149–153
Total alphabet, 16
Total function, 6
Track, 211
Tractable problem, 239
Transducer
finite, 59
pushdown, 125
Transitive closure, 7
Transitive relation, 10
Tree, 9
depth, 8
frontier, 8
root, 8
Truth table, 3–4
Turing computable function, 214–217
Turing decider (TD), 220–222
space complexity, 240–241
time complexity, 238–240
Turing machine (TM), 22, 199
acceptance, 199
as a computational model, 213
configuration, 200
deterministic, 203
equivalence of, 248–249
formal description of, 201
informal description of, 201
k-head, 210–211
as a language acceptor, 199–200, 213
long-reading, 210
restrictions, 202
computational, 203–205
size, 205–206
simple, 210
theory of computation, *See* Theory of computation
time complexity, 238–240
two-way, 210
undecidable problems, 227
diagonalization, 228–230
reduction, 230–232
universal, 206
codes, 206–208
construction, 208–209
variations, 199
Two-pushdown automaton, 125, 211, 212
Two-way
finite automaton, 58–59
infinite tape, 210

U

Unambiguousness, 94
Unary languages, 189
Unary operators, 162
Unary representation, 15
Uncomputable function, 214, 219
Undecidability, 24, 234–238
Undecidable problems, 24, 227
diagonalization, 228–230
not concerning Turing machine, 233
reduction, 230–232
Undirected graphs, 11
Union, 5
of CFLs, 190
FA for, 49
of languages, 14
of regular languages, 77
of sets, 5
Universal language, 13
Universal Turing machines, 206
codes, 206–208
construction, 208–209
Unreachability, 39
Useful symbol, 99
Useless symbol, 96–99

V

Value, 6
false, 3–4
true, 3–4

Milton Keynes UK
Ingram Content Group UK Ltd.
UKHW051948071024
449327UK00026B/2215

9 780367 378875